Lecture Notes in Computer Science　15549

Founding Editors

Gerhard Goos
Juris Hartmanis

The series Lecture Notes in Computer Science (LNCS), including its subseries Lecture Notes in Artificial Intelligence (LNAI) and Lecture Notes in Bioinformatics (LNBI), has established itself as a medium for the publication of new developments in computer science and information technology research, teaching, and education.

LNCS enjoys close cooperation with the computer science R & D community, the series counts many renowned academics among its volume editors and paper authors, and collaborates with prestigious societies. Its mission is to serve this international community by providing an invaluable service, mainly focused on the publication of conference and workshop proceedings and postproceedings. LNCS commenced publication in 1973.

Gabriele Oliva · Stefano Panzieri ·
Bernhard Hämmerli · Federica Pascucci ·
Luca Faramondi
Editors

Critical Information Infrastructures Security

19th International Conference, CRITIS 2024
Rome, Italy, September 18–20, 2024
Revised Selected Papers

 Springer

Editors
Gabriele Oliva ⓘ
University Campus Bio-Medico of Rome
Rome, Italy

Stefano Panzieri ⓘ
University Roma Tre
Rome, Italy

Bernhard Hämmerli ⓘ
Lucerne University of Applied Sciences
Lucerne, Switzerland

Federica Pascucci ⓘ
University Roma Tre
Rome, Italy

Luca Faramondi ⓘ
University Campus Bio-Medico of Rome
Rome, Italy

ISSN 0302-9743   ISSN 1611-3349 (electronic)
Lecture Notes in Computer Science
ISBN 978-3-031-84259-7   ISBN 978-3-031-84260-3 (eBook)
https://doi.org/10.1007/978-3-031-84260-3

This Springer imprint is published by the registered company Springer Nature Switzerland AG
The registered company address is: Gewerbestrasse 11, 6330 Cham, Switzerland

If disposing of this product, please recycle the paper.

Preface

The 19th International Conference on Critical Information Infrastructures Security, CRITIS 2024, was held on September 18–20, 2023 at Roma Tre University in Rome, Italy. CRITIS 2024 was organized as a cooperation between the team at Roma Tre University, led by Stefano Panzieri, and the team at University Campus Bio-Medico of Rome, led by Gabriele Oliva. The Honorary Chair was Fabio Pistella.

Alessandro Micarelli, Director of the Department of Civil, Computer Science and Aeronautical Technologies Engineering, and Salvatore Andrea Sciuto, Director of the Department of Industrial, Electronical and Mechanical Engineering of Roma Tre University welcomed ca. 60 participants from academia, industry, defense, and government, and especially critical infrastructure practitioners.

This year the presentations mainly revolved around cyber security, cyber-physical systems, climate change, and natural threats. These proceedings document an account of the topics that were discussed during the three interesting conference days. The conference papers were selected according to a two-round peer review process. In the first round the review was conducted as double blind and at least three peer reviewers reviewed each paper. In the second round the peer review was conducted as single blind, and one or two persons reviewed each paper. Finally, we were happy to accept 24 full papers.

In the CRITIS 2024 keynote, Lieutenant General Franco Federici, Military Advisor to the Italian President of the Council, examined Italy's resilience framework in response to threats targeting critical infrastructures, providing an overview of both national and European regulatory frameworks, with a particular emphasis on Directive 2022/2557 concerning the resilience of critical entities and its transposition into Italian law. A special emphasis was posed on the protection of critical undersea infrastructures.

This theme was further expanded by the plenary talk by Johanna Karvonen, Laurea University of Applied Sciences, Finland, which revolved around the need to enhance the resilience of underwater critical assets, and the presentation of the recently funded VIGIMARE European Project. Andrea Guarino, ACEA, Italy, highlighted the development and impact of The CISO Game, an interactive gamified tool by the ECHO project, designed to enhance cybersecurity and decision-making skills for CISOs and IT professionals. The event concluded with a speech by Riccardo Croce, Director of the Italian National Anti-Cybercrime Center for the Protection of Critical Infrastructures (CNAIPIC). He discussed his institution's activities and the emerging cyber challenges in light of Directive 2022/2557.

Speakers at the conference highlighted pivotal challenges and shared innovative strategies to address them. The editors extend heartfelt gratitude to all CRITIS 2024 participants for their invaluable contributions in navigating the dynamic and ever-changing realm of technology and security.

December 2024

Gabriele Oliva
Stefano Panzieri
Bernhard Hämmerli
Federica Pascucci
Luca Faramondi

Organization

General Chairs

Stefano Panzieri   Università Roma Tre, Italy
Gabriele Oliva   University Campus Bio-Medico of Rome, Italy

Honorary Chair

Fabio Pistella   ENR, former Università Roma Tre, Italy

Program Co-chairs

Federica Pascucci   Università Roma Tre, Italy
Luca Faramondi   University Campus Bio-Medico of Rome, Italy

Steering Committee

Chairs

Bernhard M. Hämmerli   Lucerne University of Applied Sciences/Acris GmbH, Switzerland
Javier Lopez   University of Málaga, Spain
Stephen D. Wolthusen   Royal Holloway, University of London, UK/NTNU, Norway

Members

Sandro Bologna   AIIC, Italy
Gregorio D'Agostino   ENEA, Italy
Eric Luiijf   Luiijf Consultancy, The Netherlands
Roberto Setola   Università Campus Bio-Medico di Roma, Italy
Stefan Pickl   Universität der Bundeswehr München, Germany
Alain Mermoud   Cyber-Defence Campus, armasuisse S+T, Switzerland

Program Committee

Cristina Alcaraz	University of Málaga, Spain
Magnus Almagren	Chalmers University of Technology, Sweden
Sandro Bologna	AIIC, Italy
Valeria Bonagura	Università degli Studi Roma Tre, Italy
Graziana Cavone	Università degli Studi Roma Tre, Italy
Gregorio D'Agostino	ENEA, Italy
Antonio Di Pietro	ENEA, Italy
Camilla Fioravanti	Campus Bio-Medico University of Rome, Italy
Chiara Foglietta	Università degli Studi Roma Tre, Italy
Joseph Gardiner	University of Bristol, UK
Dimitris Gritzalis	Athens University of Economics & Business, Greece
Simone Guarino	Campus Bio-Medico University of Rome, Italy
Chris Hankin	Imperial College London, UK
Jukka Heikkenen	University of Turku, Finland
Mikel Iturbe	Mondragon Unibersitatea, Spain
Panayiotis Kotzanikolaou	University of Piraeus, Greece
Linas Martišauskas	Lithuanian Energy Institute, Lithuania
Päivi Mattila	Laurea University of Applied Sciences, Finland
Simin Nadjm-Tehrani	Linköping University, Sweden
Gabriele Oliva	University Campus Bio-Medico of Rome, Italy
Stefano Panzieri	Università degli Studi Roma Tre, Italy
Federica Pascucci	Università degli Studi Roma Tre, Italy
Maurizio Pollino	ENEA, Italy
Peter Popov	City St. George's, University of London, UK
Vladimir Stankovic	City St. George's, University of London, UK
Alberto Tofani	ENEA, Italy

Contents

Resilience of Critical Infrastructures and Climate Change

Silvano Bari, Glauco Bertocchi, Sandro Bologna$^{(\boxtimes)}$, Luigi Carrozzi,
Gianluca Cipriani, Elenio Dursi, Luisa Franchina, Alberto Stefanini,
and Alberto Traballesi

AIIC Associazione Italiana Esperti in Infrastrutture Critiche, Rome, Italy
s.bologna@infrastrutturecritiche.it

Abstract. The paper addresses the theme of physical risks resulting from climate change. Physical risk is linked to the properties of the physical infrastructure of the complex technologies that make up modern Cyber-Physical systems. The paper is derived from a larger Report co-authored by the same authors, where they assess the impacts, on a limited number of infrastructures, resulting from "acute" events, which are one-time events such as floods or hurricanes, as well as "chronic" events, which are long-term changes in climate parameters such as temperature. The assessment is based on the authors' experience, concerning the systems that make up the reference infrastructure. In this regard, knowledge of the physical nature of infrastructural components that could be destroyed or disrupted in their operation by specific threats arising from climate change is essential, resulting in the decay of the services provided by the infrastructures or an increase in the cost of such services.

Keywords: climate change · critical infrastructures · socio-economic impact

1 Ecosystem of a Critical Infrastructure

Analyzing recent adverse events (meteorologically speaking), weak signals are noticed on how the ecosystem of critical infrastructures (IC) has been designed without considering climate change. In doing so, a series of factors are evaluated that, at first glance, may not seem relevant to the functioning of the IC itself. However, upon closer inspection, these factors are integral to anticipating the adverse effects of climate change and adopting appropriate measures for climate change mitigation and/or adaptation. The aim is to prevent or minimize the damage caused by these changes to the entire ecosystem in which the infrastructure is located.

For a comprehensive understanding and to ensure a holistic view of the project, also on the climate-resistant side, in addition to analyzing the territory and environment in which the critical infrastructure is located (whether it is a data center or a transmission tower), one must assess the availability and continuous accessibility to sources of energy supply even in worst-case scenarios. This is based on a good understanding of the climate and the territory involved. Figures with expertise in climate change mitigation and adaptation will conduct evaluations regarding climate resilience (i.e., making infrastructure resilient to climate change).

This expanded team ensures that, by necessity, the project must be conceived holistically, considering the entire supply chain. A meticulous analysis of each link is required, as each link identifies a potential fault point. Therefore, the entire chain must be verified and validated for both the supply and the supplier to ensure resilience even from a climate-proof perspective.

Considering these aspects, potentially susceptible to climate change even in a very short time frame, must inevitably prompt us to update the algorithm of various faults that have occurred in the past years concerning weather conditions and energy flows needed to power the equipment.

To achieve good climate resilience in a critical infrastructure and its entire ecosystem, it is necessary to develop an emergency management plan that also ensures the operational continuity of the infrastructure itself. Defining this plan starts by identifying the most critical processes for the entire ecosystem in which the infrastructure is located and listing possible emergency scenarios and/or recovery solutions.

For a critical infrastructure designed in the late 90s to remain operational for a decade, updates to this plan might be needed, considering alternative scenarios if its energy chain were impacted by a flooding event like the one that devastated the Emilia region in Italy, sparing nothing but the IC directly.

While a critical infrastructure is designed to have redundancy (preferably in sites far apart), on certain fault points, such as energy supply and connectivity, adjustments may be needed, thinking beyond the infrastructure's placement and elevating the perspective to the entire supporting ecosystem.

An adverse climatic event of significant relevance can certainly impact the supply chain or suppliers located even several tens of kilometers away from the IC. Distributors may be unable to store (and therefore dispense) fuel as they secure their facilities through controlled emptying of their tanks to avoid potential spills into floodwaters.

A good emergency continuity plan must list all these aspects with cause/effect relationships, providing a comprehensive view of the entire supply chain and all its ramifications that can be significantly impacted on operational continuity.

This meteorological variability tends to be a climatic phenomenon that seems to accelerate (it certainly will not stop), where time has assumed a determining position. It is our task to quickly bring these elements together to have a clear understanding of what might happen, not if, but when.

2   Objectives of the Work

The purpose of this work is to provide an overview and evaluation of resilience measures that should be considered in national policies and regulations for protecting critical infrastructures against natural disasters and the negative impacts of climate change.

Referring to the UNDRR 2020 Report "Making Critical Infrastructure Resilient" [1]the areas requiring more attention and resources are:

- Measurement and monitoring of vulnerability, sensitivity, interdependence, and exposure to climate risk of assets constituting critical infrastructures.
- Promoting periodic tests to ensure the correct functioning of infrastructure under different climatic conditions than those envisaged at the time of design and construction.
- Strengthening rules aimed at promoting greater development of solutions to minimize the risk of disasters attributable to climate change.
- Improving the knowledge of all stakeholders playing a critical role in the development and maintenance of certain infrastructure.
- Developing a public-private partnership that can promote benefits and sustainability for both parties.

The complexity of the problem is increased by the fact that the systems characterizing these sectors are not individual systems but networks of systems and are becoming increasingly interdependent, especially with the digitalization of services.

For this work, referring to Directive (EU) 2022/2557 of the European Parliament and of the Council of December 14, 2022, on the resilience of critical entities, repealing Council Directive 2008/114/EC, the considered sectors are: energy, water supply, wastewater treatment, telecommunications, and health services.

The work is organized as follows:

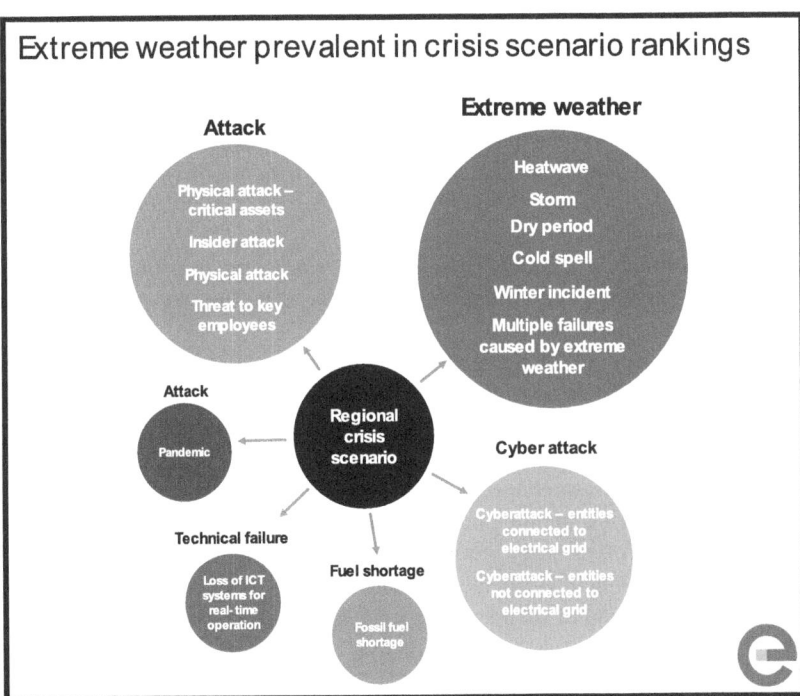

Fig. 1. Ranking of threat factors in power system (from Eurelectric, "The Coming Storm")

Threats attributable to climate change considered are listed and for each treated Critical Infrastructure (CI), possible impacts on the CI are associated with each threat.

It is necessary to be aware that no Critical Infrastructure can operate in isolation but rather as a "system of systems" so the failure of one infrastructure could result in a severe disruption of services offered by others. In this regard, the Eurelectric 2022 document "The Coming Storm" [2] reports the interdependencies among different factors that can generate a crisis, including, for example, the weight of extreme climatic events and physical or cyberattacks. As observed in Fig. 1, the power system is most affected by climatic conditions than by other factors. The present paper is derived from updating a larger Report co-authored by the same authors. The Report is titled "Resilienza delle Infrastrutture Critiche e Cambiamenti Climatici" and was published by AIIC (Italian Association of Critical Infrastructure Experts) in the year 2023 and is available only in Italian [34].

3   Methodological Considerations

Climate change is characterized, oversimplifying, by two distinct types of temporal developments.

The first type, which we might call long-term, relates to changes that take effect on a timespan scale of more than ten years and generally affect the entire planet or substantial parts of it; examples of this type are increases in average temperature, rising sea levels, and increases in the greenhouse effect. Some of those changes are consequences of others, and it is not easy to distinguish the primary causes given their interdependence.

The second type of temporal development relates to the "local" consequences of climate change of the first type and last hours, days, or months. In addition, these phenomena affect limited geographical areas even though they may include entire nations or parts thereof; examples are floods, monsoons of increased intensity, periods of drought, sudden weather phenomena of exceptional severity, etc.

It seems clear that we should try to eliminate, as far as possible, the underlying causes of long-term changes and prepare to live on a different planet than the one we know today.

It is also necessary to adopt measures that mitigate "local" effects and increase resilience by considering the possible evolution (likely worsening) that will occur over time. These measures should, possibly, also contribute to addressing the causes of climate change.

Addressing both types of changes implies the definition of a strategy articulated on very different time scales and implemented by very diverse actors (nations, regions, and local communities). This strategy requires defining and implementing an international coordination (on the political, financial, and realization levels) that is brand new in human history. The determination of such a strategy is beyond the scope of our work, which is limited to analyzing issues to improve the resilience of critical infrastructures to threats arising from ongoing climate change.

The resilience of CIs to threats from climate change requires the design and implementation of a coordinated set of technical and organizational measures with some fundamental characteristics:

1. formulation of long-term programs with "strategic" objectives, i.e., capable of possibly also affecting the causes of climate change or at least providing resilience criteria that are valid on a multi-year or better multi-decade basis,
2. formulation of "tactical" type programs, i.e., immediate or short-term programs to mitigate the effects of climate change at the local level, gradually reducing the impact of extreme events,
3. continuous risk analysis based on long-term trends, used to produce adjustments to strategy-type programs and on the short-term ability to forecast extreme events to implement targeted "tactical" interventions,
4. a governance structure capable of coordinating, on a multi-year basis and synergistically, the design and implementation of both types of interventions (strategic and tactical) and constantly adjusting objectives based on risk analysis.

An appropriate methodology is necessary to ensure the coherence of activities with short-term and strategic objectives, given the uncertainties about the capability for multi-year risk analysis of climate change.

A choice of methodologies [3–6] can be used for managing a project of such duration and complexity. It might be interesting to highlight the essential characteristics that should be present in the methodology to be adopted. A relevant initial requirement is the organization's knowledge of the methods and procedures it must adopt and adequate training of personnel who will manage the project. Furthermore, the methodology must allow the integration of continuous risk analysis, and the modification of objectives based on forecasts and lessons learned from events.

Another essential requirement of the methodology is the integration of an adequate governance structure that allows both the coordination of various project levels and the effective modification of objectives.

An appropriate methodology represents an indispensable tool, but as explained below, it should be complemented by other tools and "innovative" approaches.

The first consideration is that the resilience of critical infrastructures also involves assessing interdependencies with other structures (critical or not) that can contribute to normal functioning and overcoming adverse climate events. Meteorological events occur regardless of administrative subdivisions (municipalities, provinces, regions, or nations) in which territory has been divided or to which governance has been attributed.

In summary, the nature of climate change "requires" a paradigm shift that involves overcoming the division of administrative responsibilities in favor of an approach based on defining climatic areas subject to the same type of evolution. Adopting coordination and intervention mechanisms that surpass administrative divisions, not only for emergencies but also for daily management of resilience-enhancement projects, could allow addressing climate threats according to the natural patterns in which they occur.

The second consideration is related to risk analysis. It is necessary to improve risk analysis methods for better forecasting the evolution of climate events; these methods should use "continuous" updating of data and dynamic analysis of phenomena, rather than considering the events that have occurred. There is also a growing trend toward the adoption of quantitative methods of risk analysis as they allow comparison of impacts resulting from heterogeneous causes [7].

The complexity of interactions between critical infrastructures and climate events requires adopting a multifactorial risk approach to the extent of factors not considered in the past [8]. These aspects make it urgent to strengthen studies and research in this area.

A paradigm shift is also desirable to evolve from the concept of resilience of individual critical infrastructures to that of service resilience ensured by critical infrastructures or multiple critical infrastructures. This change would allow greater flexibility in addressing critical infrastructures' resilience issues. This paradigm shift should be associated with governance capable of "absorbing" inevitable adjustments and maximizing results.

Finally, it is necessary to emphasize that all the previous considerations presuppose the existence of adequate funds to plan and implement interventions within the expected timeframes and methods. The allocation of funds, public and/or private, to counter the effects of climate change on critical infrastructures goes beyond the scope of this work but, it is necessary to highlight it as the first prerequisite.

4   Classification of Threats Related to Climate Change

To manage risks related to climate threats, it is essential to have a reference classification of these threats, at least of the fundamental ones as we know them today. This awareness will assist competent entities (infrastructure managers, security managers) in considering the impacts that each of these threats could have on specific infrastructure and in managing related prevention and mitigation activities for potential events that degrade the availability and quality of service.

Below is a functional table schema for analyzing impacts in the face of threats attributable to climate change. The first column presents a list of threats based on Appendix A of Delegated Regulation (EU) 2021/2139, [9] which provides a classification of climate-related hazards. For each type of CI (analyzed in the following sections) the second column will associate potential impacts that these threats can generate on the infrastructure (Table 1).

Table 1. Classification of Climate-Related Hazards

CLIMATE-RELATED HAZARDS	POTENTIAL IMPACTS (to be specified for each sector)
TEMPERATURE	
CHRONIC	
CHANGING TEMPERATURE (AIR, FRESHWATER, MARINE WATER)	
HEAT STRESS	
TEMPERATURE VARIABILITY	
PERMAFROST THAWING	

(continued)

Table 1. (*continued*)

CLIMATE-RELATED HAZARDS	POTENTIAL IMPACTS (to be specified for each sector)
ACUTE	
HEAT WAVE	
COLD WAVE/FROST	
WILDFIRE	
WIND	
CHRONIC	
CHANGING WIND PATTERNS	
ACUTE	
CYCLONE, HURRICANE, TYPHOON	
STORM (INCLUDING BLIZZARDS, DUST AND SANDSTORMS)	
TORNADO	
WATER	
CHRONIC	
CHANGING PRECIPITATION PATTERNS AND TYPES (RAIN, HAIL, SNOW/ICE)	
PRECIPITATION OR HYDROLOGICAL VARIABILITY	
OCEAN ACIDIFICATION	
SALINE INTRUSION	
SEA LEVEL RISE	
WATER STRESS	
ACUTE	
DROUGHT	
HEAVY PRECIPITATION (RAIN, HAIL, SNOW/ICE)	
FLOOD (COASTAL, FLUVIAL, PLUVIAL, GROUND WATER)	
GLACIAL LAKE OUTBURST	
SOIL (SOLID-MASS)	
CHRONIC	
COASTAL EROSION	
SOIL DEGRADATION	
SOIL EROSION	

(*continued*)

Table 1. (*continued*)

CLIMATE-RELATED HAZARDS	POTENTIAL IMPACTS (to be specified for each sector)
SOLIFLUCTION	
ACUTE	
AVALANCHE	
LANDSLIDE	
SUBSIDENCE	

In managing climate risks it is crucial to be able to address both chronic and acute events, which can be known from recent history, and consider phenomena characterized by a broader temporal development, requiring continuous monitoring of their growth intensity. Identification, where applicable, of the threshold beyond which the respective threats can manifest with impacts of various scales, also needs to be established.

In this context, activities related to the construction, development, and maintenance of infrastructure providing these services can integrate the temporal dynamics of climate threats and their forecasts concerning critical thresholds, ensuring the resilience of the service.

Awareness of threats attributable to climate change affecting critical infrastructures that provide essential services is undoubtedly the first step in increasing the resilience of such infrastructure. To develop appropriate approaches to climate risk management, it is necessary to:

– Possess a data collection and processing system for climate change to continuously monitor potential threats.
– Develop analysis and forecasting capabilities for phenomena that contribute to knowledge influencing the design of new infrastructure or adaptation of existing ones (materials, processes, implementation techniques, anomaly monitoring and management systems) and planning for their development (construction criteria, secure settlement areas, etc.).

5   Climate Change and Digital Infrastructures

This paragraph endeavors to undertake an examination of the present state of digital infrastructures concerning the theme of climate change. These infrastructures assume a pivotal role in furnishing services to both public and private organizations, proffering indispensable systems for communication, data processing and management, and service control.

A data center, also referred to as a Data Processing Center (DPC), serves as the nucleus of an organization's digital infrastructure. The security of such structures is foundational, given their management of data integral to business operations. Measures encompassing information safeguarding, prevention of unauthorized access, and mitigation of cyber threats are accorded priority to ensure the dependability and uninterrupted functionality of data center operations.

The foundations of such a structure rest upon several key components:

- **Network Infrastructure**
- **Storage Infrastructure**
- **Computing Resources**

Notably, climate change poses potential detrimental impacts on data centers; the effects of such phenomena may compromise the physical integrity of structures and the continuous operational functionality of systems.

Before delineating the primary strategies implemented within these parameters, it is imperative to possess a clear comprehension of the climatic phenomena that could significantly impede the operation of a data center. With escalating temperatures, the efficacy of building cooling systems diminishes, resulting in heightened energy consumption [10]. Moreover, drought conditions pose challenges to the operation of cooling systems, particularly for larger data centers. Systems employing cooling towers necessitate substantial water usage, and extended periods of drought could severely challenge the management of the water resources that sustain them [11]. Noteworthy efforts have been undertaken by companies such as Google, Microsoft, and Apple to ensure augmented water supply to their data centers through water treatment plants. Collaboration with water services, water recycling initiatives, and the adoption of cooling systems with reduced water consumption have been proposed for this purpose.

Furthermore, an overheated data center could render itself more susceptible to cyberattacks: findings from a study conducted in 2015 [12] suggest that heat emissions could be exploited to breach computer systems. Conversely, abrupt temperature drops may lead to performance deterioration owing to phenomena like freezing rain, which occurs when temperatures plummet significantly below zero, resulting in the freezing of electrical infrastructure and transmission cables.

Such disruptions could exert a substantial impact on the operation of a data center, leading to sudden halts in activity and potential data loss. Another noteworthy impact associated with rainfall pertains to the disconnection of high-frequency wireless networks due to rain shading. This phenomenon occurs when intense precipitation interferes with the signal frequencies employed in wireless communications, thereby disrupting data transmission, and causing connectivity interruptions. In addition to the damage inflicted upon data centers by climate change, there exists a mounting environmental impact, thereby engendering a sort of self-perpetuating cycle. Moreover, owing to the heat generated by server operations, data centers can contribute to urban heat accumulation in their vicinity, thereby fostering the emergence of 'heat islands'—regions characterized by higher temperatures compared to their surrounding areas.

The energy efficiency of a data center can be gauged through an internationally recognized standard indicator termed Power Usage Effectiveness (PUE) [13], formulated by The Green Grid. This metric assesses the ratio between the total energy consumption of a data center, inclusive of cooling, and the energy usage attributed solely to IT equipment. Mitigating the ecological footprint of Data Processing Centers (DPCs) by reducing the PUE index of a data center could constitute a commendable objective, particularly because average PUE levels have remained stagnant over the past four years. Within a context wherein the European Union has prioritized the transition towards more sustainable structures, the issue of energy efficiency within data centers assumes prominence, aligning with the broader theme of ecological transition as a strategic imperative. In response to this imperative, the European Commission has, over several years, been exploring a suite of measures aimed at enhancing the energy efficiency of data centers.

In response to the escalating energy consumption witnessed within data centers and the ensuing environmental, economic, and energy security ramifications, the Joint Research Center (JRC) [14] of the Commission has formulated a "Code of Conduct for Energy Efficiency in Data Center" (EU DC CoC) [15]. This framework aims to guide operators and proprietors of Data Processing Centers (DPCs) towards judicious reduction of energy consumption, thereby realizing economic benefits without compromising the functionality of these structures.

Within this initiative, three pivotal areas of interest have been identified as foundational for delineating criteria for Green Public Procurement:

The first area, the Performance of ICT Systems, focuses on the performance of computer systems and information technologies deployed within data centers. Aspects encompassing energy efficiency, workload management, and waste reduction are deemed critical to fostering a positive environmental impact. Reducing greenhouse gas emissions stemming from data center activities assumes paramount significance in contributing towards global mitigation endeavors. The objective is to empower clients to select suppliers and bidders evincing a tangible commitment to environmental sustainability and concentrating efforts on areas where the most substantial improvements can be realized both in terms of environmental impact and economic feasibility. The ensuing table offers a summarized perspective of plausible impacts of threats arising from climate change on critical infrastructures within the telecommunications sector. Hence, for this endeavor, threats deemed likely to impact operability and costs are duly considered. It is underscored that, given the ongoing evolution of this domain, the table presented below should be perceived as a dynamic tool, subject to periodic revision to incorporate any emerging threats pertinent to digital infrastructures [14, 12] (Table 2).

Table 2. Climate Change Impacts on Digital Infrastructure

Climate Change-Related Threats -	Impacts on IT and Telecommunications Services
TEMPERATURE	
CHRONIC	
TEMPERATURE CHANGES (AIR, FRESHWATER, SEAWATER)	• *Increased cooling costs for data centers* • *Increased operating temperature of network equipment, with possible malfunctions or premature failures* • *Reduced lifespan of equipment*
HEAT STRESS	• *Increased cooling costs for data centers* • *Increased operating temperature of network equipment, with possible malfunctions or premature failures* • *Reduced lifespan of equipment*

(*continued*)

Table 2. (*continued*)

Climate Change-Related Threats -	Impacts on IT and Telecommunications Services
VARIABILITY IN TEMPERATURE	*N.A*
THAWING OF PERMAFROST	*N.A*
ACUTE	
HEATWAVES	• *Increased cooling costs for data centers* • *Increased operating temperature of network equipment, with possible malfunctions or premature failures* • *Reduced lifespan of equipment*
COLD WAVES/FROST	• *Performance degradation (icing)* • *Risks due to impact on the electrical grid*
WILDFIRE	• *Structural damage to equipment (fibers, mobile stations, data centers)* • *Possible disconnections due to deterioration of cables and/or equipment*
WIND	
CHRONIC	
CHANGE IN WIND PATTERNS	• *Structural damage to cell towers and telephone poles due to wind pressure or impact with debris* • *Reduced operability* • *Deterioration of service quality (for example, due to misalignment of microwave receivers)*
ACUTE	
CYCLONES, HURRICANES, TYPHOONS	• *Structural damage to cell towers and telephone poles due to wind pressure or impact with debris* • *Reduced operability* • *Deterioration of service quality (for example, due to misalignment of microwave receivers)*
STORMS (INCLUDES SNOWSTORMS, DUST, AND SANDSTORMS)	• *Structural damage to cell towers and telephone poles due to wind pressure or impact with debris* • *Reduced operability* • *Deterioration of service quality (for example, due to misalignment of microwave receivers)*
TORNADOES	• *Structural damage to cell towers and telephone poles due to wind pressure or impact with debris* • *Reduced operability* • *Deterioration of service quality (for example, due to misalignment of microwave receivers)*
WATER	
CHRONIC	
CHANGE IN PRECIPITATION PATTERNS AND TYPES (RAIN, HAIL, SNOW/ICE)	
RAINFALL AND/OR HYDROLOGICAL VARIABILITY	• *Structural damage to equipment (cables, mobile stations, data centers) due to flooding, corrosion, etc* • *Disconnections on very high-frequency wireless networks due to "rain shading"*
OCEAN ACIDIFICATION	*N.A*
SALINE INTRUSION	*N.A*

(*continued*)

Table 2. (*continued*)

Climate Change-Related Threats -	Impacts on IT and Telecommunications Services
SEA-LEVEL RISE	*N.A*
WATER STRESS	*N.A*
ACUTE	
DROUGHT	• *Lower water availability for cooling data centers* • *Soil subsidence and infrastructure instability*
HEAVY PRECIPITATION (RAIN, HAIL, SNOW/ICE)	• *Structural damage to equipment (cables, mobile stations, data centers) due to flooding, corrosion, etc* • *Disconnections on very high frequency wireless networks due to "rain shading"*
FLOOD (COASTAL, RIVER, PLUVIAL, UNDERGROUND)	• *Structural damage to equipment (cables, mobile stations, data centers) due to flooding, corrosion, etc*
GLACIAL LAKES COLLAPSE	*N.A*
SOIL (SOLID MASS)	
CHRONIC	
COASTAL EROSION	*N.A*
SOIL DEGRADATION	*N.A*
SOIL EROSION	*N.A*
SOLIFLUCTION	*N.A*
ACUTE	
AVALANCHES	*N.A*
LANDSLIDES	• *Structural damage to equipment (fibers, mobile stations, data centres)*
SUBSIDENCE	*N.A*

6   Climate Change and Electricity Infrastructures

Although assessing the impact of climate change on the Energy sector is considered a priority activity, many gaps persist in understanding the impact of climate change threats on this infrastructure. Some believe that extreme weather events have become more frequent since the beginning of this millennium, while others paradoxically argue the opposite: the statistics reported by Eurelectric [2] seem to dispel any doubts.

All documents produced by stakeholders on climate impact and its effects tend to emphasize this impact. The report by [16] is quite clear in judging American electrical infrastructure as obsolete in the face of climate impact: '*The country's stressed and aging electrical infrastructure was built for the climate of the past, experts say*'. The impact of fires, heatwaves, cold spells, and severe storms induced by climate change can destroy power grids, continues the source, citing Hurricane Ida in Louisiana and the winter storm in Texas (2021) as demarcating events, leading to the collapse of the electrical infrastructure and the consequent loss of lifestyle and human lives. According to this source, 96% of the electrical losses in 2020 were due to weather events; moreover, the growth of electrical disruptions from 2000 to 2019 is around 96% and can be attributed almost exclusively to climate effects.

Despite the proclamations of some experts, there are gaps in understanding how natural disasters and climate change will impact renewable energy sources, as well as the potential environmental impacts of the growing demand for water for cooling. For example, in Italy, the concept of a Security Operation Center (SOC) for managing cybersecurity risks has been introduced, while emergencies related to threats from climate change are handled on a case-by-case basis depending on the nature of the threat, using civil protection authorities.

In the period 2007—2015, Italy, along with Spain, recorded the lowest level of infrastructure spending among the major European countries. Referring to electrical infrastructure [16] points out that adverse weather conditions and natural disasters tend to expose different weaknesses in electrical systems. Three of these main influences - heat, cold, and severe storms - are particularly affecting the southern areas of the temperate belt of the planet and have the potential to cause much more damage in the future. For example [17], notes that last winter in Texas, temperatures reached record lows below zero in some cities, and 4.5 million customers across the state were left without electricity.

For the outlined risks, the OECD [17] recommends that disclosing climate risks can help raise awareness and encourage efforts to reduce climate-related risks for infrastructure but must be adapted to national circumstances. "Climate change risks are diverse, vary depending on national circumstances, and there are multiple possible metrics for measuring progress in addressing such risks… Public policies promoting resilience include public procurement processes that consider climate resilience when comparing competing bids, taking into account costs over the life of the asset in alternative scenarios… Public finances can be used to mobilize private financing for climate-resilient infrastructure. For example, a publicly funded analysis of the risks faced by the port of Cartagena in Colombia has motivated investments to manage climate risks. Public finances can thus be used to mobilize private financing for climate-resilient infrastructure".

An authoritative and fairly recent review of the resilience of the electrical system in conditions far from normality was carried out by RSE [18]. In the words of the preface author of this report, Stefano Besseghini, *'Resilience comes into play when the operating conditions of the system are far from ordinary and calls on all possible resources that the system can draw upon to ensure the fulfillment of its functions'*. The report has been deliberately extended with a popular science approach, given the lack of a complete and accessible text on the subject and presents some specific tools that RSE has developed to support the resilience of the Italian electrical system.

According to Besseghini, the climate emergency is 'an exogenous cause of anthropic origin… Particularly dangerous for its ability to undermine system security in a very unpredictable way and with the potential to inflict damage simultaneously on multiple fronts… Perhaps the worst-case scenario even for a resilient system'. Consequently, the System Research will have to make great efforts in the field of resilience and promote dialogue among operators [17].

7 Climate Change and the Healthcare System

The healthcare system is part of critical infrastructures, which includes systems providing essential services for the economy, security, and stability of a nation (such as communication services, energy, information technology, transportation, and water systems) and, therefore, must be safeguarded from disasters [19, 20].

The main direct impacts on the healthcare system, in terms of operability and costs, resulting from threats related to climate change, often shared with other infrastructures and frequently stemming from them, are listed in their table.

The healthcare system has the particularity of being extensively interconnected with all other critical infrastructures. Therefore, climate change can have strong impacts on the healthcare system, both directly and indirectly, through a series of interdependencies as illustrated in the following diagram (Fig. 2).

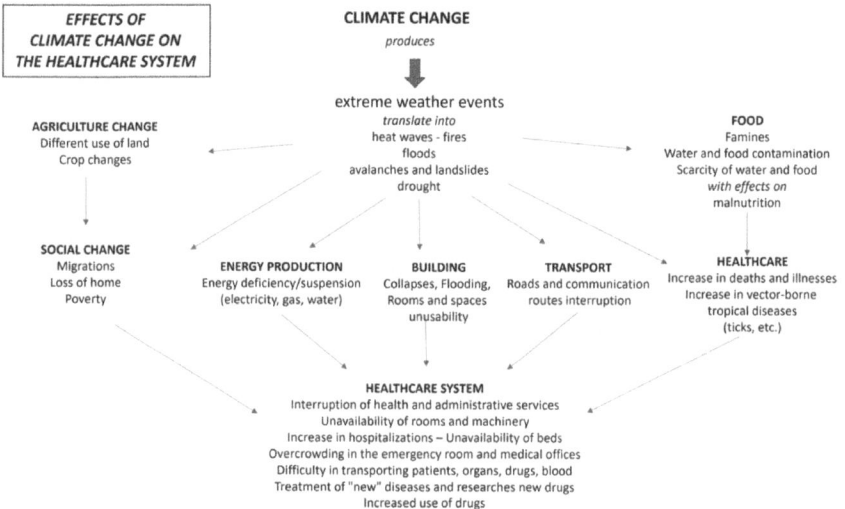

Fig. 2. Effects of Climate Change on the Healthcare System

Indirect impacts are primarily due to the close interconnection with other critical infrastructures, the effects produced by climate change on human health, the consequences of social changes, and the repercussions due to the effects transmitted by other infrastructures that are in turn impacted by changes, in a sort of "domino effect": for example, extreme events such as floods, storms, etc., can interrupt communication routes (roads, railways, planes, ships, etc.), and this, in turn, can cause difficulties in transporting patients, organs, blood, medicine, as well as the interruption of energy sources and telecommunication, leading to the halt or suspension of hospital activities [21].

The effects on human health produced by climate change have a significant direct impact on the healthcare system, such as diseases related to heatwaves, unexpected cold spells, and vectors favored by such conditions (e.g., ticks) [22].

Furthermore, it is essential to consider that a significant fallout of indirect effects is linked to social change, including migrations, food, and energy issues.

To mitigate the individual impacts represented, appropriate countermeasures can be implemented. However, it is evident that the simultaneous occurrence of all events, in a kind of "swiss cheese" effect according to the James Reason model, would lead to a collapse of the healthcare system. As mentioned earlier, following "acute" climatic events and the persistence of "chronic" events, the hospital structure can suffer physical and structural damage, resulting in a reduction or even a blockage of normal activities.

Some actions taken to mitigate climate change in various fields, from energy to transportation to urban environments, bring direct benefits such as reducing greenhouse gas emissions but can also have repercussions in terms of human health:

– Increasing green spaces in urban areas, leads to a decrease in air pollution, improved air quality, and higher levels of physical activity (with benefits for physical and mental health) [23].
– Changing nutrition patterns (reducing meat consumption) leads to the prevention of diseases transmitted by animals (zoonoses) and a decrease in the burden of chronic diseases (e.g., cardiovascular).

On the other hand, the healthcare system can be responsible for significant climate-altering emissions. For example, in a hospital, thermal energy represents about 2/3 of total energy consumption, being used to meet the needs of medical activities (operation of medical equipment, sterilization, etc.). Architecture can contribute to mitigating this situation and reduce environmental impact while saving energy: measures can be taken to reduce emissions [24–27].

8   Climate Change Impact on Drinking Water and Wastewater Infrastructures

This type of critical infrastructure is particularly relevant because water is one of the essential components for life on planet Earth, and humans depend on it for all their activities [28, 29]. Drinking water resources are internationally relevant because they can lead to tensions and conflicts among countries [30].

When defining the types of infrastructures concerning drinking water and wastewater, simplifications must be made because the infrastructures are complex and extend over vast territories, sometimes involving several countries.

Drinking water distribution plants are subject to specific regulations to ensure the absence of health risks for users. These requirements are out of the scope of the present work, and the focus is on climatic threats that could alter the quality and availability of water.

Similar considerations are also valid for wastewater treatment plants, regulated in almost all countries to reduce pollution that in this case, could pose significant health risks. The focus is on the potential impacts of climate change on these types of facilities and consequently increased risks. The classification of climate threats for this critical infrastructure type is chronic and acute.

Regarding the risk analysis of this infrastructure type, drinking water and wastewater have constantly been monitored to verify compliance with parameters set by regulations. Monitoring allows for "continuous" risk analysis, albeit limited to some parameters required for correct operation. Integration of other risk indicators related to climate threats may be "easier" for these facilities. As a purely illustrative example, monitoring the increase of certain pollutants, such as soil or plants, could be premonitory of an acute event such as a landslide.

The determination of these new risk indicators depends on the type of facility and its location in the territory, but it fits into a context that is already sensitive to risk management and its evolutions.

For this type of critical infrastructure, one can hope for the convergence of measures to reduce the effects of acute events, thus enhancing infrastructure resilience, with the possibility of using the same interventions for improvements related to chronic climate threats. For example, building reservoirs to contain excess water in the event of floods would also, if properly implemented, provide water reserves for use during drought. Similarly, in the long term, water reservoirs and other interventions, such as creating green areas, can mitigate climate evolution in a region.

Drinking water and wastewater infrastructures are facilities characterized by a constant need for maintenance that must always be ensured because breakdowns and malfunctions can threaten human health. High priority should be given to all those maintenance operations that are useful in counteracting climate-related threats, chronic or acute. For example, the scheduling of maintenance interventions should consider the possible concomitance of acute events, such as droughts or periods with an elevated risk of flooding. The increasing frequency of acute events makes it necessary to plan differently from what is scheduled since increasing the number of acute events accelerates and modifies the wear and tear of the systems and the frequency of extraordinary maintenance operations [31]. All this entails a higher cost, which must be anticipated and appropriately financed.

In addition, implementation of measures to reduce the impacts of climate threats also requires, in most cases, complex works that often cover large areas, have relevant costs, and lead times. The last two characteristics represent relevant constraints for the timely implementation of adaptation measures. Therefore, it is important to adopt a strategy that allows to proceed within the framework of an overall project of all interventions, by successive implementations, each representing a positive result in risk reduction. The strategy depends on the specific contexts (national, regional, etc.) in which these critical infrastructures are present. The availability of economic and/or technical resources and regulatory constraints that may hinder the implementation of interventions is highly dependent on context factors.

In designing and implementing retrofitting or new installations, it is remarkable to consider that climatic changes can lead to a significant variation in the operating parameters of the installations. Shifting climatic zones, for example, the placement of large areas of the Mediterranean zone in the subtropical or tropical area as opposed to the previous temperate zone classification, determines a rise in temperature, an increase in wind strength, and an increase in the intensity and frequency of rainfall. These changes require design parameters that partially derive from the experience of known climate zones (e.g. subtropical or tropical). Some design parameters will be determined in new ways considering the speed of climate change.

A detailed list of interventions to counter climate threats highlights that various measures are recommendable to address multiple types of threats, which is of significant interest to planners of interventions that, as already emphasized, incur high costs and substantial implementation times. Another approach criterion is the assurance of the continuity of the service provided by these CIs; impacts can be expressed in terms of discontinuity and alteration of essential parameters to ensure the service itself. Service continuity also makes it possible to highlight the suggestion of alternative measures to deal with several types of threats, and this is of interest to the planners of the interventions that, as already highlighted, have relevant costs and significant timeframes for their implementation.

9 Direct and Indirect Interdependence Among Different Infrastructures as a Consequence of Climatic Threats

To understand the cascading impacts of events related to climatic threats on interconnected infrastructure systems, it is necessary to identify the interdependencies among various infrastructures. The modeling of interdependencies among different infrastructures began in the early 2000s. Of historical significance is the work "Identifying, Understanding, and Analyzing Critical Infrastructure Interdependencies", Rinaldi et al. 2001 [32]. The degree to which infrastructures are coupled or connected strongly influences their operational characteristics. Some connections are weak and thus relatively flexible, while others are strong, providing little or no flexibility for the system's response to changing conditions or failures that may exacerbate problems or transfer from one infrastructure to another. These connections can be physical, informational, related to geographical location, or of a logical nature. Interdependencies and resulting infrastructure topologies can create subtle interactions and feedback mechanisms that often lead to unintended behaviors and consequences during disruptions to the proper functioning of an infrastructure.

Updating the risk assessment to include mitigation and adaptation actions to threats related to climate change, once identified, and ensuring that the new risks that may arise are reflected in the risk analysis methods for better forecasting the consequences of climate events. It is also essential to consider the use of a series of climate risk scenarios as a tool to identify these cascading risks. A further complication arises from the fact that in recent years, as extensively discussed in previous paragraphs, threats and consequently possible impacts are mainly attributable to climate change, as shown in Fig. 3 [33].

By facilitating the development of a common and shared understanding of collective risks related to climate change, it is possible to establish the foundations for cooperation and coordination among the various organizations that characterize them. A common approach to managing the uncertainty of the failure of infrastructure systems in the face of climate change hazards is to try to characterize the cause-and-effect behavior of interdependencies. Therefore, to better prepare for an uncertain future that includes climate change, managers should consider the complexity of cascading service failures and implement additional strategies appropriate for the intricate landscape of the framework.

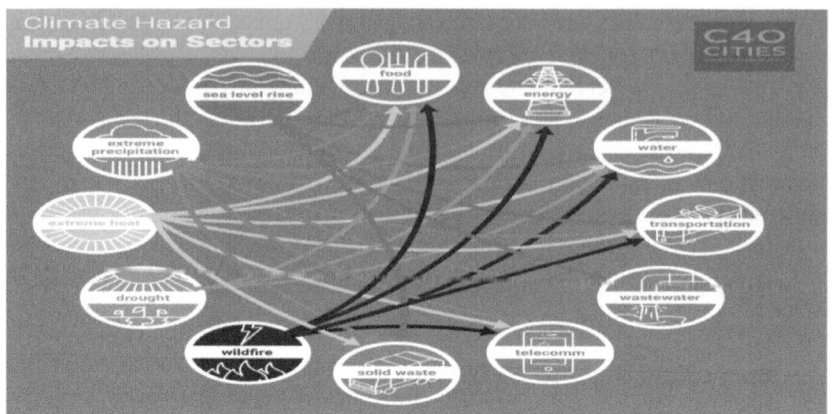

Fig. 3. Impact of Climatic Threats on CIs in different sectors – (from C40 Cities Report)

10   Conclusions

This work aims to qualitatively list the effects of individual climatic threats on the referenced Critical Infrastructures (CIs), omitting the chain effects of direct physical impacts of climate change due to the complexity of socioeconomic systems. The theme of chain effects has been addressed only in generic terms. Another aspect treated generically is that of CI design parameters. With a changing climate, what constitutes an "acute" or "chronic" event today may have different characteristics over time, necessitating different design parameters or a comprehensive revision of CI design.

This work represents an initial attempt to address the topic of CI Resilience to climate change. As outlined in paragraph 1, the distinctive feature of climate resilience is that infrastructure must be planned, designed, constructed, and operated to anticipate and adapt to changing climate conditions. The ideal solution requires withstanding, responding to, and recovering quickly from disruptions caused by climatic conditions, but achieving this is challenging due to the uncertainty of future climatic and socioeconomic conditions. Ensuring climate resilience is an ongoing process throughout the infrastructure's lifespan.

References

1. UNDRR, «Making Critical Infrastructure Resilient,» https://www.undrr.org/media/48327/download?startDownload=true, 2020
2. Eurelectric, The Coming Storm, Eurelectric, December 2022
3. Axelos, «Prince2 -Project management,» https://www.axelos.com/certifications/propath/prince2-project-management
4. ISACA, «COBIT 5 Control Objectives for Information and related Technology,» https://www.isaca.org/resources/cobit
5. European Commission, «PM2 Project management Methodology,» https://pm2.europa.eu/index_en
6. ISO, «ISO 21500:2021 Project Programme and Portfolio management- Context and concepts,» https://www.iso.org/standard/75704.html

7. Vose, D.: Risk Analysis: a quantitative guide, 3rd Ed., Wiley (2009)
8. Amos, N., Krausmann, E.: «How to use RAPID-N methodology models, technical information and tutorials,» Ufficio delle pubblicazioni dell'Unione eurpoea (2022)
9. EU COMMISSION, «Commission delegated Regulation (EU) 2021/2139 of 4 June 2021 supplementing Regulation 2020/852 of European Parliament,» https://eur-lex.europa.eu/legal-content/EN/TXT/PDF/?uri=CELEX:32021R2139, (2021)
10. SemiconductorEngineering,«https://semiengineering.com/mapping-heat-across-a-system/,»
11. IOPScience «The environmental footprint of data centers in the United States (iop-science.iop.org), »
12. Scientific American «A Computer's Heat Could Divulge Top Secrets - Scientific American, » (2015)
13. Statista «Data center average annual PUE worldwide 2022 | Statista, »
14. Joint Research Centre «JRC Publications Repository - Development of the EU Green Public Procurement (GPP) Criteria for Data Centres, Server Rooms and Cloud Services (europa.eu), »
15. EU COMMISSION«https://green-business.ec.europa.eu/green-public-procurement/gpp-criteria-and-requirements_en,»
16. Sypher, C.: «Designing for the future: power grids must adapt to climate change,» American Public Media, Saint Paul, Minnesota (2021)
17. OECD, «Climate-resilient Infrastructure, Policy Perspectives,» OECD, December 2018
18. Ricerca sul Sistema Elettrico, «Resilienza del Sistema Elettrico,» Alkes, S. Giuliano Milanese (2017)
19. Comunicazione della Commissione al Parlamento europeo, «Strategia dell'UE di adattamento ai cambiamenti climatici,». http://eurlex.europa.eu/legal-content/it/TXT/?uri=CELEX%3A5 2013DC0216
20. Ministero dell'Ambiente e della Tutela del Territorio e del Mare, «Strategia nazionale di adattamento ai cambiamenti climatici,». http://www.minambiente.it/notizie/strategia-nazion ale-di-adattamento-aicambiamenti-climatici-0
21. Cataldo, A.: «Gestione ospedaliera nella pianificazione dell'emergenza in caso di catastrofi,». https://nursetimes.org/gestione-ospedaliera-nella-pianificazione-dellemergenza-caso-catastrofi/20594
22. P. Michelozzi, «Cambiamenti climatici e salute: gli interventi di adattamento e mitigazione,». https://www.politichesanitarie.it/archivio/752/articoli/8506
23. Biblus, «Edifici mangia smog, cosa sono? Un esempio concreto,» 10 December 2018. https://biblus.acca.it/edifici-mangia-smog/
24. N. P. Beatley T., «Biophilic cities are sustainable, resilient cities,» https://www.researchgate.net/publication/277377188_Biophilic_Cities_Are_Sustainable_Resilient_Cities
25. CostruireBio, «L'Architettura Bioclimatica: Caratteristiche e Progettazione,» 13 December 2021. https://www.costruirebio.it/architettura-bioclimatica/
26. CMCC, «I cambiamenti climatici minacciano la sicurezza di edifici e infrastrutture in Europa,» https://www.cmcc.it/it/articolo/i-cambiamenti-climatici-minacciano-la-sicurezza-di-edifici-e-infrastrutture-in-europa
27. L. Rollino, «La complessa progettazione impiantistica degli ospedali: qualche consiglio in ottica post-covid,» 07 July 2020. https://www.ingenio-web.it/articoli/la-complessa-progettaz ione-impiantistica-degli-ospedali-qualche-consiglio-in-ottica-post-covid/
28. UNESCO, «The United Nations World Water Development Report 2021: valuing water; facts and figures,» https://unesdoc.unesco.org/ark:/48223/pf0000375751, (2021)
29. UNESCO, «The United Nations World Water Development Report 2021: valuing water,» https://unesdoc.unesco.org/ark:/48223/pf0000375975, 2021

30. U. N. W. W. A. P. o. UNESCO, «Transboundary water governance and climate change adaptation,» https://unesdoc.unesco.org/ark:/48223/pf0000235678/PDF/235678eng.pdf.multi, (2015)

31. Kirchoff, C., Peter, G., Mullin, C., Watson, P.: «Resilience of Wastewater and Drinking Water Systems,» UCONN, Mansfield, TN, USA (2018)

32. Steven, M.R., Rinaldi, M., Peerenboim, P.J., Kelly, T.K.: «Identifying, understanding, and analyzing critical infrastructure interdependencies,» IEEE Control Syst. Mag. **21**(6), 11–25 (2001)

33. C40 Cities Climate Leadership Group, AECOM, «C40 Infrastructure Interdependencies and Climate Risks report,» AECOM (2017)

34. Bologna, S., et al.: https://infrastrutturecritiche.it/resilienza-delle-infrastrutture-critiche-e-cambiamenti-climatici-2, Accessed Nov 2024

Questioning the Myth: Investigating ICS Traffic Homogeneity from an Anomaly Detection Perspective

Franka Schuster[(✉)] and Hartmut König

Brandenburg University of Technology Cottbus-Senftenberg, Cottbus, Germany
{franka.schuster,hartmut.koenig}@b-tu.de

Abstract. Attack detection in industrial control systems (ICS) using machine learning (ML) is a frequently addressed problem. Due to the lack of real-world traffic data in this area, the design and evaluation of attack detection approaches for operational technology (OT) traffic often exclusively rely on public datasets generated from testbeds. A frequently pursued approach is anomaly detection identifying attacks as deviations from normal activities. Its potential is usually motivated by the homogeneity of ICS communication, although this assumption has hardly been proven. In this work, we examine how representative currently available OT traffic datasets are by comparing detection-relevant characteristics with OT traffic captured in three real OT networks. Furthermore, we quantify the homogeneity degree of all datasets from the perspective of self-learning anomaly detection systems when applied to this traffic. From both analyses, we derive implications for the design and evaluation of such systems and their reliable operation in real OT networks.

Keywords: ICS/CPS Traffic Homogeneity · Public Dataset Representativeness · Anomaly Detection Requirements

1 Motivation

Critical infrastructures have become an important target for attacks [37]. Accordingly, identifying malicious activity in these networks, which mainly rely on operational technology (OT)[1] to manage complex physical processes, is of paramount importance. For this reason, a variety of detection approaches for OT networks have been proposed in research. Unfortunately, scientists usually do not have access to real OT facilities. They use data from testbeds that are either already available or generated by them. Due to a lack of real data they cannot assess the quality of the selected testbed data. In the worst case, they develop a detection approach that works well on the generated data, but will fail with realistic input data. As a result, there is now a plethora of approaches that neither were

---

[1] In the following, we use OT as a generic name for terms such as cyber-physical systems(CPS) and industrial control systems (ICS), which are defined differently.

© The Author(s), under exclusive license to Springer Nature Switzerland AG 2025
G. Oliva et al. (Eds.): CRITIS 2024, LNCS 15549, pp. 21–42, 2025.
https://doi.org/10.1007/978-3-031-84260-3_2

evaluated on real data nor applied in real scenarios [58]. One important app-roach for the identification of attacks in OT networks are anomaly detection systems. Their great potential for OT in difference to information technology (IT) networks is often motivated by the assumption that OT events and traffic are of very homogeneous[2] nature [10, 16, 58]. This myth, however, has never been properly questioned or even quantified. At the same time, anomaly detection sys-tems directly applied on network traffic play a minor role in research [58]. Most approaches depend on the availability of pre-extracted and well-structured pro-cess data that in general cannot be found in real-world infrastructures[3]. Direct network traffic analyses with only normal communication required for configu-ration is a tremendous advantage for detection systems. Thus, they can operate independently of other pre-processing systems and do not rely on attack samples for training. This makes the approach particularly suitable for critical infras-tructure networks whose high availability requirements usually neither allow the reconfiguration of current network settings nor accept the initiation of intrusions to produce training traffic including attacks. Therefore, the scope of this work is to support the development of such one-class trained anomaly detection systems directly applied to network traffic.

Contribution. For this, we examine the following:

- We evaluate how *representative* currently available OT datasets are by com-paring their traffic with captures from three real networks. The measurements from the real networks can serve as a reference for future approaches.
- We quantify the *homogeneity* of traffic over time from the anomaly detection perspective defining a specific measure. The measure can be used to assess and express the difficulty to model a given traffic dataset for an anomaly detection purpose and in future to relate the degree of homogeneity of new public datasets to previous ones and real OT traffic.
- From the observed findings of representativeness and homogeneity we work out *implications* for the design and evaluation of traffic-based anomaly detec-tion systems to help developers to reason and assess their systems regarding the application in real-world OT networks.

Remainder. In Sect. 2, we introduce the considered datasets. Thereafter in Sect. 3, we explore the characteristics of testbed traffic and real OT commu-nication. In Sect. 4, we take the perspective of anomaly detection systems and examine the traffic homogeneity by means of the saturation of feature samples derived from the traffic as usual input for such detection systems. We conclude in Sect. 5 by outlining the main implications drawn from our findings for creating OT anomaly detection systems applicable also to real-world infrastructures.

---

[2] or *regular*.

[3] This is a fundamental finding of the authors after reviewing the existence and capabilities of log systems (historians) in numerous real-world critical OT networks including power plants, energy distribution networks, and railway systems.

2   Datasets

The selection of the datasets is determined by the goals of our investigations, which are (1) to assess how representative available OT datasets are for real OT traffic characteristics and (2) to give insights in real OT traffic that are relevant for the design and evaluation of anomaly detection systems. Our analysis is therefore based on both public datasets and traffic from three real OT networks.

2.1   Public Datasets

We reviewed existing datasets with regard to (1) providing unpreprocessed (raw) network traffic, (2) including anomalous traffic additional to normal traffic necessary for researchers to evaluate the performance of their detection system, and (3) a labeling of these anomalies on sufficient granularity[4], so that the dataset is indeed usable for the evaluation of detection systems. The results are summarized in Table 1. We identified four datasets relevant for our analysis.

Table 1. Public datasets with OT traffic (selected ones in bold, reused from [48]).

	year	labeled	OT protocol(s)		year	labeled	OT protocol(s)
CyberCity [23]	2013		Modbus, Ethernet/IP	SCADA #1 [13]	2018		Modbus
4SICS [40]	2015		Modbus	QUT S7 (Myers) [38]	2018	●[a]	S7comm
S4x15 ICS [41]	2015		Modbus, BACnet	HVAC [39]	2019		S7comm
Lemay [28]	2016	●	**Modbus**	SWaT [52]	2020		EtherNet/IP, CIP
QUT S7comm [54]	2017	●	**S7comm**	EPIC [52]	2021		Modbus, IEC61850
QUT DNP3 [53]	2018	●	**DNP3, GOOSE**	**WDT** [22]	2021	●	**Modbus**

[a] We omit this dataset because timestamp deviations do not allow a reliable use.

Lemay Dataset (Lemay). These captures [28] have been collected from a simulation of a power grid control system. From the six normal capture files, we analyze the one called `Run1_6RTU` because it is taken from the setting with six Remote Terminal Units (RTUs) for which the attack traffic is generated for. This is the actual relevant normal traffic for researchers to train their detection systems since also in a real-world scenario one would apply a detector in a similar network setup in which it was trained before.

Water Distribution Testbed (WDT) Dataset. This dataset comes from a testbed that emulates a water distribution process by connecting a real subsystem to a simulated one using hardware-in-the-loop technology [22]. The core activity of the process is the water flowing among eight tanks using four programmable logical controllers (PLCs), valves, pumps, pressure and flow sensors. We analyze the entire normal traffic capture from this dataset.

DNP3 Dataset. This traffic collection published by the Queensland University of Technology of Brisbane (QUT) [53] is taken from a testbed of energy transmission stations communicating via the protocols DNP3 and GOOSE. We used control/testing/frequent/slave.pcap as purely normal traffic.

---

[4] We consider a dataset as *sufficiently labeled* if the authors of the dataset either provide a flag for each network packet of the traffic or attack periods are given so precisely that such a labeling can be derived directly by users of the data.

S7comm Dataset. This dataset, also published by QUT, [54] originates from a testbed rebuilding a subprocess of a mining refinery based on communications using the S7comm protocol. Our experiments were conducted on the traffic captured in the file called master.pcap.

ICT Dataset (CIC-IDS17). For also drawing relations to more human-driven IT networks, we use the prominent ICT dataset CIC-IDS17 [42]. Here, the 2017 data is used instead of the 2018 version because the device number is more comparable to the size of the real OT networks. It further includes a designated (and well-documented) normal traffic phase.

2.2   Real-World Datasets

We also focus on three datasets from real OT networks. The traces were recorded in January 2023 in three different networks of a productive lignite-fired power generation infrastructure, which belongs to the class of 500 MW units. For each capture, the tool `tcpdump`[5] was installed on a separated device and attached to a central switch of each network with activated port mirroring[6]. The infrastructure consists of several power plants protected by a demilitarized zone (DMZ). Each plant involes a high number of subprocesses. Figure 1 shows the three capture points. All three traces were recorded in parallel during full and normal power plant operation.

DMZ Dataset (DMZ). This trace was captured in the DMZ of the power generation site. It serves as perimeter network between the individual power plants and the non-OT networks belonging to the overall infrastructure.

Plant Control Dataset (Plant). This capture reflects OT traffic at plant level. It was taken from the network at that point where the data streams of all generation sub-networks are combined and prepared for the process monitoring in the plant's control room.

Steam Production Dataset (Steam). A subprocess of the power generation is the steam production to drive a turbine. The third trace is taken from the network controlling this process. Devices in the respective subnetwork interact as part of the steam control system to regulate and optimize the firing of several steam generators. The steam is then fed into a turbine to generate electricity.

Although the three networks belong to the same infrastructure, they differ fundamentally in the physical processes, the OT equipment, and network organization. In contrast to networks of different infrastructures, this allows not only cross-network comparisons but also level-specific observations within a site.

Two of the public datasets (Lemay and WDT) and one real OT dataset contain communications over the OT protocol Modbus (using port 502), which can be considered as both a widely applied protocol in real networks and the dominant OT protocol considered in academia [12].

---

[5] www.tcpdump.org.

[6] High security regulations of this critical infrastructure do not allow us to publish the traffic due to non-disclosure agreements.

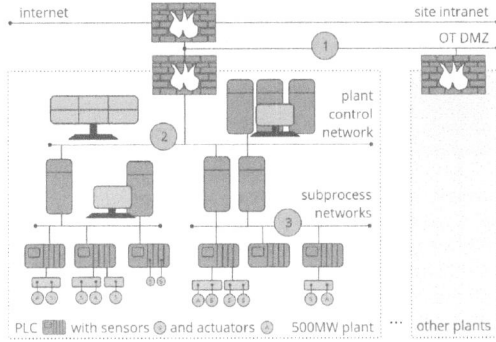

Fig. 1. Real infrastructure with three capture points (reused from [48]).

Normal Network Traffic Only. We emphasize that only normal network traffic is treated in this work for two reasons: (1) This is the traffic part presented to anomaly detection systems in a training phase to configure the detection. (2) Attack traffic provided by public datasets is always provoked by the dataset authors, which is a bias that shall not affect the outcome of our paper.

For a fair comparison, we trimmed all traces to the period of 54 min, which is the duration of the shortest capture used (S7comm dataset). For the sake of reproducibility, we provide the concrete periods at the end of the paper.

3   Real OT Traffic vs. Public Captures

As a first step, we measured basic properties relevant for traffic processing. They are compiled in Table 2. A *network packet* is a containing information to transport a piece of data with the data themselves being called *payload*. A *network flow* is a top view on network traffic. It characterizes and quantifies a communication stream as a sequence of packets defined by five attributes (source and destination IP addresses and ports with IP protocol). The measurements allow us to relate traffic from different OT levels, from OT to IT networks, and to assess the representativeness of public OT datasets for traffic from real sites.

3.1   Real OT Level Findings

From a bottom-up perspective, the real traces contain (a) a dataset with communications of a specific subprocess (steam), which is the steam production as part of driving a turbine for power generation, (b) another set from the highest plant level (plant), in which all subprocesses of the plant, such as lignite preparation, firing, steam production, and turbine regulation, are coordinated to control the overall generation purpose, and (c) traffic from the inter-plant level (DMZ), in which communications from and to the individual plants are regulated.

The steam traffic is the most challenging one regarding flow rate, packet rate, byte rate, and mean packet size. Although it is taken from a single subprocess,

Table 2. Dataset characteristics

	traffic from public OT testbeds or simulations				traffic from real OT networks			IT network
	Lemay	WDT	DNP3	S7comm	DMZ	plant	steam	CIC-IDS17
entire traffic								
# flows	12,397	17,029	23	23	18,473	3,815	253,176	42,982
# packets	123,052	7,341,840	15,843	45,541	4,635,168	131,058	20,118,001	5,809,082
# bytes	14,157,547	479,609,532	2,164,106	6,250,847	1,359,962,189	19,812,716	28,637,438,769	7,212,468,973
∅ packet size	115	65	137	137	293	151	1,423	1,242
# flows / sec	3.826	5.256	0.007	0.007	5.702	1.177	78.141	13.266
# packets / sec	38	2,266	5	14	1,431	40	6,209	1,793
# bytes / sec	4,370	148,028	668	1,929	419,741	6,115	8,838,716	2,226,071
# MAC addresses	18	7	9	15	107	44	55	51
% non-IP packets	0	0	67.44	4.63	0.15	5.11	0.01	1
OT protocol traffic	Modbus	S7comm	DNP3, GOOSE	Modbus	–		Modbus	–
# flows	11,726	17,027	2	2			74,113	
# packets	105,182	7,341,826	13,526	42,460			542,043	
# bytes	6,501,976	479,608,548	1,973,735	5,897,615			42,005,011	
∅ packet size	62	65	146	139			77	
# flows / sec	3.619	5.255	0.001	0.001			22.874	
# packets / sec	32	2,266	4	13			167	
# bytes / sec	2,007	148,027	609	1,820			12,965	
# MAC addresses	8	7	5	2			11	

Fig. 2. Protocol share among the IP packets indicated by the top 6 ports.

the traffic amount is significantly higher compared to the other two infrastructure levels. In the plant level network, several processes interact, but the communication for inter-process coordination only shows 1–11% of the intensity of the steam network. One perspective level higher, in the DMZ network, the traffic volume is larger than at plant level. Although traffic is transmitted to and from several plants, the parameters indicate an intensity of only 5–23% of the traffic of the steam network. These observations show that the diversity of traffic in real OT networks is quite high even within a single infrastructure.

3.2   Real OT Versus IT Traffic

This diversity is also reflected in the comparison with IT traffic from the public dataset CIC-IDS17. Real OT DMZ traffic with twice the number of MAC addresses (indicating the number of communicating devices) has about half as many flows, a fraction of the mean packet size (25%), but a similar number of packets. Plant-level traffic is also lower, despite containing a similar number of MAC addresses as the IT dataset (44 to 51 devices). In the steam network, however, the number of flows, packets, and bytes of the OT traffic significantly exceeds (three to about six times) the IT traffic. These observations contradict two expectations: (1) DMZ traffic as a perimeter network to non-OT networks does not have most similarities to IT networks. (2) Highly specific OT communications at the subprocess level can have larger dimensions than those observed in a general IT network of similar size.

3.3   Public OT Traffic Representativeness

We discuss the representativeness of public OT traffic based on the protocol mix, number of flows, packets, and the average packet size, since each aspect can have different relevance depending on the design of traffic-based anomaly detection systems. For this, we refer to the measurements of the whole analyzed period summarized in Table 2. We summarize the findings in Table 3.

Protocol Mix. The datasets Lemay and WDT contain mainly Modbus flows via port 502 (95–99%) with a correspondingly high packet share (85–99%). The S7comm dataset has a similar dominance of one OT protocol reflected by 97% packets using port 102. In the DNP3 dataset two OT protocols dominate the protocol mix. The DNP3 protocol transmitted through port 20000 dominates the IP-based traffic, as it can be seen in Fig. 2. While IP-based communications comprise 95–100% in all other datasets, it only represents 32% here. The remaining traffic consists almost entirely of communications using the Ethernet-based protocol GOOSE, which has a total share of 62%. Consequently, also the fourth public datasets is clearly dominated (combined share of 94%) by maximum two protocols, both of which are OT protocols. With respect to the three real infrastructure captures, the public data shares contradict two main obsevations in real OT traffic. (1) there is no such dominance of a single (or two) protocols under realistic traffic conditions. Real OT traffic shows a more diverse mix of protocols, whereby the most dominant protocol does not reach a share larger 13–29%. (2) there are not necessarily OT protocols in the real datasets DMZ and plant or their share is extremely low. They do not appear among the top six protocols (2.7% Modbus traffic in the steam dataset). As a result, none of the public OT datasets exhibit a protocol mix of IT and OT protocols observable in real OT networks. They are therefore not representative regarding this aspect.

Network Flows. Anomaly detection can be implemented using *flow analysis* [50]. In this way the traffic monitoring is limited to the meta attributes of the packets, but it allows for a very efficient monitoring. By the volume-based analysis of traffic, load-based attacks (Denial-of-Service attacks) can be identified, which are hardly detectable by packet-based analyses. On the other hand, false data injection attacks [19] cannot be detected without analyzing packet contents. The only similarity regarding the number of flows between public and real captures can be observed between the WDT dataset and the DMZ level (○).

Table 3. Representativeness of public OT datasets in terms of similar (○) or more intensive (●) traffic characteristics compared per real OT dataset. The maximum value results from the number of aspects (a) and the number of real datasets (r) applicable ($max = a \cdot r$, cf. Table 2).

	entire traffic				OT protocol traffic			
	Lemay	WDT	DNP3	S7comm	Lemay	WDT	DNP3	S7comm
protocol mix								
# flows / sec	●	○●						
# packets / sec	○	●●				●		
# bytes / sec		●				●		
∅packet size			○	○	○	○	●	●
representativeness	**2**	**5**	**1**	**1**	**1**	**3**	**1**	**1**
		(max=**15**)				(max=**5**)		

Although not similar, the Lemay and WDT datasets are more extensive than the plant dataset. Consequently, they would cover also the plant level characteristics if considered as flow number benchmark (●). The public datasets S7comm and DNP3 contain very few flows which are not representative for real OT traffic.

Network Packets. The limitations of flow analysis additionally require packet analysis for attack detection. Packet-based analysis enables a very precise monitoring, which in turn usually involves considerable effort for packet decoding. This can be challenging, potentially a bottleneck at high packet rates. However, to detect Man-in-the-Middle attacks [43] or the manipulation of process data encapsulated in packets, such an analysis is essential. The only observable similarity regarding the number of packets is between the Lemay dataset and the plant-level capture (○). Given the real captures, the S7comm and DNP3 dataset cannot be considered as representative regarding the packet rate recorded at the real OT networks. WDT offers, in contrast, a packet rate that clearly exceeds the total rate of two of the real network captures ($2 \times$ ●, regarding DMZ and plant level) as well as the Modbus packet rate of the third real capture steam (further ● for OT protocol traffic). Therefore, it can be used as benchmark for packet-pased detection systems for Modbus traffic.

Mean Packet Size. This measure is directly associated to the amount of payload carried in a network. It is of high relevance for the design of a detection system monitoring packet payloads. The payload size varies from packet to packet, while for implementation reasons a fixed size is usually prepared and analysed per packet. This size should be chosen in a way that it represents a sufficiently large portion of the payload to detect attacks. On the other hand, it should not be too large, as this increases the decoding and processing effort. Considering the complete traffic, the S7comm and DNP3 datasets show a mean packet size of 137 bytes, which is *quite* similar to the real capture from the plant level (○). The average packet sizes observed in the DMZ and subprocess networks, which are larger by a factor of 2 and 9 compared to the plant network, are not observed in any of the public datasets. If we focus on OT protocol traffic, the public Modbus datasets Lemay and WDT show a similar mean size of Modbus packets (62 to 65 bytes) as also given in the real Modbus capture, which is 77 bytes on subprocess level ($\bigcirc$). Therefore, the public Modbus datasets can at least be considered as representative regarding Modbus packet sizes. The mean packet sizes of the OT protocol traffic in the S7comm and DNP3 datasets is twice that of the Modbus traffic, which is why these datasets can serve as benchmarks for systems analyzing payloads of OT protocol packets ($\bullet$).

4   Traffic Homogeneity

After considering the representativeness of OT datasets used in research compared to real traffic, we now challenge the myth of OT traffic homogeneity. The latter is usually assumed to motivate anomaly detection in OT networks to identify attacks as deviations from normal traffic observations gathered in a previous training phase. The more homogeneous normal traffic is, the easier it is to model it as a class using machine learning, rules, or state machines to later distinguish deviations. Consequently, the quantification of homogeneity can serve as a measure to express the difficulty to model given traffic for anomaly detection. It can help to design such systems and to assess their performance on given datasets.

We first explore the distribution of per-second measurements of the traffic characteristics already discussed. Thereafter, we present a method for measuring traffic homogeneity with regard to the traffic contents, i.e., the payloads. The latter directly corresponds to a detection system's monitoring perspective on network activities and can therefore express the diversity of monitoring data that a detection system has to model effectively.

4.1   Homogeneity of Quantitative Properties

In Sect. 3 we used the flow and packet numbers, the mean packet size, and the byte number to compare these quantities transmitted in average per second during the whole capture period. We also analyzed their individual counts per second to investigate their homogeneity over time. The distribution of the measures is depicted in Fig. 3. It gives an impression of the homogeneity degree among the different datasets (inter-dataset homogeneity). The dispersion normalized to the individual measurement ranges, which represents the intra-dataset homogeneity, is given in Fig. 4.

Limitations. Using these traffic properties as indicator for the homogeneity of network communication is very limited. It completely neglects the measurement of content diversity. This leads to the more refined approach of measuring traffic homogeneity through the eye of an anomaly detection system.

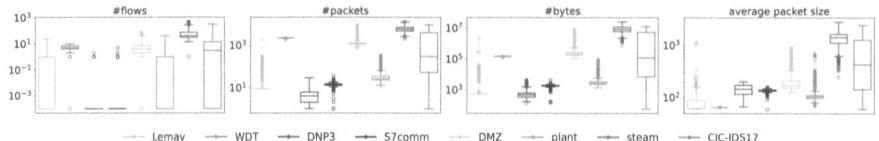

Fig. 3. Traffic aspect distribution indicating inter-network homogeneity.

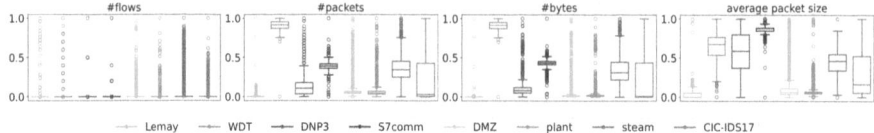

Fig. 4. Traffic aspect distribution normalized by the feature data range indicating intra-network homogeneity.

4.2 Homogeneity of Detection Aspects

In the context of detection systems configured during a certain training phase, input instances for the detection system, which consist of a collection of observed information in traffic, can be referred to as *samples*. During the training phase, a certain number of traffic samples are presented to the detection system.

Sample-Based Homogeneity Quantification. In OT traffic, the assumed homogeneity should be reflected in a comparatively strong decrease of new, not yet seen samples during the training phase. To investigate this point, we interpret the traffic of each dataset introduced in Sect. 2, which is completely normal traffic, as communications observed in a 54-minute training phase. The traffic is continuously transferred to samples and the occurence of new samples is measured. In the area of network monitoring and attack detection, there are two traditional views on network traffic reflected by the two different approaches of *flow analysis* and *packet analysis*. Both are taken into account when creating samples due to their different strenghts in attack detection (cf. Section 3.3).

Flow Samples. For each identified flow (cf. Section 3), we collect 33 typical flow features to create a flow sample. They consist of eleven parameters measured per (bidirectional) flow, as well as separately per forward and backward direction: *duration* in milliseconds, *number of packets, number of bytes, minimum, mean, and maximum packet size, standard deviation of the packet size, minimum, mean, and maximum packet inter-arrival time,* and the *standard deviation of the packet inter-arrival time* in milliseconds.

Packet Samples. Deep packet inspection (DPI) is used to extract meta and payload data from each Ethernet frame transmitted on the network. This enables very precise analyses of the traffic. We compose single-packet samples using seven packet features. These are *packet size, number of packet layers, source* and *destination MAC address, Ethertype, payload size* and *payload identifier*. For our homogeneity analysis through packet similarity, it is sufficient to distinguish the payloads instead of analyzing the payload content. Therefore, packet payloads are mapped onto hashed values. Two packet sample sets are then continuously created, one set with the payload as sample attribute $(+)$ and one without it $(-)$. The idea of using two sets stems from the fact that not every packet-based detection system analyzes the payload. The detection is often limited to meta-data analysis only to circumvent the effort and lack of knowledge required to extract application-specific payload from OT network packets with a comparatively high number of proprietary or undocumented protocols.

Multi-packet Samples. We also consider sample construction based on a sequence of packets. Information from packet sequences serves as input to anomaly detection systems that attempt to identify attacks where the individual packets are normal and only certain sequences of these normal packets indicate attacks[7]. We create n-packet samples by concatenating the n samples from each packet. In the case of seven-dimensional packet samples including the payload feature, a sequence of three packets is assigned to a multi-packet sample of dimension $21 = (7 \times 3)$. We refer to an n-packet sample as *n-gram* in the following.

4.3   Sample Saturation

In order to express homogeneity we introduce a measure that we call *sample saturation*. This allows us (1) to characterize a dataset by a single value and (2) to compare the degree of homogeneity between different datasets. It is determined by the following procedure: First, the time span of the examined captures is divided into equal time slots. Data traffic is continuously mapped onto flow and packet samples using the features specified in Sect. 4.2. By continuously monitoring the generated samples, the number of new samples that have not yet been generated in the previous time slots can be determined in each slot. This number of new samples can be related to the overall number of flows or (sequences of) packets seen in the same time slot. Consequently, the proportion of new samples to all samples in the slot can be expressed as a value between 0 and 1. This value is an indicator of the achieved proportion (saturation) of the sample set derived from the normal traffic up to this time slot. This directly corresponds to the knowledge extracted so far by an anomaly detection system trained on the monitored traffic based on the respective sample type. As an example, the measured sample saturation of single-packet samples (1-grams) for all datasets is depicted in Fig. 5. From these series of ratios the *area under the curve* (AUC) is calculated using the trapezoidal rule

$$AUC = \int_a^b f(x)\,\mathrm{d}x \approx \frac{s}{2}\left(f(a) + 2\sum_{i=1}^{n-1} f(a + ih) + f(b) \right)$$

---

[7] Man-in-the-Middle attacks or Replay attacks a. o.

where $s = x_i - x_{i-1}$ for all $i \in \{1, .., n\}$. Since this measure reflects the variability of traffic, consequently the reciprocal value $(1-AUC)$, the *area above the curve* (AAC), can be defined as a measure of homogeneity:

$$h = AAC = 1 - AUC.$$

For each of the eight analyzed datasets, we mapped the features specified in Sect. 4.2 to flow and packet samples, compiled the 3-gram and 5-gram sets as explained in 4.2, continuously recorded the sample saturation over a period of 54 min and used it to calculate the AAC.

4.4   Results

The results of the approach are summarized in Table 4. We discuss them by referring to the h value identifiers (IDs) given there.

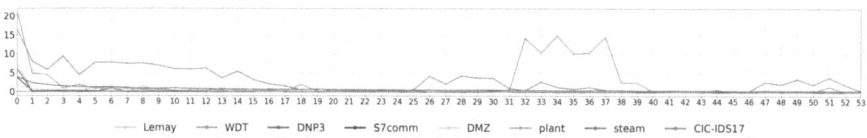

Fig. 5. Share of newly observed 1-grams in % per 1-minute slot in all observed samples in the same slot.

Public OT Traffic Versus Real Captures. If non-payload mappings are applied (h measures 0–3), the public traffic is constantly more homogeneous than the one in the real networks plant and steam. This is different as soon as payload data is included in the sample creation. Two public datasets show less homogeneity here than all others. Among the real datasets, the DMZ capture is the most homogeneous one with the highest h measure in 4/7 cases (h measures 0–6) and similar values like the Lemay dataset. What stands out in the measured values is the overall homogeneity of the S7comm traffic.

Public Modbus Traffic to Real Modbus Traffic. For this aspect, the measurements on the protocol-specific traffic of the datasets Lemay, WDT, and steam are relevant. Here, too, the observations can be divided into two parts. Without payload data handling the public Modbus traffic traces Lemay and WDT are more homogeneity whereas the incorporation of the actual Modbus communication content leads to less homogeneity than in the real network steam. A major difference between public Modbus traffic and real Modbus traffic can be observed for flow samples (h measure 7), whereby the homogeneity of Lemay and WDT is 55% higher than that of the real steam capture. Consequently, an evaluation of a flow-based anomaly detection system on the Lemay or WDT dataset should not be used to draw conclusions about the potential of flow-based anomaly detection on real Modbus traffic. This should also be avoided if the detection system operates on payload-less packet sequences of more than five packets (h measure 10). Here, the degree of homogeneity differs by 38% between the public datasets and the real one.

Relevance of Payload Inclusion. If the traffic from WDT and DNP is converted into sequences of 1, 3 or 5 packets and payload is taken into account (h measures 4–6), this results in a significantly more diverse sample quantity than with all three real datasets. This means that detection systems working on such a traffic mapping and are evaluated on WDT or DNP3 are also well-suited for the use in real networks. This also applies to the protocol-specific case on the Modbus protocol (h measures 11–13). Here, the two public datasets Lemay and WDT are a good base for evaluations on Modbus traffic. The opposite is true if payloads are omitted for multi-packet samples (h measures 2 and 3). Since the homogeneity of the public datasets is significantly higher in most cases, it is possible to achieve very good results with the public datasets without being able to draw any conclusions about their usability under real conditions, such as those in the plant and steam network. Only the traffic in the DMZ capture has similar characteristics to the Lemay and DNP3 datasets.

Flow-Based Versus Packet-Based Analysis. Traffic on flow-level generally exhibits a lower homogeneity expressed by a lower h measure compared to single- and multi-packet samples. From 1- to 5-grams, there is a steady decrease of homogeneity. This is an expected observation, as the variants seen in individual packets are amplified by the concatenation of several packets. Interesting is the degree of reduction per dataset. For the public datasets, it is the most extreme (at over 50%) when including payload data (h measures 4–6 and 11–13). Regarding the real datasets, the drop is most noticeable for the plant capture with 43% on the overall traffic (h measures 4–6) and over 60% on the Modbus traffic (h measures 11–13). Consequently, the configuration of an anomaly detection system on packet sequences is challenging. The longer the sequence length, the more sophisticated the modeling has to be designed to reflect normality.

Real OT Versus IT Traffic. For 3/7 mapping types (h measures 0, 2, and 3), each of the public datasets is more homogeneous than at least two of the real captures. This is clear evidence that OT traffic cannot per se be described as more homogeneous than IT traffic. This result has a number of implications for the design and evaluation of anomaly detection systems.

Table 4. Homogeneity h for different sample types with red indicating low and blue indicating high homogeneity.

ID	scope	mapping	payload	n-grams	Lemay	WDT	DNP3	S7comm	DMZ	plant	steam	CIC-IDS17
0	all	flows		1-grams	0.856	0.725	0.828	0.792	0.606	0.308	0.202	0.353
1	all	packets	-	1-grams	0.999	1.000	0.999	0.999	0.998	0.995	0.996	0.975
2	all	packets	-	3-grams	0.936	0.999	0.959	0.991	0.952	0.701	0.672	0.785
3	all	packets	-	5-grams	0.853	0.985	0.836	0.982	0.874	0.372	0.489	0.645
4	all	packets	+	1-grams	0.751	0.577	0.196	0.916	0.668	0.758	0.641	0.530
5	all	packets	+	3-grams	0.410	0.026	0.023	0.737	0.284	0.184	0.313	0.138
6	all	packets	+	5-grams	0.231	0.021	0.019	0.584	0.202	0.109	0.213	0.084
7	proto	flows		1-grams	0.887	0.725	0.972	0.972			0.173	
8	proto	packets	-	1-grams	1.000	1.000	0.999	1.000			1.000	
9	proto	packets	-	3-grams	0.937	0.999	0.986	0.998			0.826	
10	proto	packets	-	5-grams	0.853	0.985	0.949	0.997			0.466	
11	proto	packets	+	1-grams	0.783	0.577	0.154	0.939			0.973	
12	proto	packets	+	3-grams	0.433	0.026	0.019	0.791			0.664	
13	proto	packets	+	5-grams	0.244	0.021	0.019	0.676			0.309	

5 Implications for Anomaly Detection on OT Traffic

The representativeness of public OT datasets and the comparison of homogeneity of public and real OT traffic in Sect. 3.3 reveal implications for the design and evaluation of OT anomaly detection systems.

1. Real OT traffic is not necessarily more homogeneous than IT traffic. As argued above, the prevailing perception in attack detection for OT is that events and traffic are particularly homogeneous here [10,16,58]. Our measurements show that this assumption does not hold for real OT networks. In 2/3 of these networks, the regularity of the traffic is for 3/6 of the examined traffic perspectives actually lower than in the IT network (cf. perspectives 0, 2 and 3 in Table 4 for plant and steam). If we already observe this in 2/3 of the real networks analyzed, we must generally assume that there is a very large proportion of real traffic in practice that is not characterized by increased homogeneity. Accordingly, the potential of anomaly detection should not be justified by the homogeneity of OT traffic, as this depends strongly on the network and the traffic perspective. Rather, the main reason for the application of anomaly detection in this area lies in the restrictions, high availability requirements, and often low fault tolerance of OT networks, which simply do not allow the development of a detection system based on attack activities. Due to the lack of homogeneity, developing a reliable anomaly detection system is challenging. Therefore, the following points should be taken into account.

2. Protocol mixes in real OT networks require protocol-agnostic analysis approaches. In research, most approaches focus the detection on a specific OT protocol. We reviewed research in the field using the collection of [58] supplemented by eight approaches recently published at top security venues, summarized in Table 5. Only 5/19 of the anomaly detection methods (one-class approaches) were evaluated on heterogeneous traffic with different OT protocols. Among the five, only one can be considered protocol-agnostic being applicable to a wide range of protocols. Our analysis shows that a high number of IT protocols is also used in OT networks, so that traffic based on dedicated OT protocols either does not exist (cf. the real DMZ and plant captures), or, as in the steam capture, plays only a minor role. Protocol-specific detection approaches designed for the Modbus protocol, for instance, would be useless for the DMZ and plant traffic. They would also be blind regarding all non-Modbus communications in the steam network, which accounts to over 97% (cf. Section 3.3) of the traffic. Therefore, reliable anomaly detection systems should be designed to cover potentially every protocol mix. Such systems have a higher local detection effectiveness by analyzing the whole traffic of a network and better global effectiveness by being applicable to a wide range of OT networks regardless of the OT technology used. As shown in the related work in Table 5, there is a research gap here.

3. Numerous OT protocols that are not based on IP require a communication analysis at Ethernet level. Many OT protocols are not transmitted using the IP protocol, but are transferred directly using Ethernet. The analyzed public dataset DNP3 contains such a protocol, GOOSE, with a share of 62% non-IP packets. All flow-based detection systems are limited to the analysis of network flows transmitted over IP. Consequently, the entire group of flow-based approaches in Table 5 is blind regarding any non-IP traffic, which means over 60% blindness in case of the DNP3 dataset. Many non-experts are not aware of this limitation or potential blindness. As a result, there is a high risk that such flow-based systems give a false sense of security to users that can have fatal consequences, especially in critical infrastructures. This implies that anomaly detection for OT networks, in contrast to detection systems for Internet traffic, must not be limited to flow analysis only. Likewise, the decoding of network packets should start at the Ethernet level and not at the IP level.

4. The choice of the monitored traffic features rules out the success of some detection procedures from the outset. For the detection of some attack types [43], the analysis of sequences of network packets is necessary because they cannot be detected neither by flow nor single-packet analysis. We worked out that the configuration of an anomaly detection system operating on packet sequences is challenging (cf. 4.4) because the variants seen in individual packets are amplified by the concatenation to packet sequences and the homogeneity constantly decreases from single packets to 5-packet sequences. While in the past rules and state machines were proposed for the protocol-specific analysis of OT protocols [8,16], which were already very complex for only that single protocol, these approaches cannot help to design protocol-agnostic detection schemes to analyze the entire communication including all protocols (as motivated in point 2). There is a wide range of machine learning algorithms meanwhile, whose strength is the automated extraction of knowledge from complex input data. They can operate efficiently and effectively on a large number of inputs. In our opinion, they are the only feasible approach to develop reliable detection schemes for the demonstrated diversity of OT traffic. As soon as developers not only provide users with the trained (black-box) detection models, but also with an analysis about how they make decisions, their usability can be better assessed and their acceptance by network operators will increase.

5. Creating a reliable anomaly detection approach requires an evaluation on several datasets with divergent characteristics. As we worked out in Sect. 3, the diverse nature of OT networks is not only evident in protocol mixes but also in the large differences in the flow rate, packet rate, and data volume. This diversity must not only be assumed among infrastructures, it can even be proven across different networks of the same infrastructure, as our real traffic captures reflect it. Consequently, the general suitability of a detection approach cannot be inferred from the evaluation of one or similar datasets. If possible, it should be evaluated on real traffic. If there is no access to real networks, available public datasets with as many different characteristics as possible should be used to complete an evaluation on sufficiently diverse inputs. The four public datasets we analyzed represent a very good collection for this purpose due to their different characteristics regarding the protocol mix, flow and packet rate, the data amount transmitted, the relation of non-IP to IP-based traffic, and the degree of homogeneity.

6. For proving a reliable system, the detection speed must also be evaluated. Another finding of our review of related work in the area of traffic-based attack detection for OT (cf. Table 5) has been the neglect of performance analyses regarding detection speed. Only 8/19 of the approaches partially performed such an evaluation, which is actually a compelling point for demonstrating the reliability of a system for the detection purpose. In Sect. 3, we have provided traffic characteristics of real OT networks. These statistics can be used in future to demonstrate and to argue whether or to what extent a newly proposed detection system could analyze these transmission rates in real time.

7. To cover a wide range of attacks, flow and packet analysis must be combined. Apart from the implications drawn from the results of our experiments, we conclude the implications by this independent fact. The types of available attacks [37] require the combination of flow-based analysis, the monitoring of single packets, and also the detection in packet sequences, which is why we have considered all three perspectives in our investigations. If one kind of analysis is neglected, the effectiveness of the anomaly detection system is limited from the outset. For example, if flow-based analysis is omitted, load-based Denial-of-Service attacks may not be detectable through packet analysis alone. Man-in-the-Middle attacks [43] or the manipulation of process data encapsulated in packets [19], on the other hand, only become apparent through detailed analysis of packets and sequences. Existing approaches (cf. Table 5) focus on a single type of analysis instead of using all three kinds.

Table 5. Traffic-based detection schemes with evaluation aspects indicating local (# OT protocols) and global effectiveness (# datasets), adapted from [48]. *Options* is the number coverable using the four public datasets.

	two-class approaches								one-class approaches																			
	[45]	[49]	[17]	[55]	[44]	[1]	[11]	[46]	[57]	[4]	[21]	[60]	[8]	[9]	[56]	[7]	[31]	[15]	[35]	[16]	[29]	[61]	[47]	[59]	[30]	[32]	[6]	options
flows	•		•	•				•	•	•							•			•			•					•
single packets		•		•	•																		•	•		•	•	•
packet sequences													•	•	•	•	•	•		•	•	•						•
# public data			1	1^a	1			1							1^b		1	1						2		3		4
# real data					1				1				1	3	1	2	1			1	1		9	2	1			
# OT protocols	1	1	1	2	1	2	1	1	1	x^c	1	1	1	1	2	1	3	1	1	1	1	1	2	6	1	1	3	4
speed eval.	•				•	•			•						•					•	•		•			•		•

^{a} This work was evaluated on two datasets but one [24] is not accessible anymore.
^{b} This work was evaluated on the SWaT network [20] but the traffic is not public.
^{c} The protocol(s) are not named.

6   Related Work

Previous research on OT traffic characterization can be divided into two groups: aggregated and structural ones. Here, we refer to the terms SCADA and DCS (distributed control systems) [51].

Aggregated Traffic Characterization. This group quantifies traffic meta information. The approaches first elaborate differences between SCADA and ICT networks by measuring the periodicity in terms of the frame rate and the number of active connections [2] and, thereafter, compare the results with standard IT traffic models. It was found out that they are different from SCADA communications [3]. Later investigations characterized OT communications (for the protocol DNP3) in terms of polling intervals, inter-arrival times, idle and round-trip times per device, (temporal and byte) duration of TCP flows, retransmission rates, and timeouts [18]. A quantification of distribution changes of event inter-arrival periods over time (for the SCADA protocol IEC 60870-5-104) led to a categorization of traffic into strongly cyclic, weakly cyclic, stable, bursty, and phase transitional [29,30]. A recent work proposed a five-step approach [27] to quantify communication intensity and repeated communication patterns to use this profiling for recognizing work-cycles' states. In [36] the feasibility to distinguish proprietary protocols by clustering traffic based on the inter-arrival times and frame header data has been demonstrated for DCS. A rich protocol mix was identified, contrary to what is usually stated for SCADA networks.

Structural Traffic Profiling. The second group tries to model periodic communication patterns. This was first investigated for single protocols [21,25]. Later a protocol-independent modeling of concrete periodic traffic patterns [5,26] was proposed to explore message repetition and timing information. The approaches were analyzed for DCS (protocols Siemens S7 and MMS, respectively) and for SCADA (Modbus). Also deep packet inspection has been applied [14] to OT protocols to especially generate communication models for device pairs. This was shown for SCADA and DCS networks (for the protocols Modbus/TCP, DNP3, and EtherNet/IP). Other approaches [33] focused on the analysis of TCP flow dynamics and different OT header and message types (for IEC 60870-5-104) as a prerequisite for a future attack detection using whitelists. In [34], an investigation of a power distribution backbone network (referring to the protocol IEC 60870-5-104) was presented. In addition to physical network changes and communication flow lengths, structural traffic analyses are applied by clustering session variants and determining the number and semantics of message types.

Research Gap. The first group abstracts network activities to aggregated traffic observations. This allows only a topview on OT traffic quantities. The latter type of investigations analyzes communication frames, but goes too deeply into the perspective of the process (modeling of process variables), thereby losing track of network transactions and running into a state explosion. None of the approaches examines traffic characteristics from the perspective of sampling traffic through a combination of flow or packet features. This investigation, however, directly relates to the degree of variability or homogeneity of traffic that a security system based on modeling normal traffic for detection must handle.

7 Summary and Subsequent Activities

In order to support developers of anomaly detection systems regarding reasoning, designing, and evaluating their systems, we have compared public OT traffic datasets with communication captured in real OT networks. We worked out in which aspects the public datasets are representative and in which they are not. We further introduced a measure for the homogeneity of traffic and used it to express and compare the homogeneity of public and real OT traffic. With regard to the investigated myth of homogeneous OT traffic reflected in the title of this paper, we must note that this assumption cannot be confirmed for real networks. From the analyses regarding representativeness and homogeneity, we finally identified a number of implications for the design and evaluation of traffic-based anomaly detection systems for OT networks that also can operate reliably under real traffic conditions. Once we had identified these requirements, the next step for us was to develop a corresponding anomaly detection system. We implemented and evaluated it according to the identified implications [48].

Reproducibility. With the exception of the real OT captures, all necessary information is given to reproduce results without any further material or code. This includes the testbed files, the examined periods of the testbed data (cf. Table 6), their mapping to flow and packet features, and the calculation of the homogeneity measure h.

Table 6. First and last packet timestamps of the examined capture periods.

	first packet timestamp	last packet timestamp
Lemay	2015-02-23 18:46:43.192	2015-02-23 19:40:38.509
WDT	2021-04-09 09:30:52.716	2021-04-09 10:24:52.716
DNP3	2016-08-23 08:03:48.553	2016-08-23 08:57:47.937
S7comm	2016-12-19 03:28:14.069	2016-12-19 04:22:13.687
CIC-IDS17	2017-07-03 11:55:58.598	2017-07-03 12:49:58.597

Acknowledgments. We like to thank Andreas Paul for fruitful discussions. Special thanks go to Heiko Kanisch for his trust and relentless efforts to bridge the gap between science and real world. Without him, this research would not have been possible. Nor would this be the case without Franka's muse and favorites.

References

1. Anton, S.D.D., Sinha, S., Schotten, H.D.: Anomaly-based intrusion detection in industrial data with SVM and random forests. In: SoftCOM, IEEE (2019)
2. Barbosa, R.R.R., Sadre, R., Pras, A.: A first look into SCADA network traffic. In: NOMS, IEEE (2012)
3. Barbosa, R.R.R., Sadre, R., Pras, A.: Difficulties in modeling SCADA traffic: a comparative analysis. In: Taft, N., Ricciato, F. (eds.) PAM 2012. LNCS, vol. 7192, pp. 126–135. Springer, Heidelberg (2012). https://doi.org/10.1007/978-3-642-28537-0_13
4. Barbosa, R.R.R., Sadre, R., Pras, A.: Towards periodicity based anomaly detection in SCADA networks. In: ETFA, IEEE (2012)
5. Barbosa, R.R.R., Sadre, R., Pras, A.: Exploiting traffic periodicity in industrial control networks. In: IJCIP, vol. 13 (2016)
6. Cai, J., Wang, Q., Luo, J., Liu, Y., Liao, L.: CapBad: content-agnostic, payload-based anomaly detector for industrial control protocols. Internet Things J. 9(14) (2021)
7. Caselli, M., Zambon, E., Amann, J., Sommer, R., Kargl, F.: Specification mining for intrusion detection in networked control systems. In: USENIX Security (2016)
8. Caselli, M., Zambon, E., Kargl, F.: Sequence-aware intrusion detection in industrial control systems. In: ACM CPSS (2015)
9. Caselli, M., Zambon, E., Petit, J., Kargl, F.: Modeling message sequences for intrusion detection in industrial control systems. In: IFIP ICCIP, Springer (2015)
10. Cheung, S., Dutertre, B., Fong, M., Lindqvist, U., Skinner, K., Valdes, A.: Using model-based intrusion detection for SCADA networks. In: SCADA Security Scientific Symposium 2007 (2007)
11. Chu, A., Lai, Y., Liu, J.: Industrial control intrusion detection approach based on multiclassification GoogLeNet-LSTM model. Secur. Commun. Netw. **2019** (2019)
12. Conti, M., Donadel, D., Turrin, F.: A survey on industrial control system testbeds and,datasets for security research. Commun. Surv. Tutorials **23** (2021)
13. Cruz, T.: Modbus TCP SCADA #1 dataset (2018). https://github.com/tjcruz-dei/ICS_PCAPS/releases/tag/MODBUSTCP%231

14. Faisal, M.A., Cárdenas, A.A., Wool, A.: Profiling communications in industrial IP networks: model complexity and anomaly detection. In: Security and Privacy Trends in the Industrial Internet of Things, Springer (2019)
15. Feng, C., Li, T., Chana, D.: Multi-level anomaly detection in industrial control systems via package signatures and LSTM networks. In: SDSN, IEEE (2017)
16. Ferling, B., Chromik, J., Caselli, M., Remke, A.: Intrusion detection for sequence-based attacks with reduced traffic models. In: Measurement, Modelling and Evaluation of Computing Systems, Springer (2018)
17. Formby, D., Srinivasan, P., Leonard, A.M., Rogers, J.D., Beyah, R.A.: Who's in control of your control system? Device Fingerprinting for Cyber-Physical Systems. In: NDSS (2016)
18. Formby, D., Walid, A.I., Beyah, R.A.: A case study in power substation network dynamics. In: SIGMETRICS, ACM (2017)
19. Gao, W., Morris, T.H.: On cyber attacks and signature based intrusion detection for modbus based industrial control systems. J. Digit. Forensics Secur. Law 9(1) (2014)
20. Goh, J., Adepu, S., Junejo, K.N., Mathur, A.: A dataset to support research in the design of secure water treatment systems. In: CRITIS, LNCS, vol. 10242. Springer (2016)
21. Goldenberg, N., Wool, A.: Accurate modeling of modbus/TCP for intrusion detection in SCADA systems. CIP 6(2) (2013)
22. Guarino, S., Faramondi, L., Setola, R., Flammini, F.: A hardware-in-the-loop water distribution testbed (WDT). Dataset for Cyber-physical Security Testing. IEEE Dataport (2021). https://dx.doi.org/10.21227/rbvf-2h90
23. Institute, S.: CyberCity dataset (2013). https://assets.contentstack.io/v3/assets/blt36c2e63521272fdc/bltff8e7c1232f3bcbc/5fbd7be072a3526f28dbed75/sansholidayhack2013.pcap
24. Kaiserslautern, D.: IUNO project website with datasets (not online anymore) (2023). https://projects.dfki.uni-kl.de/IUNO
25. Kleinmann, A., Wool, A.: Accurate modeling of the siemens S7 SCADA protocol for intrusion detection and digital forensic. J. Digit. Forensics Secur. Law 9(2) (2014)
26. Kleinmann, A., Wool, A.: Automatic construction of Statechart-based anomaly detection models for multi-threaded SCADA via spectral analysis. In: ACM CPS-SPC@CCS, ACM (2016)
27. Lavassani, M., Åkerberg, J., Björkman, M.: Modeling and profiling of aggregated industrial network traffic. Appl. Sci. 12(2) (2022)
28. Lemay, A.: Modbus dataset from CSET 2016 (2016). https://github.com/antoine-lemay/Modbus_dataset
29. Lin, C.Y., Nadjm-Tehrani, S.: Understanding IEC-60870-5-104 traffic patterns in SCADA networks. In: ACM CPSS (2018)
30. Lin, C.Y., Nadjm-Tehrani, S.: Timing patterns and correlations in spontaneous SCADA traffic for anomaly detection. In: RAID (2019)
31. Lin, C.Y., Nadjm-Tehrani, S., Asplund, M.: Timing-based anomaly detection in SCADA networks. In: CRITIS, Springer (2018)
32. Maglaras, L.A., Jiang, J.: Intrusion detection in SCADA systems using machine learning techniques. In: Science & Information Conference, IEEE (2014)
33. Mai, K., Qin, X., Silva, N.O., Cardenas, A.A.: IEC 60870-5-104 network characterization of a large-scale operational power grid. In: SPW, IEEE (2019)
34. Mai, K., Qin, X., Silva, N.O., Molina, J., Cárdenas, A.A.: Uncharted networks: a first measurement study of the bulk power system. In: IMC, ACM (2020)

35. Markman, C., Wool, A., Cardenas, A.A.: A new burst-DFA model for SCADA anomaly detection. In: Workshop on CPS Security and Privacy (2017)
36. Mehner, S., Schuster, F., Hohlfeld, O.: Lights on power plant control networks. In: PAM, LNCS, vol. 13210, Springer (2022)
37. Miller, T., Staves, A., Maesschalck, S., Sturdee, M., Green, B.: Looking back to look forward: lessons learnt from cyber-attacks on industrial control systems. IJCIP **35** (2021)
38. Myers, D.: QUT S7 Communication (not online anymore) (2018). https://cloudstor.aarnet.edu.au/plus/index.php/s/9qFfeVmfX7K5IDH
39. Ndonda, G.K.: HVAC data (2019). https://github.com/gkabasele/HVAC_Traces
40. NETRESEC: Capture files from 4SICS Geek Lounge (2015). https://www.netresec.com/?page=PCAP4SICS
41. NETRESEC: S4x15 ICS Village PCAP files (2015). https://www.netresec.com/?page=DigitalBond_S4
42. of New Brunswick, U.: Intrusion detection evaluation dataset (CIC-IDS2017) (2022). https://www.unb.ca/cic/datasets/ids-2017.html
43. Paul, A., Schuster, F., König, H.: Towards the protection of industrial control systems – conclusions of a vulnerability analysis of Profinet IO. In: DIMVA, Springer (2013)
44. Perez, R.L., Adamsky, F., Soua, R., Engel, T.: Machine learning for reliable network attack detection in SCADA systems. In: TrustCom, IEEE (2018)
45. Ponomarev, S., Atkison, T.: Industrial control system network intrusion detection by telemetry analysis. Trans. Dependable Secure Comput. **13** (2015)
46. Radoglou-Grammatikis, P., Sarigiannidis, P., Efstathopoulos, G., Karypidis, P.A., Sarigiannidis, A.: DIDEROT: an intrusion detection and prevention system for DNP3-based SCADA systems. In: ARES (2020)
47. Schneider, P., Böttinger, K.: High-performance unsupervised anomaly detection for cyber-physical system networks. In: Workshop on Cyber-physical Systems Security and Privacy (2018)
48. Schuster, F., König, H.: No need for details: effective anomaly detection for process control traffic in absence of protocol and attack knowledge. In: RAID, ACM (2024)
49. Shang, W., Cui, J., Wan, M., An, P., Zeng, P.: Modbus communication behavior modeling and SVM intrusion detection method. In: ICCNS (2016)
50. Sperotto, A., Schaffrath, G., Sadre, R., Morariu, C., Pras, A., Stiller, B.: An overview of IP flow-based intrusion detection. Commun. Surv. Tutorials **12**(3) (2010)
51. Stouffer, K., Pillitteri, V., Lightman, S., Abrams, M., Hahn, A.: Guide to industrial control systems (ICS) security. NIST Special Publication 800-82 Rev. 2 (2015)
52. SUTD: datasets collection inlcuding electric power and intelligent control (EPIC) and secure water treatment (SWaT) (2021). https://itrust.sutd.edu.sg/itrust-labs_datasets/dataset_info/
53. of Technology Information Security, Q.U.: DNP3 cyber-attack datasets (2017). https://github.com/qut-infosec/2017QUT_DNP3
54. of Technology Information Security, Q.U.: SCADA network attack datasets and process logs (2017). https://github.com/qut-infosec/2017QUT_S7comm
55. Terai, A., Abe, S., Kojima, S., Takano, Y., Koshijima, I.: Cyber-attack detection for industrial control system monitoring with support vector machine based on communication profile. In: EuroS&PW, IEEE (2017)
56. Urbina, D.I., et al.: Limiting the impact of stealthy attacks on industrial control systems. In: ACM CCS (2016)

57. Valdes, A., Cheung, S.: Communication pattern anomaly detection in process control systems. In: Conference on Technologies for Homeland Security, IEEE (2009)
58. Wolsing, K., Wagner, E., Saillard, A., Henze, M.: IPAL: Breaking up silos of protocol-dependent and domain-specific industrial intrusion detection systems. In: RAID, ACM (2022)
59. Wressnegger, C., Kellner, A., Rieck, K.: Zoe: content-based anomaly detection for industrial control systems. In: IEEE/IFIP DSN, IEEE (2018)
60. Yoon, M.K., Ciocarlie, G.F.: Communication pattern monitoring: improving the utility of anomaly detection for industrial control systems. In: NDSS (2014)
61. Yun, J.H., Hwang, Y., Lee, W., Ahn, H.K., Kim, S.K.: Statistical similarity of critical infrastructure network traffic based on nearest neighbor distances. In: RAID. Springer (2018)

Enhancing Long-Term Storage Security in Critical Infrastructures Under NIS2 Directive: Addressing Post-quantum Cryptography Challenges

Nino Ricchizzi[1,2]([⊠]), Andrea Langner[3], and Jan Pelzl[4]

[1] Computer Science, Lucerne University of Applied Sciences and Arts,
Lucerne, Switzerland
nino.ricchizzi@hslu.ch
[2] Ruhr University Bochum, Bochum, Germany
[3] Indexing and Digitization, Hessian State Archives, Marburg, Germany
andrea.langner@hla.hessen.de
[4] Computer Security, Hamm-Lippstadt University of Applied Sciences,
Hamm, Germany
jan.pelzl@hshl.de

Abstract. This study explores integrating Post-Quantum Cryptography (PQC) into the Open Archival Information System (OAIS) to enhance data security in critical infrastructures under the NIS2 directive. Emphasizing the need for quantum-resistant archives, it develops a threat model to outline quantum vulnerabilities and strategic protective measures. The goal is to safeguard digital archives against current and future cryptographic threats, ensuring the integrity and confidentiality of critical data.

Keywords: CRITIS (Critical Infrastructures) · Long-term data preservation · Post-Quantum Cryptography (PQC) · Quantum-resistant storage · OAIS (Open Archival Information System)

1 Introduction

Critical infrastructures (CRITIS) are essential for the functioning of modern societies, as they provide vital services such as energy supply, healthcare, and transportation. The consequences of disruptions or failures of these facilities can have severe repercussions for public welfare and safety. At the European level, the new NIS2 directive introduces stricter requirements for the security of these infrastructures and extends national regulations. This directive differentiates between two categories of CRITIS companies: sectors of high criticality and other critical sectors [24], shown in 1. Entities of high criticality are those whose impairment would have direct and extensive negative effects on national security, the economy, or public order. Important entities are those whose disruptions are severe but are more limited in scope and impact.

© The Author(s), under exclusive license to Springer Nature Switzerland AG 2025
G. Oliva et al. (Eds.): CRITIS 2024, LNCS 15549, pp. 43–63, 2025.
https://doi.org/10.1007/978-3-031-84260-3_3

Article 21 of the NIS2 directive requires essential and important facilities to take appropriate technical, operational, and organizational measures to manage risks to the security of their network and information systems [24]. This includes measures to minimize the impact of security incidents on service recipients and other services. Furthermore, Article 21(2) demands the maintenance of critical operational processes, including backup management and recovery measures after emergencies, as well as crisis management.

Table 1. NIS2: Critical Sectors [24]

Sectors of High Criticality	Other Critical Sectors
Energy	Postal and Courier Services
Transport	Waste Management
Banking	Manufacture, Production and Distribution of Chemicals
Financial Market Infrastructures	Production, Processing and Distribution of Food
Health	Manufacturing
Drinking Water	Digital Providers
Waste Water	Research
Digital Infrastructure	
ICT Services Management (B2B)	
Public Administration	
Space	

Secure documentation of established processes and standards, which are both protected and accessible, is crucial. According to Paragraph 8a of the German IT Security Act [10], critical infrastructures must be able to provide documentation for audits. The Open Archival Information System (OAIS) [1] offers a framework for the long-term preservation and accessibility of digital information, which has already been successfully implemented by various companies and authorities [13,16,56]. In compliance with the German CRITIS regulation, archives implement the OAIS to ensure long-term security. This paper introduces an archival framework for long-term storage and its application in the CRITIS sector, examining its suitability for long-term security and data preservation in light of the development of quantum computers.

2   Methodology

This study explores adapting the OAIS model for critical infrastructures, assessing document types and storage purposes. We investigate CRITIS use cases needing robust security and identify quantum computing vulnerabilities. A threat model is developed, leading to protective strategies with Post-Quantum Cryptography (PQC) for enhancing archive resilience.

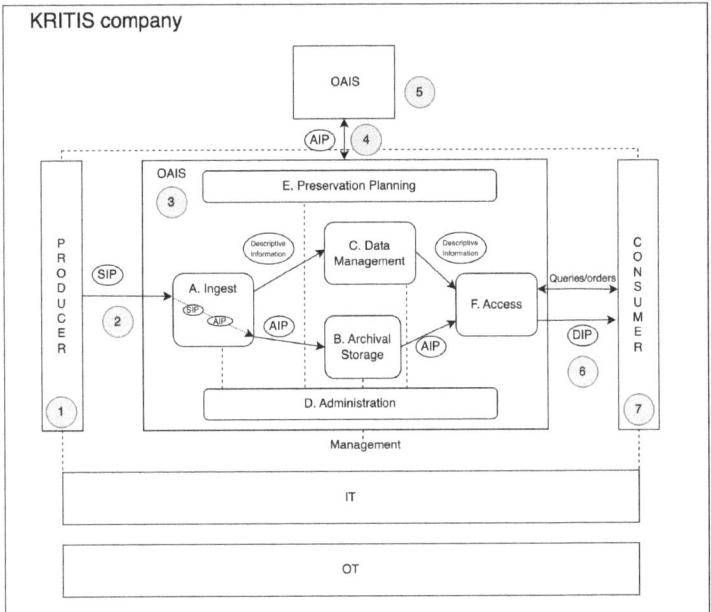

Fig. 1. OAIS Architecture [1]

3 Use Cases in Critical Environments

In the realm of Critical Infrastructure, specific use cases for long-term secure storage emerge due to regulatory, security, and forensic requirements. Firstly, Information Security Management Systems (ISMS) require the documentation and archiving of processes such as risk analyses and security audits, as mandated by A.17.1.2 of ISO/IEC 27001:2022 [2]. This is facilitated by the OAIS, which ensures secure storage with change tracking and efficient search capabilities Secondly, compliance and legal mandates require CRITIS entities to demonstrate continual adherence to statutory and regulatory obligations, making the long-term preservation of compliance documents critical [24]. Additionally, in the event of security incidents, entities must be able to demonstrate the implementation of adequate technical and organizational measures as per current technological standards; here, long-term archiving of operational logs and security incidents is crucial for effective legal response post-attack. Moreover, industries such as energy and water need to store operational data over extended periods to analyze long-term trends or meet regulatory demands [49,62]. Finally, protecting critical business data and intellectual property, including patents and design documents, against data loss from technological changes or cyber-attacks is imperative. These use cases summarize the necessity of long-term secure storage solutions in CRITIS sectors to address operational, legal, and security challenges. Archives, classified as part of the critical infrastructure sector, widely employ the Open Archival Information System (OAIS) model [1]. Developed by the Consultative Committee for Space Data Systems (CCSDS), this model provides a framework for the long-term preservation of digital information. Additionally, there are specific standards for preserving electronic documents, such as ISO 31644 [19] to DIN 31646 [29].

4   Functional Components and Structure of an Archival Framework

In this section, we present OAIS with the roles of the functional units [1]. Respective examples of use cases are provided in order to gain a basic understanding. Subsequently, possible attack models for the long-term security of an long-term secure storage are derived based on the functions. It is important to note that while an archive can be integrated into a company, it requires specific roles and permissions to operate effectively. Although the archive is closely linked to IT, it should be technically and physically separated in terms of security to prevent unauthorized access and ensure data integrity. Additionally, from an organizational standpoint, management should ensure that the archive operations are distinct and independent, providing clear guidelines and control mechanisms that uphold the integrity and security of the archived information.

Before diving into the functions and roles of an archive framework, it is essential to understand three key concepts within this model: the Submission Information Package (SIP), the Archival Information Package (AIP), and the Dissemination Information Package (DIP).

A SIP is a collection of files and metadata submitted by producers to an OAIS for long-term preservation. The SIP serves as the initial package that enters the archive environment, containing all necessary documentation and data required for processing and archiving [1]. For instance, in the context of CRITIS, this could include Information Security Management System (ISMS) documents, which are crucial for ensuring the security and resilience of critical infrastructure services. An AIP is the result of processing a SIP within the archive. It includes the data to be archived along with the metadata necessary for its management and preservation. The AIP is stored in the archive storage and is managed over time to ensure its long-term accessibility and readability [1].

A DIP is then created from the AIP to facilitate data access and distribution, tailored to meet the specific needs of the user or consumer, ensuring that the archived data remains unchanged and retrievable as needed.

Within the framework of the OAIS reference model (shown in Fig. 1), digital data undergoes a sequential chain of processes, from submission by the producer to provisioning for the consumer. These processes involve specific transformations of the data packages: from SIPs (Submission Information Packages) to AIPs (Archival Information Packages), and finally to DIPs (Dissemination Information Packages), as detailed in [1].

- **From Producer to Ingest:** Producers submit data in the form of an SIP, which contains both the digital data and the associated metadata for archiving. It is important to note that there can be restrictions on the formats allowed in the SIP to ensure compatibility and long-term preservation within the archive system.

- **Ingest:** In the ingest process, the SIP is validated and transformed into an AIP. This transformation includes the enrichment of metadata and the preparation of data for long-term storage and preservation.
- **Data Management:** During the data management phase, the AIP metadata is managed to ensure persistence, findability, and accessibility. Key information about the archived contents is cataloged and indexed.
- **Archival Storage:** The AIPs are stored for the long term during this phase, which includes maintaining data integrity and implementing strategies for data migration and preservation.
- **Access:** Upon request, DIPs are generated from the AIPs, tailored specifically to the information needs and permissions of the consumers. This step adjusts the archived data for delivery to end-users.
- **To the Consumer:** The DIPs are eventually provided to the consumers, completing the information flow from the original data producer to the end-user.

5   Quantum Threats and Attack Model

Quantum computers introduce profound security challenges, primarily due to the advent of Grover's [34] and Shor's [57] algorithms. In particular, Shor's algorithm poses a critical threat to the foundations of asymmetric cryptography which supports most of our current digital security infrastructure, including digital signatures [44]. Asymmetric encryption methods, relying on the computational difficulty of problems such as integer factorization and computation of discrete logarithms, are vulnerable to being efficiently solved by quantum computers, rendering traditional cryptographic safeguards obsolete.

In contrast, symmetric encryption appears to be less vulnerable to quantum attacks. Although, Grover's algorithm can theoretically halve the effective security of symmetric keys by enabling a quadratic speedup of attacks, doubling the key length can mitigate this threat, making symmetric cryptography more resilient in the quantum era.

Given these considerations, the attack model developed in the subsequent chapter will specifically focus on the vulnerabilities introduced by quantum computing. We will examine the application and reliance on digital signatures and asymmetric encryption across our digital infrastructure, identifying critical areas and proposing respective mitigations.

In the following step, potential threats posed by quantum computing to the CRITIS archival model, as illustrated in 1, will be analyzed. A notable feature depicted in the figure is the connection between the given company's archive and a second company's archive for the purpose of data exchange. This scenario is also mentioned in the reference model [1]. Among various interconnected models, this particular model was chosen due to its unique vulnerabilities to specific threats. CIRITS companies can establish archival systems at various locations and exchange Archival Information Packages (AIPs) among themselves. The highlighted numbers in red in 1 have been added to identify typical objects and communication paths, serving as the basis for the attack models discussed herein.

In this discussion, it is assumed that the archival system is physically and organizationally separated from IT and OT systems. Data transferred from IT or OT via a conventional communication channel is directed solely to the producer interface, which does not have direct access to the internal archive. Furthermore, the internal archive management, including the ingest phase, is logically and physically isolated from the rest of the infrastructure.

1. **Producer:** The transmission of data for long-term storage by the producer might involve different formats, including PDFs [54, 60]. For critical infrastructure companies, these documents could be part of an ISMS or required by legal regulations. It's important to note that PDFs are vulnerable to attacks, such as malware embedding [52]. Typically, the producer, located within the company or network, manages and secures the transmission process. Since this attack vector is not new in the context of quantum computers, it will not be further discussed.

2. **Connection Between Producer and Ingest:**
   Assuming the internal archive, including the ingest phase, is a physically isolated area within a critical infrastructure company: Data transfer can occur through direct physical delivery, involving a personal handover from the producer to an OAIS-compliant archival system, ensuring a controlled exchange of media like CD-ROMs or USB drives. Alternatively, data can be conveyed over unsecured IP-based channels like the internet [41] or through the local company network. Data loss, destruction, or theft can occur during physical handover but are not considered in this paper, which focuses on quantum computing threats. Over an unsecured channel, data integrity is at risk from attackers who might alter data during transit. Signatures and checksums cannot prevent alterations but can detect tampering [51]. Although quantum computers capable of breaking classical cryptography do not yet exist [7], the risk of future decryption of harvested, classically encrypted data is significant [50] [42]. This threat is particularly relevant when transporting archival information over the internet, including VPN connections. CRITIS companies must consider various data transfer scenarios, with producers possibly within the same network, across a corporate network, via VPN, or solely through the internet.

3. **Archive Framework:** For this model, it is assumed that organizational units, roles, and functions in the reference model do not distribute data over unsecured connections (internet), avoiding equivalent risks mentioned previously. We focus on attackers from within the archive or intruders, limited to physical breaches. External attacks, such as malware, are classical threats and not quantum-specific. Insider threats span various operational stages: Ingest, Data Management, Archival Storage, and Access. This section outlines potential insider attack models across these functions, emphasizing

classical security concerns critical to maintaining archival integrity.

Organizations with archival systems alongside primary operations face unique challenges. Unlike dedicated archival institutions, these environments require a complex arrangement of roles and permissions. ISO 14721:2012 emphasizes establishing a robust organizational framework to segregate the archive framework from other systems, preventing unauthorized access and ensuring archival integrity [1].

Ingest: Unauthorized modification of metadata or content in Submission Information Packages (SIPs) either prior to or during the ingestion process, endangering the integrity and authenticity of the archived data. Additionally, there is the risk of introducing malicious code within digital objects, potentially compromising the security of the archiving system at a subsequent stage.

Data Management: Manipulation or deletion of metadata within Archival Information Packages, impacting the retrievability and utility of the archived content. Illicit access to sensitive or restricted data through the exploitation of permissions or vulnerabilities within the data management framework is another concern.

Archival Storage: Acts of physical or digital sabotage can lead to the degradation or loss of AIPs, such as through malware or physical harm to storage mediums. Alteration of storage management systems to modify or eliminate data undermines data longevity and integrity.

Access: Unauthorized release of sensitive information to unqualified users can result in data breaches. Furthermore, modification or eradication of Dissemination Information Packages (DIPs) can deceive users or obstruct legitimate access requests.

These models illustrate a range of insider threats within classical risk parameters. A common principle across all archive functions is that only authorized users can create, edit, or alter data or metadata in the long-term archive, such as during signature renewal.

The advent of powerful quantum computers introduces new risks, enabling insiders to create legitimate AIPs, alter existing AIPs, and generate valid signatures, thereby extending beyond classical threat models [44].

4. **Communication Between CRITIS Archives:** Inter-archive communication poses similar threats to producer-to-archive data transmission, with added complexity from potential eavesdropping and data interception. Attackers who decrypt an AIP and become insider threats can selectively manipulate data within the archival system.

5. **Other Connected Archives or other Company Locations:** Equivalent to points 3 and 4.

6. **Connection Between Archive and Consumer:** Building upon the threats discussed in Sect. 2, the interception of encrypted DIPs presents a distinct scenario. Attackers intercepting encrypted communication (e.g., during an https transmission) could potentially decrypt this data at a later time, specifically once quantum computing capabilities become available, thus accessing the information contained within. However, since a DIP is not re-incorporated back into the archive and therefore does not compromise long-term security, this situation is considered less critical compared to the one presented in Sect. 2. Nonetheless, Sect. 6 involves the authentication process for retrieving information. Data intercepted now could be decrypted in the future, which would render current credentials insecure. This prospect highlights the need for forward-looking security measures that anticipate the advent of quantum computing, ensuring that current authentication mechanisms remain robust against future decryption capabilities.

7. **Consumer** Attacker targeting authentication processes to gain unauthorized access to DIPs can use methods ranging from traditional username and password to advanced e-ID services, enhancing convenience and security. However, despite efforts to establish robust Public Key Infrastructures (PKI) [33], these systems are not immune to quantum computing threats, potentially allowing attackers to exploit vulnerabilities and bypass authentication, posing significant risks to data security and access control. In a business context, consumers within the infrastructure may be located on-site at the company but could also potentially be external, accessing resources over the internet.

6 Post-Quantum Cryptography

Due to the potential threats posed by quantum computers, the field of Post-Quantum Cryptography (PQC) has gained importance, encompassing algorithms resistant to both classical and quantum computing attacks. The National Institute of Standards and Technology (NIST) initiated a program to evaluate such algorithms [11], introducing various candidates. These differ in their application areas, like key transmission and digital signatures, and are based on distinct mathematical problems, moving away from traditional factorization-based methods. Instead, these new approaches rely on problems such as lattice-based, multivariate polynomial, and isogeny-based problems. For a detailed overview of the different mathematical foundations of these algorithms, see Table 2.

The Open Quantum Safe (OQS) [4] project aims to support the development and prototyping of quantum-resistant cryptography. The OQS project provides libraries and implementations for various protocols, including MQTT, facilitating the integration of post-quantum cryptographic algorithms into existing digital communication systems. Despite these advancements and the adoption of initial PQC methods by NIST after several years of evaluation [11], these algorithms are not as time-tested as classical cryptographic methods and may contain unknown security risks.

Various companies, including Google [48], Cloudflare [43], and Apple [23], have adopted different approaches to migrate towards quantum-resistant cryptographic methods.

Quantum-resistant algorithms have been extensively tested in standard protocols such as TLS [58,59] and VPN [38], as well as within X.509 [39] and PKI [53] environments. Despite these advancements, PQC methods face diverse challenges, such as the use of longer key lengths and reduced performance compared to classical cryptographic algorithms. In a comprehensive literature review, [63] succinctly summarizes the challenges, migrations and open questions associated with the migration to Post-Quantum Cryptography (PQC) algorithms.

Implementing secure communications involves various approaches such as hybrid, combiner, and composite methods. Hybrid models blend classical and quantum-resistant algorithms to enhance security; combiner approaches use multiple algorithms to create a single, more secure protocol; and composite methods integrate different cryptographic techniques within the same system for robustness. Challenges arise across software, hardware, infrastructure, as well as internal and external processes, standards, and regulations. Therefore, the feasibility of PQC integration must be carefully evaluated for each use case. Here, T_{prep} is the preparation time for PQC integration, T_{migr} is the migration time to PQC, and T_{quantum} is the Quantum Deadline for completing this transition [46]. The essential condition for successful implementation is:

$$T_{\text{prep}} + T_{\text{migr}} < T_{\text{quantum}}.$$

This equation highlights the need to ensure that the total time for preparation and migration to quantum-resistant systems is less than the time before powerful quantum computers are expected to emerge.

Table 2. Promising PQC families and cryptosystems [12]

PQC Family	Supported Services	Cryptosystems
Lattice-based	key transport digital signatures	LWE, KYBER, FRODO DILITHIUM, FALCON
Code-based	key transport	McEliece, Niederreiter
Hash-based	digital signatures	MSS, XMSS, LMS, SPHINCS+

7 Recommendations for Migration

From the previous chapter, we derive two scenarios: data transmission over the internet for archival activities and attacks within the archive of CRITIS. This subsection is organized into three parts: internet-based communications, long-term security within internal archival practices, and other recommendations. These sections provide a comprehensive overview of options for integrating PQC.

To align with security requirements, organizations are required to classify information as part of their compliance with standards such as ISO 27001 [2] and the requirements of the NIS2 directive [24]. While these frameworks do not specify the classification criteria, they mandate the establishment of a classification system to manage information security effectively.

The classifications for the confidentiality of information from [47] are shown in Table 3.

Table 3. Classification of information

TOP SECRET	Information at the highest security level, where unauthorized disclosure could cause exceptionally grave damage to national security
SECRET	Indicates information whose unauthorized disclosure could cause serious damage to national security
CONFIDENTIAL	Refers to information whose unauthorized disclosure could damage national security
RESTRICTED	Information whose unauthorized disclosure could harm national security (lesser extent than CONFIDENTIAL)
UNCLASSIFIED/ Public	Information that can be made public without any harm to national security

Additionally, it's important to note that specific and further regulations may apply depending on the country, such as the VS-Verschlussklassifizierung in Germany [15]. Moreover, the chosen classification level can change after the expiration of a data embargo period. This means that information initially classified as CONFIDENTIAL can become publicly accessible after the embargo period has elapsed.

Standards require the categorization of data to determine appropriate security measures, akin to the classifications of *normal, high,* and *very high* used in the implementation of IT-Grundschutz [35], which assesses the security objectives of confidentiality, integrity, and availability of information. While the classification Table 3 primarily addresses confidentiality, it is crucial to also consider the integrity and authenticity of the data, especially in the context of long-term security. The implementation of PQC aims not only to protect the confidentiality of information but also to ensure its integrity and authenticity over extended periods.

Given the potential threats posed by quantum computing, adaptive measures must be established based on specific preconditions. Considering the handling of confidential data that is subject to a 30-year embargo period, a scenario frequently encountered in archival practices [9,14]. In CRITIS sectors such as chemicals, finance, and healthcare, statutory retention periods are prescribed, too. In the chemical industry, this is regulated by the REACH regulation, which mandates a ten-year retention of safety-relevant information [25]. In the financial sector, the Fourth EU Anti-Money Laundering Directive (AMLD) requires the retention of customer identification and transaction data for at least 10 years to support efforts to combat money laundering and terrorist financing [27]. In the European healthcare sector, specifically in France, the "Code de la santé publique" prescribes a retention period of at least 20 years for medical records to ensure continuous patient care and compliance with legal requirements [55]. In this embargo period, quantum computer probable and proactive measures are essential. In its report, "Quantum-safe cryptography - fundamentals, current developments, and recommendations," the Federal Office for Information Security (BSI) references two political hypotheses [17, 18], which state that "relevant quantum computers will be available in the early 2030 s" [22]. In a FAQ within the context of the 'Commercial National Security Algorithm Suite 2.0', it is stated that the National Security Systems will be quantum-resistant by 2035 [61].

Internet-Based Communications. Transfers from consumer to archive system, archive system to consumer, and company-archive-to-company-archive involving standard IT components, where the performance of cryptographic algorithms is not critical and can be managed through various strategies, including encapsulation:

1. In this approach, Transport Layer Security (TLS) is implemented using a hybrid method that integrates both PQC and classical cryptographic techniques. Specifically, two separate transport keys are employed: k_{pqc}, which is derived from PQC methods, and k_{classic}, which is generated using traditional cryptographic algorithms. Data t is encrypted (enc) using a two-layer encryption process where the inner layer uses the classical key and the outer layer uses the PQC key: $enc_{k_{\mathrm{pqc}}}(enc_{k_{\mathrm{classic}}}(t))$. This dual approach ensures that the data transmission benefits from the robustness of classical methods while gaining an additional layer of security from the quantum-resistant properties of PQC.

   The advantage of this setup is that it incorporates PQC as an extra security layer without completely abandoning the well-tested and familiar classical cryptographic protocols. This hybrid approach minimizes disruption to existing systems and allows for a smoother transition towards full quantum resistance. However, there are challenges to consider: the hybrid method introduces additional computational overhead due to the dual encryption process and PQC-PKI, and since PQC techniques are less mature and standardized compared to classical methods, there may be potential security risks and performance issues that are not yet fully understood. Ensuring compatibility and interoperability between classical and PQC-based systems remains a primary challenge, necessitating careful implementation and ongoing evaluation.

2. Symmetric encryption methods, used in exchanges between confidential producers and company archives, remain quantum-resistant. However, they require careful management and renewal of keys. In critical infrastructure companies, producers and consumers are usually within the internal network, activating established key management processes and facilitating symmetric

key distribution at OAIS access points. Key distribution must not occur over the internet; all internet connections to and from producer and consumer units must be secured with post-quantum resistant strategies to protect against cryptographic threats.

3. Although the physical handover of data carriers ensures direct control over data transfer, thus enhancing security, it requires stringent physical security measures and can be logistically challenging and less scalable compared to digital methods.

Given that quantum computers are not expected to decrypt data streams, including certificate structures, in real-time [32] in the foreseeable future to significantly compromise integrity, this scenario has not been considered in the context of data transmission over public connections.

Within the Archive Framework. In an *AIP* within the OAIS model, **Content Information** (the digital object) and **Representation Information** form the core, crucial for understanding and using the stored data. AIPs also include **Preservation Descriptive Information**:

- **Reference Information:** Unique identifiers for retrieval.
- **Provenance Information:** Data origin and history.
- **Context Information:** Context for data's original environment.
- **Fixity Information:** Integrity checks (hash values, digital signatures).
- **Representation Information:** Technical details for content use.
- **Access Rights Information:** Access permissions and conditions.

Michael Factor et al. simplify the contents of an AIP as shown in Fig. 2 [28].

According to DIN 31647 "Information and Documentation - Preservation of Evidence of Cryptographically Signed Documents", fixity information includes what are known as evidential data and evidence-relevant data [21]. To secure evidential value in archiving, these key steps are necessary according to [21]:

- Identification of data objects for integrity and authenticity protection through cryptographic evidence.
- Determination of all relevant cryptographic safeguards for these objects.
- Verification and, if necessary, supplementation of the safeguards with necessary validation data for comprehensive evidential value.
- Generation and integration of additional evidential data to document integrity and the time of archiving.

In addition it must meet legal standards for evidence preservation as it may be subject to authenticity checks in court [8]. Integrity is therefore closely linked with authenticity, non-repudiation and traceability. In Germany, the Signature Ordinance, supplementing the Signature Act, established the legal basis for re-signing data that must be preserved longer than the time for which the used algorithms are considered secure [30]. Although this ordinance has been superseded by the eIDAS Regulation, which slightly relaxed these rules, it continues

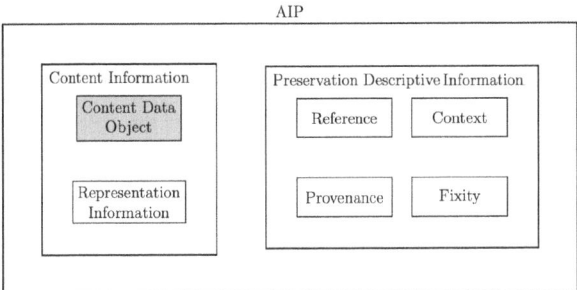

Fig. 2. Possible content of an AIP [28]

to stress the importance of preserving information long-term to uphold the legal validity of electronic signatures and seals amidst technological evolution [26]. Additionally, the more detailed Trust Services Act (Vertrauensdienstegesetz - VDG) specifies, that if necessary, qualified electronically signed, sealed, or time-stamped data must be re-secured by appropriate measures before the security value of the existing signatures, seals, or time stamps is reduced due to the passage of time. The new security measures must be implemented according to the current state of technology [31].

Table 4. Impact of large-scale quantum computers on cryptographic algorithms

Cryptographic Algorithm	Type	Purpose	Impact from large-scale quantum computer
AES	Symmetric key	Encryption	Larger key sizes needed
SHA-2, SHA-3	Hash function	Hash functions	Larger output needed
RSA	Public key	Signatures, key establishment	No longer secure
ECDSA, ECDH	Public key	Signatures, key exchange	No longer secure
DSA	Public key	Signatures, key exchange	No longer secure

To ensure data integrity, cryptographic hash functions generate checksums to detect alterations, but hashes alone can't track who made changes since they can be easily replaced. Digital signatures enhance this by guaranteeing authenticity and non-repudiation, attributing modifications to a specific source. However, these signatures, based on classical cryptographic methods, are vulnerable to quantum computing attacks (Table 4).

Digital certificates and public keys are managed using a Public Key Infrastructure (PKI), which involves the generation, distribution, verification, and revocation of certificates by a trusted Certification Authority (CA). PKI links public keys to user identities through signed digital certificates, ensuring authenticity with the CA's signature and data integrity through signature mechanisms using private keys [3]. Figure 3 illustrates a simple PKI with a RootCA and several SubCAs signing the AIPs. The PKI's structure can vary based on the use case and serves as an example.

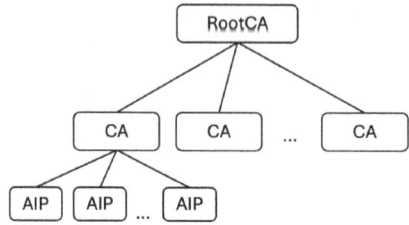

Fig. 3. Tier 2 PKI with RootCA and SubCAs

In the context of a PKI, the signature and verification process could be structured as follows:

Signature Process

1. During the ingest process or in case of modifications of the AIP, a cryptographic hash value of the AIP is generated (excluding certain fixity information).
2. This hash value then is signed with the private key of an archive CA, resulting in a digital signature.
3. The digital signature is associated with the AIP file, either by adding it to the AIP or by storing it separately.

Verification Process

1. To verify the AIP file, a user generates a new hash value of the file.
2. The archive's public key is used to decrypt the received signature and extracts the hash value.
3. If the extracted hash value matches the newly calculated hash value, the authenticity and integrity of the AIP file are confirmed.

Upon closer examination, the AIP format within the fixity data includes the signature along with all additional information. Thus, the signature is part of the AIP and integrated into the fixity data, as illustrated in Fig. 4. This additional information should comply with the criteria specified in DIN 31647. Consequently, the structure of the evidential information for the signature could be modeled on the Cryptographic Message Syntax (CMS), as defined in RFC 8933 [36]. In the context of a legally qualified signature, for example, [37] has depicted CMS as one variant.

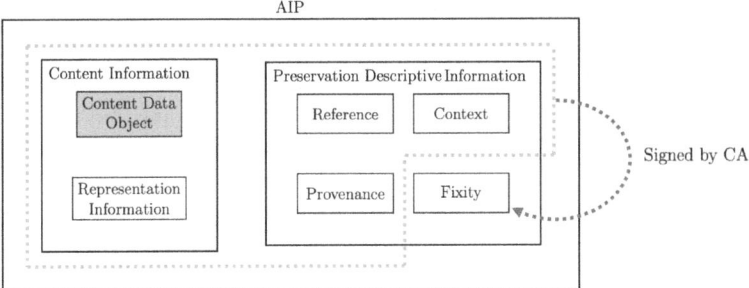

Fig. 4. Signing an API.

To maintain the structure of an AIP, a detached signature is created, meaning the data is separated from the signature information. Since the Cryptographic Message Syntax (CMS) is applicable across various applications, we provide an example of how it could be implemented in an archival context in Table 5.

Table 5. Components of a Possible CMS-based Digital Signature

Component	Description
Version	Version of the SignerInfo structure
Signer Identifier	Identifies the signer via a PKI certificate
Digest Algorithm	Hashing method used before signing
Signature Algorithm	Signature algorithm used
Signature	Signature generated by the CA
Signed Attributes (optional)	Time of the signature, expiration date
Certificate	Certificate chain
Digest Algorithm Identifiers	List of hashing algorithms used
ContentInfo	Reference to the signed data (not the files themselves)
Timestamp Token (optional)	Timestamp of the ingest
Archival Information (optional)	Additional optional information

This CMS container is integrated into the fixity information and meets the previously mentioned requirements of DIN 31646 [21]. Integrity and authenticity are assured by the signature originating from a trusted authority. All cryptographic methods and validation data used are cited within the container or in the certificate chain under an X.509 certificate framework. Furthermore, the CMS format allows for additional options, such as appending timestamps that can denote the ingestion of the SIP or the creation of the AIP.

8   Long-Term Archiving Using PQC

We aim to present two variants for the integration of PQC into such a PKI framework. A method of double signing is described in [6] and suggests the establishment of a second PKI with PQC methods along the existing PKI utilizing classical cryptography. This scenario is illustrated in Fig. 5. Obviously, an advantage is the ability to apply existing processes to a second PKI with quantum-resistant procedures in parallel by, e.g., adding a second signature to the AIP within the fixity data. A disadvantage is the additional overhead of the second signature which is larger in general [40,53]. During the verification phase of double signing, uncertainties may arise if a failure occurs, as it often remains unclear which of the two signatures – classical or post-quantum – has been compromised. This could be due to the potential vulnerability of classical methods to quantum computer attacks or undiscovered weaknesses in the arising PQC algorithms. A solution could be found in establishing multiple PQC-PKIs using various algorithms.

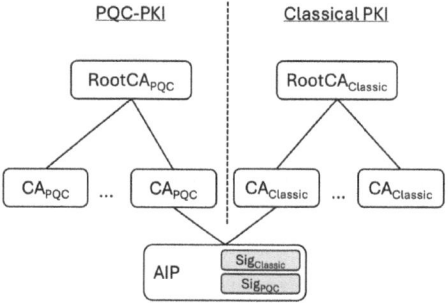

Fig. 5. Signing with two PKIs

Another structure for a PKI is given by hybrid certificates: within an X.509 certificate, corresponding classical and quantum-resistant methods are concatenated [20]. This leaner variant has the disadvantage of not yet being an established method. Furthermore, interoperability between such certificates only is possible within the same application. This means that in the archival area of an CRITIS company, it would be required to be standardized. As another disadvantage, an existing PKI must be completely replaced by a new hybrid PKI. Although the storage requirements of this solution are lower, the organizational effort is greater. In addition, in the example from [20], only one quantum-resistant method is combined with the classical method. The addition of many methods should be considered when creating the PKI which may lead to potentially confusing X.509 certificates.

Further Approaches and Considerations

The topic of establishing and migrating PQC in classical environments is widely discussed and presents solutions beyond those we have presented. Another approach could be, e.g., the decentralization of the PKI through a blockchain [5]. Additionally, intensively tested mechanisms such as Merkle Trees can also be used [45]. Either the hash values of multiple AIPs can be constructed into a Merkle Tree, or only the Merkle Root needs to be signed, minimizing the effort for the PQC-PKI. DIN 31644 and the OAIS Reference Model emphasize observing the latest technological developments that could influence the long-term preservation of data archived in a long-term archive and integrating appropriate measures [1,19]. ISO 14721 further states that a periodic risk analysis should take place within the model.

9   Future Work

This paper analyzed potential future threats to CRITIS archives, focusing on long-term secure document storage. However, proof-of-concept and reference implementations are lacking in data transport and evidence preservation. Future work should develop a proof-of-concept to integrate long-term storage archives into CRITIS companies, addressing both current and future security needs across management, IT, and OT.

10   Conclusion

Archives are crucial for critical infrastructures, with the OAIS model providing a framework for regulatory compliance. Quantum computing introduces new archiving challenges, risking confidentiality and data integrity. We propose strategies like secure hash trees and quantum-resistant signatures. However, establishing a Public Key Infrastructure (PKI) remains complex, requiring comprehensive approaches to ensure long-term data security.

References

1. ISO/TC 20/SC 13. ISO 14721:2012 space data and information transfer systems - open archival information system (OAIS) - Reference model. Standard, International Organization for Standardization (ISO), Geneva, CH, September 2012
2. ISO/IEC JTC 1/SC 27. ISO/IEC 27001: information technology – security techniques – information security management systems – requirements. ISO Standard, October 2022. http://www.iso.org/iso/home/standards/management-standards/iso27001.htm
3. Carlisle Adams and Steve Lloyd. Understanding PKI: Concepts, Standards, and Deployment Considerations. Addison-Wesley Professional, 2 edition, November 2002

4. Linux Foundation's Post-Quantum Cryptography Alliance. Open Quantum Safe: software for the transition to quantum-resistant cryptography. webpage
5. An, H. and Kim, K.: QChain: quantum-resistant and decentralized PKI using blockchain. In: 2018 Symposium on Cryptography and Information Security (SCIS), Niigata, Japan, January 2018. The Institute of Electronics, Information and Communication Engineers. Graduate School of Information Security, KAIST, 291, Daehak-ro, Yuseong-gu, Daejeon, South Korea 34141
6. Bernstein, D.J., Hülsing, A., Lange, T., Rekleitis, E.: Post-quantum cryptography integration study. Technical report, European Union Agency for Cybersecurity (ENISA), October 2022. ISBN: 978-92-9204-590-6, https://doi.org/10.2824/151162, Catalogue Number: TP-03-22-080-EN-N
7. Bundesamt für Sicherheit in der Informationstechnik (BSI). Status of quantum computer development. Technical Report 2.0, Bundesamt für Sicherheit in der Informationstechnik, August 2023. Accessed 17 Mar 2024
8. Bundesrepublik Deutschland. *Zivilprozessordnung.* Bundesgesetzblatt (BGBl. I S. 3202), December 2005. letzte Änderung durch Art. 5 und 6 G vom 8. Oktober 2023
9. Bundesrepublik Deutschland. Personenstandsgesetz (PStG). Bundesgesetzblatt, Februar 2007. Vom 19. Februar 2007 (BGBl. I S. 122), zuletzt geändert durch Artikel 3 des Gesetzes vom 17. Juli 2023 (BGBl. 2023 I Nr. 190)
10. Bundesrepublik Deutschland. Gesetz über das Bundesamt für Sicherheit in der Informationstechnik (BSI-Gesetz - BSIG), volume BGBl. I S. 2821. Bundesrepublik Deutschland, 2009. Zuletzt geändert durch Artikel 12 des Gesetzes vom 23. Juni 2021 (BGBl. I S. 1982)
11. Chen, L., et al.: Report on post-quantum cryptography. Technical report, National Institute of Standards and Technology, http://dx.doi.org/10.6028/NIST.IR.8105, April 2016
12. Paar, C., Pelzl, J., Güneysu, T.: Understanding cryptography: from established symmetric and asymmetric ciphers to post-quantum algorithms. Springer Verlag (2024)
13. Consultative Committee for Space Data Systems (CCSDS). Recommendation for Space Data System Practices: Reference Model for an Open Archival Information System (OAIS). Recommended Practice CCSDS 650.0-P-3, CCSDS Secretariat, Space Communications and Navigation Office, NASA Headquarters, Washington, DC, USA, April 2019. PINK (PRE-MAGENTA) BOOK
14. Der Grosse Rat des Kantons Basel-Stadt. Gesetz über das Archivwesen (Archivgesetz), September 1996. Vom 11. September 1996, Stand 1. Januar 2012
15. Hessisches Ministerium des Innern und für Sport. Verschlusssachenanweisung (VS-Anweisung, VSA) für das Land Hessen. Verwaltungsvorschrift des Hessischen Ministeriums des Innern und für Sport, February 2010. Gültig ab 01. Mai 2010, Aktenzeichen Z 1 - 03 a 08.08
16. Deutsche Nationalbibliothek. Langzeitarchivierungssystem koala. online, 2019. Unser kooperatives Langzeitarchivierungssystem koala übernimmt die Aufgabe der dauerhaften Speicherung digitaler Objekte. Das System wurde in Kooperation mit der Gesellschaft für wissenschaftliche Datenverarbeitung mbH Göttingen (GWDG) entwickelt und löste 2017 das Digital Information Archiving System (DIAS) ab. Die Deutsche Nationalbibliothek ist als vertrauenswürdiges digitales Langzeitarchiv geprüft und zertifiziert
17. Deutscher Bundestag. Antwort der Bundesregierung auf die Kleine Anfrage der Abgeordneten Dr. Anna Christmann, Kai Gehring, Margit Stumpp, weiterer Abgeordneter und der Fraktion BÜNDNIS 90 / DIE GRÜNEN. Drucksache 19/24762, 2021. Zugriff auf Dokumente des Deutschen Bundestages

18. Deutscher Bundestag. Antwort der Bundesregierung auf die Kleine Anfrage der Abgeordneten Dr. Konstantin von Notz, Tabea Rößner, Dr. Irene Mihalic, weiterer Abgeordneter und der Fraktion BÜNDNIS 90 / DIE GRÜNEN. Drucksache 19/25549, 2021. Zugriff auf Dokumente des Deutschen Bundestages

19. Deutsches Institut für Normung, Berlin, Germany. *Information und Dokumentation – Kriterien für vertrauenswürdige digitale Langzeitarchive*, 2012-04 edition, April 2012. Available from Beuth Verlag GmbH

20. Dimitrios Chatziamanetoglou and Konstantinos Rantos. On the implementation of x509-compliant quantum-safe hybrid certificates. Technical Report STO-MP-IST-SET-198-A1-02, NATO Communications and Information Agency, Obourg, 7034, Hainaut, Belgium; Ag. Loukas, 65404, Kavala, Greece (2022)

21. DIN-Normenausschuss Bibliotheks- und Dokumentationswesen (NABD). DIN 31647: Information und Dokumentation – Beweiserterhaltung kryptographisch signierter Dokumente. Beuth Verlag GmbH, May 2015

22. Ehlen, S., et al.: Quantum-safe cryptography – fundamentals, current developments and recommendation. Federal Office for Information Security (BSI), Godesberger Allee 185–189, 53175 Bonn, Germany, October 2021. This brochure is part of the Federal Office for Information Security's public relations work. It is provided free of charge and is not intended for sale

23. Apple Security Engineering and Architecture (SEAR). iMessage with PQ3: The new state of the art in quantum-secure messaging at scale. webpage, Februar 2024

24. European Parliament and Council of the European Union. Directive (EU) 2022/2555 on measures for a high common level of cybersccurity across the Union, amending Regulation (EU) No 910/2014 and Directive (EU) 2018/1972, and repealing Directive (EU) 2016/1148. Official Journal of the European Union, 2022. OJ L 333, 27.12.2022, p. 80

25. European Parliament and the Council of the European Union. Regulation (EC) No 1907/2006 concerning the Registration, Evaluation, Authorisation and Restriction of Chemicals (REACH), establishing a European Chemicals Agency, amending Directive 1999/45/EC and repealing Council Regulation (EEC) No 793/93 and Commission Regulation (EC) No 1488/94 as well as Council Directive 76/769/EEC and Commission Directives 91/155/EEC, 93/67/EEC, 93/105/EC and 2000/21/EC. Official Journal of the European Union, 2006. Accessed on 01/12/2023

26. European Parliament and the Council of the European Union. Regulation (EU) No 910/2014 of the European Parliament and of the Council of 23 July 2014 on electronic identification and trust services for electronic transactions in the internal market and repealing Directive 1999/93/EC. http://data.europa.eu/eli/reg/2014/910/oj, July 2014. Document 32014R0910, In force

27. European Parliament and the Council of the European Union. Directive (EU) 2015/849 of the European Parliament and of the Council of 20 May 2015 on the prevention of the use of the financial system for the purposes of money laundering or terrorist financing, amending Regulation (EU) No 648/2012 of the European Parliament and of the Council, and repealing Directive 2005/60/EC of the European Parliament and of the Council and Commission Directive 2006/70/EC. Official Journal of the European Union, 2015. Accessed 01 Dec 2023

28. Factor, M., et al.: Preservation DataStores: architecture for preservation aware storage. In: 24th IEEE Conference on Mass Storage Systems and Technologies (MSST 2007), pp. 3 – 15, October 2007

29. DIN Deutsches Institut für Normung e. V. DIN 31646: Preservation of archival and library materials - Requirements for storage in libraries, archives and museums, December 2023. DIN 31646:2023-12

30. Germany. Signaturverordnung (SigV), 2001. Repealed by the law from 18.07.2017, BGBl. I S. 2745

31. Germany. Vertrauensdienstegesetz (VDG). Bundesgesetzblatt Teil I, July 2017. "Vertrauensdienstegesetz vom 18. Juli 2017 (BGBl. I S. 2745), geändert durch Artikel 2 des Gesetzes vom 18. Juli 2017 (BGBl. I S. 2745)"

32. Gidney, C., Ekerå, M.: How to factor 2048 bit RSA integers in 8 hours using 20 million noisy qubits. Quantum **5**, 433 (2021)

33. Gorniak, S., Koerting, S., Ombelli, D., Tirtea, R., Ikonomou, D. :National eIDs in pan-European e-Government Services, https://www.enisa.europa.eu/, January 2010. Accessed 18 Mar 2024

34. Grover, L.K.: A fast quantum mechanical algorithm for database search. In: Proceedings of the Twenty-Eighth Annual ACM Symposium on Theory of Computing, STOC 1996, pp. 212–219, New York, NY, USA, 1996. Association for Computing Machinery

35. Schildt, S.H., Hoffmann, B., Oppelt, J., Welticke, J. (eds.) IT-Grundschutz-Kompendium. Reguvis Fachmedien GmbH, Köln, 6 edition, 2023. Erscheinungsdatum (2023)

36. Housley, R.: Update to the Cryptographic Message Syntax (CMS) for Algorithm Identifier Protection. RFC 8933, Internet Engineering Task Force (IETF), October 2020. Updates RFC 5652

37. Hühnlein, D., Korte, U.: Rechtliche Rahmenbedingungen der elektronischen Rechnung. In Jana Dittmann, editor, *Sicherheit 2006: Sicherheit - Schutz und Zuverlässigkeit, Beiträge der 3. Jahrestagung des Fachbereichs Sicherheit der Gesellschaft für Informatik e.v. (GI), 20.-22. Februar 2006 in Magdeburg*, vol. P-77, pp. 256–269. GI, January 2006

38. Hülsing, A., Ning, K.-C., Schwabe, P., Weber, F.J., Zimmermann, P.R.: Postquantum WireGuard. In: 2021 IEEE Symposium on Security and Privacy (SP), pp. 304–321 (2021)

39. Kampanakis, P., Panburana, P., Daw, E., Van Geest, D.: The Viability of Postquantum X.509 Certificates. Cryptology ePrint Archive, Paper 2018/063 (2018)

40. Kampanakis, P., Sikeridis, D.: Two PQ signature use-cases: non-issues, challenges and potential solutions. Cryptology ePrint Archive, Paper 2019/1276 (2019)

41. Kärberg, T., et al.: Hans Fredrik Berg, Björn Skog, Henrik Ek, and Karin Bredenberg. SIP specification, records export requirements, transfer and ingest, Best Practice (2018)

42. Kong, I.: Transitioning towards quantum-safe government: examining stages of growth models for quantum-safe public key infrastructure systems. In: Proceedings of the 15th International Conference on Theory and Practice of Electronic Governance, ICEGOV 2022, pp. 499–503, New York, NY, USA, Association for Computing Machinery (2022)

43. Kwiatkowski, K., Valenta, L.: The TLS post-quantum experiment. webpage, October 2019

44. Mavroeidis, V., Vishi, K., Zych, M.D., Jøsang, A.: the impact of quantum computing on present cryptography. *CoRR*, abs/1804.00200 (2018)

45. Merkle., R.C.: A digital signature based on a conventional encryption function. In: Pomerance, C. (ed.), Advances in Cryptology — CRYPTO 1987, pp. 369–378, Berlin, Heidelberg (1988)

46. Mosca, M.: Cybersecurity in a quantum world: will we be ready? April 2015. University of Waterloo, Institute for Quantum Computing, CryptoWorks21
47. North Atlantic Treaty Organization. Security Within the North Atlantic Treaty Organization (NATO). Note by the Secretary General, November 2020. Revision 1 to C-M(2002)49 dated 17 June 2002
48. O'Brien, D.: Protecting chrome traffic with hybrid Kyber KEM. webpage, August 2023
49. Office of Parliamentary Counsel, editor. National Greenhouse and Energy Reporting Act 2007. No. 175, 2007. Office of Parliamentary Counsel, Canberra, compilation no. 25 edition, 2024. Compilation date: 20 March 2024, Includes amendments: Act No. 74, 2023, Registered: 3 April 2024
50. Ott, D., Peikert, C., and other workshop participants. Identifying research challenges in post quantum cryptography migration and cryptographic agility 2019
51. Paar, C., Pelzl, J.: Understanding Cryptography: A Textbook for Students and Practitioners, 1st edn. Springer Publishing Company, Incorporated (2009)
52. Singh, S.T.P., Gupta, S.: Malware detection in PDF and office documents: a survey. Inf. Secur. J. Global Perspect. **29**(3), 134–153 (2020)
53. Raavi, M., Chandramouli, P., Wuthier, S., Zhou, X., Chang, S.-Y.: Performance characterization of post-quantum digital certificates. In: 2021 International Conference on Computer Communications and Networks (ICCCN), pp. 1–9 (2021)
54. Rahmanto, K.N., Riasetiawan, M.: Data preservation process in big data environment using open archival information system. In: 2018 4th International Conference on Science and Technology (ICST), pp. 1–5 (2018)
55. Française, R.: Code de la santé publique. Légifrance, 2023. Accessed 01 Dec 2023
56. SCOPE. OAIS-Conform Archive Solutions. Website (2024). Accessed 13 May 2024
57. Shor, P.W.: Algorithms for quantum computation: discrete logarithms and factoring. In: Proceedings 35th Annual Symposium on Foundations of Computer Science, pp. 124–134 (1994)
58. Sikeridis, D., Kampanakis, P., Devetsikiotis, M.: Post-quantum authentication in TLS 1.3: a performance study. IACR Cryptol. ePrint Arch., 2020:71, 2020
59. Sosnowski, M., et al.: The performance of post-quantum TLS 1.3. In: Companion of the 19th International Conference on Emerging Networking EXperiments and Technologies, CoNEXT 2023, pp. 19–27, New York, NY, USA, Association for Computing Machinery (2023)
60. Todd, M.: File formats for preservation. DPC Technology Watch Report. Accessed December 1:2014, 2009
61. U.S. Department of Defense. Csi cnsa 2.0 faq. online, Sep 2022. Frequently Asked Questions for the Commercial Solutions for Classified Program National Security Agency (NSA) Commercial National Security Algorithm Suite (CNSA) 2.0
62. U.S. environmental protection agency. National primary drinking water regulations. Technical report, U.S. Environmental Protection Agency, 2003. Accessed 14 May 2024
63. Wiesmaier, A., Alnahawi, N., Grasmeyer, T.: Julian Geißler. Pia Bauspieß, and Andreas Heinemann. On PQC Migration and Crypto-Agility, Alexander Zeier (2021)

Exploratory Trend Analysis of Supply Chain Cybersecurity Management

Hyunwoo Yoo[(✉)] [iD], Manhyun Chung, Moonsu Jang, and Woo-Nyon Kim

Affiliated Institute of Electronics and Telecommunications Research Institute, Daejeon, Korea
{uwill,manhyun,moonsujang,wnkim}@nsr.re.kr

Abstract. As critical supply chain cybersecurity threats increase, so does the importance of a systematic supply chain cybersecurity management strategy. Managing risk factors in the supply chains is particularly important to ensure the safe, reliable, and secure operation of critical systems such as infrastructure, cyber-physical systems, and industrial control systems, whose breach can extend to significant physical, economic and environmental damage. This paper presents case studies of thirteen supply chain cybersecurity management practices from public and private industrial sectors, and an exploratory trend analysis. The case studies concentrate on the practices of critical system operators in managing the security of their suppliers from a comprehensive supply chain cybersecurity risk management perspective. While the thirteen cases are not representative enough to draw clear trends, the results of the exploratory trend analysis are still valuable in that they provide insights for organizations operating critical systems to formulate supply chain cybersecurity management strategies and plans.

Keywords: Cybersecurity supply chain risk management · procurement · supplier management · supply chain cybersecurity · third-party security

1 Introduction

Supply chain cybersecurity has emerged as a critical issue since a large number of reports and articles have emphasized its importance [1–3]. In particular, numerous critical supply chain cybersecurity issues, such as the SolarWinds Orion Platform attack (2020), Log4j security vulnerability (2021), MOVEit transfer data breaches (2023), and xz-utils backdoor (2024) have highlighted the significance of cybersecurity to a great extent [4, 5].

The supply chain has been around since ancient times for distributing products and services. However, contemporary supply chains are exhibiting an increased vulnerability to a multitude of risks and disruptions [6]. Cybersecurity threats to supply chains are constantly evolving for two main reasons. First, the complexity and interdependencies of supply chains are increasing as they have expanded globally based on advancements in industrial technologies. Another is new threat vectors and increased attack surfaces introduced by rapid convergence between industrial fields and the digitalization of fundamental technologies.

G. Oliva et al. (Eds.): CRITIS 2024, LNCS 15549, pp. 64–83, 2025.
https://doi.org/10.1007/978-3-031-84260-3_4

Managing risk factors in the supply chains is particularly important to ensure the safe, reliable, and secure operation of critical systems such as critical infrastructure, cyber-physical systems, and industrial control systems (ICS). Given the potential for severe physical, economic and environmental harm from a breach, these systems are generally well protected. In contrast, a considerable number of suppliers still lack the human and financial resources to adequately address cybersecurity concerns [7].

While various studies related to supply chain cybersecurity have been conducted [8–12], there is relatively little research on the systematic risk management of supply chains throughout its entire lifecycle. In particular, software supply chain threats have recently received considerable attention, with activities to introduce software bill-of-materials and vulnerability exploitability exchange being a focus.

This paper presents thirteen supply chain cybersecurity management cases from public and private industrial sectors and an exploratory trend analysis. While the cases are not representative enough to draw clear trends, the results of the exploratory trend analysis are still valuable in that they provide insights and ideas for organizations operating critical systems to formulate supply chain cybersecurity management strategies and plans. The case studies concentrate on the practices of critical system operators in managing the security of their suppliers from a comprehensive supply chain cybersecurity risk management perspective (which is why we do not focus on techniques or cases related to software supply chain security management).

The public sector cases from the US and UK have been selected for analysis. In the private sector, we endeavored to select companies from a variety of industries, including major ICS manufacturers (Siemens, General Electrics, and unnamed companies), global information and communications technology (ICT) companies (Microsoft, Seagate, and unnamed companies), and an oil and gas infrastructure operating company (Saudi Aramco).

2 Supply Chain Cybersecurity Management

2.1 Overview of Supply Chain Cybersecurity Management

To build and operate critical systems comprised of information technology (IT) and/or operational technology (OT) systems, various types of suppliers are required, and complex interconnections are established between organizations. As a result, the supply chain of the system is constructed in the form of a network, as shown in Fig. 1 [13, 14]. The suppliers include system integrators, service providers (such as outsourced development, maintenance, communication network services, cloud, and data center services), component suppliers (including manufacturers, wholesalers, retailers), and so forth. The connection types between organizations include ICT linkages, where data are transferred, and logistics linkages, where physical transportation occurs [15].

It is necessary to implement supply chain cybersecurity management to protect the system operator node of a supply chain network. The Protection of a specific node within a network necessitates security management activities not only for the corresponding node, but also all nodes and linkages connected to it. Therefore, supply chain cybersecurity management involves activities for ensuring the security of all organizations and linkages within the supply chain. Moreover, it is also essential to apply this management approach throughout the entire lifecycle. The goal of secure operation of the critical system is only fully achieved when the system is securely deployed, operated, and ultimately decommissioned [16]. Taken together, from a critical system operator's perspective, supply chain cybersecurity management is a set of activities for verifying and ensuring the trustworthiness of every node and linkage in the supply chain throughout its entire lifecycle.

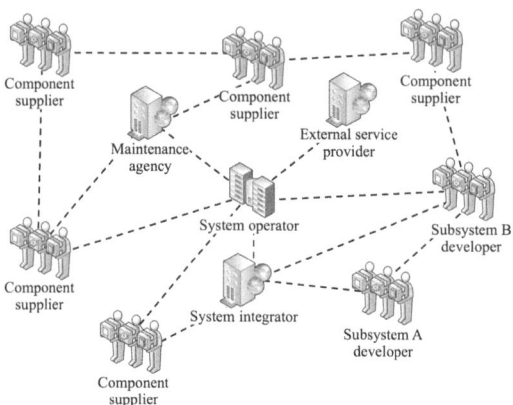

Fig. 1. Simplified structure of a typical supply chain.

2.2   Fundamental Considerations for Supply Chain Cybersecurity Management

The supply chain cybersecurity management has a multitude of target entities, a significantly broad scope, and long time period (the entire lifecycle) that it's practically impossible to cover comprehensively, thus necessitating selection and focus when establishing a management system. We have identified fundamental considerations that critical system operators should take into account while establishing or enhancing their supply chain cybersecurity management systems.

Table 1 presents a summary of the considerations, comprising five management elements and the taxonomy of types for each element. The initial three considerations—management entity, management scope, and management step—determine the extent of supply chain cybersecurity management and account for its comprehensive nature, thus it's nearly impossible to plan management for every system and component, for the full scope, and for the entire lifecycle. Initially recognizing the significance of the supply chain cybersecurity, it is easy to feel discouraged by the lack of resources and the overwhelming workload. Hence, the operators should identify the entities, scope and steps that need to be managed first, taking into account the national regulations, the industry environment and the organizational context. The following two considerations—management standard and verification method—are important factors that determine how practitioners manage, and should be determined based on the management entity, scope, and step considered earlier.

Table 1. Fundamental considerations for supply chain cybersecurity management system.

Code	Management Element	Type of Element
ENT	Management Entity	• **ENT.1** ICT/OT product and service providers • **ENT.2** Critical data processors
SCP	Management Scope	• **SCP.1** Supplier organizational security - **SCP.1.1** General organizational security of suppliers - **SCP.1.2** Development organizational security of suppliers - **SCP.1.3** Operational organizational security of suppliers • **SCP.2** Supplier linkage security - **SCP.2.1** ICT linkage security of suppliers - **SCP.2.2** Logistics linkage security of suppliers • **SCP.3** Comprehensive cybersecurity supply chain risk management (includes SCP.1 and SCP.2)
STP	Management Step	• **STP.1** Pre-acquisition (design, development, and production) • **STP.2** Acquisition (distribution, acquisition, and deployment) • **STP.3** Post-acquisition (operation and maintenance) • **STP.4** Disposal • **STP.5** Entire lifecycle (includes STP.1 through STP.4)
STD	Management Standard	• **STD.1** International standards • **STD.2** National standards • **STD.3** Entity's self-standards
MTD	Verification Method	• **MTD.1** Verification upon acquisition - **MTD.1.1** First-party verification upon acquisition - **MTD.1.2** s-party verification upon acquisition - **MTD.1.3** Third-party verification upon acquisition • **MTD.2** Audit before and after acquisition - **MTD.2.1** First-party audit - **MTD.2.2** s-party audit - **MTD.2.3** Third-party audit

These considerations are useful for organizations that are newly establishing a supply chain cybersecurity management system. They are effective for assessing the current status of practical cases and are also useful for organizations that already have a management system to determine reasonable enhancements and supplementary directions. Additionally, they can be utilized to evaluate supply chain cybersecurity management trends.

3   Case Studies on Supply Chain Cybersecurity Management

This section presents the results of case studies conducted to gain insight into the current status of supply chain cybersecurity management in practice and to establish a path forward. We have emphasized cases that implement supply chain cybersecurity management using international or national standards. This emphasis stems from our recognition that the standards frequently underpin certification programs, providing an efficient means of substantiating supplier security. Nevertheless, the studies also include several cases of leading global companies utilizing self-standards that are closely aligned with critical infrastructure construction and management. These include major ICS manufacturers (Siemens, General Electrics, and unnamed companies), global ICT companies (Microsoft, Seagate, and unnamed companies), and an oil and gas infrastructure operating company (Saudi Aramco).

3.1 Supply Chain Management Using ISO 27001 Certification

The International Organization for Standardization (ISO)/International Electrotechnical Commission (IEC) 27001 certification, commonly referred as ISO 27001, is widely used internationally in industries when the security management level of a contract partner must be inspected or when suppliers need to publicize their security status. For example, major ICS manufacturers (Siemens and General Electric) and a global ICT company (Microsoft) require ISO 27001 certification from suppliers for supply chain cybersecurity risk management. Sections 3.7, 3.8, and 3.9 detail the management cases of these companies.

In addition to the private industrial sector, the government procurement processes of various countries demand ISO 27001 certification for suppliers or additional points are awarded to certified suppliers to strengthen supply chain security.

The evaluation factors of suppliers for each procurement conducted by the General Services Administration (GSA) of the US are determined based on the characteristics of supplied products or services. However, additional points are awarded for ISO 27001 certification when evaluating a request for proposal (RFP) in of most cases of procuring ICT systems [17]. "Cybersecurity and SCRM assessment" is an RFP evaluation criterion for ITES-3S, which is a contract vehicle for providing IT services and solutions to the US army, Department of Defense (DoD), and other federal agencies, as well as for 8(a) STARS III, Alliant 2, VETS 2, and Polaris, which are GSA government-wide acquisition contracts (GWACs) for providing IT solutions to federal agencies efficiently and economically. This factor is used to evaluate cybersecurity and supply chain risk mitigation measures, and additional points are awarded to suppliers with related certifications such as ISO 27001 and ISO 28000.

In the UK, suppliers handling critical data in the process of procuring ICT products and services for government agencies are required to obtain the Cyber Essentials (CE) certification. However, the ISO 27001 certification includes all the requirements of CE that can be substituted [18]. Section 3.4 covers the specifics of supply chain cybersecurity management cases using CE in the UK.

3.2 Supply Chain Management Using O-TTPS Certification

The Open-Trusted Technology Provider™ (O-TTPS) certification based on ISO/IEC 20243 standards is used to promote the security and integrity of commercial off-the-shelf ICT products throughout their lifecycles.

Seagate was previously experiencing excessive manpower consumption due to the varying types of cybersecurity evidence required by customers. However, Seagate announced that the submission of their O-TTPS certification efficiently demonstrated that their supplied products satisfy supply chain security requirements from various clients, including OEM and cloud service providers [19].

The Solutions for Enterprise-Wide Procurement (SEWP), which is a GWAC process operated by National Aeronautics and Space Administration (NASA) in the US, manages prime contract holders with sufficient supply capacity and performance based on a preliminary competition, thereby enabling the efficient supply of ICT and audio-visual products. The proportion of suppliers with O-TTPS certification is continuously increasing with 83 of 139 suppliers as of May of 2024 [20]. NASA advises that acquirers can lessen the risk of purchasing products that have been contaminated during the supply chain lifecycle by choosing suppliers with this certification.

3.3 Supply Chain Management by The US Federal Government

US Federal agencies must implement supply chain cybersecurity management by complying with National Institute of Standards and Technology (NIST) standards such as NIST special publication (SP) 800–161, NIST SP 800–171, NIST SP 800–172, and NIST Cybersecurity Framework (CSF). The authority and responsibility of managing and overseeing compliance with these standards for federal information systems remain with the secretary of homeland security and director of the Office of Management and Budget (OMB) [21]. All federal agencies must independently perform annual evaluations of their compliance with the regulations through the Office of Inspector General (OIG) or through an external audit agency and must report the results to the OMB and congress. Noncompliance results in penalties to corresponding organizations, including censure by congress, loss of work for several agency employees, reduction in federal funding, increased government oversight, and reputation damage [22].

a. C-SCRM with NIST SP 800–161. All US federal agencies must perform cybersecurity supply chain risk management (C-SCRM) as part of their information resource management activities and comply with NIST SP 800–161 as minimum requirements [23]. Federal agencies can define security requirements using the controls of the standard with which suppliers must comply and demand compliance from suppliers when acquiring ICT products and services.

Especially, in response to Executive Order (EO) 14028 on Improving the Nation's Cybersecurity [24], NIST revised NIST SP 800–161 to Revision 1 in May 2022. It does not address software supply chain risk alone; rather, it also provides guidance on identifying, assessing, and responding to supply chain cybersecurity risks at all levels of an organization [13].

b. Safeguarding CUI from Suppliers. In accordance with the Federal Acquisition Regulation (FAR) 52.204 of the US, nonfederal systems and organizations handling controlled unclassified information (CUI) from federal agencies must comply with the requirements of NIST SP 800–171 [25]. The subjects of this regulation include manufacturers and service providers within the federal agencies' supply chains, as well as consultants and universities who perform research using federal funds.

In accordance with the Defense FAR Supplement 252.204, all DoD suppliers are required to obtain a Cybersecurity Maturity Model Certification (CMMC), because they consistently handle CUI [26, 27]. In November, 2021, CMMC 2.0 was released with updated program structure and requirements. The model has been streamlined from five to three compliance levels as detailed in Table 2, with a focus on the most critical requirements to ensure reliable assessments with reduced costs [28].

Table 2. CMMC 2.0 requirements and assessment methods

Levels	Requirements	Assessment
Level 1	15 requirements	Annual self-assessment and annual affirmation
Level 2	110 requirements with NIST SP 800–171	Triennial third-party assessment and annual affirmation; Triennial self-assessment and annual affirmation for select programs
Level 3	110 + requirements with NIST SP 800–171 and 800–172	Triennial government-led assessment and annual affirmation

The CMMC assessments includes a Supplier Performance Risk System (SPRS) score. SPRS, which is provided by the US Navy, is a web application that gathers, processes and displays data about supplier performance, and analyzes the risk that supplier represents, among other things. All contractors of the DoD must register their assessment results for the requirements through the SPRS and submit the registered information for the CMMC assessment [29].

c. C-SCRM Using NIST Cybersecurity Framework. According to EO 13800 on Strengthening the Cybersecurity of Federal Networks and Critical Infrastructures, operators and owners of national critical infrastructure and all federal agencies operating IT systems are required to perform cybersecurity risk management with NIST CSF [30].

The CSF supports federal agencies to interact with their suppliers. The framework profile can be incorporated into the acquisition process as a foundation for evaluation criteria, solicitation responses, proposal/quote reviews, and minimum contract requirements. The use of profiles allows suppliers the flexibility to select from various standards and practices to meet federal agency-specific requirements while communicating their cybersecurity posture in a consistent way [31].

Compliance with the CSF, including supply chain risk management, is verified through periodic audits [32]. Agencies whose information security risk is high based on an assessment of cybersecurity preparedness are audited annually and all other agencies are audited biennially. Audits are conducted by the inspector generals of the OIG and the audit reports are transmitted to the OMB, Office of Science and Technology Policy, Government Accountability Office, and congress.

3.4 Supply Chain Management Using Cyber Essentials in the UK

Since October 2014, the Crown Commercial Service (CCS), which is the central procurement agency of the UK government, has required CE certification from the National Cyber Security Centre if companies supplying ICT products and services to the central government handle critical data [18].

The subjects are suppliers who handle personal information, and provide ICT systems and services designed to store or process official-level data in the Government Protective Marking scheme. The certification is also required for individual procurement cases if the CE are considered to be an appropriate measure for mitigating security risks, such as when critical data are stored outside the UK or at the US-EU Safe Harbor, as well as separate disaster recovery locations [18].

The CE scheme used for certifications includes only five key controls (firewalls, secure configurations, user access control, malware protection, and security update management) for protecting the IT infrastructure of each organization from internet-based attacks [33]. Two levels of certification are available: CE, which is based on self-evaluation, and CE Plus (CE +), which is based on a third-party assessment. Given that CE and CE + certifications have a 12-month validity period, they must be renewed on an annual basis [34].

The UK Ministry of Defence (MoD) demands CE certification in addition to different compliance requirements for security management based on the cyber risk profile (CRP) of each procurement contract [35]. Contracted suppliers who have received "very low" for their CRP rating must obtain CE certification, whereas those who have received "low," "moderate," or "high" ratings must obtain the CE + certification and comply with additional requirements in different degrees depending on the CRP.

3.5 UL Supplier Cyber Trust Level

In 2020, Underwriters Laboratories (UL) launched the Supplier Cyber Trust Level (SCTL) program as a supply chain cybersecurity evaluation service. The SCTL is a document-based supplier trust level evaluation solution that provides consultations to establish appropriate documents and evidence for a desired trust level [36]. Trust levels are divided into five categories: levels 1 (Nascent), 2 (Developing), 3 (Challenger), 4 (Contender), and 5 (Leader). The requirements for evaluation are determined based on various industrial standards such as ISO 9001, ISO 27001, ISO 20243, CMMC, IEC 62443–4-1, European Telecommunications Standards Institute (ETSI) technical specification (TS) 103 645, North American Electric Reliability Corporation (NERC) Critical Infrastructure Protection (CIP)-013, NIST SP 800–171, and NIST SP 800–53, as well as best practices.

The SCTL is an evaluation and consultation service, rather than an official certification program. As such, service applicants have exclusive authority to disclose evaluation results, and no significant related information has been disclosed. However, we have observed several companies utilize this service to enhance their comprehensive supply chain cybersecurity posture since its inception [37]. As an example, a leading ICS manufacturer "A" have demanded vendors to obtain a security rating using the SCTL and submit their evaluation results. In another case, semiconductor manufacturers "B" and

"C" autonomously decided to use the SCTL to secure competitiveness as suppliers, raising the trust level of their development and maintenance processes for specific products to 3 (Challenger) and 2 (Developing), respectively.

3.6 Supply Chain Management in the Electric Power Sector with NERC CIP-013

The Federal Energy Regulatory Commission established the NERC as a non-profit regulatory agency for the reliable operation of electric power systems, which are critical infrastructures operated through private companies in North America. The NERC regulates the owners and operators of bulk electric systems (BESs) to comply with the CIP standards [38]. This is a case of supply chain cybersecurity management, as a federal agency tasked with overseeing the national electric grid is responsible for ensuring the security and reliability of each electric power supplier. Additionally, CIP-013 covers the requirements for the C-SCRM of BES cyber systems and their associated systems, such as electronic access control or monitoring systems, and physical access control systems.

3.7 Supplier Management by Siemens

Siemens, which is a major ICS manufacturer, specifies in the "Siemens General Terms and Conditions of Purchase" that organizational and technical security measures must be established to ensure the confidentiality, authenticity, integrity, and availability of all assets, processes, systems, data, personnel, and sites of suppliers, as well as goods and services [39]. Such requirements are applied to suppliers who wish to provide Siemens with products and services, including software, firmware, and chipsets. ISO/IEC 27001 and IEC 62443 are suggested as normative references for organizational and technical security measures.

Information related to the verification of compliance with requirements at the time of concluding a supply contract was unavailable. However, suppliers are obligated to provide evidence of their compliance when requested by Siemens. Generally accepted audit reports such as SOC 2 Type 2 can be provided as evidence.

3.8 Supplier Management by General Electric

GE, which operates businesses in diverse industrial fields with significant social impacts, such as electric power, aerospace, and healthcare, has defined and demanded compliance with the "Third-party Cyber Security Requirements, Ver. 2.0," which consist of 12 categories for mitigating risks in supply chains [40].

Third-party organizations, including suppliers and joint ventures, must comply with requirements that include managerial security measures for organizations and technical security measures for IT and OT systems used in production and supply, and cover all controls of ISO/IEC 27001. Requirements are applied differentially according to the type of data processed by suppliers, type of supplied products and services, and network connectivity.

Information related to the verification of compliance with requirements when concluding a supply contract was unavailable. However, GE has the authority to conduct an audit to assess the security of suppliers according to related guidelines and is obligated to notify a supplier 30 days before conducting the audit [41].

3.9 Microsoft Supplier Data Protection Regulations

Microsoft operates the Supplier Security and Privacy Assurance (SSPA) program for safe procurement. All suppliers handling personal information or confidential information owned by Microsoft must comply with the Data Protection Requirements (DPR) specified by Microsoft to ensure that data are protected [42, 43]. The DPR consists of 10 sections, encompassing both the managerial domain, which includes policies and procedures for data collection and processing, and the technical domain, which covers the security of all assets and development environments of suppliers.

Suppliers can submit either ISO 27001 or SOC 2 certification to indicate their compliance with security requirements. However, software-as-a-service suppliers, who directly store and process critical data, are obligated to submit ISO 27001 certification.

3.10 Supplier Management Using Site Certification

Bundesamt für Sicherheit in der Informationstechnik (BSI, Federal Office of Information Security) in Germany has taken the lead on a Common Criteria (CC) project to develop and validate a procedure to perform reusable evaluations of ALC-related aspects. ACL is an assurance class for life-cycle support. As a result of this project, the BSI currently operates the CC Site Certification (SiteCert) Program for the development and production sites of IT products [44, 45].

The SiteCert certification of the BSI in Germany cannot be recognized by all signatories of the CC Recognition Arrangement as a CC certification issued by certificate-authorizing schemes. However, the on-site assessment results of the ALC class of Site-Cert can be reused if CC certification is obtained within the member countries of the Senior Officials Group-Information Systems Security, which is an institution formed by the EU Council for the standardization of CC protection profiles and certification policies between European Certification Bodies.

SiteCert is utilized to streamline the overall CC certification process by reusing the ALC class certification result in the following cases: 1) when multiple IT products are developed and manufactured in the same environment; 2) when one IT product is developed and manufactured at multiple sites; 3) when one product is developed and manufactured, and specialized companies are involved in each process [45].

An example of supplier management using SiteCert is that a global semiconductor manufacturer "D". The manufacturer requires its vendors in the production process to obtain SiteCert certification, provides support for their certification procedure, and awards additional points to certified vendors when renewing the contract. Accordingly, the security of the vendors in the supply chain of manufacturer "D" are enhanced and the CC certification of various products using the same processes is obtained more efficiently [46].

3.11 Supplier Management Using CCC by Saudi Aramco

Saudi Aramco, who experienced serious cyberattacks in 2012 and 2017 [47], published the Third Party Cybersecurity Standard (SACS-002) in 2020, which demands that all third-party companies in their supply chain obtain the Cybersecurity Compliance Certificate (CCC) [48]. The CCC is mandatory for Saudi Aramco's supplier registration and even suppliers that have already engaged in transactions must obtain the CCC for further business agreements.

SACS-002, which defines the minimum cybersecurity requirements for third parties, was developed based on the NIST CSF and their own security regulations, such as Computer Use_6969 and Supplier Code of Conduct_9677.

Companies subject to certification must first perform company classification as suppliers of network connectivity, outsourced infrastructure, critical data processing, customized software, or cloud computing service based on their activities within Aramco's supply chain. These classes can overlap. Different requirements are applied based on the classification result and the required certification type also vary, as shown in Table 3 [49].

Table 3. CCC certificate types by third party class

3rd party class	Description	Cert. Type	Assessment approach
Outsourced Infrastructure	Third party that is managing, maintaining, and/or supporting a computing infrastructure on behalf of Saudi Aramco	CCC	Self-compliance assessment completed by the company and verified remotely by the authorized audit firm
Customized Software	Third party that is developing and/or hosting a customized software, application, website, or solution for Saudi Aramco		
Cloud Computing	Third party that is providing public cloud computing services to host, store, and/or process Saudi Aramco data		
Network Connectivity	Third party whose computing infrastructure is provided with network connectivity to the Saudi Aramco Corporate Network	CCC +	On-site compliance assessment conducted by the authorized audit firm
Critical Data Processor	Third party that is developing, accessing, and/or processing Saudi Aramco critical data		

4 Exploratory Trend Analysis of Supply Chain Cybersecurity Management Cases

This section presents the results of an exploratory trend analysis of the cases that were previously examined in Sect. 3. While the thirteen cases are not representative enough to draw clear trends, the results of the exploratory trend analysis are still useful and valuable in that they provide insights and ideas for organizations operating critical systems to formulate future supply chain cybersecurity management strategies and plans.

Firstly, the types of the five management elements (entity, scope, step, standard, and verification method) of each case was analyzed in accordance with the taxonomy presented in Table 1. These elements are fundamental considerations identified in Sect. 2.2. The full analysis is presented in Table 5 in the Appendix. Subsequently, in order to identify trends in supply chain cybersecurity, the analysis results were reorganized in a visual format, as illustrated in Table 4. The rows represent the management elements and their types, and the columns represent studied cases. The types of the elements corresponding to each case are indicated by a circle (○). "SCP.3 Comprehensive cybersecurity supply chain risk management" signifies that all scopes are managed, thus all SCP fields of the case whose SCP.3 is circled are marked with dotted circles (⊙). The same is true for "STP.5 Entire lifecycle." To gain an intuitive understanding of overall trends and the relative management status of each case, we have color-coded them as follows: green indicates that more than 70% is managed, yellow indicates that 70–30% is managed, and light red indicates that less than 30% is managed. For the rows, the percentage was calculated as the proportion of cases corresponding to each type out of the total 13 cases. For the columns, the percentage was calculated as the proportion of types managed by each case out of the total 11 ENT, SCP, and STP types (excluding SCP.3 and STP.5).

The overall trends for each consideration element are as follows.

Management Entity. Most cases indicate that supply chain cybersecurity management is performed for ICT products and service suppliers (ENT.1). However, these cases do not necessarily indicate a lack of interest in protecting critical information within a supply chain because many organizations consider that it is also possible to protect critical information by managing critical digital products and service suppliers.

Management Scope. In most cases, management is not performed within the entire scope, but only partially examined and managed. Despite differences in depth, general organizational security (SCP.1.1) and ICT linkage security (SCP.2.1) are managed in all cases. Furthermore, development organizational security (SCP.1.2) is adequately addressed. Because numerous useful frameworks and tools have been disclosed and the relevant culture is mature. In contrast, cases of performing operational organizational security (SCP.1.3) and logistics linkage (SCP.2.2) security are relatively rare. Certain suppliers may not have operational organizations or physical supply routes, but when introducing a management system, their priorities may have been evaluated to be lower compared to other management scope, or the construction of a management system could have been more difficult based on a lack of reference standards or practices.

Table 4. Exploratory trend analysis of supply chain cybersecurity management cases.

Management Elements		3.1 Contract Vehicles in the US Using ISO 27001	3.2 SEWP, US GWAC by NASA	3.3 US Federal Government Regulations			3.4 UK Government and MoD Procurement	3.5 UL SCTL	3.6 NERC CIP-013 in the Electric Power Sector	3.7 Siemens Supplier Management	3.8 GE Supplier Management	3.9 Microsoft Supplier Management	3.10 Supplier Management using Site Certification	3.11 Saudi Aramco Supplier Management Using CCC
				a. C-SCRM with NIST SP 800-161	b. CUI Regulations	c. C-CSRM Using NIST CSF								
Mgmt. Entity	ENT.1	O	O	O		O		O	O	O	O		O	O
	ENT.2				O		O				O	O		O
Mgmt. Scope	SCP.1.1	O	O	⋮	O	⋮	O	O	⋮	O	O	O	O	O
	SCP.1.2	O	O	⋮	O	⋮		O	⋮	O	O		O	O
	SCP.1.3		O	⋮		⋮		O	⋮	O	O		O	
	SCP.2.1	O	O	⋮	O	⋮	O	O	⋮	O	O	O	O	O
	SCP.2.2	O	O	⋮		⋮		O	⋮		O		O	
	SCP.3		O	O			O		O					
Mgmt. Step	STP.1	⋮	⋮	⋮	⋮	⋮			⋮		⋮	⋮	O	O
	STP.2	⋮	⋮	⋮	⋮	⋮	O		⋮	O	⋮	⋮	O	O
	STP.3	⋮	⋮	⋮	⋮	⋮	O		O	⋮	⋮	O	O	O
	STP.4	⋮	⋮	⋮	⋮	⋮			⋮		⋮	⋮		
	STP.5	O	O	O	O	O		O	O		O	O		
Mgmt. Standard	STD.1	O	O								O		O	
	STD.2			O	O	O	O		O					
	STD.3							O			O	O		O
Verification Method	MTD.1.1				O		O							
	MTD.1.2											O		
	MTD.1.3	O	O				O	O	O			O	O	O
	MTD.2.1													
	MTD.2.2			O	O	O					O	O	O	
	MTD.2.3								O					

▮ : >70% is managed   ▮ : 70~30% is managed   : <30% is managed

Management Step. Most cases indicate that management is conducted throughout the entire lifecycle (STP.5), because most management standards include security requirements for the entire lifecycle. However, not all standards have the same level of security requirements for all lifecycle steps, as the requirements for certain steps may be concise or abstract. Therefore, further analysis is required to evaluate the management level at each stage. Management for the disposal step (STP.4) is highly inadequate because the idea of supply chain cybersecurity management having to focus on operating systems remains prevalent. Even if supply chain cybersecurity risks in the disposal step are not encountered for now, proper measures should be prepared and a relevant system should be established in advance.

Management Standard. International standards (STD.1) and national standards (STD.2), as well as organizations' self-standards (STD.3), have been effectively applied according to the environment. Notably, even when an organization employs their self-standards, fully new standards are rarely used. Instead, their self-standards are largely established by quoting relevant international or national standards.

Verification Method. The verification methods employed depend on the industrial and regulatory environment of each case. In most cases, organizations verify compliance with standards upon acquisition (MTD.1) by integrating the procurement process. Although the cases of Siemens and GE led to the conclusion that an audit is solely conducted during operation (MTD.2) because reference data regarding the acquisition process were unavailable, this does not indicate that they do not have any verification procedure upon acquisition.

5 Insight from the Case Studies and Trend Analysis

5.1 Once Again, Risk Assessment is the First

The initial step in the implementation of a supply chain cybersecurity management system is to identify the supply chain and determine the management entities. Managing all suppliers of critical systems such as control systems for electric power generation and railways, is difficult because of the numerous ICT/OT products and services comprising the systems. Therefore, management entities must be selected by performing risk assessment and examining the importance of each product, service, and data as well as the impact of security incidents. In the US, the first activity for enhancing software supply chain security according to EO 14028 was also defining EO-critical software as management entities [24, 50].

5.2 It is Imperative to Be Explicit About the Objective

The scope of supply chain cybersecurity is so extensive and comprehensive that it is virtually impossible to fully manage. It is therefore crucial to implement a supply chain cybersecurity management system in a sequential manner, focusing on a detailed scope according to reasonable priorities, particularly in the initial stages of its introduction.

A clear set of criteria is necessary to rationally prioritize the management scope, and the criteria are determined based on the objective of supply chain cybersecurity management. The more detailed and clear objectives are, the more reasonable the prioritization will be. Examples of objectives may include complying government regulations, protecting specific functions of a critical systems, and protecting operational data with potentially high economic impact.

5.3 Supply Chain Cybersecurity Risk is Bidirectional

It is a fallacy to assume that cybersecurity risks within a supply chain is unidirectionally caused from suppliers to acquirers. For risk management, acquirers may be involved in suppliers' supply processes (such as development, production, and distribution), and have access to their critical information. Consequently, acquirers can also pose risks to suppliers [51]. Therefore, a management system must be established in which suppliers also request appropriate security measures from acquirers and demand them to comply. In practice, however, it is challenging for suppliers to require and verify cybersecurity measures from acquirers. Indeed, none of the cases presented in this paper were applicable. It is crucial for critical system operators to be aware that any compromise of their supplier's systems or intellectual property will have an impact on them again.

In many cases, third-party certification programs are used for supplier verification due to advantages of the reliability and procedural efficiency. While suppliers may perceive it as a cost and procedural burden (see Sect. 5.5), it is an effective method for guaranteeing that operators do not have excessive direct access to the supplier's processes and information.

5.4   There Are Many Standards You Can Refer to

There are standards that explicitly address supply chain cybersecurity, such as NIST SP 800–161, ISO/IEC 20243, and IEC 62443-2-4. However, as long as the concept of supply chain cybersecurity management (see Sect. 2.1) is kept in mind, it is possible to leverage a greater number of standards. That is, any standard pertaining to the security management of organizations or pathways, such as ISO/IEC 27000 family and IEC 62443 series, can be leveraged.

5.5   No Single Correct Answer for the Standard and Verifying Method

It is also important to determine the standard and verification method for supply chain cybersecurity management. The management standard includes requirements that are appropriate for the scope and steps to be managed. The standard also determines the relevant certification programs and verification methods that are available. While there are optimal types of standards and verification methods in terms of security, they may require considerable resources including time, money, and personnel, or the industrial and regulatory environment may not support them.

International and national standards are commonly considered the optimal choices, because they are already widely recognized and have a high degree of credibility. In addition, demonstrating compliance with the standards is relatively straightforward through relevant third-party certification programs. Nevertheless, supply chain cybersecurity management can be accomplished by independently defining an entity's self-standards. This approach is suitable when international or national standards do not completely reflect the unique characteristics of a specific industry or when applying international or national standards may be excessively burdensome.

Third-party verification is preferable due to the reliable verification results and the efficient process from the operator's perspective. In accordance with the concept that supply chain cybersecurity management should be continuous throughout the entire lifecycle, it is recommended that both verification upon acquisition (MTD.1) and audit before and after acquisition (MTD.2) be employed. However, continuous third-party verification may not be feasible due to the high cost or the absence of an independent verification body in the immature ecosystem. In such instances, first- or second-party verification remains a viable option, despite inherent trade-offs. For first-party verification, legal frameworks must ensure accountability for the results. For second-party verification, it is essential that the acquirer possesses the technical capabilities to verify the evidence.

6   Conclusion

This paper presents thirteen supply chain cybersecurity management cases from public and private industrial sectors and an exploratory trend analysis. While the cases are not representative enough to draw clear trends, the analysis is still valuable in that they provide insights for critical systems operators to formulate supply chain cybersecurity management strategies and plans.

Synthesizing the analysis results, we found an overview of the trends that systematic management remains lacking because supply chain cybersecurity management is in the initial stages of its introduction. However, a variety of activities, though not necessarily systematic, are underway to ensure the security of suppliers and supply paths with diverse management entities, scope, steps, standards, and verification methods. This is because, from an administrative perspective, supply chain cybersecurity management is not a standalone process; rather, it is an integrated one with the organization's procurement, quality assurance, and risk management processes.

Several key insights were gained from the analysis. Critical system operators should 1) prioritize management entities based on risk assessment; 2) recognize that it is virtually impossible to fully manage the risks, therefore it is essential to set clear objectives and prioritize the management scope accordingly, 3) keep in mind that supply chain cybersecurity risks are bidirectional, 4) alleviate the burden by utilizing appropriate international or national standards for the scope and lifecycle steps to be managed, and 5) apply management standards and verification methods flexibly, depending on the industrial and regulatory environment.

As future work, we have a plan to develop a framework for critical system operators to systematically establish supply chain cybersecurity management systems. The framework will take into account national regulations, industry environments, and insights presented in this paper.

Acknowledgments. This work was supported by the Nuclear Safety Research Program through the Korea Foundation of Nuclear Safety (KoFONS) using financial resources granted by the Nuclear Safety and Security Commission (NSSC) of the Republic of Korea (No. 2106044).

Appendix: Analysis Results of Supply Chain Cybersecurity Management Cases

Table 5. Analysis Results of Supply Chain Cybersecurity Management Cases

Case	Management entity (ENT)	Management scope (SCP)	Management step (STP)	Management standard (STD)	Verification method (MTD) Method and timing	Verification method (MTD) Type	Note
3.1 US Contract Vehicles Using ISO 27001	**ENT.1** ICT products and services suppliers	**SCP.1.1, SCP.1.2, SCP.2** General and development organizational security, linkage security	**STP.5** Entire lifecycle	**STD.1** ISO/IEC 27001	**MTD.1.3** Submit a certificate during the acquisition process	Third-party verification	Additional points awarded in RFP evaluation for certified suppliers
3.2 SEWP, US GWAC by NASA	**ENT.1** ICT/AV products suppliers	**SCP.1, SCP.2, SCP.3** Organizational and linkage security, (entire or partial) supply chain risk management	**STP.5** Entire lifecycle	**STD.1** ISO/IEC 20243	**MTD.1.3** Submit a certificate during the pre-competition process	Third-party verification	Management scope varies depending on supplier type
3.3.a C-SCRM in the US	**ENT.1** ICT/OT products and services suppliers	**SCP.3** Comprehensive supply chain risk management	**STP.5** Entire lifecycle	**STD.2** NIST SP 800-161, Rev. 1	**MTD.2.2** Conduct an audit annually	Second-party verification	Federal agencies are regulated in accordance with legislation and each agency requires suppliers to comply with the requirements of the standards
3.3.b CUI Regulations in the US	**ENT.2** CUI handling suppliers	**SCP.1.1, SCP.1.2, SCP.2.1** General and development organizational security, ICT linkage security	**STP.5** Entire lifecycle	**STD.2** NIST SP 800-171, Rev. 2	**MTD.1.1** Submit self-evaluation results during the acquisition process **MTD.2.2** Conduct an audit annually	First-party verification Second-party verification	
3.3.c C-SCRM Using CSF in the US	**ENT.1** ICT/OT products and services suppliers	**SCP.3** Comprehensive supply chain risk management	**STP.5** Entire lifecycle	**STD.2** NIST CSF 2.0	**MTD.2.2** Conduct an audit annually or every other year depending on the risk level	Second-party verification	
3.4 UK Government and MoD Procurement	**ENT.2** Critical data handling suppliers	**SCP.1.1, SCP.2.1** General organizational security, ICT linkage security (specified for IT infrastructure)	**STP.2, STP.3** Acquisition, post-acquisition	**STD.2** Cyber Essentials	**MTD.1.1, MTD.1.3** Submit a certificate during the acquisition process (ISO 27001 certificate can be submitted instead)	**(CE)** First-, **(CE+)** Third-party verification	CE or CE+ certificate is required differentially and substitutable with ISO 27001, which includes all CE requirements
3.5 UL SCTL	**ENT.1** ICT products and services suppliers	**SCP.1, SCP.2** Organizational security, linkage security	**STP.5** Entire lifecycle	**STD.3** UL SCTL	**MTD.1.3** Submit evaluation results during the acquisition process	Third-party verification	An evaluation and consultation service to mitigate supply chain risks, not an official certification program

(continued)

Table 5. *(continued)*

Case	Management entity (ENT)	Management scope (SCP)	Management step (STP)	Management standard (STD)	Verification method (MTD) Method and timing	Type	Note
3.6 NERC CIP-013 in the Electric Power Sector	ENT.1 ICT products and services suppliers	SCP.3 Comprehensive supply chain risk management	STP.2, STP.3 Acquisition, post-acquisition	STD.2 NERC CIP-013	MTD.1.3, MTD.2.3 Verify the compliance when new entity registration process, and conduct an audit every three years	Third-party verification	Mid/High-risk BES operators require suppliers to comply with the supply chain cyber security risk management plan(s) devised according to CIP-013
3.7 Siemens Supplier Management	ENT.1 Digital products and services (including software, firmware, and chipsets) suppliers	SCP.1.1, SCP.1.2, SCP.2.1 General and development organizational security, ICT linkage security	STP.5 Entire lifecycle	STD.1 ISO 27001	MTD.2.2 Submit evidence of compliance when Siemens request	Second-party verification	Reference data on the acquisition process were unavailable
		SCP.1.2, SCP.1.3, SCP.2.1 Development and Operational organizational security, ICT linkage security	STP.5 Entire lifecycle	STD.1 IEC 62443			
3.8 GE Supplier Management	ENT.1, ENT.2 ICT/OT services and products suppliers, Sensitive information handling suppliers	SCP.1, SCP.2 Organizational and linkage security	STP.5 Entire lifecycle	STD.3 GE Third-party Cyber Security Requirements (including ISO 27001)	MTD.2.2 GE holds the right to audit	Second-party verification	Reference data on the acquisition process were unavailable
3.9 Microsoft Supplier Management	ENT.2 Personal information or confidential information handling suppliers	SCP.1.1, SCP.2.1 General organizational security, ICT linkage security	STP.2, STP.3 Acquisition, post-acquisition	STD.3 MS SSPA, DPR (Including ISO 27001, SOC 2)	MTD.1.2 Submit evidence of compliance during the acquisition process	Second-party verification	Evidence for "Section J: Security" of the DPR can be replaced by submitting ISO 27001 or SOC 2 certificates
					MTD.1.3 Submit ISO 27001 or SOC 2 certificate during the acquisition process	Third-party verification	
					MTD.2.2 Conduct an audit annually	Second-party verification	
3.10 Supplier Management Using Site Certification	ENT.1 Product lifecycle-related suppliers	SCP.1, SCP.2 Organizational and linkage security	STP.1, STP.2, STP.3 Pre-acquisition, acquisition, post-acquisition	STD.1 CC Part 3	MTD.1.3 Submit a certificate during the contract process	Third-party verification	
3.11 Saudi Aramco Supplier Management Using CCC	ENT.1, ENT.2 All types of suppliers	SCP.1.1, SCP.1.2, SCP.2.1 General and development organizational security, ICT linkage security	STP.1, STP.2, STP.3 Pre-acquisition, acquisition, post-acquisition	STD.3 SACS-002 (based on NIST CSF)	MTD.1.3 Submit a certificate during the vendor registration process	Third-party verification	

References

1. Gartner Top 9 trends in cybersecurity 2024. https://www.gartner.com/en/cybersecurity/top ics/cybersecurity-trends. Accessed 13 May 2024
2. Fier, J.: The future of cyber security: Software supply chain attacks become a given in 2022. https://darktrace.com/blog/the-future-of-cyber-security-software-supply-chain-att acks-become-a-given-in-2022. Accessed 13 May 2024
3. George, R.: Why we should worry about the supply chain. Int. J. Crit. Infrastruct. Protect. **11**, 22–23 (2015). https://doi.org/10.1016/j.ijcip.2015.05.002
4. Check Point: From SolarWinds to Log4j: The global impact of today's cybersecurity vulnerabilities. https://blog.checkpoint.com/2022/04/05/from-solarwinds-to-log4j-the-global-impact-of-todays-cybersecurity-vulnerabilities/. Accessed 13 May 2024
5. Banach, Z.: The xz-utils backdoor: the supply chain RCE that got caught. https://www.invicti.com/blog/web-security/xz-utils-backdoor-supply-chain-rce-that-got-caught/. Accessed 13 May 2024
6. Sonatype: 2021 state of the software supply chain report, 2022. https://www.sonatype.com/res ources/white-paper-2021-state-of-the-software-supply-chain-report-2021. Accessed 13 May 2024
7. Windelberg, M.: Objectives for managing cyber supply chain risk. Int. J. Crit. Infrastruct. Protect. **12**, 4–11 (2024). https://doi.org/10.1016/j.ijcip.2015.11.003
8. Durooju, O., Chan, H.K., Wang, X.: Investigation of the effect of e-platform information security breaches: a small and medium enterprise supply chain perspective. IEEE Trans. Eng. Manage. **69**(6), 3694–3709 (2022). https://doi.org/10.1109/TEM.2020.3008827
9. Gupta, N., Tiwari, A., Bukkapatnam, S.T.S., Karri, R.: Additive manufacturing cyber-physical system: supply chain cybersecurity and risks. IEEE Access **8**, 47322–47333 (2020). https://doi.org/10.1109/ACCESS.2020.2978815
10. Asante, M., et al.: Distributed ledger technologies in supply chain security management: a comprehensive survey. IEEE Trans. Eng. Manage. **70**(2), 713–739 (2023). https://doi.org/10.1109/TEM.2021.3053655
11. Enck, W., Williams, L.: Top five challenges in software supply chain security: observations from 30 industry and government organizations. IEEE Secur. Privacy. **20**, 96–100 (2022). https://doi.org/10.1109/MSEC.2022.3142338
12. Jang, J., Kang, B.B.: 3rdParTEE: Securing third-party IoT services using the trusted execution environment. IEEE Internet Things J. **9**, 15814–15826 (2022). https://doi.org/10.1109/JIOT.2022.3152555
13. Boyens, J., et al.: Cybersecurity supply chain risk management practices for systems and organizations. NIST SP 800–161, Rev. 1 (2022)
14. Security management systems for the supply chain – Best practices for implementing supply chain security, assessments and plans – Requirements and guidance, ISO 28001 (2012)
15. Reed, M., Miller, J.F., Popick, P.: Supply chain attack patterns: Framework and catalog, Office of the Deputy Assistant Secretary of Defense Systems Engineering (2014)
16. Eggers, S.: A novel approach for analyzing the nuclear supply chain cyber-attack surface. Nucl. Eng. and Technol. **53**(3), 879–887 (2021)
17. ISMS solution: government contractors. https://ismssolutions.com/iso_gov.php. Accessed 13 May 2024
18. Procurement policy note – Cyber essentials scheme. CCS, UK (2016)
19. Szakal, A.R., et al.: The road to adopting ISO 20243 & a new practitioner standard. Software and Supply Chain Assurance Fall Forum 2019, McLean, VA, US (2019)
20. NASA: SEWP contract holders. https://www.sewp.nasa.gov/sewp5public/contractholders. Accessed 13 May 2024

21. Federal Information Security Modernization Act of 2014. Public Law 113–283 (2014)
22. Jatheon: FISMA compliance: Requirements, penalties and email archiving (2021). https://jat
    heon.com/blog/fisma-compliance-email-archiving/. Accessed 13 May 2024
23. Managing Information as a Strategic Resource. OMB Circular No. A-130 (2016)
24. Improving the Nation's Cybersecurity. Exec. Order No. 14028, 86 F.R. 26633 (2021)
25. Basic Safeguarding of Covered Contractor Information Systems. FAR 52.204–21 (2021)
26. Safeguarding covered defense information and cyber incident reporting. DFARS 252.204-
    7012 (2023)
27. Cybersecurity maturity model certification requirements. DFARS 252.204-7021 (2023)
28. Cybersecurity maturity model certification model overview, version 2.0. Carnegie Mellon
    University and Johns Hopkins University (2021)
29. US Navy: Supplier performance risk system. https://www.sprs.csd.disa.mil/. Accessed 13
    May 2024
30. Strengthening the cybersecurity of federal networks and critical infrastructure. Exec. Order
    No. 13800, 82 FR 22391 (2017)
31. Barrett, M., et al.: Approaches for federal agencies to use the cybersecurity framework. NIST,
    NISTIR 8170 (2020)
32. NIST Cybersecurity Framework, Assessment, and Auditing ACT of 2017. H.R.1224 (2017)
33. Cyber Essentials: Requirements for IT infrastructure, v3.1. NCSC, UK (2023)
34. The IASME Consortium Ltd.: Cyber essentials frequently asked questions. https://iasme.co.
    uk/cyber-essentials/faq-cyber-essentials/. Accessed 13 May 2024
35. Cyber Security for Defence Suppliers. MoD, UK, DEF Stan 05–138, Issue 3 (2021)
36. Managing cybersecurity risk in the supply chain: UL supplier cyber trust level. UL,
    Northbrook, IL, US (2020)
37. Jo, B.: private communication. May 2021
38. Enforcement of Reliability Standards. 18 CFR 39.7 (2010)
39. Siemens General Terms and Conditions of Purchase Rev. No. 4.9. Siemens, Munich, Germany
    (2021)
40. Third-Party Cyber Security Requirements Version 2.0. GE, Boston, MA, US (2020)
41. Product Cybersecurity Appendix. GE, Boston, MA, US (2016)
42. Microsoft Procurement – Supplier Security & Privacy Assurance (SSPA) Program Guide
    Version 9. Microsoft, Redmond, WA, US (2023)
43. Microsoft Supplier Data Protection Requirements, Version 9. Microsoft, Redmond, WA, US
    (2023)
44. Supporting document guidance: site certification, Version 1.0, Revision 1. BSI, Germany,
    CCDB-2007-11-001 (2007)
45. Guidance for Site Certification, Version 1.1. BSI, Germany (2013)
46. Choi, M.: private communication. November 2022
47. Independent: a cyber attack in Saudi Arabia failed to cause carnage, but the next attempt could
    be deadly. https://www.independent.co.uk/news/long_reads/cyber-warfare-saudi-arabia-pet
    rochemical-security-america-a8258636.html. Accessed 13 May 2024
48. Third Party Cybersecurity Standard. Saudi Aramco, SACS-002 (2022)
49. Cybersecurity Compliance Certification (CCC) Third Party Manual. Saudi Aramco (2021)
50. NIST: critical software definition. https://www.nist.gov/itl/executive-order-improving-nat
    ions-cybersecurity/critical-software-definition. Accessed 13 May 2024
51. Information technology – security techniques – information security for supplier relation-
    ships – Part 1: Overview and concepts. ISO/IEC 27036-1 (2014)

A Cooperative Feature Removal Mechanism for Cell Outage Detection in Wireless Telecommunication Networks

Andrea Wrona[1]([✉]) , Simone Gentile[1,2] , Emanuele De Santis[1] ,
Alessandro Giuseppi[1] , Antonio Pietrabissa[1] ,
and Francesco Delli Priscoli[1]

[1] Department of Computer, Control, and Management Engineering "Antonio Ruberti" Sapienza University of Rome, via Ariosto 25, 00185 Rome, Lazio, Italy
wrona@diag.uniroma1.it
[2] Department of Electrical and Information Engineering, Polytechnic of Bari, via Re David 200, 70125 Bari, Puglia, Italy

Abstract. In the domain of crisis management for telecommunications infrastructures, the autonomous detection of cell outages within cellular networks is of paramount importance for prompt identification and resolution in ensuring uninterrupted connectivity to users. Traditional methods usually involve data aggregation at the core network, which is responsible for identifying cell failures. Proposing a novel approach, we leverage a Machine Learning-based distributed and cooperative feature removal mechanism in order to preserve the privacy of data and avoid any degradation in classification performance. Simulations carried out on a dataset retrieved from a real 4G-LTE rollout demonstrate that the proposed approach, through a cooperation among agents, maintains or even slightly improves accuracy, precision, recall, and F1-score in outage prediction compared to other conventional methods, showcasing its efficacy for cell outage detection purposes while maintaining data privacy.

Keywords: Anomaly Detection · Random Forest · Federated Learning

1 Introduction

Fifth-generation (5G) networks are the cornerstone for the development of new-generation telecommunication systems [23] as their unmatched data rates, extremely low latency, and widespread device connections allow the provision of new and more advanced services that further stress the importance of the telecommunication network as a critical infrastructure fundamental for the society of the future. Due to the critical nature of modern ICT services (e.g., e-health, security and augmented reality) the 5G technology has been specifically designed to provide ubiquitous and uninterrupted connectivity. However, unforeseen events such as equipment failures, natural disasters, malicious attacks, or

G. Oliva et al. (Eds.): CRITIS 2024, LNCS 15549, pp. 84–95, 2025.
https://doi.org/10.1007/978-3-031-84260-3_5

base stations' (BSs) capacity saturation can lead to cell outages and faults, disrupting service for users within the affected area [20,27]. Cell outage detection (COD) mechanisms are essential to promptly identify and mitigate these disruptions, ensuring that users experience consistent and reliable connectivity, in compliance with stringent requirements imposed by nowadays applications.

Proactive COD is necessary for wireless networks to operate efficiently. Network operators should reduce the impact on overall network performance by implementing mitigation methods, such as rerouting traffic or providing interim solutions, as soon as cell failures are identified. In addition to maintaining service quality, this proactive approach aids in the effective use of network resources.

In literature, several approaches to solve the problem have been proposed.

COD has previously been accomplished through the application of algorithms based on the geographical correlations among users [30] or through handover statistics [6]. Authors in [19] exploit neighbor cell list reports and observe changes in topology produced by visibility graphs to identify outage cells. A composite hypothesis based on the Channel Quality Indicator (CQI) has been applied in [16] to identify outages.

During the last years, the intelligent management of communication networks is becoming more and more dependent on Machine Learning (ML) techniques [1,3], which allow for automatic detection, prediction, and mitigation of complicated problems like cell failures. Clustering methods and Bayesian networks have been used for COD in [14], where authors provide an automated diagnostic model for Universal Mobile Telecommunications System (UMTS) networks based on a Naive Bayesian classifier. The model makes use of both real UMTS network data and network simulator, offering a comparable method. Another well-known classifier, Hidden Markov Models (HMM), was also investigated in COD by training data on both outage and healthy cells to predict the outage state of eNodeBs [5].

A study on the K-Nearest Neighbors approach for COD in multi-tier networks was carried out in [22]. A technique for detecting anomalies based on the analysis of large data derived from Key Performance Indicators (KPI) was presented in [7] as an alternative to ML processes.

Specifically, [9] offers an approach based on clustering diffusion map that may identify abnormal behaviors produced by a sleeping cell. On the contrary, authors in [15] design a fuzzy logic-based method for an automated troubleshooting system diagnostic. The authors suggest a controller that takes a collection of typical KPIs as input and uses them to decide if a failure has occurred.

The work in [11] covers the situation in which the cell can deliver a certain degree of service, but is unable to meet the needs of the expected user agent. In order to teach KPIs that are retrieved by human operators to make defensible judgments, the strategy depends on ensemble approaches. The authors of [28] examine big data sets in order to find anomalous BS behavior. They suggested an approach that included stages for preprocessing, detection, and analysis. The findings demonstrate that abnormally behaved BSs may be found in a self-organized fashion by employing dimensionality reduction and anomaly detection approaches. Additionally, the k-NN method is used in the works of [10,31,32] to provide a self-healing solution, specifically addressing the fault detection area.

Moreover, in [17] authors propose a COD method using the Autoencoder, a neural network that is trained by unsupervised learning. The data for the network training comes from the Reference Signals Received Power (RSRP) and Reference Signals Received Quality (RSRQ) values from the measurement reports. Later on, the same authors improved the performance of their COD mechanism, introducing a more robust deep convolutional autoencoder [25]. A similar work has been carried out in [18], where authors show the superiority of deep autoencoders over support vector machines for COD. Finally, another unsupervised method combining SOM-BP and genetic algorithms has been proposed in [26], with the input features being extracted from four characteristic dimensions, including accessibility, retainability, mobility and quality.

In [21] authors make use of neural networks classifier, and in particular Multi–Layer Perceptrons (MLP), having as inputs different KPI metrics at users' level, like SINR, CQI, and RSRQ.

As seen, faults identification in a single cell is accomplished by state-of-the-art literature using feedforward deep neural networks or other classifiers at core network (CN). However, said technique is not practical as it would overload the CN that monitors thousands of cells at a time. In recent times, research works in [12,13] have proposed a novel approach, through which the network is divided into multiple cell regions, each under the supervision of an edge server (ES), exploiting the Mobile Edge Computing paradigm [4] and deep convolutional neural networks (CNNs) as classifiers [24]. After an aberrant cell has been found by the ES, an alert signal is sent from the server to the CN for additional corrective actions under self-healing mechanism. In this way, this distributed approach eases computational load on the CN, speeding up data analysis and training.

However, the latter approach does not allow exchanging data and information among the ESs within the network. This means that each server trains the classifier on its own data and is not aware of the situation within other cells. Moreover, it may happen that a specific area served by an ES is lacking training data (as en example because few users are active in those cells), thus leading to poor anomaly detection performance.

To overcome these existing limitations, this work introduces a Random Forest–based cooperative feature selection paradigm, called FedRF, for solving the COD problem in a distributed, private, and collaborative way. In ML literature, the Random Forest algorithm is a popular ensemble learning technique, firstly introduced in [8], that can be applied to both regression and classification problems. Said algorithm builds a collection, or *ensemble*, of decision trees and leverages their combined predictions to achieve improved accuracy, stability, and robustness compared to individual trees. This paradigm reminds the Federated Learning one [2], in which classifiers are typically artificial neural networks. The proposed FedRF approach, in contrast to standard centralized models or local distributed training, uses the combined intelligence of edge devices in order to progressively remove unnecessary features within the training set for anomaly detection while maintaining raw data private. The innovation is in the capacity to combine insights from several sources without sending raw data to a central server or to other peers, which reduces communication costs and addresses privacy issues. This method improves the network's resilience and response to dynamic changes by fostering a more scalable and adaptable cell outage detection system.

Hence, the original contribution of this work resides in the fact that the proposed collaborative distributed COD mechanism relies on local Random Forests' ensemble instead of raw data or alert signals, as the ESs share the feature importance scores only. This innovation ensures that sensitive users' data remain localized, addressing privacy concerns and complying with stringent data protection regulations. To ensure a rigorous evaluation, a labeled COD dataset obtained from a real multi–BS 4G–LTE deployment was employed, with different metrics about (i) uplink and downlink throughput, and (ii) number of active User Equipments (UEs). The dataset was used to train the proposed algorithm and to favourably evaluate it by comparing its performance against two other state-of-the-art classifiers, considering four different classification metrics.

The remainder of this paper is organized as follows: Section 2 illustrates the wireless network system scenario, defining logical and physical relationships between the various network entities. Section 3 introduces the proposed distributed and cooperative framework for autonomous cell outage detection, detailing the algorithm and the rationale behind its choice. Experimental results and performance evaluations are presented in Sect. 4, and, eventually, the paper is concluded in Sect. 5, summarizing the contributions and outlining potential avenues for future research in the distributed COD domain.

2   Wireless Network Scenario

The reference scenario is depicted in Fig. 1.

The cellular network comprises $N \in \mathbb{Z}^+$ BSs, also referred to eNB (evolved NodeB), indexed by i. The generic eNB_i monitors $C_i \in \mathbb{Z}^+$ cells and is responsible for providing wireless connectivity to the attached cells. It is worth highlighting that each eNB may serve a different number of cells. Hence, in general

$$C_i \neq C_j, \quad i \neq j. \tag{1}$$

Each eNB_i is equipped with an edge server ES_i, designed for carrying out the anomaly detection task. For this purpose, each edge server has a dataset $\mathcal{D}_i$ containing various information related to each cell managed by the BS to which it is connected. Cell data may contain information about (i) date time, (ii) BSs' Physical Resource Block (PRB) utilization, (iii) amount of users connected, and (iv) user activities, like Call Detail Records [13].

The fundamental assumption in this work relies on the fact that each ES only handles private data belonging to its cells and cannot share raw data with other edge servers or with the core network itself.

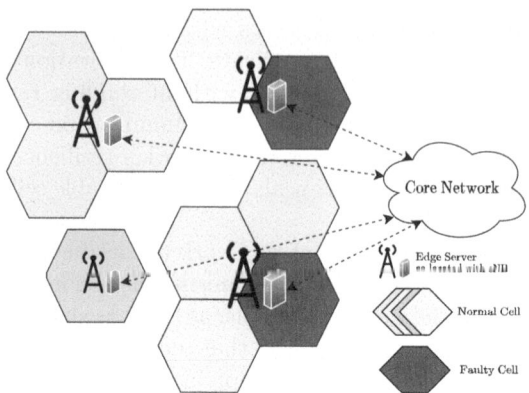

Fig. 1. Cellular Network Scenario.

3   Collaborative Feature Selection Framework

One of the main problems related to the anomaly detection process in cellular networks is the identification of the best set of features guaranteeing good classification performance. Feature selection or removal actions is crucial when dealing with large amounts of data, especially data are noisy and come from numerous users. As already stated, this work introduces a collaborative and privacy-preserving approach for feature selection based on Decision Trees and Random Forests.

As already introduced, Random Forest algorithms build a collection, or ensemble, of decision trees. A decision tree is a hierarchical structure made up of nodes. Each leaf node is an output and represents a prediction, whereas each internal node reflects a choice based on a certain trait. Each decision tree is trained on a subset of the training set, sampled randomly (bagging technique).

For classification problems like anomaly detection in cellular networks, the Random Forest ensemble usually uses a majority voting method. In this mechanism, each tree *votes* for a class, and the final prediction relies on the class with the highest rating.

One of the merits of the Random Forest ensemble is that, based on how frequently a feature is chosen for splitting throughout the ensemble, the algorithm calculates the relevance of that feature, assigning to it an importance score. This can help with feature selection and determining the significance of the dataset's variables.

In this work, importance scores computed at local level are aggregated and exploited to improve the overall anomaly detection performance.

The iterative FedRF algorithm for anomaly detection is described by the pseudocode of Algorithm 1.

Initially, all the edge servers are included in the federation and independently train on their own datasets, computing the feature importance scores. Similarly, the initial feature set of the federation includes all the features. At each iteration, the scores of each ES within the federation are transmitted to the CN, where they are aggregated and averaged. The CN identifies the feature with the lowest average importance score, designating it as the least significant feature. This decision is communicated back to the ESs, instructing them to remove the identified feature and retrain their Random Forest models. The ESs experiencing a deterioration in performance exit the federation without removing the identified feature, whereas the other ones start a new iteration by communicating to the central core network the new score obtained with the reduced set of features. The iterative process continues until the federation is empty. This collaborative and adaptive approach aims to enhance anomaly detection accuracy in cellular networks.

Algorithm 1. Distributed Feature Selection using Random Forest (FedRF)

Require: Individual datasets $\mathcal{D}_1, \mathcal{D}_2, \ldots, \mathcal{D}_N$ from N clients
Require: Federation: $\mathfrak{F} = \langle \text{ES}_1, \ldots, \text{ES}_N \rangle$
Ensure: Final selected features $\mathcal{F}_{\text{final}}$
 1: Initialize $\mathcal{F}_{\text{final}}$ as the full feature set
 2: **repeat**
 3:     **for** each client i in $\mathfrak{F}$ **do**
 4:         Train Random Forest on $\mathcal{D}_i$ with features $\mathcal{F}_{\text{final}}$
 5:         Compute feature importance scores $(\mathcal{I}_j^i)$ for each feature j
 6:         Send feature importance scores to the server
 7:     **end for**
 8:     Server computes average importance scores $\mathcal{I}_j^{\text{avg}}$ for each feature j
 9:     Identify the least significant feature $j^* = \arg\min_j(\mathcal{I}_j^{\text{avg}})$
10:     **for** each client i in $1, 2, \ldots, N$ **do**
11:         Communicate j^* to client i
12:         Retrain Random Forest on $\mathcal{D}_i$ excluding j^*
13:         **if** Client i worsens its performance **then**
14:             Client i rejects server's decision and exits $\mathfrak{F}$
15:         **end if**
16:     **end for**
17:     Update $\mathcal{F}_{\text{final}}$ by removing j^*
18: **until** $\mathfrak{F} \neq \varnothing$
19: **return** $\mathcal{F}_{\text{final}}$

In the next section, the proposed federated approach will be tested over an anomaly detection dataset.

4   Experimental Results

4.1   Dataset and Metrics

The anomaly detection dataset has been taken from [29] and represents an actual LTE rollout. Every 15 min for two weeks, various radio and connectivity metrics were collected from a group of $N = 10$ BSs, each with a different number of cells. The dataset contains 36905 samples. Features and label for classification are listed in Table 1. Based on the *CellName* feature, the dataset has been split among the 10 ESs. Specifically, 80% of each private dataset $\mathcal{D}_i$ has been allocated for training purposes, serving as the primary input for the model optimization process. Subsequently, the remaining 20% has been earmarked for testing, thereby facilitating the rigorous evaluation of the model's performance and generalization capabilities on unseen data.

Table 1. Features of the 4G cell outage detection dataset.

Feature	Description	Measurement Unit
Time	Hour of the day (hh:mm)	–
CellName	Unique identifier for eNB and cell	Text String
PRBUsageUL	Resource utilization in uplink	%
PRBUsageDL	Resource utilization in downlink	%
meanThr_UL	Average carried traffic in uplink	Mbps
meanThr_DL	Average carried traffic in downlink	Mbps
maxThr_UL	Maximum carried traffic in uplink	Mbps
maxThr_DL	Maximum carried traffic in downlink	Mbps
meanUE_UL	Average number of active UEs in uplink	–
meanUE_DL	Average number of active UEs in downlink	–
maxUE_UL	Maximum number of active UEs in uplink	–
maxUE_DL	Maximum number of active UEs in downlink	–
maxUE_UL+DL	Maximum number of active UEs (UL + DL)	–
Anomaly	Label for supervised learning	0 or 1

The proposed approach has been compared against two benchmark solutions for classification:

1. **DisNN**. Local Neural Network classifier without collaboration among ESs.
2. **DisRF**. Local Random Forest without collaborative feature selection.

Moreover, the comparison has been carried out in terms of four classification metrics evaluated over the private test sets. Let TP, TN, FP, FN be the number of true anomalies, true normal, false anomalies and false normal samples, respectively. The metrics are as follows:

– **Test Accuracy**. It measures the overall correctness of predictions:

$$A = \frac{TP + TN}{TP + TN + FP + FN}. \tag{2}$$

- **Precision**. It is a measure of the accuracy of predictions about anomalies:

$$P = \frac{\text{TP}}{\text{TP} + \text{FP}}. \tag{3}$$

- **Recall**. It represents the capability of the model in classifying correctly all anomalies:

$$R = \frac{\text{TP}}{\text{TP} + \text{FN}}. \tag{4}$$

- **F1–Score**. It is the harmonic mean of precision and recall, providing a balance between the two metrics:

$$F_1 = 2\frac{PR}{P + R}. \tag{5}$$

4.2   Results

Simulations results are shown using histograms in Figs. 2 to 5 It is evident that the NN classifier achieves worse results with respect to Random Forest in terms of all the four defined metrics.

Looking at the plots, it is possible to check that the proposed collaborative approach for feature selection leads to local improvements over the non–cooperative RF ensemble, thanks to the feature space reduction carried out in eight rounds. In particular, the algorithm proceeds as follows::

- eNB_1 and eNB_9 exit the federation $\mathfrak{F}$ after the first round, thus keeping all the initial features.
- eNB_3, eNB_4 and eNB_5 eliminate the feature $maxUE\_UL$ and exit $\mathfrak{F}$ after the second round.
- eNB_8, eNB_{10} eliminate the features $maxUE\_UL$ and $maxUE\_DL$ and exit $\mathfrak{F}$ after the third round.
- eNB_7 eliminates the features $maxUE\_UL$, $maxUE\_DL$ and $meanThr\_DL$ and exit $\mathfrak{F}$ after the fourth round.
- eNB_6 eliminates the features $maxUE\_UL$, $maxUE\_DL$, $meanThr\_DL$, $maxThr\_UL$ and $meanThr\_UL$ and exit $\mathfrak{F}$ after the sixth round.
- eNB_2 eliminates the features $maxUE\_UL$, $maxUE\_DL$, $meanThr\_DL$, $maxThr\_UL$, $meanThr\_UL$, $maxUE\_UL+DL$ and $maxThr\_DL$ and exit $\mathfrak{F}$ after the eighth round.

Hence, after performing the proposed algorithm, 6 out of 10 ESs gained significant improvements with respect to F1-score. Although a marginal decrease in Precision is noted for two ESs, this is counterbalanced by improvements observed in two others, and notably, by an overall enhancement in Recall, in particularly for 7 ESs. Consequently, there is also a corresponding improvement in test accuracy. It is important to notice that this improvement could not be achieved following a purely private feature removal mechanism guided by feature importance assessment by RF. This is due to the fact that the less significant features pointed out at local level by each ES in general do not correspond to the one chosen by the core network through averaging.

The exploitation of the proposed ML cooperative approach among eNBs yielded a an improved balance between accuracy and recall, implied by a higher F1-score. As a result, there will be fewer false negatives, which means that when a real cell outage happens, network operators will get more accurate alert signals, thus quickly identifying real cell failures and avoiding unnecessary interventions (Figs. 3 and 4).

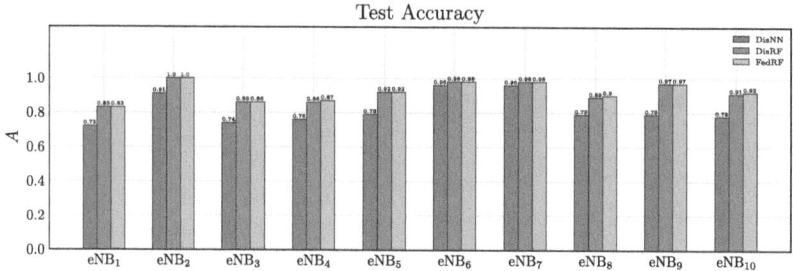

Fig. 2. Test Accuracy Comparison.

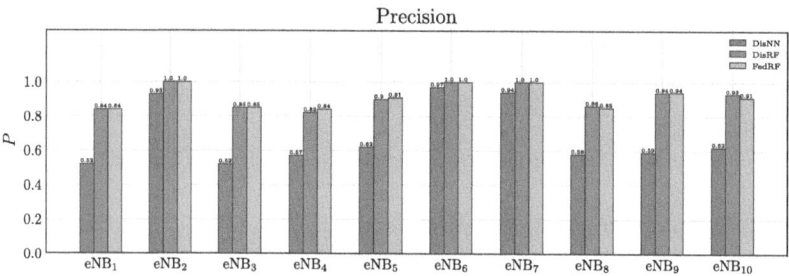

Fig. 3. Precision Comparison.

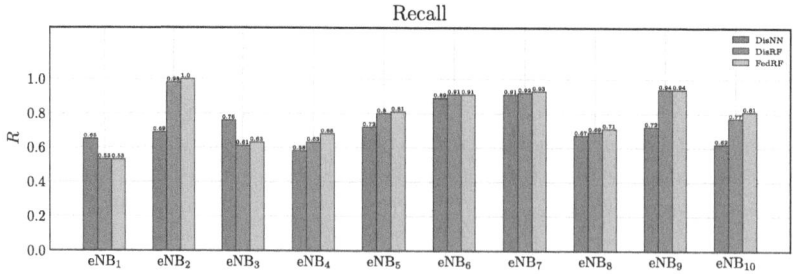

Fig. 4. Recall Comparison

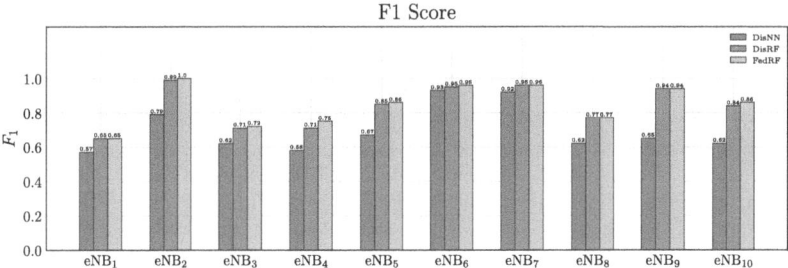

Fig. 5. F1-Score Comparison

5   Conclusion

In this work, a COD problem has been successfully tackled by leveraging a cooperative distributed algorithm based on Random Forests and a feature removal approach. It has been proven how it is possible to keep raw data containing information about radio and connectivity metrics private while sharing local knowledge about feature importance scores. The proposed mechanism allows not to deteriorate (and, in some cases, to improve) performance in terms of test accuracy and F1–score, while guaranteeing that each BS keeps its data completely private, without sharing them with the other access points within the network.

The integration of the proposed algorithm within each access point of the communication network may provide telecommunication providers with a powerful tool to proactively identify faults or attacks at cell level in the critical infrastructure, resulting in a considerable reduction of the mean time to repair. As network disturbances are quickly detected and fixed, this decrease in mean time to repair immediately translates into improved service dependability and a better end-user experience.

Future works may extend the COD problem considering a multi–class classification scenario, in which the dataset labels differentiate with respect to the type of internal fault or external attack happening within that specific cell. Eventually, the federated method proposed in this work may be tested and validated in large-scale scenarios, envisaging a greater number of base stations and cells.

Acknowledgment. This work has been partially supported by the EU in the scope of the NANCY project, which has received funding from the Smart Networks and Services Joint Undertaking (SNS JU) under the European Union's Horizon Europe research and innovation programme under Grant Agreement No 101096456, and the FSE REACT-EU, PON Ricerca e Innovazione 2014–2020, programme. Project co-funded by the European Union - Next Generation Eu - under the National Recovery and Resilience Plan (NRRP), Mission 4 Component 1 Investment 4.1 - Decree No. 118 (2nd March 2023) of Italian Ministry of University and Research - Concession Decree No. 2333 (22nd December 2023) of the Italian Ministry of University and Research, Project code D93C23000450005, within the Italian National Program PhD Programme in Autonomous Systems (DAuSy).

References

1. Wrona, A., Tantucci, A.: Artificial intelligence-based data path control in low Earth orbit satellites-driven optical communications. Int. J. Satell Commun Network. **42**, 425–443 (2024)
2. Giuseppi, A., Manfredi, S., Menegatti, D., Pietrabissa, A., Poli, C.: Decentralized federated learning for nonintrusive load monitoring in smart energy communities. In: 2022 30th Mediterranean Conference on Control and Automation (MED), pp 312–317. IEEE (2022)
3. Wrona, A., De Santis, E., Priscoli, F.D., Lavacca, F.G.: An intelligent ground station selection algorithm in satellite optical communications via deep learning. In: 2023 31st Mediterranean Conference on Control and Automation (MED), pp 493–499. IEEE (2023)
4. Ahmed, E., Rehmani, M.H.: Mobile edge computing: opportunities, solutions, and challenges (2017)
5. Alias, M., Saxena, N., Roy, A.: Efficient cell outage detection in 5g hetnets using hidden markov model. IEEE Commun. Lett. **20**(3), 562–565 (2016)
6. de-la Bandera, I., Barco, R., Munoz, P., Serrano, I.: Cell outage detection based on handover statistics. IEEE Commun. Lett. **19**(7), 1189–1192 (2015)
7. Bodrog, L., Kajo, M., Kocsis, S., Schultz, B.: A robust algorithm for anomaly detection in mobile networks. In: 2016 IEEE 27th Annual International Symposium on Personal, Indoor, and Mobile Radio Communications (PIMRC), pp. 1–6. IEEE (2016)
8. Breiman, L.: Random forests. Mach. Learn. **45**, 5–32 (2001)
9. Chernogorov, F., Turkka, J., Ristaniemi, T., Averbuch, A.: Detection of sleeping cells in lte networks using diffusion maps. In: 2011 IEEE 73rd Vehicular Technology Conference (VTC Spring), pp. 1–5. IEEE (2011)
10. Chernov, S., Chernogorov, F., Petrov, D., Ristaniemi, T.: Data mining framework for random access failure detection in lte networks. In: 2014 IEEE 25th Annual International Symposium on Personal, Indoor, and Mobile Radio Communication (PIMRC), pp. 1321–1326. IEEE (2014)
11. Ciocarlie, G.F., Lindqvist, U., Nováczki, S., Sanneck, H.: Detecting anomalies in cellular networks using an ensemble method. In: Proceedings of the 9th International Conference on Network and Service Management (CNSM 2013), pp. 171–174. IEEE (2013)
12. Hussain, B., Du, Q., Imran, A., Imran, M.A.: Artificial intelligence-powered mobile edge computing-based anomaly detection in cellular networks. IEEE Trans. Industr. Inf. **16**(8), 4986–4996 (2019)
13. Hussain, B., Du, Q., Zhang, S., Imran, A., Imran, M.A.: Mobile edge computing-based data-driven deep learning framework for anomaly detection. IEEE Access **7**, 137656–137667 (2019)
14. Khanafer, R.M., et al.: Automated diagnosis for umts networks using bayesian network approach. IEEE Trans. Veh. Technol. **57**(4), 2451–2461 (2008)
15. Khatib, E.J., Barco, R., Gómez-Andrades, A., Serrano, I.: Diagnosis based on genetic fuzzy algorithms for lte self-healing. IEEE Trans. Veh. Technol. **65**(3), 1639–1651 (2015)
16. Liao, Q., Wiczanowski, M., Stańczak, S.: Toward cell outage detection with composite hypothesis testing. In: 2012 IEEE International Conference on Communications (ICC), pp. 4883–4887. IEEE (2012)

17. Lin, P.C.: Large-scale and high-dimensional cell outage detection in 5g self-organizing networks. In: 2019 Asia-Pacific Signal and Information Processing Association Annual Summit and Conference (APSIPA ASC), pp. 8–12. IEEE (2019)
18. Masood, U., Asghar, A., Imran, A., Mian, A.N.: Deep learning based detection of sleeping cells in next generation cellular networks. In: 2018 IEEE Global Communications Conference (GLOBECOM), pp. 206–212. IEEE (2018)
19. Mueller, C.M., Kaschub, M., Blankenhorn, C., Wanke, S.: A cell outage detection algorithm using neighbor cell list reports. In: Hummel, K.A., Sterbenz, J.P.G. (eds.) IWSOS 2008. LNCS, vol. 5343, pp. 218–229. Springer, Heidelberg (2008). https://doi.org/10.1007/978-3-540-92157-8_19
20. Mulvey, D., Foh, C.H., Imran, M.A., Tafazolli, R.: Cell fault management using machine learning techniques. IEEE Access **7**, 124514–124539 (2019)
21. Oğuz, H.T., Kalaycioğlu, A.: Cell outage detection in lte-a cellular systems using neural networks. Commun. Faculty Sci. Univ. Ankara Series A2-A3 Phys. Sci. Eng. **60**(1), 31–40 (2018)
22. Onireti, O., et al.: A cell outage management framework for dense heterogeneous networks. IEEE Trans. Veh. Technol. **65**(4), 2097–2113 (2015)
23. Pana, V.S., Babalola, O.P., Balyan, V.: 5g radio access networks: a survey. Array **14**, 100170 (2022)
24. Pinaya, W.H.L., Vieira, S., Garcia-Dias, R., Mechelli, A.: Convolutional neural networks. In: Machine learning, pp. 173–191. Elsevier (2020)
25. Ping, Y.H., Lin, P.C.: Cell outage detection using deep convolutional autoencoder in mobile communication networks. In: 2020 Asia-Pacific Signal and Information Processing Association Annual Summit and Conference (APSIPA ASC), pp. 1557–1560. IEEE (2020)
26. Ruan, Y., Wang, Y., Tang, Y.: An intelligent cell outage detection method in cellular networks. In: 2021 16th International Conference on Computer Science & Education (ICCSE), pp. 548–553. IEEE (2021)
27. Sangaiah, A.K., Rezaei, S., Javadpour, A., Miri, F., Zhang, W., Wang, D.: Automatic fault detection and diagnosis in cellular networks and beyond 5g: Intelligent network management. Algorithms **15**(11), 432 (2022)
28. Turkka, J., Ristaniemi, T., David, G., Averbuch, A.: Anomaly detection framework for tracing problems in radio networks. In: Proceedings of to ICN, vol. 2011 (2011)
29. Vidal, J.: Anomaly detection in 4g cellular networks (2020)
30. Wang, W., Liao, Q., Zhang, Q.: Cod: a cooperative cell outage detection architecture for self-organizing femtocell networks. IEEE Trans. Wireless Commun. **13**(11), 6007–6014 (2014)
31. Xue, W., Peng, M., Ma, Y., Zhang, H.: Classification-based approach for cell outage detection in self-healing heterogeneous networks. In: 2014 IEEE Wireless Communications and Networking Conference (WCNC), pp. 2822–2826. IEEE (2014)
32. Zoha, A., Saeed, A., Imran, A., Imran, M.A., Abu-Dayya, A.: A son solution for sleeping cell detection using low-dimensional embedding of mdt measurements. In: 2014 IEEE 25th Annual International Symposium on Personal, Indoor, and Mobile Radio Communication (PIMRC), pp. 1626–1630. IEEE (2014)

"Paying the Rent" A Formal Methods Riposte to "Living Off the Land" Attacks

Thomas Richard McEvoy[1] and Stephen D. Wolthusen[1,2](✉)

[1] Center for Cyber and Information Security(CCIS), Faculty of Information Technology and Electrical Engineering, NTNU I Gjøvik, Trondheim, Norway
{Thomarm,stephen.wolthusen}@ntnu.no
[2] Information Security Group, Department of Mathematics Royal Holloway, University of London, London, UK

Abstract. "Living off the land" attacks make use of legitimate, preexisting code in combination with stolen credentials, rather than by adding malicious code infiltrate and launch attacks including on industrial control (ICS) systems. Lacking the usual indicators of compromise (IoC), detecting attacks requires engineering knowledge of the system, which may not be within possession of SOC analysts or their tool sets. To counter this deficit, we propose using a formal model of the cyber-physical system, coded as a "digital shadow", to reference the behavior of the underlying system. A divergence in the probability of messaging behavior between the shadowed systems highlights where an intrusion may have occurred. We model this approach using identically defined systems and then illustrate via a simulated attack. As a secondary contribution, we demonstrate that stateful applied pi calculus, with minimal and commonly used process algebraic extensions, is sufficient to model cyber-physical (hybrid) systems without the need to introduce "alien" syntax and semantics, allowing for more straightforward verification.

1 Introduction

"Living off the land" attacks make use of the existing, legitimate codebase, relying on existing variability and scope for coding in combination with stolen credentials rather than malware, to carry out attacks on ICS systems. Such attacks are not readily amenable to discovery by conventional intrusion detection methods. Instead, it requires engineering knowledge of the systems to detect when an intrusion has occurred or an attack commenced [1], but this would need to be available to SOC tools and analysts in addition to more general insights into the security of systems.

The level of difficulty is increased when the attack does not consist of an immediately obvious breakdown in operational capacity, but takes place over a longer period of time, resulting in degraded production, wear and tear, and breakage of misused equipment, or unacceptable externalities such as levels of pollution – all of which which make it economically or possibly politically unfeasible to operate the system [1,2]. Current threat levels for this type of attack

G. Oliva et al. (Eds.): CRITIS 2024, LNCS 15549, pp. 96–115, 2025.
https://doi.org/10.1007/978-3-031-84260-3_6

are increasing as malicious software developers seek to automate these types of attack [3], making them available to low-skilled threat actors.

We propose making use of a *digital shadow*, defined using formal methods, to close the detection gap, not by exactly replicating the behavior of the system, but by reproducing its *likely* behavior and bounds on this over time. We can model both physical and cyber behavior and also distinguish between different modes of operation and the likely and, more importantly, unfeasible transitions between them. This makes each phase of operational amenable to statistical analysis and proofs of soundness, reducing the search of the state space required for detection purposes.

In this paper we use the simple example of a heater to demonstrate our approach. We show how to build a model of a cyber-physical system in the stateful applied π calculus using a modular approach which is easily scalable to larger and more complex examples. We use two copies of the model to simulate the action of the real-world system and digital shadow and subject one of them to a simulated attack.

Initially, for simplicity, we assume the adversary is not actively falsifying messages, but is relying on the apparent normalcy of the malicious commands to achieve their goals. We show the output of each system where both are operating normally, and where one is under attack. Our analysis shows distinct differences in stochastic behavior over time but also enables detection over much shorter timescales as well as validation of behavioral differences which are acceptable within the confines of the model.

An advantage of our approach is that it is feasible even in the absence of security protocols which are frequently not implemented on OT systems for economic, or operational, or even regulatory reasons [1,4] and only relies on the operation of SCADA protocols for its success.

As a secondary contribution, we demonstrate the stateful applied π calculus, with minimal extensions, is sufficient to model cyber-physical ("hybrid") systems without the need to introduce additional syntax and semantics.

Section 2 provides a summary of related research where Sect. 3 sets out the problem of "living off the land" attacks. Section 4 describes our approach. Section 5 shows how we can specify a system and modularize its design before defining it in the π calculus. Section 6 summarizes the features of the stateful applied π calculus, our extensions and our approach to bisimulation. In Sect. 7, we sketch the model of the heater and show its behavior under attack; in Sect. 8 we briefly discuss our results before concluding with Sect. 9 also setting out future work.

2   Literature Review

Modern "Living off the land" attacks are e.g. described in [1]. These attacks are becoming more accessible to lesser skilled attackers as they are automated [3]. The "CrashOverride" attack on the Ukrainian power system is an early example of this kind of attack [5]. Both "Stuxnet" and "Trisis" are examples of attacks with longer-term aims rather than ones simply trying to cause immediate destruction [1,2]. It is the combination of these type of attacks which we seek to address.

The π calculus was originally developed by Milner [6] as a process algebra for mobile systems and subsequently extended by Abadí et al.for the purposes of security analysis [7] and further extended to include state cells for the purposes of analyzing hardware states by Arapini et al. [8]. Our extensions to it represent commonly used features of process algebra [9] to describe cyber-physical (also known as "hybrid") environments. We depart from previous attempts to create hybrid calculi—for example, [10–12]—by adhering more rigidly to the philosophy and idiom of process calculi. Our work falls into the research stream on modeling cyber-physical systems which is surveyed by [13]. Our approach enables traceability and conformance analysis by the application of formal methods.

Digital shadows (or twins) have been developed as a cost-effective way of monitoring critical systems, including cyber-physical systems. They are usually in communication with their twin and use this to mirror operations or even to intervene and take over from a degraded "real-world" system [14]. Our aim differs somewhat. We seek to provide the operator with a means of checking the current validity of system operations and that any divergence between the virtual and physical shadows is within acceptable limits in stochastic terms. This is similar to the idea of "distance" developed in [10] but we have made use of the theory of hybrid automata [15] as an underlying structure to allow us to modularize the approach for more complex systems while simplifying the detection method through approximation.

The adversary model we use is based on the account of "living off the land" attacks [1] and could be regarded as unusual because the adversary does not make use of malware in the traditional sense, except to build legitimate-appearing command streams during the final attack phase. For our purposes also, for the moment, we assume the adversary does not engage in MITM type message falsification techniques. This is a simplification which we are using in our initial phase of research, but does represent a genuine paradox for these kinds of attack in that adversaries employing malware instantly become more detectable by conventional means while the goal of such attacks is to achieve the opposite result [1].

3   Motivation

As "living off the land" attacks are difficult to detect using conventional indicators of compromise, particularly in the case of hybrid IT/OT systems, knowledge of the operating parameters and their relation is required for detection [1].

This problem bifurcates into two parts. The first part concerns infiltration and lateral movement in the IT system and is out of scope for our study as it has been covered extensively by other researchers. However, once the attacker has reached the target system, the attack methods rely on custom-made malicious scripts to craft and attack which appears to consist of legitimate commands using OT protocols in the case of hybrid systems. Only an intimate knowledge of system operations and current state would show that the commands lack validity but the system behavior induced by the attacker can lead to severe consequences, and attackers must conversely be able to identify state sub-spaces in which attacks can have the desired effect. Alternatively, attacker actions may result long term physical damage to the system or a material reduction in production values, or unacceptable externalities during production runs [1, 2, 16]. We focus on the last problem.

We seek to provide the security operations staff, who lack an engineering knowledge of the systems, with a ready means of detecting anomalous behavior. The approach also needs to work in the absence of protocols with extensive security guarantees, both because they are often not implemented on SCADA systems and also because conventional security techniques have already shown themselves unable to detect such attacks [1, 4]. As a further motivation, we note that the commodification of such attacks considerably increases the likelihood of their frequency in the future [3].

4 Approach

We mimic the use of a digital shadow of the cyber-physical system which simulates, but due to aleatory factors, does not exactly match the behavior of the real-world system by using identical system models. The shadow is defined in the stateful applied π-calculus, with some well-known process algebraic extensions to incorporate temporal and stochastic features. It can subsequently be translated into a suitable model-checking or verification framework. Our contention is that bisimilar systems exhibit invariant behavior with regard to event probability and the timing of transitions between operating modes and changes to state variables. We can therefore use the timing and probability of events to detect deviations in system performance, which may be indicative of a potential attack.

We illustrate our approach using a simple system (a heater) with a view to demonstrating that more complex models may be readily constructed using a modular approach to system design, helping to reduce the state space under analysis at any one point in time. This may then also be captured in a combination of simulation environments such as Matlab/Simulink and verification environments such as Isabelle/HOL provided suitable embeddings.

Our approach assumes, at this stage, that the adversary is not trying to falsify information, but is relying on the apparent "normalcy" of the malicious command stream to hide attacks. This is a somewhat arbitrary constraint, and we will address the issue of message falsification in the next stage of research. However, it should be recognized that if the adversary does make use of malware to inject or alter messages, that this would make these more detectable by conventional means.

5   System Architecture

Cyber-physical systems can be relatively complex and go through various modes of operation, traversing different state sub-spaces. Initially, to represent these, we can model them using a hybrid automaton – see Fig. 1 in Sect. 7.

Using a hybrid automaton to define the initial architecture has the advantage of providing a relatively easy way to understand a view of the system with its main parameters which is modular and allows us to build up a complex system architecture   see [15] for further examples. The modular approach also reduces the state space under consideration at any point in time.

We can subsequently take each mode of the system (represented by a node on the graph in Fig. 1) and define the behavior of that node using the π-calculus. We can also define the conditions under which new modes are invoked and, based on define system limits, alarm conditions. This subdivides the state space under consideration.

In addition, we can move beyond the model provided by the hybrid automaton and define the cyber behavior of each system, e.g. commands issued to actuators, sensor readings, data sent to the operator. We can also explicitly synchronize the behavior of the system over time and represent concurrency in the model, along with external factors – such as the influence of the external environment on system behavior (e.g. weather, feed stock).

Finally, we can represent attack behavior and exhibit its results, either by defining new modes of operation, or divergent behavior in current modes of operation. Attack behavior can, for example, consist of altering parameters in the gain function or changing safety conditions.

The system is validated through a formal proof of its operation. This makes it possible to confidently analyze its behavior using a statistical approach, resorting to formal proofs where necessary to demonstrate where one system has unfeasibly diverged in behavior from its shadow. The difference between this and a straightforward statistical analysis is that we use the model of the system to help us take account of the varying modes of operation and transitions between them. So we analyze both the occurrence and feasibility of transitions between modes and also behavior within modes. We may also resort to more formal proofs during forensic analysis of apparent incidents.

6   The Applied Pi Calculus

We use the stateful applied π-calculus [7,17] with a small set of temporal and stochastic extensions to represent cyber-physical (sometimes called "hybrid") systems.

Temporal extensions allow us to deal win change over time in the physical environment, while stochastic extensions allow to take account of aleatory factors in those environments such as external disturbances to processes and measurement uncertainty.

6.1   Syntax and Informal Semantics

A signature Σ consists of a finite set of function symbols, each with an arity m. A function symbol with arity 0 is a constant.

Given a signature Σ, an infinite set of names, and an infinite set of variables, we define the set of terms using the grammar –

$$L, M, N, T, U, V ::= \qquad\qquad\qquad\qquad \text{terms}$$

$$a, b, c, k, m, n, s \qquad\qquad \text{names}$$
$$x, y, z \qquad\qquad \text{variables}$$
$$f(M_1, \ldots, M_l) \quad \text{function application}$$

where f ranges over the functions of Σ and l matches the arity of f. u, v, w are used as meta-variables to range over both names and variables. Tuples $u_1, \ldots, u_l$ and $M_1, \ldots, M_l$ are abbreviated to $\tilde{u}$ and $\tilde{M}$ respectively.

We rely on a sort system for names and variables which includes a sort Channel for channels and a sort Cell for cells and may include other sorts such as Integer, Real, or (more simply) a universal Data. We assume names, variables and functions are well-sorted and constrain actions within the calculus appropriately. Sorts may be specified explicitly, if required, using the notation $x : \tau$, but are usually defined implicitly in our examples.

The grammar for processes is similar to the pi calculus, but messages may contain terms, not just names and names need not just be channel names (e.g., cell names). We extend the grammar with non-deterministic choice over the sum of capabilities.

$$P, Q, R ::= \qquad\qquad\qquad \text{processes (or plain processes}$$

0	null process
$P \mid Q$	parallel composition
P	replication
$\nu n.P$	name restriction ("new")
if $M = N$ then P else Q	conditional statement
$\alpha.P + \beta.Q$	non-deterministic choice
$N(x).P$	message input
$\bar{N}\langle M \rangle.P$	message output
$[s \longmapsto M]$	cell s containing term M
$s := M.P$	writing a cell
read s as $x.P$	reading a cell
locks $s.P$	locking a cell
unlocks $s.P$	unlocking a cell

The null process **0** does nothing. $P \mid Q$ is parallel composition. $!P$ behaves as an infinite number of copies of P working in parallel. $\nu n.P$ makes a new private name n and then continues as P. The conditional construct if $M = N$then Pelse Q runs P if M and N are equal and Q otherwise. The construct $\alpha.P + \beta.Q$ offers a non-deterministic choice for branching behavior, where either branch may be chosen to the exclusion of the other. $\sum_i \alpha_i.P$ is sometimes used to stand for an extended set of such choices, where α_i stands for any process capability. $N(x).P$ receives x on N and $\bar{N}\langle M \rangle.P$ sends the term M on N.

Regarding cells, the following requirements apply:

- x, M, N are not of cell sort; additionally, M is of sort data.
- for every $locks/s.P$, the part P of the process must not include parallel or replication unless it is after an $unlocks/s.P$
- for a given cell name, s the replication operator ! must not occur between νs and $[s \longmapsto M]$.

For a process term $A + B$, either A or B may be chosen, but the choice of one excludes the other. Modified by a boolean term, we may also have $[s]A + [t]B$, then A or B may only be selected if s or t are true. If the boolean terms are non-exclusive such that $s = t = TRUE$ we revert to a non-deterministic choice between them.

We further extend this notion of non-deterministic choice by introducing probability functions(including constants), replacing each boolean term in the sum $\sum_i [s_i]A_i$, $i = 1 \ldots n$ with a probability s_i' such that $\sum s_i' = 1$. The probability functions may vary depending on the state of the system. Each process term $[s_i]A_i$ is active where $s_i > 0$ and deadlocked otherwise. Non-deterministic choice occurs as before but the likelihood of the event is an input to the proof process. A run of low probability events may trigger some limit $k < l$ on the validity of the process.

Processes are extended with *active substitutions*:

$$A, B, C ::= \qquad \text{extended processes}$$
$$P \qquad \text{plain process}$$
$$A | B \qquad \text{parallel composition}$$
$$\nu n.A \qquad \text{name restriction}$$
$$\nu x.A \qquad \text{variable restriction}$$
$$\{M/_x\} \qquad \text{active substitution}$$

$\{M/_x\}$ is a substitution that replaces the variable x with a term M. It acts like *let $x = M$ in* ... except that it works on any process it comes in contact with unless x is restricted in the process. Larger substitutions using multiple variables are possible and we write $\sigma.\{M/_x\}, \{M/_{\tilde{x}}\}$ for substitutions; $x\sigma$ for the image of x by σ; and $T\sigma$ for the result of applying σ to the free variables of T. We may also write $\{M_1/_{x_1}, \ldots, M_l/_{x_l}\}$ for $\{M_1/_{x_1}\} | \ldots | \{M_l/_{x_l}\}$. We identify the empty substitution and the null process $\mathbf{0}$.

Names and variables have scopes, defined by restrictions and inputs. We write $fv(A)$ and $fn(A)$ for sets of free variables and free names of A which are not bound, respectively, $bv(A)$ and $bn(A)$ for those which are bound. The domain $dom(A)$ of an extended process A is the set of variables x for which A contains a substitution $\{M/_x\}$. Substitutions are assumed to be cycle-free. An extended process is *closed* when its free variables are all defined $dom(A) = fv(A)$. The abbreviation $\nu \tilde{u}$ is used for the, possibly empty, set of distinct restrictions $\nu u_1, \ldots, \nu u_l$.

A frame is an extended process built up from **0** and actives substitutions of the form $\{^M\_x\}$. We use ϕ and φ to range over frames. We map an extended process A to a frame $\varphi(A)$ by replacing every plain process with **0**.

A frame accounts for the static knowledge exposed by an extended process A to its environment. It does not explain the dynamic behavior of A. But we will extend the notion of frames to include substitution of functions (see Sect. 6.4) which does open the door to explaining the dynamic behavior of A using frames.

6.2 Temporal Representation

We represent the passing of time using a discrete framework. Discrete time is represented by using a process or function of type $tick(n)$ where where n is the number of units of time which pass for the operation of the function. A function of type $tick(n)$ is not strictly part of the grammar of the calculus, but it is useful to give it its own reduction relationship in operational semantics – see Sect. 6.3.

For convenience, computational steps are normally assumed to take no time (but we can specify where this is not the case) and processes in physical states take, at least, $tick(1)$.

We can synchronize actions in time across the system by communicating using a $\overline{tick(n)}, tick(n)$ function as interactive terms. Alternatively, we can use the function to write implicitly or explicitly to one or more state cells representing local and/or global time and use these as timestamps to mark messages. This should subsequently allows us to consider attacks which specifically target timing in the system .

6.3 Operational Semantics

Central to the operational semantics of the π-calculus is the reduction relation $\rightarrow$ which models computational steps. The axioms for reduction rely on auxiliary rules for a structural equivalence relation $\equiv$. Both rely on an underlying equational theory.

Terms are equipped with an equivalence relation $=_\Sigma$, based on an equational theory, which is closed under substitution, re-namings and function applications. We require that the equational theory respect the sort system. We write $\sigma \vdash M = N$ when $M = N$ is the theory associated with σ, otherwise $\sigma \nvdash M = N$.

An evaluation context is an expression with a hole which is not under a replication, a conditional, an input, or an output. A context $E[\cdot]$ closes A when $E[A]$ is closed.

Structural equivalence $\equiv$ is the smallest equivalence relation on extended processes that is closed by application of evaluation contexts such that –

| SUM-0 | $A \equiv A + \mathbf{0}$ |
| SUM | $M + N \equiv N + M$ |

PAR-0	$A \equiv A	\mathbf{0}$
PAR-A	$A|(B|C) \equiv (A|B)|C$
PAR-C	$A|B \equiv B|A$
REPL	$!P \equiv P	!P$

NEW-0	$\nu u.\mathbf{0} \equiv \mathbf{0}$	
NEW-C	$\nu u.\nu v.A \equiv \nu.v.\nu.u.A$	
NEW-PAR	$A|\nu v.B \equiv \nu v(A|B)$	when $u \notin fv(A) \cup fn(A)$
ALIAS	$\nu x.\{^M/_x\} \equiv \mathbf{0}$	
SUBST	$\{^M/_x\}|A \equiv \{^M/_x\}|A\{^M/_x\}$	
REWRITE	$\{^M/_x\} \equiv \{^N/_x\}$ when $\Sigma \vdash M = N$	

The rules for parallel composition and restriction are as usual. ALIAS allows the introduction of arbitrary active substitutions. SUBST describes the application of an active substitution. Their combination allows for the substitution of variables for processes in a frame. REWRITE deals with equational re-writing and assumes the sort system is enforced.

The *internal reduction* relation $\rightarrow$ is defined such that

| COMM | $\bar{N}\langle x \rangle.P|N(x).Q \rightarrow P|Q$ |

| THEN | if $M = N$ then P *else* $Q \rightarrow P$ |

| ELSE | if $M = N$ then P else $Q \rightarrow P$ |
| | for any ground terms M and N such that $\sigma \nvdash M = N$ |

| CHOICE(+) | $P + Q \rightarrow P$ or $P + Q \rightarrow Q$ |

| TICK | $f : tick(0) \equiv 0, g : tick(n) \rightarrow g : tick(n - 1)$ |

As well as the reduction relationship, we also make use of labeled transitions to indicate interaction between a process and the external world.

6.4 Bisimilarity

If two processes cannot be distinguished by any context, then they are observationally equivalent [7]. In the spi calculus, this equivalence captures the security properties authenticity and secrecy where the context is an active attacker.

This argument may be transposed to the security property of system integrity in cyber-physical systems, but it requires more work to create a suitable context to distinguish sound from unsound systems because of aleatory factors in cyber-physical systems, inter alia.

We begin with the standard definition of observational equivalence [7]. We write $A \Downarrow a$ when A can send a message on name a, i.e., $A \to * \equiv E[\bar{a}\langle M \rangle . P]$ for some evaluation context $E[\cdot]$ that does not bind a.

Definition 1. *Observational Bisimulation*

An observational bisimulation is a symmetric relation R between closed extended processes with the same domain such at $A/R/B$ implies:

1. *if $A \Downarrow a$, then $B \Downarrow b$;*
2. *if $A \to *A'$ and A' is closed, then $B \to B'$ and $A'/R/B'$ for some B';*
3. *$E[A]/R/E[B]$ for all closing contexts $E[]$.*

Observational equivalence ($\approx$) is the largest such relation.

$\Downarrow a$ is called a *barb* on a, where $\approx$ is one of two notions of weak barbed bisimulation congruence. Usefully, this notion can be extended to arbitrary terms in the applied π-calculus. This includes the application to functions, including constants, and variables along with their values.

In a cyber (IT) system, this allows us to define a potential detection event as a breach of observational equivalence. But disturbances associated with physical (OT) processes and measurement inaccuracy mean that system behavior, even between two identical systems may diverge and merge over time.

We hence have to take account of a probabilistic distribution over process capabilities, using a notion of weak stochastic bisimulation.

By extending the grammar of processes to include non-deterministic choice and using stochastic functions to distribute the probability of action non-deterministically over process choices, we create a (weak) transition from a process to a probability distribution over sub-processes $P \xrightarrow{\alpha} \gamma$ where $\gamma = \sum_i [p_i] P_i'$ as proposed also by Lanotte et al. [10].

Clearly, if we have a process Q such that $P \, R \, Q$ and $Q \xrightarrow{\alpha} \gamma'$ where $\gamma' = \sum_j [q_j] Q_j'$ and each $[p_i] P_i' \, R \, [q_j] Q_j'$ for all $i = j$ (re-ordering, if necessary) then the systems are weakly stochastically bisimilar. But even this is not sufficiently useful as probabilities generated by functions which vary their output dependent on state are very unlikely to correspond so neatly for even a single transition.

Instead, using a concept from open bisimulation [18], we treat the processes (and the system as a whole) as tree structures. two trees are claimed to be stochastically branching bisimilar, if the expectation of a branch (process transition representing a stochastic choice) occurring in each tree is within a narrow range of values.

Definition 2. *Expectation of Branching Behavior*

Let s be a conditional probability which varies over time. For a stochastic process transition $[s]P \xrightarrow{\alpha} P'$, the expectation of P', written $Ex(P')$ is the average conditional probability of branching behavior.

For deterministic transitions and non-deterministic choices, the expectation of branching behavior is not a meaningful concept, although the bisimilarity of branching behavior is. However, for stochastic processes, the selection of a transition will be conditionally dependent on the state of the system and the outcome of measurement processes. The expectation of a transition is therefore derived from the conditional probability of its occurring. Where a transition represents a choice over outcomes, each with a different probability, this leads to a notion of stochastic branching bisimilarity:

Definition 3. *Stochastic Branching (Barbed) Bisimilarity*

Let S and T be process trees representing cyber-physical systems. For a given transition, $P \xrightarrow{\alpha} \gamma$ where $\gamma = \sum_i [p_i] P'_i$, let $Ex(P_i)$ be the expectation of choice P_i occurring in tree S. If there exists a tree T and a transition $Q \xrightarrow{\alpha} \gamma'$ where $\gamma' = \sum_i [q_i] Q'_i$ such that each $Q'_i = P'_i$ (re-ordering as required). Then if for all closing contexts, $E[S]$ and $E[T]$, the expectation of each Q_i and P_i matches within a given limit – written $Ex(Q'_i) \approx_l Ex(P'_i)$ – where l represents the limit of divergence then S R T is a stochastic branching bisimilarity and S is weakly stochastically bisimilar to T written $S \approx_p T$.

Weakly stochastic branching (barbed) bisimulation ($\approx_p$) is the largest such relation.

Showing how to prove this formally for a set of systems would be out of scope for this paper, but requires us to do two things. First, demonstrate the branching structure of the system is the same for a non-deterministic version of the system where branches are selected arbitrarily and not associated with stochastic functions and, second, extend the definition of a frame to allow functions as well as variables to be introduced to the model by a "let" construct, introducing the idea that two differently constructed functions may be bisimilar in terms of their behavior. As a byproduct, this introduces the interesting notion that two cyber-physical systems may be bisimilar, even though they deal with different physical systems because their disparate functions produce the same expectation over branching behavior.

We believe that the notion of weakly stochastic branching (barbed) bisimulation encompasses the idea of "distance" put forward in [10] as a metric of bisimilarity in cyber-physical systems. But this, again, is outside the scope of the paper to show.

7   Example - A Heating System

In this section we illustrate the construction of a simple cyber-physical system. We subsequently show how we can simulate an attack on this system and its detection.

7.1   Cyber-Physical System

To illustrate using the applied π-calculus in the context of a cyber-physical system, we use the example of a heating system under control of a thermostat, based on [15].

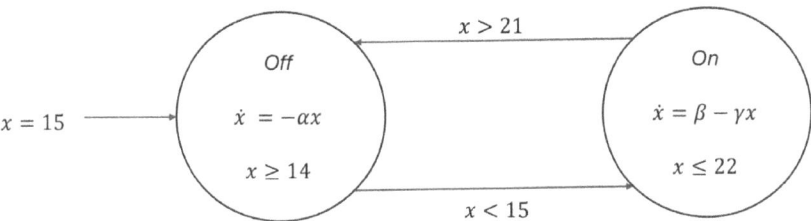

Fig. 1. Hybrid automaton of a thermostat

The initial temperature x is set to 15. The first parameter shows the mode (or state) of operation currently in place. The initial mode of operation is OFF. While in OFF mode, the system temperature falls at a rate of γx where we γ is an operator-defined parameter. If the temperature falls below 15 the system switches to ON mode and the temperature begins to rise following the gain function $\dot{x} = \alpha - \beta x$ where α and β are again operator defined. The arrows show the boolean conditions under which modes based on the value of the state variables (here, the temperature x) should change between OFF and ON and the third parameter shows the invariant behavior of the temperature x in the system. It should not fall between 14 nor rise above 22. We identify these invariants with safety parameters which may lead to alarms being sounded, if violated.

7.2   Transposition to the π-Calculus

In the π-calculus we are representing not only the physical actions of the system but also the cyber aspects of its control. Hence we need to represent communication with the operator – both commands and telemetry, the explicit passing of time rather than ordering only, and concurrent actions. Hence a more complex representation is needed, even for a single cyber-physical process. A system can be represented by the following *types* of process. We provide examples of each type in the following.

$$HeatingSystem := Operations|Actuators|Sensors|SafetySystems|$$
$$GainFunctions|Main\_Process|SystemParameters|$$
$$Clock|State\_Variables|Measurements|Reporting$$

Operations are the commands which the operator may carry out. For example, altering *SystemParameters* or changing the setting on an actuator. The nature of the commands is determined by the SCADA protocol which is being simulated by the model. We assume a simplified version of the IEC 60870-5-104 protocol which allows us, for example, to request multiple sensor readings simultaneously. There will be several possible operations, e.g., to switch on the heater we could use the process $SwitchOn := \bar{s}$. We assume a command input process exists with a defined language for issuing commands.

The *Actuators* are defined by a state variable and a process which allows its value to be altered by an operation. For the heating system, the two states are Off and On which can be represented by a binary switch. A more complex system may require a menu of options to set different modes.

$$Switch := \ !s.\text{read } Mode \text{ as } m.\text{lock } Mode.$$
$$\quad\quad\quad \text{if } m = 1 \text{ then } Mode := 0 \text{ else } Mode := 1.\text{unlock } Mode$$
$$Mode := \ [Mode \longmapsto m]$$

The *Sensors* are processes which read the values of the *StateVariables* state variables, which are cells and store these values in *Measurements*, which are also cells. However, to represent measurement inaccuracy, a function is used to skew the reading before it is stored. In our system, the temperature is read and stored as a measurement by the thermometer. There is a continuous uniform probability that the temperature may be up to 0.5 degrees higher or lower than its reading. This level of inaccuracy is in line with the performance of industrial equipment "in the wild". The operator and other parts of the system use the stored value, not the state value, to make control decisions.

$$ReadTemperature := \ !r.\text{read } Temperature \text{ as } x.\text{lock } Thermometer.$$
$$\quad\quad\quad Thermometer := skew(x).\text{unlock } Thermometer.\bar{r} |$$
$$\quad\quad\quad [Thermometer \longmapsto h] | [Temperature \longmapsto x]$$

SafetySystems are processes which may make independent readings of the state variables and either sound alarms or institute safety procedures if the measurements exceed the limits of the system. For example, in our system, the alarm system sounds if the thermometer reading exceeds either the low temperature limit or the high temperature limit.

$$Alarm := \nu \ s \ !a.\text{read } Thermometer \text{ as } s.\text{read } LowL \text{ as } ll.$$
$$\quad\quad\quad \text{read } HighL \text{ as } hh.[s > hh]alarm(hh) + [s < ll]alarm(ll).\bar{a}$$

The *gain* functions determine how much the state variable changes depending on the mode of operation. For complex systems, encoding each gain function separately can simplify the understanding of the system. But, for the purposes of economy of space, we have encoded gain function which alters the temperature depending on the current mode of operation as a single function.

$$gain\colon mode = 1 \longmapsto \alpha - \beta x$$
$$mode = 0 \longmapsto \beta - \gamma x$$

The main control process is the heating system which seeks to maintain the temperature inside a specified range by switching on and off the heater in a timely fashion. Due to external conditions, the operation of the *gain* function is perturbed. To represent this, we assume there exists a continuous uniform probability that the temperature gain may be up to 0.3 degrees higher or lower than the outcome of the *gain* function.

$$Heater(1) := !h.\text{read } Mode \text{ as } m.\text{read } Temperature \text{ as } x.\text{lock } Temperature.$$
$$Temperature := x + perturb(gain(x, m, \alpha, \beta)).$$
$$\text{unlock} Temperature.\bar{h}$$

Note, we explicitly model a global clock as a state cell $[Clock \longmapsto t]$ which we implicitly update by declaring the *Heater* process to be of type $tick(1)$. Any messages to processes with a time dependency (e.g., operations) are marked with the time stamp t.

The *SwitchMode* process reads the current temperature measurement and determines whether to change the operational mode. But there is a difference in how this process is defined in an encoding of the system and in the π calculus. In an encoding of the system, the function behaves deterministically. It switches mode when the thermometer reading exceeds either the high or low limit.

$$SwitchMode := !m.\text{read } Thermometer \text{ as } s.\text{read } Low \text{ as } l.$$
$$\text{read } High \text{ as } h.\text{lock } Mode.$$
$$[s > h]Mode := 0 + [s < l]Mode := 1.$$
$$\text{unlock } Mode.\bar{m}$$

However, in the π-calculus model, the *SwitchMode* process is defined stochastically and uses the actual temperature of the system to calculate the probability of a switch in mode occurring by estimating the range of possible thermometer readings. Hence two identical systems can diverge in behavior over time, but the expectation of their behavior should be bisimilar for identical functionality (see Sect. 6.4).

$$SwitchMode := !m.\text{read } Temperature \text{ as } x.\text{read } Low \text{ as } l.$$
$$\text{read } High \text{ as } h.\text{lock } Mode.$$
$$[p(fuzz(x) > h)]Mode := 1 + [p(fuzz(x) < l)]Mode :=$$
$$1.\text{unlock } Mode.\bar{m}$$

For a mode to be capable of being activated, the probability of activation must be greater than 0 or else some pre-determined positive limit $0 < i \leq 1$. The function $fuzz(s)$ calculates the spread of possible thermometer values (in this case, $+/-0.5^{o}$ celsius)

The heating system (the main process) is defined by –

$$HeatingSystem := \nu \; x, m, s, l, h \; (Heater(1)|Switch)$$

The system is controlled by the operator(or the adversary) using a SCADA protocol to reset values. We model a simplified version of the IEC 60870-5-104 protocol. This allows the operator to learn the current mode of operation, the current sensor reading for temperature, and read or write to the current set points of the system.

For example, the process to read the thermometer by the operator may be defined by –

$$ReadTemp .- !u.read\ Thermometer\ as\ s.u\langle s, t\rangle$$

The process to change one of the set points may be defined by –

$$WriteLow := !x(s).lock\ Low.Low := s.unlock\ Low$$

and similarly for other parameters.

Significant changes to systems operation are notified to the operator. For example, if the temperature drops or rises by 2 degrees and if the system switches between *on* and *off* modes. The latter process is shown.

$$NotifyModeChange := !w.\text{read}\ Mode\ as\ m.\text{read}\ Lastmode\ as\ p.$$
$$\text{if}\ m \neq p.\ \text{then}\ \bar{o}\langle m, t\rangle.$$
$$\text{lock}\ Lastmode.Lastmode := m.\text{unlock}\ Lastmode.\bar{w}$$

Additional layers of unreliability (beyond physical disturbance and measurement inaccuracy) in both the physical and cyber environment may be introduced by using a stochastic process. For example, if resetting the set points occasionally fails, this can be modeled by –

$$WriteLowFails := !l.lock\ Low.[.96]Low := s.unlockLow$$

The process *WriteLowFails* will fail .04 of the time since where the alternative choice is 0 we can omit the remainder of the sum.

We have described the operation of the thermostat using what we label a *brittle* model with two operating modes which it switches (i.e., "snaps") between based on temperature (as may be found in some primitive controllers). However, many SCADA systems, such as pumps, rely on systems which vary set point values, while the gain function remains fixed.

This is not difficult to model. It is simply a matter of altering the operation of the *gain* function: For example, assume we wanted the thermostat to maintain a constant temperature. We would alter the gain function as follows, while the *Switch* function would be replaced by a function to vary the set point value.

$$gain\colon x = sp \longmapsto 0$$
$$x > sp \longmapsto \alpha - \beta x$$
$$x < sp \longmapsto \beta - \gamma x$$

The parameters for positive and negative gain, respectively, α and β, γ (which might, for example, represent changes to voltage or resistance or the flow of cooling fluid) can subsequently be varied by the operator to determine how fast temperature is restored to the desired level. Additional state cells are added to the model along with associated read and write functions.

7.3   Simulating Attack Detection

We model the twinned systems in with a simple numerical model for illustration. A more elaborate model would require capturing physical effects, and should also include proof of the model conforming to the π-calculus definition (with the exception of being deterministic rather than non-deterministic as already mentioned in Sect. 7.2. However, for the purposes of this brief illustration we omit this somewhat lengthy step. The action of the replicating (i.e., continuously repeating) processes of reporting the current mode of operation and significant change to temperature where we will use differences in behavior to find indicators of compromise are trivially proven.

Bisimilar systems can be modeled by simply creating a copy of the current system. A non-bisimilar twin is created by making a change to a copy, in this case altering the α parameter from 2.5 to 3 causing the system to heat more rapidly than planned. In a real-world system, this kind of attack could result in increased fatigue to the heating elements over time, resulting in breakage. However, normal temperature ranges are respected, so only the frequency and not the amplitude of the system output is altered which makes distinguishing the behavior of the systems visually hard to do. Figure 2 show the respective outputs for bisimilar (top) and non-bisimilar (bottom) systems.

Using the invariant features of the operation we selected, we can show differences in the stochastic behavior of the system. The probability values vary $+/-0.1$ even between the bisimilar models but their range is constrained with $P(\text{ON})\ 0.02 + /-0.01$ and $P(\text{OFF})\ 0.05 + /-1$ (reflecting the fact the system heats faster and has to switch off more often). In the non-bisimilar model, $P(\text{OFF})\ 0.9 + /-0.1$ while $P(\text{ON})$ remains the same. This shows how mode dependent the probabilities are. Reported differences in temperature also provide a (somewhat weaker) signal with probabilities in the system under attack being consistently up to 0.03 points higher in their range over different runs of the system. This is not a significant difference but reflects that a cruder reporting threshold is being used. At the same time, the temperature ranges are not affected and graphs of system behavior do not show obvious features of an attack.

A further means of analysis is to condition on the current state of the system at any point and determine the likelihood that it could have reached the next point reported under normal operations. This stepped analysis allows us to uncover low probability or even unfeasible transactions. To do this properly, we would need to make use of estimation techniques, such as a Kalman filter, but crudely we can use the measured temperature for the valid system, recalculate the gain and measurement inaccuracy using the same parameters as for the non-

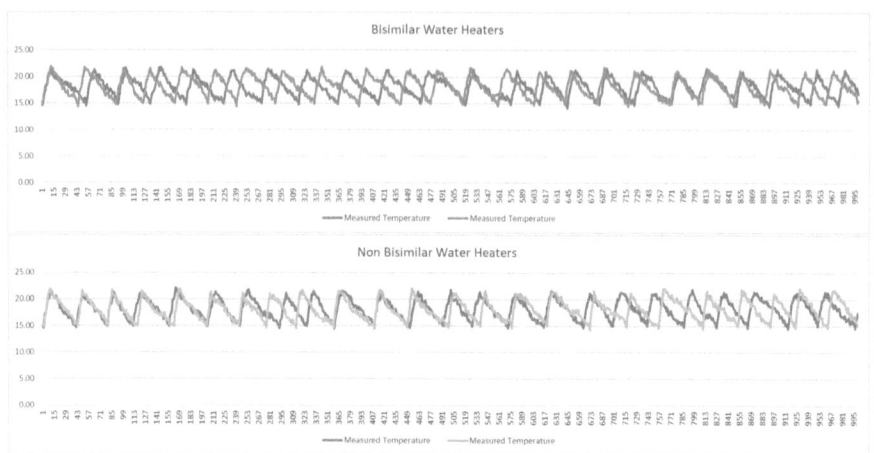

Fig. 2. Heating Systems Output

bisimilar system and compare the temperature gain and subsequent behavior of the system.

It is subsequently easy to see even across a short time slice of system behavior where significant breaches in branching behavior have occurred (noting that in an ICS these would be mutually influencing loops, however). This is illustrated in the diagram by a light blue area in the first page showing a clear deviation in branching behavior. Practically, this would be accomplished by reproducing a set of starting conditions over the period of a suspected breach in a copy of the system. For bisimilar systems, starting from the same place, the differences in behavior are much smaller.

This can also be shown formally by assigning intervals and probabilities over these to give estimated temperature range (from the measured temperature), applying the *gain* function, disturbance and measurement inaccuracies and using the subsequent measured temperature range to estimate the probability of a transition in operational mode. However, we omit this consideration here.

8   Discussion

"Living off the land" attacks represent a very real threat to SCADA systems which are difficult to detect by conventional means. Nor is it feasible to endow SOC analysts with the engineering knowledge of the system needed to detect such attacks, any more than it is practical for SCADA operators to be alert for potential malware attacks where the cyber behavior of the system appears to be normal.

To resolve this conjoint dilemma, we propose making use of a "digital shadow" of the system which is to track its behavior over time and is characterized by invariant probabilities for systems events such as message reporting or transitions in mode of operation without necessarily replicating the behavior of the real-world system exactly.

We provide a "proof of concept" by using identical models and subject one to a simulated attack to demonstrate the change to probable behavior. The advantage of our approach is that it simplifies detection for both SCADA and SOC operators. It provides the basis for a simplified form of statistical analysis and behavioral validation by considering different modes of system operation and also feasible transitions between modes of operation.

Disadvantages of the approach are that it takes some initial effort to properly define system behavior and to formally prove the model as well as to determine an appropriate set of invariant behavior to analyze. Also, as an initial arbitrary constraint on the adversary model, we have assumed that no message falsification is taking place, so we have yet to show that the system can reveal attacks where the adversary is actively altering messages. We note, however, that any such alterations would make adversary presence detectable by already existing conventional means.

It may be argued that similar results could be achieved by artificial intelligence learning the behavior of the system over time. But we would argue that our approach immediately reduces the state-space which needs to be searched and would accelerate any such learning process. Similarly, a complete search of the phase space of the system's behavior would be computationally unfeasible. Finally, while we have not shown it here but only implied it in our discussion of command failure (see Sect. 6), our search for invalid system behavior can be conducted in both the cyber and physical aspects of the system's behavior at the same time.

Finally, our paper illustrates that it is possible to approximately model cyber-physical systems in the applied π-calculus without resorting to additional syntactical and semantic devices outside the usual idiom of process calculi.

9   Conclusion

In this paper we have shown that by capturing the behavior of cyber-physical systems in the framework of the applied π-calculus, we can reduce the search space for detecting attack behaviors for both physical and cyber aspects of system operation by defining the different phases of operation of the systems and subjecting those to suitable statistical and formal analyzes. Our paper also illustrates that it is possible to model cyber-physical systems in the applied π calculus without necessarily resorting to additional syntactical and semantic devices outside the usual idiom of process calculi and represents a minor advance in modeling techniques, which is relevant for the use of tools for verification and model checking that would otherwise need to be amended as well.

This approach should enable SOC operators to better detect anomalous behavior in SCADA systems which may be the result of longer-term attacks, where other traditional indicators of compromise have failed – without the requirement to train operators to become SCADA engineers.

Future work will concentrate on models with explicit interactions and loops between the cyber- and physical subsystems to demonstrate the feasibility of approach particularly related to the effective state space reductions achievable. This may allow us to uncover additional techniques for measuring divergence in operations. We also need to determine the effects of message falsification on detection and determine how difficult it would be for an adversary to (stealthily) falsify messages while acting within the parameters of event probability, which will also require the consideration of message semantics for satisfying the stealth condition on adversaries. Finally, we are currently also considering the mapping of hybrid calculi on our approach and are particularly considering a more robust characterization of weak stochastic (barbed) branching bisimilarity.

References

1. Slowik, J.: Evolution of ICS attacks and the prospects for future disruptive events. Threat Intelligence Centre Dragos Inc (2019)
2. Farwell, J.P., Rohozinski, R.: Stuxnet and the future of cyber war. Survival **53**(1), 23–40 (2011)
3. Bergset, S., Nyland, A.J.: Ensuring safe and secure operations in the norwegian petroleum industry: a study on assessing trends in cyber risk levels. Master's thesis, NTNU (2023)
4. Yadav, G., Paul, K.: Architecture and security of scada systems: a review. Int. J. Crit. Infrastruct. Prot. **34**, 100433 (2021)
5. Slowik, J.: Crashoverride: reassessing the 2016 ukraine electric power event as a protection-focused attack. Dragos Inc (2019)
6. Sangiorgi, D., Walker, D.: The Pi-Calculus: a Theory of Mobile Processes. Cambridge University Press (2003)
7. Abadi, M., Blanchet, B., Fournet, C.: The applied pi calculus: mobile values, new names, and secure communication. J. ACM **65**(1) (2017)
8. Arapinis, M., Liu, J., Ritter, E., Ryan, M.: Stateful applied pi calculus. In: Abadi, M., Kremer, S. (eds.) Principles of Security and Trust, pp. 22–41. Heidelberg, Springer, Berlin Heidelberg, Berlin (2014)
9. Baeten, J.C.M., Basten, T., Reniers, M.A.: Process Algebra: Equational Theories of Communicating Processes. Cambridge Tracts in Theoretical Computer Science. Cambridge University Press (2009)
10. Lanotte, R., Merro, M., Tini, S.: A probabilistic calculus of cyber-physical systems. Inf. Comput. **279**, 104618 (2021)
11. Lanotte, R., Merro, M., Munteanu, A., Viganò, L.: A formal approach to physics-based attacks in cyber-physical systems. ACM Trans. Priv. Secur. (TOPS) **23**(1), 1–41 (2020)
12. Rounds, W.C., Song, H.: The φ-calculus-a hybrid extension of the π-calculus to embedded systems. In: Eighteenth Workshop on the Mathematical Foundations of Programming Semantics (2002)
13. Roehm, H., Oehlerking, J., Woehrle, M., Althoff, M.: Model conformance for cyber-physical systems: a survey. ACM Trans. Cyber-Phys. Syst. **3**(3) (2019)
14. Becker, F., et al.: A conceptual model for digital shadows in industry and its application. In: Ghose, A., Horkoff, J., Silva Souza, V.E., Parsons, J., Evermann, J. (eds.) Conceptual Modeling, pp. 271–281. Springer International Publishing, Cham (2021)

15. Henzinger, T.: The theory of hybrid automata. In: Proceedings 11th Annual IEEE Symposium on Logic in Computer Science, pp. 278–292 (1996)
16. McEvoy, T.R., Wolthusen, S.D.: An attack analysis of managed pressure drilling systems on oil drilling platforms. In: Panayiotou, C.G., Ellinas, G., Kyriakides, E., Polycarpou, M.M. (eds.) Critical Information Infrastructures Security, pp. 109–121. Springer International Publishing, Cham (2016)
17. Arapinis, M., Liu, J., Ritter, E., Ryan, M.: Stateful applied pi calculus: observational equivalence and labelled bisimilarity. J. Logical Algebraic Methods Program. **89**, 95–149 (2017)
18. Sangiorgi, D.: A theory of bisimulation for the π-calculus. Acta Informatica **33**, 69–97 (1996)

Lyapunov-Based Performance Oriented Switching Strategies for Linear Systems

Simone Mattogno[1]([✉]) [ID], Matteo Vulcano[1] [ID], Fabrizio Schiano[2],
Domenico Cappello[2], and Daniele Carnevale[1]

[1] University of Rome Tor Vergata, Viale del Politecnico 1, 00133 Rome, Italy
simone.mattogno@uniroma2.it
[2] Leonardo Innovation Labs, Leonardo S.p.a., Rome, Italy

Abstract. The last frontiers of robotic applications present increasingly restrictive constraints of control robustness and performance. Concerning this critical requirement, we provide a simple approach leveraging on a switching control policy that we propose optimizing a quadratic performance index that relates to the $\mathcal{L}_2$ norm of the tracking error. The approach allows the definition of an optimal switching strategy orchestrating the agent controller, bumpless transfer and reference governor filters, combined with state resets enhancing the performances of the resulting closed-loop hybrid system, which is guaranteed to be globally asymptotically stable while robustness is guaranteed by Lyapunov arguments. We also provide the dual formulation applied to the estimation problem.

Keywords: Switching Controller and Filter · Bumpless Transfer · Reference Governor · Lyapunov

1 Introduction

In today's interconnected world, the security of Critical Information Infrastructure (CII) stands as a paramount concern. With the increasing sophistication of cyber threats, safeguarding these infrastructures against potential breaches and disruptions is a pressing necessity. Traditional security measures often fail to address the dynamic and evolving nature of modern cyber threats. Consequently, there arises a crucial demand for innovative solutions capable of mitigating risks and fortifying the resilience of CII systems.

In response to this imperative, our paper presents a simple approach leveraging switching controller techniques to enhance the security of critical information infrastructure. In this sense, switching controller techniques offer a versatile framework for orchestrating dynamic adjustments and responses within CII systems, thereby enhancing their resilience improving control tracking performances and robustness. Furthermore, similar solutions can be considered to robustify autonomous systems trajectories. In such a situation, the control system needs to

G. Oliva et al. (Eds.): CRITIS 2024, LNCS 15549, pp. 116–132, 2025.
https://doi.org/10.1007/978-3-031-84260-3_7

achieve various control objectives such as maneuverability, energy saving, security, emergency, and so on, and the system's parameters, including engine thrust, flight control surfaces, and fuel distribution, may need to be rapidly adjusted to ensure the safe navigation as for an aerial vehicles. By employing switching controller techniques, the aircraft's onboard systems can autonomously adapt to the evolving circumstances, optimizing performance, and minimizing risks in real-time. Then, we present a novel approach that combines switching control with the optimization of a performance index, leveraging bumpless transfer and reference governor strategies to ensure continuous transition between different operational modes and ensure desired system performance. As a primary approach to this problem, we decide to consider linear systems. The discontinuities of control signal and the reset state strategy, introduced by the switching policy, require techniques such as bumpless transfer and reference governor. Bumpless transfer control is a method originally used to seamlessly transition between manual and automatic control modes [1] but, in a general context, it could be considered between different controllers [2,3] to avoid introducing sudden changes to the plant and excite poorly modeled high-frequency or non-linear dynamics as well as meet input derivative saturation constraints. This technique ensures continuity and stability by adjusting the controller output [3,4]. A reference governor is a mechanism that regulates the reference signal provided to a control system in order to prevent violations of constraints and ensure optimal performance. It dynamically adjusts the reference signal based on system states and constraints, ensuring that control actions remain within acceptable bounds [5].

In this work we provide a unifying framework orchestrating switching of controller (output filter in the dual problem), bumpless transfer and reference governor filters as well as state resets to optimize a quadratic cost function.

Notation: the set of positive (non negative) real numbers is denoted by $\mathbb{R}_+$ ($\mathbb{R}_{0+} = \mathbb{R}_+ \cup \{0\}$); $\mathbb{R}^n$ represents the set of n-dimensional real vectors and $\mathbb{R}^{n \times m}$ denotes the set of real matrices with n rows and m columns; a matrix A is positive definite (semidefinite) if denoted by $A \succ 0$ ($A \succeq 0$); $\mathbb{H}$ denotes the set of Hurwitz matrix (all eigenvalues have negative real part); $\mathcal{C}^0(\mathcal{D})$ is the space of piecewise continuous function with domain $\mathcal{D}$.

2 Preliminaries

We must introduce the concept of norm in order to measure the size of a signal [6] (e.g. the tracking error e of a system) and in particular we consider the space $\mathcal{L}_2$ defined as the set of signals $u(\cdot)$ such that

$$u \in \mathcal{C}^0([t_0, +\infty)) : \|u\|_{\mathcal{L}_2} \triangleq \left(\int_{t_0}^{+\infty} u^T(t)u(t)dt \right)^{\frac{1}{2}} < +\infty. \tag{1}$$

We define as a *Lyapunov function* a continuously differentiable function $V : \mathcal{D} \subset \mathbb{R}^n \to \mathbb{R}_{0+}$ such that [6]:

$$V(x_e) = 0 \quad \text{and} \quad V(x) > 0 \quad \forall x \in \mathcal{D}\backslash\{x_e\} \tag{2}$$

$$\dot{V}(x) \le 0 \quad \forall x \in \mathcal{D} \tag{3}$$

where $\mathcal{D}$ is the domain containing the equilibrium point x_e. In conclusion, it is worth of highlight the difference between the regulation problem and the tracking one: the former has got the goal to make the output track a family of signals (e.g. constant); the latter is specific to a particular time-varying reference signal.

Given the family of sufficiently smooth function $f_{\sigma(t)} : \mathbb{R}^n \to \mathbb{R}^n$ with $\sigma(t) \in \mathcal{Q} \subset \mathbb{N} \, \forall t \geq t_0$, we define time-dependent switching system as:

$$\dot{x}(t) = f_{\sigma(t)}(x(t)). \tag{4}$$

In the linear time-invariant (LTI) case, we have $f_{\sigma(t)}(x(t)) = A_{\sigma(t)}x(t)$ with $A_{\sigma(t)} \in \mathbb{R}^{n \times n}$. We refer to the signal $\sigma(t)$ as the *switching signal* and, for simplicity, its argument will often be omitted.

3   Control Scheme

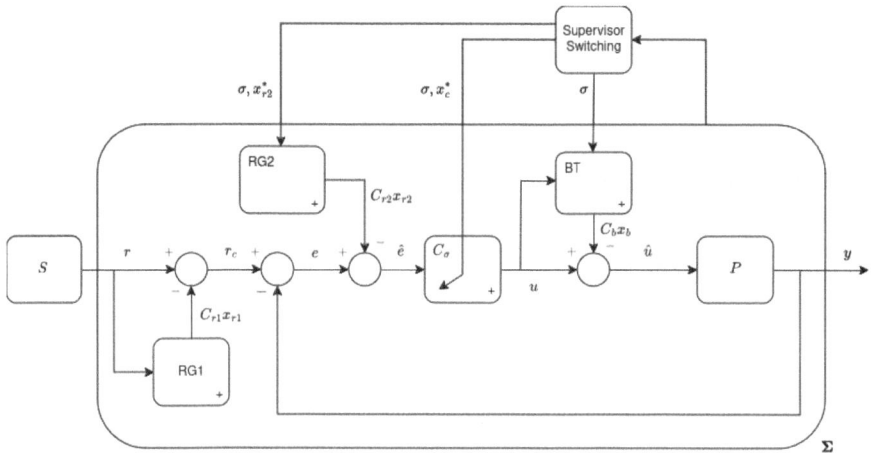

Fig. 1. The proposed control scheme; "+" blocks are systems with state resets at switching times; "⤵" blocks are switched system.

Consider the switching control system depicted in Fig. 1 and the regulation problem where the output y of the LTI plant Σ_p, with state space matrices (A_p, B_p, C_p, D_p), state $x_p(t) \in \mathbb{R}^{n_p}$ and scalar output $y = C_p x_p + D_p \hat{u}$, has to track the desired scalar reference r, which is the output of an autonomous exogenous LTI system S with state space matrices (A_s, C_s), state $x_s(t) \in \mathbb{R}^{n_s}$ and $r = C_s x_s$. We propose a supervisor that at given switching (jumping) time instants t_k, $k \in \mathbb{N}$ either can select the LTI controller C_σ, with $\sigma \in \mathcal{Q}$ and $\mathcal{Q}$ the index set of available stabilizing controllers with state space matrices $(A_{c,\sigma}, B_{c,\sigma}, C_{c,\sigma}, D_{c,\sigma})$, or sets a jump in the state $x_c(t) \in \mathbb{R}^{n_c}$ of the controller and the state of the hybrid subsystems Σ_{r2} to minimize a quadratic cost index of the tracking error that will be defined later. The hybrid system Σ_{r1} with state $x_{r1}(t) \in \mathbb{R}^{n_{r1}}$ and state space matrices (A_{r1}, C_{r1}) is an exponentially stable scalar LTI system whose state resets are selected in order to render continuous the signal r, yielding r_c. The second exponentially stable LTI system Σ_{r2}, with state $x_{r2}(t) \in \mathbb{R}^{n_{r2}}$ and state space matrices $(A_{r2}, B_{r2}, C_{r2}, D_{r2})$, acts as a reference governor with state resets managed by the supervisor. Similarly, we also introduce the bumpless transfer hybrid system Σ_b (exponentially stable LTI) with state $x_b(t) \in \mathbb{R}^{n_b}$ and data (A_b, C_b) whose state resets are selected by the supervisor in order to guarantee continuity of the control signal $\hat{u}$.

Let the tracking error [7] be defined as $e = r_c - y$, i.e. $e = C_s x_s - C_{r1} x_{r1} - C_p x_p = C_s x_s + C_e x$ where $x = [x_p^T, x_c^T, x_{r1}^T, x_{r2}^T, x_b^T]^T$ is the state of the overall closed-loop system Σ. To solve the tracking problem [8], assume that for any controller C_σ there exist matrices $\Pi_\sigma \in \mathbb{R}^{n \times n_s}$ such that:

$$A_\sigma \Pi_\sigma - \Pi_\sigma A_s = -B_\sigma, \tag{5}$$

$$C_e \Pi_\sigma + C_s = 0, \tag{6}$$

where A_σ is the dynamic matrix of the closed-loop system Σ of order n shown in Fig. 1 and B_σ is its input matrix related to the state of S. In particular:

$$A_\sigma = \begin{bmatrix} A_p - B_p D_{c,\sigma} C_p & B_p C_{c,\sigma} & -B_p D_{c,\sigma} & -B_p D_{c,\sigma} & -B_p \\ -B_{c,\sigma} C_p & A_{c,\sigma} & -B_{c,\sigma} & -B_{c,\sigma} & 0 \\ 0 & 0 & A_{r1} & 0 & 0 \\ 0 & 0 & 0 & A_{r2} & 0 \\ 0 & 0 & 0 & 0 & A_b \end{bmatrix} \quad B_\sigma = \begin{bmatrix} B_p D_{c,\sigma} C_s \\ B_{c,\sigma} C_s \\ 0 \\ 0 \\ 0 \end{bmatrix}$$

Consider the coordinate transformation $\hat{x} = x - \Pi_\sigma x_s$, then it holds:

$$\dot{\hat{x}} = A_\sigma x + B_\sigma x_s - \Pi_\sigma A_s x_s \overset{(5)}{=} A_\sigma \hat{x} \tag{7}$$

$$e = C_s x_s + C_e x \overset{(6)}{=} C_e \hat{x} \tag{8}$$

In this way, it is easy to verify that $e^{(k)} = C_e A_\sigma^k \hat{x}$, where $e^{(k)}$ is the k-th derivative of the tracking error with respect to time. Furthermore, consider the change of coordinates:

$$E = \begin{bmatrix} e \\ \dot{e} \\ \dots \\ e^{(n)} \end{bmatrix} = T_q \hat{x} \quad \text{with} \quad T_q = \begin{bmatrix} C_e \\ C_e A_q \\ \dots \\ C_e A_q^n \end{bmatrix} \in \mathbb{R}^{n \times n} \tag{9}$$

where the change of coordinates matrix T_q is invertible under observability condition and such that $\dot{E} = A_{e,q} E$ with $A_{e,q} = T_q A_q T_q^{-1}$.

3.1 Switching Controller Design

We now present the main result of the paper dealing with controller switching and reset strategies in order to improve an $\mathcal{L}_2$ cost index of the tracking error

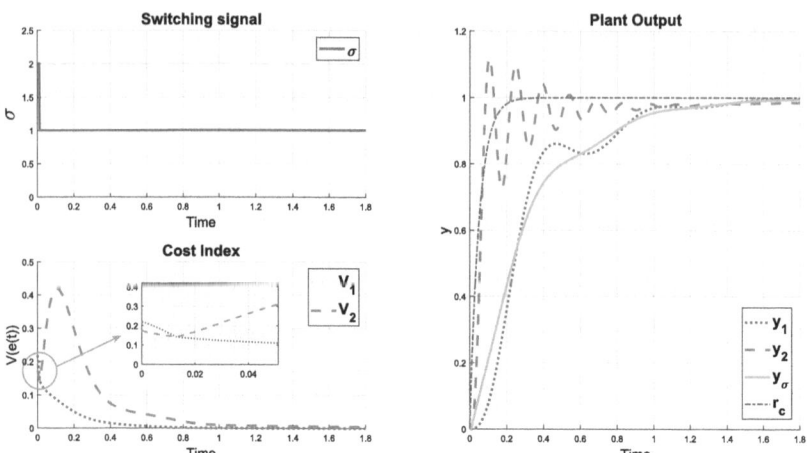

Fig. 2. On the right: comparison between the outputs obtained using the controllers individually (dash and dots) and the proposed switching scheme without reset events (solid).

and its first time derivative, providing stability arguments of the switching error system Σ_e, with state $\chi = [E^T, \sigma]^T$ and dynamics [9]

$$\begin{cases} \dot{E} = A_{e,\sigma}E, \\ \dot{\sigma} = 0, \end{cases} \quad \text{if } \chi \in \mathcal{C}, \tag{10a}$$

$$\begin{cases} E^+ = G_{e,\sigma}(E), \\ \sigma^+ = H(E), \end{cases} \quad \text{if } \chi \in \mathcal{D}, \tag{10b}$$

with flow set $\mathcal{C}$ and the jump set $\mathcal{D}$, $(t, k) \in \text{dom}(\chi)$ is the hybrid time domain of Σ_e and t_k are the switching time instants (jump times). The proof of the stability of the closed-loop system with switches and resets can be proven via Lyapunov, as we show in the follow, which is somehow similar to [10, 11] but, given the specific case considered here, with less stringent assumptions and improved performances thanks to the state reset map $G_{e,\sigma}(E)$ and $H(E)$ that is proposed in the next Theorem.

Theorem 1. *Consider the cost index*

$$J_\sigma(t) = \int_t^{+\infty} \|e(\tau)\|_2^2 + \lambda\|\dot{e}(\tau)\|_2^2 \, d\tau = \int_t^{+\infty} E(\tau)^T Q_\lambda E(\tau) \, d\tau, \tag{11}$$

with $\lambda \in \mathbb{R}_+$, $Q_\lambda \triangleq \text{diag}\{1, \lambda, 0, ..., 0\} \succeq 0$, $Q_\lambda \in \mathbb{R}^{n \times n}$. *Assume that* $\text{rank}(T_q) = n$ *and that the pair* $(A_{e,q}, C_\lambda)$ *is detectable for all* $q \in \mathcal{Q}$, *with* C_λ *such that* $C_\lambda^T C_\lambda = Q_\lambda$. *Select the jump (reset) map of* E *in (10) as*

$$G_{e,\sigma}(E) = T_\sigma \left([x_p^T, x_c^{\star T}, x_{r1}^T, x_{r2}^{\star T}, x_b^T]^T - \Pi_\sigma x_s \right), \tag{12}$$

where

$$\{x_c^\star(q), x_{r2}^\star(q)\} = \underset{x_c, x_{r2}}{\operatorname{argmin}} V_q(t), \quad V_q = E^T P_q E, \tag{13}$$

with $P_q = P_q^T \succ 0$ *such that*

$$A_{e,q}^T P_q + P_q A_{e,q} = -Q_\lambda, \forall q \in \mathcal{Q}. \tag{14}$$

Then, defining the jump map $H(\cdot)$ *in (10) with the switching policy*

$$\sigma^\star = \underset{q \in \mathcal{Q}}{\operatorname{argmin}} \{J_q(t)\} \Big|_{\substack{x_c = x_c^\star(q) \\ x_{r2} = x_{r2}^\star(q)}}, \tag{15}$$

i.e. $H(E) = \sigma^\star$, *and the definition of the flow and jump sets as below*

$$\mathcal{C} = \{\chi \in \mathbb{R}^n \times \mathbb{N} \times \mathbb{R}_{\geq 0} : V_\sigma - V_\sigma^\star < \varepsilon\} \tag{16a}$$

$$\mathcal{D} = \{\chi \in \mathbb{R}^n \times \mathbb{N} \times \mathbb{R}_{\geq 0} : V_\sigma - V_\sigma^\star \geq \varepsilon\} \tag{16b}$$

for any $\varepsilon > 0$, *yield the origin of the hybrid closed-loop system (10) globally exponentially stable (GES).*

Proof. The time derivative of the tracking error $\dot{E} = A_e E$ can be rewritten by (14) as $\dot{V}_q = E^T(A_{e,q}^T P_q + P_q A_{e,q})E = -E^T Q_\lambda E$, and the existence and uniqueness of such P_q is provided by Theorem 4.6 in [6] since $A_{c,q}$ is Hurwitz for all $q \in \mathcal{Q}$ (only stabilizing controllers are considered). The cost index (11) can be rewritten exploiting the definition of the Lyapunov function, i.e. the following holds

$$J_q(t) = -\int_t^{+\infty} \dot{V}_q \, d\tau = -V_q(E(\infty)) + V_q(E(t)) = V_q(t), \tag{17}$$

since $E = T_q \hat{x}$ and $\hat{P}_q = T_q^T P_q T_q$ is a congruent transformation of P_q (in fact $V_q = E^T P_q E = \hat{x}^T T_q^T P_q T_q \hat{x} = \hat{x} \hat{P}_q \hat{x}$), it follows that $\hat{P}_q \succ 0$ as stated in the Sylvester's Law of Inertia [12]. Consequently the minimum of V_q with respect to the component of the closed-loop state that can be reset, such as the controller state x_c and the reference governor state x_{r2}, can be analytically solved for all $q \in \mathcal{Q}$, i.e. $\{x_c^\star(q), x_{r2}^\star(q)\}$ in (13) can be easily computed. The selection of the flow and jump set in (16), and the switching policy (15), is such that jumps (resets) occur only if the newly selected controller q guarantees an ε decrease of the cost index (11), indeed as stated in (16b) the flow is not allowed and a jump (switch) occurs if $V_\sigma^\star \leq V_\sigma - \varepsilon$, then since $\sigma^+ = H(E) = \sigma^\star$ it holds

$$V_{\sigma^+}^+ = E^{+T} P_{\sigma^+} E^+ = V_{\sigma^\star(t_k, k+1)} \leq V_{\sigma(t_k, k)} - \varepsilon, \quad \forall(t, k) \in \operatorname{dom} \chi.$$

Moreover, since during the flow $\dot{V}_\sigma = -E^T Q_\lambda E$, V_σ does never grow, which implies simple stability of the origin $E = 0$, i.e. $e(t)$ and $\dot{e}(t)$ are bounded and since $\int_t^{+\infty} E^T Q_\lambda E$ is finite, by linearity of the flow dynamics $\dot{E}$, it necessarily implies that $\lim_{t \to \infty} e = 0$, and $\lim_{t \to \infty} \dot{e} = 0$ by Barbalat's Lemma [13]. Furthermore, the detectability assumption of $(A_{e,q}, C_\lambda) \forall q \in \mathcal{Q}$, implies that $\lim_{t \to \infty} E(t, k) = 0$. Finally, since V_q is radially unbounded and quadratic, global exponential stability of the origin $E = 0$ is proved. $\qquad \square$

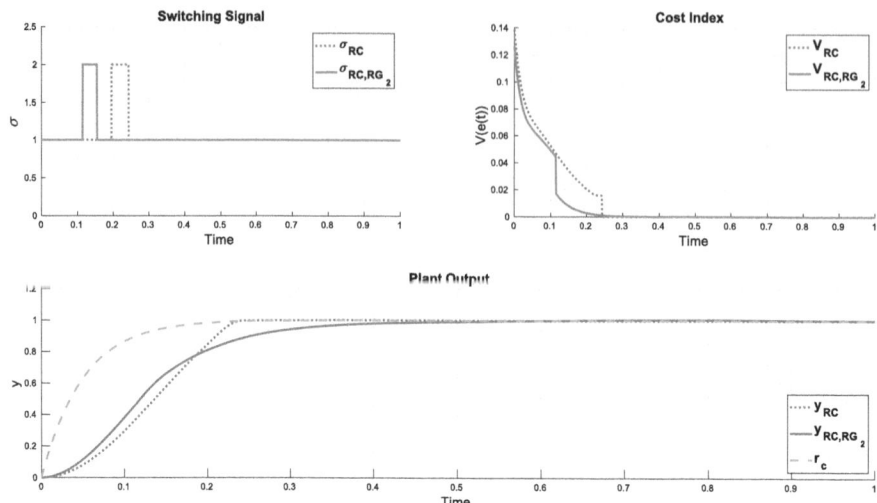

Fig. 3. Bottom: plant output y and other signals obtained using control reset (solid) and also adding the action of RG_2 (dots).

Remark 1. The selection $\varepsilon > 0$ in the definition of $\mathcal{C}$ and $\mathcal{D}$ implies that no Zeno phenomenon can occurs. Furthermore, a finite initial value $E(0)$ implies that a finite number of switches (jump) occurs and is less than $k_{\max} = \lceil V_{\sigma(0,0)}(E(0,0))/\varepsilon \rceil$.

Remark 2. Given the cumulative cost index $J(t)$ defined as:

$$J(t) = \int_0^t E(\tau)^T Q_\lambda E(\tau)\, d\tau = \sum_{k=0}^{\overline{k}-1} \left(V_{\sigma(t_k,k)} - V_{\sigma(t_{k+1},k)} \right) + V_{\sigma(t_{\overline{k}},\overline{k})}, \qquad (18)$$

for some $\overline{k} \leq k_{\max}$. In case at least a switch has occurred, i.e. $\overline{k} \geq 1$ the cumulative cost index related to the switching policy (15) is less than the one associated the any fixed initial controller $\sigma(0,0) \in \mathcal{Q}$.

3.2   Simulation Results

Consider a second-order system described by the transfer function $P(s) = 100/(s^2 + 9s + 100)$. The desired reference signal is given by $r(t) = 1\delta_{-1}(t)$, where $\delta_{-1}(t)$ is the Heaviside function, and assume that there are two PI controllers $C_1(s)$ and $C_2(s)$ with $K_{P,1} = 0.3855, K_{P,2} = 17.77, K_{I,1} = 3.497, K_{I,2} = 13.32$. Let $\lambda = 8.5e - 3$ and Σ_{r1} always active to suitably define the cost index described in Eq. (11). In Fig. 2 the time traces of the signals are depicted showing the switching logic based solely on the comparison of the cost indices evaluated at each time instant.

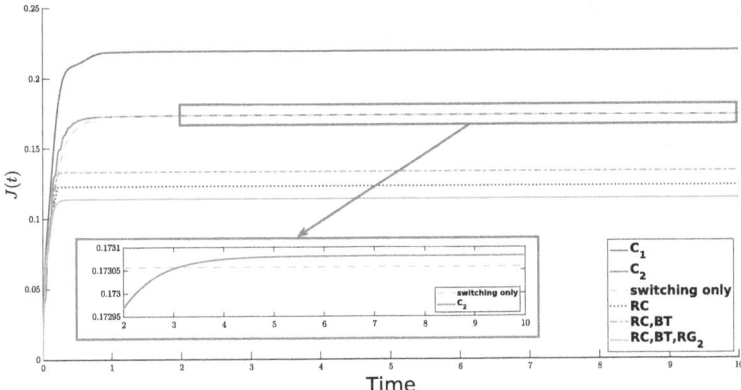

Fig. 4. As expected the switching policy (dashed yellow curve) gets better performance in terms of cost index respect to the best single controller policy (second solid curve from the top). (Color figure online)

Figure 3 shows how the action of resetting the state of the controller and of Σ_{r2} improves the performance in terms of settling time compared to the previous case reported in Fig. 2.

Figure 4 shows the switching cost index (11) in the range $[0, T_{sim}]$, where T_{sim} is the duration of the whole simulation. Its lowest value is reached by applying all the previously described mechanisms, as shown by the lowest solid curve in Fig. 4. Furthermore it shows that the simple switching logic yields a slightly smaller final value of the cost index than the single controller scenarios.

Figure 5 illustrates how the final value of the cost index changes with respect to the parameter λ for various policies. The inclusion of mechanisms such as RC and RG_2 reduces the cost index value for a fixed λ, as expected. In contrast, the implementation of BT increases the cost index value because this mechanism imposes a continuous constraint on the input signal, which adversely affects performance.

4   Dual Problem

Consider the closed-loop system depicted in Fig. 6, the state space representations of the plant and the controller are analogous to those introduced in Sect. 3. Assume also that the controller stabilizes the plant and regulates the plant output with respect to a specified class of reference signals generated by the exosystem S.

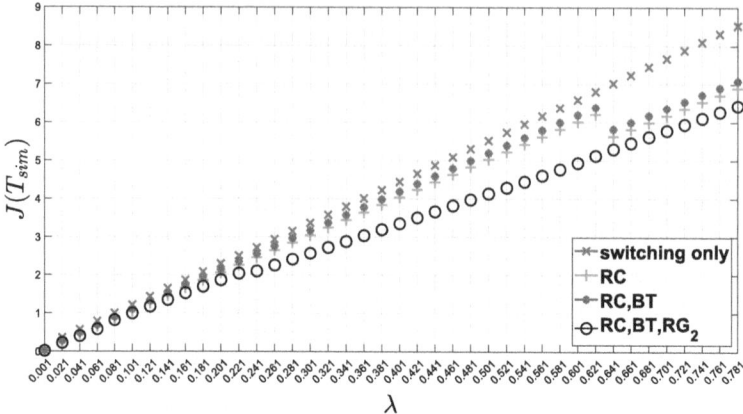

Fig. 5. For some λ we can see a drastic change in the signal because the switching signal significantly changes its time evolution.

We now consider a collection of LTI filters $\mathcal{F}$, where each filter is denoted by $\Sigma_{F,q} \; \forall q \in \mathcal{Q}$, with $\mathcal{Q}$ as the index set associated with $\mathcal{F}$; the state space representation of $\Sigma_{F,q}$ is given by the following equations:

$$\dot{x}_o = A_{o,q}x_o + B_{o,q}\tilde{y}$$
$$\tilde{y} = C_{o,q}x_o + D_{o,q}\tilde{y} \tag{19}$$

where $x_o(t) \in \mathbb{R}^{n_o}$ is the state vector of the filter, and $\tilde{y}(t) \in \mathbb{R}^p$ is the input vector. Additionally, $A_{o,q}$, $B_{o,q}$, $C_{o,q}$, and $D_{o,q}$ are constant, appropriately sized real matrices. The signal $\tilde{y}$ is given by the sum of the plant output signal y and a sinusoidal disturbance v, indexed by the signal $\nu \in N$ with N as the collection of sinusoidal signals with amplitude α_ν and angular velocity $\bar{\omega}_\nu$.

The goal is to design a supervisor which selects at each time instant a filter $\Sigma_{F,q} \in \mathcal{F}$ associated to the smallest value of a predefined cost functional, denoted by $J_{q,\nu}$. Additionally, when switching from the i-th filter to the j-th filter, with $i \neq j$, the supervisor can reset the state x_o in the same manner as the controller state reset described in Sect. 3.

The closed-loop system $\Sigma_{q,\nu}$ of order n is represented in state space form as follows:

$$\dot{x} = A_{q,\nu}x + Bx_s \tag{20}$$

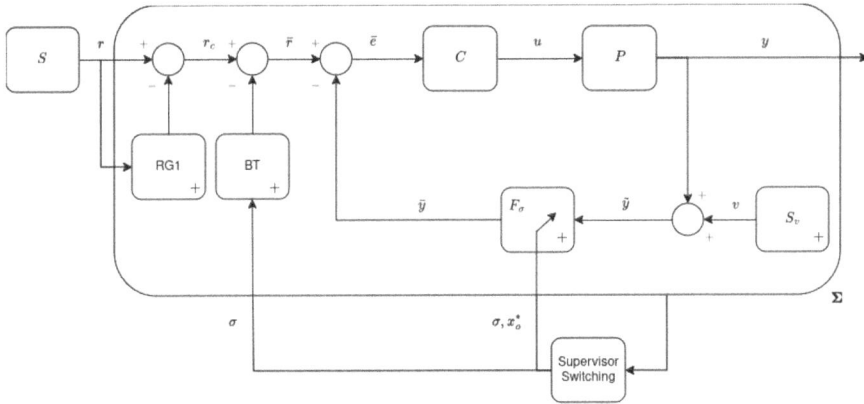

Fig. 6. The dual problem refers to switches among filters of a disturbed plant output.

where:

$$x = \begin{bmatrix} x_p \\ x_c \\ x_o \\ x_{r1} \\ x_b \\ x_v \end{bmatrix}$$

$$A_{q,\nu} = \begin{bmatrix} A_p - B_p D_c D_{o,q} C_p & B_p C_c & -B_p D_c C_{o,q} & -B_p D_c C_{r1} & -B_p D_c C_b & -B_p D_c D_{o,q} C_{v,\nu} \\ -B_r D_{o,q} C_p & A_c & -B_r C_{o,q} & -B_r C_{r1} & -B_r C_b & -B_r D_{o,q} C_{v,\nu} \\ B_{o,q} C_p & 0 & A_{o,q} & 0 & 0 & B_{o,q} C_{v,\nu} \\ 0 & 0 & 0 & A_{r1} & 0 & 0 \\ 0 & 0 & 0 & 0 & A_b & 0 \\ 0 & 0 & 0 & 0 & 0 & A_{v,\nu} \end{bmatrix} \quad B = \begin{bmatrix} B_p D_c C_s \\ B_r C_s \\ 0 \\ 0 \\ 0 \\ 0 \end{bmatrix}$$

The definition of the tracking error and its management are analogous to the ones of Sect. 3.

4.1 Performance Index Design

Given $\lambda \in \mathbb{R}_+$ and a filter indexed by $q \in \mathcal{Q}$ with active noise of index $\nu \in N$, consider the following finite-horizon cost functional:

$$J_{q,\nu}(t) = \int_t^T \|e(\tau)\|_2^2 + \frac{\lambda}{\bar{\omega}_\nu} \|\dot{e}(\tau)\|_2^2, d\tau \quad \forall t \in \mathbb{R}_{0+} \tag{21}$$

where $T \in \mathbb{R}_+$ is the system observation time and the parameter λ is normalized by $\bar{\omega}_\nu$ to allow the cost index to assume more comparable values across different types of noise. A finite-horizon cost functional is used because the overall system is stable due to the dynamics of the sinusoidal noise generator. We aim to express the cost index as a time-varying quadratic function $V_{q,\nu}$, while explicitly showing its dependency on x. Therefore, the cost index can be expressed as follows:

$$J_{q,\nu}(t) = \int_t^T E(\tau)^T Q_{\lambda,\nu} E(\tau), d\tau$$

Given $V_{q,\nu} = E^T P_{q,\nu}(t) E$ with $P_{q,\nu}(t) = P_{q,\nu}(t)^T$ and $P_{q,\nu}(T) = 0$, we impose:

$$\dot{V}_{q,\nu} = E^T (A_{e,q,\nu}^T P_{q,\nu} + P_{q,\nu} A_{e,q,\nu} + \dot{P}_{q,\nu}) E \overset{!}{=} -E^T Q_{\lambda,\nu} E \quad \forall E \qquad (22)$$

The computation of the time-varying coefficient matrix, $P_{q,\nu}(t)\ \forall q \in \mathcal{Q}\ \forall \nu \in N$, was carried out as follows:

1. Offline backward computation of $P_{q,\nu}(0)$ using MATLAB's ode23tb function;
2. Online resolution on Simulink of the following ODE:

$$\dot{\tilde{P}}_{q,\nu}(t) = A_{e,q,\nu}^T \tilde{P}_{q,\nu} + \tilde{P}_{q,\nu} A_{e,q,\nu} + Q_{\lambda,\nu}$$
$$\tilde{P}_{q,\nu}(0) = 0 \qquad\qquad (23)$$

3. Online computation on Simulink of $P_{q,\nu}(t) = P_{q,\nu}(0) - \tilde{P}_{q,\nu}(t)$.

Given $E = T_{q,\nu}\hat{x}$, the computation are analogous to the ones of Sect. 3.

4.2 Luenberger Observer

As depicted in Fig. 7, a Luenberger observer [14] is introduced to estimate either the state of the plant and the one of the noise generator because these are systems for which the state in general cannot be directly measured. Since we are dealing with LTI systems, we can assume the initial time t_0 equal to 0 without loss of generality and initial condition of the estimate given by $\hat{x}_u(0) = 0^{n_u}$ where $n_u = n_p + n_v$ is the order of the system Σ_u, whose state space representation is given by:

$$\begin{cases} \dot{\hat{x}}_u = A_u \hat{x}_u + B_u u + L(\tilde{y} - \hat{y}) \\ \hat{y} = C_u \hat{x}_u \end{cases}$$

where $A_u \in \mathbb{R}^{n_u \times n_u}$, $B_u \in \mathbb{R}^{n_u \times 1}$, $C_u \in \mathbb{R}^{1 \times n_u}$ and $L \in \mathbb{R}^{n_u \times 1}$ such that $A_u - LC_u$ is Hurwitz.

In occasion of a change in the noise type, we change L and A_u accordingly because we assume the knowledge of the possible noise frequencies (but not about its amplitudes).

4.3 Simulation Results

Given the plant of Sect. 3, we now consider a controller represented by the input-output transfer function $C(s) = 0.5 + 3/s$, which is, in the nominal case, stabilizing and capable of regulating the system output in response to a constant signal.

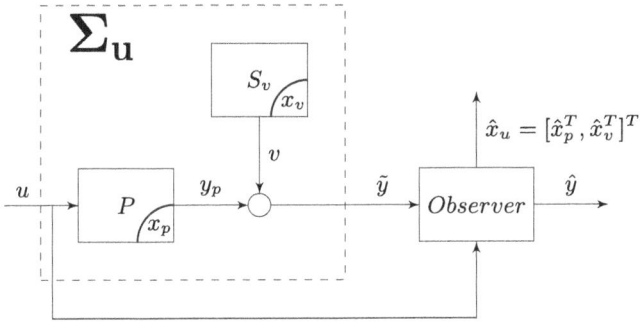

Fig. 7. The observer estimates the Σ_u state $x_u = [x_p^T, x_v^T]^T$.

Additionally, we consider a collection of first order low-pass filters represented by the following input-output transfer functions:

$$F_1 = \frac{1}{0.1\,s + 1} \qquad\qquad F_2 = \frac{1}{15\,s + 1}$$

The noise index set N contains two entries related to sinusoidal signals, each with its own unique set of parameters reported in Table 1. Furthermore we have $\lambda = 1$ and a simulation step size of 0.005 s. In Fig. 8 the evolution of the noise signal added to the plant output throughout the simulation is shown. This noise consists of two components: a low-frequency noise that can be related to positional tracking, and a high-frequency noise associated with a GPS/RTK sensor.

Table 1. Parameter values associated to the different types of noise

ν	α_ν	$\bar{\omega}_\nu$
1	0.02	$2\pi \cdot 5$
2	0.5	$2\pi \cdot 0.4$

The effectiveness of switching between multiple filters, as opposed to employing a single filter, is distinctly illustrated in Fig. 9. Notably, the solid purple curve lacks the overshoots that are noticeable in the other signals.

Figure 10 illustrates the advantage of switching activities over the single-filter policy in terms of the final value of cumulative cost index and Fig. 11 its time evolution in function of λ, remarking the results obtained in Sect. 3; besides, numerical errors have been encountered in the computation of the optimal reset value for the filter state, denoted by x_o^*, which depends on the simulation step size and solver algorithm.

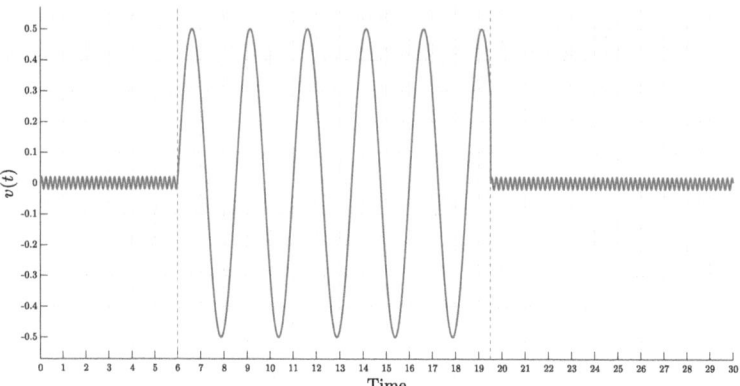

Fig. 8. The noise evolution corresponds to a scenario in which two types of measuring instruments are available, chosen accordingly to the working conditions.

We now consider the simulation results using the Luenberger observer, for which we have chosen the matrix L such that:

$$\sigma(A_u - LC_u) = \{-5, -5, -5, -5\} \tag{24}$$

The introduction of a Luenberger state observer does not compromise the switching filter architecture as shown for example by the Fig. 12 and 14. Figure 13 shows the correctness of the Luenberger observer activities in a scenario without reset and bumpless transfer mechanisms.

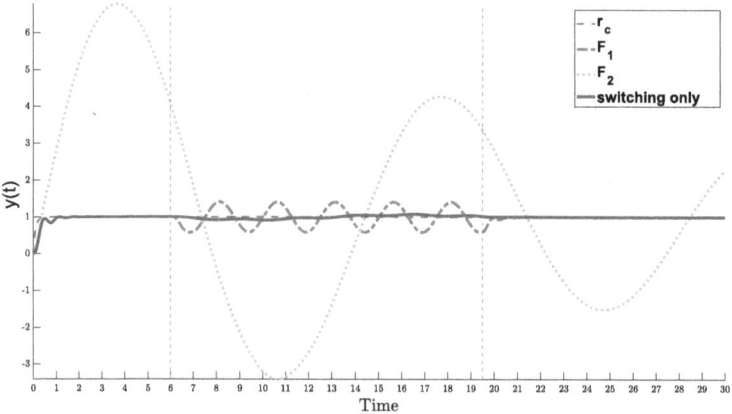

Fig. 9. The switching among filters significantly improves performances as shown by the solid purple curve. (Color figure online)

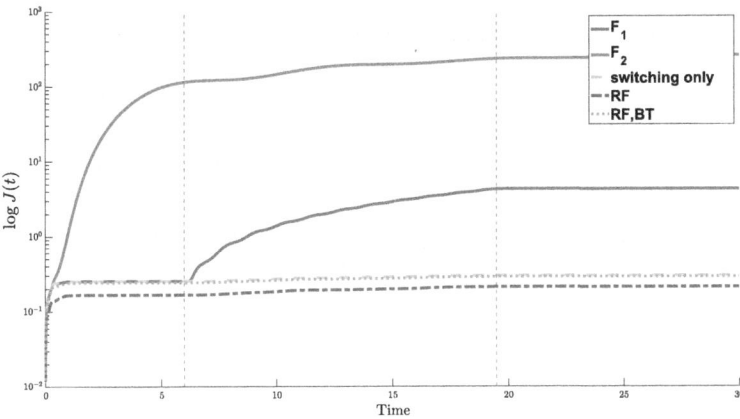

Fig. 10. The logarithmic scale of the y-axis allows to show the results more clearly.

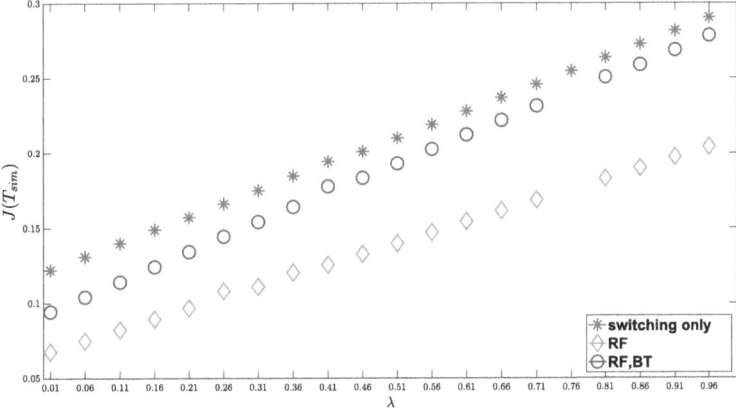

Fig. 11. Study of the final value of the cumulative cost index in function of λ.

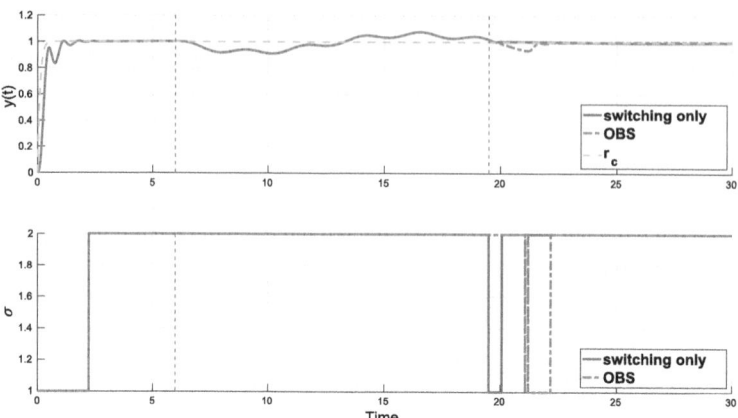

Fig. 12. Observer's introduction slightly deprecates performances as shown near the instant $20s$; this fact carries over to an increasing in the final value of the cumulative cost index.

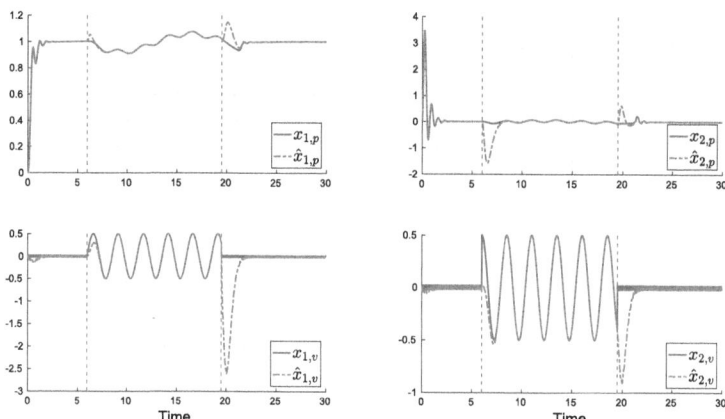

Fig. 13. The transient behavior of the state estimate depends on the choice of the eigenvalues of the matrix $A_u - LC_u$.

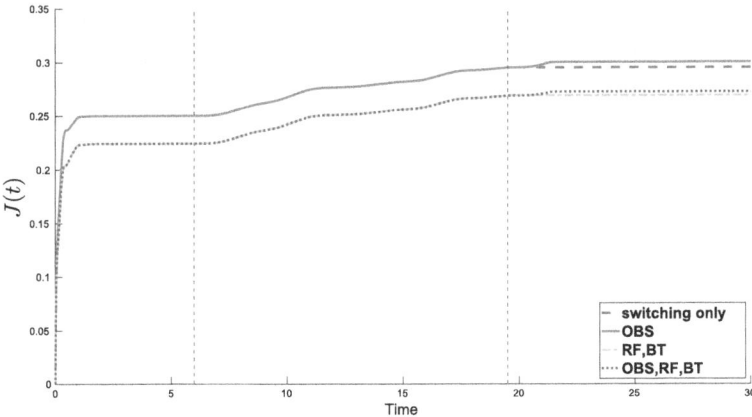

Fig. 14. In order to get this result we needed to decrease the fixed step size to 0.0001 s because of numerical errors.

5   Conclusions

In this work, we have introduced a methodology based on hybrid system optimization to increase robustness of control and estimation that might play a fundamental role for critical systems. This method could be used considering a larger set of controllers, that is to say, considering a larger set of the system configurations.

Additionally we presented the dual approach about switching among filters of the plant output in order to let the system automatically choose the way to mitigate the action of noise with time-varying parameters. This scenario addresses the one in which multiple redundant sensors are employed to estimate the system state. For simplicity we have been assuming at first a full state information for the supervisor activities but it is easy to add a Luenberger observer considering the properties of linear systems as shown in Sect. 4.

Looking ahead, we envision the development of a switching filter framework capable of dynamically evaluating the optimal sensor fusion strategy, thereby optimizing state estimation and enhancing overall system reliability, using the method presented in [15].

This work was supported in part by the Italian Ministry for Research in the framework of the 2020 Program for Research Projects of National Interest, Grant No. 2020RTWES4.

References

1. Hanus, R., et al.: Conditioning technique, a general anti-windup and bumpless transfer method. Automatica **23**(6), 729–739 (1987)
2. Shi, Y., et al.: Bumpless transfer control for switched linear systems and its application to aero-engines. IEEE Trans. Circuits Syst. I: Regular Pap. 1–12 (2021)

3. Cheong, S.-Y., and et al.: Bumpless transfer for adaptive switching controls. In: 17th IFAC World Congress, vol. 41, no. 2, pp. 14415–14420 (2008)
4. Bianchi, L., et al.: Efficient visual sensor fusion for autonomous agents. In: 2023 International Conference on Control, Automation and Diagnosis (ICCAD), pp. 01–06 (2023)
5. Garone, E., et al.: Explicit reference governor for linear systems. Int. J. Control **91**, 1415–1430 (2018)
6. Khalil, H.K.: Nonlinear Systems, 3rd edn. Prentice-Hall, Upper Saddle River (2002)
7. Trentelman, H.L., et al.: Tracking and regulation. In: Control Theory for Linear Systems, pp. 195–209 (2001)
8. Isidori, A. (ed.): Nonlinear Control Systems: An Introduction. Lecture Notes in Control and Information Sciences, vol. 72 (1985)
9. Goebel, R., Sanfelice, R.G., Teel, A.R.: Hybrid dynamical systems. IEEE Control Syst. Mag. **29**(2), 28–93 (2009)
10. Colaneri, P., et al.: Stability and stabilization of continuous-time switched linear systems. SIAM J. Control Optim. **45**(5), 1915–1930 (2006)
11. Liberzon, D.: Switching in Systems and Control. Systems & Control: Foundations & Applications. Birkhäuser, Boston (2003)
12. Carrell, J.: Groups, Matrices, and Vector Spaces: A Group Theoretic Approach to Linear Algebra. Springer, New York (2017)
13. Farkas, B., Wegner, S.-A.: Variations on Barbalat's Lemma, vol. 123, no. 8, p. 825 (2016)
14. Zeitz, M.: The extended Luenberger observer for nonlinear systems. Syst. Control Lett. **9**(2), 149–156 (1987)
15. Oliva, F., et al.: A trajectory based optimization approach for hybrid observer design. In: 62nd IEEE Conference on Decision and Control, pp. 1873–1878 (2023)

A Re-transmission Algorithm for Phasor Data Concentrators for Resilience Enhancement of State Estimation

James G. Wright[1]([✉]) and Stephen D. Wolthusen[1,2][iD]

[1] Department of Information Security and Communication Technology,
Norwegian University of Science and Technology, Trondheim, Norway
{james.g.wright,stephen.wolthusen}@ntnu.no
[2] Department of Information Security Royal Holloway, University of London,
London, UK
stephen.wolthusen@rhul.ac.uk

Abstract. To maintain the current safety standards expected within power grids whilst incorporating new functionalities, such as distributed power generation, an increase in the precision of control and sensing devices is needed. A critical element for achieving this goal is the incorporation of phasor measurement units (PMUs) across the grid. However, the greater precision offered by PMUs is dependent on *all* them being synchronised to the same time source. This could be achieve through civilian GNSS time signals, however these are easily jammed. An adversary could exploit this vulnerability to manipulate or delay PMU measurements that are used in state estimation (SE) calculations, which estimate the current state of the power grid.

The consequence of injecting malicious data in the SE calculation have been studied in depth, but less attention has been given to the attack vectors that could be used for their introduction. There has been some attention paid to how the manipulation of an individual PMU's data can be used to facilitate a SE attack, but none has be given to the phasor data concentrators (PDC), the intermediate device which aggregates the PMU measurements before they are used in SE calculations.

This paper presents an initial result that shows how a PDC can be utilised to *lessen* the chances that an adversary can successfully implement a SE attack, through the proposal of a PDC re-transmission algorithm. The proposal shows how a PDC can integrate the retransmission of data that it has discerned as corrupted or maliciously delayed. The proposal is formalised in applied π-calculus.

Keywords: Phasor Measurement Unit · Phasor Data Concentrator · Re-transmission Algorithm · Applied π-calculus

1 Introduction

The greater adoption of renewable energy sources and electrical storage technologies, along side more dynamic loads in the power grids, must be met by providing

G. Oliva et al. (Eds.): CRITIS 2024, LNCS 15549, pp. 133–150, 2025.
https://doi.org/10.1007/978-3-031-84260-3_8

grid operators with as close to real-time control of these systems as possible to ensure the stability of the grid. This improved regime of real-time control will be supported by more granular measurement of the grid's state, which also reduce errors in the measurements. One important element for meeting these new sensing and control requirements will be the mass deployment of PMUs. A PMU has the ability to directly measure the phase angle and amplitude of the electrical signal, which provides the increased precision and sampling rate needed for the integration of these new power generation technologies. They also allow for faster line fault location as well as the implementation of distributed out-of-step protection between two different grids [1,11,14].

PMUs also provide significant improvement in the SE of the power grid, as they reduce the amount of imperfect and asynchronous data that is relied upon during calculations. Instead of having to derive the grid's state from the measurement of voltage and active/reactive power flow, the PMU takes direct measurements of the electrical signal. This increased precision in the SE calculations allows for an improved real time image of the grid, and gives operators more granular control [14].

All of these new and improved functionalities that the PMUs facilitates are contingent on all of the devices being synchronised to the same time source. This mass time synchronisation is expected to be primarily achieved through the use of civilian GNSS time signals, which are easy to jam or spoof [7].

The use of delayed or subtly malicious data introduced to influence SE calculations to force a grid's energy management system (EMS) to perform unsafe actions has long been theorised [12]. The adversary's maliciously delayed or injected data compromises the EMS's ability to observe the state vector or current topology of the grid, if it can pass the bad data detection algorithm. Given the hard real-time quality of service (QoS) requirements of SE calculation that ensures the safety of the grid, there is little time to detect and respond to these kinds of attacks in a power system environment. While there have been proposals for using individual PMUs to *detect* this class of attack, little work has been done on preventing their use in instigating SE attacks. Primarily the study of PMU security has been as a attack vector for malicious data into grid SE calculations, with a focus on the undermining of their timing synchronisation assumption leading to inaccurate or delayed measurements being used by the SE calculations. This malicious data can either be used to directly target the EMS, or can disrupt a specific region of the grid through one of the proposed distributed protect mechanisms.

In most proposed uses of a PMU a PDC is required to mediate between a group of PMUs and the EMS. It is responsible for batching together, and thus ensuring the synchronous arrival of, a collection PMU data. However, they are surprisingly understudied in their contribution to the security of the SE calculations, and currently only contribute to the integrity of the SE calculation by flagging late or absent PMU data. This paper proposes a PDC re-transmission algorithm that can be used to detect and respond to adversarial attempts to influence SE calculations due to the malicious delaying or omitting PMU data to a PDC. The re-transmission algorithm provides the system with *a last chance* to correct an error that the adversary has introduced before it compromises the EMS's observability and controllability of the grid, which would require the EMS needing to reset their knowledge of the grid's state vector if the attack is successful. This proposal builds begins to construct another layer of defence into security of the grid's SE calculations, as well as fulfilling a desired communication model that is stated, but not realised, in the PDC standard. The standard IEEE C37.244-2013 states that *'there is a need for the implementation of such a function to recover data. While presently there is no standard, proprietary mechanisms exist in the industry* [2]'.

This work presents a formalised proposal for a re-transmission algorithm that works in tandem with, and inside of, a PDC's PMU relative measurement aggregation window, with the PMU using the IEC 61850-7 Sample Value (SV) communication model [3] which sends periodic measurements. The re-transmission algorithm responds in one of two ways. If the PDC receives a measurement from a known PMU that fails the data integrity, but not bad data detection, then it will send a unicast message to the PMU asking for a re-transmission. The second mode is when a timing threshold, within the aggregation window, is reached, then the PDC will multicast to all devices who have failed to have an accepted measurement this aggregation window asking for a re-transmission. This proposal gives the PDC the *chance* to detect and correct any malicious or erroneous measurement in the current aggregation window, which will *reduce* the chances of error propagating in the EMS's SE calculations. This will lessen the likelihood that an unauthorised safety actions or a loss of observability from occurring will occur.

The PMU SV communication model and the PDC C37.244 standard are modelled in an applied *pi*-calculus, before being modified to incorporate the proposed re-transmission algorithm. The work then presents a series of structural congruence proofs to show that the additional processes required to implement the proposed algorithm *will not modify* the already verified correct and safe C37.244 communication models.

The rest of the paper has the following structure. The next section present an overview of SE attacks along with the literature regarding the security of PMUs & PDCs. Section 3 presents the main contribution of the paper: **A re-transmission algorithm that allows for a PDC to respond to PMUs whose periodic measurements are either delayed or corrupted.** The algorithm is formalised in an applied π-calculus. In Sect. 4 a series structural congruence proofs are given, which shows that the additional re-transmission algorithm processes *do not modify* the formal models of the PMU and the PDC. The paper concludes in Sect. 5 with a brief summary and an outlook towards ongoing work.

2   Literature Review

This section presents an overview of SE attacks, and how PMUs can be used as an attack vector for their introduction. It then looks at the research regarding the cybersecurity of PMUs and PDCs.

2.1   An Overview of State Estimation Attacks

First theorised by Liu et al., the field of SE attacks is concerned with adversaries injecting malicious data into power grid SE calculations to force the EMS into an unsafe state. In their paper they formalise how an adversary, with limited access to measurements, can utilise the approximations used in the SE calculations, so long as they circumvent the (rudimentary) bad data detection algorithms, to compromise the observability of the grid's state vector [12]. Since this seminal paper, researchers have theorised extensively about different aspects of this attack vector.

Various adversarial objectives have been explored beyond forcing the EMS to lose knowledge of the state vector. Yuan et al. showed that by manipulating line flow measurements, it is possible to force the EMS into provisioning a line with more power than it has capacity for, which would trigger load shedding [19]. Kim & Tong theorised that an adversary could use an SE attack to manipulate the EMS current knowledge of the grid topology, not just power flow [10].

Work has also explored the various kinds, and amount, of knowledge of the grid state an adversary needs to successfully orchestrate an SE attack. Sandberg et al. developed an algorithm that uses grid topology and sensor coverage to identify the critical power flow input data which requires the least manipulation to corrupt the SE calculations [15]. Baiocco et al. showed how an adversary manipulating the communication channel, to expand the range of possible jitter values, can increase the error in the EMS' knowledge of bus bar amplitudes [6].

Finally, Deka et al. compared the strategies of jamming measurements with injecting false data into SE calculations, and showed that the same loss of EMS observability can be achieved while requiring less access to meters and knowledge of the grid's state vector.

There has been some work into how an adversary can abuse PMUs to compromise the grid's EMS. Shereen et al. showed that an adversary can inject small message delays by disrupting the time synchronisation between PMUs, which would compromise the SE calculations [17]. Zhang et al. demonstrated that in the case of the IEEE 118-bus systems that an adversary can us PMUs to circumvent a low-rank decomposition integrity checker [20]. Almas & Vanfretti performed an experiment to show that it is not just the traditional EMS that are under threat from data errors created by loss of PMU time synchronisation. They showed that a loss of synchronisation can trigger both anti-islanding and oscillation dampening control functions [5], which are proposed functionalities that the introduction of PMUs would facilitate.

2.2   PMU Security

The research community has developed several taxonomies regarding the insecurity of PMUs. Sundararajan *et al.* did a thorough analysis of how the degradation and/or compromise of the traditional CIA(A) security properties can affect the safety and QoS of the PMU, as well as how this would undermine SE calculations [18]. They then presented a list of traditional IT security measures to secure PMUs. In contrast, Beasley *et al.* sparser taxonomy discusses how a limited set of IT attack vectors can easily DoS a PMU. They do briefly also consider physical damage to PMUs.

Kahn *et al.* performed a penetration test on a PMU and demonstrated that they could easily inject commands, drop packets, replay messages, and manipulate PMU data [9].

2.3   PDC Security

The authors found only two papers regarding the security of PDCs. The first by D'Antonio *et al.* discusses how an adversary could use the unencrypted communications between a PMU and PDC to perform an SQL injections on the PDC to undermine their data validation and aggregation functions [8]. Moussa *et al.* proved how manipulating the timing of PMU can be used to exclude data from the PDC's alignment window, leading to legitimate packets not being aggregated for the EMS [13]. They then modelled how this could lead to a loss of observability for various IEEE test systems.

3   The PDC Re-transmission Algorithm

This section presents the proposed re-transmission algorithm which corrects for errors in the SV messages that are sent *periodically* between PMUs to their PDC across an idealised reliable channel. Given the hard real-time requirements it will be presumed that the devices will be communicating on a unencrypted channel, as is the case with most power system communication networks. Whilst this proposal will not prevent sustained denial of service attacks, it will *lessen* the probability of success of adversaries who are trying to stealthily delay/inject malicious messages into the SE calculations. This will force adversaries to be more aggressive in their interference, and thus make them more detectable.

The rest of this section will present the formalised PDC re-transmission algorithm in applied π-calculus. The first section states the applied π-calculus and equational theory that is used in this work. The work provides a formal model of the PDC aggregation procedure, with respect to a relative aggregation window, as described in Sect. 6.1.2.3 of the PDC standard C37.244 [2], before declaring the adversary model used in this work. The final section concludes by modifying the PDC aggregation procedure with the proposed re-transmission function to handle errors.

3.1   The Applied π-Calculus Used in This Work

This paper will not provide an introduction to π-calculus or the applied π-calculus. For a thorough treatment of these abstractions the authors recommend Sangiorgi & Walker [16] and Abadi *et al.* [4].

$$
\begin{aligned}
L, M, N ::= & \quad \text{Terms} \\
a, b, c... & \quad \text{Names} \\
\text{x, y, z...} & \quad \text{Variables} \\
f(M_1, ..., M_n) & \text{ Functions}
\end{aligned}
\tag{1}
$$

The applied π-calculus, defined in Eq. 1, is an abstraction that represents the evolution of terms across concurrent processes in a distributed system. These terms can be an infinite amount of names and variables, or a finite amount of functions. The names can be either variables themselves or represent communication channels, and the functions are primarily used to represent encryption operations. The applied π-calculus operations used in this work are expressed in Eq. 2.

$$
\begin{aligned}
P ::= P.Q \mid x < y > .P \mid x(z).P \mid \nu z\ z.P \mid P|P' \mid \\
P + P' \mid [x = y].xP \mid P! \mid \{P/x\} \mid \emptyset
\end{aligned}
\tag{2}
$$

where P can represent a processes or the underlying state machine of a device. The operations presented in Eq. 2 are:

- $P.Q$: Sequential processes can occur.
- $x < y > .P$: The process will send the name or variable y along channel x.
- $x(z).P$: The process will receive the name or variable z from channel x. Any subsequent z names/variables in the process will be replaced by this input via a substitution process $\{y/z\}$.
- $\nu z\ z.P$: A restriction of the name or variable z, where sending or receiving along z can only occur if the involved processes already know of z's existence. This operation is used to make explicit restriction of a name or variable, or to represent the generation of a fresh name or variable. In this paper multiple names and variables will be stated with a single ν. Each will be separated by comma.
- $P|P'$: The composition of P and P' which represents two processes that can occur concurrently.
- $P + P'$: The summation of P and P' represent the selection of one of the two processes.
- $[x = y].xP$: The matching of names x and y represent an *if-then* statement within the distributed systems.
- $P!$: The replication of P is used to generate infinite copies of the process.
- $\{P/x\}$: The substitution process, where all instances of process P are replaced with the name or variable x.
- $\emptyset$: The null process, where no further process transitions occur.

The processes evolve through either the communication with other intra-agent processes, or with the environment (processes external to the one being analysed).

The functions used in a model have an associated equational theory that defines how they are treated in process reductions and equivalence proofs. This work builds upon the the symmetric encryption equational theory defined by Abadi *et al.* [4]. The equational theory used in this work is presented in Eq. 3:

$$
\begin{aligned}
R, S, T &: List \\
\nu R &: List \\
Rx :: List \times variable &\rightarrow List \\
del\|x &\rightarrow List \\
ret(R, i) &\rightarrow r \\
is\_in(R, x) &\rightarrow true \\
is\_empty(R) &\rightarrow true \\
len(R) &\rightarrow int
\end{aligned}
\tag{3}
$$

where

- νR : It the initialising of an empty list.
- :: : Appends a variable or name to a list function.
- $del\|x$: Removes the name or variable from the list.
- $ret(R, i)$: Is a function that returns the ith (starting from 1) member of the list of a variable
- $is\_in(R, x)$: Returns a boolean 'true' if a name/variable is in a list.
- $is\_empty(R, x)$: Returns a boolean 'true' if there are no names/variables is in a list.
- $len(R)$: Returns the integer length of the list

3.2   The Data Aggregation Model

This section presents a formal model of multiple PMUs sending their measurements to a PDC to aggregate, before they are passed onto the EMS. The C37.224 standard [2] offers two models of aggregation windows which can accept either IEC 61850 GOOSE or SV (SV) messages [3]. The first modes is an absolute window, where the window opens and closes at a set time, and the second is a relative window, where the window opens after the arrival of the first message and then closes after a set period of time. This model will use the relative window, but it can easily be modified to model the absolute window. This work will also use the IEC 61850 SV communication model, where the new PMU data is transmitted with a known periodicity, because this communication model has less semantic content to encapsulate.

Figures 1 and 2 demonstrate the mechanics of the C37.224 relative aggregation window. The window begins at the arrival of the first packet, and closes after a set amount of time. However, if there is a packet that is being processed when the window is closing, that packet is rejected as shown in Fig. 2.

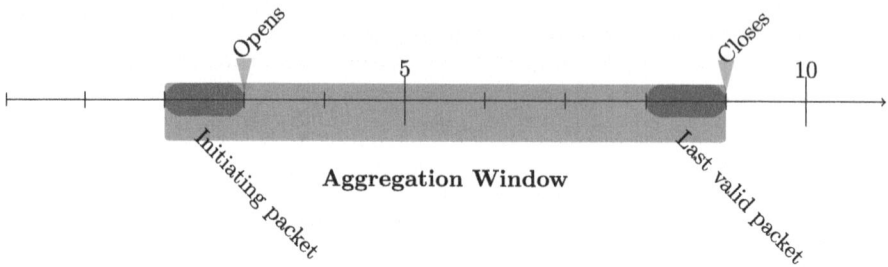

Fig. 1. The generation of an C37.244 [2] PDC aggregation window where the last packet is accepted

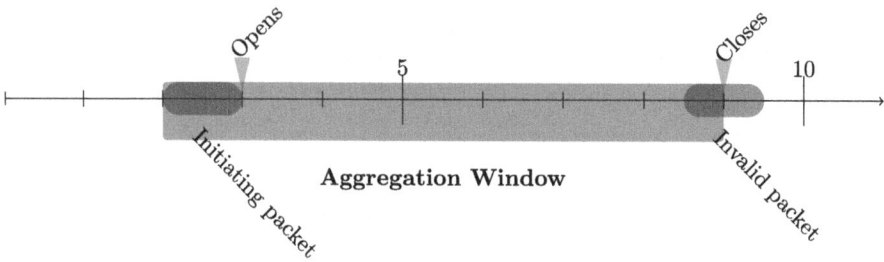

Fig. 2. The generation of an C37.244 [2] PDC aggregation window where the last packet is rejected

There will be some processes in this section where there is an *implicit* real-time component to them. However, modelling an explicit real-time clock is beyond the scope of this work, and so the authors are assuming that process will *eventually* transition state.

The format of the names and variables used throughout this work is shown in Eq. 4.

$$a_{\text{sender index}}^{\text{function label}} \tag{4}$$

where function label represents any additional information needed to distinguish the name, and sender index distinguishes which PMU sent their SV to the PDC.

The PMU Model. The SV communication model mandates that the PMU transmits the measurements at a set and expected period dictated by its internal clock, which is synchronised with an external time source (e.g. GNSS). The PMU process initialises in Eq. 5

$$\text{PMU} ::= \nu\text{m SEND}_{PMU}! \tag{5}$$

where m represents the MAC address of the PMU. The periodic sampling and sending the data to the PDC is represented by Eq. 6.

$$\text{SEND}_{PMU} ::= \nu\text{Value}, \textit{Sample Samplem.SampleValue.} \tag{6}$$
$$s_{\text{m}} < \textit{Sample} >$$

The PDC Model. Equation 7 provides an overview of the processes PDC uses in the aggregation.

$$\text{PDC} ::= \nu PMU - List \; B < \text{Start} > .(\text{RECEIVE!}|\text{CLOCK!}| \\ \text{AGGREGATE!}|\text{CHECK!}|\text{SEND}_{SE}!) \tag{7}$$

where $PMU - List$ is the list of all the PMUs the PDC expects to receive SV messages from, and the $B < \text{Start} >$ process is to initialise the RECEIVE_{PMU} process waiting to hear from the first measurement for the initial aggregation window.

The below equation represents how the PDC sorts receiving PMU measurements.

$$\text{RECEIVE} ::= (B(s)|s_{\text{m}}(S_m)).(t^b < \text{Start} > |K < \text{Going} > |c < S_m >)| \\ ((K(g)|s_{\text{m}}(S_m)).((c < S_m > |K < \text{Going} >) + t^s(\text{h})))! \tag{8}$$

The first line describes how the aggregation window is initialised upon the receipt of the first measurement. The $B(s)$ primes the process to listen for the first PMU packet. When it is received the PDC starts the aggregation window clock, and passes the received message on to be checked for errors. The $K < \text{Going} >$ is to ensure the replication of the process that listens for subsequent PMU messages. The second line listens for subsequent PMU packets until receives the $t^s(\text{h})$ variable from the CLOCK. This maps to the PDC standard [2], as the PDC should drop any data that hasn't been processed when the aggregation window closes.

The CLOCK process, which is implicitly real-time, marks the opening of the measurement aggregation window, when the first PMU measurement arrives, and the closing of the window. This is shown in Eq. 9.

$$\text{CLOCK} ::= t^b(s).t^s < \text{close-window} > \tag{9}$$

The implicit real-time clock begins when the clock receives notification of the first measurement, and then it will *eventually* announce to the rest of the PDC processes when the aggregation window is closed with the close-window variable.

The integrity requirements that a PDC must abide are ensure that the measurement "correct source" and "data integrity checks". It *does not* perform bad data detection [2]. The integrity function of the model is shown in Eq. 10.

$$\text{CHECK} ::= c(s).(ret(s,1) \rightarrow \text{sm}.c^m < \text{sm} > |ret(s,2) \rightarrow \text{sv}.c^v < \text{sv} >)| \\ c^m(\text{a}).[is\_in(PMU - List, \text{a}) = true]c^{sm} < \text{a} > +c^{sm} < \emptyset > | \\ c^v(\text{b}).[\text{b} \neq error]c^{sv}(\text{b}) + c^{sv}(\emptyset)| \\ (c^{sm}(\text{fm})|c^{sv}(\text{fv})).[fm \neq \emptyset][fv \neq \emptyset]c^s < \text{fm, fv} > \tag{10}$$

The integrity process receives the list containing the measurements, and unpacks it. It checks that PMU is in the list of devices it should receive a sample from and that the measurement hasn't been 'corrupted'. The tests are shown in the second and third line. If it has it discards the value. In the final line, if both variables have passed their integrity checks, they are passed to the window aggregator process, which is shown in Eq. 11

$$\text{AGGREGATE} ::= \nu\,Window\ t^b(\text{s}).la < Window > |$$
$$(la(w).(c^s(\text{am}, \text{av}).wam.wav.la < w > +t^s(\text{cl}).ems < w >))! \tag{11}$$

The aggregation process initialises a list to store the measurements generated in this window, when the start variable is received when the first packet is received. It passes the new list to the new instance of the process that appends the list with variables that have passed the integrity checker. The append process terminates when it receives the end variable from the CLOCK process and then passes this window's list to the process that will send it to the EMS.

The sending of the aggregated PMU data is shown Eq. 12.

$$\text{SEND}_{SE} ::= s(w).(SE < w > |B < \text{Start} >) \tag{12}$$

The process receives this aggregation window's list of aggregated PMU data, and then proceeds to send it to the EMS, while initialising the PDC to listen for the first measurement of the next aggregation window.

3.3   The Adversary Model

The goal of adversary model is to introduce subtle errors into the SE calculation through either delaying the transmission of PMU measurements, corrupting the data integrity of the packet, or having legitimate measurements rejected by compromising the messages MAC address. With these corrupted messages the adversary is aiming to increase the likelihood that the EMS to instigate an inappropriate safety action.

This model is based upon the objectives presented in the work of Shereen *et al.* [17]. The adversary has gained their ability to generate malicious messages through compromising, either by manipulating the GPS signal or compromising the PMU itself [18]. The adversary *does not* occupy a man in the middle position, which is common in the SE attack literature. However, this model is not focused on how the adversary achieves these manipulations but on different kinds of compromised messages the adversary can generate and providing the proposed re-transmission algorithm for the PDC to *have a chance* of remedying them.

In this model, the adversary is only able to edit *one* SV message per aggregation window, and is not allowed to edit the subsequent re-transmission request, to limit the chance of their detection. An iterative adversary shall be considered in future work. As attackers are able to perform passive reconnaissance, we must assume that they are able to learn the semantic structure of the SV messages and have no restriction on their memory. The kinds of error messages the adversary can inject into communications are given in table 1. The adversary has the ability to orchestrate multiple PMUs within a particular PDC group, as has been theorised in some some of the models SE adversaries discussed in Sect. 2.1.

Table 1. The three kinds of erroneous the adversary model can generate.

Address	Value
e	Value
m	e
e	e

The adversary process can be represented as a version of equation is given by Eq. 5,

$$\text{PMU}^{\text{comp}} ::= \nu m \ \text{SEND}^{\text{comp}}_{PMU} \tag{13}$$

The modification to the send process is given in Eq. 14.

$$\text{SEND}^{\text{comp}}_{PMU} ::= \nu \text{Value}, Mal - list$$
$$(\nu \text{em} \ Mal - list :: \text{em}.Mal - list :: \text{Value}$$
$$+ \nu \text{ev} \ Mal - list :: \text{m}.Mal - list :: \text{ev} \tag{14}$$
$$+ \nu \text{em}, \text{ev} \ Mal - list :: \text{em}.Mal - list :: \text{ev}).$$
$$s_m < Mal - list >$$

where em and ev are the malicious variables that the adversary generates. They generate a malicious MAC address and/or measurement, represented by the options in Table 1, and encapsulate them into their list $Mal - list$. They send this new list off to the receiver via PMU's communication channel name r_m.

3.4   The Re-transmission Algorithm

This section lays out the principal contribution of this paper. It willmodify the PMU and PDC models from earlier in this section to allow for are-transmission algorithm. This gives the PDC a *chance* to correct any malicious perturbations that the adversary, from the previous subsection, wishes to introduce to undermine the SE calculations. This proposal give the PDC a *chance* to respond to the adversaries' interference by giving the PDC the ability to *demand* the PMUs under its ageis to resend its measurements immediately. This model provides two forms of re-transmission algorithm.

Firstly a unicast option if a PMU's measurement is corrupted in transmission, but the device identity is still known. This option will be used until a last-chance re-transmission threshold.

The second option is a multicast where the PMUs whose measurements either haven't arrived or a whose identity isn't verifiable are asked to retransmit their measurement. This threshold can be set out the most optimistic value of network jitter.

The process additions have been implemented in a way that they can not interfere with the original PMU and PDC processes. Figure 3 illustrates the additional sub-window that the re-transmission algorithm introduces into the

PDC aggregation window. Once the predefined threshold has been crossed, the PDC will accept re-transmitted measurements and multicast an urgent retransmission request to any PMU it believes hasn't received a measurement from in this window. In the following, additions to the PMU and PDC models will use the font abcABC.

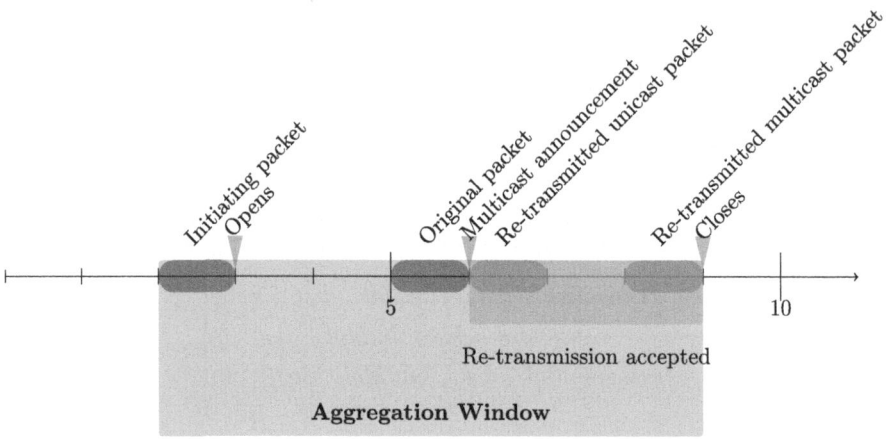

Fig. 3. The generation of a modified C37.244 [2] PDC aggregation window with a sub window for tagged packets that have been as re-transmitted

The Modified PMU. The PMU now has two process. The additional one to handle the retransmission of the last SV. The new process structure is shown in Eq. 15.

$$\text{PMU}^{\text{mod}} ::= \nu\text{m } \text{SEND}^{\text{mod}}_{PMU}!|\text{RESEND}_{\text{PMU}}! \tag{15}$$

The SEND process is modified as follows

$$\text{SEND}^{\text{mod}}_{PMU} ::= (\text{s} < \text{Halt} > |\nu\text{Value}, Sample).$$
$$(\text{ca} < \text{Value} > |Sample :: m.Sample :: Value). \tag{16}$$
$$s_{\text{m}} < Sample >$$

The additional $s < \text{Halt} >$ signals to the $\text{RESEND}_{\text{PMU}}$ process that the next SV has been prepared and so it is no longer permitted to resend the last Value variable. The $\text{ca} < \text{Value} >$ process caches the newly measured value in case a re-transmission request is received.

$$\text{RESEND}_{\text{PMU}} ::= \nu R - List \ R - List :: \text{m.ca}(\text{v}).R - List :: \text{v}.$$
$$R - List :: \text{flag.prep} < R - List > |$$
$$K(\text{R}).\text{rel} < \text{Go} > | \tag{17}$$
$$\text{prep}(\text{RL}).(\text{rel}(\text{g}).s_{\text{m}} < \text{RL} > +\text{s(h)})$$

The RESEND$_{PMU}$ process creates a list and appends the PMU address before receiving the latest cached measurement value. It appends the measurement and then appends a flag to the list to identify the message is a re-transmission. Line three of Eq. 17 shows the process that receives the re-transmission variable from the PDC and instructs the prepared list to be sent. The final line terminates either by sending the prepared re-transmission list or halting, because it received the Halt variable as the next PMU measurement has begun.

The Modified PDC. Equation 18 provides an overview of the modified PDC processes which incorporates the re-transmission algorithm into the aggregation window. The ^{mod} superscript shows which processes have been modified and third line shows the additional processes required for the re-transmission window. The additional cp $< PMU\text{-}List >$ process is to facilitate the duplication of the list of PDCs, which will be explained in Eq. 22.

$$PDC^{\text{mod}} ::= PMU\text{-}List\ (B < \text{Start} > |\text{cp} < PMU\text{-}List >).(\text{RECEIVE}^{\text{mod}}_{PMU}!|$$
$$\text{CLOCK}!|\text{AGGREGATE}!|\text{CHECK}^{\text{mod}}!|\text{SEND}_{SE}!|$$
$$\text{SUB} - \text{CLOCK}!|\text{COPY}!|\text{UPDATE}!|\text{RE}_{\text{UNI}}!|\text{RE}_{\text{MULTI}}|\text{RECEIVE}_{\text{re-transmit}}!)$$
$$(18)$$

The PDC's RECEIVE process has been modified to handle the receipt of re-transmitted measurements. If a received list has three elements then it is a re-transmitted packet. It will be passed to the RECEIVE$_{\text{re-transmit}}$ process via the addition of np $< S_m >$.

$$\text{RECEIVE}^{\text{mod}} ::= (B(\text{s})|s_{\text{m}}(S_m)).$$
$$[len(S_m) = 2]((t^b < \text{Start} > |K < \text{Going} > |c < S_m >) + \text{np} < S_m >)|$$
$$((K(\text{g})|s_{\text{m}}(S_m)).[len(S_m) = 2]((c < S_m > |K < \text{Going} > +t^s(\text{h})) + \text{np} < S_m >))!$$
$$(19)$$

The only addition to the CHECK process, in Eq. 20, is the addition of rm $< \text{fm} >$ & ru $< \text{fm} >$ processes. The first masses the MAC of a successful PMU to the UPDATE process, so it can be removed from the copy of list that will be used in the re-transmission multicast, and is sending the MAC of erroneous SV for a unicast re-transmission request.

$$\text{CHECK}^{\text{mod}} ::= c(s).(ret(s, 1) \to \text{sm}.c^m < \text{sm} > |ret(s, 2) \to \text{sv}.c^v < \text{sv} >)|$$
$$c^m(\text{a}).[is\_in(PMU\text{-}List, \text{a}) = true]c^{sm} < \text{a} > +c^{sm} < \emptyset > |$$
$$c^v(\text{b}).[\text{b} \neq error]c^{sv}(\text{b}) + c^{sv}(\emptyset)|$$
$$(c^{sm}(\text{fm})|c^{sv}(\text{fv})).[fm \neq \emptyset][fv \neq \emptyset]((c^s < \text{fm}, \text{fv} > |\text{rm} < \text{fm} >) + \text{ru} < \text{fm} >)$$
$$(20)$$

When the aggregation window opens a second clock now begins that will *eventually* announce the beginning of the sub-window indicated by the process t$^{\text{lc}} < \text{Last-Chance} >$. Both the sub-window and the aggregation are terminated with signal in the CLOCK process

$$\text{SUB-CLOCK} ::= t^b(\text{s}).t^{\text{lc}} < \text{Last-Chance} > \qquad (21)$$

The COPY process duplicates the list of PMUs and passes a copy onto the next aggregation window, as the re-transmission algorithm will delete PMUs who have successfully transmitted their measurements from a copy of the list.

$$\texttt{COPY} ::= \texttt{cp}(PL).\texttt{mv} < PL > .\texttt{cp} < PL > |\texttt{mv}(ML).\texttt{ml} < ML > \qquad (22)$$

Equation 23 shows the manipulation of a copy of the PMU list when a measurement has successfully arrived and been processed. The first part of the first line receives the windows copy of the list, and the forwarding of the list of unsuccessful PMUs when the multicast process is activated when the re-transmission window is opened. The second line shows the removal of any successful PMUs from the list when their measurement has passed the integrity checker in Eq. 20.

$$\texttt{UPDATE} ::= \texttt{ml}(LC\text{-}List).\texttt{ul} < LC\text{-}List > |\texttt{t}^{1c}(\texttt{LC}).\texttt{hm} < \texttt{Multicast} > |$$
$$((\texttt{ul}(ML)|\texttt{rm}(\texttt{m})).(ul||m.\texttt{ul} < ul > +\texttt{hm}(MC).\texttt{co} < ul >))! \qquad (23)$$

When a measurement from an identifiable PMU has been flagged as erroneous, the modified integrity checker it will be passed to the $\texttt{RE}_{\texttt{UNI}}$ process. If the re-transmission subwindow hasn't begun, the process will send a re-transmission request to the flagged PMU. Lines two and three are there to prevent any further unicast requests once the sub-window has begun:

$$\texttt{RE}_{\texttt{UNI}} ::= (\texttt{ru} < \texttt{m} > .(\texttt{s}_\texttt{m} < \texttt{Retransmit} > +\texttt{no}(\texttt{uh})))!|$$
$$\texttt{t}^{1c}(\texttt{lc}).\texttt{us} < \texttt{start} > | \qquad (24)$$
$$(\texttt{us}(\texttt{s}).((\texttt{no} < \texttt{uni} - \texttt{halt} > |\texttt{us} < \texttt{start} >) + \texttt{t}^\texttt{s}(\texttt{cw})))!$$

Once the sub-window has opened the $\texttt{RE}_{\texttt{MULTI}}$ process willreceive the list of missing measurements and send a re-transmission request to each one. Once the request is sent the PMU MAC is removed from the list. This is done until the list is empty. No matter how many of the list the process has messaged for re-transmission, the multicast process terminates if it receives $t^s(\texttt{h})$ from the CLOCK process.

$$\texttt{RE}_{\texttt{MULTI}} ::= (\texttt{co}(re\text{-}list).[is\_empty(re\text{-}list) = false]ret(re\text{-}list, 1) \rightarrow \texttt{m}.$$
$$\texttt{s}_\texttt{m} < \texttt{Retransmit} > .re - list||\texttt{m} + t^s(\texttt{h}))! \qquad (25)$$

Finally, the process in Eq. 26 ensures thatre-transmitted packets are only accepted during the re-transmission sub-window. The first and second lines keep track of when the sub-window begins and ends. The first is listening for the variable that signals the opening of the sub-window. When the sub-window opens, the second line will signal that re-transmitted packets can be accepted, until the aggregation window closes. The final line passes on any re-transmitted measurements to the $\texttt{CHECK}^{\text{mod}}$ process, when the sub-window is open, and just loops round if it is outside the sub-window.

$$\texttt{RECEIVE}_{\texttt{re-transmit}} ::= \texttt{t}^{1c}(\texttt{lc}).\texttt{bt} < \texttt{begin-last-chance} > |$$
$$(\texttt{bt}(\texttt{blc}).\texttt{clo} < \texttt{allow-three} > .\texttt{bt} < \texttt{begin-last-chance} > +\texttt{t}^\texttt{s}(\texttt{clc}))!| \quad (26)$$
$$((\texttt{sy}(\texttt{y})|\texttt{np}(R_m)).(\texttt{clo}(\texttt{at}).(\texttt{c} < R_m > |\texttt{sy} < \texttt{yes} >) + \texttt{sy} < \texttt{yes} >))!$$

4 The Re-transmission Algorithm's Correctness

This section lays out the formal proofs that show that the proposed re-transmission algorithm executes after receiving erroneous inputs without interfering subsequent with verified safe PDC functions stated in C37.244 [2]. This section presents the applied *pi*-calculus structural congruence proofs that show that additional processes proposed in Sect. 3.4 are separate from the original PMU and PDC models in Sect. 3.2.

Applied π-calculus has various formalised equivalences and relations to formally state how process are related. This work is in interested in the structural congruence equivalence, represented by $\equiv$. This equivalence is used to formally state the kinds of modifications to process that do not affect the evolution of the original process. The list of axiomatic modifications that do not affect the original process are given in Table 2. Here, $fn(P_1)$ is the set of free names in process P_1 [16]. The $\emptyset$ processes in Table 2 are non-degenerate null sets, which can be transformed into contexts, $[\bullet]$, that explicitly indicate where new processes can be inserted without affecting the original process.

4.1 PMU Proofs

This section presents the structural congruence proofs that prove that the additional processes required for the PMU to re-transmit its measurements will not interfere with the mandated C37.244 functionality.

Proposition 1. $\text{SEND}_{PMU} \equiv \text{SEND}_{PMU}^{\text{mod}}$

Table 2. List of structural congruence axioms [16]

Index	Label	Axiom	
1	**SC-MAT**	$[x = x]\pi.P$	$\equiv \pi.P$
2	**SC-SUM-ASSOC**	$M_1 + (M_2 + M_3)$	$\equiv (M_1 + M_2) + M_3$
3	**SC-SUM-COMM**	$M_1 + M_2$	$\equiv M_2 + M_1$
4	**SC-SUM-INACT**	$M + \emptyset$	$\equiv M$
5	**SC-COMP-ASSOC**	$P_1|(P_2|P_3)$	$\equiv (P_1|P_2)|P_3$
6	**SC-COMP-COMM**	$P_1|P_2$	$\equiv P_2|P_1$
7	**SC-COMP-INACT**	$P|\emptyset$	$\equiv P$
8	**SC-RES**	$\nu z \nu w\ P$	$\equiv \nu w \nu z\ P$
9	**SC-RES-INACT**	$\nu z\ \emptyset$	$\equiv \emptyset$
10	**SC-RES-COMP**	$\nu z\ P_1|P_2$	$\equiv P_1|\nu z\ P_2$ if $z \notin fn(P_1)$
11	**SC-REP**	$P!$	$\equiv P|P!$

Proof. To transform the $Send_{PMU}$ process into Eq. 16 rule 7 from Table 2 is used to create two composition processes with non-degenerate $\emptyset$. This non-degenerate $\emptyset$ are transformed into contexts, which the s $<$ Halt $>$ & ca $<$ Value $>$ processes are inserted. $\square$

Theorem 1. $PMU \equiv PMU^{mod}$

Proof. Along with proposition 1 another rule 7 from table2 is used to transform PMU into PMU^{mod}. The composite $\emptyset$ is used to insert the RESEND process into the process. $\square$

4.2   PDC Proofs

This section presents the structural congruence proofs that prove that the additional processes required for the PDC to re-transmit its measurements will not interfere with the mandate C37.244 functionality.

Proposition 2. $RECEIVE \equiv RECEIVE^{mod}$

Proof. To transform the RECEIVE process into equation RECEIVE^{mod} first rule 1 is used to insert the list length matching processes. Next rule 4 inserts a summation whose $\emptyset$ becomes a context that becomes the np $< S_m >$ processes that pass any re-transmitted packets to the RECEIVE$_{re-transmit}$ process. $\square$

Proposition 3. $CHECK \equiv CHECK^{mod}$

Proof. CHECK becomes CHECK^{mod} by first using rule 7 for a composition $\emptyset$ which is used to insert rm $<$ fm $>$ that sends the MAC to theUPDATE. Then a summation rule 4 is used insert the process which is used to send measurements that had corrupted values to the to the unicast re-transmission process. $\square$

Theorem 2. $PDC \equiv PDC^{mod}$

Proof. Along with propositions 2 & 3 six instances of rule 7 are used to generate the composite non-degenerate $\emptyset$ that are used to insert the additional processes needed for PDC re-transmission algorithm. $\square$

5   Conclusion

This paper has set out a formalised proposal for a PDC re-transmission algorithm that observes the C37.244 standard [2], but offers a further resilience without affecting the semantics of C37.244 communication models. The formal model provides a re-transmission guarantee for a collection of PMUs that send their measurements, via the IEC 61850 SV communication model [3], with an expected period. It requests and accepts a re-transmission of measurements from PMUs strictly within a the particular aggregation window of the measurements. The PDC will ask for a re-transmission through either one of two ways. Firstly through unicast, if the PDC receives a measurement from a registered PMU that fails the data integrity (not bad data detection) check. And secondly through a multicast, when the aggregation window reaches a specific threshold. The multicast will message any PMU that has failed to have their measurement accepted by the threshold. In this model the PMU will receive at most two re-transmission messages, per aggregation window, but can only reply once.

The re-transmission window is implemented to respond to an adversary that has compromised either PMU(s) itself, or the PMU's access to their GPS time synchronisation signal. Whilst this will not prevent denial of service attacks, it will force manipulation to be far more easily observable, negating stealth conditions and afford operators a small grace period to adjust the SE.

The proposed re-transmission algorithm was formalised in an applied π-calculus, and using structural congruence equivalence it was proven that the proposed algorithm cannot interfere with the original C37.244 communication models.

5.1 Future Work

There are three main theoretical additions to this work that could enhance the guarantees that the proposed re-transmission algorithm can provide. Firstly, as mentioned in Sect. 3.3, is an iterative adversary model. Currently the adversary can only edit the initial measurement, and nothing else. Having a model that can detect and respond to either malicious measurements or re-transmission manipulation would provide stronger security guarantees for the PDC. An additional adversary power that could be incorporated into this model is coordination between different compromised PMU's, which could be used to model the network aspects of the SE attacks.

Secondly, there is an implicit race condition in the unicast re-transmission. The algorithm will only accept re-transmissions after the sub-window has begun. Removing this race condition would increase the soundness of the guarantee that the model provides.

Finally, timing is implicit in this protocol. Having an explicit real-time clock would allow for the testing of different sub-window timings, which may provide system implementers with a stronger foundation to work with, but is beyond the scope of this paper.

References

1. Communication networks and systems for power utility automation: Standard IEC 61850-90-5. International Electrotechnical Commission, Geneva, Switzerland (2012)
2. IEEE Guide for Phasor Data Concentrator Requirements for Power System Protection, Control, andMonitoring. Standard IEEE Std C37.244-2013, The Institute of Electrical and Electronics Engineers Standards Association, Piscataway, New Jersey, USA (2013)

3. Communication networks and systems for power utility automation - Part 7-1: Basic communication structure - Principles and models. Standard IEC 61850-7-1:2011+AMD1:2020, International Electrotechnical Commission, Geneva, Switzerland (2020)

4. Abadi, M., Blanchet, B., Fournet, C.: The applied pi calculus: mobile values, new names, and secure communication. J. ACM **65**(1), 1–41 (2017)

5. Almas, M.S., Vanfretti, L.: Impact of time-synchronization signal loss on PMU-based WAMPAC applications. In: 2016 IEEE Power and Energy Society General Meeting (PESGM), pp. 1–5 (2016)

6. Balocco, A., Foglietta, C., Wolthusen, S.D.: Delay and jitter attacks on hierarchical state estimation. In: 2015 IEEE International Conference on Smart Grid Communications (SmartGridComm), pp. 485–490 (2015)

7. Bonebrake, C., O'Neil, L.R.: Attacks on GPS time reliability. IEEE Secur. Priv. **12**(3), 82–84 (2014)

8. D'Antonio, S., Coppolino, L., Elia, I.A., Formicola, V.: Security issues of a phasor data concentrator for smart grid infrastructure. In: Proceedings of the 13th European Workshop on Dependable Computing, p. 38 (2011). https://doi.org/10.1145/1978582.1978584

9. Khan, R., McLaughlin, K., Laverty, J.H.D., David, H., Sezer, S.: Demonstrating cyber-physical attacks and defense for synchrophasor technology in smart grid. In: 2018 16th Annual Conference on Privacy, Security and Trust (PST), pp. 1–10 (2018)

10. Kim, J., Tong, L.: On topology attack of a smart grid: undetectable attacks and countermeasures. IEEE J. Sel. Areas Commun. **31**(7), 1294–1305 (2013)

11. Lee, H., Tushar, Cui, B., Mallikeswaran, A., Banerjee, P., Srivastava, A.K.: A review of synchrophasor applications in smart electric grid. WIREs Energy Environ. **6**(3), e223 (2017)

12. Liu, Y., Ning, P., Reiter, M.K.: False data injection attacks against state estimation in electric power grids. ACM Trans. Inf. Syst. Secur. **14**(1) (2011)

13. Moussa, B., Al-Barakati, A., Kassouf, M., Debbabi, M., Assi, C.: Exploiting the vulnerability of relative data alignment in phasor data concentrators to time synchronization attacks. IEEE Trans. Smart Grid **11**(3), 2541–2551 (2020)

14. Phadke, A.G., Thorp, J.S.: Synchronized Phasor Measurements and Their Applications. Power Electronics and Power Systems, Springer, New York (2008)

15. Sandberg, H., Teixeira, A., Johansson, K.: On security indices for state estimators in power networks. In: First Workshop on Secure Control Systems (2010)

16. Sangiorgi, D., Walker, D.: The Pi-Calculus: A Theory of Mobile Processes. Cambridge University Press, Cambridge (2003)

17. Shereen, E., Delcourt, M., Barreto, S., Dán, G., Boudec, J.L., Paolone, M.: Feasibility of time-synchronization attacks against PMU-based state estimation. IEEE Trans. Instrum. Meas. **69**(6), 3412–3427 (2020)

18. Sundararajan, A., Khan, T., Moghadasi, A., Sarwat, A.I.: Survey on synchrophasor data quality and cybersecurity challenges, and evaluation of their interdependencies. J. Mod. Power Syst. Clean Energy **7**(3), 449–467 (2019)

19. Yuan, Y., Li, Z., Ren, K.: Modeling load redistribution attacks in power systems. IEEE Trans. Smart Grid **2**(2), 382–390 (2011)

20. Zhang, J., Chu, Z., Sankar, L., Kosut, O.: False data injection attacks on phasor measurements that bypass low-rank decomposition. In: 2017 IEEE International Conference on Smart Grid Communications (SmartGridComm), pp. 96–101 (2017)

Locally Optimal Information Pathways in the Presence of Static Adversaries for a Hierarchical Smart Distribution Grid Model

Nataša Gajić[(✉)] and Stephen Dirk Bjørn Wolthusen

NTNU, Trondheim, Norway
{natasa.gajic,stephen.wolthusen}@ntnu.no

Abstract. Future smart grids will provide greater flexibility to both users and operators but will also inherently lessen resilience of the grid. This work deals with improving that resilience by looking into topological structure of distribution grids and providing suggestions for the improvement of the structure of the grid. Distribution grid is modeled with a hierarchical, smart, multilayer graph model. That model is then compromised by placing multiple static adversaries in the distribution grid layer of the model and contaminating the graph with their respective areas of influence. To localize the damage such adversaries can deal, a linear optimization problem of finding the shortest and least costly information path from the neighborhood of the compromised area to the top layer in the hierarchical model is presented and solved for, so that relevant information of grid contamination reaches grid operators in a timely manner. After that, suggestions for improving the structure of layers in Information Overlay of the model are presented. Lastly, Optimal Path algorithm is presented, which finds optimal paths in compromised areas and areas that are blocked off or unreliable.

Keywords: Adversary Models · Linear Optimization · Communication and Control Networks

1 Introduction

Adversaries and adversarial activities in different systems have been studied for a long time, ever since Dolev and Yao modeled two types of adversaries in 1983 in the area of communication technology [9]. Nowadays, where systems are increasingly becoming more intelligent and dynamic, opportunities for different adversarial attacks are multiplying as well. From large patient databases in health [19,33] to cyber protection of nuclear power plants [13], over communication security of ICT devices in food industry [28] to the security of critical infrastructures such as water systems [15], power grids [34] and communication networks [32]. This means that different models of all these systems and different

© The Author(s), under exclusive license to Springer Nature Switzerland AG 2025
G. Oliva et al. (Eds.): CRITIS 2024, LNCS 15549, pp. 151–170, 2025.
https://doi.org/10.1007/978-3-031-84260-3_9

types of adversaries should be and are being researched on. Depending on the needs of the researchers and the systems they are looking at, adversaries can have different capabilities.

In the case of power grids, it is convenient to model them as graphs, especially when the main goal is to study how an adversary can affect and "contaminate", or compromise, its structure. Studying which part of the grid can provide grid operators with reliable information and which part of the grid provides information which validity is uncertain provides important insight. This insight becomes increasingly more important when distribution grid is in question as it is becoming more dynamic with the rise of things like EVs (electric vehicles) or private solar panels and other small power plants. Having many input points in a network that, due to its sheer size, can't have a constant and strict overview by a grid operator makes it more vulnerable. This vulnerability can, in the worst case scenario, jeopardize the whole grid. And the trend of striving for smart neighborhoods [22] and smart cities [18,31] in the near future will make for even more of those vulnerable input points in a distribution grid.

Therefore, when planning future distribution grids, in our previous work in [20] and [21] a modelling tool is presented which generates distribution grid graph structures when given certain input variables, such as number of nodes, branching factor and number of connections, aka density of the network. This tool is imagined to be of use to the distribution grid designers while they create new sections of smart distribution grids. Therefore, the tool, or, more precisely, the topology generator, generates not only the distribution grid but it also has an information overlay which will be there to monitor the distribution grid and make some decisions instead of a grid operator, if needed. This information overlay has a multilayer structure and those layers have a hierarchy between themselves. This is done both to lower the cost of smart components in the network as well as to impose a decision hierarchy, which is important in a critical situation of an active adversarial activity.

Utilizing this generator to test the stability of such a future multilayer network under different adversary models is something of a value for the protection of future smart distribution grids.

The idea of this study is to first model an adversary that can influence distribution grid in a certain radius and then create protection algorithms that would act as countermeasure to the adversary. The plan is to model the adversary (or adversaries) as a function that can act in a provided radius from its placement (or origin node) in a multilayer graph model that is representing a smart distribution grid. That radius will be defined by neighborhoods in the graph. Lets call it adversary's area of influence. In that area, it will be assumed that the adversary has, in the worst case scenario, total control of the nodes in that area. Total control means that it can turn any nodes on and off, tell them which (false or true) measurements their sensors (which are nodes in the graph) should be showing or actually changing the voltage. If there are sensors on the edges (that is, cables) in its area of influence, it will be assumed that the adversary will also be able to change their readings as well.

Additionally, it is important to mention that the model made by the generator from [20] and [21] provides flexibility of structuring the information overlay to fit needs of different constraints.

The novelty in this work lies in its the approach. Rather then just counting nodes and labeling them, that is, rather than this work being just an exercise in enumeration, this work will take a different approach. Instead of enumeration, the idea of the approach is to identify structures in the given *distribution grid model* that will help find a way to solve the optimization problem of finding a specific shortest and least costly path from the Distribution Grid to the highest layer in the Information Overlay that also honors the structure.

1.1   Structure of the Paper

The remainder of this paper is structured as follows: After the problem statement is given in (2), a review of the related work on adversaries and linear programming and combinatorial optimization is presented. Next, the methods and algorithms used here are described in detail in (4). Detailed overview of Optimal Path algorithm (OPA in further text) is present after that in (5) as well as how it differs from the original Dijkstra algorithm. Lastly, there is a brief description of the ongoing and future work (8) as well as conclusions (7).

2   Problem Statement

A static adversary that has a reach of influence and can be comprised of multiple adversaries in a graph can be defined as

$$f(multilayerModel, locations, radius) = compromisedModel, \qquad (1)$$

where its domain will be a subset of the graph model, while its codomain will be defined as the whole graph, since its actions in its area of influence could potentially influence other parts of the graph, which can be assumed is one of its goals and something that should be prevented, if possible. This function will provide a new, partially "contaminated" version of the original graph. The idea then, is, to find a path of information from as close as possible to the contaminated area in the Distribution Grid layer to the top layer of the Information Overlay, which will then be able to signal to the grid operator that there is something wrong with the grid. This path should be the shortest possible, because, in a critical situation, time is essential. However, it will also have a cost, or a weight, because the closer its starting node is to the contaminated area, the more uncertain the information it sends forward is. But the starting node needs to be as close as possible to the contaminated area, otherwise the intelligent monitoring Information Overlay won't notice that there is a problem in the grid, since there won't be an untempered measurement from that part of the grid, and therefore, no alarms would be raised. And noticing that there *is* a problem in the grid is the main idea. Thus, finding a (locally) optimal shortest path, that is also least costly/weighty will be then the main task of this work. The optimization used will be combinatorial optimization (which is well suited for a discrete structure such as a graph). One of the things that will be available to this work are the locations of an adversary or adversaries. Their initial location is one of the initial constraints.

The core problem in this work can be defined as following:

Lets assume that there is a hierarchical multilayer graph model comprised of Distribution Grid, Information Overlay and Adaptive Layer (see [20] and [21]). Let us also assume that there are at least 2 different adversaries located in the Distribution Grid, each with a k neighbor and such that the intersection of their neighborhoods (or reach of influence) is not an empty set. We want to find the shortest and least costly path (or paths), if it exist, from a $(k+1)$ neighbor of all adversaries located in the Distribution Grid or the lowest Information Overlay layer to the top layer in the Information Overlay.

A k neighborhood can be defined as a set of neighbors which are not immediate neighbors (except in the case of $k = 1$, when they *are* immediate neighbors), but which are connected to their neighbor via k, or less, connections, or edges.

2.1   Assumptions

We will make the following assumptions:

- The hierarchical multilayer model is used as a close approximation of a future smart distribution grid (see [20] for proof).
- There are at least 2 adversaries in the graph, with the same reach of influence k and their neighborhoods intersect at least partially. These adversaries are static and they are located in the Distribution Grid layer of the model.
- Since we are concerned primarily with the neighborhoods of adversaries, the problem is localized and can therefore be approached a problem of finding a local optimum (or optimums, depending on the strictness of the constraints).
- No new cables will be added to the Distribution Grid layer, meaning, no new edges are allowed in the Distribution Grid layer.
- In searching for the shortest/least weighty/least risky path, vertical edges (that is, edges between the layers) are preferred to the horizontal edges (that is, edges that are in the same layer).

2.2   Constraints

The constraints of the problem are as follows:

- Cost, or length, of the found path has to be equal or less of a given, positive number.
- The path cannot contain adversarial nodes.
- There is an edge budget for new edges.
- New edges from (2.4) can be only be added in one of the Information Overlays or in the Adaptive Layer, since we made the assumption that no new cables would be added to the Distribution Grid layer, which leads to no new edges being allowed in that layer.

– We assume that outside of (k + 1) neighborhoods, the rest of the graph is stable. That is, the edge budget cannot be used outside of (k + 1) neighborhood.
– Only nodes located in the Distribution Grid layer and the lowest Information Overlay layer are considered as the candidates for (k + 1) neighbors.

Due to the constraints, there is a possibility that there is no solution that satisfies all of the constraints. Which can lead to either needing to relax some of the constraints (e.x. the cost constraint) or to take the approach presented in (4.2). This problem will be solved in two steps.

2.3   Step I

In this first step, all of the $(k + 1)$ neighbors are tested as possible candidates as possible starting points for the shortest path from the distribution grid to the top layer. The search for the (locally) optimal path is done using OPA (5). Then, depending on the constraints, (2.2), none, one, or multiple shortest paths can be found.

2.4   Step II

In the second step of this algorithm, let us assume that there is an edge budget. Using this edge budget, the algorithm will try to find a new shortest path, using the same OPA. This edge budget will be used only locally, close to the "contaminated" areas.

It is also important to note that while there are active components in the graph model, modelling the control behaviour is out of the scope of this work. Instead, the focus of this work is on the structure of the graph (and specifically, the "contaminated" graph) and how that structure can be used.

3   Related Work

With the development of new technologies and improvement of old, new security vulnerabilities appear constantly. And new models of systems, protocols and adversaries are constantly present. Therefore it tends to feel like both the researches and the society in general are trying to catch up with that constant wave of new vulnerabilities [12]. Some of the initial work regarding adversary modelling and protocols that concern adversaries has been done in the work of Dolev and Yao from 1983 [9]. In it, two different models are developed: The Cascade Protocols and the Name-Stamp Protocols. The important thing that those protocols have done is set up a set of rules which an adversary abides by, that is, setting up a set of all the actions which an adversary can make.

The work in [7] outlines the theory of compositional security that addresses the following challenge: While the modern systems are made of many individual components, and each of those components are constantly being improved, the security between those components isn't guaranteed. That is because even though if we assume that each of the components is, by itself, secure, the complex connections between different components are vulnerable and can be exploited by a knowledgeable adversary. This work also models security proprieties. It also states that security properties can then be modeled as formulas of a first-order temporal logic.

Compositional security approach can then further help with predicting vulnerabilities of certain attacks. For example, any specific attack that doesn't break the invariant which all of the interfaces maintain, then the attack won't break the security property of the system. Using the same logic, if even one interface doesn't maintain this invariant, the system could potentially be attacked.

An adversary can be defined as someone or something that has the intent of disturbing the expected functionality of a system o a network. The author of [23] gives a rough classification of adversaries into two categories: passive (also known as semi-honest or honest-but curious) and active (also known as malicious adversaries). An adversary model is a formalization of an adversary in a computer or network system. Depending on the formalization, an adversary may be an algorithm, program, may simply be a series of statements with regards to capabilities and goals or something else and they can have many different capabilities, depending on the need of the model. They are crucial in cryptography where they are used in the security proof of a particular cryptographic scheme or a protocol. Another one of the earliest adversary models is the Bellare-Rogaway Adversary Model (see [2,3] and [1]). This model allowed for modeling of different types of adversaries, whether it is a passive or an active one as well as whether it is a benign or a malign adversary.

Since an adversary can be so many different things, Bellare and Rogaway propose a method to model an adversary to fit the needs of a presented scenario in their work in [3] and [1]. There, they propose to model an adversary with three distinct different parts - Adversary Goals, Adversary Assumption and Adversary Capabilities. Each of these parts can be formally defined depending on the needs of the specific situation or a problem.

While this work will not be researching the types of attacks, it is important to know what types of attacks would an adversary be able or need to run. The following work [30], classifies the attack types on electric power systems in a cyber-physical environment into the three following categories:

- Physical Attack
- Cyber attack and
- Human Attack.

In this work, the focus will be mostly be on the physical attacks, as well as the measurement attacks.

We will focus on combinatorial graph optimization in this work. Hierarchical multilayer graphs as models for future distribution grids have been recently looked into in the [20] and [21]. Additionally, recent studies on multilayer graph using combonatorial optimization can be seen in this work from 2017 [24] as well as in this work from 2020 [27] which applies combinatorial optimization to the networking problem in applications. Important part of our work will play out in the terms of cut sets and edge density. So, one of the available tools is Max-Flow Min-Cut Theorem [6]. That this theorem can be useful in the environment of power systems showcases this work from 2014 [17]). Other possible approaches [4] that we will be looking into are Thresholding approach [14], Random walker for multi-class and relaxed optimization [29], Flow Metrics [16], Block Coordinate Descent [25], LASSO estimation [26], Gradient Projection, Interior Point Method [11], Alternating Direction of Multipliers [5] as well as the classic LP problem [10].

4   Methods and Algorithmic Results

Now, with all that preparation in place, this section will present detailed, step-by-step algorithms on how to solve the problem defined in the Problem Statement section (2). Lets repeat that problem statement here, for the sake of the ease of overview while presenting the solution.

Lets assume that there is a hierarchical multilayer graph model comprised of Distribution Grid, Information Overlay and Adaptive Layer. Let us also assume that there are at least 2 different adversaries located in the Distribution Grid, each with a k neighbor and such that the intersection of their neighborhoods (or reach of influence) is not an empty set. We want to find the shortest and least costly path (or paths), if it exists, from an optimal (k + 1) neighbor of all adversaries located in the Distribution Grid or the lowest Information Overlay layer to the top layer in the Information Overlay, while also fulfilling all of the constraints given in (2.2).

As a reminder, a k neighbor is defined as a neighbor which is not an immediate neighbor (except in the trivial, $k = 1$, case), but which is connected to its neighbor via k, or less, connections, or edges. Therefore, a k neighborhood is a set of all k neighbors of a given adversary. If there is more than a single adversary present, such that their respective k neighborhoods have a non-zero (that is, a non $\emptyset$ overlap), then their united k neighborhood can be defined as the intersection of their respective k neighborhoods. Let us also put it down in more mathematical terms.

Let DB be a set that contains all the nodes in Distribution Grid. Let IO_1, $IO_2, \ldots, IO_m$ be sets that contain the nodes from different Information Overlay layers, where IO_1 represent the lowest Information Overlay layer, which is also the layer closest to the Distribution Grid and IO_m represents the highest Information Overlay in the hierarchy and is, thus, the one the farthest away from the Distribution Grid and the one with most executive power. Let $A_1, A_2, \ldots A_l$ be sets that contain different adversaries as well as k neighborhoods we suppose they are (or can) influence. We shall suppose that $A_1, A_2, \ldots A_l$ must have a non-empty set intersection, otherwise the adversaries won't be close enough to influence each other areas of influence nor combine their influence on close, that is, local "un-contaminated" areas of grid. So, we suppose that

$$\bigcap_{i=1}^{l} A_i \neq \emptyset \tag{2}$$

Let us also showcase that is problem is an LP (Linear Programming or Linear Optimization) problem by additionally formulating it in the standard form of an LPP (Linear Programming Problem). *Find the shortest and least costly path (or paths)* can be formulated as

$$min \quad c^T x, \tag{3}$$

where c is a vector of weights and x is a vector of edges. Let us now look at the constraints from (Sect. ? 2). *Cost, or length, of the found path has to be equal or less of a given, positive number* can be written as $a_1^T x \leq \alpha$, where α is a given cost limit and a_1 is a vector of weights. *There is an edge budget for new edges* can similarly be written down as $a_2^T x \leq \beta$, except that β is the given budget and that many elements of a_2 are 0 because one of the constraints is that new edges are not allowed outside of (k+1) neighborhoods and also not in the Distribution Grid layer. Lastly, all of the edges are non-zero, because if they would be 0, it would mean that there is no edge. Therefore $x \geq 0$. Combining (3) with the newly observed conditions, we get a standard for of an LP problem:

$$
\begin{aligned}
min \quad & c^T x \\
& Ax \leq b, \\
& x \geq 0,
\end{aligned}
\tag{4}
$$

such that $A = [a_1^T, a_2^T]$ and $b = [\alpha, \beta]$. Therefore, it is obvious that our problem is a well defined LP problem.

Before continuing further, it might be beneficial to discuss what happens in a case where different adversaries have different reaches - $k_1, k_2, \ldots, k_l$ instead of all having the same reach k. But this is a simple case because if we find a maximum of $k_1, k_2, \ldots, k_l$, we can use that particular k as universal one. This will, obviously, change the number of "contaminated" nodes, but doesn't change the nature or the complexity of the problem because of all reaches need to be of the same order of magnitude. If they are not of the same order of magnitude, then the adversary with the highest order of magnitude would overtake the rest and simplify this problem into a problem with a single adversary.

Next, with all of the neighborhoods defined, the search/optimization algorithm can start in full. As it has been mentioned in the problem statement, solving this problem is done in two steps.

4.1   Step I

In Step I, the problem will be approached without changing the structure of the graph in any way. So, finding an optimal path (or paths, depending how strict or relaxed the first constraint in the (2.2) is) in an "contaminated" graph from a (k+1) neighbor to the top Information Overlay is the main task in Step I.

Step I starts with finding all of the $(k+1)$ neighbors. Out of all these $(k+1)$ neighbors, only those that are in Distribution Grid, or DB or in the lowest Information Overlay, aka IO_1 will be considered because a local optimum is what is being solved for. Additionally, looking for $(k + 1)$ neighbors in these two layers exclusively is important because the core idea of this problem is getting the information that something is wrong in the lowest layers to the highest layer using the fastest route. And to be able to notice that something is wrong in Distribution Grid, the starting node that will forward that information to the upper layer needs to be as close as possible to the "contaminated" area while not being contaminated itself - therefore, we are only allowing for $(k + 1)$ neighbors in those 2 lowest layers.

Next, using OPA (see (5)), find a shortest and least costly path (or paths). Lets call it $path_{min}$.

Before continuing on to the next step, it is worth discussing why there might be a need for more than one optimal path in this step. In the future work, some of the constraints (2.2) will be changed or added to. This might lead to having no solution to the problem. Therefore, relaxing the constraint of having a single shortest and least costly path might end up being quite beneficial and it is an easy constraint to relax. Also, since local solutions are what is being solved for, relaxing that constraint makes sense. And solving for local solution comes naturally from the structure of the model. [21] showcases that one of the pros of having a hierarchically structured Information Overlay layers lies in the fact that layers with more "intelligence" and more executive powers need increasingly less and less nodes, because having many nodes of same executive power in the same Information Overlay layer that are monitoring the same branches of the graph can lead to conflicts in a critical situation regarding which nodes should decide what is to be done, which could then lead to wasted time. Creating models that will waste as little time as possible in critical situation should be of high importance, since every second lost might mean a second gained for an adversary to spread its influence and damage the network. Therefore, the model in [21] adds the hierarchical structure to the Information Overlay layers from the [20] model and makes each higher layer has continuously less and less nodes with the statement that the top layer should have as few nodes as possible, but still more than one. This creates chain of command in the model.

4.2   Step II

One of the constraints in (2.2) has not been used so far. The edge budget has not been mentioned yet. It will come into play here in Step II.

Since this project (work done previously in [20,21] and here, as well as the future work) has been guided by the idea of how to help distribution grid architects and operators model future smart grids and make them as resilient as possible from adversarial influence, Step II is what is deeply concerned with that and answers the following question: *If there is a budget to add additional edges, or connections (or lines, in power grid terminology), where should such an additional edges (or edges) be located to make new shortest and least costly paths, so that the important information reaches grid operators as soon as possible in a critical situation of an adversarial appearance in the distribution grid?* Or, in mathematical terms: *In the setting and scope of the original problem in Step I (4.1), Among all of the elements of the set of possible candidates C*

$$C = \left(DB \cup IO_1 \right) \setminus \bigcup_{i=1}^{l} A_i \qquad (5)$$

does there exist a node such that if made into $(k+1)$ neighbor by using the given edge budget it provides the path from the Distribution Grid to the top layer of the Information Overlay which is shorter and less costly than a path (or paths) found in Step I? This is what is being solved for here in Step II.

Step II will be done iteratively. First, lets assume that the edge budget is a single new edge. This edge will be used to upgrade a non- $(k+1)$ neighbor node from (5) to a $(k+1)$ neighbor. While there will be a need to check new possible path for each $(k+1)$ neighbor candidate, there is a way to do the search in a slightly smarter approach rather than simply going through each candidate in the random order. To that end, candidate nodes will be put in a list of preferences, using a cost function c which will assign each candidate node a preference.

$$c : C \times \bigcup_{i=1}^{l} A_i \rightarrow \mathbb{N}, c(V, V_k) = n, \qquad (6)$$

where $V \in C$ is a possible candidate node (aka vertex), V_k is a k neighbor and $n \in N$ is its assigned cost to make V in into a $(k+1)$ neighbor. The preference will depend on two things, both of which deal with either length or cost of the path. Let us suppose that we have two possible $(k+1)$ neighbor candidates: V_1 and V_2 and lets suppose that, according to the given definition of a $k+1$ neighbor, V_1 and V_2 would be currently considered $k+q_1$ and $k+q_2$ neighbors, where $q_1, q_2 > 1$ and $q_1 > q_2$. Since $q_1 > q_2$, then V_1 would be given a larger value than V_2 and therefore be put lower on the list of preferences than V_2 for the new $(k+1)$ neighbor. Using this cost function, all of the possible candidates will be listed in accordance to the preference for them being the new $(k+1)$ neighbor.

Then, using this list, all of the candidates will be tested (multiple times, because there are different possibilities as to how they could become a $(k+1)$ neighbor). Using this list makes this approach into a greedy algorithm, which aligns well with the OPA, which is also a greedy algorithm.

There is an additional way to use this listing to lower the number of tests. An additional constraint could be made that a new edge could not have a cost larger than a given number. This constraint could, depending on the magnitude of that constraint, shorten the list. This would also work well if, instead of saying that the provided edge budget is one edge, we could provide a number instead, which would then be used as total cost available instead of number of possible new edges.

Next, for each new candidate on the list, the graph model will be changed to include the new edge, after which the OPA will be used to find a shortest and least costly path for this new graph. Comparing the old and the new shortest path will decide which shortest path, and thus, which structure to use. Of course, the original "contaminated" structure will always be remembered, but any changed ones will be only temporary unless by the end the search algorithm decides that they provide shorter path. This part will need to be iteratively repeated until each of the listed (whether the list has been shortened or not) candidates has been tested.

Since we the constraints were strictly followed in both steps and our problem is well defined as an LP problem (4), a solution, if it exists, will be a local optimum.

Using this algorithm, the grid operator can test whether adding an edge (or edges, using the cost edge budget approach) would be beneficial to heightening the resilience of a distribution grid in multitude of different scenarios.

5   Optimal Path Algorithm

In this section, the Optimal Path algorithm will be described in detail, as well as motivation behind being strongly inspired by Dijkstra's algorithm [8].

Let G be a multilayered graph for which we will want to find a shortest and least costly path from the neighboring area of contamination in Distribution Grid to the top layer of Information Overlay. Let then M be a matrix with three columns: first will contain the list of all the nodes (that is, vertices), second will contain shortest distances from the starting node and the third one will contain previous node in the shortest path. First column won't change during the run of the algorithm, while second and third will be continuously updated (see Table 1 for an example and visual representation of the matrix M). Next, lets initialize M so that it contains all nodes in the first column, second column should contain ∞ in all cells, while the third column should be empty at the start of the algorithm. After that, matrix M shall be updated to have the information about the adversarial nodes and their contamination reach, that is, their k neighborhoods. This will be done in the following manner: Let us assume that V_{i1} is an adversary node. Then, M_{i2} will become $M_{2i}NaN$ (Not-a-Number). This effectively means that adversary nodes are not allowed to be part of the shortest path, since they will certainly provide false information. Next, for each $k = 1$ neighbor of V_{i1}, their respective M_{i2} will become $M_{i2} = (|V| + |E|)^{k-1}$, where $|V|$ is the order of the graph G, aka its number of nodes and $|E|$ is the size of the graph G, aka its number of edges unless the current number is greater (but finite) than $(|V|+|E|)^{k}$. In that case, M_{i2} won't change its value. Next, each $k = j$, where $0 \leq j \leq k$ neighbor of V_{i1}, their respective M_{i2} will become $M_{i2} = (|V| + |E|)^{k-j+1}$, unless the current value of their respective M_{i2} is greater (but finite) than $(|V|+|E|)^{k-j+1}$. In that case, their respective M_{i2} won't change their values. This is done so that the cost (which in this case has the meaning of risk of using a compromised node in the information path is being searched for), showcases obvious cost difference, order of magnitude wise, when using a compromised node compared to using a non-compromised one. This will also affect the path preference because of the constraint on the path length/cost (2.2). Graph G will also be updated with these values. That is, edges connecting adversary nodes will gain the weight of NaN, and the edges connecting the their compromised neighbors will gain the weight of $(|V| + |E|)^{k-j+1}$. This updated matrices M and G are what will be used in the search. One of the main modifications of the Dijkstra algorithm lies in the idea that adversary nodes are not allowed to be a part of the shortest path. Additionally, OPA has different constraints (2.2) compared to the original Dijkstra [8] and therefore, there is a possibility of the algorithm terminating without satisfying the constraints. The last assumption from (2.1) is added to provide an intentionality of grid architects or operators into the algorithm. That intentionality being cheaper edges. This basically means that if there is a need to use the edge budget from step II (4.2), it is significantly cheaper to add an edge in a wireless space (that is, in the Adaptive Layer (see [20])) than putting down an actual cable in the ground. Additionally, having edge density be mostly concentrated between layers lessens the opportunity of an adversary contaminating many branches of the tree-like graph structure of the model. Three additional lists will be taken into account and used: a list of visited nodes, *visited*, a list of unvisited nodes, *unvisited* and the list of adversary nodes, *adversaries*. Before the first iteration of the algorithm, a list of visited nodes will be empty, while the list of unvisited nodes will contain all nodes except the adversary ones.

Table 1. An example of matrix M from Optimal Path algorithm.

Node	Shortest Distance From Node 1	Previous Node
1	0	
2	1	1
3	2	2
4	3	2
5	7	3

Next, for the starting point of the path, assign its M_{i2} value to 0, taking into account that the starting point cannot be among the list of adversaries. From the assigned starting point, visit the node from the list of unvisited nodes with the smallest known distance to the start node. Next, for the currently visited node, examine its immediate unvisited neighbors and calculate distance of each immediate neighbor to the start node. If the calculated distance is less than the value in its M_{i2}, update the M_{i2} value. Only do this if the value in M_{i2} is not NaN. Update the previous node for each of the updated M_{i2} values. Add the current node to the list of visited nodes and remove it from the list of unvisited nodes. Repeat this process until the list of unvisited nodes is empty.

Let us present the process in a more algorithmic form as well.

1: **function** OPTIMALPATHALGORITHM(G, *adversaries*, *start*)
2:    ▷ G is the input graph, *adversaries* is a list/set of adversaries and *start* is the starting node.
3:    $M \leftarrow initiate(G)$
4:    $M(start, 2) \leftarrow 0$
5:    $unvisited \leftarrow M(all, 1)$ ▷ *unvisited* gets the first column of M
6:    $visited \leftarrow \emptyset$
7:    $G \leftarrow contaminate(G, adversaries)$
8:    $M \leftarrow contaminateMatrix(M, G, adversaries)$
9:    $G \leftarrow prefVertical(G)$
10:   **while** $unvisited \neq \emptyset$ **do**
11:       $temp \leftarrow findClosestUnvisited(M, unvisited)$
12:       $(visited, unvisited) \leftarrow visit(temp, visited, unvisited)$
13:       $M \leftarrow updateM2(M, G, temp)$
14:       $M \leftarrow updateM3(M, G, temp)$
15:   **end while**
16:   **return** M
17: **end function**

Function $initiate(G)$ is an additional function that inputs all of the nodes from G into the first column of M, sets all the values in the second column to ∞ and empties the third column. $contaminate(G, adversaries)$ and *contaminateMatrix(M, G, adversaries)* are additional functions that contaminate G and M by changing the weights of edges in G according to the list of adversaries and update the second column of M according to contaminated G and the list of adversaries. Function $prefVertical(G)$ changes the weights of edges so that vertical edges are preferred to horizontal, aka edges between the layers are given smaller weights so that algorithm will choose them first, as it is a greedy algorithm. Exception to this would be if an edge is part of the contaminated neighborhood. Weights of such edges won't be changed as they are **not** considered preferable. Function $findClosestUnvisited(M, unvisited)$ is an additional function that finds and returns the node from the list of unvisited nodes with the shortest and least costly known distance to the start node. $visit(temp, visited, unvisited)$ is an additional function that updates the list of visited and unvisited node by taking out the node that is currently being visited from the list of unvisited node and putting it into the list of visited nodes. $updateM2(M, G, temp)$ is an additional function that updates M_{i2} values for every immediate neighbor of the currently visited *temp* node, in case that the new calculated distance from the starting node to the neighbor is less than the value in its M_{i2}. $updateM3(M, G, temp)$ is an additional function that updates M_{i3} of the neighbors of the currently visited node to it, in case its M_{i2} has been updated.

In Fig. 1 a visual example of areas compromised by adversaries as well as possible $(k+1)$ candidates is presented. This example shows only the Distribution Layer and the lowest Information Overlay Layer and is there to visually represent the idea of contaminated neighborhoods and possible $(k+1)$ candidates, thus it doesn't show the full model with all of its layers.

There is an additional case that should be looked into - what happens within the algorithm if there is a node whose only neighbor is an adversary? Would it make the algorithm go into an infinite it is in the list of unvisited neighbors, but its distance is and would stay $\emptyset$? This is actually one of the reasons why the introduction of NaN value was deemed as a useful addition. A node whose only neighbor is an adversary will still be visited, since it is in the list of unvisited neighbors, but it will be visited as the last node (or nodes, if there are more than one). And while its M_{i2} value won't change from ∞, since its only other updated value would be $\infty + NaN$, however, whenever an algorithm would come upon a NaN value, it would immediately stop that iteration or part of the process. Therefore, such a node will still be visited and will, therefore, leave the list of unvisited nodes, which will allow for the termination of the algorithm.

Information Overlay Layer 1

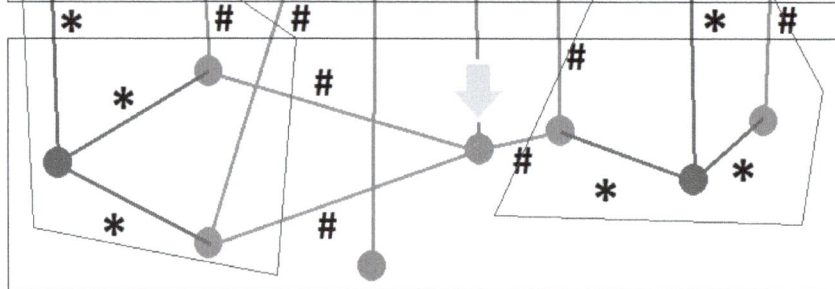

Distribution Grid

Fig. 1. Color coded example of the OPA, with k neighborhood equal to 1. Red nodes represent adversarial nodes, orange represent k neighbors of the adversarial nodes, aka "contaminated nodes" and green represent "un-contaminated" nodes. Similarly, red edges represent edges going directly from adversary nodes, orange from k neighbors and green represent edges that safe for the information flow, aka the edge a grid operator would be confident that they provide true grid information. * represents biggest cost for those edges to be used for the path the algorithm is searching for since it includes actual adversary nodes, thus they are unsuitable to be used. Therefore their cost needs to be something like $* = \infty$ or $* = NaN$. Following the same logic, # needs to be significantly larger than any regular cost of an edge. This is represented in this work by being different orders of magnitude of $(|V| + |E|)^k$, depending on its k. Blue polygons visually represent adversarial nodes and their area of influence while yellow arrows visually represent possible $(k + 1)$ candidates. (Color figure online)

5.1   Choosing Weights

As there are quite a few different order of magnitudes for different edges, it would be beneficial to have an explanation of all of them in one section. Figure 2 showcases which different orders of magnitude are used in OPA.

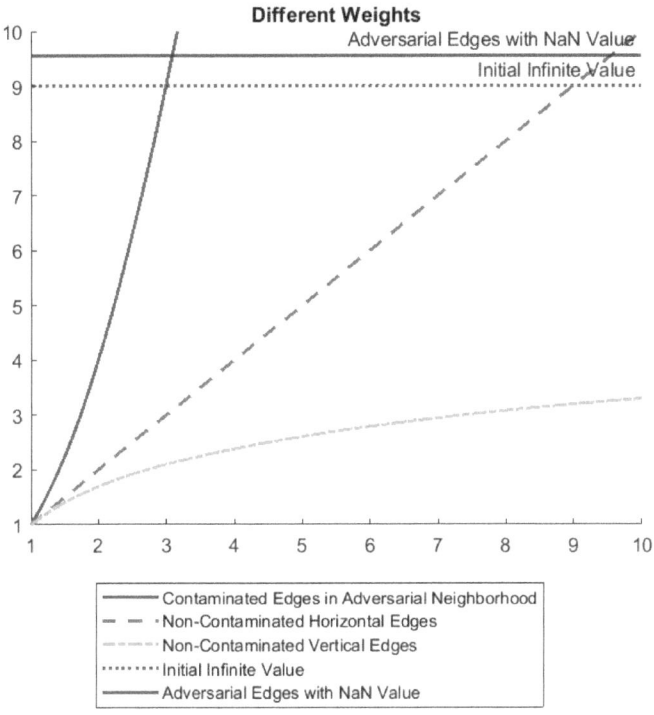

Fig. 2. Different orders of magnitude for different weights.

All edges that directly connect adversary nodes are assigned NaN as their weight. This assures that these edges won't be used in the shortest path and thus, fulfils the constraint (2.2) that adversarial nodes won't be included in the path. Next, the ∞ value is reserved for the initialization stage of OPA. Exponential values are assigned to the edges that are in contaminated areas, but not first neighbors of adversary nodes. The closer the edge is to an adversary node, the higher its exponential is. This represents non-preference for using these edges in the path, due to the risk of contaminating information. Linear values are assigned as weights for horizontal edges, that is, edges that lie on a layer. To showcase algorithm's preference for vertical edges, that is, edges that connect different layers, to horizontal edges, they are assigned logarithmic values. These values are chosen for the order of magnitude between them and can be changed if needed, so long as the difference in these orders of magnitude is preserved.

6   Having More Than 2 Adversaries

There is an inherent risk with having many adversaries whose areas of influence overlap. The risk being that the more adversaries with overlapping areas of influence, the less possible $(k + 1)$ candidates there are. That means that the OPA from (5) might end without finding a path. This is why step II from (4.2) has additional inherent importance because not only it provides possibilities for new optimal paths, it might create new paths in a situations where OPA in step I ends without a path. It is important, therefore, to provide proof that the presented two-step algorithm is valid for any $n \in \mathbf{N}$. In this section, a proof by induction will be used to showcase that.

Theorem 1. *Algorithms presented in (4.1), (4.2) and (5) are valid for any $n \in \mathbf{N}$, where n is the number of adversaries.*

Proof. **Base Case:** $n = 2$
The validity of the base case is presented by the construction of algorithms (4.1), (4.2) and (5).

Induction Step: We suppose that the statement of the theorem holds true for $n = l, l \in \mathbf{N}$ as well as any n, such that $2 \leq n \leq l$. We shall prove then that the statement of the theorem also holds true for $n = l + 1$.

So, let us suppose that the statement of the theorem holds true for $n = l, l \in \mathbf{N}$. That means that algorithms from (4.1), (4.2) and (5) are valid for $n = kl$. Next, let us add another another adversary in the Distribution Grid (second assumption (2.1)) and let $n = l + 1$. Due to the assumption that adversary neighborhoods intersect at least partially (2.1), that means that the area of influence of the newest adversary has a non-empty intersection with at least one of the previous adversaries. Let us pick a closest adversary to the new one (closest in the sense of k−neighbors previously defined) and let its area of influence be big enough so that it swallows up the newest adversary. This is a valid option because of the previous proof in section (4) regarding why the assumption that all adversaries can have the same reach k. Next, let us apply the new reach for all of the $l + 1$ adversaries. However, since the closest adversary we picked has swallowed up the newest one, they can be taken into account as a single adversary. So, the number of adversaries has gone down from $l + 1$ to l, and we assumed that the algorithms are valid for l adversaries. Therefore, the algorithms are valid for $l + 1$ adversaries.

Since we showed that the algorithms are valid for both the Base Case and Induction Step, that means that the algorithms are valid for any $n \in \mathbf{N}$ number of adversaries.   ∎

There is one more thing that should be noted. In the **Induction Step** of the proof, a new, bigger reach was used to enclose the newest adversary to its closest adversary neighbor. That new reach was then used for all of the adversaries. But in such a case, it might happen that some of other adversaries might end up swallowed up by some of the other adversaries. That is not a problem, since that would make a total new number of adversaries $\leq l$ but the assumption in the **Induction Step** states that the algorithms are valid for any n, such that $2 \leq n \leq l$. Therefore, the proof still stands.

7   Conclusions

Distribution grids will become increasingly more intelligent in the future, with the increased use of EVs, smart meters, IoT (Internet of Things) devices and similar. Therefore, they will have many points of input which a grid operator won't be able to constantly monitor, due to sheer number of the expected input points to arise in distribution grids. This multitude of input points will weaken the information security of the grid and is, therefore, something that should be planed for.

In this work, we presented a grid resilience optimization algorithm that grid architects and grid operators can use both while they are modelling future distribution grids and while they are updating and modernizing current grids with the additions of new sensors (which could be smart or not). With a multilayer grid model and multiple static adversaries in the Distribution Grid layer of the model as the input, the optimization algorithm presented in this work:

1. Finds a shortest and least uncertain path from as close as possible from the compromised area of Distribution Grid to the top layer of the Information Overlay, so that uncompromised information can reach a grid operator as soon as possible so that protective actions can be done in a timely manner and the damage, or the effect of an adversary, can be minimized.
2. Or, if the algorithm terminates without finding such a path, within a given edge budget, it proposes edge placement in Information Overlay such that the algorithm constraints can be satisfied and the shortest and least uncertain path can be found, meaning that a grid operator can get true information from the compromised part of the grid.

8   Future Work

In this work the problem was being solved for the case of static adversaries. However, adversaries can be dynamic and move around in a grid. They could also work together or against each other. They could have different goals. They could have different levels of executive powers. These are the problems we will work on in the future.

Additional complexity that will be looked into is as follows: Can the optimal path be improved and the model have more resilience if, instead of only having an edge budget (see (2.4)) there is also a sensor budget, that is, a budget for new nodes. That also immediately implies that the edge budget will have to be bigger than 1. Whether different ordering of the edge budget usage gives different results is something that will be also done in the future work.

References

1. Bellare, M., Pointcheval, D., Rogaway, P.: Authenticated key exchange secure against dictionary attacks. In: Preneel, B. (ed.) EUROCRYPT 2000. LNCS, vol. 1807, pp. 139–155. Springer, Heidelberg (2000). https://doi.org/10.1007/3-540-45539-6_11

2. Bellare, M., Rogaway, P.: Entity authentication and key distribution. In: Stinson, D.R. (ed.) CRYPTO 1993. LNCS, vol. 773, pp. 232–249. Springer, Heidelberg (1994). https://doi.org/10.1007/3-540-48329-2_21

3. Bellare, M., Rogaway, P.: Provably secure session key distribution: the three party case. In: Proceedings of the Twenty-Seventh Annual ACM Symposium on Theory of Computing, STOC 1995, pp. 57-66. Association for Computing Machinery, New York (1995). https://doi.org/10.1145/225058.225084

4. Benfenati, A., Chouzenoux, E., Duval, L., Pesquet, J.C., Pirayre, A.: A review on graph optimization and algorithmic frameworks. Research report, LIGM - Laboratoire d'Informatique Gaspard-Monge (2018). https://hal.science/hal-01901499

5. Cai, J.F., Wei, K.: Chapter 2 - exploiting the structure effectively and efficiently in low-rank matrix recovery. In: Kimmel, R., Tai, X.C. (eds.) Processing, Analyzing and Learning of Images, Shapes, and Forms: Part 1, Handbook of Numerical Analysis, vol. 19, pp. 21–51. Elsevier (2018). https://doi.org/10.1016/bs.hna.2018.09.001, https://www.sciencedirect.com/science/article/pii/S157086591830005X

6. Dantzig, G.B., Fulkerson, D.R.: 12. On the Max-flow Min-Cut Theorem of Networks, pp. 215–222. Princeton University Press, Princeton (1957). https://doi.org/10.1515/9781400881987-013

7. Datta, A., Franklin, J., Garg, D., Jia, L., Kaynar, D.: On adversary models and compositional security. IEEE Secur. Priv. **9**(3), 26–32 (2011). https://doi.org/10.1109/MSP.2010.203

8. Dijkstra, E.W.: A note on two problems in connexion with graphs. Numer. Math. **1**(1), 269–271 (1959). https://doi.org/10.1007/BF01386390

9. Dolev, D., Yao, A.: On the security of public key protocols. IEEE Trans. Inf. Theory **29**(2), 198–208 (1983). https://doi.org/10.1109/TIT.1983.1056650

10. Du, D.Z., Pardalos, P.M., Wu, W.: Linear Programming. In: Du, DZ., Pardalos, P.M., Wu, W. (eds.) Mathematical Theory of Optimization. Nonconvex Optimization and Its Applications, vol. 56, pp. 23–40. Springer, Boston (2001). https://doi.org/10.1007/978-1-4757-5795-8_2

11. Frisch, K.: The logarithmic potential method for convex programming. Institute of Economics (1955)

12. Gligor, V.D.: Position statement: on the evolution of adversary models in computer systems and networks. In: 2008 32nd Annual IEEE International Computer Software and Applications Conference, p. 10 (2008). https://doi.org/10.1109/COMPSAC.2008.237

13. Guo, Y., Yan, A., Wang, J.: Cyber security risk analysis of physical protection systems of nuclear power plants and research on the cyber security test platform using digital twin technology. In: 2021 International Conference on Power System Technology (POWERCON), pp. 1889–1892 (2021). https://doi.org/10.1109/POWERCON53785.2021.9697764

14. Hallquist, M.N., Hillary, F.G.: Graph theory approaches to functional network organization in brain disorders: a critique for a brave new small-world. Netw. Neurosci. **3**(1), 1–26 (2018). https://doi.org/10.1162/netn_a_00054

15. Hehong, H.: Construction of urban ecological water systems under perspective of information security. In: 2012 Fourth International Conference on Multimedia Information Networking and Security, pp. 580–583 (2012). https://doi.org/10.1109/MINES.2012.90

16. Kalman, L., Krauthgamer, R.: Flow metrics on graphs (2021). https://doi.org/10.48550/ARXIV.2112.06916

17. Kosut, O.: Max-flow min-cut for power system security index computation. In: 2014 IEEE 8th Sensor Array and Multichannel Signal Processing Workshop (SAM), pp. 61–64 (2014). https://doi.org/10.1109/SAM.2014.6882338

18. Kurniawan, B., Supangkat, S., Lumban Gaol, F., Ranti, B.: Framework for developing smart city models in Indonesian cities (based on Garuda smart city framework). In: 2022 International Conference on ICT for Smart Society (ICISS), pp. 01–05 (2022). https://doi.org/10.1109/ICISS55894.2022.9915073

19. Li, Z., He, Y., He, J.: Cluster construction and information security for the portal system of grade 3A traditional Chinese medicine hospitals under tertiary level protection. In: 2023 8th International Conference on Signal and Image Processing (ICSIP), pp. 1019–1023 (2023). https://doi.org/10.1109/ICSIP57908.2023.10270949

20. Gajić, N., Wolthusen, S.D.B.: Adaptable smart distribution grid topology generation for enhanced resilience. CRITIS2023 (2023)

21. Gajić, N., Wolthusen, S.D.B.: Improved topology generator with hierarchical information overlay. IFIP11.10 (2024)

22. Nickahdar, F.A., Khalifa, F.A.A.: Smart sustainable neighbourhood design: a prototype for Bahrain. In: 2nd Smart Cities Symposium (SCS 2019), pp. 1–6 (2019). https://doi.org/10.1049/cp.2019.0197

23. Oded, G.: Foundations of Cryptography: Volume 2, Basic Applications, 1st edn. Cambridge University Press, USA (2009)

24. Potebnia, A.: Construction of the comprehensive multi-layer graph model of the search spaces associated with the combinatorial optimization problems. In: 2017 4th International Scientific-Practical Conference Problems of Infocommunications. Science and Technology (PIC S&T), pp. 281–286 (2017). https://doi.org/10.1109/INFOCOMMST.2017.8246398

25. Rabanser, S., Neumann, L., Haltmeier, M.: Analysis of the block coordinate descent method for linear ill-posed problems. SIAM J. Imag. Sci. **12**(4), 1808–1832 (2019). https://doi.org/10.1137/19M1243956

26. Tibshirani, R.: Regression shrinkage and selection via the lasso. J. Roy. Stat. Soc. Ser. B (Methodol.) **58**(1), 267–288 (1996). http://www.jstor.org/stable/2346178

27. Vesselinova, N., Steinert, R., Perez-Ramirez, D.F., Boman, M.: Learning combinatorial optimization on graphs: a survey with applications to networking. IEEE Access **8**, 120388–120416 (2020). https://doi.org/10.1109/ACCESS.2020.3004964

28. Wu, Y., Takács-György, K.: Information security of food security. In: 2023 IEEE 21st World Symposium on Applied Machine Intelligence and Informatics (SAMI), pp. 000261–000266 (2023). https://doi.org/10.1109/SAMI58000.2023.10044492

29. Xia, F., Liu, J., Nie, H., Fu, Y., Wan, L., Kong, X.: Random walks: a review of algorithms and applications. IEEE Trans. Emerg. Top. Comput. Intell. 1–13 (2019). https://doi.org/10.1109/TETCI.2019.2952908

30. Xiang, Y., Wang, L., Liu, N.: Coordinated attacks on electric power systems in a cyber-physical environment. Electr. Power Syst. Res. **149**, 156–168 (2017). https://doi.org/10.1016/j.epsr.2017.04.023, https://www.sciencedirect.com/science/article/pii/S0378779617301700

31. Yang, J., Kwon, Y., Kim, D.: Regional smart city development focus: the South Korean national strategic smart city program. IEEE Access **9**, 7193–7210 (2021). https://doi.org/10.1109/ACCESS.2020.3047139
32. Yang, Y., Zhang, W., Dang, F., Yan, L., Liang, H.: Research on computer network information security and protection strategy based on internet of things. In: 2020 IEEE 3rd International Conference of Safe Production and Informatization (IICSPI), pp. 688–691 (2020). https://doi.org/10.1109/IICSPI51290.2020.9332399
33. Yimei, Y., Yujun, Y., Wang, Z., Hongbo, X., Wei, L.: A privacy protection mechanism for health big data based on XML. In: 2021 18th International Computer Conference on Wavelet Active Media Technology and Information Processing (ICCWAMTIP), pp. 450–455 (2021). https://doi.org/10.1109/ICCWAMTIP53232.2021.9674143
34. Zhang, H., Yang, H., Cao, X.: Design of real-time information security monitoring system for power grid. In: 2022 2nd International Conference on Electrical Engineering and Control Science (IC2ECS), pp. 366–371 (2022). https://doi.org/10.1109/IC2ECS57645.2022.10088039

Inoperability Propagation in Networks with Coupled Logistic Dynamics

Antonio Scala[1], Camilla Fioravanti[2], and Gabriele Oliva[2]([✉]) [ID]

[1] APPLICO Lab, CNR Institute for Complex Systems, Rome, Italy
antonio.scala@cnr.it
[2] Università Campus Bio-Medico di Roma, via Álvaro del Portillo 21,
00128 Rome, Italy
{c.fioravanti,g.oliva}@unicampus.it

Abstract. Networked infrastructures are essential for modern society but are vulnerable to various threats that can lead to significant disruptions. Traditional models often fail to capture the complex dynamics of these systems. To address this issue, we propose a novel framework based on coupled logistic dynamics, where each unit is represented as a node in a coupled logistic system. In this model, damage growth within individual nodes follows logistic patterns and propagates through interdependent units via coupling mechanisms. Our analysis demonstrates that degradation spreads radially across the network, with delays in damage that scale logarithmically with respect to the coupling strength and the distance from the initial failure. We conclude with numerical results that support our theoretical findings, offering insights into the resilience and vulnerability of networked infrastructures.

Keywords: Logistic growth · Cascading failures · Interdependent networks · System resilience · Damage propagation

1 Introduction

In modern society, networked infrastructures play a critical role in sustaining essential services, facilitating economic activities, and ensuring the well-being of communities. However, these infrastructures are vulnerable to various threats, including natural disasters, cyberattacks, equipment failures, and operational errors, which can lead to disruptions, downtime, and cascading failures with far-reaching consequences [1,4,11]. Understanding the dynamics of failures and inoperabilities in network infrastructures is essential for enhancing resilience, mitigating risks, and maintaining the reliability of critical systems.

Traditional approaches to modelling failures and inoperabilities in network infrastructures often rely on simplistic assumptions or linear frameworks that fail to capture the complex interdependencies and nonlinear dynamics inherent in these systems [5,10,12]. To address this limitation, we propose a novel modelling framework based on coupled logistic dynamics [6,9], which offers a more realistic

G. Oliva et al. (Eds.): CRITIS 2024, LNCS 15549, pp. 171–182, 2025.
https://doi.org/10.1007/978-3-031-84260-3_10

representation of the propagation and growth of damage within interconnected infrastructures.

Examples of logistic growth of damage within individual units or components of larger infrastructure systems include:

- **Transformer in a Power Grid:** A fault in a transformer can initially cause gradual increases in temperature or vibration. As the fault progresses, the degradation rate accelerates due to thermal runaway or insulation breakdown, leading to rapid damage growth. Eventually, the rate stabilizes as the trans former fails catastrophically or protective mechanisms, such as overcurrent relays or automatic shutdown systems, activate.
- **Critical Component in a Transportation System:** Components like bridges or tunnels can suffer damage from corrosion, fatigue, or structural deficiencies. Corrosion in a bridge, for example, may start slowly but accelerate as the structure's integrity deteriorates. The damage growth eventually stabilizes when the bridge approaches collapse or remediation measures, such as repairs or load restrictions, are implemented.
- **Network Router in a Communication Network:** Routers can experience faults from hardware malfunctions, software bugs, or cyberattacks. Initial faults may cause minor network disruptions, but as the faults propagate, the impact on performance escalates rapidly, leading to congestion and service outages. The damage growth stabilizes as failover mechanisms or redundancy features activate to restore normal operation or isolate the affected component.
- **Pump in a Water Distribution System:** Pumps can experience wear, mechanical failures, or cavitation issues. A fault may initially cause a gradual decrease in efficiency, but as it worsens, it leads to accelerated deterioration due to increased vibrations or overheating. The damage growth stabilizes as protective measures, such as automatic shutdown systems or maintenance protocols, activate.

In these examples, damage growth within a single unit or component typically follows a logistic pattern: slow initial progression, accelerating deterioration, and eventual stabilization as critical thresholds are reached or intervention measures are implemented.

Notice that, although to the best of our knowledge this work is the first modelling failure/inoperability propagation via coupled logistic dynamical networks, in recent literature logistic functions have been adopted as a convenient tool in the context of the study of cascading effects: in [2] a simulation-based model for the spread of failures is provided where the breakdown of the elements is modelled as a logistic function; in [13] the influence of the stress-dependent wear out on the failure propagation dynamics is modelled as a logistic function; in [7] a model for cascading failures in a network is developed where the probability that an overloaded node fails as a logistic function.

In our proposed framework, each unit or component within the network is modelled as a node in a coupled logistic system, where the growth of damage within a unit follows logistic patterns once it exceeds a certain threshold.

Moreover, the damage can propagate to interdependent units through coupling mechanisms, triggering logistic growth of damage in those units as well. This coupling captures the feedback loops, dependencies, and interactions present in networked infrastructures, where failures in one component can propagate and amplify throughout the system.

Specifically, under the assumption of logistic growth and considering a small coupling among the subsystems, an initial failure or damage affecting one unit leads to degradations in other systems that follow a similar logistic pattern. These degradations are essentially delayed versions of the original damage, with the same growth shape but shifted in time. Moreover, such degradation propagates radially in the network and the delay experienced by the units scales with the product of the logarithm of the coupling strength and the distance from the initiator in terms of the number of hops in the graph. Numerical results confirm the theoretical findings.

2   Materials and Methods

In this section, we present a comprehensive modeling framework to understand the dynamics of failures and inoperabilities in networked infrastructures characterized by logistic-like failure dynamics, which provide a realistic representation of damage propagation within interdependent systems.

This section is structured as follows:

1. After introducing some necessary preliminary definitions, we examine the dynamics of two interdependent systems governed by coupled logistic equations. This initial analysis allows us to understand the basic interactions and propagation mechanisms between a pair of systems. We identify the fixed points, analyze the stability, and derive the conditions under which the growth of damage follows logistic patterns.
2. Next, we extend the model to n interdependent systems. We generalize the coupled logistic equations to accommodate multiple systems, each influenced by its neighbours through a defined adjacency matrix. By applying perturbation theory, we derive the equations governing the evolution of damage in this multi-system framework. We explore the propagation of initial perturbations across the network and establish the scaling relationships for the delay in the spread of damage.
3. Finally, we introduce an algorithm for calculating the *path degeneracy*, z_{ii_0}, which measures the number of shortest paths from the initially perturbed node to other nodes in the network. This metric is crucial for understanding the distribution of dependencies and the potential for cascading failures. We provide a step-by-step procedure to compute z_{ii_0} using matrix operations and illustrate its application within the context of our coupled logistic framework.

2.1   Notation and Graph Theory

We denote vectors with boldface lowercase letters and matrices with uppercase letters.

Let $\mathcal{G} = \{\mathcal{V}, \mathcal{E}\}$ be a graph with N nodes $\mathcal{V} = \{v_1, v_2, \ldots, v_N\}$ and e edges $\mathcal{E} \subseteq \mathcal{V} \times \mathcal{V}$, where $(v_j, v_i) \in \mathcal{E}$ captures the existence of a link from node v_i to node v_j. A graph is said to be undirected if $(v_j, v_i) \in E$ whenever $(v_i, v_j) \in E$, while is said to be directed otherwise. In the following, we consider an undirected graph. An undirected graph is *connected* if each node can be reached by every other node via the edges. Let the neighbourhood $\mathcal{D}_i$ of a node $v_i \in \mathcal{V}$ be the set of nodes $v_j \in \mathcal{V}$ such that $(v_i, v_j) \in \mathcal{E}$; similarly, the p-neighborhood $\mathcal{D}_i^p$ of a node $v_i \in \mathcal{V}$ is the set of nodes $v_j \in \mathcal{V}$ such that the length of the minimum path from v_i to v_j is p. The *degree* d_i of a node v_i is the number of its incoming edges, i.e., $d_i = |\mathcal{D}_i|$. The *adjacency matrix* associated to a graph $\mathcal{G}$ with n nodes is the $n \times n$ matrix A such that its (i,j)-th entry a_{ij} is $a_{ij} = 1$ if $(v_j, v_i) \in E$ and $A_{ij} = 0$, otherwise.

2.2   Two Coupled Systems

Let us analyze the dynamics of two interdependent systems (referred to as system X and system Y) governed by coupled logistic equations:

$$\begin{cases} \dfrac{d\,y(t)}{dt} = y(t)(1 - y(t)) + \epsilon\, x(t)(1 - y(t)) \\[2mm] \dfrac{d\,x(t)}{dt} = x(t)(1 - x(t)) + \epsilon\, y(t)(1 - x(t)) \end{cases} \tag{1}$$

Here, $0 \le \epsilon \ll 1$ quantifies the interaction between systems X and Y. The system exhibits two fixed points: $(x, y) = (0, 0)$ (unstable) and $(x, y) = (1, 1)$ (stable).

Notice that when $x \gg \epsilon$ and $1 - x \gg \epsilon$, we can approximate its dynamics as $\frac{d\,x(t)}{dt} \approx x(t)(1 - x(t))$ (a similar result holds for for $\frac{d\,y(t)}{dt}$). This means that in a range $\Delta < x, y < 1 - \Delta$ with $\epsilon \ll \Delta \ll 1$, the growth of x has the same shape as the growth of y since $\epsilon \ll 1$; in particular, as clarified later in the text, they both exhibit logistic growth and will therefore appear as time-shifted versions of each other.

Suppose that at $t = 0$, $x(t)$ starts at 0 while $y(t)$ starts at a very small $y_0 \to 0$. When $y(t)$ is small, the term $y(t)(1 - y(t)) \approx y(t)$ dominates, leading to an initial exponential growth of $y(t)$. As $y(t)$ grows, the term $\epsilon y(t)$ becomes increasingly significant in the equation for $\frac{d\,x(t)}{dt}$; thus, $x(t)$ will also start growing, but since $\epsilon \ll 1$, $x(t)$ will remain relatively small compared to exponentially growing $y(t)$. Eventually, $x(t)$ will grow "almost logistically" in the region $[\Delta, 1 - \Delta]$, mirroring the previous growth of $y(t)$ in the same region.

To calculate the time shift, we need to understand how $x(t), y(t)$ reach values $\overline{x}, \overline{y} \approx \Delta$ with $\epsilon \ll \Delta \ll 1$ so that the approximation $\frac{d\,x(t)}{dt} \approx x(t)(1 - x(t))$, $\frac{d\,y(t)}{dt} \approx y(t)(1 - y(t))$ holds. To consider the growth away from the unstable fixed point, we analyze the linearized system:

$$\begin{cases} \frac{d\,y(t)}{dt} = y(t) + \epsilon\,x(t) \\[2mm] \frac{d\,x(t)}{dt} = x(t) + \epsilon\,y(t) \end{cases} \tag{2}$$

One approach to understanding this system's behaviour is to resort to perturbation theory: by expanding our functions in powers of ϵ,

$$\begin{cases} y(t,\epsilon) = y^{(0)}(t) + \epsilon y^{(1)}(t) + \dots \\ x(t,\epsilon) = x^{(0)}(t) + \epsilon x^{(1)}(t) + \dots \end{cases}$$

Equation (2) becomes

$$\begin{cases} \frac{d}{dt}\left(y^{(0)}(t) + \epsilon y^{(1)}(t) + \dots\right) = \left(y^{(0)}(t) + \epsilon y^{(1)}(t) + \dots\right) + \epsilon\left(x^{(0)}(t) + \epsilon x^{(1)}(t) + \dots\right) \\[2mm] \frac{d}{dt}\left(x^{(0)}(t) + \epsilon x^{(1)}(t) + \dots\right) = \left(x^{(0)}(t) + \epsilon x^{(1)}(t) + \dots\right) + \epsilon\left(y^{(0)}(t) + \epsilon y^{(1)}(t) + \dots\right) \end{cases}$$

This system is satisfied for every ϵ if all the terms corresponding to the same power in ϵ are equal, leading to:

$$\begin{cases} \dfrac{dy^{(0)}}{dt} = y^{(0)} \\[3mm] \dfrac{dx^{(0)}}{dt} = x^{(0)} \\[3mm] \dfrac{dy^{(1)}}{dt} = y^{(1)} + x^{(0)} \\[3mm] \dfrac{dx^{(1)}}{dt} = x^{(1)} + y^{(0)} \\[3mm] \dots \end{cases} \tag{3}$$

Notice that considering terms only up to the first order, the perturbation expansions of Eq. (1) and Eq. (2) yield the same equations for the evolution of $x^{(0)}$, $y^{(0)}$, $x^{(1)}$, and $y^{(1)}$; however, working with the linearised system facilitates keeping track of combinatorial factors. To satisfy the initial conditions $x(t = 0, \epsilon) = x_0$, $y(t = 0, \epsilon) = y_0$ for all ϵ, we impose the initial conditions $x^{(0)}(t = 0) = x_0$, $y^{(0)}(t = 0) = y_0$, and $x^{(k)}(t = 0) = y^{(k)}(t = 0) = 0$ for all $k > 0$.

Now, suppose the perturbation starts in system Y, i.e., $x(t = 0) = x_0 = 0$ and $y(t = 0) = y_0 \ll 1$. With the given initial conditions, we have that

$$y^{(0)}(t) = e^t y_0$$

and thus

$$y(t) = e^t y_0 + \mathcal{O}(\epsilon).$$

With the given initial conditions, $x^{(0)}(t) = 0$; thus, the first non-vanishing term is $x^{(1)}$ with initial condition $x^{(1)}(t = 0) = 0$:

$$\frac{dx^{(1)}(t)}{dt} = x^{(1)}(t) + y^{(0)}(t) = x^{(1)}(t) + e^t y_0$$

Thus, by solving the above differential equation, we have that

$$x^{(1)}(t) = \int_0^t e^{t-\tau} e^\tau y_0 \, d\tau = t e^t y_0$$

and hence

$$x(t) = \epsilon t e^t y_0 + O(\epsilon^2) \approx \epsilon t y(t) + O(\epsilon^2).$$

Since both $x(t)$ and $y(t)$ are growing, system X will reach the same state as system Y after a delay τ such that $x(t + \tau) = y(t)$.

Let us now characterize such delay τ. Considering only the smallest non-vanishing terms, we solve the following system of equations:

$$\begin{cases} x(t + \tau) = y(t) \\ x(t) \approx \epsilon y_0 t e^t = \epsilon y_0 f(t) \\ y(t) \approx y_0 e^t \end{cases} \tag{4}$$

where $f(w) = we^w$ and its inverse function is typically referred to as the *Lambert function* W [8]. In particular, for z real with $z \geq 3$, a reasonably accurate estimation[1] W_0 for the Lambert function is given by [3]:

$$W_0(z) = \ln z - \ln \ln z + \underbrace{\sum_{k=0}^{\infty} \sum_{m=0}^{\infty} c_{km} (\ln \ln z)^{m+1} (\ln z)^{-k-m-1}}_{\omega_{k,m}(z)}$$

For large real values of z, the term $\omega_{k,m}(z)$ in the above expression becomes negligible and we have that

$$W_0(z) \approx \ln(z) - \ln(\ln(z)) + o(1).$$

We are now in a position to characterize the delay τ. In particular, the equation $x(t + \tau) = y(t)$ yields

$$\epsilon(t + \tau)e^{t+\tau} = e^t,$$

i.e.,

$$(t + \tau)e^{t+\tau} = \frac{e^t}{\epsilon}.$$

At this point applying the Lambert function $W(\cdot)$ on both sides, and by considering the approximation $W_0(\cdot)$ we obtain

$$t + \tau = W\left(\frac{e^t}{\epsilon}\right) \approx W_0\left(\frac{e^t}{\epsilon}\right) \approx \ln\left(\frac{e^t}{\epsilon}\right) - \ln \ln\left(\frac{e^t}{\epsilon}\right) + o(1)$$

$$= t - \ln(\epsilon) - \ln(t - \ln(\epsilon)) + o(1)$$

---

[1] This term is the principal branch, see [3] for details.

and thus

$$\tau \approx -\ln(\epsilon) - \ln(t - \ln(\epsilon)) + o(1).$$

The above expression, apart from a logarithmic correction term $\ln(t - \ln(\epsilon))$, which is negligible for small ϵ, follows the scaling

$$\tau \sim -\ln(\epsilon). \tag{5}$$

2.3   Extension to n Subsystems

This reasoning can be extended to the dynamics of $i = 1, \ldots, n$ interdependent systems governed by coupled logistic equations:

$$\frac{d\, y_i(t)}{dt} = y_i(t)(1 - y_i(t)) + \left(\epsilon \sum_j a_{ij}\, y_j(t)\right)(1 - y_i(t)). \tag{6}$$

Here, the $n \times n$ adjacency matrix A with entries $a_{ij} \in \{0, 1\}$ represents dependencies among nodes ($a_{ij} = 1$ if system i depends on system j; $a_{ij} = 0$ otherwise) while ϵ measures the strength of the dependencies. The unperturbed system has two fixed points, one featuring $y_i = 0$ (unstable) and one with $y_i = 1$ (stable). Also in the perturbed case, the fixed points for the coupled systems are $y_i = 0\ \forall i$ (unstable) and $y_i = 1\ \forall i$ (stable).

To understand the growth away from the unstable fixed point, we linearize Eq. (6), obtaining

$$\frac{d\, y_i(t)}{dt} = y_i(t) + \epsilon \sum_j a_{ij} y_j(t). \tag{7}$$

Then, applying perturbation theory with $y_i(t) = \sum_{k=0}^{\infty} \epsilon^k y_i^{(k)}(t)$, we get:

$$\begin{cases} \dfrac{dy_i^{(0)}(t)}{dt} &= y_i^{(0)}(t) \\[2mm] \dfrac{dy_i^{(1)}(t)}{dt} &= y_i^{(1)}(t) + \sum_j a_{ij} y_j^{(0)}(t) \\[2mm] &\vdots \\[2mm] \dfrac{dy_i^{(k+1)}(t)}{dt} &= y_i^{(k+1)}(t) + \sum_j a_{ij} y_j^{(k)}(t) \\[2mm] &\vdots \end{cases} \tag{8}$$

Considering an initial scenario where only one node i_0 is perturbed (i.e., $y_k(0) = y_0$ if $k = i_0$, $y_k(0) = 0$ otherwise), we have that all the zero-th terms are null $y_k^{(0)}(t = 0) = 0$ for $k \neq i_0$ while only $y_{i_0}^{(0)}(t)$ is non-zero and equal to

$$y_{i_0}^{(0)}(t) = y_0 e^t.$$

Thus, the only nodes with a non-zero first term in the equation

$$\frac{dy_i^{(1)}}{dt} = y_i^{(1)} + \sum_j a_{ij} y_j^{(0)}$$

are the immediate neighbors of i_0, collected in the set $\mathcal{D}^1$ i.e.,

$$\begin{cases} \dfrac{d\, y_{i_1}^{(1)}(t)}{dt} &= y_{i_1}^{(1)} + y_0 e^t \\ y_{i_1}^{(1)}(t) &= y_0 t e^t \\ i_1 \in \mathcal{D}^1; \end{cases} \tag{9}$$

for all the other nodes, $y_i^{(1)}(t) = 0$. Similarly, nodes with a first non-vanishing term of second order in ϵ are in $\mathcal{D}^2$, with equations:

$$\begin{cases} \dfrac{d\, y_{i_2}^{(2)}(t)}{dt} &= y_{i_2}^{(2)} + \displaystyle\sum_{i_1 \in \mathcal{D}^1} y_{i_1}^{(1)} \\ y_{i_2}^{(2)}(t) &= y_0 \dfrac{t^2}{2} e^t \sum_{i_1 \in \mathcal{D}^1} a_{i_1 i_2} \\ i_2 \in \mathcal{D}^2 \end{cases} \tag{10}$$

Generalizing, nodes at distance k from the source have equations of the form:

$$\begin{cases} \dfrac{d\, y_{i_k}^{(k)}(t)}{dt} &= y_{i_k}^{(k)} + \displaystyle\sum_{i_{k-1} \in \mathcal{D}^{k-1}} a_{i_k i_{k-1}} y_{i_{k-1}}^{(k-1)} \\ y_{i_k}^{(k)}(t) &= y_0 \dfrac{t^k}{k!} e^t z_{i_k i_0} \\ z_{i_k i_0} &= \displaystyle\sum_{i_{k-1} \in \mathcal{D}^{k-1}} \cdots \sum_{i_1 \in \mathcal{D}^1} \sum_{i_0 \in \mathcal{D}^0} a_{i_k i_{k-1}} \cdots a_{i_2 i_1} a_{i_1 i_0} \\ i_k \in \mathcal{D}^k, \end{cases} \tag{11}$$

where $z_{i_k i_0}$ accounts for the number of shortest paths of the same length from i_0 to i_k.

Similarly to the case of two coupled subsystems, let us now identify the delay τ_{i_k} such that $y_{i_k}(t + \tau_{i_k}) = y_{i_1}(t)$. To this end, we observe that it holds

$$y_{i_k}(t) \approx \epsilon^k y_{i_k}^{(k)}(t) + \mathcal{O}(\epsilon^{k+1}) = \epsilon^k y_0 \frac{t^k}{k!} e^t z_{i_k i_0} + \mathcal{O}(\epsilon^{k+1}).$$

Therfore, the delay τ_{i_k} is such that

$$\epsilon^k y_0 \frac{(t + \tau_{i_k})^k}{k!} e^{t + \tau_{i_k}} z_{i_k i_0} = y_0 e^t.$$

At this point, let us assume that τ_{i_k} is large enough to have that $k \ln \tau_{i_k} \ll \tau_{i_k}$; thus we can also assume that $k \ln(t + \tau_{i_k}) \ll t + \tau_{i_k}$ since $t / \ln t$ is an increasing function. Therefore, applying $\ln(\cdot)$ to both members and using

$$\ln\left((t + \tau_{i_k})^k e^{t + \tau_{i_k}} \right) \approx t + \tau_{i_k}$$

for $\tau_{i_k} \gg 1$, we obtain

$$\tau_{i_k} \sim -k \ln \epsilon + \ln k! - \ln z_{i_k i_0}.$$

Notice that $A(x) \sim B(x)$ is used here to mean that A scales like B for large x, i.e., $A(x) - B(x) = f(x)$ with $f(x) \ll A(x)$, $f(x) \ll B(x)$. Thus, if the dynamics start from an operating/non-failed system with a small failure $y_0 \ll 1$ in the system i_0, the delay of the i-th system scales as

$$\tau_{i i_0} \sim -d_{i i_0} \ln(\epsilon) - \ln(z_{i i_0}) + \ln(d_{i i_0}!) \tag{12}$$

where $d_{i i_0}$ is the *chemical distance* (i.e., the length of the shortest path) from i_0 to i and $z_{i i_0}$ counts the number of shortest paths from i to i_0 with distance $d_{i i_0}$.

2.4 Algorithm for Calculating the Path Degeneracy

To calculate $z_{i i_0}$, note that the first term is simply $z_{i i_0} = a_{i i_0}$ for all i that are neighbours of i_0. By defining

$$\left[B^{(d)} \right]_{ij} = \begin{cases} a_{ij} & \text{for } i \in \mathcal{D}^d \wedge j \in \mathcal{D}^{d-1} \\ 0 & \text{otherwise} \end{cases} \tag{13}$$

and $Z^{(d)} = \prod_{k=1}^{d} B^{(k)}$, we have that the matrix coefficients (even without the tree approximation) for elements at minimum distance $k + 1$ are:

$$\sum_{j_k \in \mathcal{D}^k, \ldots, j_2 \in \mathcal{D}^2, j_1 \in \mathcal{D}^1} a_{i j_k} a_{j_k j_{k-1}} \cdots a_{j_2 j_1} a_{j_1 0} = \left[Z^{(k+1)} \right]_{i i_0}. \tag{14}$$

Thus, the algorithm for computing $z_{i i_0}$ (using just for short the case of the dynamics starting from site 0) can be summarized as follows.

Algorithm 1. Compute $z_{i i_0}$ for all nodes

Calculate the minimum distance matrix $d_{i i_0}$
Calculate the diameter $D = \max_i d_{i i_0}$
$\mathcal{D}^0 \leftarrow \{i_0\}$
$z_{i_0 i_0} \leftarrow 1$
for $k = 1 \ldots D$ **do**
    $\mathcal{D}^k \leftarrow \{i : d_{i i_0} = k\}$
    for $i \in \mathcal{D}^k$ **do**
        $z_{i i_0} \leftarrow \sum_{j \in \mathcal{D}^{k-1}} a_{ij} z_{j i_0}$
    end for
end for

---

3 Results

In this section, we present the results of numerical simulations validating the theoretical predictions derived from our modeling framework. We focus on two scenarios: the dynamics of two interdependent systems governed by coupled logistic equations and the dynamics of a network of interdependent systems.

3.1   Interdependent Systems

First, we investigate the dynamics of two interdependent systems described by coupled logistic equations. Our theoretical analysis predicted that the delay in the failure of one system, given the failure of the other, scales logarithmically with the coupling strength. To verify this prediction, we performed numerical simulations varying the coupling strength ϵ over a range of values.

Figure 1 illustrates the relationship between the coupling strength ϵ and the corresponding delay τ in the failure of the second system, given the failure of the first. The numerical results align closely with the theoretical prediction, confirming that the delay indeed scales logarithmically with ϵ. Linear fits to the numerical data further support the validity of our theoretical analysis.

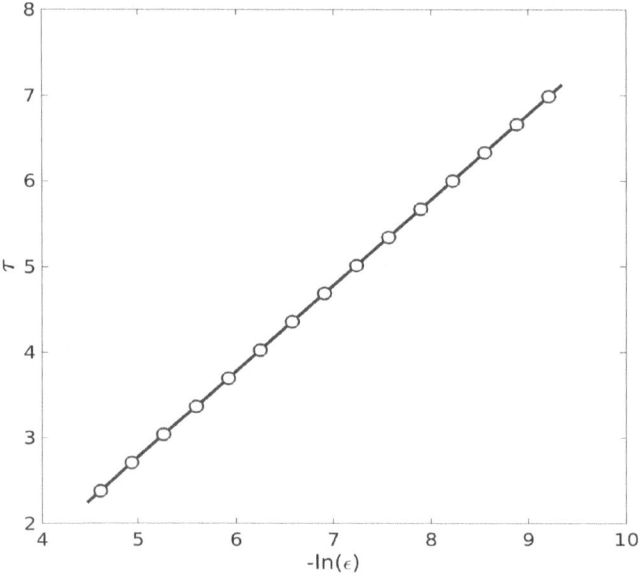

Fig. 1. By numerical solutions of the model, it is possible to estimate the delays τ as a function of the coupling ε. The numerical delays τ follows the theoretical prediction of Eq. 5 that assert that if a system Y fails, a system X dependent with intensity ε on X will fail with a delay τ that scales as $\tau \sim -\ln \epsilon$. We consider values of ε in $[10^{-4}, 10^{-2}]$ with initial conditions $y(t = 0) = 10^{-6}$. Continuous lines are linear fit to the numerical data.

3.2   Network of Interdependent Systems

Next, we extend our analysis to a network of interdependent systems, where the failure of one system can propagate through the network, affecting interconnected systems. Our theoretical framework predicted that the delay in the failure of a system within the network scales logarithmically with the number of shortest paths connecting it to the initially failed system, as well as with the coupling strength.

Figure 2 presents the results of numerical simulations conducted on 100 random networks of interdependent systems. The plot demonstrates the logarithmic scaling of the delay τ with both the number of shortest paths connecting the failed system to the target system and the coupling strength ϵ. Linear fits to the numerical data confirm the consistency of our theoretical predictions with the simulated results.

Overall, our numerical simulations validate the theoretical framework proposed in this study, providing empirical evidence for the logarithmic scaling of delays in the failure of interdependent systems. These results underscore the importance of understanding system interdependencies and dynamics in enhancing the resilience and reliability of networked infrastructures.

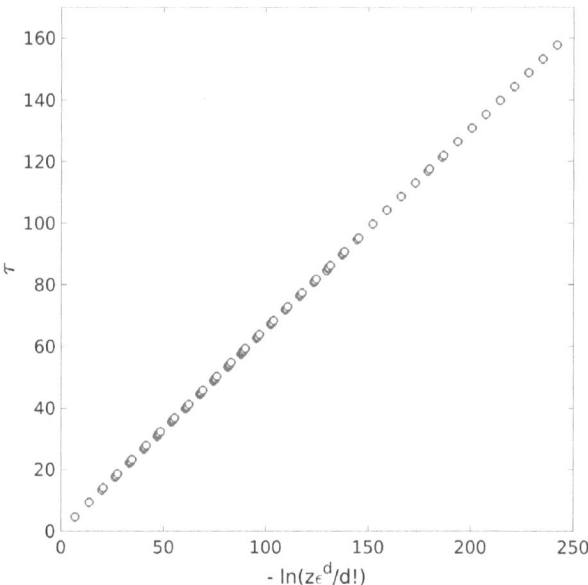

Fig. 2. By numerical solutions of the model, it is possible to estimate the delays τ as a function of the coupling ε. The numerical delays τ follows the theoretical prediction of Eq. (12) that assert in a network of n elements where the i_0-th system fails, a system i connected by z shortest paths of length d to i_0 fails with a delay τ that scales as $\tau \sim -\ln(z\epsilon^d/d!)$. We plot the results for 100 networks of $n = 50$ interdependent systems with average degree $k = 2.4$, coupling strength $\varepsilon = 10^{-3}$ and initial conditions $y_{i_0}(t = 0) = 10^{-6}$.

4   Conclusion

This study introduces a novel framework using coupled logistic dynamics to model the propagation and growth of damage in networked infrastructures. Traditional models often fail to capture the complexity of these systems, but our approach provides a more realistic representation by considering interdependencies and nonlinear dynamics.

Key findings include:

1. **Logarithmic Scaling:** The delay in failure propagation scales logarithmically with both the coupling strength and the number of shortest paths connecting the initial failure to the affected system.
2. **Radial Propagation:** Damage spreads radially, with delays increasing with the coupling strength and distance from the initial failure.

Numerical simulations support these theoretical results, emphasizing the importance of understanding interdependencies for enhancing system resilience. Future research should focus on incorporating real-world data and exploring advanced modeling techniques to improve predictive capabilities and risk management strategies.

References

1. Andrew, L., et al.: The vulnerability of vital systems: how 'critical infrastructure' became a security problem. In: Securing 'the Homeland', pp. 17–39. Routledge (2020)
2. Buzna, L., Peters, K., Helbing, D.: Modelling the dynamics of disaster spreading in networks. Phys. A **363**(1), 132–140 (2006)
3. Corless, R.M., Gonnet, G.H., Hare, D.E.G., Jeffrey, D.J., Knuth, D.E.: On the LambertW function. Adv. Comput. Math. **5**(1), 329–359 (1996). https://doi.org/10.1007/BF02124750
4. De Felice, F., Baffo, I., Petrillo, A.: Critical infrastructures overview: past, present and future. Sustainability **14**(4), 2233 (2022)
5. Haimes, Y.Y., Horowitz, B.M., Lambert, J.H., Santos, J.R., Lian, C., Crowther, K.G.: Inoperability input-output model for interdependent infrastructure sectors. I: Theory Methodol. J. Infrastruct. Syst. **11**(2), 67–79 (2005)
6. Hastings, A.: Complex interactions between dispersal and dynamics: lessons from coupled logistic equations. Ecology **74**(5), 1362–1372 (1993)
7. Kim, M., Kim, J.S.: A model for cascading failures with the probability of failure described as a logistic function. Sci. Rep. **12**(1), 989 (2022)
8. Lehtonen, J.: The Lambert W function in ecological and evolutionary models. Methods Ecol. Evol. **7**(9), 1110–1118 (2016)
9. Marti, A., Masoller, C.: Delay-induced synchronization phenomena in an array of globally coupled logistic maps. Phys. Rev. E **67**(5), 056219 (2003)
10. Oliva, G., Panzieri, S., Setola, R.: Agent-based input-output interdependency model. Int. J. Crit. Infrastruct. Prot. **3**(2), 76–82 (2010)
11. Pescaroli, G., Nones, M., Galbusera, L., Alexander, D.: Understanding and mitigating cascading crises in the global interconnected system (2018)
12. Santos, J., Roquel, K.I.D.Z., Lamberte, A., Tan, R.R., Aviso, K.B., Tapia, J.F.D., Solis, C.A., Yu, K.D.S.: Assessing the economic ripple effects of critical infrastructure failures using the dynamic inoperability input-output model: a case study of the Taal Volcano eruption. Sustain. Resilient Infrast. **8**(sup1), 68–84 (2023)
13. Schläpfer, M., Shapiro, J.L.: Modeling failure propagation in large-scale engineering networks. In: Zhou, J. (ed.) Complex 2009, Part 2. LNICSSITE, vol. 5, pp. 2127–2138. Springer, Heidelberg (2009). https://doi.org/10.1007/978-3-642-02469-6_89

Resilience Analysis of Naval Vessels with i2SIM

Kirollos M. Morcos[2] , Andrea T. J. Martí[1] , and José R. Martí[2(✉)]

[1] Department of Civil Engineering, The University of British Columbia,
Vancouver, B.C. V6T 1Z4, Canada
[2] Department of Electrical and Computer Engineering, The University of British Columbia,
Vancouver, B.C. V6T 1Z4, Canada
`jrms@ece.ubc.ca`

Abstract. Naval vessels are complex systems operating under stress and critical conditions. The interdependencies among the ship systems make the optimal paths to repair to be not obvious. The Infrastructures Interdependencies Simulator (i2SIM) is used to evaluate the resilience of naval vessels during mission-critical operations when faults occur in their electrical system. Through modelling the interdependencies, i2SIM finds the optimum restoration pathway that will bring back as much of the vessel's functionality as possible as fast as possible, therefore enhancing the ship's resilience. This paper presents a systematic methodology to set up the i2SIM model of a ship. Use cases are presented comparing response pathways without and with i2SIM.

Keywords: Naval Vessels · Resilience · Interdependencies

1 Introduction

Given the severe consequences of failures, resilient design is critical for naval fleets. The ship's propulsion system is a key element of this resilience. Traditionally, the focus when designing the propulsion system has been performance and operational efficiency. However, as modern naval vessels grow in complexity, understanding the system's interdependencies has become essential to restoring the ship's operability as much as possible and as quickly as possible after a fault [1–4]. This paper presents a number of ship systems' failure scenarios to show the importance of interdependencies and of optimizing the allocation of resources. The Infrastructures Interdependencies Simulator, i2SIM, and its optimization capabilities are used for the analysis of these cases. The analysis of the ship systems' integration is becoming an important part of naval architecture disciplines as it directly impacts the vessel cost, capability, and survivability. The optimizations presented here apply to the operation of a single ship. For a group of vessels, the individual roles of the ships can be integrated using i2SIM into a global combined objective for which each ship becomes a subsystem. However, this is beyond the scope of this paper.

© The Author(s), under exclusive license to Springer Nature Switzerland AG 2025
G. Oliva et al. (Eds.): CRITIS 2024, LNCS 15549, pp. 183–194, 2025.
https://doi.org/10.1007/978-3-031-84260-3_11

1.1 Resilience of Naval Ships

Interdependence modelling has yet to be widely used in naval vessel systems [10–12]. Most studies focus on individual components and individual subsystems without considering interdependencies and optimal restoration paths. Among the subsystems that are essential for the ship's integrity are the propulsion system, the communication system, the controllers, and the human factors [4–7].

Naval Ship Codes. Merchant vessels operate under international regulations governed by the International Maritime Organization (IMO), and safety is a major concern. On the other hand, naval forces strive to strike a balance between safety and military capabilities, ensuring that their peacetime operations meet an acceptable standard of safety. In contrast, military applications are focused on the success of the mission. The peacetime operations are normally aligned with the safety standards applied to merchant ships and civilian regulations.

However, the primary safety document issued by the IMO, the *Safety of Life at Sea* (SOLAS) [8], is not fully suitable for many naval vessels due to the unique design and operational requirements of military operations. The military operation requirements often conflict with SOLAS provisions, and in certain instances, adhering to SOLAS can compromise the ship's military capabilities.

Recognizing these challenges, NATO established in 2004 a specialized team consisting of naval forces and classification societies. Their goal was to develop a naval equivalent to SOLAS. After four years of collaborative effort, they produced the *Naval Ship Code* [9]. This code was designed to provide safety assurance in line with legal standards while still employing universally recognized common standards that acknowledge the specific operational needs of military vessels.

The Naval Ship Code warns against using certain chapters and topics of SOLAS because "many hazards are interdependent" [9]. This warning highlights the importance of developing a comprehensive approach to studying these interdependencies. The work presented in this document attempts to contribute to this task.

Disaster Recovery Plans. Disaster recovery plans are needed to make quick decisions in remote mission vessels and military vessels during emergencies, redirect the use of undamaged resources quickly and effectively, and promptly repair the damaged systems. A number of methodologies have been proposed to analyze system interdependencies and develop *realistic* disaster response plans [10–20]. In this paper, the Infrastructure Interdependencies Simulator i2SIM [21–23] is used to evaluate proposed restoration strategies for naval vessels.

2 Methodology

The first step to developing disaster response plans is to understand and collect data describing the systems, subsystems, and their interdependencies [3, 29]. For decisions at the operational level, it is not necessary to understand the physics of the behaviour of individual components such as generators, electrical circuits, control systems, etc., but how these systems interact with each other, such as how the output of one system or component is needed at the input of another system or component. These relationships can be shown in high-level operability diagrams or Entity Relationship Diagrams (ERD), such as the one in Fig. 2 for the ship systems. The next step in studying the behaviour of the combined system is to quantify how much of the output from one entity is needed to operate another entity. Often, these relationships are nonlinear but can be represented in a general interdependencies simulator like i2SIM [23].

For our study of naval vessels, we first identified the critical specific components and subsystems. We then collected data on their input-output characteristics, such as size, weight, and power requirements [24]. Ship models and manufacturer data sheets were used to develop the relationships among system components. Incident reports were used to identify how these components interact with the social and cyber systems.

Probabilistic data was used for two purposes. One is to prioritize the type of faults and events that are most likely to occur. The second is to establish the granularity of the relationships between input and output transfer blocks in the i2SIM simulator. If historical or probabilistic data is unavailable, high-level design parameters and component limits can be used to estimate these relationships [28].

Key subsystems in the naval vessel propulsion system include engines and their auxiliary subsystems, like the lubrication and cooling subsystems. Other major systems include communications, navigation, and combat systems.

2.1   The i2SIM Simulator

The i2SIM simulator [21] is a mathematical implementation of the high-level concept of the Input-Output production model proposed by Leontief for economic production sectors [25], extended to consider nonlinear relationships and non-physics relationships like component ageing and human factors. i2SIM has been used for a number of disaster response studies [14, 19, 20, 22] and, more recently, for resilience evaluation of climate-change-related resilience during disasters [26]. In i2SIM, the Input-Output production units are called Cells. The functional relationship between the inputs and output of a Cell is defined by physics (e.g., electricity laws) or experience (e.g., how many patients per hour a physician can work on a shift before getting tired). The links that connect the output of Cells to the inputs of other Cells are called Channels. Channels can have delays associated with transportation time (e.g., a vehicle) or with the time needed to carry out an action (e.g., time to repair a damaged unit).

Figure 1 is an example of an HRT for a Cell. The cell's output is the electrical power needed for the ship. The inputs are the fuel (Diesel Oil), the Lubricant System, and the Cooling System. When Oil, Lubricant, and Cooling are at their maximum values, the power output is 10 MW. If, due to a problem, the oil is limited to 712 kg, the Lubricant System is still 100% of its normal value, but the Cooling System is 50% of its normal value due to a mechanical failure. As a consequence of the cooling system failure, the output of the Power-Generated HRT (Fig. 1) has to be limited to 5 MW so as not to overheat the generators. The output becomes limited by the least available input, which is the health of the cooling jacket. The value of the other inputs does not matter as long as they are greater or equal to their value in the output row (475 kg for the oil and 50% for the lubricant system). To prioritize the system restoration when the outputs are limited by least-available resources, i2SIM has an optimizer that will determine which limiting resource needs to be improved first, second, etc. For each Cell, the optimizer algorithm will increase the limiting resource until the next limiting resource is reached. For example, in Fig. 1, the Cooling System health will be increased to the next row above, to 75%, when Diesel Oil becomes a co-limiting factor. The same principle is used for the other Cells in the system. We call this method "Pari Passu" or "with synchronized step". This strategy achieves very fast convergence, and it is suited for real-time applications.

The inputs and the output of an HRT can be physical quantities. In addition, they can also be component states (e.g., how old the component is or how often maintenance is performed) and human states (for example, the amount of training of a specialist in the lubrication subsystem).

The entities exchanged among Cells are called Tokens. Examples of Tokens are electricity, lubricant, cooling, or repair personnel. Output Tokens, such as electricity, can be split into "slices" and sent to the Cells that use electricity. The Distributors do this splitting, and the percentage of the split can be controlled externally by the user or automatically by the software during resource optimization. Using the automatic option of splitting the resources at the Distributors allows the software to find an allocation that results in the largest output of the Objective Cell (optimum solution). Inputs of the same type, such as electric power from different sources, can be aggregated in Aggregators before they are delivered to Cells.

Power Generated MW (Output)	Diesel Oil kg	Lubricant System Health %	Cooling System Health %
10	950	**100**	100
7.5	**712**	80	75
5	475	50	50
2.5	237	20	25
0	0	0	0

Fig. 1. Human Readable Table (HRT) for the Diesel Engine Cell, where the power generated (5 MW) is the available output; the Cooling System Health is the limiting input, and the Lubricant system health and Diesel oil are the non-limiting inputs.

The relationships between inputs and outputs and the connections among Cells form a system of algebraic nonlinear equations. For a given Cell, the relationship between inputs and output is first established as a Table ("The Human Readable Table," HRT). Because these relationships are defined in a table form, it is possible to relate physical variables (for example, the number of transformers needed to transfer a certain amount of electrical power) and human variables (for example, the time that will be required to repair a certain component in terms of the level of training and skill of the repair technician). The number of rows in this table depends on the certainty we have of the specific value of this relationship. For example, if we have five rows (Fig. 1), this means that we know the value of the quantities in each row with a certainty of at least 20%.

The input-output relationships in the HRT table are translated into mathematical functions by fitting the discrete relationships with nonlinear, continuous, rational, and exponential functions (poles and zeroes). After this fitting, the values between rows in the HRT become "known" by interpolation. An important mathematical/physical concept in this interpolation is the concept of analyticity. The interpolating functions are nonlinear but monotonical and analytical. They have a well-defined slope at each point and satisfy the Cauchy-Riemann condition. The system of algebraic equations is then solved by numerical iterations and numerical optimization.

3 Case Study: Combined Diesel and Gas Propulsion System

3.1 I2SIM Model

As an example of the methodology, we consider a simplified system of a combined diesel and gas (CODAG) ship and how to recover from a contingency optimally. The example can be extended to other ship systems and topologies, such as fully electric propulsion systems, hybrid propulsion, or traditional mixed fuel systems.

Figure 2 below shows the Entity Relationship Diagram (ERD) used to build the i2SIM Schematic model shown in Fig. 3. Tables 1 and 2 below show examples of cell HRTs for this case.

As shown in Fig. 3, the prime movers' combined power output is distributed to various ship subsystems. When there is a failure, this output can decrease and needs to be redistributed to obtain a maximum value of the Operability Cell. The Operability Cell needs to be maintained at its maximum possible value. In our case study, we define this operability based on three factors: the propulsion system health, the control system health, and the combat system health. The three factors are modelled as cells feeding into the Operability Cell. Their relative weight is modelled in the HRT for the Operability Cell.

The i2SIM Schematic diagram of Fig. 3 implements the functions of the ERD diagram of Fig. 2.

In addition to Cells, Channels, Aggregators, and Distributors, an i2SIM schematic has external inputs, called Sources, and external outputs, called Sinks. Sources allow the connection to the system of external tokens or control signals in real-time. In this example, we use Sources to supply Diesel and Natural Gas fuel tokens and to provide manual control to distributors. In the i2SIM schematic (Fig. 3), there must be a global output cell that represents the global objective function of the i2SIM optimization. In this case, the global objective is the ship's operability. This objective can change, for instance, from a peacetime operation to a combat operation.

The output of the Operability Cell in the schematic is a Sink (what goes "out of the diagram"). In this case, it is information on how close the optimum state is achieved.

Another Sink represents the Auxiliary Systems, which are not directly part of the Operability Objective and include the hotel loads, such as non-emergency lighting, heating, and entertainment loads. The Manual Override Source is used to represent different integrity states, such as when a part needs servicing or has been damaged by an attack. Similarly, the system's topology can be altered manually.

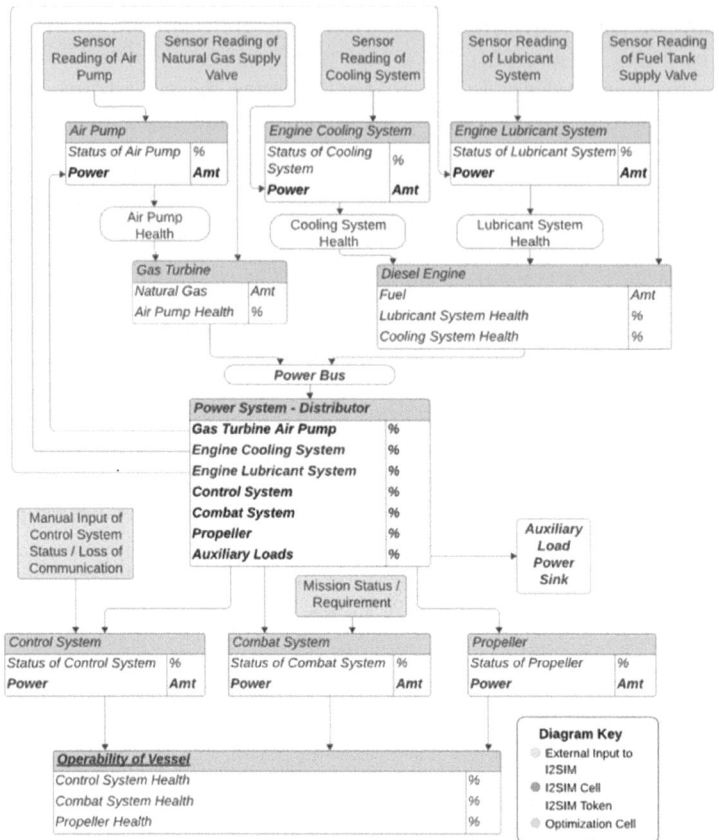

Fig. 2. Entity Relationship Diagram (ERD) for the i2SIM Model

3.2 Failure Scenarios

Five failure scenarios were simulated to demonstrate the capability of using i2SIM to achieve optimal functionality with reduced resources after each failure.

The results of i2SIM's optimization on these scenarios are shown in Table 1. Tables 2 and 3 show the HRTs affected by the failure before i2SIM's optimization. The details in these tables are further discussed following this general description. In Table 1, the first column (a) shows the case without i2SIM when the resource distribution is not changed, while the second column (b) shows the result when the distribution of resources is optimized by i2SIM.

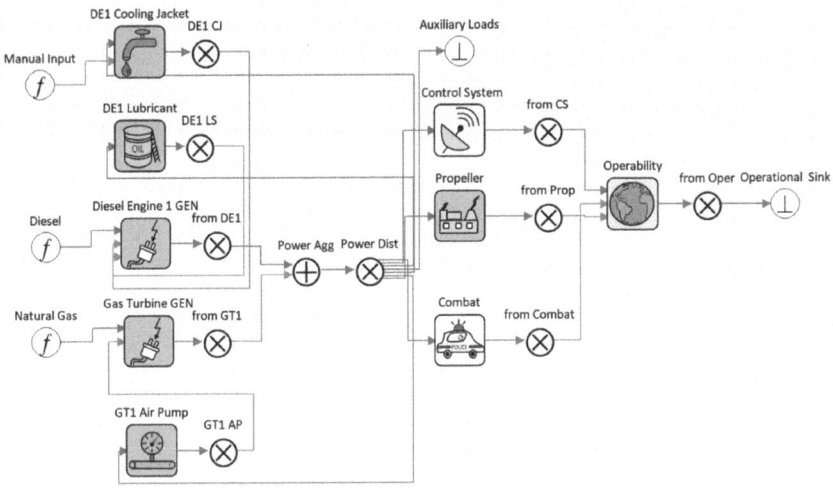

Fig. 3. i2SIM Schematic for the Ship System

Scenario #1 considers a partial failure of one of the major subsystems in the engine room, *the cooling jacket*. Due to clogging in the tubes, the water circulation capacity is limited to 50% of the original flow. This scenario highlights the effect of an unseeingly minor failure and how it causes strong cascading failures across the system. Table 1 shows that i2SIM's optimization resulted in a 15% higher Operability.

Scenario #2 looks at a *cyber-attack*. Often, cyber-attacks target the sensor systems of the vessel. In this scenario, the attackers feed incorrect readings to the integrated bridge system (IBS). (In other scenarios, the attackers could "steal" information so that the operators would be left wondering what the status of critical systems is [27]). As a result of the IBS receiving incorrect data from the cooling jacket sensors, an incorrect action will be taken. However, with i2SIM in place, in real-time mode, the internal algorithm detects that this reading is inconsistent with the other readings as related by the input-output relationships given by i2SIM. Using the manual override function in i2SIM, the incorrect data is ignored, and (after manually verifying the information) operation is resumed, assuming correct data from the cooling jacket. Table 1 shows that i2SIM's optimization resulted in a 15% higher Operability.

Scenario #3 emulates a *combat scenario* in which the demand for power for the combat system is increased due to a change in the vessel's normal operational functional profile to a combat profile. Table 1 shows that i2SIM's optimization resulted in a 30% higher Operability.

Scenario #4 involves two *simultaneous failures*. In this scenario, the diesel engine's cooling jacket and the gas turbine's air pump are partially damaged due to an attack on the ship. Both subsystems now operate at 75% capacity. In this case, i2SIM's optimization did not change the results.

Scenario #5 also considers two simultaneous failures. Only this time, the damage is to the cooling jacket and the lubricating system. Both systems serve the same power source, the diesel engine. Both subsystems are now operating at 50% capacity. I2SIM's optimization resulted in an improvement of 10% in the operability.

Table 1. Failure Scenarios. Operability Output: (a) No Redistribution vs (b) i2SIM Optimized

Failure Scenario	(a) Operability Not Redistributing Resources	(b) Operability with i2SIM Optimized Redistribution	Improvement
Scenario 1	62%	77%	15%
Scenario 2	85%	100%	15%
Scenario 3	60%	90%	30%
Scenario 4	83%	83%	0%
Scenario 5	62%	72%	10%

HRTs for the Scenarios. Tables 2 and 3 below show the HRTs for the Scenarios. Under normal operating conditions, at full capacity, these tables operate on Row 1 (100%). During the contingency considered, the output of the tables drops to less than 100% (italic) due to the limitation in input resources (bold). Notice that the lowest percent-value column (least available resource) determines the output value (Operating row).

The HRT tables affected by the contingencies in the scenarios are described next.

In scenario #1, the power initially delivered to the cooling jacket is reduced to 50% since the jacket's operability is capped at 50%. The optimizer also reduced the amount of power going to the lubricant. This action is because the output of the cooling jacket will still limit the diesel engine's performance. The excess power was routed to the Sink (the auxiliary loads). i2SIM successfully identified waste and optimally redistributed the useful power.

In scenario #2, we show that when the tampered-with sensor gives incorrect information, the users can manually override the data. For example, the attack showed that the available power input was 0.75 MW instead of 1 MW, limiting the control system output to 75%. The i2SIM model detected the inconsistency in the data, and the operator manually applied the correct setting.

In scenario #3, the combat system's power demand is doubled. If the system were to continue distributing power as before, the ship's operability would have dropped to 60%. In this case, i2SIM reduces the power given to the control system and raises the power supplied to the combat system. This allocation ensures that the other systems are still operational at reasonable values and optimizes the ship's combat capability.

In scenario #4, the two subsystems that generate electricity are equally affected, and changing the input to one of the systems is detrimental to the other system and results in a lower value of the global objective function. The i2SIM optimizer correctly identified this situation and did not redistribute the resource.

In scenario #5, unlike scenario #4, both subsystems affected by the fault affect only one of the power suppliers, the diesel engine. The power sent to the cooling jacket

Table 2. HRT Cells for Failure Scenarios 1, 2, and 3

Cooling System Health % (Output)	Operability from Sensor Reading %	Power Required MW	Control System Health % (Output)	Power Required MW
100	100	1	100	1
75	75	0.75	75	0.75
50	50	0.5	50	0.5
25	25	0.25	25	0.25
0	0	0	0	0
Scenario 1			**Scenario 2**	

Combat System % (Output)	Power Required MW
100	1
80	0.8
60	0.6
40	0.4
20	0.2
0	0
Scenario 3	

Table 3. HRT Cells for Failure Scenarios 4 and 5

Cooling System Health % (Output)	Operability from Sensor Reading %	Power Required MW	Air-Pump Health % (Output)	Operability from Sensor Reading %	Power Required MW
100	100	1	100	100	4
75	75	0.75	75	75	3
50	50	0.5	50	50	2
25	25	0.25	25	25	1
0	0	0	0	0	0
Scenario 4					

Cooling System Health % (Output)	Operability from Sensor Reading %	Power Required MW	Lubricant System Health % (Output)	Operability from Sensor Reading %	Power Required MW
100	100	1	100	100	3
75	75	0.75	75	75	2.3
50	50	0.5	50	50	1.5
25	25	0.25	25	25	0.75
0	0	0	0	0	0
Scenario 5					

and lubricating system serving the diesel engine is rerouted to the air pump, allowing a maximum output for the gas turbine.

4 Conclusion

Due to their isolation from rescue operations, the vital systems in maritime vessels need to be very resilient, particularly in high-sea or mission-critical operations. The systems must be capable of resuming operations as fast as possible and make optimum use of the undamaged systems and resources. The work in this paper has been sponsored by a grant to develop optimized resilience approaches for commercial and navy vessels equipped with the next generation of propulsion, communications, and control resources.

The Infrastructures Interdependencies Simulator i2SIM has been used for these studies because it can represent complex systems interdependencies. I2SIM also includes an Optimizer that can automatically redistribute the available input resources to the operating units based on the Pari Passu principle of increasing the limiting resource one row at a time. This optimizer is very fast and can find the optimum path in real-time.

Multiple failure scenarios were analyzed, showing that alternative paths can restore performance optimally automatically after a failure. In the failure scenarios presented, the i2SIM Optimizer increased the ship's operability by as much as 30%.

The knowledge of the critical failure and recovery paths during the phase of ship design will indicate where more investment should be placed and eventually lead to better and more economical designs. For example, reducing repair times by using more skilled personnel or carrying certain spare parts can make a significant difference.

Acknowledgments. This study was funded with support from the NSERC Alliance Grant "Integrated Design and Operation of Efficient and Resilient Shipboard Electric Power Systems." (Grant number 431401578).

References

1. Brefort, D., Shields, C.P., et al.: An architectural framework for distributed naval ship systems. Ocean Eng. **147**, 375–385 (2018). https://doi.org/10.1016/j.oceaneng.2017.10.028
2. Van Leeuwen, S.: Estimating the vulnerability of ship distributed system topologies. Master of Science in Marine Engineering, Delft University of Technology (2017)
3. Løvmo, S.A.: Analysis of potential critical equipment and technical system on a modern PSV. Recommending a method for Troms Offshore Management AS. Master thesis in Technology and Safety in the High North, The Arctic University of Norway (2016)
4. Worlton, T.J., Shwayhat, A.F., et al.: US navy ship-based disaster response: lessons learned. Current Trauma Rep. **8**, 138–146 (2022). https://doi.org/10.1007/s40719-022-00227-3
5. Allensworth, T.J., Schuster, J.G.: Adding resilience to naval systems for mission success. Johns Hopkins APL Tech. Digest **34**(4) (2019)
6. Hasanspahić, N., Vujičić, S., et al.: The role of the human factor in marine accidents. J. Marine Sci. Eng. **9**, 261 (2021). https://doi.org/10.3390/jmse9030261
7. Rumawas, V.: Human factors in ship design and operation. Ph.D. thesis, Norwegian University of Science and Technology NTNU (2016)

8. The International Naval Safety Association: Naval Ship Code (2004) https://navalshipcode. org/publiccodes. Accessed 26 May 2024
9. The International Naval Safety Association, Part 1: Naval Ship Code, ANEP-77 (2022)
10. Mussington, D.: Concepts for enhancing critical infrastructure protection: relating Y2K to CIP research and development. Rand's RAND's Science and Technology Policy Institute for the Office of Science and Technology, Contract ENG-9812731 (2002)
11. Han, Y., Chen, W., Liu, F.: The interdependence ranking method and failure mitigation strategy for cyber-physical power system. In: 3rd International Conference on Advanced Electrical and Energy Systems (AEES), pp. 297–302 (2022). https://doi.org/10.1109/AEES56284.2022. 10079308
12. Parshani, R., Rozenblat, C., et al.: Inter-similarity between coupled networks. EPL (Europhys. Lett.) **92**, 68002 (2010). https://doi.org/10.1209/0295-5075/92/68002
13. Arghandeh, R., Meier, A.V., et al.: On the definition of cyber-physical resilience in power systems. Renew. Sustain. Energy Rev. **58**, 1060–1069 (2016). https://doi.org/10.1016/j.rser. 2015.12.193
14. Yang, Z., Martí, J.R.: Resilience of electrical distribution systems with critical load prioritization. In: D'Agostino, G., Scala, A. (eds.) 12th International Conference on Critical Information Infrastructures Security, CRITIS 2017, Lucca, Italy (2017). https://doi.org/10.1007/ 978-3-319-99843-5_1
15. Henry, D., Ramirez, J.E.: Generic metrics and quantitative approaches for system resilience as a function of time. Reliab. Eng. Syst. Saf. **99**, 114–122 (2012). https://doi.org/10.1016/j. ress.2011.09.002
16. Foglietta, C., Panzieri, S.: CISIApro critical infrastructures modeling technique for an effective decision-making support. In: Soldatos, J., Philpot, J., Giunta, G. (eds.) Chapter 21, Cyber-Physical Threat Intelligence for Critical Infrastructures Security. Now Publishers, Hanover (2020). https://doi.org/10.1561/9781680836875.ch21
17. Sarker, P.S., Lester, H.D.: Post-disaster recovery associations of power systems dependent critical infrastructures. Infrastructures **4**, 30 (2019). https://doi.org/10.3390/infrastructures 4020030
18. Raoufi, H., Vahidinasab, V., Mehran, K.: Power systems resilience metrics: a comprehensive review of challenges and outlook. Sustainability **12**(22), 9698 (2020). https://doi.org/10.3390/ su12229698
19. Khouj, M.T., Alsubaie, A., et al.: Intelligent decision system for responsive crisis management. Int. J. Crit. Infrastruct. **14**, 375–399 (2018)
20. Alutaibe, K, Alsubaie, A., Martí, J.R.: A fire management decision support system to minimize economic losses: a case study in a petrochemical complex. Int. J. Crit. Infrastruct. (IJCIS) **14**(2), 120–139 (2018). https://doi.org/10.1504/IJCIS.2018.10013026
21. Martí, J.R., Ventura, C.E., et al.: I2Sim modelling and simulation framework for scenario development, training, and real-time decision support of multiple interdependent critical infrastructures during large emergencies. In: NATO RTO Modelling and Simulation Group Conference, Vancouver, BC, Canada, vol. 16, no. 1, p. 16-13 (2008)
22. Martí, J.R., et al.: Modelling critical infrastructure interdependencies in support of the security operations for the Vancouver 2010 Olympics. Report to Defence Research and Development Canada (DRDC), pp. 1–120 (2010)
23. i2SIM-RT Technologies: i2SIM Reference Manual. Vancouver, BC, Canada (2023)
24. Song, Z., Ren, G., et al.: A resilience metric and its calculation for ship automation systems. In: 2016 Resilience Week (RWS), Chicago, IL, USA, pp. 194–199 (2016). https://doi.org/10. 1109/RWEEK.2016.7573332
25. Leontief, W.: Input-Output Economics, 2nd edn. Oxford University Press, Oxford (1966)

26. Martí, A., Martí, J.R.: Climate change risk framework using complex interdependent critical systems. In: 18th International Conference on Critical Information Infrastructures Security CRITIS 2023, Helsinki, Finland (2023). https://doi.org/10.1007/978-3-031-62139-0_14

27. Lanouette, J.M.: Master of Defence Studies Maîtrise En Études de La Défense. JCSP 42 PCEMI 42 (2016)

28. Xiong, Z., Lv, J., Xie, Z., Xu, Y.: Influence factor of naval vessel's equipment under an optimized sailing strategy. Math. Probl. Eng. 1–11 (2023). https://doi.org/10.1155/2023/590 6332

29. Paul, D.: A history of electric ship propulsion systems. IEEE Ind. Appl. Mag. **26**, 9–19 (2020). https://doi.org/10.1109/MIAS.2020.3014837

Gender Gap in the Critical Infrastructure Research Community

Maria Guariglia Migliore[1,2,3] (ID), Gregorio D'Agostino[3] (ID),
and Antonio De Nicola[3(✉)] (ID)

[1] Network of Networks (NEToNETS), Rome, Italy
[2] Sapienza University of Rome, Department of Mechanical and Aerospace
Engineering, Via Eudossiana, 18, 00184 Rome, Italy
`maria.guarigliamigliore@uniroma1.it`
[3] Italian National Agency for New Technologies Energy and Sustainable Economic
Development (ENEA), Rome, Italy
`{gregorio.dagostino,antonio.denicola}@enea.it`

Abstract. A significant gender gap persists in STEM fields across many developed countries, despite encouraging policies. To develop effective solutions that narrow the gender gap in these fields, a deeper understanding of the root causes is essential. Quantifying the disparity is a crucial first step in any analysis. Specifically, we focus on the critical infrastructure sector. Our research delves into the participation of women in this domain by examining articles and conference proceedings published between 2006 and 2022 in the CRITIS conference. We meticulously analyzed the presence of women and their roles in these events to gain insights into gender representation, dynamics, and contribution within this field. To perform an automated gender identification based on names, we used a software called Cerbero-Lite. This takes names from dblp (developed at University of Trier in 1993) as input, extracts the first names, and, then, uses the Harvard Dataset to predict their genders. Subsequently, we performed a gendered assessment of the community by means of advanced social network analysis techniques. The research shows that, while a significant gender gap in favor of males exists in terms of participation, it does not reflect a difference in the ability of females to contribute to the development of the field.

Keywords: Critical Infrastructure · Gender · Social Network Analysis

1 Introduction

Throughout history, women have always been discriminated against compared to men. Unfortunately, even today in the 21st century, even in so-called developed societies, we witness all sorts of discrimination and prejudiced attitudes towards women, despite the fact that they are an integral and indispensable part of society. Even by looking at simple statistical data, it is easy to see that female employment rates are lower than male ones. Certain fields, particularly in

G. Oliva et al. (Eds.): CRITIS 2024, LNCS 15549, pp. 195–211, 2025.
https://doi.org/10.1007/978-3-031-84260-3_12

the scientific realm, which were historically dominated by men, such as engineering, medicine, and science in general, now categorized under STEM (acronym of Science Technology Engineering Mathematics), were once off-limits to women. Those few women who managed to enroll in universities had to fight against immense challenges and deep-rooted prejudices. This was partly due to the prevailing notion, still held by some today, that men and women possess different abilities and aptitudes, making some fields more suitable for one gender than the other. Indeed, a glance at labor data reveals a stark disparity: women are heavily represented in the fields of care and education, while men dominate domains like politics, science, computer science, and mathematics.

In this paper, we analyze the role of women in the critical infrastructure (CI) field, which heavily relies on STEM subjects. Our primary objective is to determine whether a gender gap exists in this field by analyzing data and identifying disparities in representation, opportunities, and roles. Additionally, we aim to evaluate the evolution of the gender gap in the sector over the years. We used data from the International Conference on Critical Information Infrastructures Security (CRITIS), a leading event for CI practitioners and researchers, covering the period from 2006 to 2022. Our analysis identifies trends and assesses whether the gender gap has been widening, narrowing, or remaining stagnant.

We can identify the following five research questions. (RQ1) As a group, are females and males equally contributing to the development of the CI field? (RQ2) As a group, are females and males equally essential to the larger CI community, (RQ3) As a group, have females and males different sources of inspiration? (RQ4) As a group, are females and males equally successful? (RQ5) As a group, are females and males equally creative?

Let us not forget that an equitable society is one of the core objectives of the Sustainable Development Goals (SDGs). A society that provides equal opportunities for all fosters an environment brimming with diverse perspectives and inputs, which in turn facilitates breakthroughs and problem-solving. The aim of this paper is to examine the prevalence of the gender equity issue and bring it to light, thereby prompting governments to implement effective policies for its resolution. To this purpose, in our research, we used Cerbero-lite, a name-based gender disambiguation software created for the gEneSys European project [6], along with the gender divide assessment framework described in [7].

The rest of this paper is organized as it follows. Section 2 presents the related work. Section 3 discusses the methodology and software for gender gap assessment. The data analyzed and the results are described in Sect. 4. The discussion is provided in Sect. 5 and, finally, Sect. 6 concludes the paper with some recommendations for the future.

2   Related Works

Several studies have examined the participation of women in communities. For example, Di Tommaso et al. [8] used social network analysis to study gender disparities in enterprises. Similarly, De Nicola & De Agostino [7,9] defined and applied a gender divide assessment framework based on social network analysis to evaluate four scientific communities within computer science and information systems. The proposed framework considers three dimensions: context, discipline, and community. Context refers to the operating environment of community members. Discipline defines the specific domain being analyzed. Community encompasses characteristics derived from social relationships, collaborations, and the ratio of females to males. A study by Kane et al. [13] examines gender bias on Wikipedia by analyzing data on profiles of female and male Fortune 1000 CEOs. The researchers specifically looked at how editors on Wikipedia, a collaborative online encyclopedia, interacted with these pages. Their findings were unexpected: gender bias on Wikipedia seemed to favor feminine CEOs over their male counterparts. This research (by Kane et al.) presents a method of analysis using real-world data collected from publicly available web information and editor behavior on Wikipedia. Continuing our exploration of gender and online collaboration, a study by Mennecke et al. [14] examines how gender differences manifest in virtual environments during creative tasks. This research explores how gender might influence teamwork and creative outcomes within virtual spaces.

Abramo et al [1] investigated the impact of Covid-19 on scientific production. These studies primarily focused on changes in preprint submissions (arXiv, bioRxiv, medRxiv) before and after the pandemic. Notably, Abramo et al. found a similar decrease in research output for both females and males, particularly in Europe and North America. Social network analysis, as evidenced by research in this field, offers a valuable tool to study both these aspects - people's behavior in online collaboration and the evolution of creative fields within social network platforms. D'Agostino & De Nicola [4] studied researcher's resilience during the Covid-19 pandemic. The resilience is defined as the capacity or ability of a researcher to adapt, recover, and bounce back from challenges, setbacks, or adversity. This allows them to continue pursuing their scientific activities. Specifically, the study aimed to investigate whether there was a gender gap in resilience, and no significant differences were observed. A recent report by the EU Commission [10] explored the broader impact of Covid-19 on academic activities. Their findings highlighted a concerning gender disparity: women submitted manuscripts at a lower rate than expected compared to their pre-pandemic submissions in the same period of 2018 and 2019. Additionally, the number of female first authors decreased by 19% compared to publications in the same journals during 2019. This resulted in a widening gender gap of 14 percentage points for first authorship.

With respect to the cited papers, the study in this article aims to investigate the gender gap in the field of critical infrastructure, an area that has not yet been addressed by other studies.

3   Methodology and Software for Gender Gap Assessment

3.1   Gender Assessment Framework

In a study of De Nicola & D'Agostino [7], the authors defined the gender divide assessment framework, which is structured in three dimensions: the context, the attitude, and the success. The first dimension, the context, regards the environment in which community members engage. Examples of the corresponding indicators are gender ratio, degree, and network centrality indices The gender ratio and degree measure, respectively, the percentage of females and males and the number of coauthors. Other examples of network centrality indices are betweenness, closeness, and eigenvector centrality (see Table 1). The second dimension is the attitude and examples of the indicators are susceptibility of authors to the topics treated in the papers of their co-authors or in the conference papers as a whole, novelty, and combinational creativity. Novelty measures the researcher's capacity to generate innovative and relevant work. Combinational creativity measures a researcher's ability to integrate diverse topics. For the third dimension, the success, which pertains to the attainment of objectives, examples of indicators are the number of papers, charges, and authority. The number of papers measures the average number of papers authored or co-authored by a researcher. The authority quantifies the degree to which the topics discussed in an author's paper exert influence on the topics explored in the papers of their coauthors.

A summary of a selection of the indices used in this analysis is presented in Table 1.

3.2   A Software for Name-Based Gender Disambiguation

In this work, we analyzed a set of articles extracted from dblp[1] by using a gender automated disambiguation software called Cerbero-Lite. The software takes as input a list of names, determines which is the first name and through Harvard Dataset [15] assigns a gender probability. Figure 1 represents the architecture of Cerbero Lite. From a software standpoint, the Cerbero-Lite process operates as illustrated in Fig. 1 and elaborated below. Bibliometric data for a sample of papers are retrieved from a scientific online database, i.e., DBLP. The data are then cleaned and imported (1) into the disambiguation manager. Subsequently, the disambiguation manager extracts the name from the full name. The previously acquired HARVARD World Gender Name Dictionary (WGND 2.0) [15] is employed (2) to correlate the name with a gender probability. The WGND 2.0 is a compilation of names from various countries, categorized by gender. For each author, the software can assign (3) three gender likelihoods: the likelihood that the author is male, female, or of undetermined gender. This system has been used to analyze female participation in the CRITIS conference and to assess overall conference participation.

---

[1] dblp computer science bibliography url: https://dblp.org.

Table 1. Summary of a selection of the indices presented in [7].

Index	Description
Authority	Authority measures to what extent the topics in an author's papers influence the topics in his/her coauthors' papers
Betweennes	Betweenness (B) [11] measures how important were a node if all of them would try to communicate along the network by the shortest path. That is, supposing anyone sends a message to anyone, how many of such messages pass through a node
Charges	Number of positions of responsibility for controlling or caring for something. Examples could be the role of a scientist inside an organization (e.g., Full Professor) or a community
Closeness	Closeness measures the average harmonic distance for a member to reach any other member of the community [2]
Combinational creativity	Combinational creativity measures the ability of a researcher to combine different topics [12]. It is given by the number of times he/she has been the one that combined two topics for the first time
Degree	Number of coauthors of a member of the community
EigenCentrality	EigenCentrality [3] can be interpreted as the probability of news to reach a node upon spreading on the network
Gender ratio	Gender ratio allows to measure the female to male ratio
Neighbour susceptibility	This index measures to what extent the topics in an author's papers are influenced by the topics in his/her coauthors' papers
Novelty	Novelty measures the ability of a researcher to produce work that is both novel (i.e., original, unexpected) and appropriate (i.e., useful, adaptive concerning task constraints) [16]. It is given by the number of times he/she has been the one that introduced a topic for the first time
Number of papers	Number of papers written by a researcher
Trend susceptibility	Trend susceptibility measures to what extent the topics in an author's papers are influenced by the topics in the conference papers as a whole

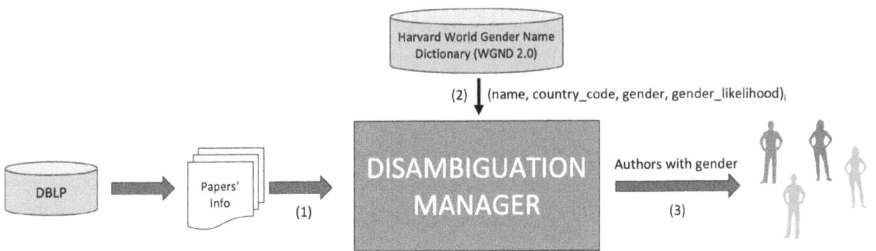

Fig. 1. Architecture of Cerbero Lite

4   Analysis of Data

4.1   Gender Dynamics in the CRITIS Community

To capture the evolving dynamics of gender representation, our study spans a substantial timeframe, encompassing articles published between 2006 and 2022. This extensive time range enables us to identify trends and patterns in females' participation and roles within the critical infrastructure sector over nearly two decades.

As outlined in Sect. 3, the procedure was conducted as follows. First, data were extracted using dblp that provides open access to bibliographic information for major computer science publications (journals and conference and workshop proceedings). Then, they were filtered using a software program. Once the files with the names were obtained, Cerbero-Lite was used to disambiguate the gender. After, we computed the percentages of participation by men, women, and undeterminated individuals, year by year from 2006 to 2022.

Table 2 shows the number and the corresponding rates of males, females, and undetermined by year. There is a significant gender gap and a consistent trend over time. Similarly, Fig. 2 depicts the gender rates by year. Upon examining it, a significant gender gap becomes evident. The rate for males remains around 80% and stays consistent throughout the examined period, except for a slight dip between 2008 and 2010. Regarding females, the rate remains around 18%. For authors with undetermined gender, the rate is insignificant, demonstrating Cerbero-lite's capability in name-based gender disambiguation.

Table 2. Number and rates of males (n_m, $\%_{Males}$), females (n_f, $\%_{Females}$), undetermined (n_u, $\%_{Undet.}$) scientists participating at the CRITIS conference by year.

Years	n_m	n_f	n_u	%Males	%Females	%Undet.
2006	57	6	2	87.69%	9.23%	3.08%
2007	118	18	4	84.29%	12.86%	2.86%
2008	198	45	6	79.52%	18.07%	2.41%
2009	244	52	7	80.53%	17.16%	2.31%
2010	272	55	7	81.44%	16.47%	2.10%
2011	298	66	7	80.32%	17.79%	1.89%
2012	335	72	10	80.34%	17.27%	2.40%
2013	374	80	11	80.43%	17.20%	2.37%
2014	458	99	15	80.07%	17.31%	2.62%
2015	508	107	17	80.38%	16.93%	2.69%
2016	552	125	21	79.08%	17.91%	3.01%
2017	602	134	24	79.21%	17.63%	3.16%
2018	642	141	25	79.46%	17.45%	3.09%
2019	692	154	25	79.45%	17.68%	2.87%
2020	698	156	27	79.23%	17.71%	3.06%
2021	723	162	29	79.10%	17.72%	3.17%
2022	782	169	31	79.63%	17.21%	3.16%

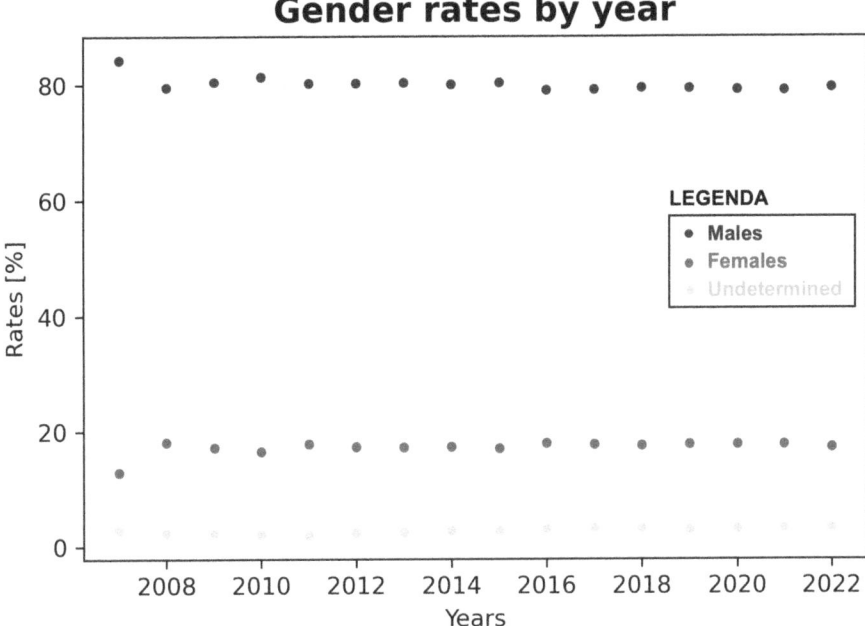

Fig. 2. Gender rates of scientists participating at the CRITIS conference by year.

4.2   Centrality of CRITIS Scientists in the Community

By exploiting the coauthorship relationship emerging from the papers written together by authors, a community of scientists can be represented as a social network [7,8]. For the CRITIS community, the emerging social network is depicted in Fig. 3. Blue circles represent males while purple circles females. The size of each circle is proportional to the node degree. The figure clearly shows a large group of 202 researchers working together in this field, along with several smaller ones. There are three prominent groups consisting of more than 20 scientists: 23, 28, and 34 individuals, respectively. It is worth noting that the proportions of males and females in these groups are 74,75% and 25,25%, respectively. Hence, the representation of females in the largest group is better compared to that in the broader CRITIS community.

A network representation allows for the application of advanced techniques typically used in complex network analysis. Specifically, we measured four indicators to capture different aspects of network centrality: average betweenness ($\bar{B}$), average closeness ($\bar{Cl}$), average degree ($\bar{D}$), and average eigenvector centrality ($\bar{E}$). Table 3 presents the corresponding values. Although $\bar{B}$ for females is higher than for males, these differences are not statistically significant, as shown in Subsect. 4.6. The average degree, $\bar{D}$, favors females when considering either all authors or only the semantically treatable ones (see, respectively, $\bar{D}_A$ and $\bar{D}_T$ in Table 3). Semantically treatable (T) authors are defined as those who have

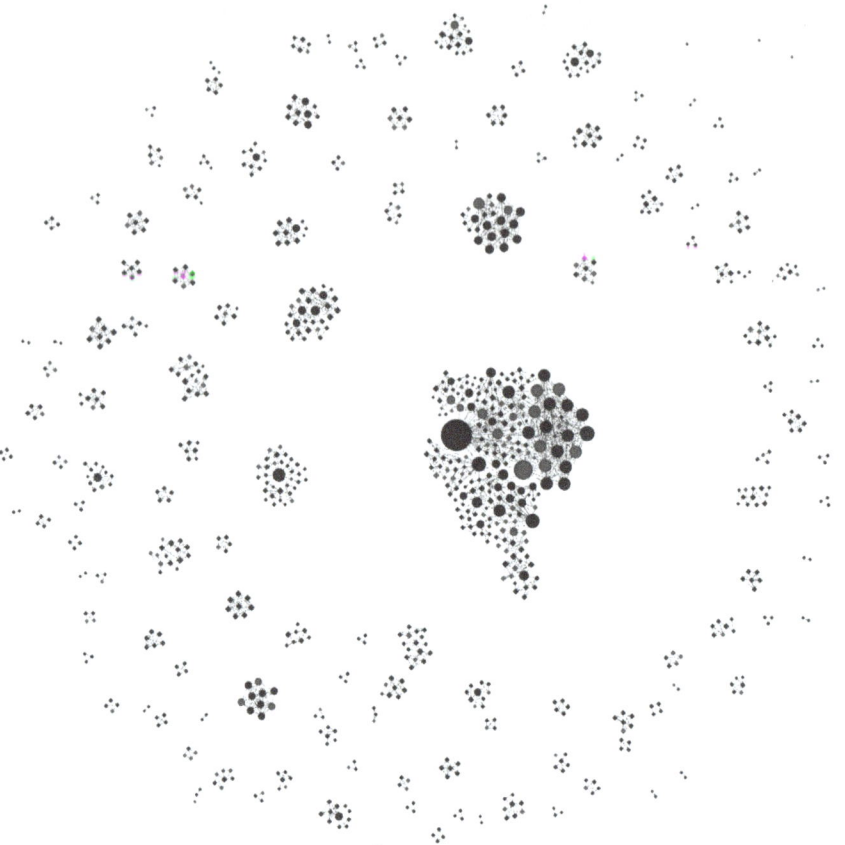

Fig. 3. CRITIS social network emerging from coauthorship relationships (Color figure online)

written at least two papers in two different years [5]. However, the differences between the average values for males and females are only weakly statistically significant. In contrast, both closeness ($\bar{Cl}$) and eigenvector centrality ($\bar{E}$) favor females and these differences are highly statistically significant.

Table 3. Comparison of the average values of the main centrality indices.

Gender	$\bar{B}$	$\bar{Cl}$	$\bar{D}_A$	$\bar{D}_T$	$\bar{E}$
Females	0.000147	0.0197	5.04	8.00	0.0108
Males	0.000134	0.0142	4.55	7.04	0.0045

4.3   Susceptible Scientists

By following the approach presented in [5], we analyzed the diffusion of interests in various topics and estimated neighbour susceptibility (x_i) and trend susceptibility (x_{si}) for each semantically treatable member of the CRITIS community. Table 4 presents the obtained values. For x_i, the average value for females is 0.042, while for males, it is 0.059. This suggests that females are generally less influenced by their coauthors compared to males, although the difference is only weakly statistically significant. Conversely, the average trend susceptibility value is higher for females, with this difference also being weakly statistically significant.

Table 4. Comparison of the average values of the susceptibility indices and authority for semantically treatable values. Average susceptibility to neighbours: $\bar{x}$; average susceptibility to trends: $\bar{x}_s$; average authority: $\bar{a}$.

Gender	$\bar{x}$	$\bar{x}_s$	$\bar{a}$
Females	0.042	0.114	0.132
Males	0.059	0.088	0.108

4.4   Success of CRITIS Scientists

Success of authors can be assessed by checking their scientific production, and the recognition by the community. Here, we have identified some indicators that can be used for the purpose. Table 5 includes the average number of papers of males $(\overline{p_m})$, of females $(\overline{p_f})$, and of undetermined $(\overline{p_u})$ authors as well as the average number of papers of semantically treatable masculine $(\overline{p_{T,m}})$ and of feminine authors $(\overline{p_{T,f}})$. $\overline{p_m}$ is 1.415 while $\overline{p_f}$ is 1.408. These values are similar and there is not a statistically significant difference. Similarly, for semantically treatable authors, we can note a value of 3.059 for males and 2.889 for females. Even if this suggests that males tend to write more articles over the years also this difference is no statistically significant.

Table 5. Average number of papers of males $(\overline{p_m})$, average number of papers of females $(\overline{p_f})$, and average number of papers of undetermined $(\overline{p_u})$, average number of papers of T (semantically treatable) males $(\overline{p_{T,m}})$, and average number of papers of T females $(\overline{p_{T,f}})$.

$\overline{p_m}$	$\overline{p_f}$	$\overline{p_u}$	$\overline{p_{T,m}}$	$\overline{p_{T,f}}$
1.415	1.408	1.354	3.059	2.889

After analyzing the average of written papers for each author categorized by gender, we investigated if there is gender gap in the organizational roles of

CRITIS conference. The information was extracted from the Springer proceedings books, after cleaning the data. Particularly, we considered the program committees, the chairs roles, and some other secondary roles, such as participation to the local organization committee.

Table 6. Number of males (n_m), females (n_f), and undetermined (n_u) and corresponding rates (%Males, %Females, and %Undet), respectively, for chairs, members, and secondary roles.

	n_m	n_f	n_u	%Males	%Females	%Undet
Chairs	65	15	0	85.52%	14.47%	0.00%
Members	216	42	13	79.70%	15.49%	4.79%
Secondary	56	34	4	59.57%	36.17%	4.25%

Table 6 clearly demonstrates that the number of females is consistently far lower than that of males. Moreover, the gap widens when considering leadership positions such as chairs, where females represent only 14%. This presents a significant challenge, as achieving equity is one of the fundamental goals towards a more progressive and sustainable society.

Figure 4 presents the number of memberships on the x-axis and the number of chairs on the y-axis. The graph uses circles that increase in size as the number of people filling those roles increases. Blue circles represent males, purple circles represent females, and gray circles represent an equal number of males and females in those roles. We observe that in most cases, the largest circle is always the one representing males, with the purple circle represented within it. Furthermore, if we look at the people who have most frequently held the roles of chairs and members, we always see blue spheres indicating males. This indicates a clear presence of a gender gap in all these conference roles.

Finally, the average authority of semantically treatable authors is in favor of females (see Table 4). However, the difference between the average value for females and for males is weakly statistically significant.

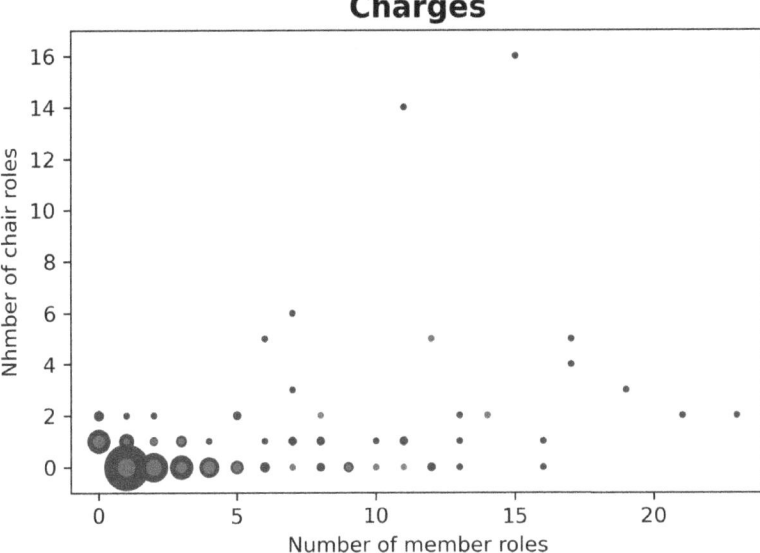

Fig. 4. Relationships between number of member roles and number of chair roles. The size of the balls is proportional to number of masculine (blue) and feminine (purple) scientists. (Color figure online)

4.5   Creativity of CRITIS Scientists

Creativity in conceiving new ideas and technology is one of the elements required to disrupt science and technology. To assess creativity of CRITIS members, we measured four indicators: the number of scientists that were the first to introduce a topic, the number of scientists that were the first to combine two topics, the novelty index ($\bar{\mathcal{N}}$), and the combinational creativity index ($\bar{\mathcal{C}}$) [7]. We recall that $\mathcal{N}_{h_i} = \frac{1}{N_{c_k}} \cdot \sum_{c_k} \frac{\delta_{k,i}}{n_{c_k}}$ where $\delta_{k,i} = 1$ if the author h_i was one of the first authors to propose the topic c_k; $\delta_{k,i} = 0$ if the author h_i was not one of the first authors to propose the topic c_k; n_{c_k} is the number of the authors that first proposed the topic c_k; and N_{c_k} is the overall number of topics. This index spans the $[0,1]$ range. Then, $\mathcal{C}_{h_i} = \frac{1}{N_{p_{kl}}} \cdot \sum_{p_{kl}} \frac{\delta_{p_{kl},i}}{n_{p_{kl}}}$, where p_{kl} is the pair of topics (c_k, c_l); $\delta_{p_{kl},i} = 1$ if the author h_i was one of the first authors to propose p_{kl}; $\delta_{p_{kl},i} = 0$ if the author h_i was not one of the first authors to propose p_{kl}; $n_{p_{kl}}$ is the number of the authors that first proposed p_{kl}; and $N_{p_{kl}}$ is the overall number of detected pairs of topics. Also this index spans the $[0,1]$ range. While the first pairs of indicators measure how many authors are creative, $\bar{\mathcal{N}}$ and $\bar{\mathcal{C}}$ measure the extent of their creativity.

Table 7 presents the values for the above-mentioned indicators. Considering only the disambiguated authors, males are 82,23% and females 17,7%. The percentage of masculine scientists that were the first to introduce a topic is 79.29%

whereas the percentage of feminine ones is 20.71%. The percentage of feminine scientists that were the first to combine two topics is 18.36% whereas the percentage of masculine ones is 81.64%. Finally, both $\bar{\mathcal{N}}$ and $\bar{\mathcal{C}}$ are in favor of males. However, the differences of $\bar{\mathcal{N}}$ are not statistically significant while the differences of $\bar{\mathcal{C}}$ are weakly statistically significant.

Table 7. Results of the creativity analysis and average number of papers for the CRITIS community. $\mathcal{N}$ authors are the authors introducing novel topics. $\mathcal{C}$ authors are the authors introducing novel combinations of topics. $\bar{\mathcal{N}}$ is the average novelty index. $\bar{\mathcal{C}}$ is the average combinational creativity index.

Gender	Ratio	$\mathcal{N}$ authors	$\mathcal{C}$ authors	$\bar{\mathcal{N}}$	$\bar{\mathcal{C}}$
Females	17.77%	20.71%	18.36%	0.00101	0.0009
Males	82.23%	79.29%	81.64%	0.00103	0.0010

4.6   Note on the Statistical Significance of Results

Figures 5 and 6 illustrate the distribution of the average number of papers in random samples for both females and males. This helps estimate the likelihood that the observed deviations in the female group are not due to chance. To create these figures, we randomly sampled authors 100,000 times. The figures use vertical lines to represent the average indicator values for different groups: purple (F) for females (ind_F), blue (M) for males (ind_M), and gray (U) for authors with undetermined gender (ind_U). The black line (R) represents the average value for random samples (ind_R). To generate the control group results, we first calculated the average value for each of the 100,000 random samples. The control group's mean is then the average of all these individual sample averages, with the standard deviation (σ) reflecting the spread of values within this distribution of sample averages. The hypothesis was considered highly significant if the deviation of the female average value was greater than $5/2 \cdot \sigma$, significant if the deviation was between $3/2 \cdot \sigma$ and $5/2 \cdot \sigma$, and weakly significant if the deviation was between $\sigma/2$ and $3/2 \cdot \sigma$. It was rejected if the deviation was less than $\sigma/2$.

   It is important to note that if the hypothesis of a gender gap for an indicator is not statistically significant, this does not mean the findings are invalid. Instead, it indicates that there is no gender gap for that particular indicator.

5   Discussion

(RQ1) As a group, are females and males equally contributing to the development of the critical infrastructure field?
Based on the analyzed data, we can observe the presence of significant gender gap. Males are contributing much more than females, since most of the authors

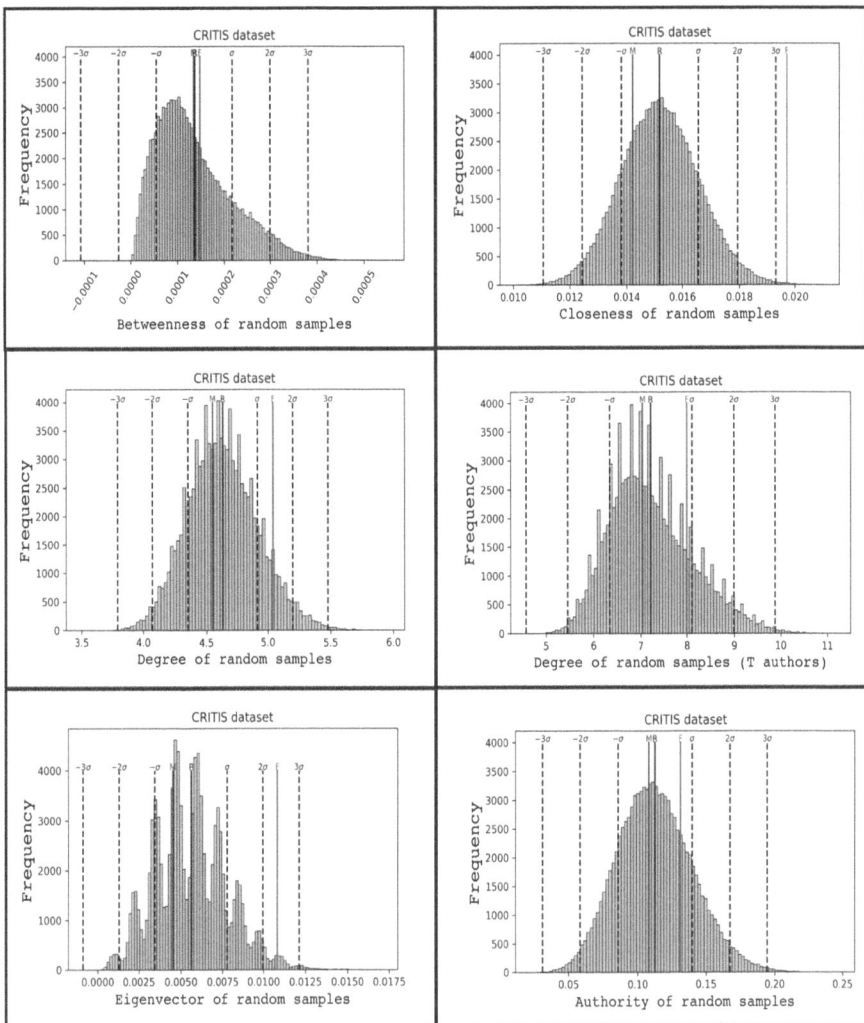

Fig. 5. Distribution of sample averages of the betweenness, closeness, degree of random samples for all the authors and for semantically treatable (T) ones, eigenvector centrality, and authority.

are males. Particularly, analyzing the set of articles published between 2006 and 2022, the rate of males remains about 80% while the rate for females is about 18%. Over the years, the gap has remained constant or has experienced only a slight temporary decline.

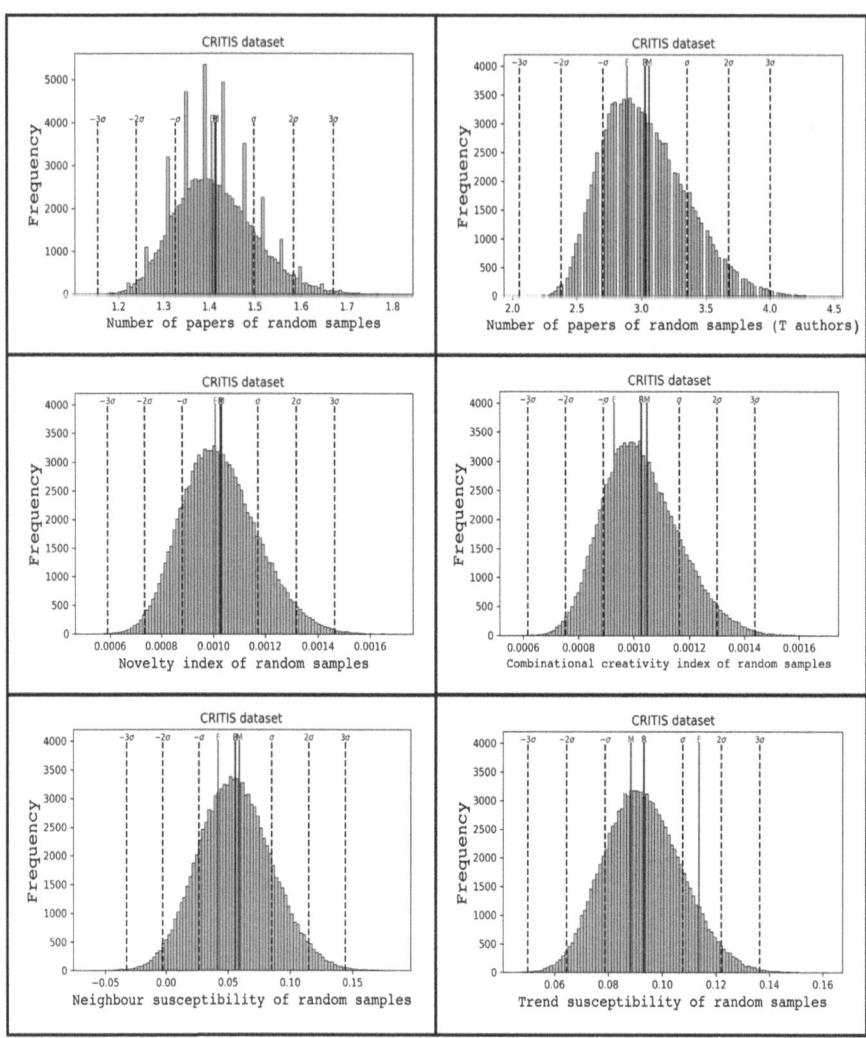

Fig. 6. Distribution of sample averages of the number of papers for all the authors and for semantically treatable (T) ones, novelty, combinational creativity, neighbour susceptibility, and trend susceptibility.

(RQ2) As a group, are females and males equally essential to the larger CI community?

While degree simply tells us how many connections a member of a community has, other measures like betweenness, eigencentrality, and closeness go beyond that. These latter metrics focus on the likelihood of new information, like a topic, reaching a particular member. They achieve this by considering the network's structure and how a member is positioned within it. In essence, these measures tell us how important a member's position is for the spread of information within the community. To answer this question we can observe Table 3. Indeed, we have to consider four indicators, respectively: betweenness ($\bar{B}$), closeness ($\bar{Cl}$), degree ($\bar{D}$), and eigenvector centrality ($\bar{E}$). $\bar{Cl}$, $\bar{D}$, $\bar{D}_T$, and $\bar{E}$ are in favor of females. This means that, despite they are fewer, females are more central than males.

(RQ3) As a group, have females and males different sources of inspiration?
Observing Table 4, we note that while the values of neighbour susceptibility (x_i) are lower for females, those of trend susceptibility (x_{si}) are higher. This indicates that females tend to be more influenced by trends than by their coauthors compared to males.

(RQ4) As a group, are females and males equally successful?
The issue of success within the CRITIS community is somewhat controversial. The differences in productivity, measured by the average number of papers published, are not statistically significant when considering either the entire CRITIS community or the most regular conference participants. However, leadership roles tend to favor males. Key positions such as chair and member roles are predominantly held by males, and although the situation is somewhat better for females in secondary organizational roles, a significant gender gap still exists. Interestingly, among the most regular participants, females are perceived as more authoritative. This suggests that despite their lower numbers, the females who do regularly participate are highly respected and considered leaders within the community.

(RQ5) As a group, are females and males equally creative?
Considering the proportions of males and females, as well as the number of scientists who were the first to introduce a new topic or combine two topics, the data reveal that the number of creative females is higher than expected. In terms of the extent of creativity, we did not find significant differences between males and females for novelty. However, we found weakly statistically significant differences favoring males in their ability to combine topics.

6 Conclusion

In this paper, we presented a study on the participation of females and males in the critical infrastructure field. We posed five research questions to analyze the potential gender gap, focusing on three dimensions of scientific activities: context, success, and attitude. Our dataset was extracted from the CRITIS conference proceedings, covering the period from the conference's inception in 2006 to 2022. We specifically considered the papers, their authors, the committees, and the various chairs. We employed Cerbero-lite, a software for name-based gender disambiguation developed as part of the European project gEneSys, and the gender divide assessment framework presented in [7]. Despite an ongoing imbalance in participation favoring males, our research indicates that females have equal potential to contribute to the development of this field. To increase the presence of females in the critical infrastructure field, we suggest implementing policies such as special awards for females and mandatory quotas in committees and chair roles. These measures would ensure more proportionate female representation at conferences, thereby raising their visibility and profile in the field and bringing new perspectives for the advancement of security of critical information infrastructures.

Acknowledgments. We gratefully acknowledge the partial support of the gEneSys (Transforming Gendered Interrelations of Power and Inequalities in Transition Pathways to Sustainable Energy Systems) project, which has received funding from the European Union's Horizon Europe - Culture, creativity and inclusive society - under grant agreement no. 101094326.

Disclosure of Interests. The authors have no competing interests to declare that are relevant to the content of this article.

References

1. Abramo, G., D'Angelo, C.A., Mele, I.: Impact of Covid-19 on research output by gender across countries. Scientometrics **127**(12), 6811–6826 (2022). https://doi.org/10.1007/s11192-021-04245-x
2. Bavelas, A.: Communication patterns in task-oriented groups. J. Acoust. Soc. Am. **22**(6), 725–730 (1950)
3. Bonacich, P.: Power and centrality: a family of measures. Am. J. Sociol. **92**(5), 1170–1182 (1987)
4. D'Agostino, G., De Nicola, A.: Women's resilience in the time of Covid-19. In: Agrifoglio, R., Lazazzara, A., Za, S. (eds.), Navigating Digital Transformation: Organizational Change, Digital Work, and Individual Behavior, Lecture Notes in Information Systems and Organisation (LNISO), vol. 73. Springer International Publishing, Cham (2025). https://doi.org/10.1007/978-3-031-76970-2_19
5. D'Agostino, G., D'Antonio, F., De Nicola, A., Tucci, S.: Interests diffusion in social networks. Phys. A: Stat. Mech. Appl. **436**, 443–461 (2015). https://doi.org/10.1016/j.physa.2015.05.062
6. De Nicola, A., et al.: D.1.2 - Report on Gendered assessment of the energy systems knowledge community and EU policies for sustainable energy systems - Horizon Europe Project gEneSys - Transforming Gendered Interrelations of Power and Inequalities in Transition Pathways to Sustainable Energy Systems, grant agreement no. 101094326 (March 2024). https://doi.org/10.5281/zenodo.11566948
7. De Nicola, A., D'Agostino, G.: Assessment of gender divide in scientific communities. Scientometrics **126**(5), 3807–3840 (2021). https://doi.org/10.1007/s11192-021-03885-3
8. Di Tommaso, G., Gatti, M., Iannotta, M., Mehra, A., Stilo, G., Velardi, P.: Gender, rank, and social networks on an enterprise social media platform. Soc. Netw. **62**, 58–67 (2020)
9. D'Agostino, G., De Nicola, A.: Analysis of gender diversity in the Italian community of information systems. In: Lazazzara, A., Nacamulli, R.C.D., Rossignoli, R.C.D., Za, S. (eds.), Organizing for Digital Innovation: At the Interface Between Social Media, Human Behavior and Inclusion, LNISO, vol. 27, pp. 97–109. Springer International Publishing, Cham (2019). https://doi.org/10.1007/978-3-319-90500-6_8

10. European Commission: Impact on gender equality in research & innovation (2023). https://research-and-innovation.ec.europa.eu/strategy/strategy-2020-2024/democracy-and-rights/gender-equality-research-and-innovation_en

11. Freeman, L.C.: Centrality in social networks conceptual clarification. Soc. Netw. **1**(3), 215–239 (1978)

12. Gero, J.S.: Computational models of innovative and creative design processes. Technol. Forecast. Soc. Change **64**(2), 183–196 (2000). https://doi.org/10.1016/S0040-1625(99)00105-5

13. Kane, G., Wigdor, A., Young, A.: It's not what you think: gender bias in information about fortune 1000 CEOs on Wikipedia. In: Proceedings of the ICIS Conference (2016)

14. Mennecke, B., Nah, F., Schiller, S., Siau, K.: Gender differences in virtual collaboration on a creative design task. In: Proceedings of the ICIS Conference (2011)

15. Raffo, J.: WGND 2.0 (2021). https://doi.org/10.7910/DVN/MSEGSJ

16. Sternberg, R.J., Lubart, T.I.: The concept of creativity: prospects and paradigms. Handb. Creat. **1**, 3–15 (1999)

Centrality-Based Security Allocation in Networked Control Systems

Anh Tung Nguyen$^{(\boxtimes)}$ (iD), Andreas Hertzberg, and André M. H. Teixeira (iD)

Department of Information Technology, Uppsala University,
PO Box 337, 75105 Uppsala, Sweden
{anh.tung.nguyen,andre.teixeira}@it.uu.se,
andreas.hertzberg.0811@student.uu.se

Abstract. This paper addresses the security allocation problem within networked control systems, which consist of multiple interconnected control systems under the influence of two opposing agents: a defender and a malicious adversary. The adversary aims to maximize the worst-case attack impact on system performance while remaining undetected by launching stealthy data injection attacks on one or several interconnected control systems. Conversely, the defender's objective is to allocate security resources to detect and mitigate these worst-case attacks. A novel centrality-based approach is proposed to guide the allocation of security resources to the most connected or influential subsystems within the network. The methodology involves comparing the worst-case attack impact for both the optimal and centrality-based security allocation solutions. The results demonstrate that the centrality measure approach enables significantly faster allocation of security resources with acceptable levels of performance loss compared to the optimal solution, making it suitable for large-scale networks. The proposed method is validated through numerical examples using Erdős-Rényi graphs.

Keywords: Security metric · networked control systems · centrality measures · stealthy attacks · cyber-physical security

1 Introduction

Networked control systems are integral to modern infrastructure, which are prominently featured in power grids, transportation networks, and water distribution systems. These systems leverage open and widely-used information and communication technologies, including the public Internet and wireless communication [3,8,24]. However, using unprotected wireless communication channels may expose them to cyber threats, which can lead to severe financial losses and societal disruptions. Notable examples include the Iranian industrial control system, which suffered from the Stuxnet malware in 2010 [3], and the Ukrainian power grid, which was compromised by the Industroyer malware in 2016 [8].

G. Oliva et al. (Eds.): CRITIS 2024, LNCS 15549, pp. 212–230, 2025.
https://doi.org/10.1007/978-3-031-84260-3_13

These incidents underscore the critical importance of bolstering security measures within control systems to protect against such potentially devastating cyber attacks.

The issue of cybersecurity has garnered significant attention from researchers within the Information Technology community. Solutions in this area are critical for maintaining the core principles of the Confidentiality, Integrity, and Availability (CIA) triad for data and IT services. These principles are defined as follows: 1) Confidentiality: ensures that data stored, transmitted, and processed remains private and accessible only to authorized individuals; 2) Integrity: ensures that data is reliable and cannot be modified by unauthorized means; and 3) Availability: ensures that the system provides timely access to data when requested. Among these, integrity is particularly emphasized, as any breach directly impacts system performance [24]. In exploring potential threats to control systems, Zhang et al. [30] introduced the concept of controlled invariant subspace, derived from geometric control theory, which remains independent of system outputs and nonlinear functions, to propose a covert attack on certain classes of nonlinear systems. Addressing nonlinear systems presents considerable challenges, requiring attackers to gain deep system knowledge and intercept real-time transmitted data. Rather than focusing on nonlinear system models, Park et al. [21] examined potential threats in linear systems with uncertainties. By thoroughly analyzing system dynamics and conventional anomaly detection mechanisms, these sophisticated stealthy data injection attacks significantly disrupt control systems without being detected. This highlights the need for more advanced detection methods. Least squares-based fusion techniques are widely employed to identify and mitigate the harmful effects of false data injection attacks on state estimation [10,11]. Physical watermarking, initially designed to detect replay attacks, has been adapted to signal the presence of false data injection attacks [15]. Recent advancements have further reduced the average detection delay time [16]. However, physical watermarking can increase control costs and reduce actuator lifespan in control systems. Multiplicative watermarking [4,5,25] offers an effective solution to these challenges. Additionally, reallocating defensive resources can help mitigate the adverse effects of attackers [1], enhancing the system's resilience against stealthy false data injection attacks. Nevertheless, it is important to acknowledge that contemporary intelligent adversaries can learn and adapt to these mitigation strategies, refining their attack methods to maintain stealth. Therefore, this paper emphasizes the need for a comprehensive investigation of networked control systems under the influence of stealthy false data injection attacks.

Upon review of the above existing studies [1,4,5,10,11,15,16,21,25,30], it becomes evident that the literature has primarily focused on secure estimation and control from the viewpoint of either the defender or the adversary. However, it is important to acknowledge that both parties encounter similar challenges. While the defender confronts resource limitations in countering malicious activities, the adversary also faces energy constraints during attack execution. Therefore, it is highly pertinent to address this matter within a comprehensive framework that encompasses both the defender and the adversary. Fortunately, the security allocation problem between the defender and the malicious adversary fits well within the framework of game theory, which is one of the most efficient frameworks addressing the challenge of optimal decision-making among non-cooperative parties [2]. In an attempt to apply game theory to deal with the security allocation problem, the authors in [9] seek the Stackelberg equilibrium by formulating the optimization problems in [9, Theorem 3.3] where all the attack scenarios are considered in their constraints. To solve those optimization problems in [9, Theorem 3.3], the authors use a linear mapping from action space to the game payoff (see more in [9, Section III.B]), removing the complexity of computing game payoff. In the same line with [9], the authors in [29] also seek the Stackelberg equilibrium by considering all the attack scenarios in [29, Theorem 1]. The study in [22] has a similar game setup to ours where the defender and the adversary have discrete action spaces. They also conduct the traditional backward induction to find the Stackelberg equilibrium [22, Algorithm 1]. To be able to proceed with the algorithm, the authors in [22] need to investigate all the possible action scenarios shown in [22], resulting in a very high computational cost [22, Section V]. Although not considering a Stackelberg game setting, the authors in [14,27] tackle an analogous problem. The authors in [27] find the Bayesian game equilibrium through solving an optimization problem [27, Section VI.A] where the game payoff matrix is employed in its constraint. Clearly, building up the game payoff matrix enumerates all the action scenarios [27, Tables 1 and 2]. Although the problem in [14] is not clearly formulated as a game between a defender and an adversary, the authors discuss the mutual formulation between theirs and a zero-sum game setting in [14, Section IV.B]. The authors in [14] find the optimal action for the operator, who has the same role as the defender in our work, through solving an optimization problem in [14, Section III.C] where they consider all the possible actions in discrete action spaces. Further, many other concepts of games describing networked systems subjected to cyber attacks such as matrix games [17–19,22,27], dynamic games [7], and stochastic games [13] have been studied. In summary, the consideration of all the action scenarios remains in recent studies [9,14,22,27,29]. Particularly, the authors in [9,14,29] deal with security problems by solving a single large optimization problem that addresses all the action scenarios. As a consequence, the computation in those existing studies is considerably heavy. We aim to address such an issue in this study.

In this paper, we consider a continuous-time networked control system, associated with an undirected connected graph, involving two strategic agents: a defender and a malicious adversary. The system consists of multiple interconnected subsystems, referred as to vertices. The aim of the adversary is to maximally disrupt the global performance of the network without being detected by the defender. Meanwhile, the defender selects several monitor vertices to measure their outputs with the purpose of alleviating the attack impact. To assist the defender in allocating the defense resources, we adopt centrality measures including degree, betweenness, and closeness centrality measures to seek the most potential monitor vertices. This approach enables us to solve less complicated optimization problems, massively alleviating the computational cost compared to finding the optimal solution.

Notation: the set of real positive numbers is denoted as $\mathbb{R}_+$; $\mathbb{R}^n$ and $\mathbb{R}^{n \times m}$ stand for sets of real n-dimensional vectors and n-row m-column matrices, respectively. A vector with the i-th element set to one and the other elements set to zero is denoted $e_i \in \mathbb{R}^n$. A positive definite matrix A and a positive semi-definite matrix B are denoted as $A \succ 0$ and $B \succeq 0$, respectively. The notations $A \prec 0$ and $B \preceq 0$ stand for $-A \succ 0$ and $-B \succeq 0$, respectively. The space of square-integrable functions is defined as $\mathcal{L}_2 \triangleq \{f : \mathbb{R}_+ \to \mathbb{R} \mid \|f\|^2_{\mathcal{L}_2[0,\infty]} < \infty\}$ and the extended space be defined as $\mathcal{L}_{2e} \triangleq \{f : \mathbb{R}_+ \to \mathbb{R} \mid \|f\|^2_{\mathcal{L}_2[0,T]} < \infty, \forall \, 0 < T < \infty\}$. The notation $\|x\|^2_{\mathcal{L}_2}$ is used as shorthand for the norm $\|x\|^2_{\mathcal{L}_2[0,T]} \triangleq \frac{1}{T} \int_0^T \|x(t)\|^2_2 \, dt$ if the time horizon $[0,T]$ is clear from the context. Let $\mathcal{G} \triangleq (\mathcal{V}, \mathcal{E}, A)$ be an undirected graph with the set of N vertices $\mathcal{V} = \{1, 2, ..., N\}$, the set of edges $\mathcal{E} \subseteq \mathcal{V} \times \mathcal{V}$, and the adjacency matrix $A = [a_{ij}]$. For any $(i,j) \in \mathcal{E}$, $i \neq j$, the element of the adjacency matrix a_{ij} is positive, and with $(i,j) \notin \mathcal{E}$ or $i = j$, $a_{ij} = 0$. The degree of vertex i is denoted as $\Delta_i = \sum_{j=1}^n a_{ij}$ and the degree matrix of graph $\mathcal{G}$ is defined as $\Delta = \mathbf{diag}(\Delta_1, \Delta_2, \ldots, \Delta_N)$, where **diag** stands for a diagonal matrix. The Laplacian matrix is defined as $L = [\ell_{ij}] = \Delta - A$. Further, $\mathcal{G}$ is called an undirected connected graph if and only if matrix A is symmetric and the algebraic multiplicity of zero as an eigenvalue of L is one. The set of all neighbours of vertex i is denoted as $\mathcal{N}_i = \{j \in \mathcal{V} \mid (i,j) \in \mathcal{E}\}$.

2   Problem Description

In this section, we present the mathematical description of a networked control system under cyber attacks. Then, the purposes and resources of the adversary and the defender are introduced.

2.1   Networked Control Systems Under False Data Injection Attacks

Consider a networked control system associated with an undirected connected graph $\mathcal{G} \triangleq (\mathcal{V}, \mathcal{E}, A)$ with N vertices where every vertex i is described by the one-dimensional state-space model:

$$\dot{x}_i(t) = u_i(t), \, i \in \{1, 2, \ldots, N\}, \tag{1}$$

where $x_i(t) \in \mathbb{R}$ represents the state variable of vertex i, and $u_i(t) \in \mathbb{R}$ denotes the control input for the same vertex. The state of the entire network will be denoted as $x(t) \triangleq [x_1(t), x_2(t), \ldots, x_N(t)]^\top \in \mathbb{R}^N$. The control law for each vertex is:

$$u_i(t) = \sum_{j \in \mathcal{N}_i} a_{ji} (x_j(t) - x_i(t)), \, \forall \, i \in \mathcal{V}. \tag{2}$$

By applying the control law (2) to the state-space model (1) for the entire network, one obtains the following closed-loop model (3) without attacks:

$$\dot{x}(t) = -Lx(t), \tag{3}$$

where L is a Laplacian matrix representing the graph $\mathcal{G}$.

When the system is in the presence of a malicious adversary, we assume that the adversary selects a set of vertices to launch false data injection attacks (says $\zeta(t)$). Let the set of attack vertices be denoted as $\mathcal{A} \triangleq \{a_1, a_2, \ldots, a_{n_a}\}$ for a given attack budget $n_a - |\mathcal{A}|$. It is worth noting that there is no benefit of choosing fewer attack vertices than the budget and therefore we ignore the case of $|\mathcal{A}| < n_a$. The N-dimensional binary vector $B(\mathcal{A}) \in \{0, 1\}^N$ stands for the chosen attack vertices where its i-th element $B(\mathcal{A})_i = 1$ if i-th vertex is attacked and $B(\mathcal{A})_i = 0$ otherwise. Then, the networked control system (3) under false data injection attacks can be rewritten as follows:

$$\dot{x}(t) = -Lx(t) + B(\mathcal{A})\zeta(t). \tag{4}$$

Let us make use of the following assumption.

Assumption 1. The networked control system (4) is at its equilibrium $x_e = 0$ before being affected by attack signals.

In the following parts, the network performance and the purposes of the adversary and the defender will be described in more detail.

2.2   Network Performance and Monitoring

In the networked control system, the overall performance of the system is the collective performance of all vertices in the system. Consequently, the cost function for the system performance can be denoted as:

$$J = \sum_{i \in \mathcal{V}} \|y_i\|_{\mathcal{L}_2}^2, \tag{5}$$

$$y_i(t) = e_i^\top x(t), \ \forall i \in \mathcal{V}. \tag{6}$$

The security challenge against the malicious adversary stems from the assumed budget limitation within the system, making it necessary to select a subset of vertices to monitor for the residual signal since it is not feasible to monitor all vertices. This security resource constraint enforces the defender chooses a subset of the vertex set $\mathcal{V}$ to serve as the monitor set $\mathcal{M} = \{m_1, m_2, \ldots, m_{n_s}\}$ for a given sensor budget $n_s = |\mathcal{M}|$. The outputs of the monitor vertices can be written as follows:

$$y_{m_k}(t) = e_{m_k}^\top x(t), \ \forall m_k \in \mathcal{M}. \tag{7}$$

By monitoring outputs (7), the defender can notify the presence of the adversary if the energy of the monitor outputs crosses a given alarm threshold δ, i.e.,

$$\|y_{m_k}\|_{\mathcal{L}_2}^2 > \delta. \tag{8}$$

Remark 1. *In this paper, we assume that the alarm threshold δ is given by the operator, which cannot be altered by the defender. Therefore, the problem of choosing the alarm threshold is not considered in this study. Instead, the defender is allowed to choose vertices, which have their given corresponding alarm thresholds, to monitor their outputs with the purpose of detecting malicious activities.*

2.3 The Purposes of Adversary and Defender

In the following, we first present the purpose of the adversary. Then, the purpose of the defender is introduced.

The purpose of the malicious adversary is to maximize the negative impact on the system performance, i.e., the adversary seeks to maximize the cost function J in (5). Furthermore, there are strong arguments as to why the malicious adversary simultaneously would seek to remain stealthy to the defender, (see the discussion in [27, Section II-E]). One can assume that the defender would quickly mitigate the attack when detected by shutting down the maliciously affected communication channels. This means there will be no payoff for the adversary, additionally one can assume that the malicious adversary has invested resources to obtain system knowledge and to infiltrate the system, which will most likely be lost when detected. Therefore, to avoid losing the investment the adversary has made, this paper considers that the malicious adversary conducts stealthy data injection attacks, which will be defined in the following.

Let us consider the networked control system under cyber attacks (4) and the monitor outputs (7). The false data injection attack $\zeta(t)$ in (4) is called a stealthy false data injection attack if, and only if, the monitor outputs $\|y_{m_k}\|_{\mathcal{L}_2}^2 < \delta$ for all $m_k \in \mathcal{M}$. If at least one monitor vertex $m_k \in \mathcal{M}$ does not satisfy this, the attack from the malicious adversary is detected.

Additionally, a realistic assumption is that the adversary has finite resources not only in the number of attack vertices but also in the energy of the attack signals. In more detail, let us denote a positive number A_e as the maximum attack energy of the attack signal $\zeta(t)$ for a given time horizon $[0, T]$, i.e.

$$\|\zeta\|_{\mathcal{L}_2[0,T]}^2 \leq A_e. \tag{9}$$

The purpose of the defender is to allocate security resources given the potential existence of a malicious adversary that seeks to negatively impact the system's performance. However, a realistic assumption is that the defender is unable to foresee the action of the adversary. Therefore, the defender needs to formulate a defense strategy without knowing the attack strategy. An approach that has not been considered in existing literature, is the utilization of centrality measures to select monitor vertices in the networked control system. This approach will be utilized and presented more thoroughly in the following sections.

3 Risk Analysis and Evaluation

Given the networked control system under cyber attacks outlined in (4), the network performance (5), and the monitor outputs (7), the attack set $\mathcal{A}$, and the monitor set $\mathcal{M}$, the worst-case attack impact (WCAI) on the network performance is formulated as follows:

$$J(\mathcal{A}, \mathcal{M}) = \sup_{\zeta \in \mathcal{L}_{2e}} \sum_{i \in \mathcal{V}} \|y_i\|_{\mathcal{L}_2}^2$$

$$\text{s.t.} \quad \|y_{m_k}\|_{\mathcal{L}_2}^2 < \delta, \; \forall m_k \in \mathcal{M}, \tag{10}$$

$$\|\zeta\|_{\mathcal{L}_2}^2 \leq A_e,$$

$$(4), (6), (7), \; x(0) = 0.$$

The following theorem presents the boundedness of the non-convex optimization problem (10) and its computation.

Theorem 1. *The worst-case impact of stealthy FDI attacks is always bounded and computed by the following semi-definite programming (SDP) problem.*

$$J(\mathcal{A}, \mathcal{M}) = \min_{P = P^\top \succeq 0, \, \beta > 0, \, \gamma_{m_k} > 0} A_e \beta + \delta \sum_{m_k \in \mathcal{M}} \gamma_{m_k} \tag{11}$$

$$\text{s.t.} \quad \begin{bmatrix} -LP - PL & PB(\mathcal{A}) \\ B(\mathcal{A})^\top P & -\beta \end{bmatrix} + \sum_{i \in \mathcal{V}} \begin{bmatrix} e_i^\top \\ 0 \end{bmatrix} \begin{bmatrix} e_i \; 0 \end{bmatrix}$$

$$- \sum_{m_k \in \mathcal{M}} \gamma_{m_k} \begin{bmatrix} e_{m_k}^\top \\ 0 \end{bmatrix} \begin{bmatrix} e_{m_k} \; 0 \end{bmatrix} \preceq 0.$$

$\triangleleft$

Proof. The networked control system (4) is stable due to the fact that matrix $-L$ is negative semi-definite. Meanwhile, the attack input ζ has bounded energy. As a result, the output performance y_i also has bounded energy for all $i \in \mathcal{V}$, leading to the boundedness of (10). Next, the computation of (10) is shown. Let us consider the dual form of (10) described in the following:

$$\inf_{\gamma_k > 0, \beta > 0} \left[\sup_{\zeta \in \mathcal{L}_{2e}} \sum_{i \in \mathcal{V}} \|y_i\|_{\mathcal{L}_2}^2 + \sum_{m_k \in \mathcal{M}} \gamma_k \left(\delta - \|y_{m_k}\|_{\mathcal{L}_2}^2 \right) + \beta \left(A_e - \|\zeta\|_{\mathcal{L}_2}^2 \right) \right] \tag{12}$$

$$\text{s.t.} \quad (4), (6), (7), \; x(0) = 0.$$

The dual form (12) is bounded if, and only if,

$$\sum_{i \in \mathcal{V}} \|y_i\|_{\mathcal{L}_2}^2 - \sum_{m_k \in \mathcal{M}} \gamma_k \|y_{m_k}\|_{\mathcal{L}_2}^2 - \beta \|\zeta\|_{\mathcal{L}_2}^2 \leq 0, \; \forall \zeta \in \mathcal{L}_{2e}, \; x(0) = 0. \tag{13}$$

As a result, the dual form can be rewritten as follows:

$$J(\mathcal{A}, \mathcal{M}) = \inf_{\gamma_k > 0, \beta > 0} \delta \sum_{m_k \in \mathcal{M}} \gamma_k + A_e \beta \tag{14}$$

$$\text{s.t.} \quad \sum_{i \in \mathcal{V}} \|y_i\|_{\mathcal{L}_2}^2 - \sum_{m_k \in \mathcal{M}} \gamma_k \|y_{m_k}\|_{\mathcal{L}_2}^2 - \beta \|\zeta\|_{\mathcal{L}_2}^2 \leq 0,$$

$$(4), (6), (7), \; x(0) = 0.$$

Recalling the key results in dissipative system theory for linear systems [26] with a non-negative storage function $V(x) = x(t)^\top P x(t)$ where $P = P^\top \succeq 0$ and a supply rate $s(\cdot, \cdot) = \sum_{m_k \in \mathcal{M}} \gamma_k \|y_{m_k}\|_{\mathcal{L}_2}^2 + \beta \|\zeta\|_{\mathcal{L}_2}^2 - \sum_{i \in \mathcal{V}} \|y_i\|_{\mathcal{L}_2}^2$, the optimization problem (14) can be computed by the SDP (11). ∎

Given that the adversary seeks to maximize the worst-case attack impact on the system, the defender selects a monitor set to minimize the worst-case attack impact. In practice, the defender seldom foresees when the adversary attacks the system. Thus, the defender should make a decision on their defense strategy before the adversary does. As a result, the optimal security allocation can be formulated as the following minimax optimization problem:

$$\min_{\mathcal{M}, |\mathcal{M}|=n_s} \left[\max_{\mathcal{A}, |\mathcal{A}|=n_a} J(\mathcal{A}, \mathcal{M}) \right]. \tag{15}$$

The above optimal security allocation can be rewritten as follows:

$$\min_{\mathcal{M}, |\mathcal{M}|=n_s} Q \tag{16}$$
$$\text{s.t.} \quad J(\mathcal{A}, \mathcal{M}) \leq Q, \ \forall \mathcal{A}, \ |\mathcal{A}| = n_a.$$

In the next section, we discuss how to compute (16) and its approximate solution based on centrality measures.

4 Security Allocation

This section outlines the methodology employed in this paper, encompassing all methods and approaches utilized to derive the results. The novel approach of selecting the monitoring set $\mathcal{M}$ utilizing centrality measures, and the approach of assessing monitoring sets.

4.1 Optimal Security Allocation

Inspired by our previous work [20, Proposition 1], the defender is able to find the optimal security allocation by solving the combinatorial problem (16). The following theorem states the computation of the optimization problem (16).

Theorem 2. *For each attack set $\mathcal{A}$, let us denote a tuple variable $(\bar{z}_{\mathcal{A}}, P_{\mathcal{A}}) \in \mathbb{R}^N \times \mathbb{S}^N$ correspondingly. Denote an N-dimensional binary vector $z_{\mathcal{M}} \in \{0, 1\}^N$ as a representation of the monitor set $\mathcal{M}$ where m-entry of $z_{\mathcal{M}}$ being equal to 1 indicates that m-th node belongs to $\mathcal{M}$. Suppose that the adversary finds an attack set $\mathcal{A}$ such that it maximizes the worst-case impact of stealthy FDI attacks (10). Then, the optimal security allocation (16) is determined by $z_{\mathcal{M}}^\star$ which is the solution to the following mixed-integer SDP problem:*

$$\min_{\bar{z}_{\mathcal{A}} \in \mathbb{R}^N, z_{\mathcal{M}} \in \{0,1\}^N, P_{\mathcal{A}} = P_{\mathcal{A}}^\top \succeq 0, \beta > 0, Q > 0} Q \tag{17}$$

$$\text{s.t.} \quad \mathbf{1}_N^\top z_{\mathcal{M}} = n_s, \ \delta \mathbf{1}_N^\top \bar{z}_{\mathcal{A}} + A_e \beta \leq Q, \ 0 \leq \bar{z}_{\mathcal{A}} \leq \tilde{M} z_{\mathcal{M}}, \ |\mathcal{A}| = n_a,$$

$$\begin{bmatrix} -L^\top P_{\mathcal{A}} - P_{\mathcal{A}} L & P_{\mathcal{A}} B(\mathcal{A}) \\ B(\mathcal{A})^\top P_{\mathcal{A}} & -\beta_{\mathcal{A}} \end{bmatrix} + \mathbf{diag}\left(\begin{bmatrix} I \\ 0 \end{bmatrix} \right) - \mathbf{diag}\left(\begin{bmatrix} \bar{z}_{\mathcal{A}} \\ 0 \end{bmatrix} \right) \leq 0, \ \forall \mathcal{A},$$

where $\mathbf{1}_N$ is an N-dimensional all-one vector, n_s is the sensor budget, n_a is the attack budget, δ is the given alarm threshold, A_e is the maximum attack energy, and $\tilde{M}$ is a given large positive number, also called a "big M" [14].

Proof. The proof directly follows [20, Proposition 1]. ∎

4.2 Centrality-Based Security Allocation

The methodology of selecting monitor sets based on the centrality measures including degree, betweenness, and closeness centrality relies on the idea that the most connected or influential vertices in the graph would be the most suitable monitor vertices. Therefore, we create all possible monitor sets for each centrality measure given the monitor budget n_s. Then, we derive the total centrality for each monitor set by summing up the calculated centrality measure for each vertex. Finally, we select the monitor set with the highest total centrality according to the specific centrality measure. Given the sensor budget, this ensures that the vertices with the highest centrality are selected as the monitor set. This process, while straightforward, often results in duplicate solutions where different monitor sets may have the same total centrality. For example, if the sensor budget is two and there are three vertices with the highest and identical centrality, there must be multiple monitor sets with the same highest total centrality. In these cases, all monitor sets are evaluated by solving (11) and selecting the monitor set with the smallest WCAI. This method is applied to all three centrality measures which are degree centrality, closeness centrality, and betweenness centrality measures. Let us make use of the following definition of the above-mentioned centrality measures.

Definition 1 (Centrality measures [6]). *Given a graph $\mathcal{G} \triangleq (\mathcal{V}, \mathcal{E}, A)$ and $d(i, j)$ as the shortest path from node i to node j, the degree centrality measure of node $i \in \mathcal{V}$, denoted as $C_D(i)$, is the total number of connections between node i and its neighbors, i.e.,*

$$C_D(i) \triangleq \Delta_i = \sum_{j \in \mathcal{N}_i} a_{ij}. \tag{18}$$

The closeness centrality measure of node $i \in \mathcal{V}$, denoted as $C_C(i)$, is the inverse-average shortest path length from the vertex to all the other vertices, i.e.,

$$C_C(i) \triangleq \frac{N-1}{\sum_{j \neq i} d(i, j)}. \tag{19}$$

The betweenness centrality measure of node $i \in \mathcal{V}$, denoted as $C_B(i)$, is the number of shortest paths that pass through vertex i of interest among all shortest paths between pairs of vertices in the graph, i.e.,

$$C_B(i) \triangleq \sum_{s \neq i \neq t} \frac{\sigma_{st}(i)}{\sigma_{st}}, \tag{20}$$

where σ_{st} is the total number of shortest paths from vertex s to t and $\sigma_{st}(i)$ is the number of shortest paths from vertex s to t that pass through vertex i.

Moreover, a combined centrality measure approach is considered where the three monitor sets (obtained from the respective centrality metrics) are first compared to each other, and the one with the smallest WCAI is selected and then compared with the optimal solution. The combined method allows us to ascertain if utilizing only one of these centrality measures would generally give a larger gap to the optimal solution than using all three and always picking the best one.

Let us denote the set of monitoring vertices founded by degree centrality measure as $z_{\mathcal{M}}^d$, closeness centrality measure as $z_{\mathcal{M}}^c$, betweenness centrality measure as $z_{\mathcal{M}}^b$, combined centrality measure as $z_{\mathcal{M}}^o$. After we obtain the set of monitoring vertices that has the highest centrality measures, denoted $z_{\mathcal{M}}^\dagger \in \{0, 1\}^N$ where $\dagger \in \{d, c, b, o\}$, we can compute the worst-case impact of stealthy FDI attacks by replacing the known value $z_{\mathcal{M}}^\dagger$ with the binary variable $z_{\mathcal{M}}$ in (17). It is worth noting that the optimization problem (17) with $z_{\mathcal{M}}^\dagger$ is an SDP problem and can be solved much faster than the mixed-integer version presented in (17) with $z_{\mathcal{M}}$ as a binary variable.

5   Results

This section describes the empirical results of centrality measure-based security allocation in networked control systems. In the first part, we show experimental results on Erdős-Rényi random graphs where an edge is included to connect two vertices with a probability of 0.5. In the second part, we present how the centrality measure assists the security allocation in an IEEE benchmark for power systems (IEEE 14-bus system).

5.1   Erdős-Rényi Random Graphs

All the experiments were performed using Matlab 2023b with YALMIP 2021 [12] and MOSEK solver on a personal computer with 2.9-GHz, 8-core Intel i7-10700 processor and 16 GB of RAM. Due to the limited hardware, the size of networks is restricted from 10 to 20. It is worth noting that not only the size of the network influence the complexity of the security allocation problem (17), but the attack scenarios also significantly contribute to its complexity. More specifically, given the attack budget n_a, the number of attack scenarios is computed by $\binom{N}{n_a}$, significantly scaling up with the network size and the attack budget. Therefore, we limit our experiment to the network size $N = \{10, 12, 14, 16, 18, 20\}$, the attack budget $n_a = \{1, 2\}$, and the monitor budget $n_s = 1$. For each network size, we did the experiment with 30 Erdős-Rényi random graphs.

The experimental results are shown in Figs. 1–2 for the relative gaps in WCAI and Figs. 3–4 for the relative gaps in solving time. As seen in Fig. 1, monitor sets chosen based on combined centrality and betweenness centrality measures perform very well where their median and 75 percentile values are kept under 10%. In particular, 75 percentile values of the combined centrality measure in case of 2 attack budget stay at zero. Regarding solving time in Fig. 3, security allocation

based on combined centrality measures reduces around 70% solving time while
the other centrality measures decrease approximately 90% solving time compared with solving the optimal value. When we increase the size of the network
up to 20 depicted in Fig. 2, the relative gaps in WCAI increase in all centrality
measures, particularly degree and closeness centrality measures. However, the
numbers for combined centrality and betweenness centrality measures are still
kept under 15%. The relative gaps in solving time are almost the same in the
case of smaller networks (see Fig. 4).

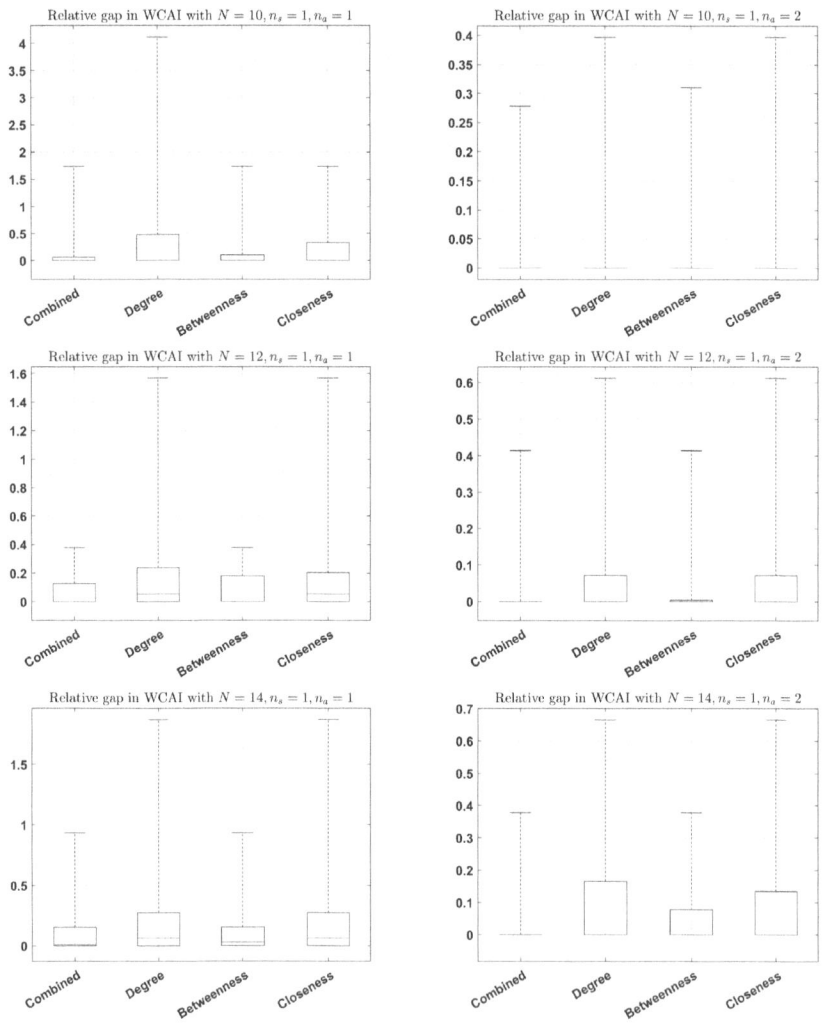

Fig. 1. Relative gap of the worst-case attack impact between the optimal value and the
value given by choosing monitor vertices based on centrality measures. The network
size $N = \{10, 12, 14\}$, the attack budget $n_a = \{1, 2\}$, and the monitor budget $n_s = 1$.
For each network size, 30 Erdős-Rényi random graphs where an edge is included to
connect two vertices with a probability of 0.5.

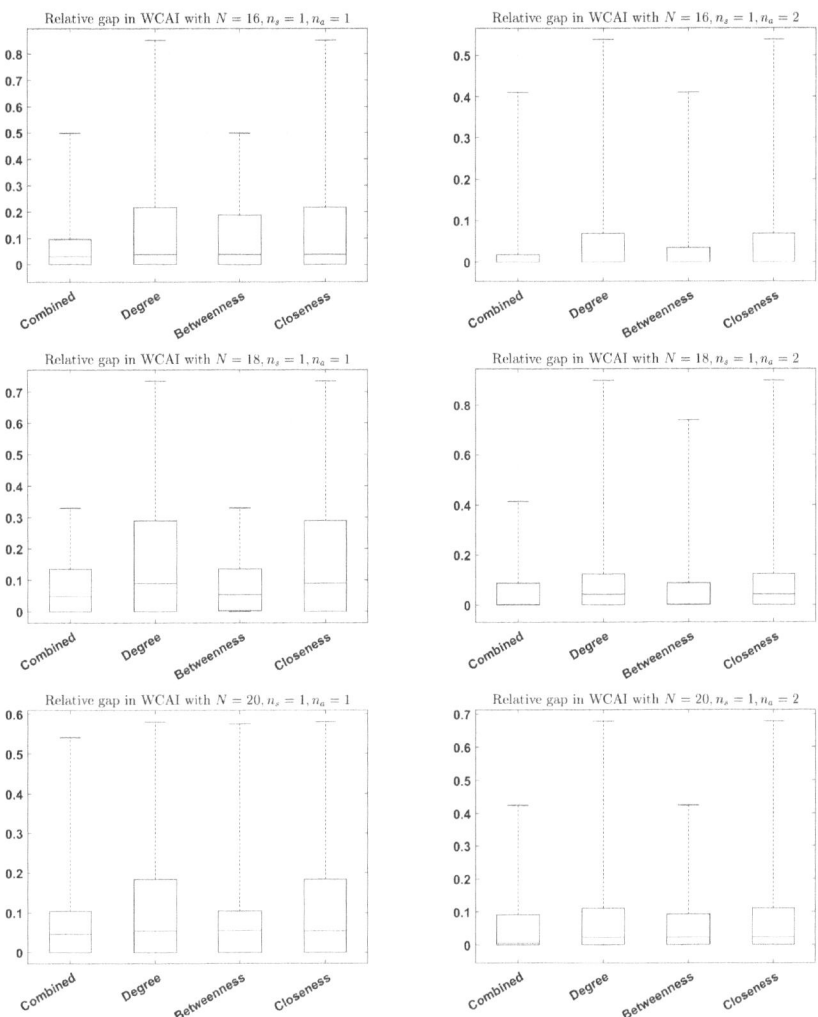

Fig. 2. Relative gap of the worst-case attack impact between the optimal value and the value given by choosing monitor vertices based on centrality measures. The network size $N = \{16, 18, 20\}$, the attack budget $n_a = \{1, 2\}$, and the monitor budget $n_s = 1$. For each network size, 30 Erdős-Rényi random graphs where an edge is included to connect two vertices with a probability of 0.5.

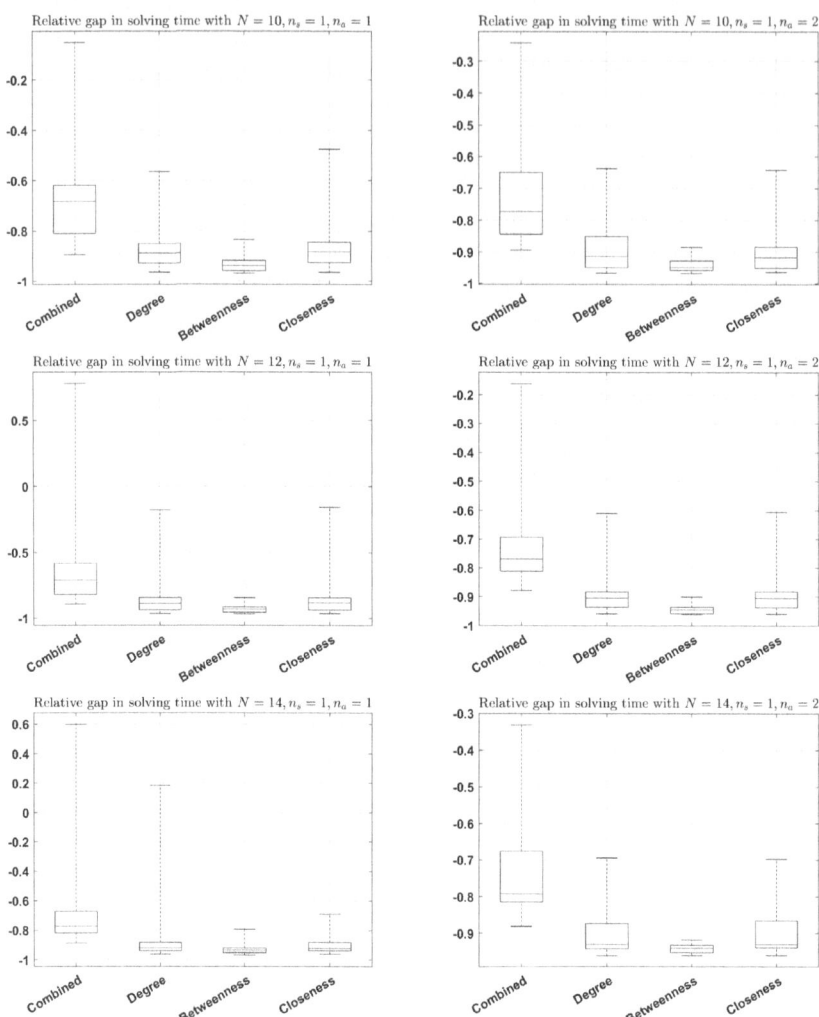

Fig. 3. Relative gap of the solving time between the optimal value and the value given by choosing monitor vertices based on centrality measures. The network size $N = \{10,\ 12,\ 14\}$, the attack budget $n_a = \{1,\ 2\}$, and the monitor budget $n_s = 1$. For each network size, 30 Erdős-Rényi random graphs where an edge is included to connect two vertices with a probability of 0.5.

5.2   IEEE 14-Bus System

In this part, we did an experiment on an IEEE benchmark of power systems which is the IEEE 14-bus system, depicted in Fig. 5. The system includes 14 buses and 20 transmission lines. The behavior of a bus $i \in \{1, 2, \ldots, 14\}$ can be described by the so-called swing equation [23]:

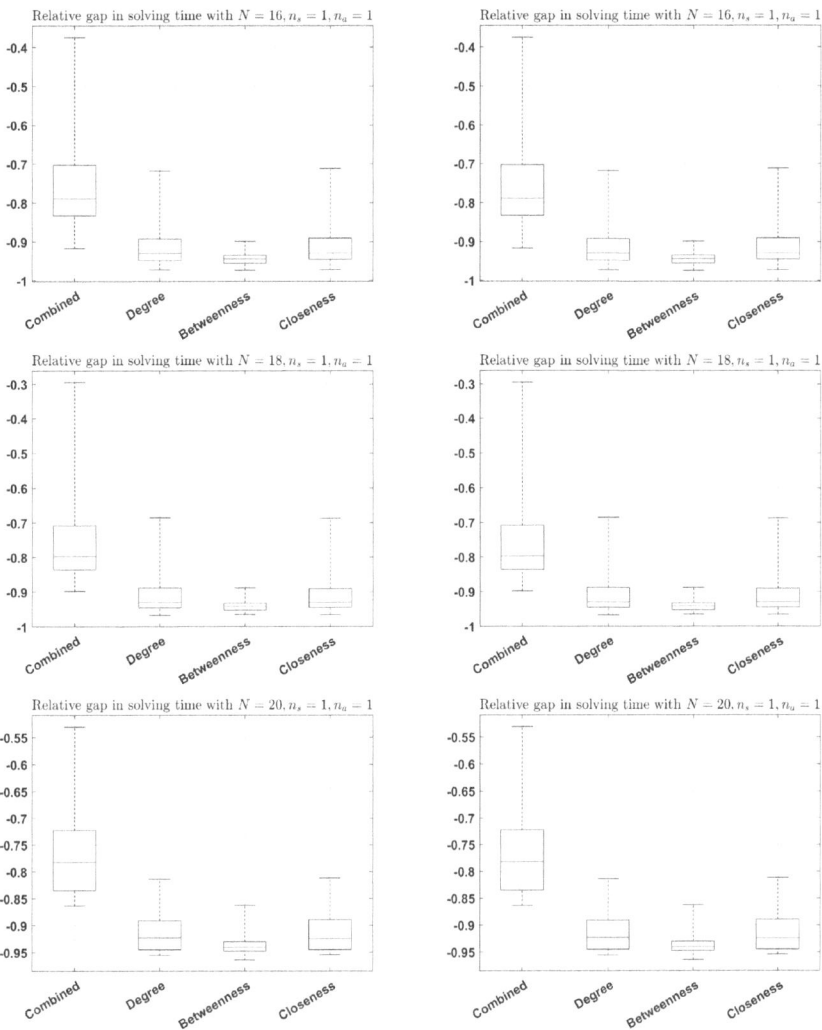

Fig. 4. Relative gap of the solving time between the optimal value and the value given by choosing monitor vertices based on centrality measures. The network size $N = \{16, 18, 20\}$, the attack budget $n_a = \{1, 2\}$, and the monitor budget $n_s = 1$. For each network size, 30 Erdős-Rényi random graphs where an edge is included to connect two vertices with a probability of 0.5.

$$I_i \ddot{\theta}_i(t) + D_i \dot{\theta}_i(t) = -\sum_{j \in \mathcal{N}_i} P_{ij}(t), \tag{21}$$

where I_i and D_i are the inertia and damping coefficients, respectively, and P_{ij} is the active power flow from bus j to bus i. Considering that there are no power losses and $V_i = |V_i|e^{jp_i}$ $(j^2 = -1)$ and θ_i be the complex voltage and the phase angle of the bus i, respectively. The active power flow $P_{ij}(t)$ from bus j to bus i is given by

$$P_{ij}(t) = -\ell_{ij}\sin(\theta_i - \theta_j), \tag{22}$$

where $-\ell_{ij} \in \mathbb{R}_+$ is the susceptance of the power transmission line connecting bus i with bus j. Those parameters consisting of line susceptance $-\ell_{ij}$, inertia I_i, and damping D_i can be found at [28] and are listed in Table 1. Since the phase angles usually are close, we can linearize (22) and rewrite the dynamics (21) of bus i as follows

$$I_i\ddot{\theta}_i(t) + D_i\dot{\theta}_i(t) = \sum_{j \in \mathcal{N}_i} \ell_{ij}\Big(\theta_i(t) - \theta_j(t)\Big), \tag{23}$$

which can be rewritten as follows:

$$\frac{\mathrm{d}}{\mathrm{d}t}\begin{bmatrix}\dot{\theta}(t)\\ \theta(t)\end{bmatrix} = \begin{bmatrix}0 & I\\ -I^{-1}L & -I^{-1}D\end{bmatrix}\begin{bmatrix}\dot{\theta}(t)\\ \theta(t)\end{bmatrix}, \tag{24}$$

where $\dot{\theta}(t) = [\dot{\theta}_1(t), \dot{\theta}_2(t), \ldots, \dot{\theta}_N(t)]^\top$, $\theta(t) = [\theta_1(t), \theta_2(t), \ldots, \theta_N(t)]^\top$. Further, L is a Laplacian matrix representing the network, $I = \mathrm{diag}(I_i)$, and $D = \mathrm{diag}(D_i)$.

By applying the computation of centrality measures in the previous section, we found that the bus number 4 always has the highest value. However, the optimal value computed by (17) gives us the optimal bus number 2. Next, we compare the WCAI of all the monitor buses depicted in Fig. 6. We observe that the relative gap in WCAI of the bus number 4 compared to the optimal bus 2 is under 2%, an acceptable value. Meanwhile, the other buses provide much higher relative gaps, for example, bus 8 gives us 10% relative gap.

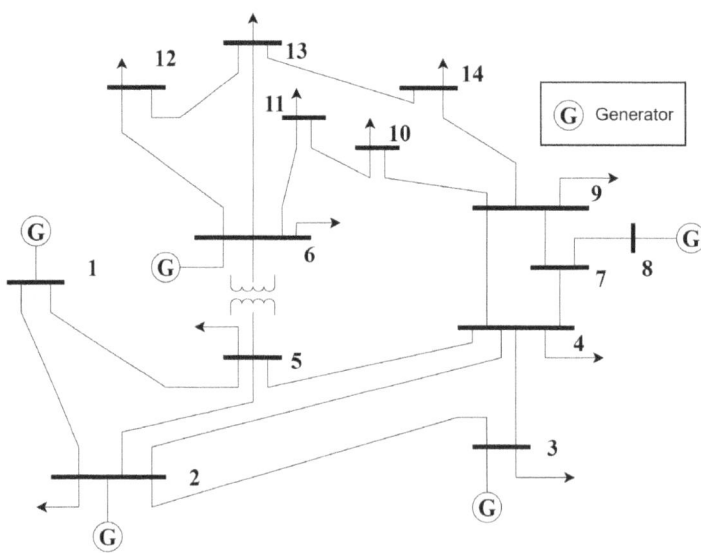

Fig. 5. IEEE 14-bus system.

Table 1. Parameters of the IEEE 14-bus system.

Susceptance	Inertial	Damping
$-\ell_{12} = 8.2838$	$I_1 = 1.060$	$D_1 = 0$
$-\ell_{15} = 31.2256$	$I_2 = 1.045$	$D_2 = 4.98$
$-\ell_{23} = 27.7158$	$I_3 = 1.010$	$D_3 = 12.72$
$-\ell_{24} = 24.6848$	$I_4 = 1.019$	$D_4 = 10.33$
$-\ell_{25} = 24.3432$	$I_5 = 1.020$	$D_5 = 8.78$
$-\ell_{34} = 23.9442$	$I_6 = 1.070$	$D_6 = 14.22$
$-\ell_{45} = 5.8954$	$I_7 = 1.062$	$D_7 = 13.37$
$-\ell_{47} = 29.2768$	$I_8 = 1.090$	$D_8 = 13.36$
$-\ell_{49} = 77.8652$	$I_9 = 1.056$	$D_9 = 14.94$
$-\ell_{56} = 35.2828$	$I_{10} = 1.051$	$D_{10} = 15.10$
$-\ell_{6,11} = 35.2828$	$I_{11} = 1.057$	$D_{11} = 14.79$
$-\ell_{6,12} = 35.8134$	$I_{12} = 1.055$	$D_{12} = 15.07$
$-\ell_{6,13} = 18.2378$	$I_{13} = 1.050$	$D_{13} = 15.16$
$-\ell_{78} = 24.6610$	$I_{14} = 1.036$	$D_{14} = 16.04$
$-\ell_{79} = 15.4014$		
$-\ell_{9,10} = 11.8300$		
$-\ell_{9,14} = 37.8532$		
$-\ell_{10,11} = 26.8898$		
$-\ell_{12,13} = 27.9832$		
$-\ell_{13,14} = 48.7228$		

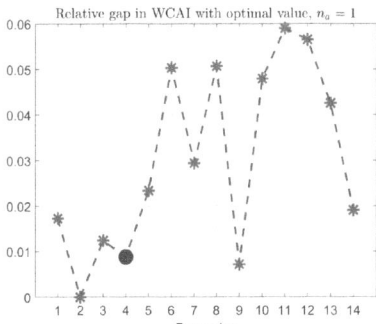 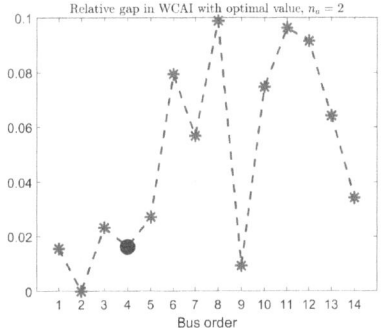

Fig. 6. Relative gap of the worst-case attack impact between the optimal value and the value given by choosing a monitor vertex based on centrality measures (blue dot at bus 4). (Color figure online)

6   Conclusion

In conclusion, we explored the security allocation problem within a networked control system featuring two opposing agents: a defender and a malicious adversary. The adversary aims to maximize the WCAI on the network performance while remaining undetected, by launching stealthy data injection attacks. Conversely, the defender's objective is to allocate security resources to minimize the WCAI. The proposed approach was centrality measures-based security allocation using degree, betweenness, and closeness centrality, in addition to a combined centrality measure approach using all three. The conclusion one can draw from this study is that the combined approach, although it could only perform as well as the best monitor set derived using the three centrality measures for each graph, outperformed them on average across the 30 Erdős-Rényi random graphs (a probability of 0.5) with 10 to 20 vertices considered in this paper. This approach can be utilized for security allocation in networks if the relative gap of 10% in terms of WCAI to the optimal solution is acceptable. We can also conclude that because the solver times are significantly shorter for the combined centrality measure approach than computing the optimal solution, this method is advantageous when hardware capabilities are limited. Additionally, among the three centrality measures investigated, the betweenness centrality performed the best. Similar to the combined centrality measure approach, we can conclude that betweenness centrality can be utilized for the security allocation in networks derived using Erdős-Rényi random graphs (a probability of 0.5) with 10 to 20 vertices. Moreover, the solver time for only using betweenness centrality is a third or shorter than the combined approach.

Acknowledgments. This work is supported by the Swedish Research Council under the grant 2021-06316 and by the Swedish Foundation for Strategic Research.

References

1. Anand, S.C., Teixeira, A.M.H., Ahlén, A.: Risk assessment and optimal allocation of security measures under stealthy false data injection attacks. In: 2022 IEEE Conference on Control Technology and Applications (CCTA), pp. 1347–1353. IEEE (2022). https://doi.org/10.1109/CCTA49430.2022.9966025
2. Başar, T., Olsder, G.J.: Dynamic noncooperative game theory. SIAM (1998)
3. Falliere, N., Murchu, L.O., Chien, E.: W32. stuxnet dossier. White Pap. Symantec Corp. Secur. Response **5**(6), 29 (2011)
4. Ferrari, R.M.G., Teixeira, A.M.H.: A switching multiplicative watermarking scheme for detection of stealthy cyber-attacks. IEEE Trans. Autom. Control **66**(6), 2558–2573 (2020). https://doi.org/10.1109/TAC.2020.3013850
5. Gallo, A.J., Anand, S.C., Teixeira, A.M.H., Ferrari, R.M.: Design of multiplicative watermarking against covert attacks. In: 2021 60th IEEE Conference on Decision and Control (CDC), pp. 4176–4181. IEEE (2021). https://doi.org/10.1109/CDC45484.2021.9683075

6. Golbeck, J.: Network structure and measures. In: Analyzing the Social Web, chap. 3, pp. 25–44. Newnes (2013)

7. Gupta, A., Langbort, C., Başar, T.: Dynamic games with asymmetric information and resource constrained players with applications to security of cyberphysical systems. IEEE Trans. Control Netw. Syst. **4**(1), 71–81 (2016). https://doi.org/10.1109/TCNS.2016.2584183

8. Kshetri, N., Voas, J.: Hacking power grids: a current problem. Computer **50**(12), 91–95 (2017). https://doi.org/10.1109/MC.2017.4451203

9. Li, Y., Shi, D., Chen, T.: False data injection attacks on networked control systems: a stackelberg game analysis. IEEE Trans. Autom. Control **63**(10), 3503–3509 (2018). https://doi.org/10.1109/TAC.2018.2798817

10. Li, Z., Mo, Y.: Secure distributed dynamic state estimation against sparse integrity attack via distributed convex optimization. IEEE Trans. Autom. Control **69**(9), 6089–6104 (2024). https://doi.org/10.1109/TAC.2024.3397158

11. Li, Z., Nguyen, A.T., Teixeira, A.M., Mo, Y., Johansson, K.H.: Secure state estimation with asynchronous measurements against malicious measurement-data and time-stamp manipulation. In: 2023 62nd IEEE Conference on Decision and Control (CDC), pp. 7073–7080. IEEE (2023). https://doi.org/10.1109/CDC49753.2023.10383571

12. Lofberg, J.: Yalmip: a toolbox for modeling and optimization in matlab. In: 2004 IEEE International Conference on Robotics and Automation (IEEE Cat. No. 04CH37508), pp. 284–289. IEEE (2004). https://doi.org/10.1109/CACSD.2004.1393890

13. Miao, F., Zhu, Q., Pajic, M., Pappas, G.J.: A hybrid stochastic game for secure control of cyber-physical systems. Automatica **93**, 55–63 (2018). https://doi.org/10.1016/j.automatica.2018.03.012

14. Milošević, J., Dahan, M., Amin, S., Sandberg, H.: Strategic monitoring of networked systems with heterogeneous security levels. IEEE Trans. Control Netw. Syst. **11**(3), 1165–1176 (2023). https://doi.org/10.1109/TCNS.2023.3333392

15. Mo, Y., Chabukswar, R., Sinopoli, B.: Detecting integrity attacks on scada systems. IEEE Trans. Control Syst. Technol. **22**(4), 1396–1407 (2013). https://doi.org/10.1109/TCST.2013.2280899

16. Naha, A., Teixeira, A., Ahlén, A., Dey, S.: Quickest physical watermarking-based detection of measurement replacement attacks in networked control systems. Eur. J. Control. **71**, 100804 (2023). https://doi.org/10.1016/j.ejcon.2023.100804

17. Nguyen, A.T., Anand, S.C., Teixeira, A.M.: A zero-sum game framework for optimal sensor placement in uncertain networked control systems under cyber-attacks. In: 2022 IEEE 61st Conference on Decision and Control (CDC), pp. 6126–6133. IEEE (2022). https://doi.org/10.1109/CDC51059.2022.9992468

18. Nguyen, A.T., Anand, S.C., Teixeira, A.M., Medvedev, A.: Optimal detector placement in networked control systems under cyber-attacks with applications to power networks. IFAC-PapersOnLine **56**(2), 1820–1826 (2023). https://doi.org/10.1016/j.ifacol.2023.10.1896

19. Nguyen, A.T., Teixeira, A.M.H., Medvedev, A.: A single-adversary-single-detector zero-sum game in networked control systems. IFAC-PapersOnLine **55**(13), 49–54 (2022). https://doi.org/10.1016/j.ifacol.2022.07.234

20. Nguyen, A.T., Teixeira, A.M., Medvedev, A.: Security allocation in networked control systems under stealthy attacks. IEEE Trans. Control Netw. Syst. (2024). https://doi.org/10.1109/TCNS.2024.3462546

21. Park, G., Lee, C., Shim, H., Eun, Y., Johansson, K.H.: Stealthy adversaries against uncertain cyber-physical systems: threat of robust zero-dynamics attack. IEEE Trans. Autom. Control **64**(12), 4907–4919 (2019). https://doi.org/10.1109/TAC.2019.2903429

22. Shukla, P., An, L., Chakrabortty, A., Duel-Hallen, A.: A robust stackelberg game for cyber-security investment in networked control systems. IEEE Trans. Control Syst. Technol. **31**(2), 856–871 (2022). https://doi.org/10.1109/TCST.2022.3207671

23. Tegling, E.: Fundamental limitations of distributed feedback control in large-scale networks. Ph.D. thesis, KTH Royal Institute of Technology (2018)

24. Teixeira, A., Shames, I., Sandberg, H., Johansson, K.H.: A secure control framework for resource-limited adversaries. Automatica **51**, 135–148 (2015). https://doi.org/10.1016/j.automatica.2014.10.067

25. Teixeira, A.M.H.: Optimal stealthy attacks on actuators for strictly proper systems. In: 2019 IEEE 58th Conference on Decision and Control (CDC), pp. 4385–4390. IEEE (2019). https://doi.org/10.1109/CDC40024.2019.9029171

26. Trentelman, H.L., Willems, J.C.: The dissipation inequality and the algebraic Riccati equation. Springer (1991)

27. Umsonst, D., Sarıtaş, S., Dán, G., Sandberg, H.: A bayesian nash equilibrium-based moving target defense against stealthy sensor attacks. IEEE Trans. Autom. Control **69**(3), 1659–1674 (2024). https://doi.org/10.1109/TAC.2023.3328754

28. UW-EE: IEEE 14-bus test case (1993). labs.ece.uw.edu/pstca/pf14/ieee14cdf.txt

29. Yuan, H., Xia, Y., Zhang, J., Yang, H., Mahmoud, M.S.: Stackelberg-game-based defense analysis against advanced persistent threats on cloud control system. IEEE Trans. Ind. Inf. **16**(3), 1571–1580 (2019). https://doi.org/10.1109/TII.2019.2925035

30. Zhang, K., Keliris, C., Parisini, T., Polycarpou, M.M.: Stealthy integrity attacks for a class of nonlinear cyber-physical systems. IEEE Trans. Autom. Control **67**(12), 6723–6730 (2021). https://doi.org/10.1109/TAC.2021.3131656

Using Tabletop Exercises to Raise Cybersecurity Awareness of Decision-Makers

Joakim Kävrestad$^{(\boxtimes)}$, Sonny Johansson , and Erik Bergström

School of Engineering, Jönköping University, Jönköping, Sweden
{joakim.kavrestad,sonny.johansson,erik.bergstrom}@ju.se

Abstract. The continuous digitalization of modern organizations leads to increased exposure to digital threats. Consequently, safeguarding digital assets is central to the organization's resiliency and cybersecurity, which are core business functions. Commitment from organizational decision-makers is crucial for good cybersecurity posture since they are responsible for allocating resources and prioritising cybersecurity. To underpin such commitment, decision-makers must be aware of the organization's cybersecurity risks and digital assets. The subsequent challenge addressed in this research is to raise awareness among decision-makers. This research draws on previous research to develop a tabletop exercise designed to raise cybersecurity awareness among decision-makers. Using a multiple-case study research approach, the tabletop exercise was conducted and evaluated on six occasions with a total of 90 decision-makers from various industrial sectors. The general view of the participants was that the tabletop exercise was a good and engaging way to learn about cybersecurity. The main contribution of this research is that it outlines tabletop exercises as a promising approach to raising cybersecurity awareness among decision-makers. However, it is important that such exercises are designed so that enough time for discussions is allowed. Furthermore, this research identifies a need for more evaluations focusing on the long-term effects of tabletop exercises.

Keywords: Cybersecurity · Awareness · Decision-makers · Tabletop exercises

1 Introduction

The modern world is highly digital, and most organizations rely heavily on their digital infrastructures for day-to-day operations. Those digital infrastructures are cornerstones in modern operations and facilitate distance working, data sharing, processing, storage, and more. While there are many potential benefits, the risks also increase. When the digital ecosystem becomes tightly integrated with the core operation of an organization, the company's resilience depends on the digital ecosystem's resilience. Subsequently, protecting the digital ecosystem is

© The Author(s), under exclusive license to Springer Nature Switzerland AG 2025
G. Oliva et al. (Eds.): CRITIS 2024, LNCS 15549, pp. 231–248, 2025.
https://doi.org/10.1007/978-3-031-84260-3_14

central to the organizations' protection at large. As such, cybersecurity is essential to any modern organization.

A part of the industry where cybersecurity demands are even greater is critical information infrastructures (CII). The European Commission describes that CIIs are essential for operating critical infrastructures that provide food, water, healthcare, and more [19]. CIIs are a big part of the total industry. The Cybersecurity and Infrastructure Security Agency (CISA) lists 16 different sectors as CIIs, while the National Institute of Standards and Technology (NIST) lists eleven [13,35]. Those include energy, emergency services, financial services and manufacturing. This research intends to cover industry in general but with an emphasis on manufacturing industries. The rationale is that while cybersecurity is crucial for all sectors, Industry 4.0 and beyond have introduced technologies such as cloud solutions and IoT into factories. Consequently, the manufacturing industry faces new threats and needs to adapt [5,33]. Employees in manufacturing often lack specialist talent, have low cybersecurity awareness, and only possess basic cybersecurity skills [4,15]. This makes them attractive targets for exploitation [23]. A study found that manufacturing scored the lowest in ISP awareness and compliance among various industries, which is unsurprising given its traditional status as a non-data-intensive sector with less emphasis on cybersecurity [11].

Cybersecurity has traditionally been seen as a technical matter, but the view of cybersecurity is moving towards becoming a criticality for the entire organization [14,46]. Seeing cybersecurity as a technical matter has led to the perception that technicians can handle cybersecurity. However, researchers are promoting a view of cybersecurity as a socio-technical property equally dependant on technology, the organization, the people in the organization, and the interplay between them [30]. Cybersecurity ensures that digital infrastructures allow people to fulfil their and the organization's goals.

A core aspect of successful cybersecurity is a commitment from the organization's decision-makers [38,46]. Decision-makers are responsible for the prioritization of tasks and for the allocation of resources that are needed for successful cybersecurity. Furthermore, recent regulations such as NIS2 and GDPR put emphasis on the management's involvement in cybersecurity matters [6]. A precursor to being invested in cybersecurity is awareness of cybersecurity. Consequently, cybersecurity awareness of decision-makers is crucial for the cybersecurity posture of their organizations [21,43]. A subsequent challenge is to raise the awareness of organizational decision-makers.

Many different approaches to cybersecurity awareness raising are discussed in the literature, with different pros and cons [9]. Chowdhury and Gkioulos [9] describe that team exercises and real-life fidelity are essential attributes, and Brilingaitė et al. [7] emphasize social interaction as important for learning. Connecting content to the participants aligns well with the principles of how to motivate adult learners [28]. Tabletop exercises are described by the National Institute of Standards and Technology (NIST) as discussion-based exercises often preceded by a scenario presented by a facilitator [34]. They are presented as a promising method for cybersecurity awareness training in recent literature [3,10,31]. To what extent they are a valuable tool for training decision-makers is, however, understudied.

To that end, this research seeks to evaluate how decision-makers in the industry, with special emphasis on the manufacturing industry, perceive the use of tabletop exercises for cybersecurity awareness training. The following research questions have been developed for this research:

- How do decision-makers perceive cybersecurity training in the form of tabletop exercises?
- What are the differences and similarities between decision-makers in general and decision-makers in manufacturing industries regarding the perception of tabletop exercises for cybersecurity awareness training?

As described by Kävrestad and Nohlberg [27], evaluating cybersecurity awareness training based on perception is important since the target group's perception of the training is central to its adoption of the same. As such, the main contribution of this research is that it demonstrates tabletop exercises potential to be widely adopted as an awareness training method.

2 Background

This section outlines the area of cybersecurity awareness, cybersecurity awareness of decision-makers, and the use of tabletop exercises for conducting cybersecurity exercises to improve cybersecurity awareness.

2.1 Cybersecurity Awareness and Training

User behaviour is often the root cause of cybersecurity incidents [16]. The awareness and behaviour of users are, therefore, one crucial aspect of cybersecurity [40]. Cybersecurity awareness can be seen as the knowledge, appreciation, and understanding of aspects regarding cybersecurity, as well as awareness of related risks and appropriate countermeasures [36]. To raise the awareness level and improve user behaviour Joinson and van Steen [24] presents Security Education, Training, and Awareness (SETA) as a solution. User perception of the training is described as a key factor for adopting the training, but more research is needed on how acceptance can differ between groups [26].

2.2 Cybersecurity Awareness of Decision-Makers

The cybersecurity awareness of decision-makers is a crucial part of cybersecurity [8,21,43]. Choi et al. [8] presents a direct correlation between decision-makers information security awareness and managerial actions toward information security and suggests strategies that raise security awareness to improve cybersecurity performance. Decision-makers' security awareness is the result of different factors, including individual security knowledge, personal prioritization, and trust in security experts [41]. Another proposition is that the organizational dimension of security awareness is key and that the industry-specific sensitivity and current security countermeasures in the organization impact cybersecurity awareness. The security awareness of decision-makers greatly influences the scope of action of cybersecurity professionals, which in turn affects the cybersecurity performance of the organization. But this affects not only top management; security awareness is important on all levels, and decision-makers at all levels of an organization need to be included for effective cybersecurity management [21,41]. The most important knowledge requirements for decision-makers identified by Garcia-Granados and Bahsi [21] are within risk management and selection of countermeasures. Even though the connection between the level of cybersecurity awareness for decision-makers and an organization's security performance is clearly proven, a recent study found that decision-makers have poor awareness of well-known threats and countermeasures [43].

2.3   Tabletop Exercises to Increase Cybersecurity Awareness

One way of conducting cybersecurity awareness training is through tabletop exercises. These are described as discussion-based exercises often preceded by a scenario presented by a facilitator [34]. They have been proposed within different fields, including emergency management [18,39], public health [17], and health-care education [20]. Tabletop exercises have also been applied for cybersecurity in multiple studies [2,3,10,31,37] with promising results.

Ottis [37] proposed already in 2014 to use lightweight tabletop exercises for raising cybersecurity awareness and evaluated the exercise on master students with good results. Brilingaitė et al. [7] presented a web-based exercise which was found to be sufficient for learning but lacking in how it promoted interaction and collaboration. Focusing specifically on cybersecurity incident response teams (CSIRTs), Angafor et al. [2,3] showed that tabletop exercises can be used to increase awareness. Tabletop exercises can be useful in teaching technical and non-technical skills and can be used to develop skills in, for instance, problem-solving, communication, and teamwork. [10] presented a framework for tabletop exercises building on the Personalized Learning Theory (PLT), including evaluation with security professionals and technical operators at an energy company, as well as master students. Their framework includes several attributes for good tabletop exercises, including ease of implementation, engaging, tailored to the target group, and flexibility.

The target groups in previous studies were mixed, and used university students for the evaluation. Vykopal et al. [44] calls for research focusing on different target groups. One interesting and important target group is decision-makers. As identified in the previous section, cybersecurity awareness of decision-makers and managers is crucial to cybersecurity. Maggio et al. [29] used a tabletop exercise with executives in academic health centers with good results. However, studies on decision-makers in industry, specifically manufacturing, remain understudied.

3   Methodology

To address the research aim, this research adopted a case study methodology described by Yin [47] as an in-depth investigation of a phenomenon in its real-life context. It is useful for exploratory research and, when employed in a multi-case fashion, allows the researchers to draw conclusions based on differences and similarities between cases [22,47]. In this research, a cybersecurity tabletop exercise was developed and tested in six distinct cases. Five workshops contained decision-makers from diverse industrial sectors, and one specifically included manufacturing industry decision-makers. Directly following each workshop, the participant's perceptions of the workshop were evaluated using a survey. The rest of this chapter will, in turn, elaborate on the workshop and cases, the data collection methods, and the data analysis.

3.1   Description of the Exercise and the Cases

The exercise was developed with the attributes presented by Chowdhury and Gkioulos [10] in mind. Chowdhury and Gkioulos [10] stress exercises that are:

- Easy to implement
- Engaging
- Tailored to the target group
- Flexible
- Able to run both physically and remotely

The tabletop exercise included two components: a presentation and a discussion-based exercise. The exercise was based on the CISA's open tabletop exercise package for Ransomware [12]. The purpose of the presentation that preceded the exercise was to inform the participants about the current cybersecurity threat landscape and recommendations on how to mitigate those threats. The presentation was developed with the assumption that the participants would have little or no expertise in cybersecurity. The presentation portion included:

- Overview of threat actors and their motivations.
- Overview of current threats such as phishing, ransomware, and supply chain attacks.
- Recommendations on how to mitigate threats using a risk-based approach to security as well as multi-factor authentication, awareness training, and backups.

The presentation was followed by a discussion-based tabletop exercise comprising two parts. In the first part, the participants were asked to reflect on their most critical assets. In the second part, the participants were asked to discuss how they would respond to a ransomware scenario. Two researchers served as instructors and were available to support the participants during the discussions.

The workshop was held on six occasions, with slight differences in time and group size. The cases are denoted Case n, and described below:

- **Case 1:** The first workshop included eight participants from a network of female decision-makers in a municipality (approximately 25,000 citizens) in Sweden. The time for the workshop was 50 min where 30 min was allocated for the presentation and 20 min for the exercise.
- **Case 2:** The second workshop included 32 participants from a network of decision-makers in the manufacturing industry in a county with approximately 750,000 citizens. The workshop was 85 min, 60 of which were allocated for the presentation and 25 for the exercise.
- **Case 3:** The third workshop included 17 participants from a network of female decision-makers in a Swedish municipality (approximately 35,000 citizens). The workshop was 90 min, 45 min of which were allocated for the presentation and 45 min for the exercise.
- **Case 4:** The fourth workshop included 12 participants who a business development organization invited. 140 min were allocated for the workshop. The presentation used 70 min, and the remaining 70 min were used for the exercise.
- **Case 5:** The fifth workshop included 17 participants and spanned 50 min evenly divided between presentation and exercise. The purpose was to evaluate the feasibility of running the tabletop exercise in a condensed format.
- **Case 6:** The sixth workshop included ten participants and was intended to span 90 min. Due to unforeseen events, the time was reduced to 60 min, of which 25 min were allocated to the presentation.

3.2   Data Collection

The participants were asked to complete a survey on their perception of the workshop after each workshop. The survey contained twelve Likert-scale statements, and the participants were asked to rate how well they agreed with the statements on a 7-point scale ranging from 1 (Completely disagree) to 7 (Completely agree). Likert-scale statements are well established for surveys measuring perceptions [25]. The statements intended to measure the participant's perception of the workshop in four categories based on Andriotis [1], Chowdhury and Gkioulos [10]. The statements included in the categories were based on Chowdhury and Gkioulos [10], Mareš et al. [31]. The categories and statements included were the following:

- Effectiveness
  - The content was relevant to me
  - I learned something new
  - We had enough time to complete the tasks
- Comprehension
  - It was easy to understand
  - The technical level was appropriate
  - The content was easy to understand

– Attractiveness
  - I enjoyed the event
  - This is a good way to inform about cybersecurity
  - The event was time well-spent
– Engagement
  - The other group members contributed to my learning
  - Discussions with peers were valuable
  - Having an instructor available was valuable

Directly following each workshop, the participating researchers filled in a brief contact summary. The contact summary was inspired by Matthew B. Miles [32] and aimed at capturing the salient points of each workshop. In practice, the contact summary was filled out on the same day as the workshop. It formed a basis for capturing our experience of the workshop that could then be related to how the participants experienced the workshop, hence helping explain the result.

3.3 Data Analysis

Using the multi-case approach, the data analysis first covered the individual cases one by one by presenting descriptive statistics from the survey and reflecting on those in relation to the experiences recorded by the researchers as salient points. Then, the cases' differences and similarities were explored to respond to the research questions. Indices reflecting the participants' mean responses in each of the four question categories were computed and compared across the six cases in response to RQ1. Cronbach's Alpha was computed to measure the internal consistency of each scale. Following the review by Taber [42], this study adopted an alpha value of at least 0.55 as the threshold of acceptance. RQ2 was explored using inferential statistics to test for differences between case 2 and the other cases. For that analysis, all cases except case 2 were considered one group, and case 2 was considered one group. Mann-Whitney U test was used to test between-group differences because of the ordinal nature of the data. The conventional 95% significance level was used for statistical tests [45].

4 Results

The results section first presents the experiences of the researchers and the results from the evaluation of each case. Then, a between-case analysis is presented.

4.1 Per Case Results

Case 1. The first workshop was intended to reserve 20 min for the presentation and 30 min for the workshop. It was held in Swedish but with English materials for the exercises and a survey in English. The participants were from companies with below 50 employees from different sectors. The researchers experienced that the workshop was well-received, and the participants appreciated both the content and the form. However, the presentation consumed too much time because a lot of discussions were sparked during the presentation. It was also clear from oral feedback that it was difficult for the participants to comprehend the material in English.

Six participants completed the survey, and the results are presented in Table 1. The participants responded to each statement with a number between 1 (Completely disagree) and 7 (Completely agree).

Table 1. Results from case 1

Category	Statement	Mean
Effectiveness	The content was relevant to me	6.7
	I learned something new	7
	We had enough time to complete the tasks	4.5
Comprehension	It was easy to understand	6.8
	The technical level was appropriate	6.2
	The content was easy to understand	6.5
Attractiveness	I enjoyed the event	7
	This is a good way to inform about cybersecurity	7
	The event was time well-spent	6.7
Engagement	The other group members contributed to my learning	6.8
	Discussions with peers were valuable	7
	Having an instructor available was valuable	7

As shown by Table 1, the participant's perception of the event was very positive, with mean values of above 6 for almost all statements. Having enough time deviated from that, and the results suggest that the workshop ran out of time. The perceptions of the participants align well with those of the researchers.

Case 2. The second workshop was extended to 85 min, during which 60 were allocated for the presentation and 25 for the exercise. Also, all the materials were translated into Swedish. It was attended by 32 participants from a network of leaders in the manufacturing industry representing companies of different sizes, from 10 to 250+ employees. The notes from the researchers again reflected the workshop was well received, and even if more time was allowed for the exercise, it was still too little. 28 participants completed the survey, and the results were positive, with most mean values around 6. The mean value for *enough time* was again lower than for the other statements. Notably, this group ranked the discussions with peers and instructors as less important than other cases but still with mean values between 5 and six. The mean results for all respondents in this case are reported in Table 2.

Table 2. Results from case 2

Category	Statement	Mean
Effectiveness	The content was relevant to me	6.2
	I learned something new	6
	We had enough time to complete the tasks	4.7
Comprehension	It was easy to understand	6.2
	The technical level was appropriate	6.2
	The content was easy to understand	6.2
Attractiveness	I enjoyed the event	6
	This is a good way to inform about cybersecurity	6.3
	The event was time well-spent	6.4
Engagement	The other group members contributed to my learning	5
	Discussions with peers were valuable	5.8
	Having an instructor available was valuable	5.7

Case 3. The third workshop was identical to workshop two but comprised 90 min, with 45 min each for the presentation and exercise. Seventeen persons from companies in different sectors and of different sizes participated. The researchers experienced that the workshop was well-received, and the participants appreciated both the content and the tabletop format. However, the time for the exercise part still felt too short. All 17 participants completed the evaluation, and the results are presented in Table 3.

Table 3. Results from case 3

Category	Statement	Mean
Effectiveness	The content was relevant to me	5.8
	I learned something new	5.8
	We had enough time to complete the tasks	4.2
Comprehension	It was easy to understand	6.7
	The technical level was appropriate	6.2
	The content was easy to understand	6.5
Attractiveness	I enjoyed the event	5.9
	This is a good way to inform about cybersecurity	6.4
	The event was time well-spent	6.5
Engagement	The other group members contributed to my learning	5.6
	Discussions with peers were valuable	6.1
	Having an instructor available was valuable	6.2

The data in Table 3 is similar to the data from the other cases presented so far. Again, an overall positive view was given, but the participants felt they had too little time for the exercise.

Case 4. The fourth workshop was structured as the previous two but lasted for 140 min, evenly divided between the presentation and the exercise. It was attended by 12 people who all completed the survey. The time for this case was significantly longer than for the previous workshops, and the intention was to test if that would remedy the time complaint from the earlier workshops while not lowering the perception of the workshop as *time well spent*. The researchers again perceived the workshop as well-received and did not experience any time constraints. As shown by the data presented in Table 4, the participants were overall content with the workshop and did feel that the allocated time was enough and that the workshop was worth the time spent.

Table 4. Results from case 4

Category	Statement	Mean
Effectiveness	The content was relevant to me	6.2
	I learned something new	5.3
	We had enough time to complete the tasks	6.5
Comprehension	It was easy to understand	6.6
	The technical level was appropriate	6.1
	The content was easy to understand	6.7
Attractiveness	I enjoyed the event	5.5
	This is a good way to inform about cybersecurity	6.6
	The event was time well-spent	6.4
Engagement	The other group members contributed to my learning	6.4
	Discussions with peers were valuable	5.8
	Having an instructor available was valuable	6.1

Case 5. Cases 1–4 all showed positive perceptions of the workshop, but the time allowed for the exercise had been perceived as low in all but one, which lasted more than two hours. This workshop intended to test if the time issue could be limited by making the presentation part more compact and if that would negatively impact the perception of the workshop in other ways. Therefore, a 50-min workshop was performed, with 30 min for the presentation and 20 min allocated for the workshop, and a more structured approach was used. The presentation was compressed, and the exercise part was more guided in an attempt to make the discussions more focused. The perception of the researchers was that the time spent on the workshop was too low but that the workshop was otherwise well revived. Seventeen participants completed the survey, and the data from the participants, as shown in Table 5, shows an overall positive perception of the workshop. Still, a negative point was that there was not enough time.

Table 5. Results from case 5

Category	Statement	Mean
Effectiveness	The content was relevant to me	5.6
	I learned something new	5.6
	We had enough time to complete the tasks	3.9
Comprehension	It was easy to understand	6.1
	The technical level was appropriate	5.6
	The content was easy to understand	5.9
Attractiveness	I enjoyed the event	5.8
	This is a good way to inform about cybersecurity	6.4
	The event was time well-spent	6.5
Engagement	The other group members contributed to my learning	5.4
	Discussions with peers were valuable	5.9
	Having an instructor available was valuable	5.5

Case 6. Following the results from case 5, the sixth workshop intended to keep the compressed format from case five but allow more time for it. Following the perception of 50 min as too little time (case 5), the rationale was to allow 90 min and evaluate if that could be sufficient. Unfortunately, the time was reduced to 60 min following technical problems which led to a room change. Twenty-five of those were used for the presentation, which left 35 min for the exercise. The perception of the participating researchers was that the event was well received but that more time would have been needed to benefit from the exercise fully. Out of ten participants, the evaluation survey was completed by nine, and the results are presented in Table 6. The results of the survey were in line with the researchers' perceptions.

Table 6. Results from case 6

Category	Statement	Mean
Effectiveness	The content was relevant to me	6.4
	I learned something new	5.8
	We had enough time to complete the tasks	4.5
Comprehension	It was easy to understand	6.6
	The technical level was appropriate	6.1
	The content was easy to understand	6.2
Attractiveness	I enjoyed the event	6.1
	This is a good way to inform about cybersecurity	6.3
	The event was time well-spent	6.2
Engagement	The other group members contributed to my learning	5.4
	Discussions with peers were valuable	5.7
	Having an instructor available was valuable	6

4.2   Between Case Analysis

The first step of the between-case analysis was to compute indices for the question categories. Each index was calculated as the mean value of all questions within a category. Cronbach's Alpha was used to evaluate the internal consistency within each category, and a threshold alpha of 0.55 was used to signify an acceptable internal consistency. During the index creation, the statement *We had enough time to complete the tasks* was removed from the *Effectiveness* index. The reason was that the Alpha for the category was 0.35 with the statement included. Further, since the time spent for the tabletop exercise differed between the cases, the consistency of the responses to that statement is expected to differ between cases. Subsequently, including it would reduce the reliability of the index. The mean index values for the six cases are presented in Table 7, which also includes the alpha values for each category. The time question is included in Table 7 on its own since it was removed from the *Effectiveness* index.

Table 7. Index means for all cases

Index	Alpha	Case1	Case2	Case3	Case4	Case5	Case6
Effectiveness	0.65	6.8	6.1	5.7	5.8	5.6	6.1
Comprehension	0.73	6.5	6.2	6.4	6.5	5.9	6.3
Engagement	0.70	6.9	5.5	6.0	6.1	5.6	5.7
Attractiveness	0.83	6.9	6.2	6.3	6.1	6.1	6.2
Time		4.5	4.7	4.2	6.5	3.9	4.5
Respondents		6	28	17	12	17	9

Data in Table 7 shows that the participants in all workshops had a positive perception of the event. The lowest index mean across all cases is 5.5, which is still 1.5 higher than 4, which was the neutral answer option. That aligns well with the researcher's salient points, which describe all workshops as well-received by the participants. The exception is the statement about having enough time, where the mean values across all cases except 4 are around 4.5, while the mean for case 4 is 6.5. The responses align well with the salient points recorded by the researchers who experienced time constraints in all cases except the fourth. It is noteworthy that case 4 had 140 min allocated while the other cases had 50 to 90 min allocated. It is also notable that the scores are low even for cases 5 and 6, where a somewhat compressed version of the tabletop exercise was used in an attempt to mitigate the time constraints.

The statements in the *effectiveness* category asked the participants if the content of the tabletop exercise was relevant to them and if they learned something new. The evaluation results suggest that the participants in all cases agreed with those statements. The *comprehension* category measured if the participants perceived the material as appropriate and easy to understand, and the results confirm that was the case. The *engagement* sought to measure the participant's perception of learning by discussing cybersecurity with peers and instructors, and the participants scored that engagement as valuable. Lastly, the *Attractiveness* category measured the participant's overall perception of the tabletop exercise, and it was found that it was well-received by participants in all cases.

The final part of the analysis sought to evaluate if the responses from case 2 differed from those from the participants in the other cases. The analysis aimed to address RQ2 by analyzing if decision-makers from the manufacturing industry perceived the tabletop exercise differently than decision-makers in general. The Mann-Whitney U test was used to test for significant differences between case 2 and the participants in the other cases for all indices, and the results are documented in Table 8, which also shows the mean values for the two groups.

Table 8. Comparison between case 2 and the others

Statistic	Effectiveness	Comprehension	Engagement	Attractiveness
Case2 mean	5.8	6.2	5.5	6.2
Other Mean	5.9	6.3	6.0	6.3
P-value	0.589	0.786	0.017	0.514

Table 8 shows that the response values for *Effectiveness, Comprehension, and Attractiveness* are very similar for the two groups, and that tendency is confirmed by the Mann-Whitney U tests, which all result in p-values over 0.5. As such, no differences between the groups can be found between those categories. The difference for *Engagement* is, however, significant and suggests that the respondents from Case 2 perceive the discussions with peers and instructors as less important than the other participants.

5 Discussion

This section first discusses the research results in relation to the research questions addressed. Then, the limitations of this work are elaborated on.

5.1 The Research Questions Addressed

The first research question addressed in this paper was *How do decision-makers perceive cybersecurity training in the form of tabletop exercises?* It was addressed by developing a cybersecurity tabletop exercise conducted and evaluated six times using a multiple-case research approach. All workshops were attended by decision-makers working in various industrial sectors. The evaluations consistently demonstrated that the participants appreciated tabletop exercises and perceived them to be an effective way to learn cybersecurity. The participants further believed that discussions with peers and instructors were beneficial for their learning. The results align with the results from Ottis [37], who evaluated similar exercises using students. While the results are similar, our research shows that the positive results apply to various industrial sectors, including the manufacturing industry. Furthermore, the results show that the social component of the exercise is important, which aligns with the results presented by Brilingaité et al. [7], who found that the social component was a missed element when evaluating a web-based exercise.

A second insight, with regard to the first research question, is that it is important to allow enough time for the tabletop exercise. Lack of time was a common theme in evaluations of exercises spanning 90 min or less, and only participants who had 140 min allocated felt that the allocated time was sufficient. While the time needed depends on the included content, it is important to emphasize that transitioning from a presentation to group discussions, providing instructions, and forming groups do take time, and an important part of developing a tabletop exercise is to investigate how much time that is needed to complete the exercise fully.

The second research question was *What are the differences and similarities between decision-makers in general and decision-makers in manufacturing industries regarding the perception of tabletop exercises for cybersecurity awareness training?* RQ 2 was addressed by grouping the sample so that case 2, which included participants from the manufacturing industry, was compared to participants from the other groups, which contained decision-makers in general. A statistical analysis suggested that the results were similar for those groups for most of the categories of questions. The exception was *Engagement*, where the participants from the manufacturing industry perceived discussions with peers and instructors to be valuable for their learning, but to a lesser extent than the other participants.

5.2   Limitations

As is typically the case, the presented research has some limitations. Most notably, the researchers in this project were substantially involved in developing and delivering the tabletop exercise, which was then evaluated. While this setup is quite typical for similar studies (e.g., [7,10,17,18]), it does introduce susceptibility to researcher bias and potentially also confirmation bias. To mitigate researcher bias the involved researchers took turns assuming different roles during the tabletop exercises. Three researchers participated in the project, and only two were present at each exercise, i.e., different exercises were conducted by different pairs of researchers. Furthermore, the tabletop exercise evaluated in this research was based on openly available material published by CISA [12]. To limit the study's susceptibility to confirmation bias, all evaluations were conducted anonymously.

A second limitation pertains to the nature of the variables included in this paper. As pointed out by Kävrestad and Nohlberg [27], cybersecurity training that participants like is not necessarily effective in driving cybersecurity decisions or behaviour. While we acknowledge that the effect of the evaluated tabletop exercise remains to be studied, perception is also important since people are more likely to attend events they perceive as valuable.

6   Conclusions

This research aimed to *evaluate how decision-makers in the industry, with special emphasis on the manufacturing industry, perceive the use of tabletop exercises for cybersecurity awareness training.* A cybersecurity tabletop exercise based on openly published materials from CISA [12] and recommendations from Chowdhury and Gkioulos [10] was developed. A multiple case study approach was used for evaluation, where the tabletop exercise was conducted six times. The participants were decision-makers from different industrial sectors. The evaluation showed that participants in all six cases found the workshop valuable. As such, the present research suggests that tabletop exercises are a promising approach for raising cybersecurity awareness among decision-makers.

The research further analyzed if the results differed between decision-makers in general and decision-makers in manufacturing industries. The results suggested that the positive perception of decision-makers in general was shared by those in the manufacturing industry. However, participants from the manufacturing industry value discussions with peers and instructors less than other participants. Furthermore, the study shows that an important aspect of planning a tabletop exercise is ensuring enough time for discussions. While the time needed in general is difficult to establish, it can be concluded that the tabletop exercise used in this research needs around two hours, including the preceding presentation.

This research provides an evaluation of using tabletop exercises to raise cybersecurity awareness among decision-makers. The results present tabletop exercises as a promising approach. What remains to be studied is the longer-term impact of tabletop exercises on decision-makers and their organizations. Such a study could be conducted as a follow-up to this study. One could imagine conducting interviews with exercise participants to review if they changed how they work and prioritize due to participating in the tabletop exercise. One could also imagine studying documents to, for instance, evaluate if cybersecurity budgets have been changed after the exercise with the rationale that an increased budget would suggest an increased commitment to security spending.

Acknowledgments. We gratefully acknowledge the grants from the Swedish Civil Contingencies Agency (MSB), projects VISKA (MSB 2021-14650) and ICANP (MSB 2023-10887).

Disclosure of Interests. The authors have no competing interests to declare.

References

1. Andriotis, N.: 5 elements to include in any post training evaluation questionnaire (2018). https://www.efrontlearning.com/blog/2017/12/element-post-evaluation-training-questionnaire.html

2. Angafor, G.N., Yevseyeva, I., He, Y.: Bridging the cyber security skills gap: using tabletop exercises to solve the cssg crisis. In: Joint International Conference on Serious Games, pp. 117–131. Springer (2020)
3. Angafor, G.N., Yevseyeva, I., He, Y.: Game-based learning: a review of tabletop exercises for cybersecurity incident response training. Secur. Priv. 3(6), e126 (2020)
4. Ani, U.D., He, H., Tiwari, A.: Human factor security: evaluating the cybersecurity capacity of the industrial workforce. J. Syst. Inf. Technol. 21(1), 2–35 (2019). ISSN 1328-7265, https://doi.org/10.1108/JSIT-02-2018-0028
5. Ani, U.P.D., He, H., Tiwari, A.: Review of cybersecurity issues in industrial critical infrastructure: manufacturing in perspective. J. Cyber Secur. Technol. 1(1), 32–74 (2017)
6. Bechara, F.R., Schuch, S.B.: Cybersecurity and global regulatory challenges. J. Financ. Crime 28(2), 359–374 (2021)
7. Brilingaitė, A., Bukauskas, L., Krinickij, V., Kutka, E.: Environment for cybersecurity tabletop exercises. In: ECGBL 2017 11th European Conference on Game-Based Learning, pp. 47–55, Academic Conferences and publishing limited (2017)
8. Choi, N., Kim, D., Goo, J., Whitmore, A.: Knowing is doing: an empirical validation of the relationship between managerial information security awareness and action. Inf. Manag. Comput. Secur. 16(5), 484–501 (2008)
9. Chowdhury, N., Gkioulos, V.: Cyber security training for critical infrastructure protection: a literature review. Comput. Sci. Rev. 40, 100361 (2021)
10. Chowdhury, N., Gkioulos, V.: A framework for developing tabletop cybersecurity exercises. In: European Symposium on Research in Computer Security, pp. 116–133. Springer (2022)
11. Chua, H.N., Wong, S.F., Low, Y.C., Chang, Y.: Impact of employees' demographic characteristics on the awareness and compliance of information security policy in organizations. Telemat. Inform. 35(6), 1770–1780 (2018). ISSN 0736-5853, https://doi.org/10.1016/j.tele.2018.05.005, https://www.sciencedirect.com/science/article/pii/S0736585318301102
12. CISA: Cybersecurity scenarios (2023). https://www.cisa.gov/resources-tools/resources/cybersecurity-scenarios
13. CISA: Critical infrastructure sectors (nd). https://www.cisa.gov/topics/critical-infrastructure-security-and-resilience/critical-infrastructure-sectors
14. Corradini, I., Corradini, I.: Building a cybersecurity culture. Building a Cybersecurity Culture in Organizations: How to Bridge the Gap Between People and Digital Technology, pp. 63–86 (2020)
15. Culot, G., Fattori, F., Podrecca, M., Sartor, M.: Addressing industry 4.0 cybersecurity challenges. IEEE Eng. Manag. Rev. 47(3), 79–86 (2019). ISSN 1937-4178, https://doi.org/10.1109/EMR.2019.2927559
16. Dada, O., Irunokhai, E., Shawulu, C., Nuhu, A., Daniel, E.: Information security awareness, a tool to mitigate information security risk: a literature review. Innov. J. Sci. 3(3), 29–54 (2021). (ISSN: 2714-3309)
17. Dausey, D.J., Buehler, J.W., Lurie, N.: Designing and conducting tabletop exercises to assess public health preparedness for manmade and naturally occurring biological threats. BMC Public Health 7, 1–9 (2007)
18. Edzén, S.: Table-top exercises for emergency management: tame solutions for wicked problems. In: 2014 47th Hawaii International Conference on System Sciences, pp. 1978–1985. IEEE (2014)
19. European Commision: Critical infrastructures (2024). https://home-affairs.ec.europa.eu/policies/internal-security/counter-terrorism-and-radicalisation/protection/critical-infrastructure-resilience_en

20. Frégeau, A., et al.: Use of tabletop exercises for healthcare education: a scoping review protocol. BMJ Open **10**(1), e032662 (2020)
21. Garcia-Granados, F.B., Bahsi, H.: Cybersecurity knowledge requirements for strategic level decision makers. In: International Conference on Cyber Warfare and Security, pp. 559–XIII, Academic Conferences International Limited (2020)
22. Gerring, J.: What is a case study and what is it good for? Am. Polit. Sci. Rev. **98**(2), 341–354 (2004)
23. Howarth, F.: The role of human error in successful security attacks. Secur. Intell. **2** (2014)
24. Joinson, A., van Steen, T.: Human aspects of cyber security: behaviour or culture change? Cyber Secur. Peer-Review. J. **1**(4), 351–360 (2018)
25. Joshi, A., Kale, S., Chandel, S., Pal, D.K.: Likert scale: explored and explained. Br. J. Appl. Sci. Technol. **7**(4), 396–403 (2015)
26. Kävrestad, J., Fallatah, W., Furnell, S.: Cybersecurity training acceptance: a literature review. In: International Symposium on Human Aspects of Information Security and Assurance, pp. 53–63. Springer (2023)
27. Kävrestad, J., Nohlberg, M.: Evaluation strategies for cybersecurity training methods: a literature review. In: Human Aspects of Information Security and Assurance: 15th IFIP WG 11.12 International Symposium, HAISA 2021, Virtual Event, 7–9 July 2021, Proceedings 15, pp. 102–112. Springer (2021)
28. Knowles, M.S.: Theory of andragogy. A Critique. International Journal of Lifelong. Cambridge, MA (1984)
29. Maggio, L.A., Dameff, C., Kanter, S.L., Woods, B., Tully, J.: Cybersecurity challenges and the academic health center: an interactive tabletop simulation for executives. Acad. Med. **96**(6), 850–853 (2021)
30. Malatji, M., Von Solms, S., Marnewick, A.: Socio-technical systems cybersecurity framework. Inf. Comput. Secur. **27**(2), 233–272 (2019)
31. Mareš, M., et al.: Assessment of performance during cybersecurity tabletop exercises. Secur. J. 1–24 (2023)
32. Miles, M.B., Michael Huberman, A.J.S.: Qualitative Data Analysis: A Methods Sourcebook, 3rd edn. SAGE Publications, Thousand Oaks (2014). ISBN 9781452257877
33. Mullet, V., Sondi, P., Ramat, E.: A review of cybersecurity guidelines for manufacturing factories in industry 4.0. IEEE Access **9**, 23235–23263 (2021)
34. NIST: Tabletop exercise (2006). https://csrc.nist.gov/glossary/term/tabletop_exercise
35. NIST: Csf 1.1 critical infrastructure resources (2024). https://www.nist.gov/cyberframework/csf-11-critical-infrastructure-resources
36. Nurse, J.R.: Cybersecurity awareness. In: Encyclopedia of Cryptography, Security and Privacy, pp. 1–4. Springer (2021)
37. Ottis, R.: Light weight tabletop exercise for cybersecurity education. J. Homel. Secur. Emerg. Manag. **11**(4), 579–592 (2014)
38. Poehlmann, N., Caramancion, K.M., Tatar, I., Li, Y., Barati, M., Merz, T.: The organizational cybersecurity success factors: an exhaustive literature review. In: Advances in Security, Networks, and Internet of Things: Proceedings from SAM'20, ICWN'20, ICOMP'20, and ESCS'20, pp. 377–395 (2021)
39. Roud, E., Gausdal, A.H., Asgary, A., Carlström, E.: Outcome of collaborative emergency exercises: differences between full-scale and tabletop exercises. J. Contingencies Crisis Manag. **29**(2), 170–184 (2021)
40. Safa, N.S., Von Solms, R.: An information security knowledge sharing model in organizations. Comput. Hum. Behav. **57**, 442–451 (2016)

41. Sonnenschein, R., Loske, A., Buxmann, P.: The role of top managers' it security awareness in organizational it security management. In: Proceedings of the Thirty Eighth International Conference on Information Systems, South Korea, Association for Information Systems (AIS) (2017)
42. Taber, K.S.: The use of cronbach's alpha when developing and reporting research instruments in science education. Res. Sci. Educ. **48**, 1273–1296 (2018)
43. Vrhovec, S., Markelj, B.: We need to aim at the top: factors associated with cybersecurity awareness of cyber and information security decision-makers. arXiv preprint arXiv:2404.04725 (2024)
44. Vykopal, J., Čeleda, P., Švábenský, V., Hofbauer, M., Horák, M.: Research and practice of delivering tabletop exercises. arXiv preprint arXiv:2404.10206 (2024)
45. Wheelan, C.: Naked Statistics: Stripping the Dread from the Data. WW Norton & Company, New York (2013)
46. Yeoh, W., Wang, S., Popovič, A., Chowdhury, N.H.: A systematic synthesis of critical success factors for cybersecurity. Comput. Secur. **118**, 102724 (2022)
47. Yin, R.K.: Case Study Research: Design and Methods, vol. 5. Sage, Los Angeles (2009)

Penetrating the Power Grid: Realistic Adversarial Attacks on Smart Grid Intrusion Detection Systems

Nelson Makau Mutua[1]([⊠]) [ID], Simin Nadjm-Tehrani[2] [ID], and Petr Matoušek[1] [ID]

[1] Brno University of Technology, Bozetechova 1, 612 66 Brno, Czech Republic
{imutua,matousp}@fit.vutbr.cz
[2] Linköping University, 581 83 Linköping, Sweden
simin.nadjm-tehrani@liu.se

Abstract. The widespread adoption and application of Machine Learning (ML) based Intrusion Detection Systems (IDS) has increased the flexibility and efficiency of automated cyber attack detection in smart grid systems. However, the emergence of such IDSes has led to a new attack vector against learning models, known as adversarial attacks. Such attacks could have serious effects in smart grid systems since adversaries can circumvent detection by IDS. This could result in detection of attacks. From the existing literature, a lot of research proposes threat models that are inappropriate for generating realistic adversarial attacks. In this research, we model realistic adversarial attacks with a focus on real attacker capabilities that are feasible to launch adversarial attacks. We discuss how adversarial learning may be used to target ML models using the Jacobian-based Saliency Map Attack (JSMA) and the Fast Gradient Sign Method (FGSM). A power system dataset generated from a smart grid testbed was used for testing the models. The performance of the trained classifiers, Random Forest, XGBoost, and Naive Bayes, dropped when adversarial instances were introduced. The outcomes of this paper are useful for helping researchers model realistic scenarios to avoid dealing with hypothetical problems.

Keywords: Intrusion Detection Systems · Adversarial Attacks · Critical Infrastructure · Machine Learning · Smart Grid Systems

1 Introduction

Smart electrical grids are essential in the digital age of hyper-connected Critical Infrastructures (CIs), providing benefits including improved grid resilience, efficient energy distribution, and smart load management [19]. The adoption of technology enablers such as machine learning (ML), the Internet of Things (IoT), 5G, and Artificial Intelligence (AI) is critical to the life cycle of smart grids. However, this technological breakthrough presents serious cybersecurity concerns, which might have fatal implications, particularly in the energy sector.

G. Oliva et al. (Eds.): CRITIS 2024, LNCS 15549, pp. 249–268, 2025.
https://doi.org/10.1007/978-3-031-84260-3_15

Given the significance of these systems, they have become a desirable target for attackers. By the fact that these systems control physical processes, cyber-attacks may have far-reaching effects on the environment in which they operate and their users [4].

Advanced Persistent Threats (APTs) and multi-step attacks against CIs, like the smart electrical grid, can cause service failures, financial losses, and sometimes tragic accidents. Examples of APT [4] campaigns include Hafnium, Industroyer, the Lazarus Group, and SolarWinds (Sunburst). In 2015, Industroyer lead to a blackout across Ukraine. The NotPetya ransomware caused significant financial damage for various energy-related organizations, making it a notable cybersecurity incident. A more recent CI attack was reported in Denmark in May 2023 where attackers compromised 22 energy organizations in the largest coordinated attack against Denmark's CI [32]. To launch the attacks, hackers exploited multiple vulnerabilities in the firewall for initial access, executing code and gaining complete control over the impacted systems. The attackers successfully compromised 11 energy organizations by executing commands on the vulnerable firewall to obtain device configurations and usernames and thus access to the CI behind it. In this light, security issues about such systems have become a serious concern globally. This prompts the development of not only a safe but also a robust technique that can effectively identify and protect CIs like smart grid networks from cyber attacks.

Although various security methods exist for traditional IT systems, integrating them into smart grid networks is difficult because the monitoring devices have limited resources and the inability to support contemporary security measures. Improvements to security are thus more likely to be brought about by passive security surveillance and other such security approaches. This has resulted in a significant rise in research into more tailor-made IDSes that monitor networks to detect attacks that could disrupt the operation of CIs [20]. IDSes are increasingly being integrated with ML due to their efficiency in attack detection attacks. However, with the introduction of these systems, a new attack vector emerges, such that even the trained models can be attacked. Adversarial Machine Learning (AdvML) refers to deploying attacks against ML systems. Small perturbations can be applied automatically to unseen data points that can result in the model crossing a decision boundary and then classify malicious data as normal.

The existence of such dynamics implies that CI, such as smart grid systems that use ML-IDSes, may be exposed to cyberattacks. AdvML can be used to manipulate data from the Intelligent Electronic Devices (IEDs) that switch circuit breakers or other devices. IEDs introduce perturbations that classify malicious data as benign, hence circumventing the IDS. As a result, there could be delays in detecting attacks, leaks of information, financial losses, or sometimes casualties. As ML-based detection methods grow more prevalent, attackers may have a stronger motive to target them. As a result, they require extensive evaluation against AdvML attacks.

1.1   Motivation and Contribution

Our research is motivated by the recognition that many research papers design, develop, and evaluate IDS in adversarial settings without considering the realism of the proposed attacks or explaining how they can be launched in reality. Many of the proposed research works assume a threat model and report the impact of the attack while providing little or no thought to the viability of the considered perturbation. Moreover, some general techniques are applied to generate adversarial attacks to manipulate the network features in a way that is inconsistent with actual network traffic [3].

Some researchers, for instance, take the view that adversaries are fully aware of the target system [16] while others assume an attacker can attempt as often as possible to breach past the Network Intrusion Detection Systems (NIDS) without getting detected [30]. When generating scenarios in cybersecurity, it is critical to concentrate on the actual problem and adversary. However, it is equally important to characterize how effective all adversarial attacks are on any ML to develop a better detector. Failing to do so could misinform defenders to allocate resources against false cases or hypothetical problems, potentially diverting attention from more critical issues. The abundance of research on adversarial attacks might inadvertently give the impression that any ML-IDS is an unreliable defensive system, contrary to the actual scenario.

Additionally, in a real communication network, manipulating an ML model does not ensure a successful cyberattack. In this study, we propose a more realistic approach to modelling adversarial attacks against ML-IDS for smart grid communication. We identify the necessary conditions and capabilities for the attacker to carry out such attacks. More importantly, this study recreates a realistic dataset gathered from a power system testbed, along with a realistic attack model and assumptions. This research will make the following contributions:

- Detailed review of the feasibility constraints needed to model valid adversarial perturbations on data used as input to an ML-IDS while preserving the network attack's fundamental logic.
- Generating evasion attacks for smart grid network communication capable of evading ML-IDS detection with limited knowledge of the target NIDS.
- Demonstrate the effectiveness of the evasion attack on ML-IDS.

2   Background and Related Work

This section introduces the fundamental ideas of adversarial machine learning. Then, we discuss related work that has utilized adversarial evasion techniques to illustrate how effective they are in evading or reducing the performance of IDS models. Finally, we outline the limitations of the network traffic and detail how the limitations can be upheld for the network to generate an adversarial flow that is valid.

2.1   Adversarial Machine Learning

An adversarial attack refers to the application of small and undetectable alterations to an ML detector [29]. In this case, the altered samples must not have a huge difference from the initial sample to maintain the basic malicious logic and avoid triggering other detection methods. In this research, we focus on evasion attacks. In the event of an evasion attack, the input is manipulated by the attacker in an attempt to trick the model and cause misclassification. There are several approaches to generating adversarial samples, and they vary in terms of their performance, generation speed, and complexity. The easiest way to create adversarial samples is by manually changing the input data points one by one. In such cases, it can take a lot of time to perturb manually, especially with large datasets, and the results could be inaccurate. Therefore, more complicated methods can be used to identify and analyze features automatically by discriminating target values.

Papernot et al. [28] and Goodfellow et al. [13] introduced Jacobian-based Saliency Map Attack (JSMA) and Fast Gradient Sign Method (FGSM) as popular methods for creating perturbed samples automatically. Both methods presume that adding small perturbations (δ) to the original sample *(X)* and can result in adversarial characteristics (X* = X + δ). This implies that X^* will be misclassified by the target model.

2.2   Fast Gradient Sign Method (FGSM)

The FGSM method for creating adversarial instances is based on the gradient sign method with backpropagation. It is an untargeted attack approach used to obtain max-norm constrained perturbation (η) expressed in Eq. 1. Here (θ) represents the model parameter, x is the input vector to the model, y is the associated label of the input, and J(θ, x, y) is the cost function. FGSM generates perturbation samples with a small noise parameter ϵ [13].

$$adv\_x = x + \epsilon * \text{sign}\left(\nabla_x J(\theta, x, y)\right) \tag{1}$$

2.3   Jacobian-Based Saliency Map Attack (JSMA)

The Jacobian matrix, on the other hand, serves as the foundation for the JSMA technique. The JSMA method is utilized to compute the forward derivative of the cost function $f(x)$. The following formula computes the Jacobian of the neural network function F using input X:

$$JF = \frac{\partial F(X)}{\partial X} \tag{2}$$

Unlike the FGSM, JSMA operates differently from other adversarial attacks by leveraging saliency maps. These maps visually represent the prediction process of a classification model for each pixel, illustrating how each pixel influences the model prediction of a specific class. JSMA has various advantages as well as disadvantages. One advantage of using JSMA is its ability to make small perturbations while maintaining high success rates. These minimal changes make it easy to control attacks based on their intensity within a specific ML-IDS. However, JSMA is more computationally intensive than FGSM [28].

2.4   Major Adversarial Attacks Against the NIDS

This section reviews existing research that used adversarial evasion methods to reduce the performance of ML-IDS models. The existing literature identifies detection methods as vulnerable to generic evasive adversarial attacks, which are considered significant threats. However, the previous research failed to evaluate the effectiveness of generated adversarial traffic for real-world attacks.

In their research, Warzyński and Kołaczek [37] demonstrated that a Deep Neural Networks (DNN) binary classifier on the NSL-KDD[1] dataset [35] was degraded by a FGSM attack. Further, they confirmed that network traffic can also be degraded by the FGSM attack, although this attack was first developed for image recognition. Using the Mirai dataset[2], Clements et al. [9] assessed Kitsune's resistance to FGSM attacks as a lightweight intrusion detection system for IoT networks. Wang [36] discovered that FGSM attacks achieve various degrees of success and use different feature patterns. The author suggested that perturbing specific features may increase the vulnerability of IDS to adversarial traffic. Nevertheless, the research does not show the features had been altered to confirm if the perturbations produced consistent traffic instances.

Asimopoulos et al. [6] introduced an AI-powered IDS for the IEC 60870-5-104 protocol. To test the model, the authors use four ML methods: (a) Decision Tree, (b) RF, (c) eXtreme Gradient Boosting (XGBoost), and (d) Multilayer Perceptron (MLP). The authors used a Conditional Tabular Generative Adversarial Network (CTGAN) adversarial attack generator and the FGSM to assess the possible impact of adversarial attacks on IDS detection performance. In comparison to the CTGAN datasets, the examined models DT, XGBoost, RF, and MLP fared better on the FGSM adversarial datasets. However, the authors did not discuss the realistic implementation of adversarial attacks in their case studies. Additionally, they did not explain how to set the optimum level of perturbations that could trigger an attack.

Huang et al. [17] evaluated the effectiveness of three port-scan attack detection models for Software Defined Networking (SDN) environments: MLP, Convolutional Neural Network (CNN), and Long Short-Term Memory (LSTM) against the FGSM attacks. Martins et al. [23] found that FGSM attacks reduced the average performance of RF, SVM, Decision Trees (DT), Naïve Bayes (NB), and Neural Network (NN) classifiers. Sriram et al. [34] evaluated the performance of DNN, RF, Support Vector Machine (SVM), NB, and DT classifiers against FGSM attacks on the NSL-KDD dataset (See footnote [1]). Debicha et al. [10]

---

[1] See https://www.unb.ca/cic/datasets/nsl.html [May 2024].
[2] See https://ieee-dataport.org/documents/nss-mirai-dataset [May 2024].

concluded that DNN detection model performance was considerably degraded by FGSM attacks.

As indicated by the existing literature, detection models fail to withstand novel adversarial attacks that are considered serious threats. The literature only demonstrates how attacks have high rates of evasion; it fails to show how real and effective the generated adversarial traffic is. In real-world attacks, it is essential to illustrate how generic evasion adversarial attacks can be done realistically. Moreover, the majority of studies have focused on the consequences of adversarial attacks within conventional IP networks [10, 11, 18, 24, 31]. Conversely, it is imperative to evaluate security threats in other networking landscapes like smart grids given their critical role of hyper-connected CIs in this digital age.

Based on the previous research, we did not find any research that has verified the realism of adversarial attacks in smart grid networks. Therefore, this paper proposes a realistic approach to modelling adversarial attacks against ML-IDS for smart grid communication by identifying the necessary conditions are required for the attacker to launch such attacks. More importantly, this research develops a reasonable attack model and assumptions and uses real power system datasets.

2.5   Limitations of Previous Research Studies

There were three specific shortcomings of the studies that had been published earlier. First, previous studies failed to observe traffic domain constraints regarding how they created adversarial attacks to maintain the validity and functionality of attack traces. Second, previous studies assumed that the adversary can manipulate or control the number of features without restraint. This would potentially lead to disruption of the semantic connections between interdependent features. Realistically, this assumption may not always hold true in some scenarios because the adversary may be an outsider or may not understand the inner operations of an IDS. Finally, previous studies worked under the conditionality that the threat model is white-box, meaning the adversary has full knowledge of all the parameters of the targeted model, which can be unrealistic in many real-world cases.

3   Case Study

For our case study, we use publicly available power system datasets developed by Mississippi State University and Oak Ridge National Laboratory[3]. Figure 1 depicts the power system framework configuration and components utilized to generate datasets for this research. The power system includes the following components:

– There are two main power generators (G1 and G2).

---

[3] See https://sites.google.com/a/uah.edu/tommy-morris-uah/ics-data-sets [05/24].

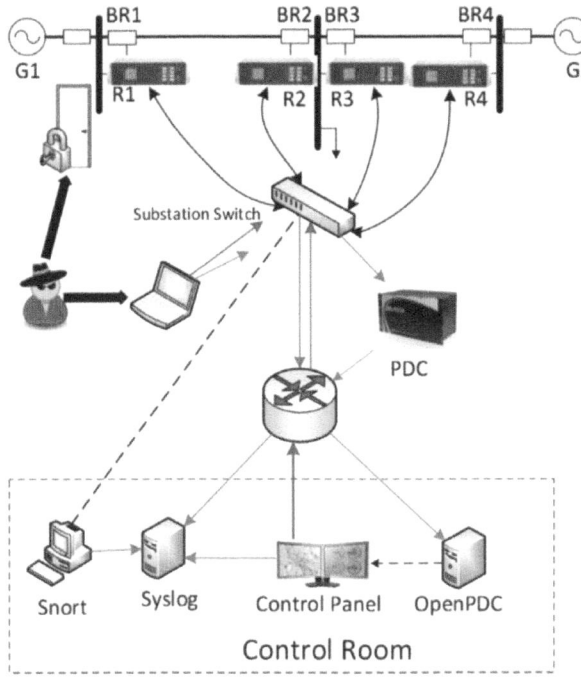

Fig. 1. Power System Testbed [2].

- The Intelligent Electronic Devices (IEDs) R1, R2, R3, and R4 activate the breakers (BR1, BR2, BR3, BR4), which automatically protect electrical circuits from short circuits.
- Each IED controls a single breaker (for example, R1 controls BR1, R2 controls BR2, and so on).
- IEDs lack internal validation; instead, they use a directional relay to trip the breaker in case a fault is detected, regardless of validity.
- System operators can manually trip the breakers by sending commands to the IEDs. To maintain lines as well as system components, operators use manual override.
- The testbed includes additional network monitoring and detection tools, like SNORT and Syslog servers.

3.1   Dataset Description

This dataset contains 128 features from two categories: 1) Phasor Measurement Units (PMU) and 2) logs from the Control Room. With a total of four PMUs, 29 measurements are obtained from each PMU, resulting in 116 features in total. The logs from the control room are categorized into SNORT, control panel, and relay logs, each category with four features. In total, the control role logs have

12 features. More details about the dataset and the description of the features can be found in the original dataset description document [2].

3.2   Simulated Attacks

From the testbed, a data set of malicious and benign data was created. Three main categories are used to classify the data: instances with 'no events', instances with 'natural events', and instances with 'attack events'. 'No event' and 'natural event' are combined to signify benign activity. During the simulation, five different attack scenarios were launched at the power system. The attacks include:

- *Short-circuit fault.* This is a power line short circuit that may occur at any distance along the length of the line. The percentage range serves as the location indicator.
- *Line maintenance.* To do maintenance on a particular line, one or more relays are disabled.
- *Remote tripping command injection.* This attack works by sending a command to a relay that will open a breaker. It is accomplished only after an attacker has penetrated through the outside defence layers.
- *Alter relay settings.* In this form of attack, relays have distance protection implemented. In order not to cause the relay to trip at the receipt of a valid command or a fault, the attacker proceeds to change the relay configuration to remove the relay functionality.
- *Data injection attack.* Data injection attacks are considered cyberattacks directed at CIs such as power grids. Attackers manipulate system sensors or use other control communication pathways to insert inaccurate data into system control. It can result in erroneous actions that precipitate problems such as instability or blackouts. For instance, an attacker can deliberately fake a power surge or a fault to compel the system to take unnecessary protective actions that interfere with the power supply or cause a blackout.

3.3   Attacker Capabilities

In this research, we model realistic adversarial attacks against Machine Learning NIDS (ML-NIDS) by adopting the taxonomies of Apruzzese et al. [5]. To model them, we evaluate the realistic capabilities of an attacker. This demonstrates how much control the attacker has over the target model. This shows how much control the attacker has over the target detection system. The attacker can have access to the following five elements, as highlighted in Fig. 2.

- *Training Data* represents the ability to obtain the dataset required to train the ML-NIDS. There are three types of access: read-only, write-only, and no access.
- *Feature Set* indicates the understanding of the features that the IDS employs to continue the detection. There are three types of it: full knowledge, partial, and none.

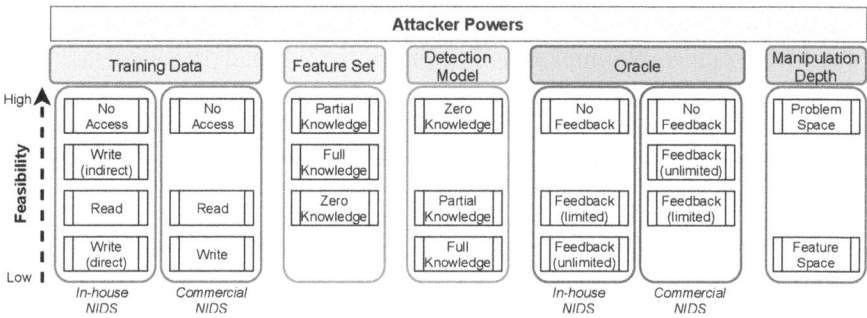

Fig. 2. Power capabilities accessible by the attacker. [5].

- **Detection Model** describes a situation whereby the trained machine learning model is employed in the NIDS and used for the detection. This information can be obtained in part, in full, or none at all.
- **Oracle** component illustrates how to obtain a response from the IDS output to an attacker manipulation input. The attacker may get no feedback, limited, or unlimited feedback.
- **Manipulation Depth** pertains to the degree or level of an adversary manipulation that can either analyse the problem space or feature space.

3.4   Threat Model

In this paper, we examine the risk posed by an insider threat actor with administrative access privileges to the network systems of the smart grid network. Insider threats represent a significant yet often overlooked danger to CI [12].

In other words, identifying and mitigating insider threats is a challenging and multifaceted endeavor due to the fact that insiders may have access to the network and often reside within enterprise-level security [22]. The German Federal Office for Information Security defines insider threats as individuals who can potentially misuse their access to information technology systems, sensitive data, or infrastructure. The following groups are specifically regarded as insider threats [1]:

- An individual who has direct access and physically interacts with control systems, such as operators or engineers.
- An individual with privileged access rights, such as system administrators.
- Anyone who has indirect access to the office network..
- Outsourced personnel or external service providers like those who develop and maintain software, suppliers, etc.

These adversaries can deploy several attacks, including:

– Social engineering can be employed to plan follow-up attacks. This involves
  identifying vulnerable employees, learning about internal processes, and mapping out the IT infrastructure to find potential weaknesses.
– Unauthorized acquisition or alteration of confidential data may occur when
  an individual accesses file servers, data storage media or historians. Primarily,
  the motives of such an attack are industrial espionage and whistle-blowing.
– Deliberate acts of sabotage against the company. This may include an attacker
  modifying control components or installing malware in the system for political
  or economical reasons. These actions, which may involve an attacker changing
  control components or installing malware in the system, may be driven by
  political or financial interests.

As shown in Fig. 3, our research is based on a realistic scenario where an
insider already possesses legitimate access to the smart grid network through
privileges such as administration and physical access. The network has an ML-
NIDS model that should be able to detect any network attack. Given the difficulties associated with analyzing individual packets, this study considers the
NIDS to be a flow-based system rather than a packet-based system in high-speed
network environments. In the power system scenario presented in Sect. 3, given
the capabilities of the attacker in Sub-Sect. 3.3, it is presumed that the adversary
is interested in launching an evasion attack. Given the adversary's position, it is
assumed that he or she is familiar with the features used by the IDS for classification; nonetheless, he or she is unfamiliar with the detector's specific algorithm
configuration. The attacker's primary objective is to identify how to circumvent
the NIDS. This will allow him/her to either launch more damaging attacks in the
future or exploit the organization for personal gain by selling this information
to competitors, ultimately leaving the organization exposed and susceptible to
harm. Due to the knowledge acquired by the adversary, this type of attack can
be classified as a grey box attack. This threat scenario presented in Fig. 3 was
used to generate adversarial data for testing on trained ML model as presented
in Sect. 5.

4   Attack Generation

This research examines the use of JSMA and FGSM attack techniques in a grey
box setting, where the attacker is aware of the complete datasets and the features
but is unaware of the target model. Even if the attacker has no information
about the target model, generating samples that will force the target model to
declassify the given model, particularly using other ML models, will be possible.
This is because adversarial samples are transferable across different ML models.
When creating adversarial traffic, there are four key steps involved, as
depicted in Fig. 4. In the first step of this attack model, the attacker generates adversarial traffic to deceive the surrogate model, which was trained by
sniffing the actual traffic flows. In step 2, adversarial traffic that goes undetected by using the surrogate model is received and analyzed by the attacker.

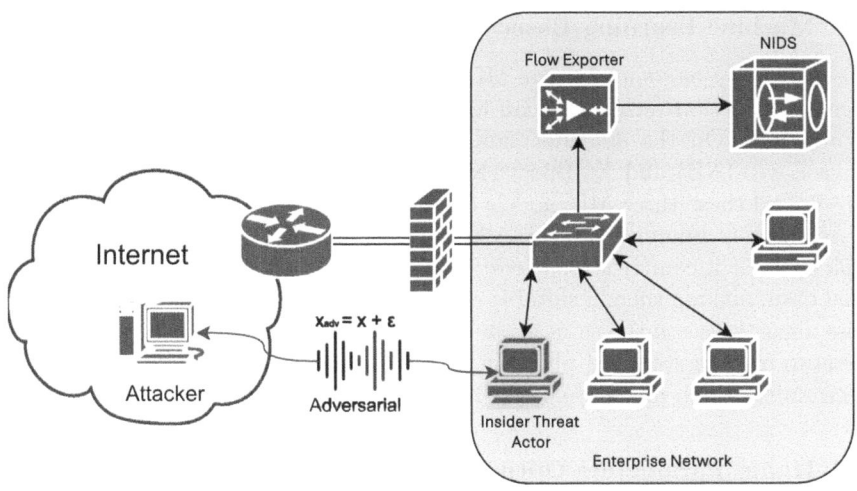

Fig. 3. Illustration of the considered threat scenario

The transferability feature is employed by the attacker in step 3 to send the adversarial traffic to defender NIDS. The adversarial traffic that managed to get past the defender NIDS will reach the insider threat actor's computer in step 4. In this research, the attacks were implemented through the Adversarial Robustness Toolbox (ART)[4]. ART is a Python tool that can generate various adversarial attacks.

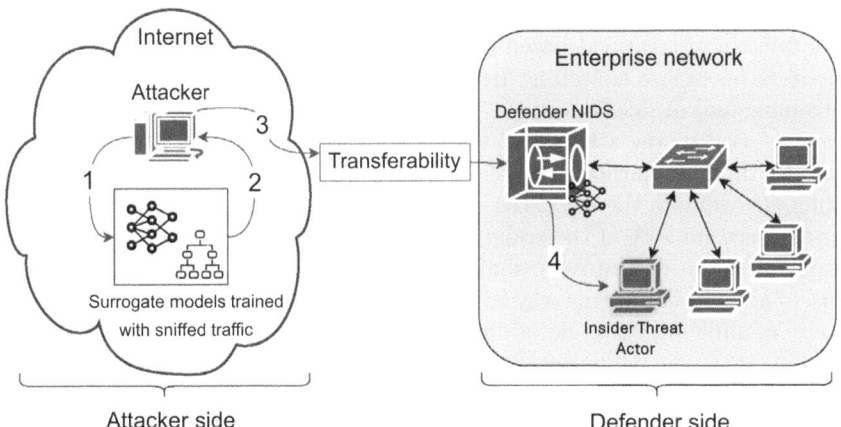

Fig. 4. Illustration of the adversarial traffic generation.

---

[4] See https://github.com/Trusted-AI/adversarial-robustness-toolbox [05/24].

4.1   Machine Learning-Based NIDS

This research uses some classical ML algorithms to assess how effectively supervised classification techniques can learn to detect cyberattacks in a smart grid environment. On the defender side, the defender uses Random Forest (RF), Naive Bayes (NB) and XGBoost (XGB) algorithms as a model for the NIDS. We selected these three ML models for our work because of their wide usage by the research community [21, 25]. Additionally, the selected methods are easy to implement, less computational cost is needed, and they work well with annotated data, making them a suitable choice for our NIDS. Figure 5 illustrates how these algorithms use the same training and testing procedures. The experimental setup offers a standard platform for performance comparison, which aids in determining which model performs the best.

4.2   Hyper Parameters Optimization

XGboost and Naive Bayes models were trained using the default parameters provided by the scikit-learn framework[5]. To ensure optimal performance of RF as recommended by Zhu et al. [38] key tunable hyperparameters were applied, including the number of trees (100), the split method (Gini), and the minimum number of samples required to split (2). Hyperparameter tuning fixes the best value from the search space for the algorithm's parameters. Even though hyperparameter tuning was not conducted in this study, it opens an opportunity for future research.

4.3   Model Training and Testing

To ensure the usability of the research results, the original dataset was divided into subsets and stratified based on their labels. Both the data subsets are the same in terms of size as well as distribution of data. The first subset is assigned for training and evaluation on the defender side. As shown in Fig. 5, the second dataset is used by the attacker to train a surrogate model. Section 3 details how an insider threat scenario can make an attacker obtain this data through network sniffing. To validate the data, the datasets of the defender and the attacker are divided based on 70% of the training data and 30% of the testing data. In both training and testing datasets, malicious traffic is equal to benign traffic. The datasets are divided in this way to be as balanced in representation as possible, thereby minimizing the issue of data imbalance.

While this is a requirement to get the most of our envisaged IDSes, it is not essential to the actual claim of the paper. We are aware of the fact that real traffic data may be rather unbalanced and tuning the IDS to work in those contexts may overcome that problem. However, our evasion attack methodology is not dependent on this aspect. As shown in Fig. 5, the threat model follows the same training and testing process. Besides, the standard ML evaluation metrics were used to measure the performance of the threat models.

---

[5] See https://scikit-learn.org/stable/ [05/24].

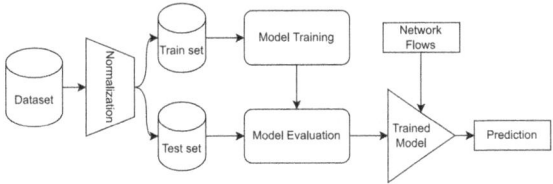

Fig. 5. The training and testing pipeline for an attacker and a defender.

4.4 Performance Metrics

Various evaluation metrics can be utilized when assessing the performance of different IDS models [15]. As shown in Table 1, all the metrics are based on the confusion matrix.

Table 1. IDS Confusion Matrix

Actual Class	Predicted Class	
	Anomaly	Normal
Anomaly	True Positive (TP)	False Negative (FN)
Normal	False Positive (FP)	True Negative (TN)

– Recall, which is sometimes called the "detection rate," helps quantify the proportion of actual positive instances that are correctly identified by the model.

$$Recall = \frac{TP}{TP + FN} \tag{3}$$

– Precision evaluates the accuracy of the positive predictions made by a model. Specifically, precision measures the proportion of predicted positive instances that are correct.

$$Precision = \frac{TP}{TP + FP} \tag{4}$$

– The F1 score provides the performance of the combined metrics and is calculated as the harmonic mean of recall and precision. In this respect, the use of the F1 score allows the system not only to offer relevant results but also to refuse the others.

$$F1 = \frac{2 * Precision * Recall}{Precision + Recall} \tag{5}$$

5   Evaluation

This section details the experimental findings. In Sub-Sect. 5.1, the performance of the attacker and defender models on the given metrics, such as F1 score, precision, and recall, is discussed. Moreover, a discussion of the model's ability to perform in an adversarial environment is discussed in Sect. 5.2. Lastly, a detailed analysis of the perturbation difference between the initial malicious instance and the adversarial instance is also provided.

5.1   ML-IDS Model Performance in Clean Settings

Different metrics are used to evaluate the model on clean settings, from both the attacker and defender perspectives. These include recall (Eq. 3), precision (Eq. 4), and F1-score (Eq. 5). In clean settings, the ML-IDS models performed binary classification to distinguish between malicious and benign traffic. As shown in Table 2, the performance of the trained ML models. XGBoost performed better compared to Naive Bayes and the Random Forest models. In general, these initial results demonstrate a good performance of the Random Forest and XGBoost. The F1 scores achieved by the classifiers were 0.845, 0.567 and 0.925 respectively.

Table 2. ML-IDS model performance in clean settings

Classifier	Accuracy	Precision	Recall	F1 Score	Time (s)
Random Forests	0.8473	0.8655	0.8473	0.8454	30
XGBoost	0.9464	0.9075	0.9464	0.9252	45
Naive Bayes	0.5742	0.5831	0.5742	0.5673	24

5.2   ML-IDS Models Performance in Adversarial Settings

In this sub-section, we demonstrate that applying the perturbations using JSMA and FGSM reduces the performance of our trained model. Further, we check whether the missed attacks (in the bigger false negative set) are still attacks and whether they will inpact the power system. To investigate how different parameter combinations can affect the model performance, multiple adversarial samples were created from the testing data using epsilon (ϵ) values ranging from 0 to 0.45 Although the current literature does not recommend a standard value for ϵ, in our research, we adopted a range between 0 to 0.45 to test attack success rates as suggested by Goodfellow et al. [14].

The adversarial dataset was then generated using different (ϵ) values. To determine how the performance of the models could be affected, the adversarial samples were then combined with the benign testing data and tested on the trained model. Figure 6 shows the overall performance for different adversarial combinations. As the (ϵ) values increased, the model accuracy decreased further. For instance, XGBoost performance decreased from 94.64% at $(\epsilon) = 0$ to 72.03% at $(\epsilon) = 0.45$. On the other hand, Random Forest performance decreased from 84.73% at $(\epsilon) = 0$ to 68.02% at $(\epsilon) = 0.45$. Lastly, the performance for Naive Bayes decreased from 57.42% at $(\epsilon) = 0$ to 32.05% at $(\epsilon) = 0.45$. For FGSM adversarial attack, the attack success rate increased with higher (ϵ) values hence the accuracy declined because to the ML model was deceived by the attack.

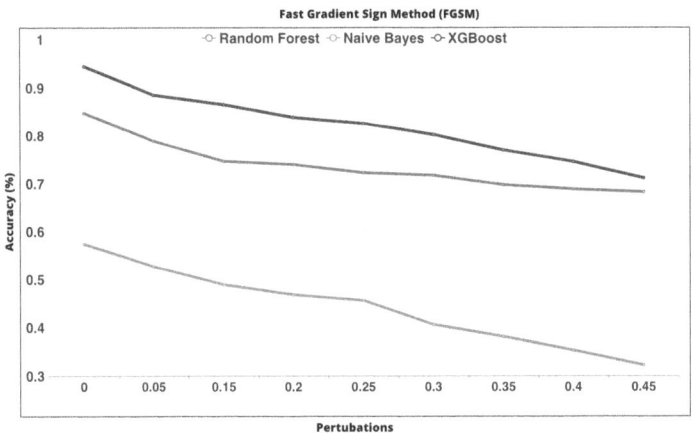

Fig. 6. Performance of trained models in adversarial settings when increasing perturbations (ϵ).

Selecting an appropriate (ϵ) value that will control the perturbation size is very crucial, as a higher (ϵ) value may increase attack success rates but may also increase the detectability of the adversarial samples. Small perturbations are ideal for launching a realistic attack and remain undetected by the IDS. For instance, when $\epsilon = 0.05$, the XGBoost accuracy dropped from 94.64% to 88.04% while Random Forest accuracy dropped from 84.73% to 78.43% and the Naive Bayes accuracy dropped from 57.42% to 52.89%. To consider another instance, when $\epsilon = 0.001$, XGBoost accuracy dropped from 94.64% to 92.36%, the Random Forest accuracy dropped from 84.73% to 82.67% and Naive Bayes accuracy dropped from 57.42% to 55.32% as detailed in Table 3. As per the adversarial performance, all the metrics declined in comparison to the performance of the original datasets in a clean setting.

Naive Bayes exhibited a greater performance drop compared to Random Forest and XGBoost. This could indicate that malicious data is misclassified by Naive Bayes due to its increased sensitivity. On the other hand, XGBoost's classification performance was better. This could suggest that XGBoost is a more reliable classifier when it comes to accurately discriminating between malicious and benign data. The first experiment focuses on JSMA, as indicated in Table 4, to investigate the effects of adversarial instances generated in our evasion attack

Table 3. Degradation of trained models in FGSM adversarial settings ($\epsilon = 0.001$).

Classifier	Accuracy	Precision	Recall	F1 Score
Random Forests	0.8267	0.6667	0.8267	0.6656
XGBoost	0.9236	0.7690	0.9236	0.7493
Naive Bayes	0.5532	0.2808	0.5532	0.2976

and the success of transferring adversarial instances generated by the attacker to the defender's trained model.

To analyze the impact of adversarial instances, recall is used as the detection rate parameter. It quantifies the number of adversarial occurrences classified by the IDS as malicious. The attacker initially creates adversarial instances for each model learned on his or her side (RF, XGBoost, and NB). The adversarial examples generated for one model are then transferred to the other models to determine the transferability of the attacker's trained models.

Table 4. Degradation of trained models in JSMA adversarial settings.

Classifier	Accuracy	Precision	Recall	F1 Score
Random Forests	0.6416	0.6605	0.6434	0.5980
XGBoost	0.7090	0.7289	0.7355	0.7234
Naive Bayes	0.2934	0.2789	0.2978	0.2784

Further, we investigated the incorrectly classified inputs to see if they could cause harm. For example, we use JSMA to alter the features of a malicious data point using various variants of θ and γ. These examples show that the greater the value of θ, the greater is the perturbation of the features. The R1-PA1:VH feature shows an increase from 0.7545 to 0.7550 for $\theta = 0.1$ and 0.5, and to 1 when $\theta = 0.9$. Similarly, the greater the value of γ, the more features are manipulated. Similarly, the higher the value of γ, the more features are perturbed. Table 5 illustrates the frequency of transmitted power features R1:F, R2:F, R3:F, and R4:F.

The frequency of transmitted power for R1:F, R2:F, R3:F, and R4:F increased significantly from an average of 60 Hz to an average of 62 Hz after perturbation. In power systems, the frequency of transmitted power from the grid is kept within a certain range, usually around 60 Hz in North America and 50 Hz in other regions of the world. Maintaining the frequency within the allowed range is critical for the power grid's reliable operation and preventing damage to connected equipment. If the frequency were to rise above 60.3 Hz, several issues could arise [7]. Therefore, from our results, we are confident that this particular attack that was undetected could damage the system, disrupt industrial processes, or cause harm.

Table 5. An example of how the frequency of transmitted power features are perturbed using JSMA.

Dataset	R1-PA1:VH	R1:F	R2:F	R3:F	R4:F
Original Test Data	0.7545	59.986	59.986	59.984	59.988
$\theta = 0.1, \gamma = 0.1$	0.7550	60.059	60.196	60.294	60.468
$\theta = 0.5, \gamma = 0.5$	0.7650	61.574	61.754	61.537	61.643
$\theta = 0.9, \gamma = 0.9$	1.0000	62.566	62.676	62.464	62.376

6   Conclusion

The increasing adoption of NIDS based on ML algorithms presents interesting security challenges. Despite their exceptional performance, these ML models are vulnerable to a wide range of adversarial techniques, including evasion attacks. This paper demonstrated the importance of realistic threat modelling in the context of adversarial attacks on smart grid systems. By highlighting real attacker capabilities and feasible attack scenarios, this research provides a more practical and applicable perspective compared to the existing literature, which often deals with hypothetical or idealized models. Moreover, this research performs an empirical evaluation using a power system dataset generated from a smart grid testbed, which adds significant value, grounding the theoretical insights in real-world data.

To our best knowledge, this is the first realistic approach that aims to evade the NIDS by leveraging on the transferability property without relying on any query methods and with a minimal understanding of the target NIDS. This approach operates within the traffic space and adheres to domain constraints. This paper demonstrates a realistic adversarial approach designed to generate valid and realistic adversarial network traffic by introducing minor perturbations. This allows for bypassing the NIDS protection with a high probability while preserving the core logic of the underlying model. The experiments detailed in this research have shown that evasion attacks can be successfully generated using JSMA and FGSM methods, impacting the classification performance of Random Forest, Naive Bayes and the XGBoost ML models.

Furthermore, our results show that the same set of adversarial examples that managed to deceive one classifier also succeeded in deceiving the other classifiers. For instance, the adversarial samples generated by FGSM managed to decrease the performance of XGBoost from 94.64% to 72.03%, Random Forest from 84.73% to 68.02% and Naive Bayes from 57.42% to 32.05%. This observation can be considered additional evidence for the transferability phenomenon first alluded to by Papernot et al. [27] within the image recognition domain and by Sheatsley et al. [33] within the network intrusion detection domain. Our work in the smart grid domain makes it clear that all three classifiers are vulnerable to adversarial perturbations.

6.1 Future Work

In this research, we have shown how adversarial attacks can be generated successfully by employing both the JSMA and FGSM methods and adversely affect how state-of-the-art supervised models are classified. However, future studies can consider how other methods, such as Carlini Wagner (CW) and Generative Adversarial Networks (GAN) can be used to generate adversarial attacks. In this regard, the current study can be extended and explored more in future works by comparing how different methods of generating adversarial attacks are different or the same. Moreover, adversarial attacks should be investigated against other ML models.

The adversarial attacks against ML models are not limited to the domain of IDS systems but to all systems where ML techniques are implemented. Future research in areas like federated learning can consider the direction of awareness, defence, and mitigation of adversarial attacks against ML [8,26]. Therefore, it would be interesting for further studies to evaluate the applicability of the proposed model in a distributed setting. As mentioned before, there is a great need for research on suitable mitigation techniques against adversarial threats.

Acknowledgments. The first and third author were supported by the Brno University of Technology project "Smart information technology for a resilient society", 2023–2025, code FIT-S-23-8209. The second author was supported by the RICS centre financed by the Swedish Civil contingencies agency (MSB) and project AIR^2 supported by the Wallenberg AI, Autonomous Systems and Software Program (WASP), funded by the Knut and Alice Wallenberg Foundation.

References

1. Industrial Control System Security. Insider threat. https://www.allianz-fuer-cybersicherheit.de/. Accessed 22 Jan 2024
2. Power system attack datasets. http://www.ece.uah.edu/thm0009/icsdatasets. Accessed 30 Jan 2024
3. Alatwi, H.A., Morisset, C.: Realism versus performance for adversarial examples against DL-based NIDS. In: Proceedings of the 38th ACM/SIGAPP Symposium on Applied Computing, pp. 1549–1557 (2023)
4. Alshamrani, A., Myneni, S., Chowdhary, A., Huang, D.: A survey on advanced persistent threats: techniques, solutions, challenges, and research opportunities. IEEE Commun. Surv. Tutor. **21**(2), 1851–1877 (2019)
5. Apruzzese, G., Andreolini, M., Ferretti, L., Marchetti, M., Colajanni, M.: Modeling realistic adversarial attacks against network intrusion detection systems. Digit. Threats Res. Pract. (DTRAP) **3**(3), 1–19 (2022)
6. Asimopoulos, D.C., et al.: Breaching the defense: investigating FGSM and CTGAN adversarial attacks on IEC 60870-5-104 AI-enabled intrusion detection systems. In: Proceedings of the 18th International Conference on Availability, Reliability and Security, pp. 1–8 (2023)
7. Barrera-Cárdenas, R., Molinas, M.: Modelling of power electronic components for evaluation of efficiency, power density and power-to-mass ratio of offshore wind power converters. In: Offshore Wind Farms, pp. 193–261. Elsevier (2016)

8. Bouacida, N., Mohapatra, P.: Vulnerabilities in federated learning. IEEE Access **9**, 63229–63249 (2021). https://doi.org/10.1109/ACCESS.2021.3075203
9. Clements, J., Yang, Y., Sharma, A.A., Hu, H., Lao, Y.: Rallying adversarial techniques against deep learning for network security. In: Symposium Series on Computational Intelligence (SSCI), pp. 01–08. IEEE (2021)
10. Debicha, I., Debate, T., Dricot, J.M., Mees, W.: Adversarial training for deep learning-based intrusion detection systems. In: The Sixteenth International Conference on Systems (ICONS) (2021)
11. Fu, X., Zhou, N., Jiao, L., Li, H., Zhang, J.: The robust deep learning-based schemes for intrusion detection in internet of things environments. Ann. Telecommun. **76**(5–6), 273–285 (2021)
12. Gollmann, D.: From insider threats to business processes that are secure-by-design. In: Third International Conference on Intelligent Networking and Collaborative Systems, pp. 627–627 (2011).https://doi.org/10.1109/INCoS.2011.175
13. Goodfellow, I., et al.: Generative adversarial nets. Adv. Neural Inf. Process. Syst. **27** (2014)
14. Goodfellow, I.J., Shlens, J., Szegedy, C.: Explaining and harnessing adversarial examples (2015). https://arxiv.org/abs/1412.6572
15. Han, J., Kamber, M., Pei, J.: Data Mining: Concepts and Techniques, 3rd edn. Morgan Kaufmann Publishers Inc., San Francisco, CA, USA (2011)
16. Hashemi, M.J., Cusack, G., Keller, E.: Towards evaluation of NIDSs in adversarial setting. In: Proceedings of the 3rd ACM CONEXT Workshop on Big Data, Machine Learning and Artificial Intelligence for Data Communication Networks, pp. 14–21 (2019)
17. Huang, C.H., Lee, T.H., Chang, L.H., Lin, J.R., Horng, G.: Adversarial attacks on SDN-based deep learning IDS system. In: International Conference on Mobile and Wireless Technology (ICMWT), pp. 181–191. Springer (2019)
18. Jeong, J., Kwon, S., Hong, M.P., Kwak, J., Shon, T.: Adversarial attack-based security vulnerability verification using deep learning library for multimedia video surveillance. Multimed. Tools Appl. **79**, 16077–16091 (2020)
19. Kravchik, M., Shabtai, A.: Detecting cyber attacks in industrial control systems using convolutional neural networks. In: Proceedings of the Workshop on Cyber-Physical Systems Security and Privacy, pp. 72–83. CPS-SPC '18, Association for Computing Machinery (2018)
20. Linda, O., Vollmer, T., Manic, M.: Neural network based intrusion detection system for critical infrastructures. In: International Joint Conference on Neural Networks, pp. 1827–1834. IEEE (2009)
21. Liu, C., Gu, Z., Wang, J.: A hybrid intrusion detection system based on scalable k-means+ random forest and deep learning. IEEE Access **9**, 75729–75740 (2021)
22. Liu, L., De Vel, O., Han, Q.L., Zhang, J., Xiang, Y.: Detecting and preventing cyber insider threats: a survey. IEEE Commun. Surv. Tutor. **20**(2), 1397–1417 (2018)
23. Martins, N., Cruz, J.M., Cruz, T., Abreu, P.H.: Analyzing the footprint of classifiers in adversarial denial of service contexts. In: 19th EPIA Conference on Artificial Intelligence, Proceedings, Part II, pp. 256–267. Springer (2019)
24. Merzouk, M.A., Cuppens, F., Boulahia-Cuppens, N., Yaich, R.: A deeper analysis of adversarial examples in intrusion detection. In: Risks and Security of Internet and Systems: 15th International Conference, CRISIS 2020, Revised Selected Papers 15, pp. 67–84. Springer (2021)

25. Min, E., Long, J., Liu, Q., Cui, J., Chen, W.: Anomaly-based intrusion detection through text-convolutional neural network and random forest. Secur. Commun. Netw. (2018)
26. Nguyen, T.D., Rieger, P., Miettinen, M., Sadeghi, A.R.: Poisoning attacks on federated learning-based IoT intrusion detection system. In: Proceedings of the Workshop Decentralized IoT System Security (DISS), vol. 79 (2020)
27. Papernot, N., McDaniel, P., Goodfellow, I.: Transferability in machine learning: from phenomena to black-box attacks using adversarial samples. arXiv preprint arXiv:1605.07277 (2016)
28. Papernot, N., McDaniel, P., Jha, S., Fredrikson, M., Celik, Z.B., Swami, A.: The limitations of deep learning in adversarial settings. In: European Symposium on Security and Privacy (EuroS&P), pp. 372–387. IEEE (2016)
29. Papernot, N., McDaniel, P., Sinha, A., Wellman, M.P.: SOK: security and privacy in machine learning. In: European Symposium on Security and Privacy (EuroS&P), pp. 399–414. IEEE (2018)
30. Peng, X., Huang, W., Shi, Z.: Adversarial attack against DOS intrusion detection: an improved boundary-based method. In: 31st International Conference on Tools with Artificial Intelligence (ICTAI), pp. 1288–1295. IEEE (2019)
31. Peng, Y., Su, J., Shi, X., Zhao, B.: Evaluating deep learning based network intrusion detection system in adversarial environment. In: 9th International Conference on Electronics Information and Emergency Communication (ICEIEC), pp. 61–66. IEEE (2019)
32. SectorCERT: The attack against Danish, critical infrastructure. https://sektorcert.dk/wp-content/uploads/2023/11/SektorCERT-The-attack-against-Danish-critical-infrastructure-TLP-CLEAR.pdf. Accessed 01 Jan 2024
33. Sheatsley, R., Papernot, N., Weisman, M., Verma, G., McDaniel, P.: Adversarial examples in constrained domains (2022). https://arxiv.org/abs/2011.01183
34. Sriram, S., Simran, K., Vinayakumar, R., Akarsh, S., Soman, K.: Towards evaluating the robustness of deep intrusion detection models in adversarial environment. In: International Symposium on Security in Computing and Communication, pp. 111–120. Springer (2019)
35. Tavallaee, M., Bagheri, E., Lu, W., Ghorbani, A.A.: A detailed analysis of the KDD CUP 99 data set. In: Symposium on Computational Intelligence for Security and Defense Applications, pp. 1–6. IEEE (2009).https://doi.org/10.1109/CISDA.2009.5356528
36. Wang, Z.: Deep learning-based intrusion detection with adversaries. IEEE Access 6, 38367–38384 (2018)
37. Warzyński, A., Kołaczek, G.: Intrusion detection systems vulnerability on adversarial examples. In: Innovations in Intelligent Systems and Applications (INISTA), pp. 1–4. IEEE (2018)
38. Zhu, N., Zhu, C., Zhou, L., Zhu, Y., Zhang, X.: Optimization of the random forest hyperparameters for power industrial control systems intrusion detection using an improved grid search algorithm. Appl. Sci. 12(20), 10456 (2022)

Cyber Resilience Using ASFA: DORA-Compliant Threat-Led Penetration Testing

Elias Seid$^{(\boxtimes)}$, Fredrik Blix , and Oliver Popov

Department of Computer and Systems Sciences, Stockholm University,
Stockholm, Sweden
elias.seid@dsv.su.se

Abstract. The financial sector is experiencing an increase in cyber incidents, prompting numerous firms to outsource IT infrastructure management. A primary factor contributing to these breaches is that the impacted systems are socio-technical systems (STSs), which include not only technical components such as software and hardware but also physical elements (e.g., robotics, mobility) and social components (e.g., human actors, business processes, and organizational units). Evaluating STS security breaches requires a holistic approach, considering human, organizational, software, and infrastructural elements. The study involves combining strategic factors, including social and organizational dynamics, with technical components such as software and physical infrastructure.

In our previous work, we developed a security attack-monitoring system to tackle these challenges. This framework was developed to monitor, analyze, and model security incidents across the social, cyber, and physical dimensions of cyber-physical systems (CPS). This paper employs the framework to conduct threat-led penetration testing in accordance with the Digital Operational Resilience Act (DORA), thus improving the financial sector's capacity to address information and communication crises. This study provides important insights into cyberattacks and their impact on the financial sector by examining security breaches reported to the Swedish Civil Contingencies Agency (MSB) by critical service providers. The experiment was performed in collaboration with a prominent Swedish financial institution.

Keywords: Incident Reporting · DORA · Cybersecurity ·
Cyber-Resilience · Risk Management · Penetration Testing

1 Introduction

The advent of digitalization has revolutionized our interactions with various aspects of life, and information communication technology has now become an integral and indispensable component of our daily existence. The process of

G. Oliva et al. (Eds.): CRITIS 2024, LNCS 15549, pp. 269–288, 2025.
https://doi.org/10.1007/978-3-031-84260-3_16

digitalization has also introduced the potential for cyber risks, which have the ability to impact us on a daily basis in various ways. Organizations are increasingly required to enhance their defense against these risks. However, considering the complex structure of digital technologies and the potential for human error, there is no straightforward solution[1].

Cyberattacks are becoming more concentrated on the financial industry, with the complexity and frequency of these threats constantly changing in response to technological improvements. The cyber-threats encompass a wide range of malicious activities, including data breaches, ransomware attacks, sophisticated phishing schemes, and distributed denial-of-service (DDoS) attacks. Each of these poses substantial dangers to the integrity, resilience, and trustworthiness of financial services (Gusiv et al., 2023). The financial services business faces complicated problems and hazards when outsourcing services to other parties, which further worsen cybersecurity concerns. Financial institutions are required to traverse a digital terrain that is becoming more vulnerable, which means they need to have strong cybersecurity frameworks in place to protect their operations and keep the trust of their customers. The dynamic nature of threats underscores the crucial requirement for adaptable and proactive cybersecurity strategies and regulations in the financial sector (Keizer et al., 2022).

The recently introduced Digital Operational Resilience Act (DORA[2]) focuses on enhancing the cyber resilience of financial entities, including banks, insurance companies, investment businesses, and crypto-asset service providers. DORA establishes a set of rules that encompass regulations on managing risks associated with Information and Communication Technology (ICT), reporting incidents linked to ICT, and conducting penetration testing (Dupont. B, et al., 2019).

1.1 Threat-Led Penetration Testing (TLPT)

Cyber Threat Intelligence (CTI): represents a systematic approach to the collection and analysis of extensive data regarding potential cyber threats, with the aim of enhancing defensive capabilities. It integrates diverse sources of information to provide a comprehensive understanding of cyber threats, including their methods of operation, indicators of compromise (IOC), and associated tactics, techniques, and procedures (TTP). Furthermore, CTI involves assessing the potential impacts of these threats and formulating evidence-based, actionable recommendations. This intelligence supports informed strategic decision-making processes to ensure the protection of networks and sensitive data (Abu et al., 2018 and Al-Tarawneh et al., 2021).

Threat-Led Penetration Testing (TLP): Threat-led penetration testing (TLPT) is a cybersecurity assessment method that emulates the tactics, techniques, and procedures of real-world threat actors to evaluate an organization's defenses. This approach leverages current threat intelligence to create realistic

---

[1] https://www.weforum.org/publications/global-risks-report-2022/in-full/chapter-3-digital-dependencies-and-cyber-vulnerabilities/?utm_source=chatgpt.com.

[2] https://www.eiopa.europa.eu/digital-operational-resilience-act-dora_en.

attack scenarios, providing a comprehensive understanding of potential vulnerabilities and the effectiveness of existing security measures. The European Union's Digital Operational Resilience Act (DORA) mandates that financial entities implement robust digital operational resilience measures, including advanced testing protocols like TLPT. DORA aims to harmonize and strengthen the ICT security framework across the EU financial sector, ensuring that institutions can withstand, respond to, and recover from all types of ICT-related disruptions and threats[3].

Once a financial institution has achieved a high level of cyber readiness, characterized by the establishment and execution of a robust and practical strategy, as well as the implementation of a resilient infrastructure, it should undergo testing. The DORA framework mandates that financial institutions conduct frequent assessments of their operational resilience and establishes uniform criteria for testing protocols(Georg Borges et al., 2023). Tests should encompass vulnerability assessments, open-source analysis, and source code reviews. DORA mandates that financial institutions of significant size must conduct a threat-led penetration test (TLPT) at least once every three years. The TLPT can be conducted in a manner that is appropriate and balanced with the size, scope, operations, and total risk of the financial institution (Clausmeier.D et al., 2023).

The G7 Fundamental Elements[4] provides a definition of TLPT as follows: "TLPT is a deliberate effort to undermine the ability of an organization to withstand cyber attacks by imitating the strategies, methods, and actions of actual malicious actors." This approach is grounded in specific and focused information about potential threats. It analyses people, procedures, and technology of a particular entity, while minimizing any prior knowledge or disruption to its activities.A targeted security analysis necessitates a methodical approach to identifying plausible attack strategies and vectors. However, the inherent unpredictability of future cyberattacks presents significant challenges in operationalizing such analyses. The absence of concrete intelligence regarding potential attacker behavior often results in inaccuracies, including false positives or negatives, during the evaluation of security measures. Conducting a comprehensive analysis of possible attack scenarios is a cornerstone of Threat-Led Penetration Testing (TLPT). This methodology not only enables the identification of critical attack pathways but also informs the development of essential security requirements. Moreover, TLPT provides a nuanced understanding of the justification and necessity for specific security controls, thereby contributing to the enhancement of organizational cybersecurity resilience and aligning with best practices in risk management.

In our prior study (Seid et al., 2023 and Seid et al., 2024), we introduced a framework named ASFA. This framework is designed to monitor security attack events across many domains. The framework provides support in monitoring

---

[3] https://www.esma.europa.eu/esmas-activities/digital-finance-and-innovation/
digital-operational-resilience-act-dora?utm_source=chatgpt.com.

[4] 2018-10-24-g-7-fundamental-elements-for-threat-led-penetration-testing-data   PDF
(www.bundesbank.de).

security attack incidents in CPS. This framework covers all three realms of a CPS. Furthermore, the framework facilitates cross-realm analysis and monitoring, allowing for the detection of security events that occur in other realms. Our models specifically target adversary that are distinct to each domain, encompassing the three realms of a CPS (cyber, physical infrastructure, and social). We also analysed the interdependent relationships among realm-specific attack models. The Attack-Mechanism Model (AM) depends on the Vulnerability Model (VM) model in revealing realm-specific vulnerabilities, and the vulnerabilities captured by (the VM) spin off and provide inputs to the next realm (AM). Thus, a suitable attack mechanism is selected by taking advantage of the weaknesses of the VM.

The framework can be employed in relation to the TLP with regards to DORA to enhance the resilience of financial sector institutions against future cyber-attacks. Cyberattacks on the cyberinfrastructure might aim at compromising processes, hardware, and users. There are other methods of cyberattacks, including syntax attacks that use malware and semantic attacks that employ social engineering tactics, with the goal of infiltrating specific cyber infrastructure (Van den Berg et al., 2022 and Wang et al., 2010). The objective of this study is to apply the ASFA framework (a framework for monitoring security attack events) to perform threat-led penetration testing, with the aim of aligning with DORA's objectives of improving digital operational resilience. Furthermore, it supports financial institutions in being prepared and resilient against advanced cyber threats, thereby fulfilling DORA objectives. The study aims to address the following research question (RQ).

– **RQ1:How can the ASFA framework be effectively employed for Threat-Led Penetration Testing to ensure compliance with the Digital Operational Resilience Act (DORA)?**

The subsequent sections of this work are arranged in the following manner. Section 2 provides the theoretical basis for our research, whereas Sect. 3 presents the ASFA framework. The paper's fourth section comprises case studies, while the fifth section is specifically focused on the experiment and its outcomes. Section 6 has discussions. Section 7 provides the conclusive summary and explores possible paths for future research.

2   Research Baseline

2.1   Digital Operational Resilience Act (DORA)

Cyber resilience refers to the "ability to continuously deliver the intended outcome despite adverse cyber events" (Fredrik et al., 2015). DORA represents a significant evolution in the regulatory landscape within the European Union, specifically tailored to bolster the information technology security of financial enterprises including banks, insurance companies, and investment businesses. This evolution is not just about enhancing the resilience of these institutions themselves but critically extends to the third-party service providers that underpin the financial sector's operational capabilities, such as cloud platforms and data analytics services[5].

The act, which came into force with final adoption by the European Parliament in November 2022, establishes a robust legal framework dedicated to ensuring that both financial institutions and their third-party partners can withstand, respond to, and recover from a broad spectrum of ICT-related threats. This unified approach across all EU member states underscores a concerted effort to mitigate cyber risks, ensuring a harmonized regulatory environment conducive to digital operational resilience (Council of the EU 2022; European Parliament, 2022).[6]

Introduced as part of a broader digital finance package by the European Commission in 2020, DORA seeks to balance the advancement of technological innovation with the imperative of maintaining financial stability and consumer safety. This balance is particularly relevant when considering the role of third-party service providers, whose integration into the financial ecosystem introduces both opportunities for innovation and potential vectors for risk. By making the existing legal framework adaptable to new digital financial instruments and technologies, DORA addresses a critical gap in EU legislation, facilitating innovation while safeguarding the operational resilience of the financial system (Council of the EU 2022; VanHoy, J. 2021).

The development and deployment of ICT technologies, while opening doors to new opportunities, also brings in new challenges and risks, particularly in times of heightened digital dependency. Recognizing this, DORA provides a comprehensive framework to enhance the digital resilience of the EU's financial institutions and, by extension, their third-party service providers. This framework includes measures for improved ICT risk management, rigorous testing of ICT systems, and enhanced oversight by financial supervisors, including the monitoring of third-party risks. Such measures aim to strengthen the financial sector's resilience by ensuring a thorough understanding and management of cyber risks and deviations (European Commission 2020; Kun, E. 2024).

In 2018, the European Central Bank (ECB) released TIBER-EU, which is a European framework that focuses on using threat intelligence to conduct ethical red-teaming[7]. The document is the inaugural EU-wide manual outlining the collaborative efforts required between authorities, entities, and providers of threat intelligence and red-team services to assess and enhance the cyber resilience of entities through the execution of controlled cyber-attacks. The framework only allows for the participation of external testers[8].

It is crucial to understand that entities coming under the scope of NIS2 will not be required to have any TLPT. Consequently, there is no possibility

---

[5] https://www.digital-operational-resilience-act.com/..

[6] https://www.cyberark.com/resources/ebooks/dora-compliance-an-identity-security-guidebook.

[7] ecb.tiber_eu_framework.en.

[8] ecb.tiber_eu_framework.en.

of conflicting regulations regarding testing requirements with DORA. Nevertheless, the DORA testing standards are exceptionally rigorous, irrespective of the tester's kind. Furthermore, smaller businesses are not required to carry out costly (TLPTs).

It is recommended to do TLPTs at a minimum frequency of once every three years (See article 23 DORA).The competent authority may require the financial company to adjust the frequency of its operations based on its risk profile and operating circumstances, as permitted by Article 23 of DORA[9] Article 23, paragraph 4aa of the DORA)

3   ASFA Framework

This section presents the ASFA framework that supports the monitoring of security attack events for CPS, and the framework spans the three realms of a CPS. Moreover, the framework supports cross-realm analysis and monitoring, which spins off security events across realms. Our models focus on realm-specific adversaries, meaning that they span the three realms of a CPS (cyber, physical infrastructure, and social). We also analysed the interdependent relationships among realm-specific attack models. The AM depends on the VM model in revealing realm-specific vulnerabilities, and the vulnerabilities captured by (the VM) spin off and provide inputs to the next realm (AM). Thus, a suitable attack mechanism is selected by taking advantage of the weaknesses of the VM (Seid et al., 2023). Figure 2 illustrates the ASFA analysis process, which includes the following steps.

Vulnerability Model (VM): This model captures the attack patterns, potential threats, and type of asset, in which an asset is a potential target for cyber attacks. The VM consists of the following sub-elements.

Threat: This is the potential for abuse of an asset that will cause harm in the context of the problem.

Vulnerability: This is a weakness in the system that an attack exploits.

Asset: This is anything that has value to an organisation, and it can be tangible (physical) or intangible (non-physical) with respect to the target of the attack.

Attack Pattern: This is defined as a generic description of a deliberate, malicious adversary that frequently occurs in a specific context (Fernandez-Buglioni, 2013). It describes the common elements and techniques used in attacks against vulnerable CPS components. These patterns generalise reusable attack knowledge from frequent adversaries to facilitate security requirements analysis for the system-to-be. An attack pattern consists of the general goal of the attack, the antecedent, the steps to carry out the attack, and the consequent (Fig. 1).

Attack-Mechanism Model (AM): This model captures design strategies for different attack pattern mechanisms. More importantly, it builds attack mechanisms by employing goal models, domain assumptions, attack mechanisms, and

---

[9] https://www.digital-operational-resilience-act.com/.

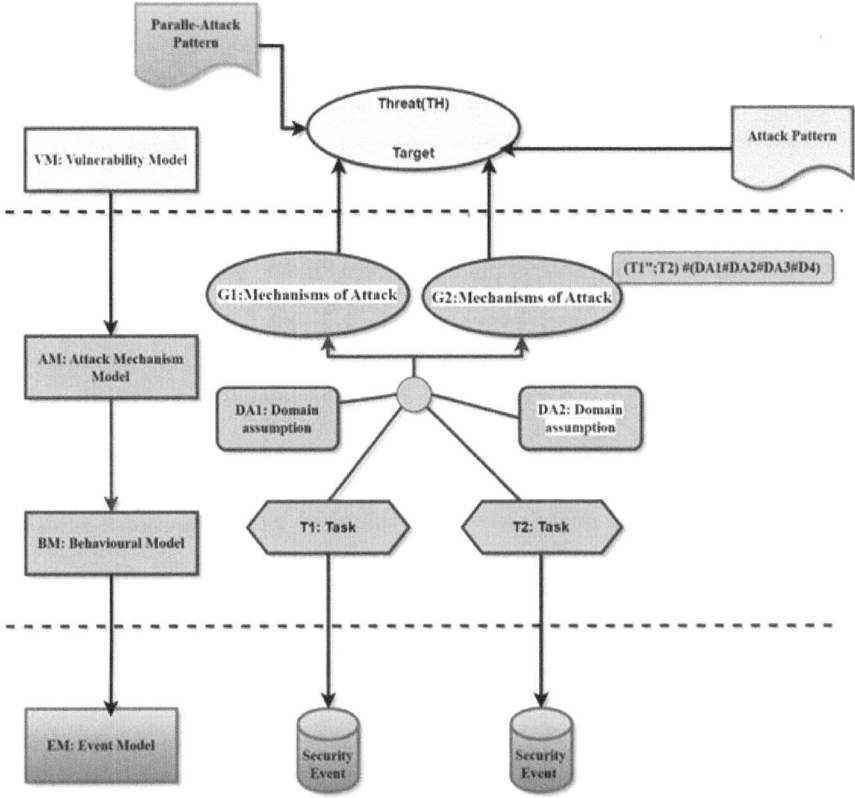

Fig. 1. Component of the Framework

task operationalisation artefacts. Each attack pattern captures knowledge about how specific parts of an attack are designed and executed, providing the adversary's perspective on the problem and the solution and guidance for mitigating the attack's effectiveness. The AM depends on the VM since it prepares its attacking mechanism based on the threat explored in the VM. However, threats can be refined not only linearly but also iteratively.

Behavioural Model (BM): Building a complete behavioural model for very complicated systems such as CPS, with many complex and heterogeneous states, is often challenging. To understand how attackers fulfill their target by compromising security concerns such as confidentiality, integrity, availability, and accountability, one has to analyse how the threat environment behaves within the system, how adversaries can compromise the system, and how the system behaves under multi-stage attacks, as well as recognise system behaviours to facilitate such analysis. This model captures fundamental system behaviours such as **sequential**, **interleaving**, **multiplicity**, and **alternative** instances of attack goal models, sub-goals, domain assumptions, and tasks.

Event Model (EM): This model captures events derived from behavioural models (BM). These events could be grouped into observable and non-observable events from an event-log perspective. We focus mainly on observable events. The application of the framework will be briefly explored in the next part, and its applicability for using TLPT will be discussed in section five of the paper.

3.1   Application of ASFA to TLPT

Threat-led penetration testing is fundamentally linked to the analysis of attack vectors and the evaluation of detection and response mechanisms within an organization's cybersecurity framework. The ASFA framework offers a structured and comprehensive methodology for the modeling, evaluating, and monitoring of security attacks, with a particular emphasis on their application in the domain of CPS. This framework can be effectively implemented for Threat-led Penetration Testing (TLPT) in accordance with the DORA (Digital Operational Resilience Act) regulations, with the objective of enhancing the resilience of financial sector entities against incidents related to Information and Communication Technology (ICT). The following elucidates how each component of our framework has been incorporated to execute TLPT.

Vulnerability Model (VM): Apply the VM to detect and prioritize vulnerabilities in financial systems that are susceptible to attacks from realistic threat actors, as mandated by DORA.

Attack-Mechanism Model (AM): Design TLPT scenarios to replicate how particular attack vectors can exploit the vulnerabilities detected in the VM.

Behavioural Model (BM): The BM is used to comprehend and replicate the dynamic interconnections and progressions of occurrences during an attack, which is crucial in evaluating the resilience and responsiveness of the financial entity's ICT systems against intricate, multi-phase attacks such as Advanced Persistent Threats.

Event Model (EM): Captures and monitors events during simulated attacks, enabling an evaluation of the organization's detection and response processes.

By using ASFA in TLPT, financial entities can ensure compliance with DORA's rigorous ICT risk management requirements and improve their ability to detect, report, and respond to ICT-related incidents. Integrating the components of the ASFA framework enables institutions to do thorough cross-realm analysis of security attacks. This capability allows for the analysis and comprehension of the interactions among cyber, physical, and social aspects of cyber-physical systems, pinpointing weaknesses and attack routes that traverse various domains. Moreover, the framework provides organisations with the essential tools to identify, report, and address cyber threats. Through rigorous monitoring and analysis of security incidents, institutions may improve their threat detection capacities and optimise their response methods to swiftly reduce the effects of cyberattacks. In the end, the convergence of these elements ensures compliance with DORA's rigorous standards for ICT risk management and incident response. Institutions can use the insights derived from the framework to formulate and execute security solutions that comply with regulatory criteria while enhancing their overall operational resilience.

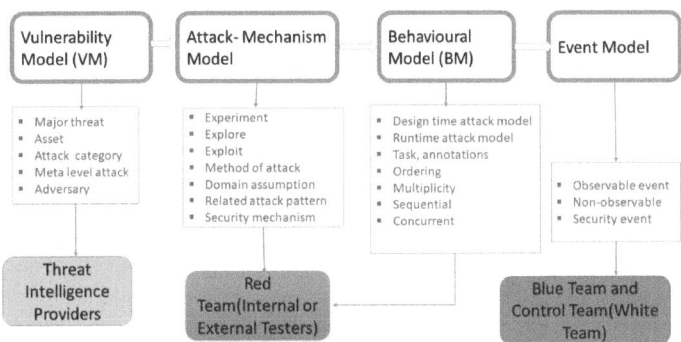

Fig. 2. TLPT Process

4   Case Study

The aim of this study was to evaluate the methods and practices currently used in the financial sector for conducting cybersecurity risk analysis. The study aimed to offer a thorough and operational understanding of the domain, with a specific emphasis on evaluating cyber risks, vulnerabilities, threats, incidents, and response strategies. Moreover, this study aims to thoroughly evaluate the techniques employed in cyber risk analysis within the financial sector. The objective is to recognize the constraints of current methods and establish the essential criteria for constructing suitable models for cyber risk analysis. To investigate the research question, it is crucial to gain a comprehensive understanding in order to establish a correlation between sub-components within the process, thereby reducing cyber security risks. The widespread availability of valuable data facilitates a comprehensive evaluation and deeper understanding of the intricate cybersecurity threats faced by the financial sector, as well as the measures implemented to mitigate cyber risks. The characteristics identified in the case study are closely aligned with the study's objectives, making it a suitable and appropriate choice for analysis. This research focuses on examining cybersecurity vulnerabilities associated with a prominent financial institution in Sweden, referred to anonymously as FI, to maintain confidentiality. The IT incident reports from the company were systematically categorized according to four key dimensions: vulnerability, attack mechanism, security events, and the target of the attack. Reports that did not contain sufficient information to meet the criteria of any classification category were designated as "unknown." In total, 44 IT incidents were analyzed, among which 8 reports provided detailed descriptions of incidents explicitly linked to intentional and malicious actions.

Our analysis revealed that social engineering is the most prevalent category of reported cyberattacks. Specifically, 32% of IT incident reports involving cyberattacks utilized social engineering tactics, such as phishing and spear phishing, as the primary method of initial entry. The second most common attack vector identified was inadequate capacity, often resulting in interruptions to information resources and system accessibility. Denial of service (DoS) attacks accounted for 43% of reported malicious incidents attributed to FI, while malicious activity overall was responsible for 50% of disruptions to information and system access. This study uses IT-incident reports as the main source of data, which were acquired from MSB (Swedish Civil Contingencies Agency). In addition, the study included a supplementary dataset comprised of written IT incident reports. The reports were submitted to MSB by various government agencies and organizations in Sweden. The dataset was chosen in accordance with the standards outlined in the European Union's NIS directive.

This study aims to advance existing knowledge by leveraging non-publicly available data, which offers a broader and more comprehensive scope compared to publicly accessible sources. Such data enables a more in-depth analysis of cybersecurity incidents, providing unique insights into the challenges faced by major service providers. However, the collection of IT incident data from these providers is often complicated by the sensitive and confidential nature of the information, posing significant barriers to access. This study's contribution lies in overcoming these challenges to deliver a nuanced understanding of cybersecurity threats and responses.

5   Simulation of Attacks: Integrating the ASFA Framework Into TLPT to Ensure Compliance with DORA Regulations

By incorporating ASFA into TLPT, financial institutions can ensure compliance with DORA's rigorous regulations for managing ICT risks, while also improving their ability to identify, report, and address incidents related to ICT. The purpose of this part is to provide a detailed security analysis of the use of ASFA, which can be used to carry out TLPT experiments.

Security Attack Analysis of XSS Through HTTP Query String: The exploitation of Cross-Site Scripting (XSS) through the HTTP Query String was analyzed using the ASFA framework. The findings are systematically presented, encompassing identified vulnerabilities, the attack mechanisms employed, and the behavioral dynamics observed following penetration testing. Additionally, the study includes detailed documentation of critical security events associated with the attack.

Vulnerability Model (VM): 1) Threat: An adversary convinces a victim to submit a malicious HTTP query string into a vulnerable web application, **2)**

Target: software (web browser), **3) attack pattern: XSS Through HTTP query strings, and 4) parallel attack: DOM-based XSS**

Attack-Mechanism Model (AM): seven attack mechanisms were captured, namely, (1) XSS through HTTP query string; (2) use a browser or an automated tool; (3) attempt variations in input parameters; (4) exploit vulnerabilities; (5) steal session IDs, credentials, page contents; (6) content spoofing; and (7) forceful browsing.

Tasks: 10 specific tasks (attack activities) have been captured, namely: (1) use spidering tool to follow and record all links, (2) use a proxy tool to record all links visited, (3) use a browser to manually explore and analyse the website, (4) use a list of XSS probe strings to inject in the parameter of known URLs; (5) use a proxy tool to record the results of the manual input of XSS probes in known URls, (6) develop malicious JavaScript that is injected through vectors and send information to the attacker, (7) develop malicious JavaScript that is injected through vectors and take and cause the browser to execute it, (8) develop malicious JavaScript that is injected through vectors and perform actions on the same website, (9) develop malicious JavaScript that is injected through vectors, and (10) cause the browser to execute requests to other websites.

Behavioural Model (BM): Alternative System Behavior expresses that the system need to satisfy a goal, and depending on the type of obstacle facing, a change in behavior is expected to happen and Multiple Instance annotates running system behaviors that could have more than once instance, and the instances can be ordered in sequence (Sequential) or they can occur concurrently (Interleaved).

Goals: represent prescriptive statements outlining the intended objectives to be achieved through the coordinated actions of the agents within a system. In this context, the term "system" encompasses not only the software but also its broader environment, including human operators, legacy systems, and physical devices such as sensors and actuators (Van Lamsweerde, 2009). Within the cybersecurity modeling framework, goals are used to define the desired outcomes of the system, contrasting with anti-goals, which represent objectives from an attacker's perspective. This distinction allows for a focused approach to identifying and mitigating threats aligned with the adversary's intent.

Security Goal Model: Is an AND/OR-graph showing how goals contribute positively or negatively to each other, and AND-refinement captures a combination of sub- goals entailing the parent goal; and OR-refinement captures an alternative way of satisfying the parent goal. A goal may be refined into sub-goals by asking How questions whereas it may be abstracted into par- ent goals by asking Why questions.

Operation (Tasks): Describe behaviors of the system-to-domain assumption. Domain Assumptions. Are properties of the domain that are assumed to hold. Normally, assumptions considered as an assertions to check the correctness of goal refinement or operationalization. In general, like goals, assumptions cannot be enforced to be refined (Feather et al., 1998). However, in our model, domain assumptions are refined together with tasks in order to satisfy the root goal as shown in Figure 3, because they are used as antecedents that supports to perform cyber attack, and facilitates to choose type of attack mechanism.

A formal behavioural annotation for the sub-attack "XSS through HTTP query String" is (G1; (G2 # G3)) #. That is, first, use a browser or automated tool, then repeatedly attempt input parameter variations and exploit vulnerabilities. A formal behavioural annotation for the sub-attack G2 (**Use a browser or an automated tool**) is T1; (T2 # T3); that is, the sub-attack G2 (use a browser or automated tool) has a formal behavioural annotation. T1 (use spidering tool to record links) should be completed first, followed by T2 (use proxy toll to record links), and T3 (use browser to manually explore and analyse website). Formal behaviour annotation for G3 sub-attack (**attempt variations on input parameters**) is (T4 # T5), which involves interleaved fulfilment (T4: inject XSS probe strings into known URL parameters) and (T5: record manual XSS probe input results in known URLs) using a proxy tool.

Formal behaviour annotation for G5 sub-attack (**steal session IDs, credentials, page content**) is (T6; T7), which involves developing malicious JavaScript that is injected through vectors and sending information to the attacker first, followed by taking and causing the browser to execute. Formal behaviour annotation for (**exploit vulnerabilities**) (G5; G6 # G7) suggests stealing session IDs, credentials, and page content first, followed by forced browsing and content spoofing.

5.1   Formal Method Representation

Definitions

- G: Set of goals.
- T: Set of tasks.
- S: System states.
- R: Rules or transitions defining behavior.

System State Representation

$$S_0 : \text{Initial state (no actions executed)}$$

S_{T1}, S_{T2}, S_{T3} : States after tasks $T1, T2, T3$ are executed sequentially or interleaved

$$S_{\text{success}} : \text{Final state where the attack is successful.}$$

Transition Rules

$$S_0 \xrightarrow{T1} S_{T1} \qquad\qquad \text{Task } T1 \text{ transitions to state } S_{T1} .$$

$$S_{T1} \xrightarrow{T2\|T3} S_{T2,T3} \qquad \text{Tasks } T2 \text{ and } T3 \text{ execute interleaved.}$$

$$S_{T2,T3} \xrightarrow{T4\|T5} S_{\text{attempt}} \qquad \text{Tasks } T4 \text{ and } T5 \text{ execute interleaved.}$$

$$S_{\text{attempt}} \xrightarrow{\text{exploit}} S_{\text{success}} \qquad\qquad \text{Exploitation leads to success.}$$

Formal Notation

$$\text{Initial State: } \quad S_0$$

$$\text{Sequential Transition: } \quad S_0 \xrightarrow{T1} S_{T1}$$

$$\text{Interleaved Execution: } \quad S_{T1} \xrightarrow{T2\|T3} S_{T2,T3}$$

$$\text{Iterative Execution: } \quad \text{while } S_{\text{success}} \notin G, \quad S_{T2,T3} \xrightarrow{T4\|T5} S_{\text{attempt}}$$

$$\text{Final State: } \quad S_{\text{success}} = \text{Goal Achieved.}$$

Event Model (EM): This model captures the security events E1: links recorded, E2: website explored, E3: visited links recorded, E4: known URLs injected, E5: results of manual input of XSS probes recorded: E6: information sent, E7: attacker's command executed by the browser, E8: action performed on the same website, E9: request executed to other website, and E8: invalid information exposed to the user. The two remaining analyses for user compromise and misconfiguration (phishing) utilise the same steps as previously explained. The framework has effectively described one attack pattern for user compromise attacks, one attack pattern for parallel attacks, four sub-attack mechanisms, and three domain assumptions.

Algorithm 1 Security Events for XSS Attack

Data: Set of security events $E = \{E_1, E_2, \ldots, E_{10}\}$
Result: Systematically identified and recorded security events
Initialization:
  Define user U, target website W, and data variables:
    L: Links identified by spidering tool
    L_v: Subset of visited links
    URL: Known URL parameters
    R: Results from XSS probes
    I: Information exfiltrated
    C: Command executed by the browser
    A_w: Actions on the same website
    URL_t: Redirected website
    C_i: Invalid information exposed
Process Events:
  foreach *Security Event E_i in E* **do**
    if $i = 1$ **then**
      Record links using spidering tool: E_1 = {recorded_links |
      use_spidering_tool(U, L)}
    else if $i = 2$ **then**
      Explore website manually: E_2 = {website_explored |
      manual_exploration(U, W)}
    else if $i = 3$ **then**
      Record visited links: E_3 = {visited_links | use_proxy_tool(U, L_v)}
    else if $i = 4$ **then**
      Inject XSS probes: E_4 = {URLs_injected | inject_XSS(U, URL)}
    else if $i = 5$ **then**
      Record results of XSS probes: E_5 = {XSS_results_recorded |
      record_proxy(U, R)}
    else if $i = 6$ **then**
      Send exfiltrated information: E_6 = {info_sent |
      malicious_JavaScript(U, I)}
    else if $i = 7$ **then**
      Execute attackers command: E_7 = {command_executed |
      browser_executes(U, C)}
    else if $i = 8$ **then**
      Perform action on the same website: E_8 = {action_performed |
      malicious_JavaScript(U, A_w)}
    else if $i = 9$ **then**
      Redirect to another website: E_9 = {request_executed |
      browser_redirect(U, URL_t)}
    else
      Expose invalid information: E_{10} = {info_exposed | invalid_content(U, C_i)}
    end
  end
Output:
  Structured set of security events $E = \{E_1, E_2, \ldots, E_{10}\}$ for analysis.

The enhancement of sub-attack scenarios enabled the systematic identification and documentation of eight discrete tasks and eight corresponding security events, underpinned by a methodical behavioral annotation process. The analysis identified two distinct attack patterns associated with the "misuse of resources" (relative path traversal) attack type, specifically one primary and one parallel pattern. Moreover, the investigation revealed one primary attack mechanism alongside three supplementary mechanisms, offering a detailed and structured insight into the operational intricacies of this attack vector. The study also identified seven tasks and articulated three domain-specific assumptions as part of the comprehensive analytical framework. In total, nine security incidents were recorded, underscoring the significance of these findings in advancing the understanding and mitigation of sophisticated cybersecurity threats.

6 Discussion

Many recorded cases of denial-of-service attacks explicitly attribute the cause to distributed denial-of-service (DDoS) attacks. Furthermore, a multitude of documented attacks suggest that the objective was to intentionally disrupt the resources of the website. Some denial-of-service attacks and disruptions have been associated with cyberinfrastructure intrusions, misuse of resources, and installation of malicious software. When evaluating the efficacy of denial of service attacks, 94% of them resulted in different levels of disruption. Our analysis indicates that a significant portion of denial-of-service (DoS) attacks comprises distributed attacks specifically targeting website resources. These disruptions often impact external accessibility to websites while leaving internal informational systems for employees largely unaffected. Additionally, these attacks have the potential to escalate into full-scale denial-of-service incidents. Despite a declining trend, social engineering attacks remain frequently reported. However, when compared to other attack vectors, social engineering and exploits leveraging insufficient authentication mechanisms demonstrated limited impact on the core cyberinfrastructure of major service providers.

Recognizing potential threats to a system is a crucial element in creating secure systems, since it enables the identification of the essential security requirements. Analyzing attacks in the financial sector is a significant problem due to their widespread prevalence. These systems comprise humans, entities, software systems, and concrete infrastructures. The ASFA framework enables the examination of security attacks on vital service providers, encompassing the three domains of Cyber-Physical Systems (CPS). Furthermore, the framework enables the study and monitoring of many worlds, enabling the identification of security incidents that occur across distinct domains. Our models are designed to explicitly address adversaries that are unique to each domain, which includes the three realms of a CPS (cyber, physical infrastructure, and social).

As a result, analysis of an attack requires scrutinizing the strategic components related to the individuals and organizations implicated, including social and organizational facets. Furthermore, it is essential to consider the technical factors that influence software systems and physical infrastructure. The process requires a considerable level of expertise in security, which presents difficulties in terms of obtaining it. At first, we concentrated on analyzing the process of identifying an attacker's methods by conducting a methodical inquiry into their malicious intentions. Each attack strategy includes one or more anti-goals, which define the malicious intentions of attackers and offer insight into what and when they might intend to carry out an attack.

Answering RQ1: This data serves as the foundation of threat-focused penetration testing, enabling cybersecurity experts to establish an authentic testing setting that accurately replicates the organization's operational and threat landscape. Conducting focused testing not only evaluates the strength of the organization's security measures but also aids in refining techniques for detecting and responding to potential attacks. The ASFA framework provides a structured approach to model, analyze, and monitor security attacks, particularly in the context of CPS. It facilitates the process of detecting, identifying, and responding to cyber attacks. Most importantly, it captures the attacking mechanism employed by adversaries.

This framework can be efficiently employed for Threat-led Penetration Testing (TLPT) in compliance with the DORA, with the objective of enhancing the resilience of financial sector firms against incidents connected to Information and Communication Technology (ICT). The framework consists of several key components that have various potential uses in TLPT. Moreover, people who have a broader understanding of security employ this framework more effectively. However, we found that manual intervention is required to identify important security incidents because the framework has limited precision and to find security Incident. Therefore, we may infer that people without proficiency in security are incapable of using this framework in its current condition.

6.1 Novelty of the Framework

Analysing attack scenarios: Numerous studies have been conducted to study and depict attack scenarios, detailing the methodologies employed by attackers in executing cyber-attacks. The current literature outlines many methodologies for illustrating assault scenarios, including attack trees (Morais et al., 2013) and graphs (Phillips and Swiler, 1998), which researchers used to represent these scenarios. In contrast to our method, existing methodologies lack in explaining the implementation of attack strategies. Further research studied threat modelling methodologies like STRIDE (Shostack, 2014), although these inadequately represent attacker motivations and fail to address intricate, multistage attacks.

In contrast, other approaches have explicitly explored the rationale of attacker behaviour through the use of anti-goals, as seen in Van Lamsweerde (2004). Our methodology has similarities with these techniques for attack models, anti-goal refining, and the formulation of attack scenarios. Our research transcends conventional approaches by exploring the behavioural models of security attack situations and applying them to construct run-time attack models.

6.2 Threats to Validity

This study considered the influential factors that impact subject performance. We assert that the competence of the individuals participating in the study was suitable for the purpose of the initial evaluation. All the authors involved in this case study have a background in cyber security and are considered experts in the field. The participants were engaged in the development and testing of security event models. It cannot be shown that our approach is suitable for non-experts in security. However, our approach does offer security patterns that can assist analysts in reusing security knowledge. For future experiment, our intention is to involve people who have limited understanding of security.

7 Conclusion

If there was a better time for DORA, it would be now. More than just the financial industry, the current state of cyber threats is extremely concerning. In the financial sector, the primary focus of DORA is to either prevent or, at the very least, better mitigate the growing number of cyber threats. The DORA framework establishes the appropriate priorities for information and communication technology governance, reporting, and testing in order to accomplish this objective. Our framework offers the benefit of aiding security analysts in the analysis of security events and the development of security solutions for financial institutions. Specifically, the VM captures the adversaries and vulnerabilities and analyses the target of the attack in terms of a realm-specific approach. The AM constructs attack model based on the adversaries specified in VM. The BM annotates system behaviours for the VM and AM. Finally in EM, the EM derives events from behavioural models.

While certain sections of DORA are notably prescriptive, its risk-based approach ensures a more balanced and adaptable application of the various requirements. The integration of ASFA in Threat-Led Penetration Testing (TLPT) holds significant promise for aiding financial institutions in enhancing their preparedness and resilience against advanced cyber threats. This alignment directly supports the operational resilience objectives outlined by DORA, enabling institutions to meet its overarching goals effectively.

References

VanHoy, J.: Third Party Risk Management, 10 January 2021

Clausmeier, D.: Regulation of the European Parliament and the Council on digital operational resilience for the financial sector (DORA). Int. Cybersecur. Law Rev. **4**, 79–90 (2023)

Fernandez-Buglioni, E.: Security Patterns in Practice: Designing Secure Architectures Using Software Patterns. John Wiley & Sons, Hoboken, NJ, USA (2013)

Abu, M.S., Selamat, S.R., Ariffin, A., Yusof, R.: Cyber threat intelligence - issue and challenges. Indones. J. Electr. Eng. Comput. Sci. **10**(1), 371–379 (2018)

Al-Tarawneh, A., Al-Saraireh, J.: Efficient detection of hacker community based on twitter data using complex networks and machine learning algorithm. J. Intell. Fuzzy Syst. **40**(6), 12321–12337 (2021)

Seid, E., Popov, O., Blix, F.: Towards security attack event monitoring for cyber physical-systems. In: ICISSP, pp. 722–732, 2023

Björck, F., Henkel, M., Stirna, J., Zdravkovic, J.: Cyber resilience - fundamentals for a definition. In: Rocha, A., Correia, A., Costanzo, S., Reis, L. (eds.) New Contributions in Information Systems and Technologies. Advances in Intelligent Systems and Computing, vol. 353. Springer, Cham (2015)

Ammann, T., Syed, I., Sanchez, V.. Exploring operational resilience in financial services-the effects of DORA on risk and regulation in top 3 financial markets. Comput. Law Rev. Int. **24**(2), 43–48 (2023)

Kun, E.: Challenges in regulating cloud service providers in EU financial regulation: from operational to systemic risks, and examining challenges of the new oversight regime for critical cloud service providers under the Digital Operational Resilience Act. Comput. Law Secur. Rev. **52**, 105931 (2024)

Seid, E., Popov, O., Blix, F.: Evaluation of ASFA, a security attack event monitoring framework. Procedia Comput. Sci. **237**, 793–802 (2024)

Dupont, B.: The cyber-resilience of financial institutions: significance and applicability. J. Cybersecur. **5**(1), tyz013 (2019)

Van den Berg, B., Kuipers, S.: Vulnerabilities and Cyberspace: A New Kind of Crises. In Oxford Research Encyclopedia of Politics; Universiteit Leiden-LUMC: Leiden, The Netherlands, 202

Pursiainen, C.: Critical infrastructure resilience: a Nordic model in the making? Int. J. Disaster Risk Reduct. **27**, 632–641 (2018)

Wang, E.K., Ye, Y., Xu, X., Yiu, S.-M., Hui, L.C.K., Chow, K.-P.: Security issues and challenges for cyber physical system. In: Proceedings of the 2010 IEEE/ACM Int'l Conference on Green Computing and Communications & Int'l Conference on Cyber, Physical and Social Computing, Hangzhou, China, 18–20 December 2010, pp. 733–738 (2010)

Uzunov, A.V., Ferncez, E.B., Falkner, K.: Engineering security into distributed systems: a survey of methodologies. J. UCS **18**, 2920–3006 (2012)

Gopstein, A., Gopstein, A., Nguyen, C., Byrnett, D.S., Worthington, K., Villarreal, C.: Framework and Roadmap for Smart Grid Interoperability Standards Regional Roundtables Summary Report; US Department of Commerce, National Institute of Standards and Technology, Gaithersburg. MD, USA (2020)

Mancuso, V.F., Strang, A.J., Funke, G.J., Finomore, V.S.: Human factors of cyber attacks: a framework for human-centered research. In: Proceedings of the Human Factors and Ergonomics Society Annual Meeting, Chicago, IL, USA, 27–31 October 2014, SAGE Publications, Los Angeles, CA, USA, vol. 58, pp. 437–441 (2014)

Urbach, N., Roeglinger, M.: Introduction to Digitalization Cases: How Organizations Rethink Their Business for the Digital Age. Springer, Berlin/Heidelberg, Germany (2019)

Ponemon, L.: Cost of Data Breach Study: Global Analysis; Technical Report; Poneomon Institute: Traverse City. MI, USA (2015)

Shostack, A.: Threat Modeling: Designing for Security. John Wiley & Sons, Hoboken, NJ, USA (2014)

Griffor, E.R., Greer, C., Wollman, D. A., Burns, M.J., et al.: Framework for cyber-physical systems: Volume 1, overview (2017)

Boyes, H., Hallaq, B., Cunningham, J., Watson, T.: The industrial internet of things (IIoT): an analysis framework (2018)

Banerjee, A., Venkatasubramanian, K.K., Mukherjee, T., Gupta, S.K.S.: Ensuring safety, security, and sustainability of mission-critical cyber-physical systems. Proc. IEEE **100**(1), 283–299 (2012)

Angelopoulos, K., Souza, V.E.S., Mylopoulos, J.: Dealing with multiple failures in zanshin: a control-theoretic approach. In: SEAMS 14, pp. 165–174. ACM, 2014

Markopoulou, D., Papakonstantinou, V.: The regulatory framework for the protection of critical infrastructures against cyberthreats: identifying shortcomings and addressing future challenges: the case of the health sector in particular. Comput. Law Secur. Rev. **41**, 105502 (2021)

Calderaro, A., Blumfelde, S.: Artificial intelligence and EU security: the false promise of digital sovereignty. Eur. Secur. **31**, 415–434 (2022)

Hsieh, H.F., Shannon, S.E.: Three approaches to qualitative content analysis. Qual. Health Res. **15**, 1277–1288 (2005)

Papakonstantinou, V.: Cybersecurity as praxis and as a state: the EU law path towards acknowledgement of a new right to cybersecurity? Comput. Law Secur. Rev. **44**, 105653 (2022)

Osei-Kyei, R., Tam, V., Ma, M., Mashiri, F.: Critical review of the threats affecting the building of critical infrastructure resilience. Int. J. Disaster Risk Reduct. **60**, 102316 (2021)

Caldarulo, M., Welch, E.W., Feeney, M.K.: Determinants of cyber-incidents among small and medium US cities. Gov. Inf. Q. **39**, 101703 (2022)

Agrafiotis, I., Nurse, J.R., Goldsmith, M., Creese, S., Upton, D.: A taxonomy of cyber-harms: defining the impacts of cyber-attacks and understanding how they propagate. J. Cybersecur. **4**, tyy006 (2018)

Kaiya, H., et al.: Security requirements analysis using knowledge in capec. In: Advanced Information Systems Engineering Workshops. Springer, Berlin/Heidelberg, Germany, pp. 343–348, 2014

Boin, A.: The transboundary crisis: why we are unprepared and the road ahead. J. Contingencies Crisis Manag. **27**, 94–99 (2019)

Harry, C., Gallagher, N.: Classifying cyber events. J. Inf. Warf. **17**, 17–31 (2018)

Syafrizal, M., Selamat, S.R., Zakaria, N.A.: AVOIDITALS: enhanced cyber-attack taxonomy in securing information technology infrastructure. Int. J. Comput. Sci. Netw. Secur. **21**, 1–12 (2021)

Mitnick, K.D., Simon, W.L.: The Art of Deception: Controlling the Human Element of Security. John Wiley & Sons, Hoboken, NJ, USA (2011)

Shevchenko, P.V., Jang, J., Malavasi, M., Peters, G.W., Sofronov, G., Trück, S.: The nature of losses from cyber-related events: risk categories and business sectors. J. Cybersecur. **9**, tyac016 (2023)

Simmons, C., Ellis, C., Shiva, S., Dasgupta, D., Wu, Q.: AVOIDIT: a cyber attack taxonomy. In: Proceedings of the 9th Annual Symposium on Information Assurance, Kyoto, Japan, pp. 12–22, 4–6 June 2014

Derbyshire, R., Green, B., Prince, D., Mauthe, A., Hutchison, D.: An analysis of cyber security attack taxonomies. In: Proceedings of the IEEE European Symposium on Security and Privacy Workshops (EuroS&PW), London, UK, pp. 153–161, 24–26 April 2018

Feather, M.S., Fickas, S., Van Lamsweerde, A., Ponsard, C.: Reconciling system requirements and runtime behavior. In: Proceedings of the 9th International Workshop on Software Specification and Design, p. 50. IEEE Computer Society (1998)

Souza, V., Lapouchnian, A., Mylopoulos, J.: Requirements-driven qualitative adaptation. On the Move to Meaningful Internet Systems: OTM 2012, volume 7565 of Lecture Notes in Computer Science, pp. 342–361. Springer, Berlin, Heidelberg (2012)

Ljung, L.: Approaches to identification of nonlinear systems. In: Control Conference (CCC), 2010 29th Chinese, pp. 1–5, July 2010

Souza, V.E.S., Lapouchnian, A., Robinson, W.N., Mylopoulos, J.: Awareness requirements for adaptive systems. In: 2011 ICSE Symposium on Software Engineering for Adaptive and Self-Managing Systems, SEAMS, pp. 60–69, 2011

Camacho, E., Bordons, C.: Model Predictive Control. Springer, London (2004)

Maciejowski, J.: Predictive Control: With Constraints. Prentice Hall, Hoboken (2002)

Cailliau, A., Lamsweerde, A.V.: Runtime monitoring and resolution of probabilistic obstacles to system goals. In: Software Engineering for Adaptive and Self- Managing Systems (SEAMS). IEEE/ACM (2017)

AdaLightLog: Enhancing Application Logs Anomaly Detection via Adaptive Federating Learning

Danilo Menegatti⬤, Emanuele De Santis$^{(\boxtimes)}$⬤, Stefano Felli⬤, and Alessandro Giuseppi⬤

Department of Computer, Control and Management Engineering 'Antonio Ruberti', Sapienza University of Rome, Rome, Italy
`edesantis@diag.uniroma1.it`

Abstract. The role of anomaly detection systems in Critical Infrastructures (CIs) is critical due to the complexity of CIs and their control systems, which are usually implemented by computer-based controllers that constantly produce logs of their activities. Moreover, many CIs, located in different locations or even belonging to different companies, may share similar application software for controlling the CIs themselves. The goal of this work is to use such logs to perform automatic anomaly detection in a federated learning (FL) paradigm, which ensures that no data is exchanged between sites to train the anomaly detection models, but each learning agent learns on its own data, leveraging the knowledge acquired by the other agents. Our proposed approach - ADALIGHTLOG - which implements a modified FL paradigm with adaptive loss functions at local servers side and weighted averaging of local server models, so to differentiate the quality of the different local servers' models in the global averaging, is tested against state-of-the-art methods and shows an improvement in performance in terms of accuracy, precision and recall with respect to the standard FL implementation (FEDAVG). Furthermore, a comparison between different metrics for the adaptive loss functions and the dynamic weights is presented.

Keywords: Federated Learning · Log Anomaly Detection · Adaptive Loss · Weighted Averaging

1 Introduction

Anomaly detection plays an important role in the framework of critical infrastructures (CIs), that is any system which is essential for providing vital economic and social functions [5]. In general, their architecture is composed of two main components, that is Industrial Control Systems (ICSs) and innovative technologies such as Internet of Things (IoT) [36] which can be seen as the means to achieve the efficient control and automation of industrial processes.

© The Author(s), under exclusive license to Springer Nature Switzerland AG 2025
G. Oliva et al. (Eds.): CRITIS 2024, LNCS 15549, pp. 289–305, 2025.
https://doi.org/10.1007/978-3-031-84260-3_17

Although such mixture proved to be effective in multiple applications [20, 37], it makes the overall framework inevitably susceptible to cyber-physical attacks, since the ICSs, which interact directly with the physical instruments and devices, also find themselves interacting with the outside environment. One of the possible strategies which proved to be effective in mitigating the risk of an attack, if not preventing it, is anomaly detection; having the frequency of malicious attacks surged in the last years due to CIs' expanded connectivity, the aforementioned techniques provide a useful tool in highlight anomalies from the expected behaviour, hence leading the way to appropriate and preventive counter-measures.

This work proposes a novel Federated Learning -based distributed anomaly detection system that analyzes application logs to detect possible anomalies at software level. The proposed algorithm makes use of Federated Learning (FL) methodology to preserve privacy among the federation. This is justified by the fact that application logs may contain sensitive and/or confidential information, that the members of the federation do not want to share for the learning purpose. Instead, the proposed approach, as in the most common FL approaches, do not share any data among the learning agents, but only the knowledge they acquired during training phases.

Moreover, application logs are usually expressed in some human-readable natural language, thus proper log parsing (based on the intuition of [6] and [45], that application logs usually follows a limited set of different templates) and embedding techniques are put in place.

In addition, this work proposes to apply weighted loss functions at learning agents level based on validation metrics, so to improve the performance of the overall FL training process. In this regard, an analysis of the performance of the presented anomaly detection system against the various validation metrics used for the custom loss functions has been performed, so to validate the overall approach.

The main highlights of the proposed approach are as follows:

– Application of an adaptive FL methodology to the log anomaly detection problem
– Introduction of a performance-based weighted averaging procedure to account for data distribution disparity and resilience of the federation
– Improvement of the training procedure via the introduction of an adaptive loss function linked to validation metrics
– Metric-based comparative analysis of the training performance

The remainder of the paper is organized as follows: Sect. 2 describes the works in the literature that are relevant to the log anomaly detection problem and its decentralisation; Sect. 3 formulates the problem and details the proposed approach; Sect. 4 presents the simulations results; Sect. 5 draws the conclusion and discussion future research directions.

2   Related Works

Although several automatic anomaly detectors have been developed during the past few years due to the massive amount of logs generated on a daily basis, some issues may arise when sensitive information about the operation of CIs is included in these data, preventing them to be shared for training purposes.

Anomaly detection in its broader sense has been the focus of many works in the last years, given the importance to gain situational awareness of the state of any CI, by giving the possibility to promptly apply adequate countermeasures in case of attacks or other anomalies. In particular, works like [19,43] make use of purely statistical methods for detecting anomalies, by exploiting statistical properties of the attack patterns. These methods, while are very suited for specific applications and attacks, may be hard to generalize to novel attacks and more complex CIs.

Machine learning methodologies started then to increase their success in the literature, given the possibility to rely much less on specific knowledge of the attack types and the CI details. Works like [1,15,18] started to use methodologies like Support Vector Machines (SVM) ad Bayesian Networks to classify anomalies on computer systems. Such methodologies has been outperformed by the advances of Deep Learning (DL) models, like in [12,32], which specialized on finding anomalies in computer networks.

As for application logs anomaly detection, other recent works are available in the literature. In particular, [14] performed anomaly detection by parsing and embedding logs as in our approach, evaluating the performances of a set of supervised and unsupervised learning techniques. This topic has been also studied by [6], which proposes a complete framework for anomaly detection of application logs, by exploiting the same parsing and embedding of the previous work, but proposing a Temporal Convolutional Network (TCN) for log key anomaly detection and a parameter-based anomaly detection of the parameters in the log keys which are considered to be normal in the first step. A lighter version of [6] is provided by [45], which does not include parameter-based anomaly detection and simplifies the parsing and embedding. The main differences between these works and our proposed work is that we apply a novel FL framework preserving logs privacy among the clients of the federation, while in the aforementioned works all the data are considered to stay on a single place.

As mentioned before, this paper leverages on the concept of FL which has emerged as a promising approach for the distributed learning of a DL model. Firstly introduced in [28] alongside the FEDERATED AVERAGING (FEDAVG) algorithm, it found application very rapidly in multiple fields, for instance within IoT and eHealth scenarios [2,31], due to its communication efficient privacy-preserving features which are associated with the complete lack of data exchange. A federation of clients learns a shared DL model, that is a neural network (NN), via an iterative procedure carried out by a server updating it by means of the weighted average of the models sent by the clients after training them over their own local data (*communication round*).

The main characteristic of the FL paradigm lies in its ability to deal with data *as-it-is*, even if non-independently and identically distributed (non-IID), without the need to collect it in a centralised fashion nor re-distribute it. Moreover, it may happen that clients could differ in terms of computational capabilities, thus performing a variable amount of local work (*stragglers*), which leads to the delay of the overall learning. Multiple strategies have been developed to mitigate the effect of such system heterogeneity; for instance, in [44] a stopping-and-weight balancing (SAWB) method is proposed with the aim of taking into account stragglers' partial model updates across the non-straggler clients, while the authors of [23] directly take into account variable computational capabilities of the federation by adding a proximal term to the loss function that each client minimizes during local training.

Over the past few years, several works have attempted to improve the original FL formulation reducing the amount of data being exchanged between the server and the clients [39,41], optimizing the loss function to achieve improved performance [9,23], and introducing privacy-preserving safeguards such as secure multiparty computation [3] and differential privacy [8].

While FEDAVG was first applied within the context of next-word prediction in [11], its $\mathcal{O}\left(\frac{1}{T}\right)$ convergence rate was demonstrated later on by the authors of [24], with T being the number of local training iterations at clients' level. The topic of convergence is also explored in [34], where a FEDAVG variant, based on the inclusion of Nesterov momentum [4], is proved to achieve a faster convergence rate in convex settings.

As mentioned before, this work envisages the use of the FL paradigm for anomaly detection purposes. To this end, [33] was one of the first works to leverage on the FL setting to train an intrusion detection model over the CIC-IDS2017 dataset. Building on top of that, the authors of [38] propose FEDSAM, a FEDAVG-like algorithm which introduces the concept of sampling size, namely the amount of data used for local training in each communication round, to deal with the presence of stragglers, and a distributed min-max scaling strategy to deal with data heterogeneity. The problem of data distribution is addressed also in [30], where clients of the federation are aggregated on the basis of the statistical properties of their local dataset and FEDAVG runs over the resulting clusters. Privacy concerns are addressed in [40] and [16]; while the former proposes a hierarchical approach together with blockchain technology to validate the model updates performed by the server, the latter envisages the use of SSL/TLS protocol.

This work aims to solve the problem of anomaly detection starting from the logs produced at application level while guaranteeing the anonymity of the collected user data leveraging on the ADAFED algorithm [9] conversely from [22] and [10] which rely on FEDAVG. In particular, we differ from the former in terms of robustness to malicious attacks by the inclusion of a model testing procedure before its update at the server level, instead of the simple addition of Gaussian noise to the clients' model parameters, and from the latter since the overall computational burden of the learning process is optimized by the introduction of an adaptive loss function instead of relying on the lottery ticket hypothesis [7] to find sparse sub-networks within the entire federation, making the corresponding clients more prone to malicious attacks.

3   Distributed Anomaly Detection

In this work, the problem of detecting anomalies on distributed log data is formulated as a binary classification problem, which envisages to decide whether each instance of a log represents a normal or abnormal activity.

Differently from standard anomaly identification procedure, we do not collect raw logs in a centralised fashion and then perform a uniform pre-processing procedure, instead we deal with scenarios where logs are stored on the source device, which is in charge of their parsing, sampling, and embedding. Figure 1 illustrates the proposed workflow.

The resulting distributed classification problem is solved via an adaptive FL procedure, emphasizing the collaboration among different devices.

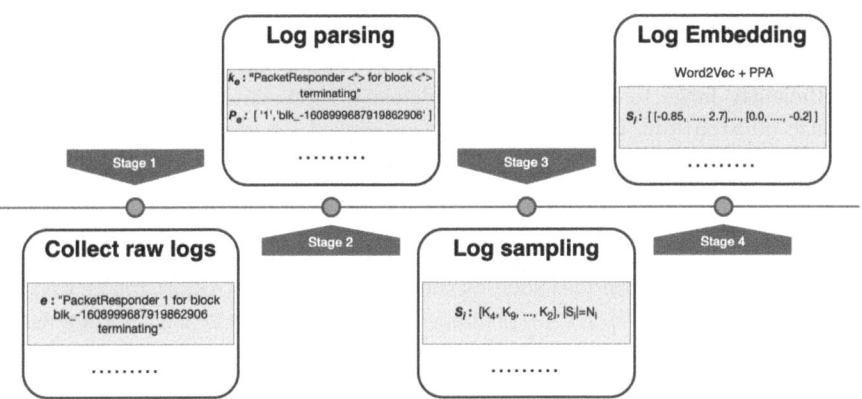

Fig. 1. Chosen log processing framework.

3.1   Log Processing Workflow

The pre-processing stage of logs is aimed at transforming raw logs into meaningful representations for the training of the learning model. We encompass the various strategies proposed in [45] which enable real-time log mapping with minimal computational resource consumption, that is processing logs in sequential phases, as depicted in Fig. 1.

Considering their entries as textual data containing various fields, such as timestamp and details regarding system processing, it is crucial to eliminate unnecessary information to isolate particular values, hence after collection (Stage 1), they undergo parsing (Stage 2).

Log parsing methods such like SPELL [29], DRAIN [13] and IPLoM [26,27] convert each raw log entry e into a structured template. This process identifies a frequently repeated portion of the log, known as log key k_e, and removes the varying parts, defined as event parameters p_e.

Once each entry e is parsed, the sampling phase takes place (Stage 3), with the log keys k_e being sampled into execution sequences S_i based on the nature of the data, each one with a different number N_i of log keys. This is achieved using session window methods, such as those applied to Hadoop Distributed File System (HDFS) logs [42] and OpenStack (OS) logs [6], which can be grouped by *block id* (HDFS) or *instance id* (OS). For logs that do not include session identifiers, like Blue Gene/L (BGL) logs [25], grouping can be done based on timestamps.

Finally, the the log embedding phase (Stage 4) concludes the pre-processing workflow. In a first step, the k-th structured sequence of log keys S_i is encoded through well-known Word2Vec model [17], a NN that generates vector representations of words, also known as word embeddings. Word2Vec trains on a large corpus of text, in this case log keys, to capture the contextual relationships between words. It represents these relationships in a continuous vector space where semantically similar words are mapped to nearby points. With this method, each log key k_e is projected into a M-dimensional vector V_e^M, with M sufficiently large to ensure a comprehensive representation of the log key's semantic information. Thus the resulting processed log sequences are composed into numerical vectors V_1^M, ..., $V_{N_i}^M$, hence these sequences can be computationally expensive to handle, particularly in tasks involving extensive training data or large vocabularies.

To overcome these computational challenges and enhance efficiency, dimensionality reduction techniques such as the Post-Processing Algorithm (PPA) are commonly employed [35]. PPA's primary objective is to decrease the dimensionality of Word2Vec embeddings while retaining as much semantic information as possible. This reduction in dimensionality substantially alleviates the computational burden associated with processing and storing the embeddings, making them more suitable for downstream tasks like natural language processing (NLP) and machine learning (ML).

The PPA, proposed in [35], utilizes techniques such as Principal Component Analysis (PCA) to achieve dimensionality reduction. PCA identifies the principal components of the high-dimensional embedding space and projects the embeddings onto a lower-dimensional subspace $n < M$ while preserving as much variance as possible. Additionally, PPA removes d dominating eigenvectors from the dimensionality-reduced embeddings. These dominating eigenvectors, which contribute the most to the variance in the data, are removed to potentially eliminate noise or irrelevant information from the embeddings. The specific number of eigenvectors to remove is typically determined empirically or through cross-validation, depending on the characteristics of the data and the specific application.

3.2   Temporal Convolutional Network Architecture for Local Training

In our work, as also proposed in [6,45], the training process for embedded data utilizes a Temporal Convolutional Network (TCN), namely a deep NN firstly introduced in [21], which proved to be effective for the log anomaly detection problem [45] due to their known capabilities in handling sequential data, that is the type of data inherent to application logs.

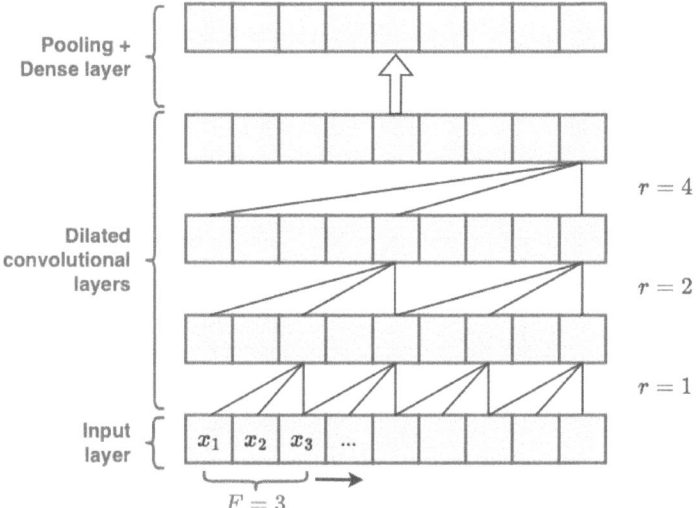

Fig. 2. Typical TCN architecture

Their ability to capture long-term dependencies relies in the usage of *dilated convolutions*, which differs from the causal convolution because of the presence of a dilation rate r. In other words, the latter can be seen as a filter envisaging to skip some input values with a certain step.

From a mathematical perspective, given an input sequence $x = \{x_{[1]}, ..., x_{[q]}\}$, with $x_{[t]} \in \mathbb{R}^n$ for the generic time $t = 1, ..., q$, a causal convolution with a filter size F only considers current and past time steps, producing an output

$$y_{[t]} = \sum_{f=0}^{F-1} w_f \, x_{[t-f]}, \tag{1}$$

with w_f the convolutional filter weights, while a dilated convolution with a dilation rate r modifies the convolution operation (1) to

$$y_{[t]} = \sum_{f=0}^{F-1} w_f \, x_{[t-rf]}. \tag{2}$$

The output of such dilation convolutional layers, which aim at capturing temporal dependencies at different scales, is handled by global pooling layers which attempt to aggregate temporal features, thus summarizing information from all time steps, across a feature map, which is then processed by fully connected layers, providing the output of the TCN as the binary classification of the log sequence. Figure 2 shows a typical architecture with three dilated convolutional layers with kernel size $F = 3$.

3.3   Proposed Federated Learning Algorithm

The proposed framework envisages a federation of K local servers in communication with a coordinating one, denoted as G, as shown in Fig. 3. Such a scenario is quite customary in CIs, where ICSs rely on devices capable of storing and processing data, such as local servers, connected to the outside environment via some secure connection. With respect to the coordinating server, it can be either one among the local ones, or may be located in the cloud and can even belong to a different party.

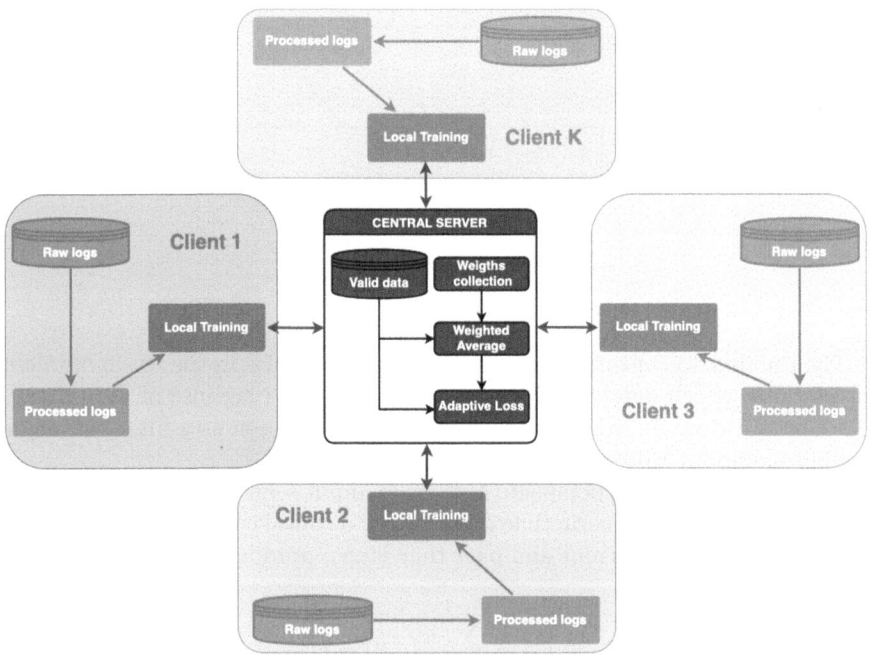

Fig. 3. Log Anomaly Detection FL

The possibility to share the same algorithm with different stakeholders, is made possible by the very nature of FL paradigm, which ensures that no logs nor embedding is shared among the federation. Hence, each local server is in charge of pre-preprocessing data independently, thus exhibiting different embedding, making the proposed scenario close to a real-world application.

Another key difference with respect to other log-related FL implementations [10, 22] lies in the use of an adaptive loss function, resulting from the employment of ADAFED [9]; while, on the one hand, the adaptive nature of the algorithm speeds up convergence, on the other hand allows to evaluate whether or not a client has been subject to a malicious attack, possibly excluding him from the training procedure, through a performance evaluation mechanism carried out by the coordinator server G.

In particular, the training procedure unfolds as follows: during the c-th *communication round*, $c = 1, \ldots, E$, the k-th client, $k = 1, \ldots, K$, receives the TCN model from G with current weights W_G^c and trains it over its own local data for T local epochs. Denoting with W_k^c the weights of its model, it sends them over to the coordinator server which evaluates its performance over a dedicated dataset, which we assume to be representative for the machine learning problem at hand, and assigns the corresponding performance weight s_k^c to it. After completing this procedure, G updated the weights of its global model W_G^{c+1} performing the weighted average of all the collected ones

$$W_g^{c+1} = \frac{\sum_{k=1}^{K} W_k^c s_k^c}{\sum_{k=1}^{K} s_k^c}. \tag{3}$$

The underlying idea under equation (3) consists in allowing the clients with an higher score to lead the learning procedure, and, consequently, the lesser performing ones to benefit from their experience, regardless of the particular reason for such behaviour; a client may own low quality data or even be subject of a malicious attack. While in the first case it can benefit from the experience of the others, in the second one it can be cut out from the learning procedure with no effect on it.

This performance evaluation strategy also envisages to link the learning of the federation with the global model performance. Due to the distributed nature of data, allowing each client to focus its training over misclassified data proved to boost the performance of shared model [9]; to do so, at the beginning of each communication round, G propagates a weighted loss function along with the newly updated TCN model.

Dealing with a binary classification problem, all the clients attempt to minimize a weighted categorical cross-entropy loss function:

$$\ell_k(D_k, c) = -\frac{1}{|D_k|} \sum_{j=1}^{|D_k|} \left[w_{normal}^c y_j^{D_k} \log(\hat{y}_j^{D_k}) + \right.$$
$$\left. + w_{abnormal}^c (1 - y_j^{D_k}) \log(1 - \hat{y}_j^{D_k}) \right], \tag{4}$$

with D_k the local dataset of the k-th client, $y_j^{D_k}$ and $\hat{y}_j^{D_k}$ its corresponding true and predicted labels, and w_{normal}^c and $w_{abnormal}^c$ representing the above mentioned weights associated to the two classes.

After initially being set to a default value, they are updated at the end of the c-th communication round on the basis of a given performance metric m describing the performance of the global model W_G^{c+1} over the dedicated test set:

$$w_{normal}^{c+1} = \frac{1}{m^{c+1} + \varepsilon}, \tag{5}$$

$$w_{abnormal}^{c+1} = \frac{1}{(1 - m^{c+1}) + \varepsilon}, \tag{6}$$

where $\varepsilon > 0$ is a arbitrarily small value to prevent numerical problems.

The complete algorithm of ADALIGHTLOG FL training is reported in Algorithm 1.

Algorithm 1. ADALIGHTLOG

1: **for** each communication round $c = 1, ..., E$ **do**
2:     **for** each client $k = 1, ..., K$ **do**
3:         train local servers with adaptive loss weights w_{normal}^c and $w_{abnormal}^c$
4:         collect model weights W_k^c
5:         evaluate and collect the score s_k^c over W_k^c on client k validation set
6:     **end for**
7:     perform weighted model average W_g^{c+1} based on the obtained scores as in (3)
8:     compute the metric m^{c+1} by evaluating W_g^{c+1} with server G validation dataset
9:     compute loss function parameters w_{normal}^{c+1} and $w_{abnormal}^{c+1}$ as in (5) and (6)
10:     propagate W_g^{c+1}, w_{normal}^{c+1} and $w_{abnormal}^{c+1}$ to the clients
11: **end for**

---

4   Simulations

Our numerical simulations are conducted over the HDFS log dataset [42], containing 11.175.629 entries, where approximately 2.58% of them contain anomalies. The chosen parsing method is SPELL [29], which has demonstrated 100% parsing accuracy on the HDFS dataset. The federated framework is depicted in Fig. 3, with the number of local servers fixed at $K = 5$ to preserve parsing accuracy as much as possible. The datasets resulting from a proportional division into K parts consist of approximately $2.235.050 \pm 50$ log entries, providing sufficient data for good parsing accuracy. Each dataset contains 21 ± 2 different log keys.

All the logs for each client are grouped into sequences by their block ID, and sessions are labeled as abnormal (i.e., 1) if there exists at least one log key labeled as abnormal; otherwise, they are labeled as normal (i.e., 0). Clients have approximately 180.000 ± 30.000 normal sessions and 4.500 ± 500 abnormal sessions, with a percentage of abnormal sessions of 2.45%, very close to that of the original database. Log embedding is then performed such that are produced vectors of dimension $M = 300$ as proposed by Wang et al. [45]. By removing $d = 7$ dominating eigenvectors, PPA reduces the embedding dimesionality to $n = N_5 = 19$, as this is the lowest number of log keys among all the local servers datasets (in particular, in this case in the fifth local server) ; indeed, the number of components used for performing PCA cannot exceed the number of log keys N_i for a given k-th client.

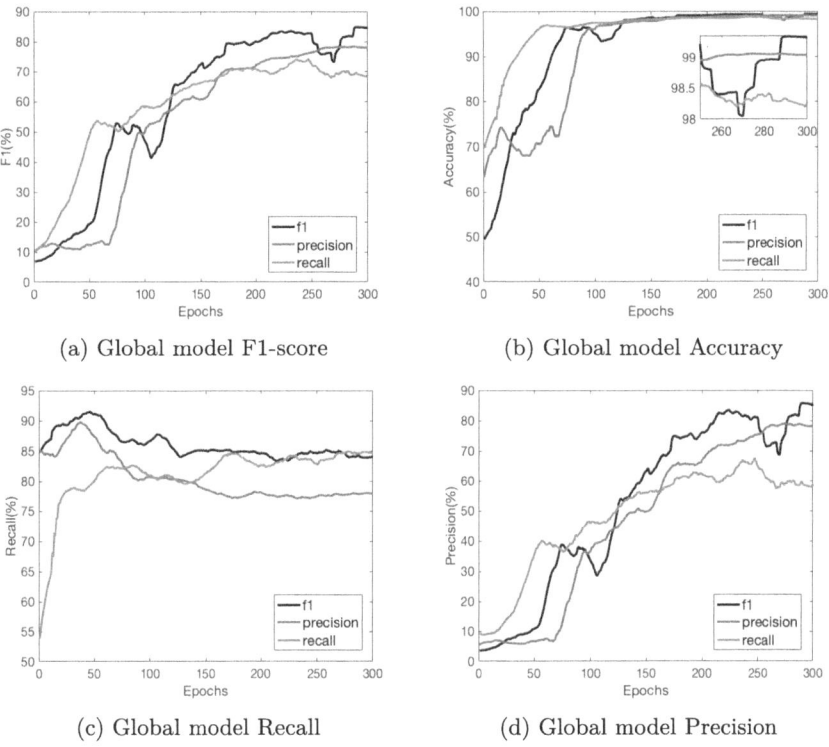

(a) Global model F1-score

(b) Global model Accuracy

(c) Global model Recall

(d) Global model Precision

Fig. 4. Comparison over four performance metrics of the m-based algorithm performance: m = F1 black line, m = Precision blue line, m = Recall orange line (Color figure online)

For what concerns the simulations, training procedures are performed over $E = 300$ global epochs. During a single communication round each local model is trained for $T = 3$ local epochs, using ADAM optimizer with learning rate $l = 0.005$ and the adaptive loss previously proposed. The local TCNs are composed by four dilated convolutional layers with dilation rates fixed respectively to the values $r = 1, 2, 4, 8$, with an Adaptive Average Pooling layer and a fully-connected linear layer outputting the binary classification of the log sequences.

The first simulation proposes a comparative analysis of the metric m used to evaluate the performance of the global model over the dedicated test set, thus to determine the weights of the adaptive loss function. Evaluating the score s_k of the k-th local client, $k = 1, \ldots, K$, as the accuracy over the test set, we compare the influence of the adaptive loss function over the learning procedure when m is set to be the precision, recall, and F1-score. Even if they are all performance metrics related to classification problems, each one of them focuses on different aspects; while accuracy describes the number of correct predictions over all predictions, precision quantifies how many instances predicted as normal are actually correct and recall measures how many instances are predicted as normal over all normal cases, the F1-score combines the former two as the harmonic mean.

In particular, Fig. 4 shows the results of such comparison, comparing the performance of the the the algorithm under a different m over four performance metrics over the dedicated test set, that is F1-score (a), accuracy (b), recall (c), and precision (d).

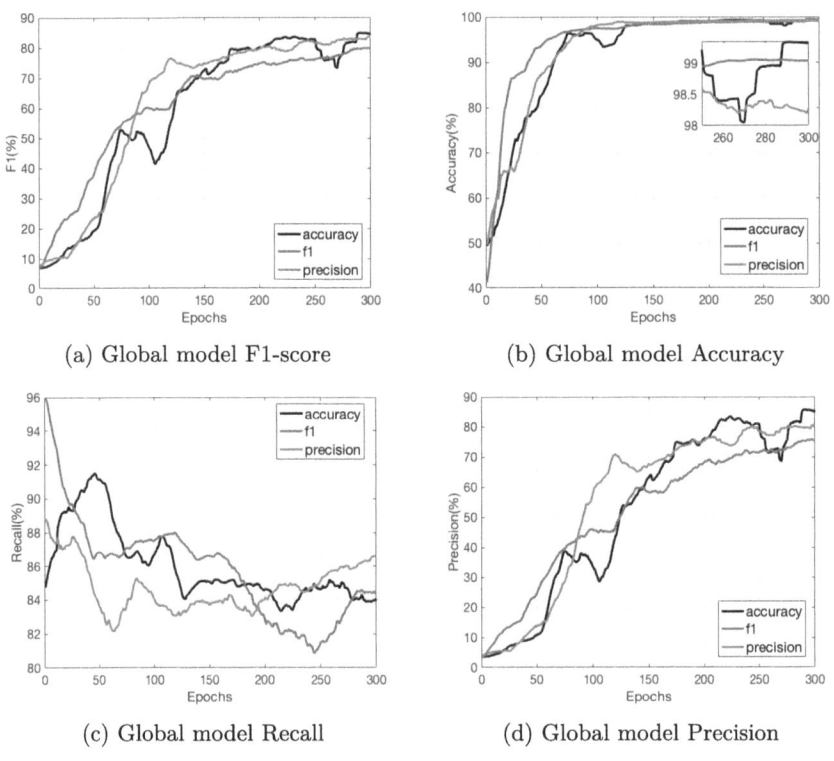

(a) Global model F1-score   (b) Global model Accuracy

(c) Global model Recall   (d) Global model Precision

Fig. 5. Comparison over four performance metrics of the s_k-based algorithm performance: s_k = Accuracy black line, s_k = F1 blue line, s_k = Precision orange line (Color figure online)

As it is possible to notice from Fig. 4b accuracy reaches values of about 99% in all cases, with the F1 metric-based model slightly outperforming the others. The model using recall metric demonstrates the quickest and most stable convergence across all metrics. It reaches high performance levels early and maintains them with fewer fluctuations. The F1 metric -based model reaches good accuracy at around $E = 100$, maintaining the highest F1-score and outperforming the other metrics also on the recall.

As the most promising performance metric m seems to be the F1-score, we perform a second comparative analysis related to the local client evaluation score s_k, $k = 1, \ldots, K$ among the accuracy, F1-score, and precision. Fixing the global model evaluation metric m to be the F1-score, Fig. 5 shows the results of such comparison, with the accuracy criteria outperforming the others over all the comparative metrics (a)-(b)-(d), except over the recall one (c), where it is outperformed by the F1-score of a 2%.

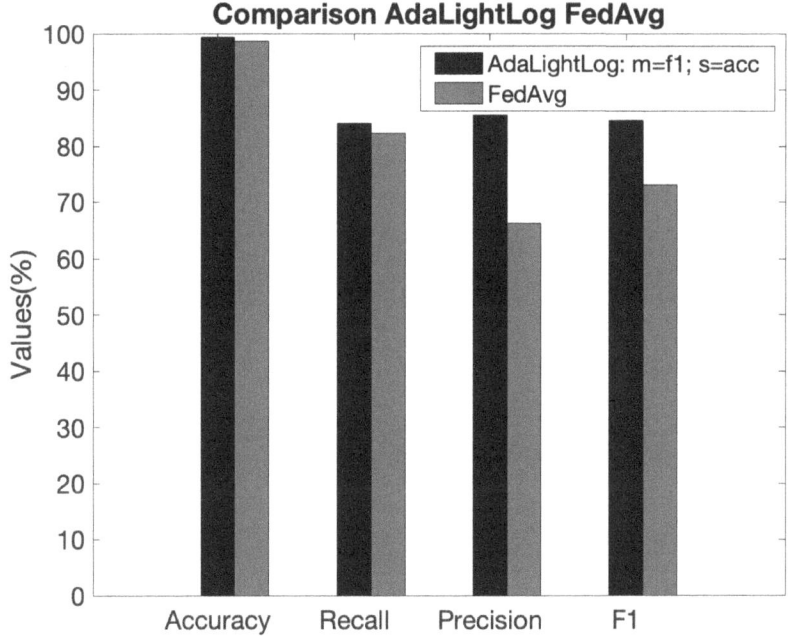

Fig. 6. Performance comparison: ADALIGHTLOG and FEDAVG

Finally, having found that the F1-score is the most promising metrics for m and accuracy for s_k, we compare the resulting proposed algorithm with FEDAVG. The results of such comparison are depicted in Fig. 6, with ADALIGHTLOG outperforming FEDAVG over all the comparative performance metrics.

5   Conclusion and Future Works

This paper has proposed a novel methodology for automatic log anomaly detection that is based on Federated Learning and that makes use of adaptive loss function driven by validation metrics computed by the central server, and dynamic weights for the weighted model averaging based on metrics from its own validation data, in order to achieve the best results, while also protecting the federation from (possibly) tampered models. The proposed approach, namely ADALIGHTLOG, has been showed to outperform traditional Federated Learning approaches like FEDAVG in terms of accuracy, precision and recall. A comparison among the results using different validation metrics both for the adaptive loss and for the dynamic weights has been presented, to achieve the best results.

Future work is aimed at achieving full decentralization of the training procedure leveraging on consensus theory, by also applying finite-time consensus guarantee the convergence of the learning of the agents in a finite-time.

Acknowledgments. This work has been partially supported by the EU in the scope of the NANCY project, which has received funding from the Smart Networks and Services Joint Undertaking (SNS JU) under the European Union's Horizon Europe research and innovation programme under Grant Agreement No 101096456, and the FSE REACT-EU, PON Ricerca e Innovazione 2014–2020, programme.

Disclosure of Interests. The authors have no competing interests to declare that are relevant to the content of this article.

References

1. Applications of Data Mining in Computer Security. Springer US (2002). https://doi.org/10.1007/978-1-4615-0953-0
2. Antunes, R.S., André da Costa, C., Küderle, A., Yari, I.A., Eskofier, B.: Federated learning for healthcare: systematic review and architecture proposal. ACM Trans. Intell. Syst. Technol. **13**(4), 1–23 (2022). https://doi.org/10.1145/3501813
3. Bonawitz, K., et al.: Practical secure aggregation for privacy-preserving machine learning. In: Proceedings of the 2017 ACM SIGSAC Conference on Computer and Communications Security, CCS 2017. ACM (2017) https://doi.org/10.1145/3133956.3133982
4. Botev, A., Lever, G., Barber, D.: Nesterov's accelerated gradient and momentum as approximations to regularised update descent (2016).https://doi.org/10.48550/ARXIV.1607.01981
5. Commission, E.: Protecting critical infrastructure in the EU - new rules (2020). https://ec.europa.eu/info/law/better-regulation/have-your-say/initiatives/12462-Protecting-critical-infrastructure-in-the-EU-new-rules_en
6. Du, M., Li, F., Zheng, G., Srikumar, V.: DeepLog: anomaly detection and diagnosis from system logs through deep learning. In: Proceedings of the 2017 ACM SIGSAC Conference on Computer and Communications Security, CCS 2017, pp. 1285–1298. ACM, New York (2017).https://doi.org/10.1145/3133956.3134015
7. Frankle, J., Carbin, M.: The lottery ticket hypothesis: finding sparse, trainable neural networks (2018). https://doi.org/10.48550/ARXIV.1803.03635

8. Geyer, R.C., Klein, T., Nabi, M.: Differentially private federated learning: a client level perspective (2017). https://doi.org/10.48550/ARXIV.1712.07557

9. Giuseppi, A., Della Torre, L., Menegatti, D., Pietrabissa, A.: AdaFed: performance-based adaptive federated learning. In: 2021 The 5th International Conference on Advances in Artificial Intelligence (ICAAI), ICAAI 2021. ACM (2021). https://doi.org/10.1145/3505711.3505717

10. Guo, Y., Wu, Y., Zhu, Y., Yang, B., Han, C.: Anomaly detection using distributed log data: a lightweight federated learning approach. In: 2021 International Joint Conference on Neural Networks (IJCNN). IEEE (2021). https://doi.org/10.1109/ijcnn52387.2021.9533294

11. Hard, A.: Federated learning for mobile keyboard prediction (2018). https://doi.org/10.48550/ARXIV.1811.03604

12. Hawkins, S., He, H., Williams, G., Baxter, R.: Outlier Detection Using Replicator Neural Networks, pp. 170–180. Springer, Berlin (2002). https://doi.org/10.1007/3-540-46145-0_17

13. He, P., Zhu, J., Zheng, Z., Lyu, M.R.: Drain: an online log parsing approach with fixed depth tree. IEEE (2017). https://doi.org/10.1109/ICWS.2017.13

14. He, S., Zhu, J., He, P., Lyu, M.R.: Experience report: system log analysis for anomaly detection. In: 2016 IEEE 27th International Symposium on Software Reliability Engineering (ISSRE). IEEE (2016). https://doi.org/10.1109/issre.2016.21

15. Hu, W., Liao, Y., Vemuri, V.R.: Robust anomaly detection using support vector machines (2003). https://api.semanticscholar.org/CorpusID:2433033

16. Jithish, J., Alangot, B., Mahalingam, N., Yeo, K.S.: Distributed anomaly detection in smart grids: a federated learning-based approach. IEEE Access **11**, 7157–7179 (2023). https://doi.org/10.1109/access.2023.3237554

17. Joulin, A., Grave, E., Bojanowski, P., Douze, M., Jégou, H., Mikolov, T.: Fasttext.zip: compressing text classification models. arXiv preprint: arXiv:1612.03651 (2016)

18. Kruegel, C., Mutz, D., Robertson, W., Valeur, F.: Bayesian event classification for intrusion detection. In: 19th Annual Computer Security Applications Conference, Proceedings. IEEE (2003). https://doi.org/10.1109/csac.2003.1254306

19. Krügel, C., Toth, T., Kirda, E.: Service specific anomaly detection for network intrusion detection. In: Proceedings of the 2002 ACM symposium on Applied computing, SAC02. ACM (2002). https://doi.org/10.1145/508791.508835

20. Kumar, M.R., Devi, B.R., Rangaswamy, K., Sangeetha, M., Kumar, K.V.R.: IoT-edge computing for efficient and effective information process on industrial automation. In: 2023 International Conference on Networking and Communications (ICNWC). IEEE (2023). https://doi.org/10.1109/icnwc57852.2023.10127492

21. Lea, C., Vidal, R., Reiter, A., Hager, G.D.: Temporal Convolutional Networks: A Unified Approach to Action Segmentation, pp. 47–54. Springer International Publishing, Cham (2016). https://doi.org/10.1007/978-3-319-49409-8_7

22. Li, B., Ma, S., Deng, R., Choo, K.K.R., Yang, J.: Federated anomaly detection on system logs for the internet of things: a customizable and communication-efficient approach. IEEE Trans. Netw. Serv. Manage. **19**(2), 1705–1716 (2022). https://doi.org/10.1109/tnsm.2022.3152620

23. Li, T., Sahu, A.K., Zaheer, M., Sanjabi, M., Talwalkar, A., Smith, V.: Federated optimization in heterogeneous networks (2018). https://doi.org/10.48550/ARXIV.1812.06127

24. Li, X., Huang, K., Yang, W., Wang, S., Zhang, Z.: On the convergence of FedAvg on Non-IID data (2019). https://doi.org/10.48550/ARXIV.1907.02189

25. Liu, X., Liu, W., Di, X., Li, J., Cai, B., Ren, W., Yang, H.: LogNADS: network anomaly detection scheme based on semantic representation. Futur. Gener. Comput. Syst. **124**, 390–405 (2021). https://doi.org/10.1016/j.future.2021.04.048

26. Makanju, A., Zincir-Heywood, A.N., Milios, E.E.: Clustering event logs using iterative partitioning. In: Proceedings of the 15th ACM SIGKDD International Conference on Knowledge Discovery and Data Mining, KDD 2009, pp. 1255–1264. ACM (2009). https://doi.org/10.1145/1557019.1557152

27. Makanju, A., Zincir-Heywood, A.N., Milios, E.E.: A lightweight algorithm for message type extraction in system application logs. IEEE Trans. Knowl. Data Eng. **24**(11), 1921–1936 (2012)

28. McMahan, H.B., Moore, E., Ramage, D., Hampson, S., Arcas, B.A.Y.: Communication-efficient learning of deep networks from decentralized data (2016). https://doi.org/10.48550/ARXIV.1602.05629

29. Min, D., Feifei, L.: Spell: streaming parsing of system event logs. IEEE (2016). https://doi.org/10.1109/ICDM.2016.160

30. Nardi, M., Valerio, L., Passarella, A.: Anomaly detection through unsupervised federated learning (2022). https://doi.org/10.48550/ARXIV.2209.04184

31. Nguyen, D.C., Ding, M., Pathirana, P.N., Seneviratne, A., Li, J., Vincent Poor, H.: Federated learning for internet of things: a comprehensive survey. IEEE Commun. Surv.; Tutorials **23**(3), 1622–1658 (2021). https://doi.org/10.1109/comst.2021.3075439

32. Poojitha, G., Kumar, K.N., Reddy, P.J.: Intrusion detection using artificial neural network. In: 2010 Second International conference on Computing, Communication and Networking Technologies. IEEE (2010). https://doi.org/10.1109/icccnt.2010.5592568

33. Preuveneers, D., Rimmer, V., Tsingenopoulos, I., Spooren, J., Joosen, W., Ilie-Zudor, E.: Chained anomaly detection models for federated learning: an intrusion detection case study. Appl. Sci. **8**(12), 2663 (2018). https://doi.org/10.3390/app8122663

34. Qu, Z., Lin, K., Li, Z., Zhou, J., Zhou, Z.: A unified linear speedup analysis of federated averaging and Nesterov FedAvg (2020). https://doi.org/10.48550/ARXIV.2007.05690

35. Raunak, V.: Effective dimensionality reduction for word embeddings. In: Proceedings of the Workshop on Representation Learning for NLP (RepL4NLP) at ACL (2019)

36. Selim, G.E.I., Hemdan, E.E.D., Shehata, A.M., El-Fishawy, N.A.: Anomaly events classification and detection system in critical industrial internet of things infrastructure using machine learning algorithms. Multimedia Tools Appl. **80**(8), 12619–12640 (2021). https://doi.org/10.1007/s11042-020-10354-1

37. Trivedi, S., Anh Tran, T., Faruqui, N., Hassan, M.M.: An exploratory analysis of effect of adversarial machine learning attack on IoT-enabled industrial control systems. In: 2023 International Conference on Smart Computing and Application (ICSCA). IEEE (2023). https://doi.org/10.1109/icsca57840.2023.10087713

38. Vucovich, M., et al.: Anomaly detection via federated learning (2022). https://doi.org/10.48550/ARXIV.2210.06614

39. Wang, H.P., Stich, S.U., He, Y., Fritz, M.: ProgFed: effective, communication, and computation efficient federated learning by progressive training (2021). https://doi.org/10.48550/ARXIV.2110.05323

40. Wang, X., Liu, W., Lin, H., Hu, J., Kaur, K., Hossain, M.S.: Ai-empowered trajectory anomaly detection for intelligent transportation systems: a hierarchical

federated learning approach. IEEE Trans. Intell. Transp. Syst. **24**(4), 4631–4640 (2023). https://doi.org/10.1109/tits.2022.3209903

41. Wu, C., Wu, F., Lyu, L., Huang, Y., Xie, X.: Communication-efficient federated learning via knowledge distillation. Nat. Commun. **13**(1) (2022). https://doi.org/10.1038/s41467-022-29763-x

42. Xu, W., Huang, L., Fox, A., Patterson, D., Jordan, M.I.: Detecting large-scale system problems by mining console logs. In: Proceedings of the ACM SIGOPS 22nd symposium on Operating systems principles (SOSP 2009), pp. 117–132. ACM, New York (2009)

43. Ye, N., Chen, Q.: An anomaly detection technique based on a chi-square statistic for detecting intrusions into information systems. Qual. Reliab. Eng. Int. **17**(2), 105–112 (2001). https://doi.org/10.1002/qre.392

44. Zhang, Y., Duan, L., Cheung, N.M.: Accelerating federated learning on Non-IID data against stragglers. In: 2022 IEEE International Conference on Sensing, Communication, and Networking (SECON Workshops). IEEE (2022). https://doi.org/10.1109/seconworkshops56311.2022.9926402

45. Zumin, W., Jiyu, T., Hui, F., Liming, C., Jing, Q.: LightLog: a lightweight temporal convolutional network for log anomaly detection on the edge. Elsevier **203** (2022).https://doi.org/10.1016/j.comnet.2021.108616

A Cost-Sensitive Approach for Managing Intrusion Alerts in OT Environments

Alex Howe[1]($\boxtimes$) (iD), Andrew Morin[2] (iD), Mauricio Papa[1] (iD), and Tyler Moore[2] (iD)

[1] Tandy School of Computer Science, The University of Tulsa, Tulsa OK, USA
{alex-howe,mauricio-papa}@utulsa.edu
[2] School of Cyber Studies, The University of Tulsa, Tulsa OK, USA
{andrew-morin,tyler-moore}@utulsa.edu

Abstract. Network Intrusion Detection Systems (NIDS) are traditionally built to minimize the total number of misclassifications without considering financial implications. However, false positives and false negatives both impose monetary costs on an organization through wasted analyst time and damage from missed attacks. This work presents an approach which uses economically informed decision making to develop a cost-sensitive intrusion detection architecture that incorporates the cost of handling such misclassifications. Specifically, we propose a cost-sensitive supervised machine learning model alongside an economically informed thresholding technique to minimize the overall cost when dealing with cyber attacks. The models are evaluated across four unique scenarios in two environments, highlighting the broad suitability of the architecture. The various scenarios allow our architecture to be evaluated across a range of notoriously difficult to determine costs. Experimental results for the two domains demonstrate an average cost reduction of 59% over traditional accuracy-based intrusion detection systems. The trade-off, measured in reduced accuracy, is minor, with an average accuracy reduction of 1.25%. Our architecture allows organizations to make detailed and informed decisions about resource allocation when implementing security tools.

Keywords: Critical infrastructure · Intrusion detection · Security economics

1 Introduction

Operational technology (OT) networks operate and manage critical infrastructures such as refineries, power plants, and water treatment facilities, where the integrity of such systems is paramount. These networks have traditionally relied on physical isolation and security through obscurity to mitigate exposure to cyber threats. However, in recent years they have become increasingly interwoven with public networks in pursuit of increased efficiency [9]. The accelerated rate at which these systems are being connected to public networks has outpaced the cyber security response. The landmark ransomware attack on several

G. Oliva et al. (Eds.): CRITIS 2024, LNCS 15549, pp. 306–325, 2025.
https://doi.org/10.1007/978-3-031-84260-3_18

Colonial Pipeline systems in May 2021 highlighted the potential consequences of continuing to integrate OT networks with public networks in the absence of sufficient cyber security polices.

To combat the expanding threat landscapes, intrusion detection systems (IDSs) are used to identify and stop attacks. The goal of the IDS is to analyze network traffic and attempt to classify incoming traffic as benign or malicious. These IDSs are predominantly evaluated on their ability to minimize false positive and false negative classifications. While both of these classification errors equally affect the accuracy of the IDS, the financial impact of false positives and false negatives can vary widely. For cyber security teams operating on a finite budget, the economic efficiency of their reaction to potential threats is of utmost importance. This paper presents a framework to incorporate economic information into the intrusion detection and response process. Specifically, we apply cost-informed weights to the machine learning process, as well as a cost-based thresholding technique, to influence the detection model's decision making.

Cost-informed weights are used to perform cost-sensitive learning, a subset of machine learning which is dedicated to scenarios with varying misclassification penalties [4]. Consider a buffer overflow attack which costs a company $10,000 if it is successfully exploited, yet only $20 for an analyst to review the traffic. The cost of a false positive, or a nonmalicious packet flagged as malicious, is inexpensive compared to the false negative, a malicious packet incorrectly labeled as nonmalicious. Thus, if the IDS generates 200 false positives in order to correctly identify 1 buffer overflow attack, the organization still saves a total of $6,000. Integrating a cost-sensitive approach into the machine learning-based IDS allows for an organization to influence the model's learning process to force it to focus on high-priority attacks.

Thresholding techniques identify optimal decision boundaries for machine learning classifiers. This work introduces a cost-based thresholding technique referred to as a *scoring manager*. This method analyzes the probability values from each of the classes as well as their associated false positive and false negative costs in order to determine thresholds for each class. The scoring manager then creates an economic filter which can be used in combination with the cost-informed weights to optimize the expected cost.

Cyber security costs are notoriously difficult to study, as they can vary widely between, and even within, industries. To combat this, we apply our framework to four scenarios across two OT environments. The scenarios represent unique salaries, expected financial impacts, and cyber security maturity levels. We find that our framework consistently reduces costs incurred by the organizations in all scenarios. The overall costs are reduced in all of the eight scenarios, with an average reduction of 59%. The loss in accuracy to achieve these reductions is minor, with an average accuracy loss of 1.25%.

In Sect. 2, we review related literature. Section 3 details the architecture used. In Sect. 4, we provide the data used, as well as detail our methodology. In Sect. 5, we detail our findings and in Sect. 6 we provide concluding remarks.

2 Related Work

The approach presented in this paper combines ideas from two fields: cost-sensitive machine learning and security economics. On the one hand there is a need to develop effective intrusion detection systems to minimize the likelihood that an attack succeeds. On the other, there is a need to develop solutions that allow stakeholders to make economically informed security decisions. This section presents work related to these two fields.

Cost-sensitive intrusion detection has emerged as one solution to handling the inherent class imbalance of network intrusion detection. One popular approach is to utilize cost-sensitive machine learning and weight the minority classes according to class distribution. For example, in [14] the authors propose an ensemble approach based on Deep Neural Networks (DNNs) which use class minority distributions to influence the training process. Specifically, they apply a bootstrap aggregation approach in which ten DNNs are trained on unique training subsets, which are balanced by weighting the minority class based on the ratio when compared to the majority class. In [6], the authors propose a cost-sensitive IDS based on the XGBoost algorithm in which attack classes are weighted based on their probabilities, or ratio compared to the majority. They compare their cost-sensitive weighting approach to the SMOTE oversampling algorithm.

In [5], the authors propose a cost-sensitive ensemble approach in which both a weighted training scheme and an oversampling method is used to identify network intrusions. Three layers, based on the cost-sensitive DNN, Random Forest, and XGBoost algorithms, are proposed which have varying levels of detection granularity. The first layer incorporates a cost-sensitive DNN in which class ratios are used to weight the minority and majority classes. The second and third layers rely on oversampling techniques to rebalance the distributions.

In all three related works, the authors rely on class distributions to derive the weights. This work proposes an economically informed weighting scheme, allowing the user to tune the IDS operations to fit the organization's requirements.

An economic approach has proved useful in understanding and managing cybersecurity risks [2]. Typically, security controls are developed and evaluated on their technical merits alone, such as their effectiveness in detecting and preventing attacks. But cybersecurity investment comes at a cost, and the interventions they introduce do too. Restricting access to networks and systems may reduce the likelihood of an attack, but it can also make completing a mission more difficult and expensive. By quantifying the costs and benefits of cybersecurity controls, it becomes possible to rationally evaluate cybersecurity investments and configure their operations in a way that optimally manages risk.

For example, many organizations balk at making investments to strengthen the cybersecurity of industrial control systems, despite the presence of long-standing weaknesses in these systems. One way to encourage investment is to demonstrate that the benefits outweigh the added costs. Papa et al. conducted a cost-benefit analysis for retrofitting wastewater facilities with an ICS attack detection system [11]. They estimated the costs associated with a successful attack using public data on harms, and then showed the circumstances under

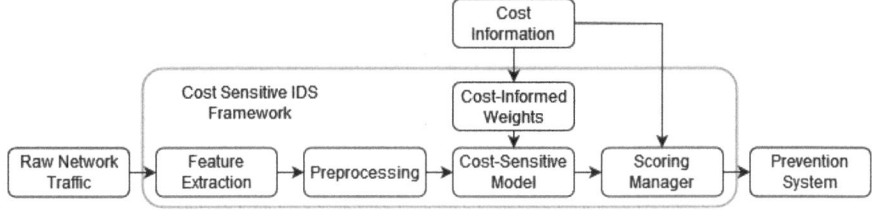

Fig. 1. Proposed cost-sensitive IDS architecture diagram.

which an investment in a detection system to reduce the likelihood of accidental or intentional overflows could be justified.

The notion that IDSs must not only optimize security but also minimize cost has been proposed before. In 2002, [7] explored the problem of building cost-sensitive IDS. Their solution considers five different types of cost: development, operation, damage (when an intrusion is successful), manual response and automated response to attacks. They define a model to formulate the total expected cost of the IDS (using all five costs) and propose cost-sensitive ML-based techniques that are designed to reduce the overall cost of intrusion detection.

Another approach is to evaluate output from binary classifiers. Receiver operating characteristic (ROC) curves are commonly used to evaluate the diagnostic ability of a binary classifier system as its discrimination threshold is varied. ROC curves have also been used to evaluate cyber security costs. [10] investigated the use of ROC curves to optimize filters that ultimately define whether there is a need to respond to an intrusion and the associated cost. The advantage of the approach is that it helps identify a more optimal allocation of resources that minimizes overall expected cost.

The proposed IDS architecture relies on cost-sensitive machine learning, but takes an entirely different financial-based approach when it comes to class weighting. Additionally, we incorporate an economically informed thresholding technique which adds an additional layer of expected cost optimization.

3   Cost-Sensitive OT IDS Architecture

The machine learning-based architecture was designed for real-time intrusion detection using the multi-stage approach shown in Fig. 1. Four sequential stages analyze incoming network traffic and generate security alerts for malicious activity: feature extraction, preprocessing, machine learning and score managing.

The detection framework uses a cost-sensitive machine learning model, which is trained offline, to generate predictions/security alerts for each packet sent over the network. Security alerts are sent to an analyst for review, thus the architecture can work asynchronously apart from the network reducing any impact on bandwidth. Each stage of the framework contains tunable parameters which can be adjusted to meet the needs of any particular network it is deployed on.

3.1   Feature Extraction

Feature extraction and engineering refers to the process of transforming raw data and creating new features or variables suitable for use in machine learning models. In this particular domain, feature extraction refers to the process of extracting meaningful features from raw packets captured on the OT network. These features convey not only the state of that particular packet but may also provide information about the overall state of the OT system.

Network packets are messages formatted and sent over an established network. These messages are formatted using a protocol stack used to give context to the data being sent. Each protocol in the stack appends a header to the packet (and sometimes a trailer), providing incrementally more information. Feature extraction is a two-step process that identifies basic and statistical features. Basic packet features are extracted directly from from packet headers, such as addresses, port numbers, and control flags. These features are crucial to understanding the context of a particular packet within a network. In contrast, statistical-based metrics provide insight about the network at-large, and help characterize communication patterns. This includes information such as transmission rates for packets as well as average packet sizes. These are calculated using a running average for variables of interest in a sliding window with a configurable time width (e.g. one second).

3.2   Pre-processing

Feature pre-processing involves the transformation of features/variables to optimize them for use with machine learning algorithms. These transformations include handling any missing values, re-scaling data to remove biases, and restructuring features to match the assumptions made by some learning algorithms. The first step of pre-processing involves handling missing values which occur when the framework attempts to extract information related to a protocol that the captured packet does not use. Missing values are imputed with zeros, which signify the absence of a particular feature from the packet. For example, a TCP related feature would be set to zero when analyzing a UDP packet.

State variables, such as TCP control flags, are one-hot encoded to binary representations in order to retain their categorical information. For discrete structured variables, such as addresses, the encoding scheme segments the variables into multiple features by a protocol define separation character. For instance, IP address 192.168.33.56 is encoded into four decimal features with individual values 192, 168, 33 and 56 respectively. These values are treated as continuous and can offer insight into additional information such as identifying subnets and unique nodes. In Shao's work [12], this splitting technique was found to be much more effective than the standard one-hot encoding method.

Continuous variables, such as statistical-based features, are individually re-scaled to have zero-mean and a unit variance. Re-scaling features to a common scale reduces bias while retaining relationships between the different variables. Finally, a basic feature selection method using a variance threshold of 0 is used during training to remove any unimportant features.

3.3   Machine Learning

Machine learning has become a promising candidate for developing robust and efficient intrusion detection systems. Three primary learning techniques are commonly used for intrusion detection: supervised, semi-supervised, and unsupervised. Supervised and semi-supervised algorithms use labeled data for training in order to predict the likelihood of a sample belonging to a class; unsupervised algorithms do not require labels and instead work to uncover latent patterns.

These detection models often interface directly with humans, thus additional performance metrics such as false positive rates and the incurred monetary costs must be considered. Ideally, the organization would take the machine learning-based IDS and implement biases into it allowing them to shape the tool to their specific requirements or security objectives. Thus, this work considers the use of supervised machine learning algorithms to create cost-sensitive intrusion detection systems that adhere to economic requirements.

Cost-Sensitive Supervised Models. Similar to traditional signature based IDSs, the supervised model is trained using labeled attack samples and attempts to classify these attacks in real-time. One assumption made in most multi-class classifications tasks is that all errors are equally undesirable. This assumption is not necessarily true for several environments including intrusion detection, where a false negative and false positive can have very different impacts.

Cost-sensitive machine learning leverages cost values to accommodate for imbalanced datasets or differences in misclassification types. Specifically, we can use economically informed weights to influence the training process of the cost-sensitive detection model forcing it to prioritize attack classes associated with higher costs/weights. Four cost-sensitive implementations of traditional supervised algorithms are explored in this work: random forest, support vector machines, XGBoost, and dense neural networks.

Cost-sensitive Random Forest involves factoring weights W into the Gini index/impurity equation:

$$1 - (w_0 * p_0^2 + w_1 * p_1^2 + ... + w_n * p_n^2) \tag{1}$$

where w_i and p_i is the economically informed weight and probability for attack class i respectively. By weighting each attack class we can adjust the impact that a misclassification for that particular class has on the model's decision making.

Cost-sensitive Support Vector Machines (SVM) factor economically informed weights into the primal objective function:

$$Min(\frac{\omega^T \omega}{2} + C \sum_i^n (w_i * \xi_i)) \quad subject\ to\ \xi_i \geq 0 \tag{2}$$

where C is a regularization parameter and ξ_i is the misclassification allowance for class i. SVM can be applied to multi-class classification by taking a "one-vs-one" approach in which multiple binary classifiers are trained to separate pairs of classes.

Both extreme gradient boosting (XGBoost) and deep neural networks (DNNs) train using a defined objective function, or loss function, which tunes the parameters based on classification errors. For multi-class classification tasks one common objective function used is the multi-class Cross Entropy loss function which minimizes the negative log-likelihood over the classes. Cost-sensitive implementations of XGBoost and DNNs can be achieved by including a weighted version of the multi-class Cross Entropy loss function.

$$-\sum w_i * y_i * \log(\hat{y}_i) \tag{3}$$

where w_i, y_i, and $\hat{y}_i$ represent the economically informed weight, true class, and predicted class for the ith sample.

Cost-Informed Weights. Traditionally, supervised detection models prescribe equal weight to all classes and train the model to minimize the total number of false positive and false negatives. To emphasize a reduction in cost over accuracy, we consider an economically informed approach which factors the financial costs incurred by the generated alerts. Specifically, we employ a cost-sensitive supervised detection model in which the class weights w_i are developed based on the misclassification cost for attack i.

By weighting the importance of alerts based on the cost of misclassification, the optimization of the model is shifted from a purely accuracy based metric, to a minimization of costs. This also introduces flexibility in the model, allowing it to adapt to different environments where the same error may have varying costs. There are several methods for developing cost-informed weights; this work proposes an approach in which the misclassification costs are normalized and applied as weights. Normalization preserves the weights association with exploitation and investigation costs.

3.4   Cost-Based Scoring Manager

When confronted with real-time network traffic, supervised and unsupervised models alike will provide a likelihood score corresponding to each attack, which represents the confidence of the model that the packet is associated with an attack. A difficulty with machine-learning based models is to choose a threshold above which alerts are considered to be valid. A threshold which is too low will result in benign traffic being caught in the filter, and a threshold too high will allow malicious traffic through.

Given a sample of network traffic alerts, there are four possible classification outcomes for each alert: false positive, false negative, true positive, and true negative. The circumstances for these outcomes are shown in Table 1, as well as the false negative rate, β, and the false positive rate, α. To identify the optimal filter threshold which minimizes both β and α, the sample traffic, with known labels, can be evaluated at a series of thresholds.

As discussed above, accuracy alone is not guaranteed to result in cost-effective configuration. In addition to the training and selection of machine-learning models, economic information can also be used to make cost-informed decisions

Table 1. Confusion matrix of all possible outcomes.

Prediction	Reality	
	Malicious	Benign
Malicious	True Positive	False Positive
Benign	False Negative	True Negative
Rate	$\beta = \frac{FN}{(FN+TP)}$	$\alpha = \frac{FP}{(FP+TN)}$

about how to respond to alerts. This is further motivated by the varying cost of false positive alerts. Certain alerts will require a more detailed and time-consuming investigation to be cleared, yet this variation in false positive cost is not accounted for in the model training phase. To incorporate economic information into alert response, we use an optimal filter configuration identification process outlined by [3]. Using this process, the cost and probability associated with classification errors can be factored into alert response for a cost-informed response. This can be done using the following equation:

$$\alpha^* = \arg\min_{\alpha} p \cdot \beta(\alpha) \cdot b + (1-p) \cdot \alpha \cdot a \tag{4}$$

where α^* represents the false positive rate associated with the minimum overall cost. The cost itself is determined by multiplying the prior probability of the malicious traffic, p, by the false negative rate, $\beta(\alpha)$, and the cost of a false negative, b. This is added to the product of the probability of the traffic being benign, $1-p$, the false positive rate, α, and the false positive cost, a. Taking the first order condition of Eq. 4 gives us the slope of the indifference line where the costs of each error are equal. That is,

$$\beta'(\alpha^*) = -\frac{1-p}{p} \cdot \frac{a}{b} \tag{5}$$

where the optimal model configuration will be where this indifference line crosses the ROC curve. By determining the optimal threshold for each alert in the training sample, the models can be compared for any alert to select the lowest expected cost response.

4   Datasets for Evaluation

One of the main challenges for intrusion detection research in the OT domain is the lack of available quality datasets. Several key works have been proposed to help mitigate the lack of available OT network data including using data captured from deployed systems, testbeds [1], and simulated environments [8]. Real time deployed environments offer the most accurate source of data when it comes to OT network behavior. However, the lack of validation when it comes to the ground truth of the data makes the data unreliable. On the other hand, simulated environments can be properly validated but can lack the characteristics of deployed OT environments. Testbeds for physical OT networks are the ideal method for generating OT security data as they can exhibit the noise and characteristics of deployed OT environments while allowing proper validation when labeling attacks. Additionally, testbeds offer the ability to implement attacks and record the results in real time, which is not possible for deployed environments as they are often used in critical infrastructure.

This work utilizes two environmental datasets of raw network captures generated using a physical testbed in the additive manufacturing domain and a simulated OT environment of an electrical network. With each dataset several types of commonly encountered attacks were implemented in real-time and the packets related to those attacks were labeled after the capture. The model is trained using labeled examples of these attacks.

Our proposed cost-sensitive IDS architecture is evaluated on four unique scenarios within each environment. These scenarios illustrate varying costs and organizational cyber security maturity, allowing us to verify consistent performance across multiple applications.

4.1 OT Environment 1: Additive Manufacturing

The additive manufacturing testbed is a 3D printing system consisting of five devices connected over a closed Ethernet network. Four of the nodes are operational and work together to manufacture parts using various metals and alloys, the fifth node is a server acting as the target of the implemented attacks. Operating over the MQTT protocol, the network utilizes the publish-subscribe method for transmitting data. The workstation, one of the operational nodes, is used by an operator to send job files and commands to the other devices on the network.

Four datasets were generated from this OT environment consisting of 24 h of normal traffic, as well as a scan attack, a MitM attack, and an anomaly attack. The scan attack was created by performing a network scan of the OT environment. The MitM attack was created by poisoning the ARP-cache allowing them to observe the network traffic. Finally, the anomaly attack is created by performing an ICMP ping sweep from a compromised server. Detailed description of the packet distribution is given in Table 2.

4.2 OT Environment 2: Electric Utility

This environment is characterized by a data set described by [8] and it corresponds to a small electrical network. The network has controllers (or RTUs) that are in charge of electrical circuits, each with a single supply branch operating at 12,000 V. Controllers provide voltage measurements on each branch to an MTU using the Modbus/TCP protocol.

Tests were conducted using datasets that involved one MTU and 6 RTUs. Separate Modbus traffic files containing both normal and malicious traffic were used in the training and evaluation of the IDS. The first file contains only polling commands from the MTU to the RTUs represents the normal operational behavior of the environment. The remote exploit attack involves an actor using Metasploit's MS08-netapi exploit to compromise an active RTU. In file transfer, the actor uses the compromised RTU to transfer files to two other RTUs. The upload executable attack records the actor using the compromised RTU to upload an executable file to another RTU. In the anomalous attack, the actor uses the compromised RTU to forge and send fake Modbus commands to other RTUs. Detailed description of the packet distribution is given in Table 2.

Table 2. Dataset packet distributions.

Additive Manufacturing					
Normal	Scan	MitM	Anomaly	-	Total
76,195	21,303	410	34	-	97,942

Electrical Utility					
Normal	File	Upload	Anomaly	Remote	Total
74,687	75	1,199	10	121	76,092

4.3   Evaluation Scenarios

The IDS architecture proposed in this paper is evaluated on its ability to reduce overall costs associated with the misclassification of alerts compared to a strictly accuracy-based IDS. Therefore, we must first assign a cost to each misclassification of a packet. Such costs are challenging to identify due to the inherent differences between organizations, environments, and the changing threat landscapes over time. Therefore, instead of constricting the IDS evaluation to a single, limited scenario, we evaluate the IDS across a variety of scenarios representing different potential organizations. In total, we introduce four scenarios to be evaluated in each of the two environments as seen in Table 3: baseline, amplified attack, uneven harms, and high salary. The purpose of these scenarios is to illustrate how varying costs can affect decision making in the model. In practice, we would expect operators to provide cost estimates reflecting their deeper knowledge of deployment realities. When calculating the expected cost we take the sum of all false positives and false negatives multiplied by their respective costs.

Baseline Scenario. First, we look to open-source data and prior work to identify the "baseline" costs for a single implementation. Morin and Moore [10] used open-source information to estimate the misclassification costs for similar OT environments. For false positives, they define the cost as the cyber security analyst time wasted investigating spurious alerts. Combining the Bureau of Labor

Table 3. The four scenarios are shown in the first column. Each row has the estimated false positive (FP) and false negative costs. The false negative costs are split into additive manufacturing above the dashed line, and the electric utilty costs below the dashed line.

Scenario	FP	Scan File	MitM Upload	Anomaly Anomaly	- Remote
Baseline	$10	$67 $2,500	$67 $2,500	$67 $2,500	- $2,500
Amplified Impact	$10	$6,667 $250,000	$6,667 $250,000	$6,667 $250,000	- $250,000
Uneven Harms	$10	$195.60 $480	$4 $8,490	$0.40 $920	- $110
High Salary	$50	$195.60 $480	$4 $8,490	$0.40 $920	- $110

Statistics median salary for a cyber security analyst with the industry reported rate of alert review by analysts, Morin and Moore estimated a single false positive would cost an organization $10.

The OT environments evaluated in [10] are specific implementations of our additive manufacturing and electric utility environments, therefore we adopt their cost estimates. For the additive manufacturing environment, they identify four 3D printers with hourly titanium alloy printing costs. The impact in this environment is captured by an hour of lost printing material. We take the average cost of all four printers, resulting in an estimated attack cost of approximately $20,000. Although a false negative alert poses a risk, not all false negatives will result in a successful attack. Therefore, we choose a 1% probability that a false negative will result in a loss, resulting in an estimated false negative cost of $200. As there are three potential attack vectors for the additive manufacturing environment (scanning, Man-in-the-Middle, and anomaly), we evenly distribute the estimated impact across each. That is, the false negative cost for each malicious packet type is $200 divided by three, or $67.

For the electric utility environment, [10] measure the impact as the financial loss resulting in a momentary electrical outage in four different U.S. cities. We again take the average cost from the four samples, which provides an estimated cyber attack cost of approximately $1,000,000. Similar to the additive manufacturing attacks, it is reasonable to assume not all false negatives will result in a successful attack, and we again take 1% of this cost. As a result, the cost of a false negative in the electric utility environment is $10,000 divided evenly across the four packet types, resulting in a false negative cost of $2,500. Note that the electric utility environment has four malicious packet types versus the three in the additive manufacturing environment.

Amplified Impact Scenario. The second scenario we evaluate is the "amplified impact" scenario. In this scenario we leave the analyst salary unchanged, while raising all attack impacts. An electric utility example of such a scenario could be the introduction of industrial and commercial losses to the outage impact. Existing literature points out that the majority of losses from an electrical outage are from industrial and commercial customers. [13] As a utility provider becomes more informed of the true cost, the impact may become amplified while the analyst salary remains unaffected. For this scenario, we take the baseline scenario false negative costs and multiply them by ten.

Uneven Harms Scenario. In the first two scenarios we have evenly distributed the estimated false negative costs across malicious packet types. The underlying assumption is that the organization is uninformed about which packet types are most likely to appear. The reality is that this is likely untrue, and certain malicious packets will appear more often. In the third scenario, "uneven harms", we consider an organization which is well informed about the appearance rate of malicious packet types. In this case, we multiply the baseline costs by the relative appearance rates of each packet type in the training data. For additive manufacturing, Man-in-the-Middle packets make up 2% of all malicious packets, and therefore we multiply the $200 original cost by 0.02 for a cost of $4.

High Salary Scenario. Finally, we consider the "high salary" scenario when analysts are paid a higher salary, resulting in costlier false positives. For this scenario we maintain the costs from the uneven harms scenario, and multiply the false positive cost by five, resulting in a false positive cost of $50. This could be a scenario in which more experienced analysts are required, or that more analysts are involved in alert remediation.

5   Evaluation

We begin our evaluation by comparing the cost-informed results of four different machine-learning classification models to identify the model best suited for cost-informed weight information. Next, we measure the relationship between accuracy and cost as the machine-learning weights are gradually adjusted to align with the relative cost of each type of misclassification. While a cost reduction in one scenario is interesting, we proceed to evaluate the consistency of these results by applying these cost-informed weights to four unique scenarios across both environments. Finally, we combine the cost-informed weights of the best model with the scoring manager to measure the overall performance of our proposed IDS architecture.

5.1   Cost-Sensitive Model Selection

The four classifier models described in Sect. 3 each incorporate the economic information differently. Because of this, we start our analysis by evaluating the cost performance differences between them. The expected cost of a model is determined by training each model on the cost-informed weights and summing up the cost of each classification error during the testing phase. We perform this test for each scenario in both environments. The results can be seen in Table 4.

The data was split using a 70/30 train-test split and the recorded values are averaged over three different controlled seeds. It is important to note that the incurred cost values are entirely dependent on the proposed scenarios, meaning that scenarios with overall low attack costs will have lower expected costs than scenarios with higher attack costs (e.g. scenarios 1 and 2).

We find the cost-informed XGBoost model achieved the best performance in terms of minimizing the overall expected cost in seven of the eight scenarios. The single outlier was the fourth scenario in the additive manufacturing environment. In this scenario the deep neural network achieved a marginally lower cost than XGBoost. Although all models had positive results, we find the XGBoost model was best suited for cost-informed weights. Therefore, any evaluations henceforth reported on will be done using the XGBoost classifier model.

Table 4. Cost comparison of the four proposed models

	SVM	Random Forest	XGBoost	DNN
Additive Manufacturing				
Baseline	$1,232.00	$1,290.10	**$1,097.55**	$1,105.42
Amplified Impact	$741,109.06	$108,376.47	**$42,631.35**	$78,980.45
Uneven Harms	$26,088.60	$26,851.32	**$9,564.45**	$13,323.30
High Salary	$27,269.10	$21,729.38	$14,130.59	**$14,059.36**
Electrical Utility				
Baseline	$181,910.00	$59,330.00	**$840.00**	$92,043.00
Amplified Impact	$10,146,493.33	$4,166,760.00	**$28,896.66**	$38,774,440.00
Uneven Harms	$61,116.44	$26,743.62	**$9,364.88**	$48,819.28
High Salary	$68,186.44	$25,176.52	**$14,011.62**	$49,712.96

5.2 Cost-Informed Weights

Before testing each scenario, we first seek to measure the interaction between the costs and accuracy as the model transitions from a purely accuracy-based model to a cost-informed model. Prior to training, the costs are normalized to a scale of $[0, 1]$ weights. The accuracy-based model, which prioritizes a minimization of misclassifications, evenly weights each error type. Specifically, for the additive manufacturing environment with four possible packet types, the weights are all 0.25. For the electric utility environment with five packet types, these weights are all 0.2. The final cost-informed weights, which will differ from the even weights to varying degrees, are also normalized to $[0,1]$. By breaking up the difference between the accuracy and cost-informed weights into a set of 100 equidistant intermediate weights, we can observe the relationship between accuracy and cost as the weights progressively become cost-informed. The result of this process can be seen in Fig. 2. The left two plots show the cost and accuracy as the weights progress from evenly weighted to cost-informed weights for the electric utility, and the right two plots show the same information for the additive manufacturing weights. For both environments we used the baseline scenario for cost estimates.

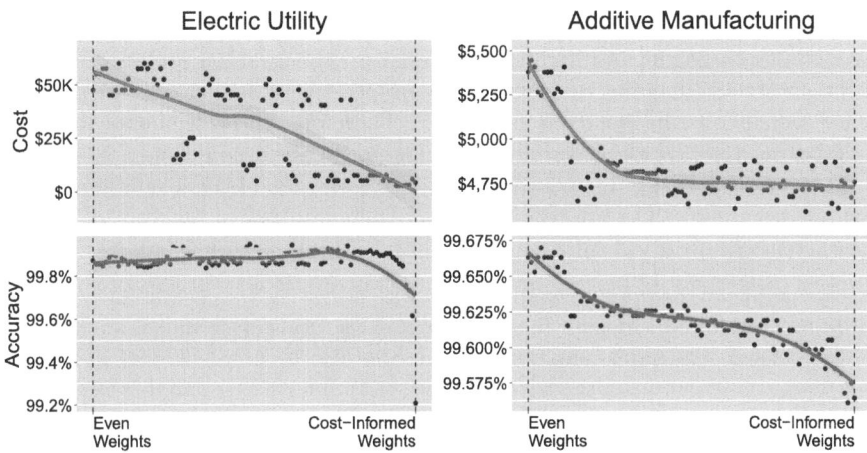

Fig. 2. The cost (top) and accuracy (bottom) for the electric utility (left) and additive manufacturing (right) environments using the baseline cost estimates. The left side of the plots are evenly weighted models, and the right side is the fully cost-informed weights.

The plots in Fig. 2 illustrate the trade-off between cost and accuracy for both environments. The electric utility costs fall steadily and significantly, from an initial cost of \$62,560 at even weights, to \$6,790 at the cost-informed weights for an 89% decrease. The change in accuracy is a noticeable, but relatively minor 0.66% decrease. For the additive manufacturing environment, the change in cost drops from \$5,487 to \$4,737, for a 14% decrease. Again, we see a relatively minor accuracy drop of 0.09%. Both sets of plots are experiencing a decrease in costs as the model permits an increase in the relatively cheaper false positives to catch more of the costly attacks. In the next section we will evaluate how these costs are handled across all scenarios.

5.3 Cost-Informed Scenarios

We now investigate how the performance of a cost-informed model changes across our four proposed scenarios. For robustness, we test our scenarios using twenty unique splits of the data for each scenario. In total, we train and test the model 80 times. While each scenario is unique, the direct comparisons between the baseline and amplified impact scenarios, as well as the uneven harms and high salary scenarios, are particularly interesting. The primary difference between the baseline and amplified impact scenarios are the general false negative costs. In both scenarios the analyst salary remains constant, and the organization remains equally uninformed about attack likelihoods, yet the relative cost of false negatives becomes larger. As such, missing a legitimate attack is amplified by a factor of ten and an organization will tolerate ten times more false positives than in the baseline scenario. This comparison highlights the false negative aversion of an organization as false negative costs increase relative to false positive costs. For the uneven harms and high salary scenarios, the analysts are well informed about packet likelihoods. However, the false positive cost increases in the high salary scenario as analyst time is costlier. Therefore, these scenarios highlight the false positive aversion introduced by higher investigation costs.

In the remainder of this section we will explore each of these relationships in both environments. The additive manufacturing results can be seen in Table 5, and the electric utility results can be seein in Table 6.

Table 5. The four scenarios for the additive manufacturing environment are shown in the first column. The second and third columns show the accuracy and cost change as a percentage compared to even weights. The last four columns show the misclassification change as a percentage compared to even weights, where a positive number represents a decrease in accuracy.

	Change(%)		Misclassification Change (%)			
Scenario	Accuracy	Cost	Normal	Scan	MitM	Anomaly
Baseline	-0.07	-15.35	1.91	-0.11	-0.25	-0.25
Amplified Impact	-9.5	-83.77	125.8	-0.56	-0.94	-0.5
Uneven Harms	-0.17	-16.96	0.33	-0.33	0.51	6.75
High Salary	-0.18	-23.44	-0.54	-0.20	0.79	6.75

Additive Manufacturing False Negative Aversion. Observing the baseline scenario from Table 5, we see a median decrease in cost of 15.35%, and a median decrease in accuracy of 0.07%. These values align with the single instance evaluated in the previous section and shown in Fig. 2. The amplified impact scenario, where the cost of a successful attack is 10 times larger, shows a larger decrease in median accuracy of 9.5%, and an 84% decrease in median cost. The last four columns highlight where the change in accuracy is most prevalent. In the baseline scenario a 1.9% increase in false positives over even weights is tolerated to reduce a minor reduction in each false negative rate. Compare this to the amplified impact scenario where false positive rates increase 126% over even weights to push the malicious scan, MitM, and anomaly false negatives down by 0.56%, 0.94% and 0.5% respectively. Because a single false negative is an overwhelming cost driver, this relatively minor decrease at the expense of a significantly higher false positive rate remains cost-effective.

Table 6. The four scenarios for the electric utility environment are shown in the first column. The second and third columns show the accuracy and cost change as a percentage compared to even weights. The last five columns show the misclassification change as a percentage compared to even weights.

Scenario	Change(%)		Misclassification Change (%)				
	Accuracy	Cost	Normal	File	Upload	Anomaly	Remote
Baseline	-0.7	-79	65	-1	-0.89	-0.75	-1
Amplified Impact	-9.96	-89.6	920.7	-1	-1	-0.86	-1
Uneven Harms	-1.08	-85.44	85.67	0.33	-1	-0.56	0
High Salary	-0.12	-77.42	12.88	0.33	-0.88	-0.56	0

Additive Manufacturing False Positive Aversion. The uneven harms and high salary scenarios are shown in the last two rows of Table 5. In both scenarios we see the median accuracy remain largely unchanged, dropping by 0.17% in the uneven harms scenario, and 0.18% in the high salary scenario. In the uneven harms scenario the well informed cyber security team is able to reduce the median costs by just under 17%, which is better than the median baseline cost from an uninformed cyber security team. This is highlighted in the misclassification columns where we see the relatively uncommon anomaly and MitM traffic is often ignored to improve the accurate classification of the much more common scanning traffic, even at the expense of increased false positives. For the high salary scenario, the analyst salary is five times higher, resulting in costlier false positives. As a result, the model improves the median cost by 23% over even weights by including the prioritization of minimizing the costly false positives in addition to the common scanning traffic.

Electric Utility False Negative Aversion. The false negative aversion within the electric utility environment can be seen in Table 6. In the first two rows we again see the median estimated costs decrease significantly for both scenarios. The costs decrease from 79% in the baseline scenario, to 89.6% in the amplified impact scenario as the attacks become costlier. The median accuracy also drops, with a 0.7% decrease in accuracy in between even weights and baseline weights, to a 10% for the amplified impact scenario. In the misclassification columns we see that this decrease in accuracy is the result of increased misclassification in the less costly false positives. In the baseline scenario false positives increase by 65% over even weights, while the amplified impact scenario results in a 920.7% increase in false positives. This increase in false positives results in a decrease in false negatives for the much more expensive upload and anomaly attacks.

Table 7. Accuracy, F1-Score and cost change (and percent change) from baseline configuration for each IDS architecture configuration across all four scenarios in the additive manufacturing environment. The best improvement in each metric is bolded.

Scenario	Metric	Cost-Informed Weights	Scoring Manager		Both	
Baseline	Accuracy	**0.9989 (-0.02%)**	0.9497	(-4.94%)	0.9987	(-0.04%)
	F1-Score	**0.9980 (-0.04%)**	0.8991	(-9.94%)	0.9974	(-0.09%)
	Cost	$1,246 (8.21%)	$15,095	(1211%)	**$1,098**	**(-4.65%)**
Amplified Impact	Accuracy	**0.9403 (1.06%)**	0.4881	(-51.15%)	0.9379	(-6.12%)
	F1-Score	**0.8810 (-11.75%)**	0.5386	(-46.04%)	0.8768	(-12.17%)
	Cost	$50,807 (-52.41%)	$172,599	(61.07%)	**$42,631**	**(-60.06%)**
Uneven Harms	Accuracy	0.9906 (-0.86%)	0.9414	(-5.78%)	**0.9939**	**(-0.52%)**
	F1-Score	0.9798 (-1.85%)	0.8829	(-11.56%)	**0.9872**	**(-1.11%)**
	Cost	$10,685 (-83.24%)	$44,709	(-29.85%)	**$9,564**	**(-84.99%)**
High Salary	Accuracy	**0.9955 (-0.36%)**	0.9494	(-4.97%)	0.9947	(-0.44%)
	F1-Score	**0.9908 (-0.76%)**	0.8986	(-9.98%)	0.9889	(-0.95%)
	Cost	$19,962 (-68.84%)	$101,610	(58.58%)	**$14,131**	**(-77.94%)**

Electric Utility False Positive Aversion. The bottom two rows of Table 6 show the uneven harms and high salary scenarios for the electric utility environment. Both show improvement in median cost reduction, again showing a decrease in false positives in the high salary scenario compared to the uneven harms scenario. However, unlike the additive manufacturing scenario, we see the median accuracy increase in the high salary scenario relative to the uneven harms scenario. As a result, the median cost reduction is lower for the high salary scenario. This is a result of the increased false negative costs in the electric utility environment. As a result, false positives are still largely preferred over false negatives and the model slightly reduces sensitivity to upload attacks to increase accuracy. Still, the median cost reduction for high salary is a 77% improvement over even weights.

5.4 Cost-Sensitive Framework Evaluation

The cost-informed weights are the first step of introducing economic information into the proposed IDS architecture. After the models are trained on these weights, the classification scores are then passed to the second economic stage:

Table 8. Accuracy, F1-Score and cost change (and percent change) from baseline configuration for each IDS architecture configuration across all four scenarios in the electric utility environment. The best improvement in each metric is bolded.

Scenario	Metric	Cost-Informed Weights		Scoring Manager		Both	
Baseline	Accuracy	**0.9993**	**-(0.04%)**	0.9989	(-0.08%)	0.9988	(-0.09%)
	F1-Score	**0.9814**	**-(1.06%)**	0.9741	(-1.80%)	0.9689	(-2.32%)
	Cost	$967	(-44.87%)	$887	(-49.43%)	**$840**	**(-52.09%)**
Amplified Impact	Accuracy	0.9799	(-1.98%)	0.5592	(-44.07%)	**0.9829**	**(-1.68%)**
	F1-Score	0.6455	(-34.92%)	0.3490	(-64.81%)	**0.7187**	**(-27.55%)**
	Cost	$46,240	(-73.58%)	$150,613	(-13.94%)	**$28,897**	**(-83.49%)**
Uneven Harms	Accuracy	0.9989	(-0.54%)	**0.9989**	**(-0.08%)**	0.9904	(-0.93)%
	F1-Score	0.8762	(-11.67%)	**0.9741**	**(-1.80%)**	0.7993	(-19.43)%
	Cost	$10,741	(-58.69%)	$12,787	(-50.82%)	**$9,365**	**(-63.98%)**
High Salary	Accuracy	**0.9989**	**(-0.07%)**	0.9989	(-0.08%)	0.9982	(-0.15%)
	F1-Score	**0.9776**	**(-1.44%)**	0.9741	(-1.80%)	0.9698	(-2.23%)
	Cost	**$13,273**	**(-48.97%)**	$13,667	(-47.46%)	$14,012	(-46.13%)

the scoring manager. The scoring manager assesses the likelihood scores and filters alerts based on the optimal filter configuration described in Sect. 3.4. In this section we add the scoring manager to the cost-informed weights to evaluate the performance of our IDS architecture. The IDS architecture is evaluated in four configurations: no economic information, cost-informed weights only, scoring manager only, and finally the combination of cost-informed weights and the scoring manager.

The first configuration is no economic influence, and uses a traditional supervised model and even weights which minimize misclassifications. The second configuration is cost-informed weights only, which takes the costs defined by the scenario, normalizes them into weights, and uses these weights during the model training process. This is the configuration used in the previous evaluation of cost-informed scenarios. The third configuration is scoring manager only, which uses a traditional supervised model using even weights as input into the scoring manager. The scoring manager then uses the scenario costs to determine the optimal filter threshold for each class based on Eq. 4. The accuracy based model will output likelihood scores for each packet class, and the largest difference between likelihood score and optimal filter threshold is selected as the predicted class. Specifically, the class which is furthest from the break-even cost is chosen as the predicted class. If no attack score exceeds its individual threshold then the packet is labeled as normal. The fourth and final configuration considers both a cost-informed weights model and the scoring manager. The cost-informed weights model produces a score for each packet. These scores are then sent to the scoring manager which uses the defined costs to find individual class-specific thresholds that result in the minimum overall cost within the training data. The combination of cost-informed weights and cost-based optimal filters are used to evaluate the testing data.

For evaluation purposes, the evenly weighted accuracy-based IDS configuration is treated as a baseline. The accuracy, cost, and F1-Score of the remaining three configurations are shown as raw values and percent change from the baseline configuration. The configurations are evaluated on each of the four scenarios in both environments. Results for the additive manufacturing environment are displayed in Table 7 and the electrical utility results are shown in Table 8.

The tables show that across all but the first scenario in the additive manufacturing environment, the inclusion of cost-informed weights leads to both significant average cost decreases and minimal average accuracy and F1-score degradation. The second configuration, where only the scoring manager is used, provided lower average costs in five of the eight scenarios. All three increased average cost scenarios were in the additive manufacturing environment. We believe this is due to the distributions for each attack class in the additive manufacturing environment. The equation used to calculate optimal threshold values relies heavily on the probability of the class appearing in the data. Thus, the scoring manager performs best in highly imbalanced environments, which the additive manufacturing environment was not.

It was found that in both environments, incorporating both the cost-informed weights model as well as the scoring manager resulted in the minimum expected cost in nearly every scenario. Scenario 4 in the electric utility environment was the single outlier where cost-informed weights outperformed the other two configurations. However, in this scenario the combination configuration did not perform poortly, rather all three configurations performed similarly well, with all three average expected cost reductions being in the range of 46%–49%.

6   Conclusion

This work demonstrates the potential benefits of including cost-sensitive learning in the development of intrusion detection systems within OT networks. By considering the financial impact of different classification errors, the detection system can make economically-informed decisions, trading minor accuracy reductions for significant cost savings. This work proposed a configurable IDS framework which incorporates two cost-sensitive techniques, including a cost-based weighting scheme which prioritizes classification errors based on their estimated cost, and a cost-based scoring manager which screens alerts based on an optimized filter. By integrating these techniques, the IDS shifts its focus from maximizing accuracy to minimizing the expected costs.

The costs used in this paper were based on prior estimates by [10]. However, these costs can be modified to accurately reflect any individual scenario. The ratio of misclassification costs drives the performance of our model, not the costs themselves. For an organization that is able to estimate their implementation specific costs, this framework offers an economically-informed alternative to accuracy based IDS techniques.

Results emphasize the importance of cost-aware decision making for cyber defense. The inclusion of cost-sensitive techniques into OT network security provides organizations with the ability to be proactive and make more informed security decisions in order to mitigate the potential operational and financial consequences associated with cyber attacks.

Acknowledgements. The authors would like to acknowledge the support from Engineer Research and Development Center (ERDC) under Contract No. W912HZ23C0011.

References

1. Ahmed, C.M., Palleti, V.R., Mathur, A.P.: WADI: a water distribution testbed for research in the design of secure cyber physical systems. In: Proceedings of the 3rd International Workshop On Cyber-Physical Systems For Smart Water Networks, pp. 25–28 (2017)
2. Anderson, R., Moore, T.: The economics of information security. Science **314**(5799), 610–613 (2006). https://doi.org/10.1126/science.1130992
3. Böhme, R., Moore, T.: Modeling optimal filter configuration (2012). https://tylermoore.utulsa.edu/courses/econsec/f12/reading/lnse-fpfn.pdf
4. Freund, Y., Schapire, R.E.: A decision-theoretic generalization of on-line learning and an application to boosting. J. Comput. Syst. Sci. **55**(1), 119–139 (1997)
5. Gupta, N., Jindal, V., Bedi, P.: CSE-IDS: using cost-sensitive deep learning and ensemble algorithms to handle class imbalance in network-based intrusion detection systems. Comput. Secur. **112**, 102499 (2022)
6. He, S., Li, B., Peng, H., Xin, J., Zhang, E.: An effective cost-sensitive XGBoost method for malicious URLs detection in imbalanced dataset. IEEE Access **9**, 93089–93096 (2021). https://doi.org/10.1109/ACCESS.2021.3093094
7. Lee, W., Fan, W., Miller, M., Stolfo, S.J., Zadok, E.: Toward cost-sensitive modeling for intrusion detection and response. J. Comput. Secur. **10**(1–2), 5–22 (2002)
8. Lemay, A., Fernandez, J.M.: Providing SCADA network data sets for intrusion detection research. In: CSET@ USENIX Security Symposium (2016)
9. Leverett, E.P.: Quantitatively assessing and visualising industrial system attack surfaces (2011)
10. Morin, A., Moore, T.: Towards cost-balanced intrusion detection in OT environments. In: 2022 IEEE Conference on Communications and Network Security (CNS), pp. 1–6. IEEE (2022)
11. Papa, S., Casper, W., Moore, T.: Securing wastewater facilities from accidental and intentional harm: a cost-benefit analysis. Int. J. Crit. Infr. Prot. **6**(2), 96–106 (2013). https://tylermoore.utulsa.edu/ijcip13.pdf
12. Shao, E.: Encoding IP address as a feature for network intrusion detection. Ph.D. thesis, Purdue University Graduate School (2019)
13. Sullivan, M., Schellenberg, J., Blundell, M.: Updated value of service reliability estimates for electric utility customers in the United States. Technical Report LBNL–6941E, 1172643 (2015).https://doi.org/10.2172/1172643
14. Thakkar, A., Lohiya, R.: Attack classification of imbalanced intrusion data for IoT network using ensemble learning-based deep neural network. IEEE Internet Things J. (2023)

Multicriteria GIS Spatial Analysis for Multi-hazard Assessment of Infrastructures in Case of Natural Events

Manuel Arduin[1] , Alberto Tofani[2] , Gregorio D'Agostino[2] ,
and Maurizio Pollino[2]([⊠])

[1] University of Rome "Sapienza", Piazzale Aldo Moro 5, 00185 Rome, Italy
arduin.1911999@studenti.uniroma1.it

[2] ENEA – Laboratory for the Analysis and Modelling of Critical Infrastructures and Essential Services, Casaccia Research Centre, Via Anguillarese, 301, 00123 Rome, Italy
{alberto.tofani,gregorio.dagostino,maurizio.pollino}@enea.it

Abstract. Earthquakes, landslides, and floods are among the natural phenomena that have been impacting the entire world in recent years, particularly Italy. This led to a significant increase in global emergencies. In this context, Geographic Information Systems (GIS) can play a pivotal role. Additionally, multi-criteria evaluation (MCE) techniques can effectively support addressing issues related to the multi-hazard (dynamical) risk assessment of critical infrastructures. In this study, GIS and MCE were integrated to evaluate and map multi-hazards across the entire Italian territory for key critical infrastructure networks, including transports, gas, and electric power. Examples of the results obtained are presented through a series of thematic maps created within the GIS environment.

Keywords: multi-hazard · spatial analysis · GIS · infrastructures

1 Introduction

In recent years, there has been an increase in environmental catastrophes and natural disasters all over the world, with the consequent enhancement of the global emergency status [1]. International bodies and national authorities have developed tools to monitor these phenomena, however prediction and predictability remain hotly debated [2].

Today, scientific knowledge is such that the impacts of natural disasters such as earthquakes, floods, volcanic eruptions, etc., can be ranked by expressing a low, medium, high degree of probability of the occurrence of the event and the extent of its consequences. In particular, through "multi-hazard" analysis, it is possible to combine different types of hazard events that can occur simultaneously in the same area or – in the worst-case scenario – link together and increase the destructive capacity of an individual, unleashing secondary and tertiary ones [3–7].

Spatial (or geospatial) analysis provides an effective perspective on the world, a kind of lens through which to examine events, patterns, and processes that operate on or near the surface of our planet [8]. Spatial analysis uses geographic information to link features

G. Oliva et al. (Eds.): CRITIS 2024, LNCS 15549, pp. 326–342, 2025.
https://doi.org/10.1007/978-3-031-84260-3_19

and phenomena on the Earth's surface to their locations. This analysis can be applied at different spatial and temporal scales, with robust methods. Therefore, in principle, there are no limits to the complexity of spatial analysis techniques. It is worth highlighting their usefulness and effectiveness, particularly upon assessing multi-hazard associated with natural calamities [9] and analysing their impacts, in particular on structures and infrastructures located in areas potentially affected by such threats [10].

The GIS (Geographic Information System) is the ideal tool to implement geospatial analyses to address and solve problems characterized by multiple criteria, offering advanced query capabilities, area and distance measurements, overlays, proximity (buffers), and more [11]. Databases integrate both spatial and non-spatial information, which can be easily visualized. Users can interactively modify solutions, facilitating feasibility studies and territorial analysis [12, 13]. GIS provides powerful data input, storage memory, retrieval, and visualization tools for decision support, but its analysis, simulation, and reasoning functions are weak. For example, to solve complex spatial decision problems, other techniques or tools (e.g., decision support systems) need to be integrated with GIS [13, 14]: in this case, we can talk about a GIS-based approach.

In this framework, the use of GIS-based approaches is fundamental to evaluate and map the multi-hazard related to the natural phenomena affecting the territory, the main of which are earthquakes, landslides, and floods. The term "multi-hazard" refers to an "all-hazard-at-a-place" concept that can be classified using qualitative, semiquantitative, and quantitative perspectives [15, 16]. In Italy, many areas are exposed to multiple natural hazards, but in this Country a homogeneous and systematic multi-hazard analysis was performed just recently [10].

In this study, our focus is on hazard assessment and protection of Critical Infrastructures (CI) across the entire Italian territory. In this context, the protection of CI is a significant task [17]. Specifically, we considered the following networks: transport (roads, bridges/viaducts), gas transmission (pipelines, storage), and power transmission (lines, plants, and primary substations).

To perform the multi-hazard assessment and produce the desired results, we developed an original approach in which the GIS-based methods are coupled with a Multi-Criteria Evaluation (MCE) technique [14]. In particular, we chose the Weighted Linear Combination (WLC) as the decision rule to aggregate the data and weighing them on the basis of the authors' expert judgment [14]. Finally, we present the results obtained through a series of thematic maps made in GIS environment.

2 Materials and Methods

Hazard analysis requires a holistic approach, with specific techniques and suitable data necessary for an accurate assessment [6]. Threats can manifest as single events or as a combination of different hazards in the same place [4]. In these contexts, multi-hazard assessment becomes crucial. In Italy, one has to deal with a variety of natural threats and only through a multi-hazard and multi-risk assessment it is possible to develop effective strategies to address and mitigate the impacts of these threats on CI [7, 10].

There are many factors that contribute to the occurrence of dangerous phenomena, related both to the environmental context (topography, geomorphology, geology, soil, etc.) and to the anthropic activities (deforestation, road construction, urbanization, etc.). The causes for these risks and hazards can be meteorological or geophysical (e.g., floods or earthquakes).

There isn't a clear definition of multiple/multi- hazard. This term is often used to refer to all relevant hazards that can occur in a given area; while in the scientific context, it frequently refers to "more than one hazard". Due to their interrelationships, multiple hazards could lead to impacts greater than the sum of the effects of the single individual hazards. As a consequence of the former non additivity, multi-hazard should be considered in disaster risk assessment and management [3] and CI protection in general [7, 10].

To cope with this complexity, tools such as GIS and Multi-Criteria Evaluation (MCE) can be employed [14]. However, each tool has its limitations, as follows. GIS, which focuses on geographic and physical analysis, struggles to integrate decision-makers' preferences; while the MCE approach, which focuses on decision analysis and evaluation for alternatives based on values and preferences, lacks spatial data management. Their integration allows to deal effectively with the aforementioned issues. To this purpose, different types of threats were analysed in spatial terms, leveraging GIS to properly process spatial data and MCE to perform a comprehensive assessment [14, 18].

2.1 Hazards

The United Nations Disaster Risk Reduction Office (UNDRR) defines hazard as a phenomenon, human activity, or condition that may result in loss of life, injury or other health impact, damage to property, loss of livelihoods and services, social and economic hardship, or environmental damage. This event has a probability of occurring within a given period and in a given area and at a given intensity [19].

Every dangerous situation requires a specific approach with a proper analysis and specific data. Hazards can occur standalone or combined/co-existing in the same place. It is essential to consider multi-hazard assessment, which analyses several threats at the same time, ensuring careful and comprehensive assessment [9].

Hazard levels vary from place to place, so it is crucial to identify areas with similar levels of hazard.

Seismic Hazard. The seismic hazard of an area is given by the frequency and magnitude of the typical earthquakes that affect it, i.e. by its seismicity. This hazard assessment takes into account several factors, including the likelihood of occurrence of seismic events in the affected area. Seismic hazard reflects the frequency and intensity of seismic events in a given region: if earthquakes of large magnitude occur frequently over a certain period of time, the area will be regarded high seismic risk [20].

In 2004 the INGV (the Italian National Institute of Geophysics and Volcanology [21]) released the Seismic Hazard Map (MPS04) [22] (Fig. 1), which provides a picture of the most dangerous areas in Italy, based on the expected ground acceleration values in the next 50 years. The MPS04 map, with its thematization, offers a simple and direct image of the distribution of seismicity in the Italian national territory.

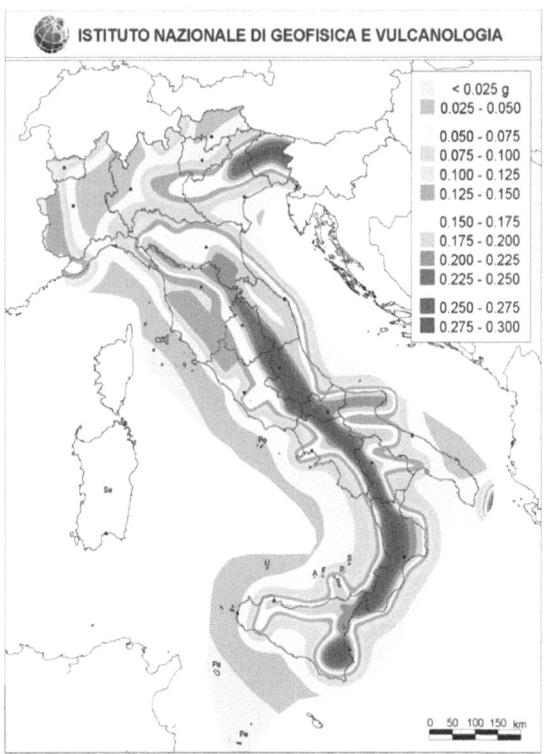

Fig. 1. Seismic hazard map MPS04 – INGV (2004). The seismic hazard is expressed in terms of PGA (Peak Ground Acceleration)

Flood Hazard. Every year, the Italian Institute for Environmental Protection and Research (ISPRA) [23], a public research body linked to the Ministry of the Environment and Energy Security (MASE), disseminates updated data showing how much the entire Italian territory is exposed to hydrogeological risk, due to landslides and floods [24]. Surveys and reports are mainly used to provide timely information to those who manage the territory, technicians, and policymakers, and in this way incentivize interventions to reduce risks.

In general, Italy, compared to several other European Countries, is naturally exposed to the risk of floods due to its geomorphological characteristics. In recent decades, this condition has worsened with the expansion of urban settlements and industrial areas that have covered a substantial part of the land. Imperviousness decreases the soil's ability to absorb rain and therefore causes the runoff of large amounts of water in areas where structures and infrastructures are located [24].

ISPRA has identified three possible scenarios related to flood hazard (Fig. 2): i) Low Probability Hazard (LPH) areas can be affected by floods with a return frequency of more than 200 years (in hydrology the return time is the average time between the occurrence of two successive events of equal or greater magnitude, and is used to express a probability); ii) Medium Probability Hazard (MPH) areas, between 100 and 200 years;

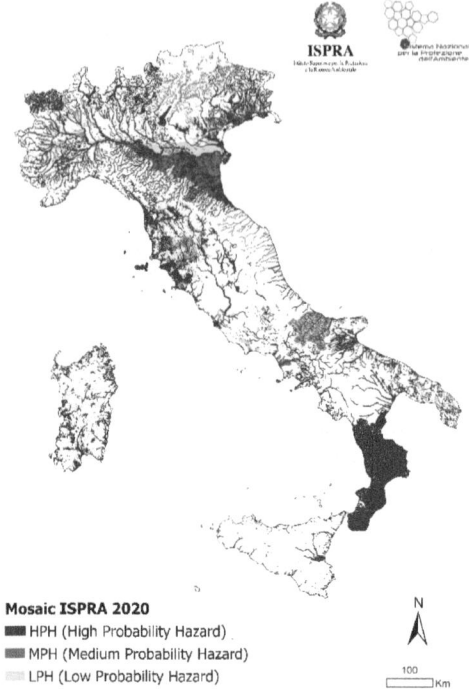

Fig. 2. Flood hazard Areas – Mosaic ISPRA (2020)

iii) High Probability Hazard (HPH) areas, between 20 and 50 years. 14% of the Italian territory is in low-hazard areas, 10% in medium-hazard areas, and 5.4% in high-hazard areas. The latest data available (2020) are fully accessible through the IdroGEO web platform [25, 26].

Landslides Hazard. Italy is a Country where exposure to hydrogeological catastrophes is particularly high. Landslides, which are extremely widespread throughout the national territory, are the natural disasters that occur most frequently and, after earthquakes, cause the greatest number of victims and damage to residential areas, infrastructures, environmental, historical, and cultural assets [24]. At the national level, ISPRA has created, in collaboration with the Regions and the Autonomous Provinces (according to the Italian Law 132/2016), the Inventory of Landslides in Italy (IFFI) [27], i.e. the national official repository of landslide events. The IFFI is a fundamental knowledge tool used to assess landslide hazard in Hydrogeological Plans (PAI), for the preliminary design of protection interventions devoted to the territory and the infrastructures, as well as for the drafting of Civil Protection Emergency Plans. Currently, the Inventory has over 620,000 landslides registered. The landslide hazard map on the entire national territory (Fig. 3) has been obtained as the mosaic of the hazard areas of the different hydrogeological plans (PAI), through the definition of 5 hazard classes: very high P4, high P3, medium P2, moderate P1 and attention areas AA. The latest data available (2020–2021) are fully accessible through the IdroGEO web platform [25, 26].

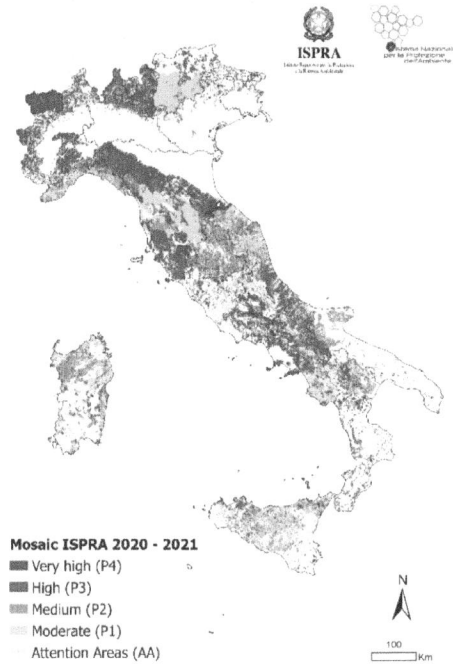

Fig. 3. Landslide hazard PAI – Mosaic ISPRA (2020–2021)

2.2 Datasets

To carry out the geospatial multi-hazard analyses described in the following, various sets of open data, i.e. publicly available, were used. Regarding seismic and hydrogeological hazards, the following data were used:

1. Seismic hazard: map of the Italian seismic hazard (MPS04) [22], Source: INGV;
2. Landslide hazard: national mosaic 2020-2021 of Hydrogeological Plans (PAI). Source: IdroGEO [26];
3. Flood Hazard: national mosaic 2020 of scenarios according to the Italian Legislative Decree 49/2010. Source: IdroGEO [26].

Then, regarding the infrastructures under analysis, the following datasets have been selected and acquired:

a. Transport Network: roads, bridges and viaducts (source: OpenStreetMap, OSM [28])
b. Gas transmission network: pipelines and storage (source: S&P Platts [29])
c. Power transmission network: lines, plants, and primary substations, (source: S&P Platts [29])

The information layers listed at point a) have been acquired (in vector shapefile format) from the Geofabrik website [30], subdivided into five macro-regions (North-West, North-East, Centre, South, and Major Islands), and made available under an open

2.3   Multi-Criteria Evaluation (MCE) Analysis

The Multi-Criteria Evaluation (MCE) analysis is a widely used methodology for assessing problems characterized by multiple criteria or factors, as this method allows quantitative and qualitative criteria to be incorporated into the evaluation of multiple alternatives [12].

Multi-criteria analysis procedures in a GIS environment require to consider several geographically defined alternatives and a series of evaluation criteria represented by geospatial data, such as the three territorial hazards considered in the present work. The main goal is to combine the criteria maps based on the values attributed to the criteria themselves and the preferences of the decision-makers, using a specific decision rule, also known as a combination rule [13].

The MCE adopts two types of procedures for the assessment of decision-making problems. The first involves Boolean overlay, where all criteria are evaluated against suitability thresholds in order to produce Boolean maps, which are obtained as a combination of the input information layers, using the logical operators intersection (AND) and union (OR). The second is a Weighted Linear Combination (WLC) [14, 31] where attributes are weighted according to their importance, if there are more than one, and they must be considered contextually to assess hazardousness. The results consist of multi-attribute geospatial features with final scores: the higher the score, the more hazardous the area. Only the WLC procedure was applied in this study.

Certain limitations are emerged in the WLC applicability in situations involving a wide range of evaluation criteria. In these situations, key aspects of the decision problem may be better specified using more sophisticated language quantifiers or fuzzy operators, such as "most criteria must be met" or "at least 80% of criteria must be met". This would require an extension of the traditional WLC, for example by using the OWA (Ordered Weighted Averaging) method [32] or the AHP (Analytical Hierarchy Process) approach [33]. In the present case study, however, limiting ourselves to only three factors (earthquakes, floods, and landslides), the WLC methodology proved to be effective and OWA or AHP were not considered.

2.4   Multi-hazard of CI Across the Italian Territory

In this section we focused on the application of the methodologies and approaches previously described. Specifically, a series of multi-hazard maps have been produced, through the GIS processing of the data described in Sect. 2.2, by exploiting the workflow depicted in Fig. 4.

Through the QGIS v.3.34 software, the various geospatial data described above (Sect. 2.2) have been structured and organized, defining the reference system of the project (RDN2008 - EPSG: 6706) [34] in a coherent and homogeneous way for all the information layers used.

All input data were pre-processed, in order to obtain for each of them a unique information layer at national level containing all the attributes useful for the analysis.

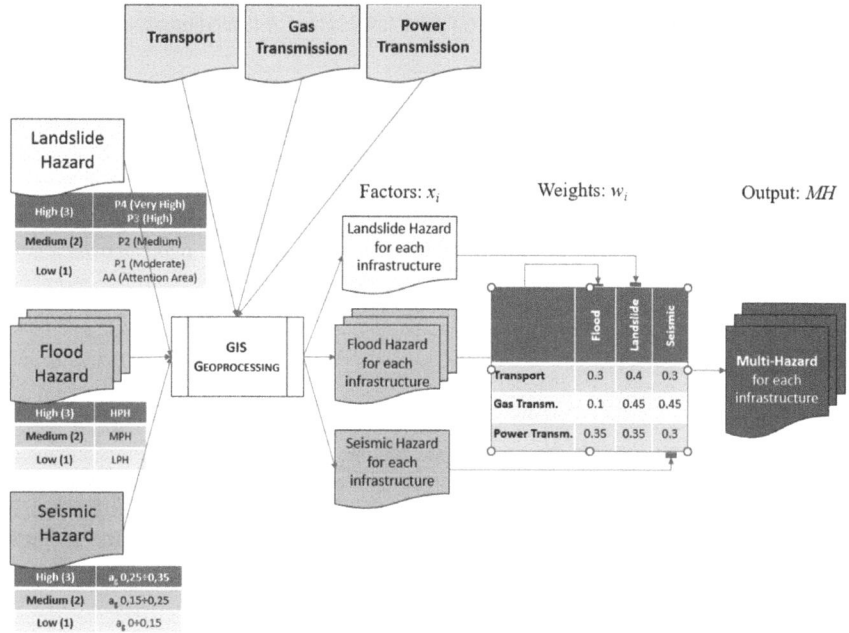

Fig. 4. Workflow implemented to evaluate and map multi-hazard for CI

The next step involved the GIS operation of intersection between each layer of the infrastructure assets (roads, bridges/viaducts, gas pipelines, gas storage, power lines, power primary substations, power plants) with those of the three hazards considered. The objective of this representation is to assign a specific single-hazard value (reclassified on three levels: low = 1, medium = 2, and high = 3) to the infrastructures of interest (Table 1), considering the three types of hazard factors most relevant in the Italian territorial context: seismicity, landslides, and floods.

Then, specific weights were assigned to each hazard. These weights were determined based on expert judgment provided by the authors and an analysis of the overall condition of the infrastructures. Additionally, the weighting values were considered based on how each type of critical infrastructure could be affected by the three types of hazard factors. For example, roads are equally susceptible to be damaged by floods, landslides, and earthquakes, so the weights were set with similar values. In contrast, pipelines are more vulnerable to landslides and earthquakes, so those weights were set higher than for floods. In summary, the weights defined for landslides, floods, and seismic activity are reported in the Table 2.

Then, by using the WLC methodology [31], it has been possible to assign to each infrastructure element its specific value of multi-hazard, according to the three classes defined (low, medium, and high). In mathematical terms, the approach implemented to assign a multi-hazard value to the *j-th* infrastructural element can be expressed as reported in the following equation:

$$MH_j = \sum_{i=1}^{n} \left(w_{ji} \cdot x_i \right) \tag{1}$$

Table 1. Single hazard h_i reclassification on three levels (low = 1, medium:2, and high = 3)

Flood[a]	Single Hazard hf	Landslide[b]	Single Hazard hl	Earthquake[c]	Single Hazard hs
HPH - High Probability Hazard	3	P4 (Very High) P3 (High)	3	a_g 0.25 ÷ 0.35	3
MPH - Medium Probability Hazard	2	P2 (medium)	2	a_g 0.15 ÷ 0.25	2
LPH - Low Probability Hazard	1	P1 (Moderate AA (Attention Area)	1	a_g 0 ÷ 0.15	1

a Classification of areas prone to hydraulic hazard, drawn up by the District Basin Authorities on the basis of three scenarios defined by Legislative Decree 49/2010.
b Classification of areas prone to landslide hazard according to the Hydrogeological Plans (PAI) issued by the District Basin Authorities,
c Acceleration values with a probability of exceeding 10% in 50 years.

Table 2. Weights w_i assigned for each specific hazard

	Flood wf	Landslide w_l	Seismic w_s
Roads/Bridges	0.3	0.4	0.3
Gas Pipelines	0.1	0.45	0.45
Power Transmission	0.35	0.35	0.3

where: n is the total number of the factors considered (in the present case three: flood, landslide, earthquake); x_i is the value of the i-th single hazard (1, 2 or 3); w_i is the weight of the i-th factor (according to Table 2).

Finally, a new attribute containing the multi-hazard values calculated according to the Eq. 1 was created for each infrastructure GIS layer. Thus, it was possible to thematize each GIS layer on the basis of this attribute and produce the thematic maps of multi-hazard. The maps obtained represent the multi-hazard assessment for the different types of CI networks considered (transport network, gas transmission network and power transmission network).

3 Results

In this Section are presented some of the most representative thematic maps produced, in which are depicted the results obtained, providing an overall representation of the Italian situation for the CI networks analysed.

As far as road network situation is concerned, Fig. 5 shows the territorial distribution of 172,305 Italian bridges/viaducts classified according to their respective multi-hazard values: 72,426 (42%) high, 18,236 (11%) medium and 81,643 (47%) low. In Fig. 6 are mapped the 5,958 km of gas pipelines, classified likewise the previous case: 3,170 km (53%) high, 606 km (10%) medium and 2,182 km (37%) low. Finally, concerning the power transmission network, in Fig. 7 are represented 3,632 primary substations: 109 (3%) high, 1,162 (32%) medium and 2,361 (65%) low.

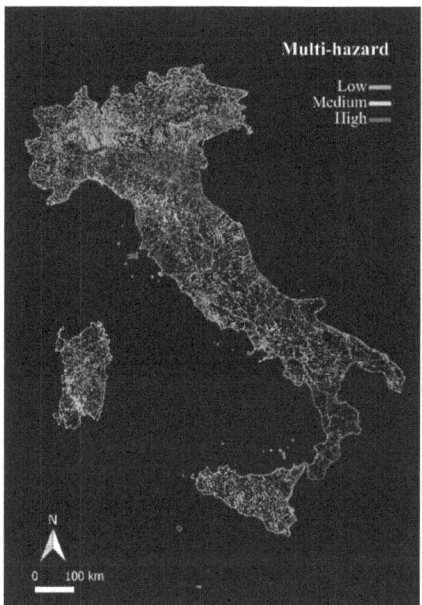

Fig. 5. Multi-hazard of Italian bridges and viaducts.

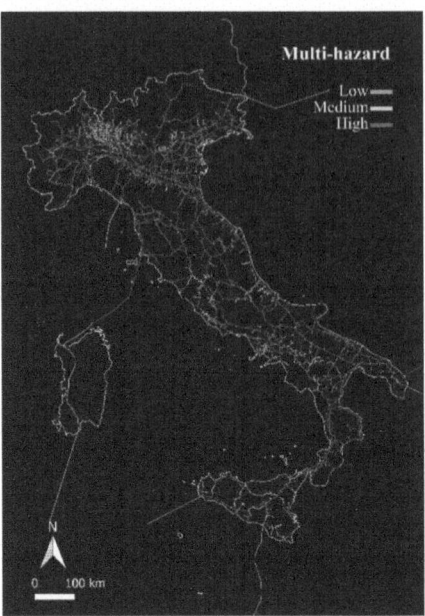

Fig. 6. Multi-hazard of Italian gas pipelines.

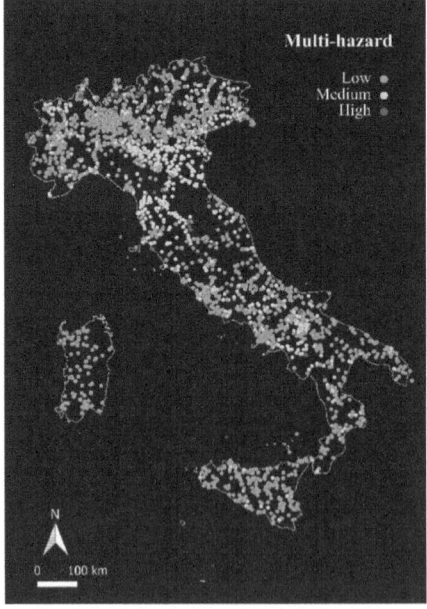

Fig. 7. Multi-hazard of Italian primary substations.

4   Discussion

Generally speaking, Italy is a territory characterized by multiple hazards. Rarely one may focus on a specific type, only. Therefore, multi-hazard analysis is strictly required. This work reflects that perspective. The following paragraphs deal with the specific features related to the different types of infrastructure.

4.1   Road Network

Concerning bridges and viaducts, the areas classified as "high multi-hazard" are mostly located in Calabria, Valle d'Aosta, Emilia-Romagna and Tuscany regions (Fig. 5). In particular, in Calabria this derives (as expected) from the very high levels of ground acceleration, observed in the Seismic Hazard Map (Fig. 1) and a predominantly medium and high value of flood and landslide hazard (Fig. 2 and Fig. 3) over a large part of the regional territory. Then, the Valle d'Aosta region exhibits high levels of hazard values. In this case, a predominant factor is represented by the contribution of landslides, with over 80% of the entire regional territory characterized by P3 and P4 risk areas (very high). More in detail, 2,671.7 km^2 (about 82%) of the region shows high and very high landslide hazard values on a total area of about 3,261 km^2. Regarding bridges and viaducts, the proposed risk assessment procedure needs to consider and integrate the Italian Guidelines for the safety of bridges. The Ministerial Decree No. 204 of 1st July 2022 adopted the "Guidelines for risk classification and management, safety assessment and monitoring of existing bridges" [35]. The Decree aims at extending the guidelines to the entire national network to grant homogeneity in the classification of risks. The most innovative aspect is the multi-level approach: in particular, a fundamental step of the approach includes the need to census and catalogue all the bridges in Italy, with unambiguous and objective procedures, thus inserting them into a single database. Due to the large number of bridges and the impossibility of intervening on all of them in the short term (for economic and logistical reasons), GIS methodologies are essential to support these first level of analysis adequately. Therefore, the approach developed and described in this work can represent a valuable tool to achieve the objectives of the guidelines.

The other areas that show high multi-hazard values are those related to Emilia Romagna and Tuscany regions. The individual hazard maps (Fig. 1, Fig. 2 and Fig. 3) show, on average, high hazard values for all the three hazards considered in this work. In particular, it is possible to distinguish among different areas: i) the Pianura Padana, where the flood hazard is the principal factor determining the final multi-hazard score for bridges, ii) the Central "Appennino" area with landslide e seismic hazards factors and iii) the northern area of Tuscany where all three hazards contribute significantly to the final multi-hazard score.

4.2   Gas Transmission Network

Focusing on the multi-hazard assessment of the Italian gas transmission network (Fig. 6), it is worth noting that more than half of the network do exhibit a high multi-hazard score. Those enhanced values are due to the assignment of higher weights to landslides (0.45) and earthquakes (0.45).

Recent data published by Snam S.p.A. [36] show that Italy imported 53.3 billion cubic metres of gas, between January and mid-November 2023. Of these huge amount, 20.2 billion m^3 came from Algeria, 8.7 billion m^3 from Azerbaijan, 5.9 billion m^3 from Northern Europe, 2.4 billion m^3 from Russia, and 2.2 billion m^3 from Libya. Imports from Russia, therefore, accounted for 4.5% in the first ten and a half months of 2023 compared to 37.9% from Algeria, 16.3% from Azerbaijan, 11.1% from Northern Europe, and 4.1% from Libya. These data are useful to drive the attention on specific areas. More in particular, the assessment focuses on the areas where there are the interconnections with the external gas pipelines. Those connections branch off from Sicily and Puglia, and from Friuli-Venezia Giulia to south and north respectively. In those cases, the multi hazard approach reveals its value.

The proposed approach gives insight also for the rest of the Italian gas network, which crosses a large part of the Italian peninsula and is located along the ridge of the Apennines; this characteristic should be taken into consideration. In fact, the network, is a unique 687 km pipeline, manged by Snam S.p.A. [36] (called "Rete Adriatica"), starting from Brindisi, in Puglia, and arriving at Minerbio, in Emilia-Romagna. That network is divided into five parts, crossing ten administrative regions, and running parallel to numerous faults or crossing them. It intercepts areas of high seismic risk in Central Italy (Fig. 1), where earthquakes of high intensity have occurred in recent years (Umbria and Marche 1997, L'Aquila 2009, Seismic sequence of Central Italy 2016–2017). Moreover, in the forthcoming years, it is planned to expand the "Adriatic Network" by the construction of a new gas pipeline. This new branch will start from Sulmona (L'Aquila) and will arrive close to Bologna, in Minerbio. It will touch five administrative regions (Abruzzo, Marche, Umbria, Toscana and Emilia-Romagna), for a total length of 425 km. The purpose is to increase transport capacity along the south-north axis of 10 billion cubic metres per year [36].

4.3   Power Transmission Network

Finally, considering the case study of the power transmission line, as an example, we have shown the multi-hazard map of the Italian primary substations (Fig. 7). Threats to the electricity grid can mainly result from critical meteo-climatic conditions, including those due to flooding that can impact power stations or power plants [37].

For electrical substations located in areas where severe conditions of flooding may occur, particular attention is required to the resulting impacts and how to counteract them. For newly built substations, it is therefore crucial, since from the feasibility phase of the project, to examine whether the interested area is prone to multi-hazard or not [38]. On the other hand, for existing substations, design and retrofit measures can be adopted to mitigate the negative impacts and increase their resilience [39].

In the case analysed in the present work (Fig. 7), the most critical areas are located in the centre-northern and northern of Italy, while high average values of multi-hazard are also observed in the Campania region. In these areas about 2% of power transmission assets have got the maximum value of the multi-hazard score. In such cases, the assets may be impacted by all the three types of considered hazards. About 29% of the assets show a score of 0.65; in these cases, two hazards need to be considered. However, most of the assets (about the 65%) are interested by a single hazard scenario, only.

5   Conclusions

Climate change is accelerating the temporal frequency of several catastrophic natural events: in our specific case, floods and landslides triggered by heavy rainfall. These events, provide clear evidence of the destructive power of nature along with earthquakes, which are not due to climate changes but purely geological cause.

The capability to superimpose information, analyse the spatial relationships between phenomena described on databases of different origins, and process large amounts of information is extremely important to highlight areas where specific conditions are present simultaneously. These are just some potentialities that a GIS system and spatial analysis can provide to contextualise the various types of hazards. The implementation of analysis tools and multi-criteria procedures specific to different territorial contexts can also facilitate a multidisciplinary approach to hazard analysis.

The combined developed approach, based on GIS and MCE, demonstrated to be able to provide an effective support in dealing with issues related to hazard analysis and mapping of various CI networks, given the intrinsic hydrogeological and seismic characteristics of the Italian territory. It allows to manage and analyse cross-referenced geoinformation on the different hazards. Furthermore, a useful systematic organization of the different information layers, (employing specific weights) allowed to evaluate the multi-hazard of the different types of CI. This resulted into the overall mapping, of the areas potentially exposed to greater multiple hazards, at national level,

As future developments, we are planning to perform the systematics and integration of further data, which, combined with the vulnerability and the exposure of specific CI, will allow the estimation of the overall risk for other networks: electrical distribution grids, water pipelines, gas distribution pipelines, et al.. Eventually, the impact of additional natural hazards, such as volcanic eruptions, fires, and tsunamis, will be accounted for. Another recurring phenomenon to be further considered is heat waves, which pose a significant risk to CI. These extreme events can cause damage to various sectors, including electricity, digital infrastructure, and transport. High temperatures can overload electrical grids, leading to blackouts and service interruptions. Additionally, digital infrastructures, such as data centres, can experience malfunctions due to overheating. The approach presented can be exploited to assess and enable preventive measures to be taken to protect infrastructures and population. Finally, more sophisticated MCE techniques will be investigated, such as the OWA (Ordered Weighted Averaging) [32] or the AHP (Analytical Hierarchy Process) [33].

Acknowledgments. This study was supported by the National Centre on HPC, Big Data and Quantum Computing project funded by Italian MUR (Ministry for Universities and Research) in the context of the National Recovery and Resilience Plan-Decreto Direttoriale n.3138 December 16th, 2021. Any opinion expressed in the paper does not necessarily reflect the view of the funders. The work, moreover, was carried-out in the framework of the internship programme set-up by ENEA and University of Rome "Sapienza", Bachelor Degree in "Geographical Sciences for environment and health".

Disclosure of Interests. The authors have no competing interests to declare that are relevant to the content of this article.

References

1. IPCC, 2023: Sections. In Climate Change 2023: Synthesis Report; Contribution of Working Groups I, II and III to the Sixth Assessment Report of the Intergovernmental Panel on Climate Change; Core Writing Team, Lee, H., Romero, J., (eds.) IPCC: Geneva, Switzerland, pp. 35–115 (2023). https://doi.org/10.59327/IPCC/AR6-9789291691647

2. UNEP Department of Economic and Social Affairs—Sustainable Development Agenda 21. https://sdgs.un.org/publications/agenda21. Accessed 2 Mar 2024

3. Kappes, M.S., Keiler, M., von Elverfeldt, K., Glade, T.: Challenges of analyzing multi-hazard risk: a review. Nat. Hazards **64**, 1925–1958 (2012)

4. Kappes, M., Keiler, M., Glade, T.: From single- to multi-hazard risk analyses: a concept addressing emerging challenges. In: Malet, J.P., Glade, T., Casagli, N., (eds.) Proceedings of the Mountains Risks: Bringing Science to Society, Florence, Italy, 1 January 2010, CERG Editions: Strasbourg, France, pp. 351–356 (2010)

5. Tarvainen, T., Jarva, J., Greiving, S.: Spatial pattern of Hazards and Hazard Interactions in Europe. In: Schmidt-Thomé, P., (ed.) Natural and Technological Hazards and Risks Affecting the Spatial Development of European Regions; Special paper 42, Geological Survey of Finland: Espoo, Finland, pp. 83–91 (2006). ISBN 978–951–690–944–1

6. Carpignano, A., Golia, E., Di Mauro, C., Bouchon, S., Nordvik, J.: A methodological approach for the definition of multi-risk maps at regional level: first application. J. Risk Res. **12**, 513–534 (2009). https://doi.org/10.1080/13669870903050269

7. Pollino, M.; Cappucci, S.; Pesaresi, C.; Farrace, M.G.; Della Morte, L., Vegliante, G.: Multi-hazard analysis and mapping of infrastructure systems at national level using gis techniques: preliminary results. In: Gervasi, O., Murgante, B., Misra, S., Rocha, A.M.A.C., Garau, C., (eds.) Computational Science and Its Applications—ICCSA 2022 Workshops; Lecture Notes in Computer, Science, vol. 13377, pp. 153–168. Springer International Publishing, Cham (2022). ISBN 978–3–031–10535–7

8. de Smith Michael, J., Goodchild Michael, F., Longley Paul & Associates: Geospatial Analysis: A Comprehensive Guide to Principles Techniques and Software Tools - 6th edition. The Winchelsea Press (2021)

9. Bell, R., Glade, T.: Multi-hazard analysis in natural risk assessments. Risk Anal. **9**, 1 (2004). https://doi.org/10.2495/978-1-84564-650-9/01

10. Cappucci, S., Pollino, M., Farrace, M.G., Della Morte, L., Baiocchi, V.: Infrastructure impact assessment through multi-hazard analysis at different scales: the 26 november 2022 flood event on the island of ischia and debris management. Land **13**(4), 500 (2024). https://doi.org/10.3390/land13040500

11. Mitchell, A.: The ESRI Guide to GIS Analysis, vol. 2. Spatial and statistical measurements, ESRI Press, Redlands, California, USA (2005)

12. Malczewski, J.: GIS and Multicriteria Decision Analysis. John Wiley & Sons (1999)

13. Triantaphyllou, E.: Multi-Criteria Decision Making: A Comparative Study. Kluwer Academic Publishers, Dordrecht (2000). ISBN 0-7923-6607-7
14. Malczewski, J., Rinner, C.: Multicriteria Decision Analysis in Geographic Information Science. Springer, New York (2015).https://doi.org/10.1007/978-3-540-74757-4, ISBN978-3-540-86875-0
15. Altenbach, T.J.: A Comparison of Risk Assessment Techniques from Qualitative to Quantitative. Lawrence Livermore National Lab. (LLNL), Livermore, CA, USA (1995)
16. Wang, J., He, Z., Weng, W.: A review of the research into the relations between hazards in multi-hazard risk analysis. Nat. Hazards **104**, 2003–2026 (2020). https://doi.org/10.1007/s11069-020-04259-3
17. Kozik, R., Choraś, M., Flizikowski, A., Theocharidou, M., Rosato, V., Rome, E.: Advanced services for critical infrastructures protection. J. Ambient Intell. Human Comput. **6**, 783–795 (2015). https://doi.org/10.1007/s12652-015-0283-x
18. Skilodimou, H.D., et al.: Multi-hazard assessment modeling via multi-criteria analysis and GIS: a case study. Environ. Earth Sci. **78**, 47 (2019). https://doi.org/10.1007/s12665-018-8003-419
19. UNDRR, Hazard definition and classification review: Technical report (2020). https://www.undrr.org/publication/hazard-definition-and-classification-review-technical-report. Accessed 6 May 2024
20. Stucchi, M., Meletti, C., Montaldo Falero, V., Crowley, H., Calvi, G., Boschi, E.: Seismic hazard assessment (2003–2009) for the italian building code. Bull. Seismol. Soc. Am. **101**, 1885–1911 (2011). https://doi.org/10.1785/0120100130
21. INGV Home Page. https://www.ingv.it/. Accessed 25 Nov 2024
22. INGV, MPS04. http://zonesismiche.mi.ingv.it/. Accessed 25 Nov 2024
23. ISPRA Home Page. https://www.isprambiente.gov.it/it. Accessed 25 Nov 2024
24. Trigila, A., Ladanza, C., Bussettini, M., Lastoria, B.: Dissesto Idrogeologico in Italia: Pericolosità e Indicatori Di Rischio; Ed. 2021 ISPRA, pp. 1–232. ISPRA, Rome, Italy (2021)
25. Iadanza, C., Trigila, A., Starace, P., Dragoni, A., Biondo, T., Roccisano, M.: IdroGEO: A collaborative web mapping application based on REST API services and open data on landslides and floods in Italy. ISPRS Int. J. Geo Inf. **10**(2), 89 (2021). https://doi.org/10.3390/ijgi10020089
26. ISPRA idrogeo. https://idrogeo.isprambiente.it/app/. Accessed 25 Nov 2024
27. IFFI, Inventario dei Fenomeni Franosi in Italia. https://idrogeo.isprambiente.it/app/iffi. Accessed 25 Nov 2024
28. OpenStreetMaps Home Page. https://www.openstreetmap.org/. Accessed 25 Nov 2024
29. S&P Platts, Power transmission network data and gas transmission network data. https://www.spglobal.com/commodityinsights/en/products-services/maps-and-geospatial. Accessed 25 Nov 2024
30. Geofabrik, OSM data. https://download.geofabrik.de/. Accessed 25 Nov 2024
31. Modica, G., et al.: Land suitability evaluation for agro-forestry: definition of a web-based multi-criteria spatial decision support system (MC-SDSS): Preliminary Results. In: Gervasi, O., et al. (eds.) Computational Science and Its Applications -- ICCSA 2016. Lecture Notes in Computer Science, vol 9788. Springer, Cham (2016). https://doi.org/10.1007/978-3-319-42111-7_31
32. Yager, R.R.: On ordered weighted averaging aggregation operators in multi-criteria decision making. IEEE Trans. Syst. Man Cybernet (1988)
33. Saaty, T.L.: The Analytic Hierarchy Process: Planning, Priority Setting. Resource Allocation. McGraw-Hill, New York (1980)
34. EPSG, Reference system. https://epsg.io/6706. Accessed on November 25th, 2024

35. Ministerial Decree 204 of 1 July 2022, Guidelines for risk classification and management, safety assessment and monitoring of existing bridges. https://www.mit.gov.it/normativa/dec reto-ministeriale-numero-204-del-1-luglio-2022. Accessed 25 Nov 2024

36. SNAM S.p.A., Gas imports in 2023. https://www.snam.it/it/trasporto/dati-operativi-business/2_Andamento_dal_2005/. Accessed 25 Nov 2024

37. Rebolini, M., Pelliccione, G., Licciardi, V.: The risks for electricity stations associated with flooding, chapter of the AEIT magazine (Italian Association of Electrical Engineering, Electronics, Automation, IT and Telecommunications) – Title: Resilience of electrical systems, vol. 103, no. 7/8 (2016)

38. Salman, A.M., Li, Y.: Multihazard risk assessment of electric power systems. J. Struct. Eng. **143**(3), 04016198 (2017)

39. Tofani, A., et al.: Operational resilience metrics for complex inter-dependent electrical networks. Appl. Sci. **11**(13), 5842 (2021). https://doi.org/10.3390/app11135842

Machine Learning Techniques for Anomaly Detection in the Hydra Testbed: A Data-Driven Defense Strategy

Valeria Bonagura$^{(\boxtimes)}$ (ID), Jacopo Pisani, Alessio Ferrato, Chiara Foglietta, Graziana Cavone, and Federica Pascucci

University Roma Tre, 00146 Rome, Italy
valeria.bonagura@uniroma3.it

Abstract. As cyber-attacks targeting Critical Infrastructures become increasingly sophisticated, successfully identifying breaches has become more challenging. Failure to detect intrusions can undermine the confidence in security services, compromising data confidentiality, integrity, and availability.

This paper introduces the HydraCPS dataset, a novel resource designed to detect cyber-physical attacks on water distribution systems. Generated through simulations on the Hydra testbed, which emulates a real-world water distribution system, the dataset includes ground truth labels essential for supervised training. Intrusion detection is framed as a classification problem, employing various Artificial Intelligence techniques to distinguish between nominal and attack conditions. The comprehensively labeled HydraCPS dataset provides a robust foundation for IDS evaluation.

The Hydra testbed's detailed simulation of a water distribution system makes it an effective tool for identifying attacks on critical infrastructure. This enhances the relevance and applicability of the HydraCPS dataset in developing and evaluating IDS models aimed at protecting vital systems. Our goal is to facilitate the design of efficient and effective intrusion detection systems by leveraging new IDS datasets and utilizing the detailed and realistic attack simulations provided by HydraCPS for improved model training and evaluation.

1 Introduction

Industrial Control Systems (ICS) are integral components of our modern infrastructure. They are used in a wide range of industries, including manufacturing, energy, water treatment, and transportation, to name just a few. These systems are responsible for monitoring and controlling physical processes, such as the flow of water through a dam, the temperature in a manufacturing plant, or the operation of a power grid.

In Critical Infrastructures (CI) context, we can think of ICSs as the "brains" behind them. They receive data from sensors, analyze it to understand the system's current state, and then send commands to actuators to control the system's operation. For example, in a power plant, an ICS might receive temperature data from a sensor in a boiler, determine if the temperature is too high, and then send a command to a valve to release some steam and lower the temperature.

The transition of ICS from traditional serial bus systems to modern TCP/IP-based systems has allowed them to be connected to existing data networks, making them more accessible and easier to manage. However, this connectivity also means they are now accessible via the Internet, introducing new vulnerabilities [19].

Cybercriminals have quickly exploited these vulnerabilities, leading to increased cyber-attacks targeting ICS and the critical infrastructure they control [32]. These attacks can cause significant disruption and damage, affecting the targeted organisation and the wider community that depends on the services provided by the critical infrastructure.

As a result, there is a growing recognition of the need for enhanced security measures to protect ICS and the critical infrastructure they control. This includes technical measures, such as firewalls and intrusion detection systems, and organizational measures, such as security policies and incident response plans.

Cyber threats affecting CI can originate from various sources and manifest in different forms. Extensive research has been conducted to address these cyber-attacks and vulnerabilities within CIs. Some researchers have focused on attacks targeting communication protocols, while others have investigated software and hardware components vulnerabilities [39].

Cyber-attacks on ICSs can be broadly categorized into two main classes [40]:

1. *Attacks on the Information Technology (IT) Layer:* These attacks target the digital infrastructure within the ICS, exploiting weaknesses in network protocols, software applications, and hardware components.
2. *Semantic Attacks:* These attacks exploit knowledge about the controlled physical processes and directly target ICS's operational technology (OT) aspects. Semantic attacks are particularly challenging to detect as they do not necessarily violate protocol specifications or generate abnormal network traffic, making traditional security approaches less effective.

While cybersecurity research within the IT domain has matured, the direct application of these approaches to ICS, is often impractical due to the substantial differences between ICS and IT systems [23]. For example, high network throughput is critical in IT, and network delays are generally acceptable and can be mitigated by increasing computing resources. In contrast, ICS's OT realm cannot tolerate even brief maintenance shutdowns or service restarts due to their potential significant societal and economic impacts. Currently, IT tools do not guarantee the three basic security properties of data and IT services - confidentiality, integrity, and availability - in the industrial domain. Unlike IT systems, which typically prioritize security objectives in the order of confidentiality, integrity, and availability (i.e., CIA paradigm), ICSs prioritize availability foremost, followed by integrity and confidentiality (i.e., AIC paradigm) [17].

The contrast in priority objectives leads to distinct cybersecurity strategies in the IT and Operational Technology (OT) domains. While the primary goal in IT is safeguarding data, in OT, the focus shifts to protecting industrial plants and critical assets. Moreover, modern industrial systems frequently have numerous connections between ICS and Information and Communication Technology (ICT) networks, increasing the risk of severe cyber-attacks. This interconnectedness necessitates robust Intrusion Detection Systems (IDS) specifically tailored for ICS.

Intrusion Detection Systems (IDS) play a crucial role in safeguarding ICS by passively monitoring events on computer networks and analyzing them for indications of potential incidents. IDSs typically consist of three main phases [16]:

1. *Data Collection:* Gathering various data types from the monitored system, such as system calls, logs, and network flows.
2. *Selection of Features:*Selecting relevant attributes necessary for decision-making and representing them as a feature vector.
3. *Decision Engine:* Processing the collected data, represented as a feature vector, to identify potentially intrusive activities.

IDS can be categorized based on detection techniques [11]:

- *Signature-based IDS:* These systems monitor all packets and events within the system, comparing them against a database of known attack signatures. They are highly effective at detecting known threats but are limited in identifying unknown threats and zero-day attacks.
- *Anomaly-based IDS:* These systems identify deviations from a system's normal behaviour model, classifying significant deviations as anomalies. They can detect new and previously unknown attacks but often suffer from a high false alarm rate.

These systems can be model-based [30] or data-driven [8]:

- *Model-based IDS* Use historical data to identify deviations. State-estimation techniques like the Kalman filter and χ^2-detector are crucial in cyber-physical intrusion detection for safety-critical Cyber-Physical Systems (CPS) like industrial control systems and power grids.
- *Data-driven IDS:* Rely on predefined behavior models to detect anomalies.

Stealthy attacks, a particularly insidious cyber threat, involve adversaries crafting actions to evade detection [37]. Integrating artificial intelligence (AI) introduces both opportunities and challenges in combating such attacks [27]. AI can empower attackers to exploit vulnerabilities without deep system knowledge, necessitating advanced detection and mitigation strategies that leverage AI to protect ICS from sophisticated threats.

Supervised machine learning techniques have shown superior detection performance against existing attack generation schemes [18]. AI offers significant opportunities to enhance efficiency, performance, and resilience within critical infrastructure by autonomously identifying cyber-attack patterns, detecting malware, and enabling better decision-making for defensive responses. However, cyber attackers can also leverage these same AI capabilities to develop advanced techniques, manipulate defender responses, create new malware, conduct network reconnaissance, and exploit social engineering tactics to infiltrate systems.

In supervised machine learning, one of the substantial technical hurdles is the creation of labelled datasets that can accurately represent various types of attacks. The process usually involves simulating attacks on the system, a practice that could potentially jeopardize the system's safety and integrity. Due to these risks, it's a common strategy to train models using data from nominal conditions [4]. This approach, while safer, may not fully capture the dynamics of an actual attack scenario. To address this, it's recommended to employ realistic testbeds for simulating system dynamics. These testbeds provide a controlled and safe environment where system behaviours under different conditions, including attack scenarios, can be studied without causing harm to the actual system. This approach allows for generating more representative datasets, thereby improving the robustness and accuracy of the supervised machine-learning models.

In this work, we utilize the HYDRA testbed, which was developed for conducting experiments, studies, and simulations on the security of Cyber-Physical Systems, to generate the HydraCPS dataset. The HYDRA testbed is part of the Models for Critical Infrastructure Protection (MCIPLab) laboratory at the Department of Civil Engineering, Informatics, and Aeronautical Technologies at the University of Roma Tre.

The HydraCPS dataset includes ground truth labels that indicate nominal (normal operation) and attack classes for binary classification. To demonstrate the effectiveness of the HydraCPS dataset in detecting intrusions, we employed several popular machine-learning methods. Our focus on binary classification aims to justify the results and ensure a clear distinguishability between normal operations and attacks.

2   Related Works

Traditional IT techniques like network traffic analysis are often enhanced in cyber-physical systems protection by monitoring physical systems through sensor readings and control inputs. Anomaly-based intrusion detection systems (IDS) are crucial in establishing a baseline for *normal* behaviour and flagging deviations as [31]. Specifically, it is possible to analyse sensor readings and control inputs to detect anomalies, such as altered sensor set-points or injected fake data. SCADA systems, integral to ICS architecture, collect data from the entire system, facilitating the integration of these specialized IDS.

Using data from sensors and actuators verifies correct system operation, providing more comprehensive and accurate threat detection. While network-based IDS have been extensively researched, there's less exploration into using machine learning algorithms for fault detection in these specialized IDS. Leveraging advanced data analysis techniques is essential for enhancing the detection capabilities of cyber-physical systems.

[7] introduced an IDS based on voltage measurement data to detect intrusions in in-vehicle controller area networks, leveraging the unique characteristics of electrical signals. However, their approach relies solely on one variable type, potentially resulting in a high rate of false positives. [25] proposed an IDS strategy combining signature-based and specification-based detection methods to safeguard electrical power transmission lines from attacks, utilizing data from relays, network security logs, and energy management system (EMS) logs. Nonetheless, their algorithm necessitates numerous captured data scenarios, posing challenges in acquisition.

[24] proposed an attack detection model utilizing state vector estimation (SVE) to detect false data injection at the physical layer of smart grids, demonstrating accuracy on various IEEE test systems but struggling to identify stealthy malicious activities. Additionally, several studies have evaluated supervised machine-learning algorithms for anomaly detection in industrial control systems. For instance, [5] compared Random Forest, SVM, and KNN classifiers on the Secure Water Treatment (SWaT) dataset, showcasing their effectiveness in identifying known attacks and anomalies.

Deploying machine learning directly on embedded ICS devices is another burgeoning research area. Commonly used techniques for anomaly detection include clustering algorithms like k-means and DBSCAN, tree-based methods such as random forests, statistical techniques like control charts and Hotelling's T2 statistic, and deep neural networks. Each technique offers unique advantages in modelling complex industrial control system data and detecting anomalies [13].

The challenges of generating a labelled dataset that accurately represents various attacks in an Industrial Control System (ICS) have led many studies to utilize normal activity datasets for training machine learning models. This approach is prevalent due to the difficulties in obtaining labelled data that effectively captures the diverse attack scenarios within an ICS environment [20]. However, overcoming this issue typically involves generating labelled datasets to train machine learning models capable of classifying attacks.

Generating such datasets often entails simulating attacks, potentially leading to irreparable damage if conducted directly on operational systems. To mitigate this risk, it is advisable to perform simulations in controlled environments. One effective approach is to use hardware-in-the-loop (HIL) simulations. In HIL simulations, the physical system is interfaced with a simulation environment, allowing for realistic testing and validation of control algorithms without damaging the system. This controlled environment provides a safe yet realistic setting for generating labelled datasets by simulating various attack scenarios while ensuring the integrity of the physical system.

Among the CI sectors defined by the Cybersecurity and Infrastructure Security Agency (CISA), only four have publicly available datasets for developing

ML-based approaches for ICS cyber attack detection [21]. In particular, seven datasets exist for the Water and Waste Water sector. Table 1 reports the main characteristics of such datasets.

Table 1. Dataset for training ML models for anomaly detection in Water and Water Waste CI sector.

Name	Classes	Type	Attacks
SWaT [38]	5	Sensors/Actuators	FDI
IUNO [2]	3	Sensors/Actuators	FDI
WST [22]	8	Network	FDI, Recon, DoS
Festo [29]	2	Sensors	FDI
WADI [1]	17	Sensors/Actuators	FDI, Spoofing
HAI [35]	2	Sensors	FDI
BADADAL [36]	15	Sensors/Actuators	FDI

The datasets summarized in Table 1 focus exclusively on specific attacks, which limits their effectiveness for early detection. The most prevalent attack type in these datasets is false data injection, which often has an immediate impact on critical infrastructure and are not stealthy. In water transportation systems, the SWaT dataset is the most frequently utilized [12,15,34].

This work introduces a labelled dataset generated using the HYDRA testbed. We aim to train machine learning models to determine whether the system is under attack by leveraging sensor readings and knowledge of control signals. We evaluate the performance of this approach by developing an experimental framework to assess the effectiveness of fault detection through monitoring measurement data in an ICS.

The contributions of this paper can be summarized as follows:

1. *Generation of a Labeled Dataset:* We create a labelled dataset based on the HYDRA testbed specifically designed for cyber and physical attacks. We differentiate between normal operating conditions and attack scenarios by collecting labelled data from sensors and actuators.
2. *Application of Machine Learning:* We apply the generated dataset to train supervised machine learning models, aiming to detect intrusions effectively.
3. *Detection of Insider and Outsider Attacks:* We utilize the measurement data to identify insider and outsider attacks. This method enhances the system's security by using sensor and control input measurements, ensuring compatibility and non-conflict with existing Network-Based IDS. Our objective is to utilize sensor measurements and control inputs to identify anomalies in the system, thereby improving the overall robustness and security of the industrial control systems.

These efforts aim to improve ICS detection capabilities by leveraging advanced machine learning techniques and realistic testbed environments.

3 Hydra Testbed

The HYDRA test-bed stands as a low-cost, open-source emulator tailored for ICSs. Crafted from the ground up, its cornerstone lies in a physical layer that mimics the behavior of a basic water distribution system, albeit excluding pressure effects. Meanwhile, the cyber layer comprises the Control System, Human Machine Interface (HMI), IDS, all interconnected via LAN to gather data from sensors and actuators, emulating real-world ICS setups. This test-bed offers versatility by enabling emulation of various scenarios. For instance, it can replicate water consumption patterns in a small city across a day or simulate cooling system operations. Thanks to the modular design of the physical layer, it can adapt to simulate different configurations and sizes of water distribution systems, catering to diverse testing and research needs within the ICS domain. ICS testbed creation plays a fundamental role in attack and defence technology to discover all vulnerabilities, enabling an attacker to infiltrate and subsequently attack the control systems. In this sense, researchers could implement, manipulate, attack and analyze testbeds to understand the implications of the vulnerability in the real world and maybe define a real and working security standard for these systems. The HYDRA testbed was realised for experiments, studies and simulations on Cyber-Physical Systems security. The design and implementation activities were conducted at the Models for Critical Infrastructure Protection (MCIPLab) laboratory of the Department of Civil Engineering, Informatics and Aeronautical Technologies - University of RomaTre. Testbed HYDRA is the scaled reproduction of the real system of the water transportation system. It's not a control system, also known as closed-loop control, in which the physical quantities tend to assume an expected reference value at each instant, but the control actions are triggered by events that occur at irregular intervals that are not known previously, such as the occurrence of an alarm or the reaching of a certain value measured by a sensor. HYDRA consists of four tanks arranged as follows: a reservoir at the base which is assumed of infinite capacity, two tanks on the same level which act as communicating vessels, and a tank on the upper level. Tank 1 (t1) is connected to tank 2 (t2) via a pipe, interrupted by a first electromechanical valve (v12), which controls the passage of water that occurs by force of gravity. Tank 2 (t2) and tank 3 (t3) are also connected by a pipe regulated by a second electromechanical valve (v23), but being placed at the same height, they behave as a pair of communicating vessels according to Stevin's law. All tanks are equipped with ultrasonic (sonar) sensors at the top measuring the height of the water surface and a pressure sensor that provides information on the water column. In Fig. 1, a picture of the testbed is shown alongside a logical schematic representation.

4 Methodology

The methodology section details the process of generating and utilizing the HydraCPS dataset to detect anomalies and intrusions in a Cyber-Physical Sys-

  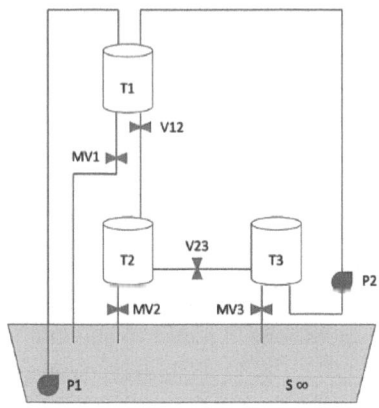

Fig. 1. HYDRA testbed structure and scheme

tem (CPS). The dataset is created using the HYDRA testbed, focusing on temporal data collected from sensors and control inputs. The primary goal is to leverage these data features to train supervised machine learning models for intrusion detection.

4.1   Data Acquisition

The HYDRA testbed is crafted to mimic the intricate dynamics of water transportation systems. At its core, HYDRA replicates a complex network of interconnected components, including tanks, sensors, valves, and a central controller orchestrating their interactions.

Central to the objective of this paper is the generation of comprehensive datasets that capture the nuances of routine operations and potential adversarial intrusions. Through simulating attacks targeting our system, we ensure that every facet of system behaviour is timestamped, guaranteeing precise alignment of events and actions.

The primary focus of data collection revolves around the sensor measurements, in particular an ultrasonic sensor meausures the height of the water surface and a pressure sensor provides information on the measurement of the height of the water column. These measurements, recorded at regular intervals, serve as the cornerstone for understanding the system's state and dynamics. Additionally, we capture the status of control signals, notably the opening and closing valves, which are pivotal in regulating fluid flow and system behaviour.

We considered a malicious agent able to modify sensor readings. We subject the testbed to various simulated attack scenarios in our quest for comprehensive anomaly detection capabilities, in particular:

- *Man in the middle attack with data modification:* In this type of attack, the adversary intercepts the sensor readings meant to the controller or control signals meant to the actuators. Once intercepted, the attacker can modify the data in real-time before they reach their intended destination.

- *False data Injection with false sensor readings:* In a false data injection attack, the attacker sends additional packets over the network that simulate false sensor readings or false control signals for the actuators.
- *Denial of Service:* In a Denial of Service (DoS) attack, the attacker blocks some packets containing sensor readings and control signals, preventing them from reaching their destination.

For each type of attack, we conduct a 20-minutes data collection session for the training dataset, and 20-minute data collection for the validation/test dataset. The attacks during data acquisition are initiated at random time points, and the duration of each attack varies randomly within a predefined interval. This approach ensures that we obtain a balanced dataset with a comparable representation of scenarios where the system is under attack and where it is not.

Each entry in our dataset comprises a timestamp and a range of sensor readings, encompassing the heights of water in Tanks 1, 2, and 3, the states of Valves V12 and V23, and the flow rate of Pump 2. Additionally, it includes a binary value indicating the operational status of the pump (active or inactive), along with a label denoting the presence or absence of an attack.

Assuming the worst-case scenario from a defence perspective, we consider that the attacker has complete access to the sensor and actuator networks and can modify both at will. This rigorous approach thoroughly evaluates our system's resilience and effectiveness (Table 2).

Table 2. Some entries of the dataset for data modification attack

Timestamp	$h1$	$h2$	$h3$	$p2$	$P2_{active}$	$V12$	$V23$	Label
03-Jun-2024 11:3...	53.45818	53.47547	53.3527	4.46656	1	1	1	0
03-Jun-2024 11:3...	53.38534	53.62693	53.38182	4.46623	1	1	1	0
$\cdots$								
03-Jun-2024 11:4...	53.58332	53.069491	52.59783	3.19328	1	1	0	1
$\cdots$								
03-Jun-2024 11:5...	61.65792	56.20523	42.50302	5.7715	1	0	1	0
$\cdots$								

Each tank in the system has two types of sensors: ultrasonic (sonar) sensors positioned at the top and pressure sensors. The ultrasonic sensors are engineered to measure the distance from the sensor to the water surface, indirectly determining the water height. Conversely, the pressure sensors gather data on the water column, providing an alternative indirect method for calculating water height expressed in millimetres.

These dual measurements offer a comprehensive view of the water height. They are harmonized to yield a more precise representation by computing the arithmetic mean of the two measurements. The resulting value, which leverages the strengths of both sensor types, is the one documented in our dataset. This methodology ensures a robust and reliable water height measurement in each tank.

The dataset is a blend of continuous and categorical data, reflecting the multifaceted operations of the HYDRA system. The continuous data primarily comes from sensor readings, providing real-time measurements of water heights in the tanks (labelled as h1, h2, and h3). The flow of Pump 2 (p2) is recorded as continuous data, expressed in units of mm^3/sec, obtained through a flowmeter located on Pump 2. Additionally, by reading the control signals, we can determine whether Pump 2 is active or not, and this information is recorded in the column $P2_{active}$. These measurements, captured at a sampling frequency of $dt = 0.1\ sec$, provide a detailed snapshot of the system's state at any moment. The categorical data in the dataset is represented by binary values. This includes the states of the valves (V12 and V23), where a value of 1 signifies an open state and 0 denotes a closed state. Similarly, the presence or absence of an attack on the system is indicated by a label, with 1 representing an attack and 0 indicating normal operation.

The data is organized in a time-series format, with each entry timestamped to ensure accurate synchronisation with the real-world operation of the HYDRA system. This structure allows for a precise understanding of the system's dynamics and the interaction between its components over time. It also aids in identifying anomalies and evaluating the system's response to potential adversarial intrusions.

A fundamental characteristic of water distribution systems, like the one simulated by the HYDRA testbed, is the principle of volume conservation. This principle dictates that the total volume of water within the system remains constant over time, barring any addition or removal of water. This principle holds true under normal operating conditions, ensuring the stability and reliability of the water distribution system. In the context of the HYDRA testbed, each tank (except Tank 4, which is conceptually considered to have infinite volume and is not relevant to our current discussion) has a capacity of approximately two litres. Given the physical dimensions of the tanks, this volume corresponds to a maximum water height of about 163 mm per tank.

Each tank's initial water height in our simulation is approximately 53.5 mm. This initial setup ensures that the total volume of water in the system is sufficient to fill the available volume of any single tank completely. In other words, if all the water in the system were directed into a single tank, it would be enough to fill that tank to its maximum capacity.

4.2 Analysis of the Dataset

In machine learning, the examination of the training dataset is paramount. The necessity for a well-organized and equitably distributed dataset is crucial to guarantee the resilience and efficiency of machine learning algorithms. The existence of a balanced data distribution across various classes or categories enables the learning algorithms to acquire a comprehensive and precise comprehension of the data patterns. This, in turn, mitigates the risk of overfitting and assures peak performance during testing and real-world application.

In addition to the balance of the dataset, feature engineering also plays a significant role in machine learning. Through the careful selection and transformation of pertinent features, practitioners can distill valuable insights from raw data, thereby augmenting the model's capacity to discern complex patterns and relationships. Thoughtful feature engineering not only enhances model performance but also bolsters interpretability and generalization across a variety of datasets. This results in the cultivation of more robust and adaptable machine learning systems (Table 3).

Table 3. Distribution of the data points during attack and non-attack conditions for the training and test sets. Additionally, in the column "Attack windows" we show the number of attacks that are performed during the whole data recording.

	Train			Test		
Attack Scenario	No attack	Attack	Attack windows	No attack	Attack	Attack windows
DM	7205	2795	7	7060	2940	8
DoS	7985	961	5	7522	1281	6
FDI	7538	9818	6	7547	9485	6

4.3   Feature Engineering

In this context, features are the measured data collected by the sensors and the control inputs. The feature engineering method plays a significant role in the performance of the model, and it should be such that the prediction is fast enough for real-time applications. We examined the impact of the attacks on the raw data captured by the sensors. As described in Sect. 4.1, these attacks alter the sensors measurements. Consequently, it is feasible to derive new features from the original data that can assist the model in distinguishing anomalies and normal behaviour. When working with time series data, it is crucial to consider the temporal dimension to identify significant patterns. Two essential feature engineering techniques for this purpose are lagging features and rolling windows [14]. Lagging features involve generating new features based on past observations of the data. For example, a lagging feature may represent the value of a specific sensor reading from a certain timestamp in the past. This approach helps the model capture temporal dependencies and relevant patterns in the data for tasks such as classifying normal behaviour and attacks. On the other hand, rolling windows entail aggregating data over a fixed time window, enabling the model to analyze not only individual data points but also trends and patterns over time. The model can capture the data's evolution and identify anomalies by sliding the window along the time series data (Fig. 2).

4.4   Machine Learning Models

Supervised anomaly detection in ICS generally uses normal activity data to build a predictive model of normal class and anomaly class. Then, any unforeseen data are compared with the generated model to detect its class. Several algorithms are applied in this study to train a machine-learning model for detecting anomalies by the MIDS. Access to a labelled dataset allows for applying supervised learning strategies by considering two classes of attack and normal activities. In this study, we employed three models that have shown their effectiveness in supervised anomaly detection of IoT Time-series [9]:

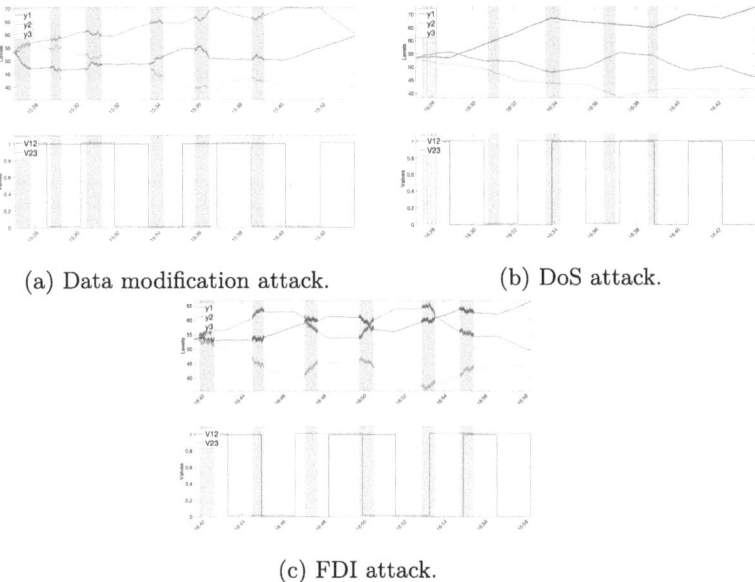

(a) Data modification attack.   (b) DoS attack.

(c) FDI attack.

Fig. 2. Training data visualization. For each attack, we show the tanks' level and the valves' binary values (1 for open and 0 otherwise). The red areas are used to show whenever the attack is performed. There is a slight shift in the valve values to avoid overlapping lines. (Color figure online)

  –   Logistic Regression
  –   Random Forest
  –   Gradient Boosting

Logistic Regression is a statistical method for modeling the relationship between one or more independent variables and a binary outcome. It functions by estimating probabilities using a logistic function. Random Forest constructs several decision trees at training time and outputs the majority class given by the mode of the individual tree predictions. Random Forest corrects decision trees' habit of overfitting to their training set, making them more reliable for anomaly detection tasks. The ensemble nature of Random Forest allows it to improve accuracy by considering the predictions of several trees to determine the final output. Gradient Boosting is a machine learning technique that produces a prediction model as an ensemble of weak prediction models, typically decision trees. In contrast to Random Forest, where a collection of decision trees is used simultaneously, Gradient Boosting constructs stage-wise decision trees, with each tree aimed at improving the results of the previous one. Random Forest and Gradient Boosting differ in their approach to constructing and combining these trees to create the final ensemble model.

4.5   Evaluation Metrics

Evaluating the performance of a chosen Machine Learning model is an essential step to ascertain its effectiveness in accomplishing the desired task. This evaluation process is not just a formality but a mandatory procedure directly influencing the model's credibility. The selection of appropriate metrics for this evaluation is of paramount importance. If the metrics are not chosen judiciously, biases could be introduced into the evaluation process. These biases could distort the assessment, leading to a misrepresentation of the model's true performance.

Performance metrics, in a broad sense, are derived from four fundamental statistics: True Positives (TP), True Negatives (TN), False Positives (FP), and False Negatives (FN). These statistics serve as the cornerstone for evaluating the effectiveness of anomaly detection classifiers.

In this context, True Positives denote the count of attack instances that have been accurately identified as such. True Negatives, on the other hand, represent the number of normal instances that have been correctly classified as non-attack instances.

False Positives refer to those normal instances incorrectly flagged as attack instances. Lastly, False Negatives correspond to the attack instances mistakenly classified as normal instances.

These four statistics form the basis for various performance metrics. Some of them are:

- *Accuracy (Acc)*: Performance metric that quantifies the degree to which the model's predictions align with the actual values. It is calculated as the ratio of correct predictions to the total number of predictions made. Mathematically, it can be expressed as:

$$Acc = \frac{TP + TN}{TP + TN + FP + FN}$$

While accuracy is a useful metric, it should be noted that it might not be the best measure for imbalanced datasets where the distribution of classes is skewed since it doesn't take into account the proportion of incorrectly detected data.

- *Precision (Prec)*: performance metric that measures the proportion of true positive predictions among all positive predictions made by the model. It is particularly useful in scenarios where the cost of false positives is high. Mathematically, precision can be defined as:

$$Prec = \frac{TP}{TP + FP}$$

A higher precision indicates that when the model predicts a positive class, it is highly likely to be correct. However, precision alone does not give a complete picture of the model's performance, and it is often used in conjunction with other metrics like recall and F1-score for a more comprehensive evaluation.

- *Recall (Rec)*: performance metric that quantifies the ability of a model to identify all relevant instances. In other words, it measures the proportion of actual positives that are correctly identified as such.
Mathematically, recall can be defined as:

$$Rec = \frac{TP}{TP + FN}$$

A higher recall indicates that the model is good at detecting positive instances and has a low false negative rate. However, recall alone does not provide a complete picture of the model's performance. It is often used in conjunction with other metrics like precision and F1-score for a more comprehensive evaluation.

- F_1-*score (F_1)*: performance metric that combines precision and recall. It provides a single score that balances both these metrics through their harmonic mean, as opposed to the arithmetic mean. This makes the F_1 score a more robust measure than accuracy, especially for imbalanced datasets.
Mathematically, the F_1 score can be defined as:

$$F_1 = 2\,\frac{Prec\,Rec}{Prec + Rec}$$

The F1 score ranges from 0 to 1, where 1 indicates perfect precision and recall, and 0 indicates that either the precision or the recall is zero.

5   Experiment

We can now describe the experiment after detailing the setting, data acquisition methods, and the chosen models and metrics in Sect. 3 and 4. First, we will explore the data preparation and the training process and its execution, and then we present and discuss the results.

5.1   Data Preparation and Training

During this phase, we decided to implement the feature engineering processes outlined in Sect. 4.3 before proceeding with training on the raw data. Specifically, for each type of attack, we identified the sliding window and lag features that could be utilized. Notably, when analyzing the DM and FDI attacks, we observed significant value fluctuations during the attack windows. Consequently, we augmented the training data for each timestamp t with new columns containing variance, standard deviation, range of change in the data, entropy levels, and correlations between the tank levels within the window spanning from t to $t - 19$ (i.e., $window = 20$). We focused on the number of packets to identify DoS attacks because they do not affect sensor readings, as packet loss occurs during the attack. Specifically, we used the same sliding window approach to account for this parameter's variance and standard deviation by filtering out sensor data that only introduced noise. Finally, we standardized the data and trained the three models described in Sect. 4.4.

5.2   Evaluation and Discussion

To evaluate the model we performed the same transformations described before on the test set and performed the prediction. Table 4 show the outcome of this process. In order to give a broader view of the achieved results we illustrate all the metrics described in Sect. 4.5.

Table 4. Test set performance across different models on DM, DoS, and FDI attacks.

Attack	Model	Accuracy	Precision	Recall	F1
DoS	Logistic Regression	0.85	0.27	0.03	0.05
	Random Forest	0.96	0.91	0.78	**0.84**
	Gradient Boosting	0.96	0.91	0.78	**0.84**
DM	Logistic Regression	0.74	0.54	0.92	0.68
	Random Forest	0.95	0.88	0.95	**0.92**
	Gradient Boosting	0.94	0.85	0.95	0.90
FDI	Logistic Regression	0.99	0.99	1.00	**0.99**
	Random Forest	0.99	0.99	1.00	**0.99**
	Gradient Boosting	0.99	0.98	1.00	**0.99**

The findings indicate that simple machine learning models, without any hyperparameter fine-tuning, can effectively detect attacks with high F1 scores, a crucial metric in this context [33]. The random forest model stands out as the top performer across various attacks, which aligns with other studies [3,28]. Specifically, the model consistently achieves values greater than 90% across different metrics for DM and FDI attacks.

However, the results for DoS attacks are less impressive than the others. This trend is attributed to the features used during the training phase. The sliding window feature promptly identifies deviations from normal behavior when the data is altered. However, it may take some time to detect such differences in cases of packet loss, leading to delayed recognition of attacks.

6   Conclusions and Future Works

While our model can detect FDI and DM attacks, there is still need of improvement for the DoS model. Future works should prioritize refining this model to more effectively capture the complex and evolving nature of DoS attacks, which may involve incorporating more sophisticated features. A major limitation of this experiment is the dependence on labeled data for supervised learning methods. Labeled data is scarce or unavailable in numerous real-world scenarios, necessitating exploring unsupervised learning approaches [10].

Furthermore, it is worthwhile to consider the potential of deep learning methods for anomaly detection [26]. Most deep anomaly detection techniques target point anomalies and demonstrate improved effectiveness over conventional approaches. Nonetheless, Pang et al. [26] underline that deep learning models research for identifying conditional or group anomalies is still underdeveloped.

This study acknowledges that the machine-learning models employed are not groundbreaking, and no fine-tuning has been conducted. However, our primary focus is on developing a labelled dataset that captures attacks on cyber-physical systems derived from data collected using the HYDRA testbed. The HYDRA testbed simulates real-world conditions, allowing us to gather valuable data without the risks associated with deploying such attacks on actual operational systems.

In many real-world applications, collecting genuine attack data is not feasible, as it could compromise the functionality and safety of the systems involved. Synthetic data is often used as an alternative to mitigate this risk. While synthetic data can be useful, our work emphasizes the importance of using data derived from realistic test environments like HYDRA, which more accurately reflects the complexities of real-world cyber-physical systems under attack. Moving forward, we plan to explore innovative deep-learning methods focusing on embedded systems [6].

References

1. Ahmed, C.M., Palleti, V.R., Mathur, A.P.: WADI: a water distribution testbed for research in the design of secure cyber physical systems. In: Proceedings of the 3rd International Workshop on Cyber-physical Systems for Smart Water Networks, pp. 25–28 (2017)
2. Anton, S.D., Gundall, M., Fraunholz, D., Schotten, H.D.: Implementing SCADA scenarios and introducing attacks to obtain training data for intrusion detection methods. In: ICCWS 2019 14th International Conference on Cyber Warfare and Security: ICCWS 2019, pp. 56. Academic Conferences and Publishing Limited (2019)

3. Anton, S.D.D., Sinha, S., Schotten, H.D.: Anomaly-based intrusion detection in industrial data with SVM and random forests. In: 2019 International Conference on Software, Telecommunications and Computer Networks (SoftCOM), pp. 1–6. IEEE (2019)
4. Ashrafuzzaman, M., Das, S., Chakhchoukh, Y., Shiva, S., Sheldon, F.T.: Detecting stealthy false data injection attacks in the smart grid using ensemble-based machine learning. Comput. Secur. **97**, 101994 (2020)
5. Bernieri, G., Conti, M., Turrin, F.: Evaluation of machine learning algorithms for anomaly detection in industrial networks. In: 2019 IEEE International Symposium on Measurements & Networking (M&N), pp. 1–6. IEEE (2019)
6. Chen, Y., Zheng, B., Zhang, Z., Wang, Q., Shen, C., Zhang, Q.: Deep learning on mobile and embedded devices: State-of-the-art, challenges, and future directions. ACM Comput. Surv. (CSUR) **53**(4), 1–37 (2020)
7. Choi, W., Joo, K., Jo, H.J., Park, M.C., Lee, D.H.: VoltageIDS: low-level communication characteristics for automotive intrusion detection system. IEEE Trans. Inf. Forensics Secur. **13**(8), 2114–2129 (2018)
8. Chou, D., Jiang, M.: A survey on data-driven network intrusion detection. ACM Comput. Surv. (CSUR) **54**(9), 1–36 (2021)
9. Cook, A.A., Mısırlı, G., Fan, Z.: Anomaly detection for IoT time-series data: a survey. IEEE Internet Things J. **7**(7), 6481–6494 (2019)
10. Goldstein, M., Uchida, S.: A comparative evaluation of unsupervised anomaly detection algorithms for multivariate data. PLoS ONE **11**(4), e0152173 (2016)
11. Han, S., Xie, M., Chen, H.H., Ling, Y.: Intrusion detection in cyber-physical systems: techniques and challenges. IEEE Syst. J. **8**(4), 1052–1062 (2014)
12. Inoue, J., Yamagata, Y., Chen, Y., Poskitt, C.M., Sun, J.: Anomaly detection for a water treatment system using unsupervised machine learning. In: 2017 IEEE International Conference on Data Mining Workshops (ICDMW), pp. 1058–1065. IEEE (2017)
13. Kumain, K.: Anomaly detection in industrial control systems using machine learning techniques. Turk. J. Comput. Math. Educ. (TURCOMAT) **10**(2), 1087–1094 (2019)
14. Lazzeri, F.: Machine Learning for Time Series Forecasting with Python. John Wiley & Sons, Hoboken (2020)
15. Li, D., Chen, D., Jin, B., Shi, L., Goh, J., Ng, S.K.: MAD-GAN: multivariate anomaly detection for time series data with generative adversarial networks. In: International Conference on Artificial Neural Networks, pp. 703–716. Springer (2019)
16. Liao, H.J., Lin, C.H.R., Lin, Y.C., Tung, K.Y.: Intrusion detection system: a comprehensive review. J. Netw. Comput. Appl. **36**(1), 16–24 (2013)
17. Lou, X., Tellabi, A.: Cybersecurity threats, vulnerability and analysis in safety critical industrial control system (ICS). Recent Developments on Industrial Control Systems Resilience, pp. 75–97 (2020)
18. Ma, M., Lahmadi, A., Chrisment, I.: Detecting a stealthy attack in distributed control for microgrids using machine learning algorithms. In: 2020 IEEE Conference on Industrial Cyberphysical Systems (ICPS), vol. 1, pp. 143–148. IEEE (2020)
19. Maleh, Y.: IT/OT convergence and cyber security. Comput. Fraud Secur. **2021**(12), 13–16 (2021)
20. Markovic, T., Dehlaghi-Ghadim, A., Leon, M., Balador, A., Punnekkat, S.: Time-series anomaly detection and classification with long short-term memory network on industrial manufacturing systems. In: 2023 18th Conference on Computer Science and Intelligence Systems (FedCSIS), pp. 171–181. IEEE (2023)

21. Maslej, N., et al.: Artificial intelligence index report 2023. arXiv preprint: arXiv:2310.03715 (2023)
22. Morris, T., Gao, W.: Industrial control system traffic data sets for intrusion detection research. In: Critical Infrastructure Protection VIII: 8th IFIP WG 11.10 International Conference, ICCIP 2014, Arlington, VA, USA, 17–19 March 2014, Revised Selected Papers 8, pp. 65–78. Springer (2014)
23. Murray, G., Johnstone, M.N., Valli, C.: The convergence of IT and OT in critical infrastructure (2017)
24. Ozay, M., Esnaola, I., Vural, F.T.Y., Kulkarni, S.R., Poor, H.V.: Machine learning methods for attack detection in the smart grid. IEEE Trans. Neural Netw. Learn. Syst. **27**(8), 1773–1786 (2015)
25. Pan, S., Morris, T., Adhikari, U.: Developing a hybrid intrusion detection system using data mining for power systems. IEEE Trans. Smart Grid **6**(6), 3104–3113 (2015)
26. Pang, G., Shen, C., Cao, L., Hengel, A.V.D.: Deep learning for anomaly detection: a review. ACM Comput. Surv. (CSUR) **54**(2), 1–38 (2021)
27. Pasetti, M., et al.: Artificial neural network-based stealth attack on battery energy storage systems. IEEE Trans. Smart Grid **12**(6), 5310–5321 (2021)
28. Primartha, R., Tama, B.A.: Anomaly detection using random forest: a performance revisited. In: 2017 International Conference on Data and Software Engineering (ICoDSE), pp. 1–6. IEEE (2017)
29. Robles-Durazno, A., Moradpoor, N., McWhinnie, J., Russell, G.: A supervised energy monitoring-based machine learning approach for anomaly detection in a clean water supply system. In: 2018 International Conference on Cyber Security and Protection of Digital Services (Cyber Security), pp. 1–8. IEEE (2018)
30. Salah, S., Maciá-Fernández, G., Díaz-Verdejo, J.E.: A model-based survey of alert correlation techniques. Comput. Netw. **57**(5), 1289–1317 (2013)
31. Samrin, R., Vasumathi, D.: Review on anomaly based network intrusion detection system. In: 2017 International Conference on Electrical, Electronics, Communication, Computer, and Optimization Techniques (ICEECCOT), pp. 141–147. IEEE (2017)
32. Santos, S., Costa, P., Rocha, A.: IT/OT convergence in industry 4.0: risks and analisy of the problems. In: 2023 18th Iberian Conference on InformationD Systems and Technologies (CISTI), pp. 1–6. IEEE (2023)
33. Schmidl, S., Wenig, P., Papenbrock, T.: Anomaly detection in time series: a comprehensive evaluation. Proc. VLDB Endow. **15**(9), 1779–1797 (2022). https://doi.org/10.14778/3538598.3538602
34. Schneider, P., Böttinger, K.: High-performance unsupervised anomaly detection for cyber-physical system networks. In: Proceedings of the 2018 Workshop on Cyber-Physical Systems Security and Privacy, pp. 1–12 (2018)
35. Shin, H.K., Lee, W., Yun, J.H., Kim, H.: {HAI} 1.0:{HIL-based} augmented {ICS} security dataset. In: 13Th USENIX Workshop on Cyber Security Experimentation and Test (CSET 20) (2020)
36. Taormina, R., et al.: Battle of the attack detection algorithms: disclosing cyber attacks on water distribution networks. J. Water Resour. Plan. Manag. **144**(8), 04018048 (2018)
37. Teixeira, A., Shames, I., Sandberg, H., Johansson, K.H.: Revealing stealthy attacks in control systems. In: 2012 50th Annual Allerton Conference on Communication, Control, and Computing (Allerton), pp. 1806–1813. IEEE (2012)
38. Wang, Y., Jiang, R., Xie, J., Zhao, Y., Yan, D., Yang, S.: Soil and water assessment tool (SWAT) model: a systemic review. J. Coast. Res. **93**(SI), 22–30 (2019)

39. Wang, Z., Liu, X.: Cyber security of railway cyber-physical system (CPS)-a risk management methodology. Commun. Transp. Res. **2**, 100078 (2022)
40. Yampolskiy, M., Horvath, P., Koutsoukos, X.D., Xue, Y., Sztipanovits, J.: Taxonomy for description of cross-domain attacks on CPS. In: Proceedings of the 2nd ACM International Conference on High Confidence Networked Systems, pp. 135–142 (2013)

Improving Impact Assessment Using Fuzzy Sets in CISIApro 2.0 Model

Chiara Foglietta[1]([envelope]) [ID], Valeria Bonagura[1] [ID], Stefano Panzieri[1] [ID], and Luisa Franchina[2]

[1] University Roma Tre, 00146 Rome, Italy
chiara.foglietta@uniroma3.it
[2] Hermes Bay S.R.L., 00143 Rome, Italy

Abstract. Cyberattacks against critical infrastructures pose a significant risk, impacting operational efficiency, economic stability, and reputation. Evaluating the domino-effect of these attacks is a challenge, especially as operators struggle to understand their impact.

In this paper, we use the proven Mixed Holistic-Reductionist (MHR) method. We focus on assessing the consequences of adverse events and recovery actions within networked infrastructures, especially in the cyber-physical domain, where interdependencies are crucial.

The CISIApro 2.0 simulator uses the MHR approach to assess the impact of negative and positive events on the functionality of different infrastructure elements. In particular, we improve the simulator by incorporating uncertainty through triangular fuzzy numbers. These numbers represent imprecise data that capture uncertainty more realistically than single crisp values. By modeling different cyber threats and attacks, we assess their effects on dimensions such as confidentiality, integrity, and availability for each element of the model. Interestingly, our results remain coherent even when the information is incomplete or inaccurate.

Keywords: Uncertainty · Fuzzy Sets · Triangular Fuzzy Numbers · Critical infrastructure Interdependency · CISIApro

1 Introduction

In the digitized world, critical infrastructures such as power grids, water supply systems, transportation networks and healthcare facilities have become deeply integrated with information technology. [18] This integration has improved operational efficiency and service delivery, but at the same time exposed these vital systems to a growing number of cyber threats. [20] Cyberattacks on critical infrastructures can have devastating consequences, disrupting services and potentially endangering lives and national security. [17,26] Operational technology (OT) refers to the hardware and software systems that monitor and control physical devices, processes, and events in industrial environments. This paper examines the impact of cyberattacks on the efficiency of these infrastructures,

G. Oliva et al. (Eds.): CRITIS 2024, LNCS 15549, pp. 362–382, 2025.
https://doi.org/10.1007/978-3-031-84260-3_21

with a particular focus on evaluating the triad of confidentiality, integrity, and availability (CIA), which are fundamental principles of information security. [13]

Confidentiality ensures that sensitive information is only accessible to authorized users. In the context of critical infrastructures, breaches of confidentiality can expose sensitive data, including citizens' personal information, strategic plans and operational details of critical systems. Cyberattacks on confidentiality can undermine public trust and provide adversaries with valuable information for further malicious activities.

Integrity refers to the accuracy and reliability of data. Maintaining the integrity of information is crucial in critical infrastructures, as tampered data can lead to incorrect decisions and actions. For example, incorrect data fed into a power grid's monitoring system can lead to inappropriate responses, potentially resulting in power outages or damage to equipment. Therefore, cyberattacks that compromise integrity can have serious operational and safety implications.

Availability is the certainty that systems and data are accessible when needed. Denial of service attacks, ransomware and other tactics aimed at disrupting the availability of critical infrastructure can bring vital services to a standstill, causing widespread chaos and economic loss. Ensuring the availability of these services is critical to maintaining societal functions and public safety.

A more detailed analysis of these terms can be found in [28] on the CIA triad. Originally conceived for information technology (IT), the CIA triad was adapted for OT, where priorities are set differently. [10] Availability comes first, as uninterrupted operation of physical processes is critical to security and functionality. Integrity is critical to ensure that data and commands sent to physical systems are correct and unaffected, as any compromise can lead to malfunction or dangerous situations. Confidentiality, while still important, often takes a back seat to availability and integrity in the OT context, as the main focus is on maintaining the safe and reliable operation of physical systems. [1]

1.1   Literature Review

Assessing the impact of cyberattacks on critical infrastructure (CI) is crucial to understanding potential consequences, improving preparedness and developing effective mitigation strategies.

Risk assessment models are an important tool for evaluating the potential impact of cyberattacks on AI. The NIST Cybersecurity Framework [8,29], which is widely used in various sectors, provides structured guidelines for identifying, assessing and managing cybersecurity risks, focusing on a comprehensive approach to understanding and mitigating the potential impact of cyber incidents. The ISO/IEC 27001 standard [21] for information security management systems also includes risk assessment as a core component and focuses on the identification of assets, threats and vulnerabilities to assess the consequences of cyberattacks.

While these approaches are general in nature, sector-specific frameworks address the specific needs of different CIs. For example, the Energy Sector Cybersecurity Framework [15] and the Healthcare Sector Cybersecurity Framework [19] provide tailored methods for assessing the impact of cyberattacks on energy networks and healthcare systems, respectively. These models enable organizations to systematically assess risks and develop robust strategies to improve their resilience to cyber threats.

Several approaches have been proposed to quantitatively measure the impact of cyberattacks, often focusing on economic metrics or Key Performance Indicators (KPIS). [2] These metrics typically include direct and indirect costs. Direct costs include repair and recovery costs as well as lost revenue due to operational downtime and service interruptions. Legal and regulatory fines may also be included. Indirect costs include intangible aspects such as reputational damage, where the long-term impact on the company's brand and public perception is assessed, which can lead to a decline in customer trust and loyalty. Opportunity costs represent missed business opportunities or delayed strategic initiatives due to the attack.

KPIs related to cyberattacks provide measurable criteria for evaluating the effectiveness of cybersecurity measures and assessing the impact of attacks on CIs. [9] Operational metrics such as mean time to recover (MTTR) measure the average time it takes to get systems and operations back to normal after a cyberattack. MTTR is critical for evaluating the efficiency of incident response processes and the company's ability to minimize downtime. System availability is another important KPI that indicates the percentage of time AI systems remain operational despite cyber threats and attacks. High system availability indicates robust cybersecurity measures and resilience to disruption.

Metrics related to human factors assess the impact on security by measuring injury and fatality rates resulting from cyberattacks and time of service disruption that impact public health and safety. [7] Cyber insurance metrics also provide insight by analyzing insurance claims data to understand the financial impact and frequency of attacks, and by monitoring changes in insurance premiums based on assessed risk levels.

Mathematical methods play an important role in assessing the impact of cyberattacks on CIs. Probability theory [25] allows modeling the probability of occurrence of different types of cyberattacks and their potential impact on CI systems. Probabilistic models enable the estimation of attack probabilities, which facilitates overall risk assessment and mitigation prioritization. risk assessment and prioritizing mitigation efforts.

Statistical analysis techniques such as regression analysis, time series analysis and hypothesis testing are used to analyze historical data on cyberattacks and their impact. [11] These statistical models help to identify trends, patterns and correlations in cyberattack data, which facilitates informed decision making regarding cybersecurity measures.

Simulation modeling creates mathematical representations of AI systems and simulates cyberattacks to assess their impact, as in [27]. Monte Carlo simulations, agent-based models and discrete event simulations are commonly used to simulate different attack scenarios and assess their impact on system performance, reliability and resilience.

Game theory provides a mathematical framework for analysing strategic interactions between attackers and defenders in cyberattack scenarios. [3] By examining the incentives and strategies of attackers and optimal defence strategies, game-theoretic models help to understand the dynamics of cyberattacks and guide defence mechanisms.

Optimization techniques such as linear programming, integer programming and dynamic programming are used to optimise resource allocation and decision making in cybersecurity risk management. [32] Optimization models identify cost-effective strategies to mitigate cyber risks and improve the resilience of AI.

Network theory is applied to analyze the topology and structure of CI networks and assess their vulnerability to cyberattacks. [24] Graph theory, centrality measures and network flow analysis techniques help identify critical nodes, paths and vulnerabilities in infrastructure networks.

Using these mathematical methods, organizations can gain insight into the impact of cyberattacks, identify vulnerabilities and develop effective strategies for managing cyber risk and improving resilience. However, the approaches described are often specific to the sector in question. It is important to find the right balance between general and sector-specific methods and the knowledge required to apply these approaches. AI can be complex and opaque even for its operators, especially in terms of communication structures that are not easily recognizable.

1.2   Contributions

The paper introduces a new method using CISIApro 2.0 to model the impact of cyberattacks and other events on critical infrastructure. It highlights the use of Triangular Fuzzy Numbers (TFNs) to manage uncertainty and improve the accuracy of risk assessments. With CISIApro 2.0, we provide a comprehensive framework that models the impact of cyberattacks and other disruptive events on CIs. This model takes into account detailed characteristics of different types of infrastructure, enabling a more accurate and tailored impact assessment.

An important innovation of our approach is the integration of TFNs to manage uncertainty. CIs are inherently complex and their detailed knowledge is often imperfect. TFNs provide a straightforward and effective way to represent uncertain data, enabling more robust and realistic modeling results. This method takes into account expert judgement and inaccurate data that is common in real-world scenarios. The use of TFNs in our modeling approach increases the accuracy of risk assessments as it provides a range of possible values instead of a single deterministic outcome. This allows decision makers to better understand the potential variability and range of impacts, leading to more informed and resilient cybersecurity strategies.

1.3   Paper Organization

The paper is structured as follows. Section 2 is dedicated to the modeling approach for assessing the impact of adverse events. Section 3 illustrates the mathematical background of TFNs and how they are integrated. The case study of eight interconnected infrastructures is described in Sect. 4 with the results. Finally, Sect. 5 discusses the conclusions and future work.

2 Modeling Approach

In this section, the proposed modeling approach is presented. We start with a presentation of the MHR approach, which serves as a comprehensive framework for modeling interdependent CIs and the consequences of different events. We then give an overview of the CISIApro 2.0 simulator, which was developed for assessing the impact of adverse events in complex scenarios.

2.1 Mixed Holistic Reductionist (MHR) Approach

We present a general framework to support the modeling process, called the mixed holistic reductionist (MHR) approach. [12] This approach integrates the strengths of reductionist and holistic thinking and provides a practical roadmap for detailed modeling of AI and its interdependencies.

In the MHR methodology, interconnected infrastructures are conceptualized as networks, each specified at multiple levels of abstraction to capture phenomena at different levels of granularity. The aim is to combine the advantages of the holistic approach, which considers infrastructures as discrete entities with well-defined boundaries and functional properties, with those of the reductionist approach, which focuses on the study of the functions and behavior of specific infrastructure components.

Holistic modeling provides a comprehensive, global view of infrastructures and facilitates the identification and description of multiple systems. It requires modest amounts of data, which are often available in open databases. In contrast, the reductionist paradigm breaks down infrastructure components into inputs and outputs and enables the identification of relationships at a more detailed level.

The assessment of service efficiency, referred to as "service", combines the holistic and reductionist methodologies. This level defines functional links between infrastructures and components across different levels of abstraction.

The MHR model enables different levels of investigation for different systems, so that a top-down or bottom-up investigation of network interactions on several levels is possible. Depending on the available data, infrastructures can be represented at different levels of abstraction. Sophisticated case studies can lose sight of system boundaries, but the MHR approach enables a structured analysis of the complex interactions within critical infrastructures.

To illustrate the practical application of the MHR (Mixed Holistic Reductionist) approach in real-life scenarios, we present an example, illustrated in Fig. 1, in which the three different levels are visualized as concentric circles. In this representation, the elements of the holistic level are primarily associated with service blocks, reflecting the arrangement within the reductionist level. Consequently, the service blocks act as links between the reductionist and holistic components.

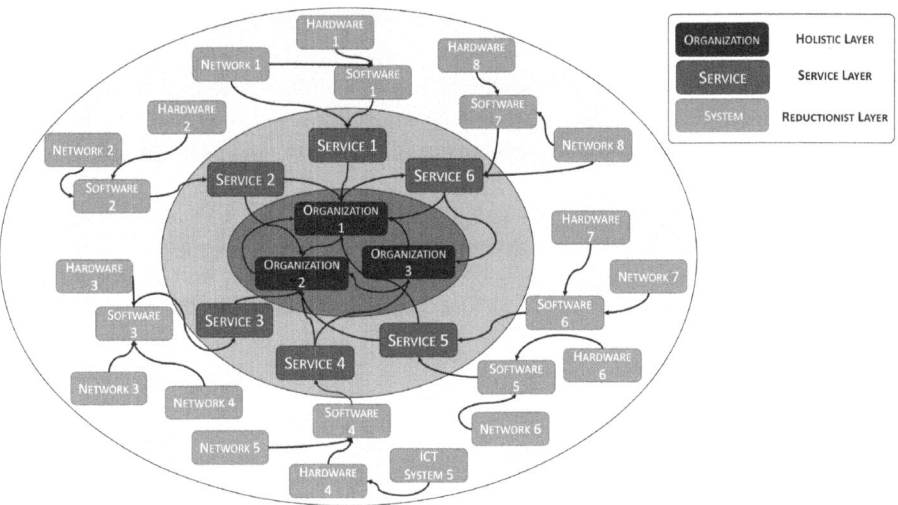

Fig. 1. The MHR representation of an example, where the dark gray nodes are in the holistic layer, the gray ones are part of an intermediate layer, and the light gray ones are in the reductionist level.

In our case study, we examine several interconnected infrastructures that are responsible for providing essential services to customers. Different types of telecommunication elements required for the provision of these essential services are considered within the reductionist layers.

The holistic layer includes all blocks representing organizations, each of which provides essential services to its customers and other organizations. The services are generated by networks, hardware and software that are interconnected in various ways, as shown in Fig. 1.

The holistic blocks exchange physical resources such as electricity or water while navigating cyber risks. This process includes an assessment of the CIA triad, i.e. confidentiality, integrity and availability, to mitigate potential cyberattacks. In our work, we use this concept to assess the impact of cyberattacks, such as ransomware, in the industrial sector. A data breach affecting a company may not have a direct impact on the availability of information, but it can significantly damage the company's reputation across the network.

In cases with limited data, the model may contain organizational blocks without additional information. The service layer includes all components required to provide the essential services. Organizational blocks are connected to services in two ways: Infrastructure services provide resources, faults, and cyberattacks to organizational blocks within the same infrastructure, and services generate specific resources (representing services) that are used by other infrastructures.

The elements required in an organisation's industrial networks, including networks, hardware, and software, are housed in the reductionist layer of Fig. 1. Certain blocks in this layer represent cyber-physical components, such as data centres, buildings, and electrical substations, even if they are not explicitly mapped. Cyber-physical systems include various components that are important for the provision of services, as well as specific elements of information and communication technology (ICT). These blocks can be interconnected to reflect the topology of the real world and facilitate the sharing of resources and information.

In our case study, we also investigate the possibility of connecting infrastructures across all model layers. For example, it is conceivable that an airport (as a reductionist component) relies on the power supply of a particular company, that ICT resources require banking services for ticket payment, and that confidentiality, integrity and availability considerations are shared at the organizational level (i.e., holistic layer).

2.2   CISIApro 2.0 Simulator

CISIApro 2.0 (Critical Infrastructure Simulator by Interdependent Agents) [6, 16] is a simulator used to assess the impact of adverse events in networked infrastructures. The agent-based modelling comprises three main components: agents, basic interaction rules and the environment in which the agents operate. Complex systems are represented by multiple agents that operate simultaneously based on basic principles without centralized control over their behavior. Instead, the agents adhere to local rules, resulting in emergent collective behaviour that adapts to the environment or reacts to negative conditions. An agent-based model means that a group of agents follow relatively simple rules to produce collective behaviour with emergent properties.

In CISIApro 2.0, each infrastructure is subdivided into agents sharing a uniform structure of inputs and outputs. These agents receive resources, faults, and cyber-attacks from upstream agents and transmit them downstream. Resources encompass materials, quantities, and other assets vital for an organization or operator's efficient functioning. Faults include malfunctions and natural disasters, whose impacts are evaluated under various circumstances stemming from initial adverse events. Cyber-attacks denote malicious operations aimed at compromising, disrupting, denying, degrading, or destroying information system resources. CISIApro 2.0 facilitates sharing resources, faults, and cyber-attacks among agents.

An agent's state is summarized at the operational level, as depicted in Fig. 2. This level represents an agent's ability to function and fulfill its responsibilities. Each agent's internal state variables determine its behavior based on resource, fault, and cyberattack assessments. Depending on its operational status, each agent distributes resources, faults, and cyberattacks to downstream agents.

In CISIApro 2.0, each infrastructure is subdivided into agents that share a uniform structure for inputs and outputs. These agents receive resources, faults, and cyberattacks from upstream agents and transmit them downstream. Resources include materials, quantities, and other assets essential for the efficient functioning of an organization or operator. Faults encompass malfunctions and natural disasters, with their impacts assessed under various scenarios originating from initial adverse events. Cyberattacks refer to malicious actions aimed at compromising, disrupting, denying, degrading, or destroying information system resources. CISIApro 2.0 facilitates the exchange of resources, faults, and cyberattacks among agents.

An agent's state is summarized at the operational level, as illustrated in Fig. 2. This level reflects the agent's capacity to operate and fulfil its responsibilities. Each agent's internal state variables determine its behavior based on the assessment of resources, faults, and cyberattacks. Depending on its operational status, the agent allocates resources, faults, and cyberattacks to downstream agents.

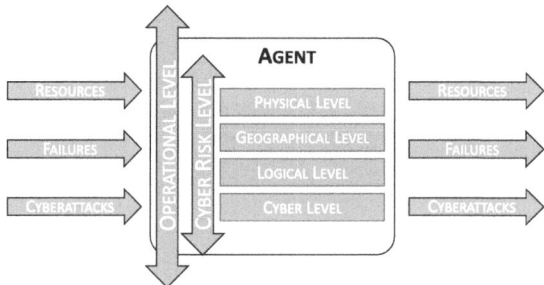

Fig. 2. The agent representation in CISIApro 2.0

In CISIApro 2.0, each agent includes an additional state variable called the "cyber-risk level" (see Fig. 2), which enhances the management of cyberattacks and enables a comprehensive analysis of their implications. This variable reflects both internal and external impacts, as illustrated in Fig. 3. Particularly significant in evaluating the effects of cyberattacks on Industrial Automation and Control Systems (IACS) connected through communication networks, the cyber-risk level leverages the CIA triad-confidentiality, integrity, and availability-as a robust framework for assessing cyber risk.

Within CISIApro 2.0, the operational level conceptually represents the availability of information transmitted via a telecommunication network. In contrast, the cyber risk level addresses aspects related to confidentiality and integrity. Although these two measures (operational and cyber risk levels) are distinct, they are interconnected and may partially overlap, reflecting the complex nature of cyber risk management (see Fig. 2).

To better reflect real-world scenarios, the model incorporates information about backup systems, redundant devices, services, or organizations. This redundancy is crucial for mitigating the risk of a single point of failure that could lead to the collapse of the entire system. Consequently, addressing uncertainties in the interconnections among devices is vital to ensuring robustness and resilience against cyber threats.

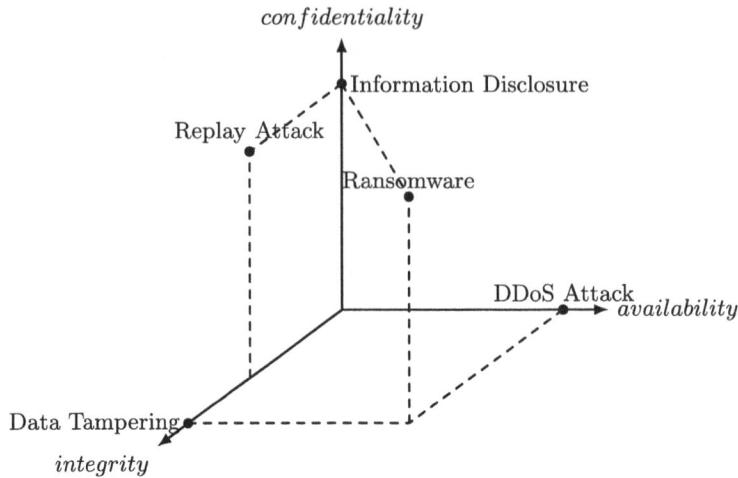

Fig. 3. Attack space based on confidentiality, integrity and availability.

3   Mathematical Background for Fuzzy Sets

Crisp (classical) sets consist of objects that strictly satisfy the properties defined by their membership functions. In crisp sets, an element either belongs to the set or does not, with no intermediate states. A crisp set A can be described using a characteristic function $M_A(x) = \{0, 1\}$.

$$M_A(x) = \begin{cases} 1 & \text{if } x \in A \\ 0 & \text{if } x \notin A \end{cases} \qquad (1)$$

where M is the characteristic function, A the crisp set, and x an element of the universe of discourse U.

Fuzzy sets, unlike crisp sets, include objects that meet imprecise criteria defined by membership functions. [14] In a fuzzy set, an object's membership can be partial, allowing for varying degrees of membership within the continuous interval $[0, 1]$, where 0 represents no membership and 1 denotes full membership. The membership function for a fuzzy set $\tilde{A}$ is mathematically expressed as:

$$\mu_{\tilde{A}}(x) : U \rightarrow [0, 1] \qquad (2)$$

Various types of membership functions (MFs) are employed for analysis, including gamma, rectangular, trapezoidal, and triangular MFs. A convex fuzzy set encompassing a specific interval of real numbers, each with a membership grade ranging from 0 to 1, is referred to as a fuzzy number. Due to their simplicity and ease of interpretation, triangular membership functions (Triangular Fuzzy Numbers, TFNs) are frequently used to calculate and analyze reliability data [4]. However, more intricate functions, such as Gaussian membership functions, provide greater precision in representing complex problems. Nonetheless, they increase computational complexity without offering a significant practical advantage [5].

A triangular membership function is represented by $\tilde{A} = (a, b, c)$ defined as follows and it is depicted in Fig. 4:

$$\mu_{\tilde{A}}(x) = \begin{cases} \dfrac{x - a}{b - a} & a \leq x \leq b, \\ \dfrac{c - x}{c - b} & b \leq x \leq c, \\ 0 & \text{otherwise.} \end{cases} \tag{3}$$

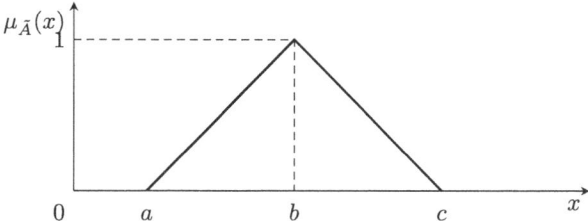

Fig. 4. Example of Triangular fuzzy membership function.

Based on the information available about the system, we consider a set of linguistic values for the CIA triad represented as:

$$T = \{\text{low}, \text{medium}, \text{high}\} \tag{4}$$

Typically, the scale is divided into three ranges, as illustrated in Fig. 5. The triangular fuzzy membership functions for these linguistic values are defined as follows: low $(0, 0, 0.4)$, medium $(0.2, 0.5, 0.8)$, and high $(0.6, 1, 1)$. Each TFN is always bounded within the interval $[0, 1]$.

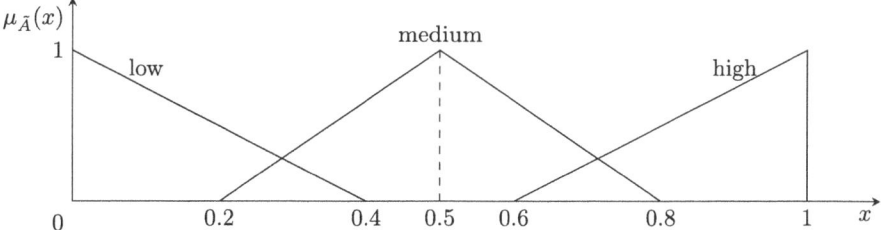

Fig. 5. The fuzzy scale for the linguistic values in T.

To represent the cyber risk for each agent, the triangular membership functions (TFNs) must be combined within the agent to obtain a single TFN. This fusion of TFNs is achieved through a convex combination, ensuring the constraints on limit values are preserved.

Given two triangular fuzzy numbers, $A = (a_1, a_2, a_3)$ and $B = (b_1, b_2, b_3)$, along with coefficients λ_1 and λ_2 such that $\lambda_1 + \lambda_2 = 1$, the convex combination of A and B is denoted as

$$C = (c_1, c_2, c_3) = \lambda_1 \cdot A + \lambda_2 \cdot B \tag{5}$$

and is calculated as:

$$\mu_C(x) = \lambda_1 \cdot \mu_A(x) + \lambda_2 \cdot \mu_B(x) \tag{6}$$

Following the method described in [31], the convex combination of medium and high, with $\lambda_1 = 0.3$ and $\lambda_2 = 0.7$, yields

$$\mu_C(x) = [0.48, 0.85, 0.94]. \tag{7}$$

For a triangular fuzzy membership function $\mu_A(x) = (a, b, c)$, the centroid defuzzification method is given as [30]

$$\bar{x}(A) = \frac{\int_a^c x\mu_A(x)dx}{\int_a^c \mu_A(x)dx} = \frac{a + b + c}{3} \tag{8}$$

where $\bar{x}(A)$ represents the centroid of the triangular fuzzy number $\mu_A(x)$.

The use of fuzzy numbers allows for the evaluation of uncertainty within individual agents of model, particularly when the collected information may be incomplete or imprecise due to limited system awareness. This is critical for analyzing the potential impact of a cyberattack or assessing the consequences of vulnerabilities within the system.

3.1   Multi-layer Graph

A graph is formally defined as a tuple $\mathcal{G} = (\mathcal{V}, \mathcal{E})$, where $\mathcal{V}$ represents the set of nodes and $\mathcal{E} = \mathcal{V} \times \mathcal{V}$ denotes the set of edges connecting pairs of nodes. Nodes connected by an edge are considered neighbors.

To model the structure of critical infrastructures, we extend the graph definition to include layers using the formalism of multilayer networks [22]. A complex system with d different types of layers is represented as $\mathbf{L} = \{\mathcal{L}_a\}_{a=1}^d$.

We define a subset $\mathcal{V}_M \subseteq \mathcal{V} \times \mathcal{L}_1 \times \cdots \times \mathcal{L}_d$, which includes node-layer combinations. For a given node u and layer $(u, \boldsymbol{\alpha}) \equiv (u, \alpha_1, \ldots, \alpha_d)$, this subset represents the topological relationship between the node u and the layer α_i.

Additionally, we introduce the edge set $\mathcal{E}_M \subseteq \mathcal{V}_M \times \mathcal{V}_M$, which comprises all possible connections between node-layer combinations. This definition accounts for alternative types of connections, such as self-node connections across different layers and connections spanning multiple layers.

Finally, we define a *multilayer network* as a quadruplet:

$$M = (\mathcal{V}_M, \mathcal{E}_M, \mathcal{V}, \mathbf{L}). \tag{9}$$

A single-layer network is a special case of a multilayer network, where $d = 0$ and $\mathcal{V}_M = \mathcal{V}$ are redundant. For a subset $D \subseteq \mathbf{L}$ of layers in a *multilayer network* M, the *neighborhood* $\Gamma(v, D)$ consists of nodes reachable by any edge starting from a node v within the layers in D.

The structure of CISIApro 2.0 is modeled as a directed multilayer network, where each agent exists in at least one layer. To ensure proper topology, CISI-Apro 2.0 avoids self-edges in the underlying graph, i.e., $((u, \boldsymbol{\alpha}), (u, \boldsymbol{\alpha})) \notin \mathcal{E}_M$. Additionally, it connects each agent with corresponding nodes identified by the same entity across different layers.

Each node $(u, \boldsymbol{\alpha})$ present in at least one layer of M is associated with a status vector $x_u(t)$, which represent the evolution of u over time t. The status changes for each u are governed by its internal state $x_i(t)$ and nearby data, following nonlinear discrete dynamical equations. These state variables are expressed using measures of possibility and necessity, capturing uncertainty and variability.

Formally, the discrete-time nonlinear dynamics of the status vectors at time k are specified as follows:

$$\begin{aligned} x_u(t+1) &= g_u\left(x_u(t), y_{\Gamma^+(u,\mathbf{L})}(t), z_u(t)\right) \\ y_u(t) &= h_u(x_u(t), z_u(t)) \end{aligned} \tag{10}$$

where g_u and h_u are nonlinear functions, $z_u(t)$ represents the external input of the node u and $y_{\Gamma^+(u,\mathbf{L})}(t)$ the data received from the incoming neighborhood. The incoming neighborhood of the node u is defined as:

$$\Gamma^+(u, \mathbf{L}) = \{v \in \mathcal{V}_M | ((v, \boldsymbol{\beta}), (u, \boldsymbol{\alpha})) \in \mathcal{E}_M, \boldsymbol{\alpha}, \boldsymbol{\beta} \in \mathbf{L}\} \tag{11}$$

Given a fixed topology for the communication network and synchronous communication among nodes (where each node exchanges information with its neighbors simultaneously), the spreading algorithm [23] for Triangular Fuzzy Numbers are defined as follows:

$$x_i(k+1) = \begin{cases} \min_{j \in \mathcal{J}_i} \{x_j(k)\} & \text{for intersection} \\ \max_{j \in \mathcal{J}_i} \{x_j(k)\} & \text{for union} \end{cases} \tag{12}$$

where $\mathcal{J}_i$ is the set of predecessor nodes of node i and k is the communication event, and $x_j(k)$ is the TFN of the agent j at time instant k. We assume that $i \in \mathcal{J}_i, \forall i \in \mathcal{V}_f$, that is, there exists a self-loop only for source nodes.

Let $A = (a_1, a_2, a_3)$ and $B = (b_1, b_2, b_3)$ two triangular membership functions. The fuzzy intersection is realized as

$$\min_{A \cap B}(x) = (\min(a_1, b_1), \min(a_2, b_2), \min(a_3, b_3)) \tag{13}$$

The notion of the fuzzy intersection denotes a scenario where all incoming elements in the neighborhood are essential for agent i to achieve its objective.

Similarly, the fuzzy union is realized as

$$\max_{A\cup B}(x) = (\max(a_1, b_1), \max(a_2, b_2), \max(a_3, b_3)) \tag{14}$$

The fuzzy union concept represents when all the elements in the incoming neighborhood are unnecessary for agent i to achieve its goal.

4   Case Study and Results

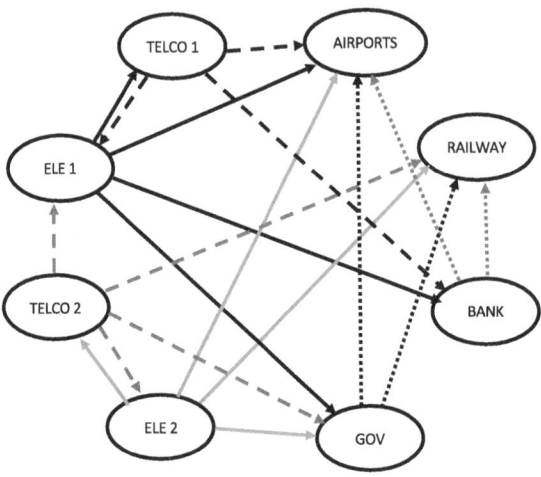

Fig. 6. The interdependency among the considered infrastructures

To illustrate the effectiveness of the proposed method, we present a scenario involving eight interconnected systems: two telecommunications providers, two electricity distribution companies, one railway corporation, one airline carrier, one bank, and one government department.

The interdependence among these systems is shown in Fig. 6. The two telecommunications carriers provide services such as internet access, mobile networks, and infrastructure to the other systems. The electricity distribution companies supply power to devices, buildings, airports, and train stations. The bank facilitates payments for both the airline and railway industries, while the government agency, the Italian Ministry of Transport, issues rail transport permits and manages air traffic rights.

4.1   Use Case 1: Impact of Vulnerability Disclosure

This use case addresses a specific vulnerability, CVE-2024-3493, which affects a device from a particular vendor. A malformed fragmented packet triggers this vulnerability, potentially leading to a major nonrecoverable fault. If exploited, the affected product becomes unavailable and requires manual intervention for recovery. Moreover, this vulnerability poses a risk of losing visibility and/or control of connected devices, significantly impacting system availability.

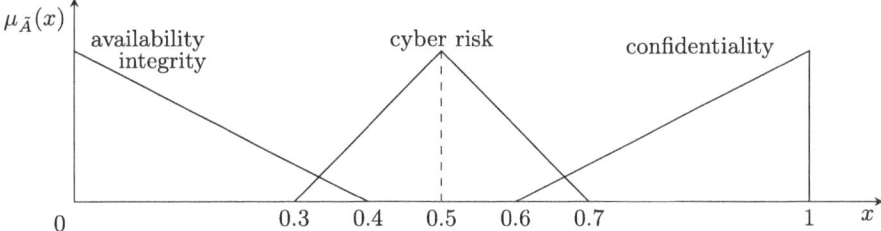

Fig. 7. The cyber risk for the second substation in the electrical distribution network 2 with the weights $(0.1, 0.4, 0.5)$ corresponding to the CIA triad.

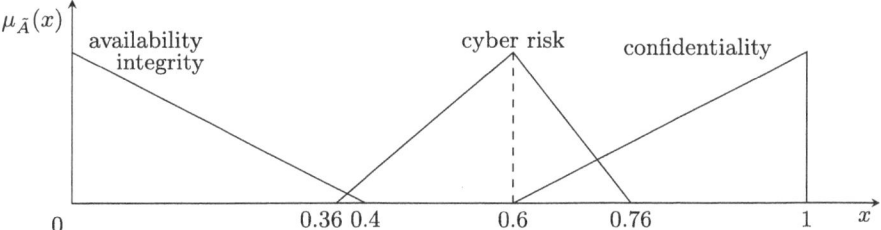

Fig. 8. The cyber risk for the node in the electrical distribution network 2 with the weights $(0.2, 0.2, 0.6)$ corresponding to the CIA triad.

In Fig. 7, we presents the values for confidentiality, integrity, and availability for one of the electrical substations affected by the identified vulnerability. The cyber risk is assessed using the weights $(0.1, 0.4, 0.5)$ for confidentiality, integrity, and availability, respectively.

Additionally, in Fig. 8, we show the assessment for one of the nodes within the same electrical grid. In this case, different weights are applied compared to the substation. With the weights $(0.2, 0.2, 0.6)$ for confidentiality, integrity, and availability, the output indicates a slightly lower operability for this node compared to the substation.

The synoptic view of one of the electrical distribution grids is depicted in Fig. 9. The color coding represents the operability of each agent, based on the centroid of the corresponding Triangular Fuzzy Number. The figure also includes the impact assessment. It is important to highlight, as illustrated in Fig. 6, that problems in power grid 2 can lead to issues in telecommunication network 2 and the railway network. This interconnectedness is also reflected in Fig. 9,

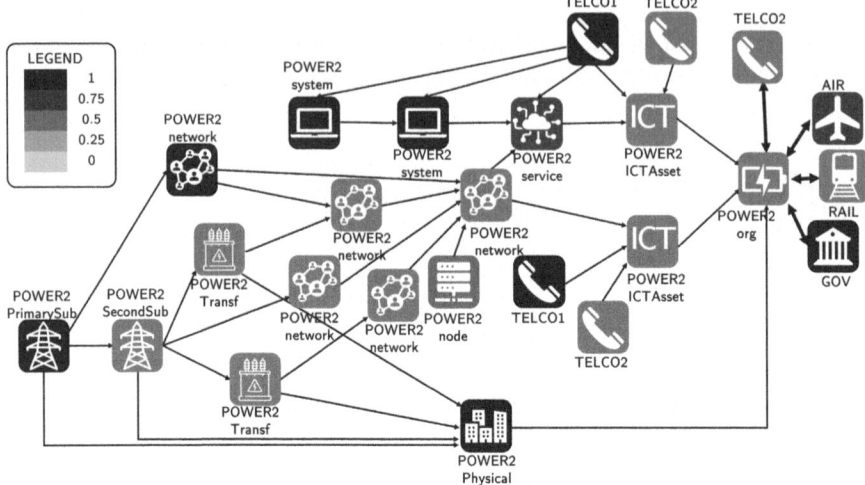

Fig. 9. The representation of the second distribution network in the use case 1.

where potential consequences from disruptions in telecommunication network 2 (Fig. 10) are shown. The initial problem is primarily related to availability, and as a result, the consequence is mainly the potential loss of electricity to the connected infrastructures.

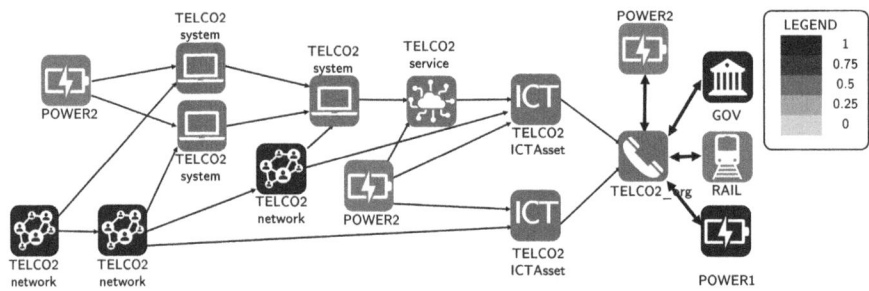

Fig. 10. The representation of the second telecommunication network in the use case 1.

In Fig. 10, the operability of the various agents in the telecommunication network is shown. In this case, potential issues in the telecommunication network may arise due to the possible absence of power feeders, which could result from the lateral disruption originating from the electrical grid.

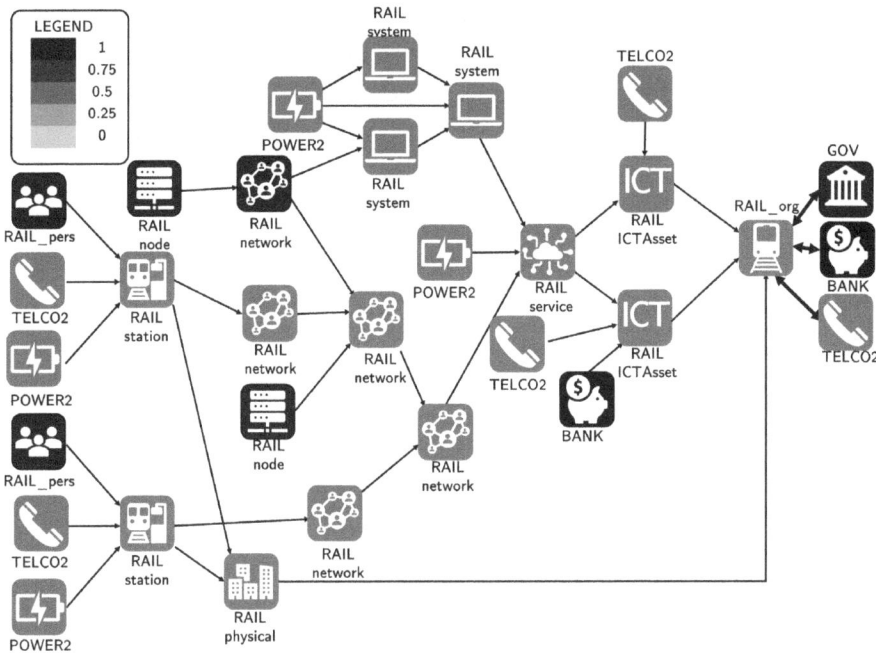

Fig. 11. The representation of the railway network in the use case 1.

The railway network depicted in Fig. 11 may face similar issues, as the two train stations rely on telecommunication network 2 and electrical distribution grid 2. This interdependence could result in widespread performance degradation across the network.

Furthermore, Fig. 12 shows the air transportation network, and Fig. 13 shows the bank company. In this case, the consequences are less severe due to the redundancy provided by the two telecommunication networks, which help mitigate the effects of cyber threats.

The other infrastructures are not significantly affected by the issue in the electrical grid. This information is concisely presented in Fig. 14. In the visual representation, the background color of each icon corresponds to the operativeness of the infrastructure, matching the organization's icon. Meanwhile, the cyber risk is depicted using Triangular Fuzzy Numbers. The second electrical distribution network, the second telecommunication network and the railway system are the most impacted by the potential consequences of the vulnerability. The airline infrastructure is affected to a lesser extent, as shown in Fig. 14, where the cyber risk is evaluated as $(0.15, 0.25, 0.35)$. The color distinction for the airline network is subtle, indicating partial operativity. The bank system faces minimal potential consequences, while the first electrical network, the first telecommunication network, and the government department remain unaffected.

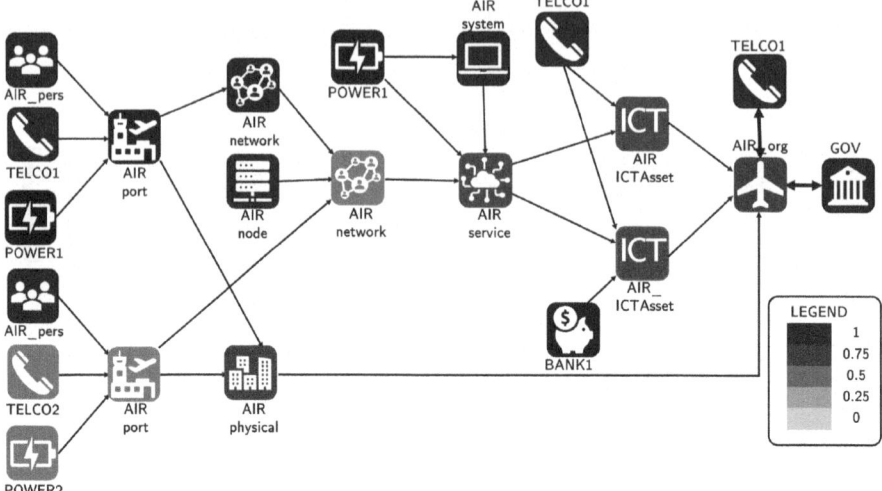

Fig. 12. The representation of the air transportation network in the use case 1.

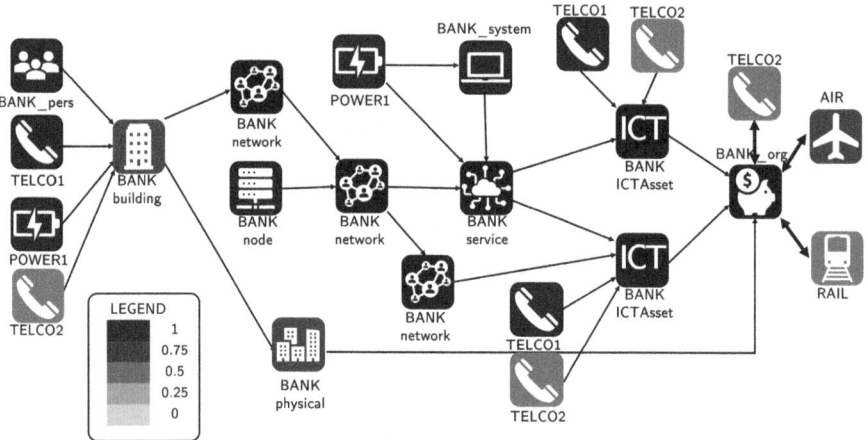

Fig. 13. The representation of the bank company in the use case 1.

4.2   Use Case 2: Impact of Data Breach

In this use case, we are examining a data breach in the network of a government department. All relevant information for this agent is presented in Fig. 15. The data breach has a significant impact on confidentiality, which outweighs the effects on integrity and availability. However, this agent prioritizes availability over integrity and confidentiality, leading to intermediate values for cyber

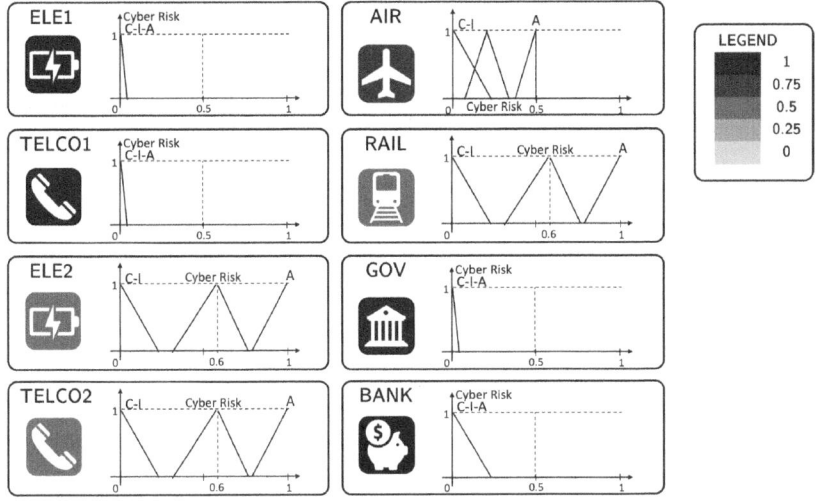

Fig. 14. Dashboard of the different infrastructures in use case 1.

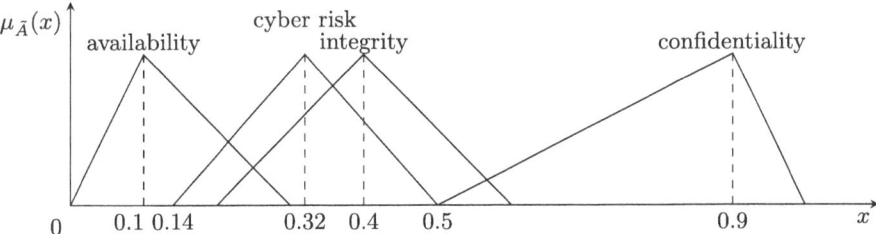

Fig. 15. The cyber risk for the government department node with the weights $(0.2, 0.2, 0.6)$ corresponding to the CIA triad.

risk. The large triangular shapes in the figure represent the uncertainty in the consequences, arising from missing information about the device.

In Fig. 16, the assessment for the entire government department model is shown. In this case, the evaluation indicates that the impact on interconnected infrastructures is minimal due to the relatively low consequences.

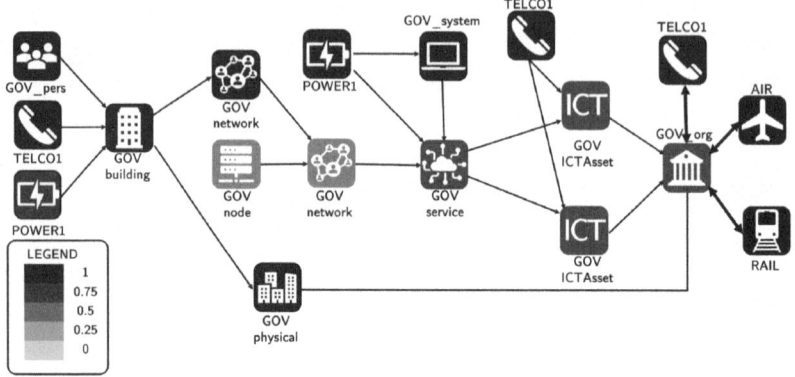

Fig. 16. The representation of the department in the use case 2.

5   Conclusions and Future Works

Cyberattacks on Critical Infrastructures (CIs) are increasingly common, leading to significant losses in operational, economic, and reputational aspects. Each infrastructure has its own regulations and best practices to mitigate such attacks. However, the situation is complicated by unintended consequences arising from the interdependencies between these critical infrastructures.

The proposed model aims to assess the consequences of adverse events or potential restoration actions. Modeling interdependent infrastructures remains a challenging task due to their inherent complexity and the absence of definitive solutions.

To address this, we employ the Mixed Holistic-Reductionist (MHR) method, which deconstructs each infrastructure into distinct abstraction layers. This approach allows us to capture the consequences of various events more effectively. In particular, we demonstrate how CISIApro 2.0, an agent-based simulator, can model complex cyber-physical scenarios using synthetic data. In CISIApro 2.0, each element functions as an agent with a common generic structure. By modeling resource exchanges, errors, and cyber-attacks among these agents, we evaluate the repercussions across interconnected infrastructures.

A case study illustrates how our proposed technique effectively measures the impact of different cyber threats on various infrastructures, especially in situations where complete knowledge is lacking. The methodology is particularly valuable in the presence of redundant devices or services. Furthermore, we have enhanced CISIApro 2.0 to handle uncertainty by incorporating fuzzy sets and Triangular Fuzzy Numbers. The results are consistent with our expectations.

Looking forward, future work will focus on refining the model to account for increasingly interconnected infrastructures. We plan to explore data propagation delays and integrate both physical processes and ICT services. Fine-tuning parameters within each block or entity will also contribute to more robust conclusions over time.

References

1. Abosata, N., Al-Rubaye, S., Inalhan, G., Emmanouilidis, C.: Internet of things for system integrity: a comprehensive survey on security, attacks and countermeasures for industrial applications. Sensors **21**(11), 3654 (2021)
2. Agrafiotis, I., Nurse, J.R., Goldsmith, M., Creese, S., Upton, D.: A taxonomy of cyber-harms: Defining the impacts of cyber-attacks and understanding how they propagate. J. Cybersecur. **4**(1), tyy006 (2018)
3. Attiah, A., Chatterjee, M., Zou, C.C.: A game theoretic approach to model cyber attack and defense strategies. In: 2018 IEEE International Conference on Communications (ICC), pp. 1–7. IEEE (2018)
4. Bai, X., Asgarpoor, S.: Fuzzy-based approaches to substation reliability evaluation. Electric Power Syst. Res. **69**(2–3), 197–204 (2004)
5. Bajpai, S., Sachdeva, A., Gupta, J.: Security risk assessment: applying the concepts of fuzzy logic. J. Hazard. Mater. **173**(1–3), 258–264 (2010)
6. Bernardini, E., Foglietta, C., Panzieri, S.: Modeling telecommunications infrastructures using the CISIApro 2.0 simulator. In: International Conference on Critical Infrastructure Protection, pp. 325–348. Springer (2020)
7. Bowen, B.M., Devarajan, R., Stolfo, S.: Measuring the human factor of cyber security. In: 2011 IEEE International Conference on Technologies for Homeland Security (HST), pp. 230–235. IEEE (2011)
8. Calder, A.: NIST Cybersecurity Framework: A pocket guide. IT Governance Publishing Ltd (2018)
9. Cheng, Y., Deng, J., Li, J., DeLoach, S.A., Singhal, A., Ou, X.: Metrics of security. Cyber Defense Situational Awareness, 263–295 (2014)
10. Conklin, W.A.: IT vs. OT security: a time to consider a change in CIA to include resilienc. In: 2016 49th Hawaii International Conference on System Sciences (HICSS), pp. 2642–2647. IEEE (2016)
11. Datta, P., Lodinger, N., Namin, A.S., Jones, K.S.: Predicting consequences of cyber-attacks. In: 2020 IEEE International Conference on Big Data (Big Data), pp. 2073–2078. IEEE (2020)
12. Digioia, G., Foglietta, C., Panzieri, S., Falleni, A.: Mixed holistic reductionistic approach for impact assessment of cyber attacks. In: 2012 European Intelligence and Security Informatics Conference, pp. 123–130. IEEE (2012)
13. Drias, Z., Serrhouchni, A., Vogel, O.: Analysis of cyber security for industrial control systems. In: 2015 International Conference on Cyber Security of Smart Cities, Industrial Control System and Communications (SSIC), pp. 1–8. IEEE (2015)
14. Dubois, D., Prade, H.: Fuzzy numbers: an overview. Readings Fuzzy Sets Intell. Syst., 112–148 (1993)
15. of Energy, U.D.: Energy sector cybersecurity framework implementation guidance (2015)
16. Foglietta, C., Panzieri, S.: Resilience in critical infrastructures: the role of modelling and simulation. In: Issues on Risk Analysis for Critical Infrastructure Protection. IntechOpen (2020)
17. Galinec, D., Steingartner, W.: Combining cybersecurity and cyber defense to achieve cyber resilience. In: 2017 IEEE 14th International Scientific Conference on Informatics, pp. 87–93. IEEE (2017)
18. Galloway, B., Hancke, G.P.: Introduction to industrial control networks. IEEE Commun. Surv. Tutorials **15**(2), 860–880 (2012)

19. of Health, U.D., Services, H.: Healthcare sector cybersecurity framework implementation guide (2016)
20. Johnson, T.A.: Cybersecurity: Protecting Critical Infrastructures From Cyber Attack and Cyber Warfare. CRC Press, Boca Raton (2015)
21. Kitsios, F., Chatzidimitriou, E., Kamariotou, M.: Developing a risk analysis strategy framework for impact assessment in information security management systems: a case study in it consulting industry. Sustainability **14**(3), 1269 (2022)
22. Kivela, M., Arenas, A., Barthelemy, M., Gleeson, J.P., Moreno, Y., Porter, M.A.: Multilayer networks. J. Complex Netw. **2**(3), 203–271 (2014)
23. Klir, G., Yuan, B.: Fuzzy Sets and Fuzzy Logic, vol. 4. Prentice Hall, New Jersey (1995)
24. Kotenko, I., Saenko, I., Lauta, O.: Modeling the impact of cyber attacks. Cyber Resilience Syst. Netw., 135–169 (2019)
25. Kumar, S., Benigni, M., Carley, K.M.: The impact of us cyber policies on cyberattacks trend. In: 2016 IEEE Conference on Intelligence and Security Informatics (ISI), pp. 181–186. IEEE (2016)
26. Lehto, M.: Cyber-attacks against critical infrastructure. In: Cyber Security: Critical Infrastructure Protection, pp. 3–42. Springer (2022)
27. Liu, R., Srivastava, A.: Integrated simulation to analyze the impact of cyber-attacks on the power grid. In: 2015 Workshop on Modeling and Simulation of Cyber-Physical Energy Systems (MSCPES), pp. 1–6. IEEE (2015)
28. Samonas, S., Coss, D.: The CIA strikes back: redefining confidentiality, integrity and availability in security. J. Inf. Syst. Secur. **10**(3) (2014)
29. Scofield, M.: Benefiting from the NIST cybersecurity framework. Inf. Manage. **50**(2), 25 (2016)
30. Wang, Y.M.: Centroid defuzzification and the maximizing set and minimizing set ranking based on alpha level sets. Comput. Ind. Eng. **57**(1), 228–236 (2009)
31. Zhang, X., et al.: New similarity of triangular fuzzy number and its application. Sci. World J. **2014** (2014)
32. Zhao, C., He, J., Wang, Q.G.: Resilient distributed optimization algorithm against adversarial attacks. IEEE Trans. Autom. Control **65**(10), 4308–4315 (2019)

A Decision Support System for the Damage and Urban Resilience Assessment of Natural Events

Antonio Di Pietro[1]([⊠])(ID), Sonia Giovinazzi[1], Valeria Leggieri[3], Michele Morici[3], Chiara Ormando[1], Maurizio Pollino[1], Alfredo Reder[2], and Giordano Vicoli[1]

[1] ENEA, Italian National Agency for New Technologies, Energy and Sustainable Economic Development, Rome, Italy
antonio.dipietro@enea.it
[2] Euro-Mediterranean Center on Climate Change, Rome, Italy
[3] University of Camerino, Rome, Italy

Abstract. This paper presents the work under development to customize a Decision Support System, called CIPCast, conceived in the framework of several international research projects, aiming to support decision makers in the event of natural events. CIPCast can acquire several types of data such as seismic events, weather forecasts, Points of Interest (POI), Critical Infrastructure (CI) components and perform a risk analysis of the vulnerable assets (e.g., buildings, electric substations, water towers) by considering the vulnerability of each asset to a specific natural event and applying a set of damage metrics taken from the literature. In order to study the effects of restoration actions when a perturbation affects one or multiple systems, a novel CIPCast feature relates the assessment of urban resilience in terms of social, economic and operational indicators in a real or simulated scenario. Thus, CIPCast DSS can support decision-makers to plan proper countermeasures to reduce the overall risk of degradation of services.

Keywords: decision support system · natural hazard · resilience · flood · heat have · earthquake · openstreetmap

1 Introduction

Resilience is defined as the ability of a system, community or society exposed to hazards to resist, absorb, accommodate, adapt to, transform, and recover from the effects of a hazard in a timely and efficient manner, including through the preservation and restoration of its essential basic structures and functions through risk management [6]. In an urban environment, resilience depends on the superimposition of policies, infrastructures and citizens, and allows the continuous supply of primary services necessary for society. All these components, however, are vulnerable to extreme natural events such as earthquakes, heat waves and floods.

G. Oliva et al. (Eds.): CRITIS 2024, LNCS 15549, pp. 383–397, 2025.
https://doi.org/10.1007/978-3-031-84260-3_22

In 2023, several natural phenomena caused victims and serious damage to structures and infrastructure. Among the most significant disasters are the Turkey-Syria earthquakes in February, which caused nearly 51 thousand casualties and a total economic loss estimated to be at least 34 billion dollars [3], the Philippine earthquake in December, the floods that struck Africa, especially the Democratic Republic of Congo, Nigeria, Somalia and the United Republic of Tanzania, the Philippines and the Italian Emilia-Romagna region. For this last event, economic damage is estimated to be nearly 9.8 billion dollars [3]. Furthermore, the extreme heat waves that hit Somalia, America, China and Europe in July caused casualties (more than 200 in Mexico [27]) and significant economic losses.

When a specific perturbation hit an infrastructure, cascading effects may occur due to systems's dependency, which propagates faults from one system to another. Thus, increasing resilience is one of the most appropriate measures for preparing cities for these hazards.

In this paper, we present an extension of CIPCast, a Decision Support System (DSS) developed by ENEA, enabling a continuous (24/7) risk assessment of large geographical areas from building up to the territorial level, where several types of assets can be simultaneously monitored. Starting from the prediction of the occurrence of natural hazards and their strength, CIPCast performs an assessment of the physical damages expected on buildings and Critical Infrastructure (CI) components. In addition, by considering the interdependency properties among CIs and the restoration actions of the different systems, CIPCast is able to evaluate the indirect effects of physical damage on the resilience in terms of economic, social and operational levels at urban and regional scales.

Considering the difficulties of focusing on real urban dependencies (e.g., lack of integration of knowledge held by different CI operators, privacy restrictions, frequent change of knowledge, lack of a unique data stakeholder), the approach to model CI dependencies was completely based on open-data. In particular, as detailed in [5], we considered Dependency Risk Graphs (DRGs) [24] whose nodes represent CI components or Points of Interest acquired from OpenStreetMap (e,.g. an electric substation, an hospital, a post office) and directed edges represent the potential risk that the destination node may suffer due to its dependency on the source node in the event of a source node failure.

The remainder of the paper is organized as follows. Section 2 presents related works in the area. In Sect. 3, we introduce the key properties of CIPCast. In Sect. 4, we present the details of the damage assessment procedure of CI components and buildings. In Sect. 5, we introduce the urban resilience assessment.

2   Related Work

Rezaei et al. [20] designed a decision support system to model urban resilience and identify resilient areas in response to natural hazards. This system takes into account demographic, infrastructure, and environmental properties, including distance from the fault, vulnerable population density, and distance from road network. The system was validated on the city of Teheran showing the low-resilient areas.

The U.S.A. Federal Highway Administration (FHWA) promoted and supported the development of REDARS[TM] 2 (Risks from Earthquake Damage to Roadway Systems) [26], a public domain software that can support the assessment of different seismic-induced hazards (surface fault rupture, liquefaction, ground motion) and the damages induced by real or simulated events on components of the highway infrastructure. Furthermore, it can assess the post-event traffic states, calculate the increased travel-time along key life-line routes, and estimate the economic losses and impacts on the served community.

3   The CIPCast Decision Support System

3.1   Objectives

CIPCast is a Decision Support System (DSS) which enables a continuous (24/7) risk assessment of large geographical areas (from city- up to the regional-level), where several types of assets can be simultaneously monitored. Natural hazard risk maps (e.g., seismic, hydrogeological) are produced on the basis of external information (e.g., sensor data, model predictions, nowcasting). In particular, earthquakes can be acquired from the Italian seismic network of the *National Institute of Geophysics and Volcanology* (INGV) or be simulated to produce the possible physical damages of buildings (including residential, Cultural Heritage and Historic that are public available or have been provided by municipalities).

CIPCast was designed and early realized in the EU FP7 CIPRNet project and then further improved through the Italian national-funded project RAFAEL. At present, CIPCast has been extended within the framework of the EU HE MULTICLIMACT project that aims at producing solutions to increase the resilience of urban environment through a set of new design standards and digital solutions. The new CIPCast properties that have been designed concern: (i) the refinement of the physical damage assessment of buildings and CI components to natural hazard; (ii) the estimation of the risk in terms of social, operational and economic indicators of an urban environment subjected to natural events; (iii) the implementation of a new user friendly Graphical User Interface (GUI) to timely alert emergency managers; (iv) the integration of aerial images provided by UASs as a support emergency managers during an emergency and (v) the implementation of an interoperability functionality among CIPCast and the other digital solutions developed in the project for collecting and monitoring harmonized datasets produced by the various sources.

In the present work, we will focus on points (i) and (ii) i.e. the main design properties of CIPCast related to the physical damage and the urban risk assessment procedures.

3.2   The CIPCast Risk Analysis Workflow

To evaluate in real time the effects of earthquakes, floods and heat waves on the urban environment, a risk analysis workflow (Fig. 1) has been designed to:

(i) acquire the latest seismic events and weather forecasts and (ii) to execute the physical damage and resilience assessment procedures.

Regarding the first point, a damage assessment is performed to estimate the damage state of buildings and Points of Interest (POI, hereafter) instances by considering the specific vulnerabilities of such components to each natural event that occurred. As for the buildings, the seismic vulnerability is expressed in terms of structural properties (including e.g., construction material, number of storeys, age [10]). The outcome of this phase is called *Damage Scenario* consisting of the set of elements affected with their specific damage state value.

In order to analyse the propagation of the estimated failures of POI instances, a dependency risk analysis model is applied to a Dependency Risk Graph (DRG) [24] whose nodes represent POI instances and directed edges represent the potential risk that the destination node may suffer due to its dependency on the source node in the event of a source node failure.

In particular, this approach allows to dynamically assess the evolution of impact and recovery over time and thus estimate the resilience of a dependency chain. The resulting set of the highest dependency chais, as well as the associated resilience values, constitute the *Resilience scenario*.

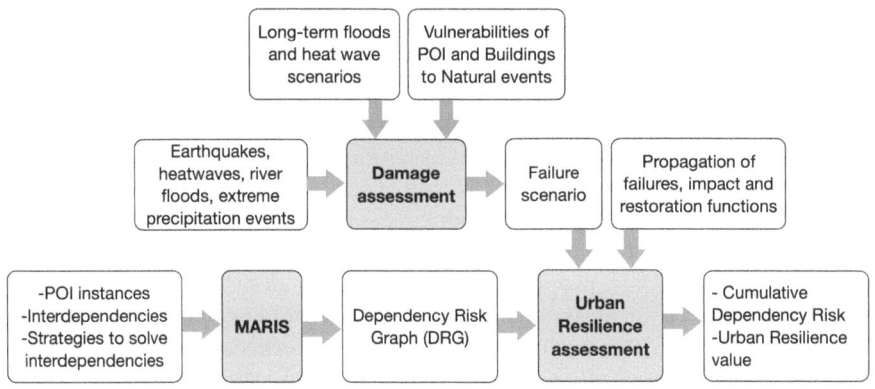

Fig. 1. The CIPCast Risk Analysis Risk Workflow.

3.3 Data Layer

The damage assessment procedure evaluates the possible physical damages applied by CIPCast on POI instances and buildings both stored locally into a geospatial database.

A POI in OpenStreetMap (OSM) refers to a specific location that someone might find useful or interesting. POIs can be various types of amenities, landmarks, or features that provide valuable information to map users. They are typically represented as nodes (single points), but can also be part of ways (lines) or areas (polygons) depending on the feature's complexity and size. In

CIPCast, we have classified POIs into three categories limiting the modeling to single-points only and associating them to a specific CI sector [5], as shown in Fig. 2:

– **Building POI**: an element that is located into a building (e.g., a post office, a university);
– **Infrastructure POI**: an element that can be an infrastructure component, a facility of a specific technological system (water tower, electric substation)
– **Generic POI**: an element which is neither a Building POI nor an Infrastructure POI.

Each POI instance contains attribute information including geographical entity name, address, affiliation type, georeference, administrative region.

At the local scale, in the areas of interest, buildings have been modelled as GIS polygon features containing structural properties required to assess the seismic vulnerability. At a larger territorial scale, in the lack of data, we modelled buildings as single point features and associated them a set of properties made available by the Italian National Institute of Statistics (ISTAT) including specific data referred to census tract areas, for the whole Italian territory in order to infer a (even if less precise) seismic vulnerability value.

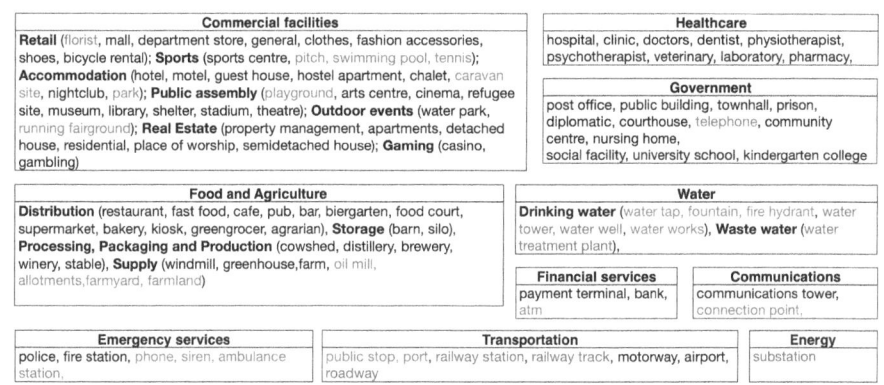

Fig. 2. List of POI modeled into CIPCast. Black color: Building POI; Red color: Infrastructure POI; Green color: General POI. (Color figure online)

4   Damage Risk Assessment

4.1   Introduction

The damage assessment procedure implemented in CIPCast aims to evaluate the possible physical damage induced on the exposed buildings and infrastructures by natural threats including earthquakes, floods and heat waves.

A natural event is generally described through one or many parameters (intensity measures, hereafter) which are used to represent the entity of the event itself. Based on the considered event, different exposure models can be considered, as far as different structures and components of infrastructures can be affected. For each element of the exposure model, the properties influencing the vulnerability, i.e. the susceptibility to suffer damage due to an event, must be known. In fact, through these properties, based on the assumption that similar components have similar behaviour, each element can be classified according to a proper taxonomy. In this way, the same fragility function or damage function can be associated with elements of the exposure model falling within the same classification. Then, the damage induced by the considered event can be estimated for each building or component of infrastructure by entering these functions through the appropriate intensity measure. In CIPCast, each component of the exposure model is characterized by default vulnerability properties, which the users can modify if necessary. As a result, different scenarios can be analyzed changing both the characteristics of the considered natural threat and the properties of the exposed elements.

The following paragraphs analyze the procedure implemented to assess the damage induced by earthquakes, heat waves and floods. To enhance understanding, in Table 1, the intensity measures, the elements of the exposure model and the vulnerability metric are shown for each considered natural threat.

Table 1. Elements of the Damage Risk Assessment. (*railway track, ** roadway, *** electric substation).

Natural threat	Intensity Measure	Elements of the exposure model	Vulnerability metric
Earthquake	Peak Ground Acceleration, Permanent Ground Displacement	Building, Building POI, Infr. POI	Probability of exceeding a specified damage level
Heat wave	Maximum Temperature	Infr. POI(*,**)	Prob. of buckling*, Maintenance Level**
Flood	Water depth	Building, Building POI, Infr. POI (**,***)	Damage level

4.2   Earthquakes

In CIPCast, damage assessment can be performed for buildings and components of infrastructures considering real or simulated earthquakes. Once the seismic event is set and the considered intensity measure is derived, fragility functions are used to obtain the probability of exceeding predefined damage levels [4] for each component of the exposure model. As said, to assign a fragility curve to an element, it must be classified according to a proper taxonomy. In the following, the classification of each element of the exposure model is described, as well as the fragility functions associated with each class of components and the related intensity measures used in the analysis.

With reference to buildings, whether they are residential ones, commercial ones or components of infrastructure, they can be classified based on material, years of construction, number of stories, state of maintenance, presence of aggregated buildings and, for reinforced concrete structures, presence of pilotis story. Using the approach proposed in [18], based on material and year of construction, a vulnerability index V is associated with each building and then modified depending on the other vulnerability properties, according to Table 2. For masonry buildings, the number of stories is "Low" for 1–2 stories, "Medium" for 3–5 stories and "High" for buildings with more than 5 stories. For reinforced concrete buildings, the number of stories is "Low" for 1–3 stories, "Medium" for 4–7 stories and "High" for buildings with more than 7 stories. To assess the damage, knowing the Peak Ground Acceleration at each building, CIPCast derives the equivalent Macroseism Intensity, considered as a continuous quantity. Then, knowing the vulnerability index and the ductility index (equal to 2.3) of each component of the exposure model, it determines the mean damage of each building. Finally, for the calculated mean damage, the probability of having one of the 5 different damage states considered by the European Macroseismic Scale (EMS98) [12] is evaluated according to the probability mass function of a binomial distribution [18].

Table 2. Vulnerability index (V) and modification factors (ΔV) according to [18].

Material	Year of const.	V	ΔV							
			Maintenance		N. of stories			Aggregates		Pilotis
			Good	Bad	Low	Medium	High	No	Yes	
Masonry	< 1919	0.79	0	0.08	−0.08	0	0.08	−0.04	0.04	–
	1919–1945	0.73	0	0.06	−0.08	0	0.08	−0.04	0.04	–
	1945–1971	0.69	0	0.04	−0.08	0	0.08	−0.04	0.04	–
	> 1971	0.65	0	0.04	−0.08	0	0.08	−0.04	0.04	–
Reinforce Concrete	< 1971	0.59	0	0.04	−0.03	0	0.03	0	0.04	0.12
	1971–1981	0.55	0	0.04	−0.03	0	0.03	0	0.04	0.12
	> 1981	0.42	0	0.04	−0.03	0	0.03	0	0	0.06

Furthermore, the user can choose to run the analysis using the fragility curves proposed by [22,23] for masonry and reinforced concrete buildings, respectively. In this case, the classification of the buildings is based on the EMS98 [12], extended considering also the building height (low-rise and mid/high-rise buildings). Based on this classification, CIPCast derives the fragility curves for the 5 different damage states considered by the EMS98 (Fig. 3). Entering the curves with the considered intensity measure (the Peak Ground Acceleration expressed in [g]), the probability of exceeding each damage state is derived.

With reference to infrastructures and their component, the taxonomy and fragility curves proposed in HAZUS^MH [9] are implemented. Considering four different damage levels (slight, moderate, extensive and complete), based on the classification of the different components of infrastructure, HAZUS^MH proposes the mean value (μ) and the standard deviation (β) to be used in a cumulative lognormal distribution to derive the probability of exceeding a damage level

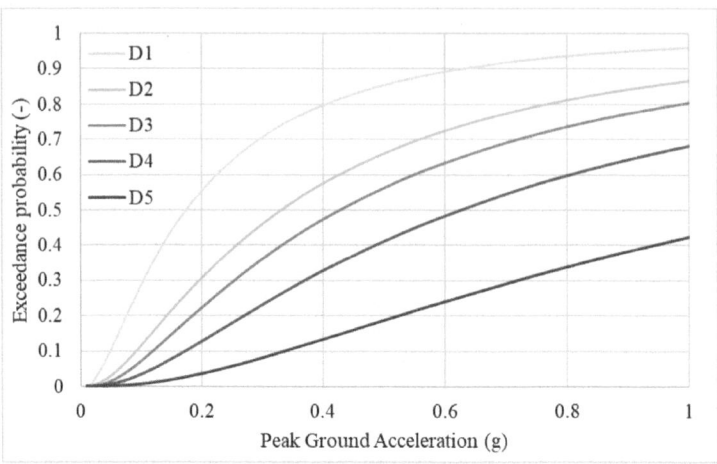

Fig. 3. Fragility curves for a medium high simple stone masonry building adapted from [22].

knowing the intensity measure at the site, expressed as Peak Ground Acceleration (PGA) and/or Permanent Ground Displacement (PGD). In Table 3 the vulnerability properties that allow the classification of each component and the intensity measures to enter the fragility curves are shown for each considered component of the infrastructures in the exposure model. It is worth noting that, in the case of the electric substation, the use of HAZUS^{MH} in some EU nations, that have aged and vulnerable infrastructure, such as in Italy, might lead to underestimation. This is due to the fact that the HAZUS^{MH} approach does not consider the possibility of having substation unenforced masonry buildings, that are very vulnerable to seismic loads, especially when bearing walls are not adequately connected [11].

4.3   Heat Waves

For the damage assessment induced by heat waves, the exposure model is composed of elements of transportation infrastructures [7]. In fact, extensive literature research highlights the vulnerability of railway tracks and roadways to extreme temperatures. The workflows implemented in CIPCast are based on the procedures described in [19] and can operate both in the short term and in the medium-long term.

Considering the railway infrastructure, extreme temperatures can induce large lateral misalignments in the rail tracks, known as railway buckling. The vulnerability to this phenomenon is related to the type of rail network (Conventional or high-Speed Rail) and the curvature of the track. Based on these properties, [19] proposes different sigmoidal functions to obtain the probability of buckling of the railway track (Fig. 4). The intensity measure to enter these functions is the rail temperature, derived from the maximum air temperature

Table 3. Vulnerability properties and Intensity measure for each considered component of infrastructures according to [9]. *Only for Buried Concrete Tank.

Infrastructure	Component	Vulnerability properties	Intensity Measure
Highway	Roadway	Road Classification (major or urban road)	PGD
Railway	Track and roadbeds	Railway Classification (major or urban railway)	PGD
Electric Power System	Substation	Voltage (low, medium or high), type of components (anchored or standard)	PGA
Potable Water Systems	Water storage tank	Material (steel, concrete, wood) and type (elevated/on-ground/buried and anchored/unanchored)	PGA; PGD*
	Well	–	PGA
Waste Water System	Water treatment plan	Dimensions (small, medium, large), type of components (anchored/unanchored)	PGA

[16]. Fixing a threshold value for the probability of railway buckling, the loss of functionality of the component can be evaluated.

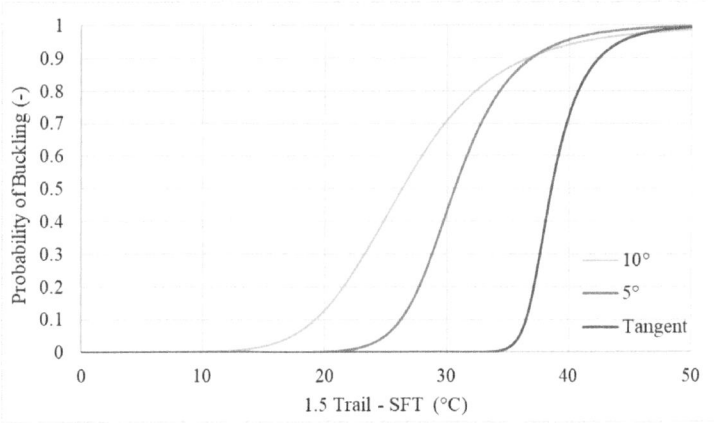

Fig. 4. Probability of buckling in function of the temperature of the rail with $SFT = 30.9\,°C$ for high-speed rail and different curvature adapted from [19].

For roadways, the damage is quantified in terms of the road's capacity to operate within or outside its built conditions, thereby requiring increased maintenance. The implemented analysis follows the workflow described in [19]. Such a workflow combines the Performance Grade (PG), characterising the grade of asphalt used for a given road to operate within a given temperature range, with exposure and vulnerability related to the level of asphalts maintenance to be operative within their built conditions. The PG is used in the US pavement design [1]. It assigns a temperature-related grade based on the maximum and minimum temperatures between which asphalt should perform adequately. In particular, in CIPCast the implemented workflow focuses on high-temperature conditions (PG_{hi}). In fact, if the pavement temperatures frequently exceeded the operating temperature range, the road would degrade faster than usual and require a higher level of maintenance. In the procedure, the intensity measure is inferred as PG_{hi} based on seven-consecutive-day average maximum pavement temperature calculated as a function of the average 7-day maximum air temperature [14]. The level of maintenance is evaluated comparing the PG_{hi} obtained considering a scenario of 7-day maximum air temperature with the reference PG_{hi}, correlated with the 7-day maximum pavement temperature associated with the current operating condition based on the 7-day maximum air temperature over a past multi-decade period (usually 30 years).

4.4   Floods

With reference to floods, damage assessment can be performed considering river floods, pluvial floods or coastal floods [8]. The damage is estimated using probability damage functions provided by [15,17], which correlate a damage factor, ranging from 0 to 1, to the water depth at the considered site. In CIPCast, these functions are implemented for buildings, roads and electric substations. In particular, for buildings, a different curve is associated based on the building's use designation, which can be residential, commercial or industrial (Fig. 5).

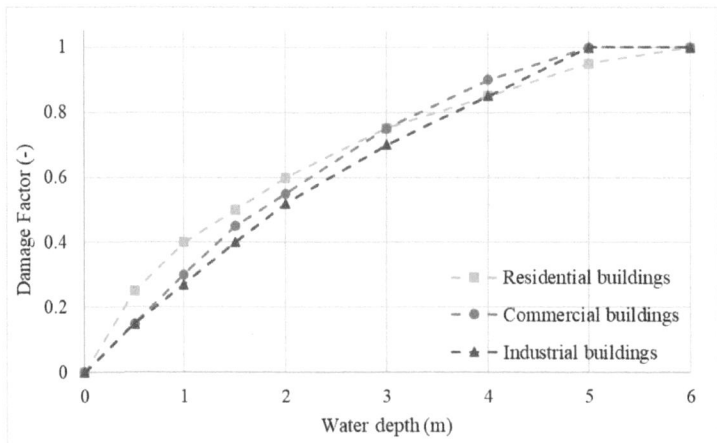

Fig. 5. Damage Factor for buildings in function of the water depth adapted from [15].

In the case of river floods, the value of the water depth is derived from two open-access maps of potential river flood extent given for different return periods. The former are maps developed by the Joint Research Centre [2] as part of the Copernicus Emergency Management Service and the maps developed by the World Resources Institute [25] are considered. These maps depict river flood extent and inundation depth under current climate conditions. The latter are maps for future periods driven by the Representative Concentration Pathways (RCP) 4.5 and 8.5. In particular, it provides maps driven by five climate models (MIROC-ESM-CHEM; IPSL-CM5A-LR; HadGEM2-ES; GFDL-ESM2M; NorESM1-M), allowing us to use the Ensemble Mean and potentially quantify the degree of uncertainty as standard deviation between the different models. It is crucial to highlight that the flood hazard maps are not official and do not consider actual river flood defences, such as levee systems, and may not completely depict flooding from smaller water bodies. If more reliable maps are available for the area of study, they can be implemented as a reference for the water depth.

Since extreme precipitations are becoming increasingly relevant, CIPCast also allows to evaluate the risk due to climate change by overlaying exposure and vulnerability with the potential variations in magnitude and frequency of these phenomena. In the medium-long term, the idea is to quantify whether the frequency of reference values calculated for the current (baseline) period is expected to change and how the magnitude of annual maximum precipitation is expected to change in the future compared to the baseline for the same return period. In this workflow, it is not possible to directly quantify the damage. Still, it is only possible to qualitatively depict whether buildings and infrastructures are potentially subject to an intensification in frequency and magnitude of extreme precipitation events. The parameter on which the analysis is based is the annual maximum precipitation values, that can be derived for different return periods. These values are calculated from climate models over a 30-year period for both current and future periods, using the Generalised Extreme Value (GEV) probability distribution model [13].

5   Urban Resilience Assessment

The MARIS [5] methodology, allowing to build a DRG of POI instances, leverages on three building blocks: (i) the mapping of POI data into relevant CI sectors; (ii) the mapping of CI sector dependencies into POI dependencies; and (iii) the application of a specific criterion to resolve the unknown dependencies among POI instances (e.g., the geographic proximity criterion). The resulting DRG consists of nodes that can be *consumer* POIs i.e. elements that are dependent on other elements to work and/or *producer* POIs i.e. elements that provide resources or services to other elements.

In order to analyse the dynamics of failure propagation, an approach extending the cumulative dependency risk model of [21] is introduced in the following.

Without loss of generality, let $\hat{G} = (V, E, W)$ be a weighted digraph where the different sets of $\hat{G}$ are described in the following:

- $V = \{v_k\}$ is the POI instance set;
- $E = \{e_{jk}\}$ is the POI instance dependency set;
- $W = \{L, I, \bar{L}, \bar{I}\}$ is the set of weights indices associated to each edge e_{jk} in $\hat{G}$ where: $L = \{L_{j,k}\}$ is the set of likelihood that a disruptive event (threat) that happened in node v_j will also affect (cascade) node v_k due to their dependency; $I = \{I_{j,k}\}$ is the set of impact (damage) caused to v_k; $\bar{L} = \{\bar{L}_{j,k}\}$ depicts the resilience influence of restoration actions implemented on node v_k that would reduce the impact on node v_j; $\bar{I} = \{\bar{I}_{j,k}\}$ is the set of impact reduction on node v_k due to the implementation of restoration actions on node v_j.

Let $v_0 \rightarrow v_1 \rightarrow \ldots \rightarrow v_n$ be a dependency chain consisting of $n + 1$ POI instances (or *nodes*) and their corresponding n dependencies. The cumulative dependency risk in the presence of resilience controls can be defined as follows:

$$\tilde{D}_{v_1 \rightarrow v_n} = \sum_{j=1}^{n} \left[\left(\prod_{k=1}^{j} L_{k-1,k} \right) \cdot I_{j-1,j} - \left(\prod_{k=1}^{j} \bar{L}_{k-1,k} \right) \cdot \bar{I}_{k-1,k} \right] \quad (1)$$

In order to incorporate a dynamic time-based analysis of the impact, the generic impact function $I_{j,k}(t)$ is defined as follows:

$$I(t) = \begin{cases} I^{\frac{t}{T}} & \text{if } G = 1 \text{ (slow evolution)} \\ I \cdot (\frac{t}{T} + 1) & \text{if } G = 2 \text{ (linear evolution)} \\ I \cdot \log_T t & \text{if } G = 3 \text{ (fast evolution)} \end{cases} \quad (2)$$

in which for any $t >= T$, impact growth caps at $I(t) = I$ is the maximum potential impact caused to v_k due to a failure to v_i. In Eq. (2), the dependency indices are omitted for simplicity. Thus, $I(t)$, I, T and G are used instead of $I_{j,k}(t)$, $I_{j,k}$, $T_{j,k}$ and $G_{j,k}$, respectively.

All the values are assigned from the following Likert scales:

- $I \in [1..9]$, where 1 is the lowest impact and 9 is the highest impact.
- $T, t \in [1..9]$, which is a granular time scale that uses the unavailability time periods: $1 = 15$ min, $2 = 1$ h, $3 = 3$ h, $4 = 12$ h, $5 = 24$ h, $6 = 48$ h, $7 = 1$ w, $8 = 2$ w, $9 = 4$ w where *min, h, w* denote minutes, hours and weeks respectively.

In Eq. (2), T denotes the time period over which a dependency between two infrastructures exhibits its maximum expected impact I, and G denotes the expected growth of the failure. The growth rates used in this model are split into three types, namely: slow, linear or fast. Finally, let t denote an examined time period after a failure. Considered the aforementioned definitions, the impact and restoration functions can be defined as follows:

$$I_{j,k}(t) = I(t, I_{j,k}, G_{j,k}, T_{j,k}) \quad (3)$$

$$\bar{I}_{j,k}(t) = \bar{I}(t, \bar{I}_{j,k}, \bar{G}_{j,k}, \bar{T}_{j,k}) \quad (4)$$

In the following, the static model described by Eq. (1) is extended to accommodate the dynamic time-related impact and restoration functions:

$$\tilde{D}_{v_1 \to v_n}(t) = \sum_{j=1}^{n} \left[\left(\prod_{k=1}^{j} L_{k-1,k} \right) \cdot I_{j-1,j}(t) - \left(\prod_{k=1}^{j} \bar{L}_{k-1,k} \right) \cdot \bar{I}_{k-1,k}(t) \right] \quad (5)$$

Each Impact value reflects a different qualitative criterion, based on the needs and threats of any given infrastructure. In particular, the impact of POI categories is expressed in terms of the indirect societal, economic and operational costs inflicted to the society by the unavailability (or partial availability) of the services (e.g., electricity, telecommunications, drinkable water, mobility) provided by the different POI categories.

Since the function $\tilde{D}_{v_1 \to v_n}(t)$ expresses the evolution over time of the impact and restoration actions performed by the dependent nodes $v_1, .., v_n$, when subjected to a perturbation, the inverse of the area of this function can be interpreted as a resilience measure. In particular, the equation for resilience proposed hereafter is represented mathematically as:

$$R_{v_1 \to v_n} = \int_{t_1}^{t_9} [D_{v_1 \to v_n}^z(t)]^{-1} dt \quad (6)$$

The presented model integrated into CIPCast allows to investigate the risk of multiple critical dependency paths affected by a natural event. In particular, the cumulative dependency risk function $\tilde{D}_{v_1 \to v_n}(t)$ expresses the time interval (and severity) where the risk of the dependency path $v_1, ..., v_n$ is higher. In addition, the resilience value R calculated allows to rank different dependency paths.

6   Conclusion

The paper provides an overview of CIPCast Decision Support System currently under development inside the EU HE MULTICLIMACT project. The system enables the damage assessment of buildings and Critical Infrastructure components due to the occurrence of earthquakes, floods and heat waves. A major component of CIPCast relates its capacity to evaluate the resilience of an urban environment in terms of social, economic and operational properties in order to minimize the effects of natural hazards. Thus, CIPCast can be valuable to critical infrastructure operators and other emergency managers involved in a crisis assessment to evaluate the effect of natural threats affecting critical assets and plan proper countermeasures to reduce the overall risk of degradation of services.

Acknowledgments. The authors wish to acknowledge the European Union who funded the MULTICLIMACT project (Grant Agreement No. 101123538). In particular, this project has supported the extension of the existing CIPCast Decision Support System.

References

1. Asphalt institute: asphalt institute superpave performance graded asphalt binder specifications and testing superpave series No. 1 (SP-1) (2003)
2. Baugh, C., et al.: River flood hazard maps for Europe and the mediterranean basin region. European Commission, Joint Research Centre (JRC) [Dataset] (2024). https://doi.org/10.2905/1D128B6C-A4EE-4858-9E34-6210707F3C81
3. CRED: 2023 disaster in numbers, 05 April 2024. https://files.emdat.be/reports/2023_EMDAT_report.pdf
4. Dall'asta, A., Morici, M., Roselli, G., Petrucci, E., Barchetta, L., Canuti,C.: ARCH D5.2. (2021). www.savingculturalheritage.eu
5. Di Pietro, A., Cavedon, F., Rosato, V., Stergiopoulos, G.: Modeling networks of interdependent infrastructure in complex urban environments using open-data. In: Proceedings of the 9th International Conference on Complexity, Future Information Systems and Risk, pp. 60–71 (2024). ISBN 978-989-758-698-9, ISSN 2184-5034
6. Disaster risk and resilience, 03 Feb 2023. https://www.un.org/en/development/desa/policy/untaskteam_undf/thinkpieces/3_disaster_risk_resilience.pdf
7. EEA: European climate risk assessment (EUCRA). EEA Report 01/2024. https://doi.org/10.2800/204249
8. Essenfelder, A.H., et al.: Probabilistic assessment of pluvial flood risk across 20 European cities: a demonstrator of the Copernicus disaster risk reduction service for pluvial flood risk in urban areas. Water Econ. Policy **08**(03), 2240007 (2022). https://doi.org/10.1142/S2382624X22400070
9. Fema: Hazus earthquake model technical manual (2022). https://www.fema.gov/sites/default/files/documents/fema_hazus-earthquake-model-technical-manual-5-1.pdf
10. Giovinazzi, A., Di Pietro, M., Mei, M., Pollino, V.: Rosato.: protection of critical infrastructure in the event of earthquakes: CIPCast-ES, in Atti del XVII Convegno ANIDIS L'ingegneria Sismica in Italia: Pistoia (2017)
11. Giovinazzi, S., Pollino, M., Tofani, A., Di Pietro, A., La Porta, L., Rosato, V.: A decision support system for mitigating the seismic risk of electric distribution networks: learnings from the Central Italy earthquake sequence 2016-2017. In: 2019 AEIT International Annual Conference (AEIT), 18–20 September 2019 (2019). https://doi.org/10.23919/AEIT.2019.8893366
12. Grünthal, G.: European Macroseismic Scale 1998, vol. 15 (1998). https://gfzpublic.gfz-potsdam.de/rest/items/item_227033_2/component/file_227032/content
13. Hosking, J.R.M., Wallis, J.R., Wood, E.F.: Estimation of the generalised extreme-value distribution by the method of probability weighted moments. Technometrics **27**(3), 251–261 (1985). https://doi.org/10.1080/00401706.1985.10488049
14. Huber, G.A.: Weather database for the superpave mix design system (1993). http://onlinepubs.trb.org/onlinepubs/shrp/SHRP-A-648A.pdf
15. Huizinga, J., De Moel, H., Szewczyk, W.: Global flood depth-damage functions: methodology and the database with guidelines. EUR 28552 EN, Publications Office of the European Union, Luxembourg, 2017, ISBN 978-92-79-67781-6, (2017). https://doi.org/10.2760/16510
16. Hunt, G.A.: An analysis of track buckling risk. Br Railw Intern Rep. **31**, 31 (1994)
17. Karagiannis, G.M., Turksezer, Z.I., Alfieri, L., Feyen, L., Krausmann, E.: Climate change and critical infrastructure: flood. EUR 28855 EN, Publications Office of the European Union, Luxembourg, 2019, ISBN 978-92-76-09552-1, (2017). https://doi.org/10.2760/007069

18. Lagomarsino, S., Giovinazzi, S.: Macroseismic and mechanical models for the vulnerability and damage assessment of current buildings. Bull Earthquake Eng. **4**, 415–443 (2006). https://doi.org/10.1007/s10518-006-9024-z

19. Mulholland, E., Feyen, L.: Increased risk of extreme heat to European roads and railways with global warming. Clim. Risk Manag. **34**, 100365 (2021). https://doi.org/10.1016/j.crm.2021.100365

20. Rezaei, H., et al.: A spatial decision support system for modeling urban resilience to natural hazards. Sustainability **15**, 877 (2023). https://doi.org/10.3390/su15118777

21. Rosato, V., Di Pietro, A., Kotzanikolaou, P., Stergiopoulos, G., Smedile, G.: Integrating resilience in time-based dependency analysis: A large-scale case study for urban critical infrastructures. In: Rosato, V., Di Pietro, A. (eds.) Issues on Risk Analysis for Critical Infrastructure Protection, chapter 5. IntechOpen, Rijeka (2021)

22. Rosti, A., Rota, M., Penna, A.: Empirical fragility curves for Italian URM buildings. Bull. Earthq. Eng. **19**(8), 3057–3076 (2021). https://doi.org/10.1007/s10518-020-00845-9

23. Rosti, A., et al.: Empirical fragility curves for Italian residential RC buildings. Bull Earthquake Eng. **19**, 3165–3183 (2021). https://doi.org/10.1007/s10518-020-00971-4

24. Stergiopoulos, G., Kotzanikolaou, P., Theocharidou, M., Gritzalis, D.: Risk mitigation strategies for critical infrastructures based on graph centrality analysis. Int. J. Crit. Infrastruct. Prot. **10**, 33–44 (2015)

25. Ward, P.J., et al: Aqueduct floods methodology. World Resour. Inst. pp. 1–28 (2020)

26. Werner, S.D., et al.: REDARS 2 methodology and software for seismic risk analysis of highway systems. federal highway administration. Special Report MCEER-06-SP08, 31 Aug 2006. https://www.eng.buffalo.edu/mceer-reports/06/06-SP08.pdf

27. World weather attribution site, https://www.worldweatherattribution.org/extreme-heat-in-north-america-europe-and-china-in-july-2023-made-much-more-likely-by-climate-change/, Accessed 05 July 2024

Urban Data Governance:
an Interoperability-Based Approach
for Monitoring Natural Threats
at Different Geographic Scales, Through
Smart City Platforms

Arianna Brutti[1]([✉])[iD], Antonio Di Pietro[1][iD], Angelo Frascella[1],
Sonia Giovinazzi[1], Cristiano Novelli[1], Gianluca D'Agosta[1], Stefano Pizzuti[1],
Maurizio Pollino[1], Ane Ferreiro Sistiaga[2], Saúl Buitrago[3],
Iñigo Lopez Villamor[4], Simone Murazzo[5], and Gian Marco Revel[6]

[1] ENEA, Italian National Agency for New Technologies, Energy and Sustainable
Economic Development, Rome, Italy
arianna.brutti@enea.it
[2] CYPE SOFT SL, Alicante, Spain
[3] Delft University of Technology, Delft, The Netherlands
[4] TECNALIA, Alicante, Spain
[5] Live Information System SRL, Ancona, Italy
[6] Università Politecnica delle Marche, Ancona, Italy

Abstract. Monitoring, preventing and managing the impacts induced
by extreme natural events requires the use of multiple and different Information Communication Technology (ICT) tools and technologies capable of collecting and processing data from various sources, and supporting public stakeholders in the planning and implementation of prompt
actions. In this perspective, the availability of platforms able to harmonize, integrate and manage heterogeneous data and to create new
knowledge, can constitute a valuable support. This article presents some
preliminary results from the EU-funded MULTICLIMACT project, part
of which is defining a reference model for customizing and adopting the
ENEA Smart City Platform to inform on the severity and extent of possible impacts induced by natural threats and on possible resilience strategies. Towards that the Smart City Platform enables the interoperability
between heterogeneous digital solutions monitoring natural threats at
different geographic scales.

Keywords: Interoperability · Smart City Platform · Ontology ·
Specifications · Smart City · Natural threat · Earthquake · Flood ·
Heat waves · Well-being · JSON

1 Introduction

Natural and man-made hazards are increasingly threatening our cities and communities. It is therefore imperative to provide readily accessible information

G. Oliva et al. (Eds.): CRITIS 2024, LNCS 15549, pp. 398–417, 2025.
https://doi.org/10.1007/978-3-031-84260-3_23

and know-how to public authorities and stakeholders on the possible impacts that such hazards might induce on different exposed elements, as well as on the opportunities of implementing resilience strategies to mitigate impacts, to adapt to long-term threats and to promptly recover and thrive in the aftermath of crisis. The on-going digital transition is posing an unprecedented opportunity towards that; cities can be digitally empowered with low-cost sensors, smart collaborative technologies, interoperable platforms that, thanks to open-science algorithms and applications, allow democratizing access to data and information and fostering knowledge [8]. The possibility to monitor in real time natural threats at different geographic scales within the city enables informed, aware and participatory decision making processes, thereby enhancing resilience.

Several definitions of resilience have been applied to urban systems and cities. The United Nations [11], defines resilience as "the measurable ability of any urban system, with its inhabitants, to maintain continuity through all shocks and stresses, while positively adapting and transforming toward sustainability" and a resilient city as the one that "valuates, plans and acts to prepare and respond to threats - natural and human-made, sudden and slow-onset, expected and unexpected - in order to protect and improve the lives of people, secure development gains, foster environment, and drive positive change" [13].

Technology, data-driven decision-making, and citizen engagement can provide a substantial contribute to build resilient cities that can withstand and recover from challenges effectively. This ability aligns with the definition provided by the United Nations Economic Commission for Europe (UNECE) for a smart city, which is described as "an inclusive, safe, resilient, sustainable, and connected city for all" [12].

In this context, the availability of multipurpose frameworks that can interconnect various heterogeneous software tools and solutions is crucial. These frameworks ensure interoperability, which is the ability of two or more networks, systems, devices, applications, or components to exchange and use information securely, effectively, and with minimal inconvenience to the user [10].

The Smart City Platform Specification and the platform based on this specification, presented in this paper, aims to: i) provide a replicable and sustainable methodology based on public specifications for interoperability communication between technological solutions, aimed at avoiding vendor lock-in; ii) interconnect resilience and smartness features both essential for urban systems; iii) unequivocally define Key Performance Indicators (KPIs) and iv) harmonize and democratize access to KPIs and data, making them comprehensible and accessible to all. [14].

The paper is organized as follows: Sect. 2 presents the problem and related works in the area. In Sect. 3, the Smart City Platform Specifications for Interoperability Layer for monitoring natural threats are presented. Section 4 outlines case studies across different geographical scales from the MULTICLIMACT project, demonstrating the implementation of Smart City Platforms Specifications for monitoring natural threats. Finally, Sect. 5 discusses conclusions and ideas for future work.

2   Related Works

The world is becoming increasingly smarter. We are building smart homes within smart buildings, connected by smart roads, all surrounded by sensors that can analyse air quality. Here people, equipped with smartphones, drive smart cars. All these smart devices are interconnected within a smart city.

The development and proliferation of such technologies presents new challenges (such as the need to avoid the vendor lock-in and to implement the data integration and harmonization), but also significant opportunities: one major opportunity is the ability to collect data to enhance security and manage natural hazards. However, to fully exploit this potential, it is crucial that all the collected data can be exchanged and readily used for forecasting and managing natural hazards. In other words, interoperability is essential.

The study [2] provides a literature review about existing research approaches in ICT for Disaster Risk Management. It highlights that "most of the selected studies focus mainly on delivering solutions regarding the prevention or reporting of a natural disaster, whereas a holistic approach is not examined" and that "this barrier in data sharing and interoperability" can hamper the "presentation of information to decision-makers".

Similarly [9], starting from a literature review, emphasizes that data interoperability in disaster risk reduction "remains a challenge due to a number of barriers that preclude exploitation of available data for disaster risk reduction before, during or after a hazard has materialized into a disaster". This paper identifies the following barriers to data interoperability:

– the high number of actors involved (civil protection, firefighters, healthcare services, municipalities and non-governmental organizations among others);
– lack of standardization in data collection, processing and distribution;
– the fact that data are collected, processed and distributed by a wide range of actors using different routines, standard and requirements.

The study [1] proposes an interoperability assessment approach "to identify the potential inter-operation in a disaster response management environment". By identifying and weighing key interoperability criteria, the framework helps entities to understand their current capabilities and areas needing improvement, thus enhancing their ability to manage and respond to crises effectively. So, this approach helps in identifying gaps, but does not arrive at a complete solution.

The issue of establishing an interoperability framework for Emergency Management Systems (EMS) across different European countries involves not only diverse IT solutions but also the variety of languages spoken in Europe. Paper [5] presents a software solution leveraging semantic and mediation technologies to tackle these challenges. The proposed solution utilizes a common, modular ontology that accounts for cultural and linguistic differences, and is built on a service-oriented architecture to ensure data interoperability. However, neither this paper address the challenge of integrating data from various sources.

As, at the best of our knowledge, there appears to be no specific solution available, we will expand our focus to consider the general approach needed to achieve data interoperability.

Interoperability is a complex attribute influenced by numerous factors, including functionality, business processes, human interaction, trustworthiness, timing, data, boundaries, composition, and lifecycle, distributed across different interoperability levels. Various layered stacks exist for interoperability, each differing in how they group concepts at each level based on the model's goals, though the underlying concepts are largely similar. From these, we can define the following layered stack: Collaboration, Functional, Semantic, Information, Communication [15].

Additionally, achieving interoperability requires on one hand the development of protocols-sets of communication rules-that comprehensively define all aspects, from the communication channel to the meaning of the exchanged data but on the other hand it also requires system stakeholders to agree to use these protocols [3].

From this, several key principles of data interoperability can be identified. [7]:

- Avoidance of semantic ambiguities in specification definitions to ensure application interoperability.
- Clear definition of the specification lifecycle, considering every stage (e.g., definition, implementation, adoption, configuration, etc.).
- Ensuring the usability of the specification for various users, including technical experts, domain experts, management personnel, and end users.

To address the challenges associated with implementing data interoperability and dismantling silos in natural threat monitoring, it is crucial to adopt a multi-tiered strategy that adheres to the following fundamental principles.

ENEA laboratories CROSS (Cross Technologies for Urban and Industrial districts) and SCC (Smart Cities and Communities) have developed, in the context of Italian National Research programs, a solution for interoperability of data coming from the different smart city applications: the "Smart City Platform Specification (SCPS) for Interoperability Layer" [4]. It is a set of specifications tackling the problem from the above explained perspective; such a solution has been adopted as the reference architecture for defining the reference model for implementing Smart City Platforms for monitoring natural threats at different geographic scales.

3   Context, Objective and Approach

3.1   Context and Objective

The reference model for implementing interoperable Smart City Platforms for monitoring natural threats at different geographic scales has been designed in the context of the EU HE MULTICLIMACT project.

One of the objective of this project is to develop a mainstreamed framework and a tool for supporting public stakeholders and citizens to assess the resilience of the built environment and its people at multiple scales (buildings, urban areas, territories) against locally relevant natural and climatic hazards, as well as to support them to enhance their preparedness and responsiveness across their life cycle. In particular, the main output of the project will be a toolkit of Design Practices, Materials, and Digital Solutions, enabling users to easily estimate the impact of their implementation on the resilience of the targeted asset, integrating a multidisciplinary approach combining socio economic, life, engineering, and climate disciplines. The Digital Solutions will enable the monitoring, detection of, and response to critical situations, improving the protecting role of the built environment for people safety and quality of living. Specifically, the following natural hazards are analyzed:

- earthquakes
- heat island and heat waves
- floods and droughts

along with the monitoring of well-being and health of people occupying buildings in areas affected by the aforementioned critical events. When the Solutions will be operational, several data will be available. New knowledge can be generated by comparing and reprocessing the data; however, this is only achievable if the data produced by the solutions are interoperable.

In this perspective, the project planned a specific Task for the identifying and validating a reference model for enabling interoperability in the data exchange among the MULTICLIMACT Digital Solutions.

3.2   The Reference Infrastructure for an Interoperable Data Exchange

The ENEA "Smart City Platform Specification (SCPS) for Interoperability Layer" and its reference implementation ("Smart City Platform" SCP) have been identified as the basis for defining the reference model for interoperability between the MULTICLIMACT digital solutions (details about SCP, SCPS and available tools can be found in [6]).

They enable the communication among heterogeneous platforms or digital solutions that speak different languages, maintaining existing technological implementations and making different data collection and management systems interoperable. The aim is to provide citizens, municipalities and various stakeholders with a valuable tool for collecting and harmonizing useful data from districts, cities and, more in general, urban environment, in order to obtain knowledge on the entire urban management. Furthermore, they are:

- **public**: everybody can adopt them to create its own smart city platform, maintaining the interoperability among the systems;
- **open**: everybody is able to propose new types of UrbanDataset, which is the common format to represent data to be exchanged between SCP and Solutions;

– **replicable**: a digital solution that adheres to the SCPS, in order to connect a platform SCPS-based, can immediately connect to another platform SCPS-based (e.g. a mobility platform connected to the platform of the municipality A, could easily connect to the platform of municipality B).

It is important to highlight that the purpose of the SCPS is not to replace the existing solutions but to allow the harmonization and recovery of data from them at a central horizontal ICT platform, the Smart City Platform (Fig. 1). This platform adopts a shared and public approach aimed at enabling interoperability between systems, preventing them from behaving as independent silos.

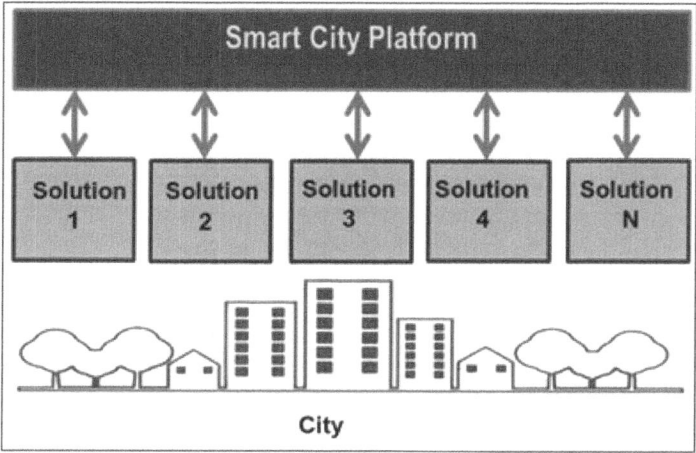

Fig. 1. SCP and Digital Solutions Communication

The SCPS is based on the following key concepts:

– **Smart City Platform (SCP)**: a city management platform that adheres to SCPS specifications. ENEA has developed an SCP prototype for demonstration purposes.
– **UrbanDataset**: the shared format to represent the data to be exchanged between SCP and Solutions, according to the SCPS; it is defined through a univocal and centralized semantic description (the Ontology component), an Abstract Model (providing a syntax-independent description of the common structure of messages) and a syntactic reference implementation (JSON, expressed through a JSON Schema). A message structured according to this format contains a set of significant urban data as well as all the information needed to understand and interpret such data. The data collection is expressed as set of properties, meant as couples key-value.
– **Ontology**: is the component defining the semantic content of the Urban-Datasets, as well as classifying them into categories and sub-categories. Concretely, it provides a shared vocabulary and terms and is expressed using

the OWL Web Ontology Language defined by W3C. Furthermore, it is a prescriptive reference for each UrbanDataset and for its semantic validation; this means that an UrbanDataset must comply with the definition given in the Ontology in order to be considered valid according to the SCPS. The ontology is a dynamic component that can evolve and grow over the time; to cover new application contexts, new terms can be added to the vocabulary and new types of UrbanDataset can be defined in the library, as happened for supporting the MULTICLIMACT scenario.

- **Registry**: internal database of the SCP acting as a register of Users, Solutions, supported UrbanDatasets and Collaborations defined between SCP and the Solutions, both to produce UrbanDatasets and to access UrbanDatasets produced by third parties.
- **UrbanDatasetGateway**: a web service to send the UrbanDataset to the SCP and to get UrbanDataset from the SCP, respecting the production and access permits stored in the Registry database of the SCP.

The Registry and the UrbanDatasetGateway will not be further discussed in this paper as it focuses on complementary aspects to them.

According to the Interoperability Reference Model, the SCPS are split into five independent modules that can be gradually adopted:

- **Functional Specification**: it describes the key concepts of the SCPS, the architecture of the SCP and its components and the functionalities.
- **Collaboration Specification**: it describes the set of information that characterizes the collaboration between a SCP and a Solution.
- **Semantic Specification**: it deals with the semantic definition of data and includes the SCPS Ontology, that ensure a single centralized definition, both of the UrbanDataset and of the properties that compose them, with the same names, formats and units of measurement;
- **Information Specification**: it deals with the syntactic definition of the data, stating the UrbanDataset format and the path to create UrbanDataset messages. The format is defined in terms of Abstract Model and a reference syntax of data exchange: JSON (expressed through JSON Schema).
- **Communication Specification**: it describes the interoperable communication protocol to enable data exchange between a SCP and one or more Vertical Solutions.

3.3   The Approach

The reference model for implementing interoperable Smart City Platforms for monitoring natural threats at different geographic scales has been conceived to be:

- applicable at three different geographic scales: building, urban, territorial;
- scalable, in order to ensure that new systems or solutions can connect to the platform without particular efforts and new services can be activated;

– replicable, meaning that the platform can be adopted in any cities or districts similar for features and needs to the ones involved in the project.

It is the result of a process aimed at extending and customizing the "Smart City Platform Specification (SCPS) for Interoperability Layer" and the ENEA "Smart City Platform" for supporting the scenario tackled by the project. Specifically, the following design and validation path has been adopted:

1. **Reference scenario definition**: identification and modelling of some Case Studies that are representative of the MULTICLIMACT digital solutions and types of exchanged information. This step has been structured in three sub-steps:
   (a) Case studies selection:
       i. Identification and description of some cases representative the MUL-TICLIMACT overall data exchange context;
       ii. Identification of solution's input and output data flow types.
   (b) Case studies analysis and modelling:
       i. Description of the main (not technical) characteristics and function-alities of the involved digital solutions;
       ii. Identification of input and output data flow types coming from dif-ferent solutions;
       iii. For each type of data flows, definition of an Abstract Data Model providing a detailed description of the exchange data and related requirements, e.g.: mandatory information, use of coded values, units of measure to be used,...
   (c) Abstract Data Models review and generalization:
       i. Checking if it includes types of information and requirements strictly tailored on the Case study; where necessary, update of the Data Model in order to make it as more general as possible;
       ii. Identification of the subset of data that which could be useful to share in an interoperable format (for example KPIs or data useful for calculating KPIs);
       iii. Release of the final generalized Abstract Data Models obtained apply-ing the i) and ii) sub-steps of this sub-step c).

   The main outputs of this step are the "Abstract Data Models" that have been the starting point for designing the UrbanDataset types that define the interoperable format for collecting data for the natural hazards monitoring.
2. **SCPS Semantic and Information analysis and improvement**: check-ing of the UrbanDataset Specifications against the identified Abstract Data Models coming from Step 1; where necessary, improvement of existing Urban-Datasets or design, development and publication of new ones. This step has produced the key component of the interoperability reference scenario: the UrbanDataset Specifications that are deeply described in Sect. 4.2.
3. **Interoperability reference model validation**: demonstration of the inter-operability among the MULTICLIMACT digital solutions involves providing one of the four demo sites in the MULTICLIMACT Project, specifically the

Municipality of Camerino, with an SCP instance and enabling interoperable communication among the solutions. It was organized in the following sub-steps:

(a) Setup of ENEA SCP and dashboard for Camerino Municipality (that is part of one of the four demo sites of the project)
(b) UrbanDatasets implementation in the Digital Solutions
(c) Configuration of the collaboration between digital solutions and SCP
(d) Communication implementation and data exchange activation
(e) Preliminary test and validation

This paper is focused on the results obtained performing the first and second steps of the path; the last one (interoperability reference model validation) will be no further treated because it is still not be implemented.

4   The Preliminary Reference Model for Interoperability

4.1   The Reference Scenario

The reference scenario is the basis for extending and customizing the "Smart City Platform Specification (SCPS) for Interoperability Layer" and enabling the interoperability in the data exchange among the digital solutions developed and targeted for MULTICLIMACT project's purposes. It is composed of some Case Studies that are representative of the MULTICLIMACT digital solutions and types of exchanged information. It does not have the ambition to depict all cases implemented in the context of the project nor all the natural hazards monitoring scenarios; rather it aims to:

- identify a set of fundamental requirements and characteristics capable of representing a subset of them;
- outline the approach to adopt for expanding the MULTICLIMACT Interoperability Reference Model in order to connect further digital solutions or replicate it in other contexts.

The Case Studies identified and analyzed for depicting the reference scenario are summarized in Table 1. Due to limited space, only one of them is explored in depth.

Earthquake Monitoring and Damage Estimation Case Study. This case study concerns the monitoring of seismic events and their impact on environment, cities, buildings and people. Data are collected or elaborated by digital solutions and shared on a Smart City Platform. It includes three types of digital solutions and two sub-case studies:

- **Earthquake detection and damages estimation**: it involves two digital solutions; a Digital Solution A, capable of collecting data on an earthquake, and a Digital Solution B, able to estimate physical damages to buildings and

Table 1. Natural threats monitoring case studies

Name	Description	Applicability scale	Abstract Data Models
Earthquake monitoring and damage estimation	Monitoring of seismic events and their impact on environment, cities, buildings, and people	- Building - Urban -Territorial	- Earthquake events - Impact Risk Indicators - Earthquake damaged buildings counter - Building structural simulation
Prediction of environmental behavior in case of heatwaves	Prediction of the critical parameters (like temperature) of outdoor urban space in case of heat waves, but also the analysis of building's energy efficiency	- Building - Urban	- Urban surface conditions prediction - Building energy consumption and demand
Flood monitoring	Monitoring of parameters useful for Decision Support Systems to warn against macro-stability failure in dikes and deformation and leakage in movable barriers under flood and drought conditions	- Urban - Territorial	- Hydrological extremes time series
Comfort and well-being indoor monitoring	Monitoring of parameters concerning comfort and healthcare of people inside buildings	- Building	- Health monitoring - Microclimate monitoring

curves of resilience (operational and socio-economical) of points of interest and critical infrastructures based on the occurrence of seismic events. When an earthquake occurs, the Digital Solution A sends the related information to the Smart City Platform where they remain available for all accredited solutions and users. Once a day the Digital Solution B send a request to SCP for receiving the last "Earthquake events" message; then, it checks if the message is different from the one received the day before and, in case, it calculates the level of damage of the buildings in the affected area and the resilience indicators. Finally, the digital solution B send this information to SCP where they remain available for all accredited solutions and users. The sequence of the exchanged messages is shown in Fig. 2.

– **Building structural behaviour simulation**: it involves one digital solutions and refers to the simulation of structural behaviour of buildings under extreme natural hazard conditions (earthquake, wind and fire). Specifically, this Digital Solution can calculate structural behaviour using an architectural BIM model of a building and is capable of comparing simulated data with the structural design codes of a specific country (National codes and Eurocode); it also allows to obtain compliance documents for the simulated structure. The Digital Solution is meant for the study of the existing building stock

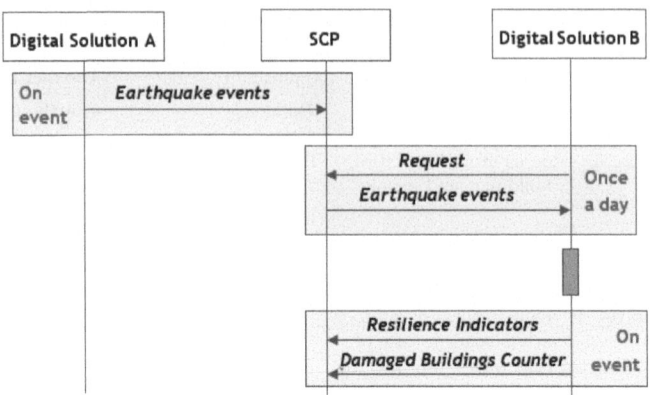

Fig. 2. "Earthquake detection and damages estimation" case study sequence diagram

and it's response to extreme natural hazard conditions with the aim of preventing future disasters. To study existing building stock can be beneficial
to apply security and correction measures in a specific building or area. The
inputs used by the Digital Solution to execute elaborations are not acquired
through the Smart City Platform which simply receives the obtained information from the Digital Solution and makes they available for all accredited
solutions and users.

The Abstract Data Models coming from this Case study are:

– **Earthquake events**: it represents data concerning one or more seismic event
  (real or simulated).
– **Impact Risk Indicators**: it represents aggregated indicators of socio-
  economic impact due to natural hazards.
– **Earthquake Damaged Building Counter**: it represents data on the number of buildings damaged in the specified geographic area due to a seismic
  event.
– **Building Structural Simulation**: it represents data related to the simulated structural behavior of buildings for earthquake conditions.

An example of connection between vertical Solution and SCP based on this
Case Study, as described also in Fig. 3, is the following:

– the "Seismic Event Monitoring" Solution implements a simple software module that
  • exports the dataset in the JSON format of the "Earthquake Events"
    UrbanDataset;
  • pushes the UrbanDataset towards the SCP (as a client, in respecting of
    the "UrbanDatasetGateway" web service interface);
– the SCP is configured to receive the "Earthquake Events" UrbanDataset from
  the "Seismic Event Monitoring" Solution, so the "UrbanDatasetGateway" web
  service is ready, waiting for UrbanDatasets from the solution;

– the connection between Solution and SCP can be enabled and automated, with the sending of the UrbanDataset, from Solution to SCP, with the configured frequency.

The other vertical solution in Fig. 3, "Impact and Resilience Assessment", works in the same way, exporting and pushing (or requesting and importing) the expected UrbanDatasets.

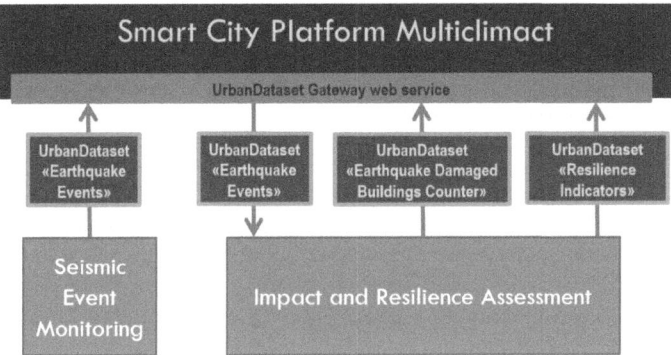

Fig. 3. Example of Reference Model implementation

"Prediction of Environmental Behavior in Case of Heatwaves" Case Study. This case study concerns the prediction of the critical parameters (like temperature) of outdoor urban space in case of heat waves, but also the analysis of building's energy efficiency. Data are collected or elaborated by digital solutions and shared on the Smart City Platform. It includes two types of digital solutions and two sub-case studies:

– **Prediction of heat mitigation KPIs**: it involves one digital solutions that, using the weather forecast as an input (currently not acquired through the Smart City Platform), can predict the surface temperature of a pavement and deduces the apparent, radiant and operative temperatures from it. The solution runs once a day predicting these KPIs for the following 24 h; these values are then sent to the Smart City Platform where they remain available for all accredited solutions and users.
– **Building energy simulation** it involves one digital solutions and refers to the prediction of building behavior (consumption and demand) under extreme weather conditions as well as the simulation of building behavior when applying correction measures such as heat mitigation pavement solution. The Digital Solution consists of a physics base simulation model with EnergyPlus simulation engine; specifically, it can simulate energy consumption and demand using an architectural BIM model of a building. It is meant for the study of the existing building stock and it's response to extreme natural hazard conditions with the aim of preventing future disasters. The inputs used by

the Digital Solution to execute elaborations are not acquired through the Smart City Platform which simply receives the obtained information from the Digital Solution and makes they available for all accredited solutions and users.

In this Case Study two Abstract Data Models have been designed:

- **Urban Surface Conditions Prediction**: it represents some KPIs concerning the predicted conditions of an urban surface (for example pavement) in a determined time horizon.
- **Building energy consumption and demand**: it defines some KPIs representing the building behavior, in terms of energy demand and consumption, under extreme weather conditions.

"Flood Monitoring" Case Study. This case study involves an early warning system that leverages surrogate models and fiber optics measurements as input to quantify the state (and early signs of failure) of two types of flood defenses: dikes and box movable barriers. The system for both scenarios operationally calculate a set of Key Performance Indicators (KPIs), consisting of time series data, which are exported to the Smart City Platform on a daily or sub-daily frequency where they remain available for all accredited solutions and users.

This Case Study has identified one Abstract Data Model, **"Hydrological extremes time series"** for representing time series relating to several types of parameters (macro stability safety factor, leakage safety factor,...) for the prevention, defence and management of floods and droughts scenarios.

"Comfort and Well-Being Indoor Monitoring" Case Study. This case study deals with the monitoring of some parameters of indoor environments (such as air quality, temperature, humidity, and physiological responses of occupants, among others) that can be useful to make evaluation for improving both comfort and energy efficiency of buildings. It involves a digital solution that not only enhance the monitoring and management of indoor environments (which are exported to the Smart City Platform where they remain available for all accredited solutions and users) but also provide actionable insights that can be used to improve both occupant well-being and energy efficiency.

In this Case Study two Abstract Data Models have been designed:

- **Microclimate Monitoring**: it represents several parameters useful for depicting the conditions of indoor environment both from the quality and energy efficiency perspectives.
- **Health Monitoring**: it defines the set of parameters able to represent the physical health condition of the occupants of an indoor environment.

4.2   The SCPS UrbanDataset for the MULTICLIMACT Reference Scenario

Starting from the Abstract Data Models identified through the reference scenario designing, the "Smart City Platform Specification (SCPS) for Interoperability Layer" has been customized and extended for supporting the monitoring of natural threads, well-being and health parameters of people occupying building in the affected areas. The results have been the design and implementation in the SCPS ontology of some new UrbanDataset types, the update of an existing one, the setting-up of their JSON implementations. Specifically:

– **"Microclimate Monitoring" UrbanDataset**, that can be used to provide comfort parameters relating to inhabited environments, has been updated to include more parameters, consistently with the Abstract Data Model defined in the "Indoor comfort and well-being" case study. This action demonstrates the flexibility and scalability of the reference infrastructure adopted and its ability to respond to new needs.

Then, the following new UrbanDatasets have been designed:

– **"Earthquake Events" UrbanDataset**: it provides data concerning one or more seismic events (timestamp of the event detection, epicenter, magnitude, depth), specifying whether the data relates to a real or simulated event. So, it can be used to share information that actually happened, as well as useful information for carrying out simulations.
– **"Impact Risk Indicators" UrbanDataset**: it gives aggregated indicators of socio-economic impact due to natural hazards, indicating the resilience evolution over time and set of the affected nodes (Points of Interest and Critical Infrastructure). The UrbanDataset is not constrained to a specific indicator calculation method neither to a specific natural hazard, and it has been designed in order to support the aggregation of the indicators at two different geographic scales: urban scale (district or town) and territorial scale (province, region or country). This UrbanDataset also allows to indicate whether the data relates to a real or simulated event.
– **"Earthquake Damaged Buildings Counter" UrbanDataset**: it deals with data on the number of buildings damaged in the specified geographic area due to a seismic event. The level of damage has to be indicated according to the European Macroseismic Scale 1998 (EMS-98) and can refer to two different geographic scales: urban scale (district or town) and territorial scale (province, region or country). This UrbanDataset also allows to indicate whether the data relates to a real or simulated event.
– **"Hydrological Extremes Time Series" UrbanDataset**: it allows to provide different types of parameters, collected as time series, useful to prevent, defend and manage floods and droughts scenarios; for example, indicators to evaluate the status of defence systems like movable barriers or dikes. Each measurement can be georeferenced by indicating the geographic coordinates of the detection point and the quality and reliability of the data can be

specified. The UrbanDataset has been designed so that the set of supported parameters can be easily expanded over time.

- **"Urban Surface Condition Prediction" UrbanDataset**: it allows to provide up to four different KPIs (surface, apparent, radiant and operative temperatures) indicating the prediction of urban surface conditions in a determined time horizon. The UrbanDataset has been designed in order to be able to be used for different kinds of surface (e.g. footpath, roads, wall,...) and materials they are composed of (e.g. pavement, asphalt,...). The set of supported surfaces and materials can be easily expanded over time. The predictions can be georeferenced by indicating the geographic coordinates where the surface is located.

- **"Health Monitoring" UrbanDataset**: it provides various parameters regarding a person's health status (e.g. blood oxygen saturation level, hear rate, heart rate variability,...). For privacy reasons, the UrbanDataset allows to identify the device/sensor that collects the data, but does not allow to identify or georeference the person.

The UrbanDatasets concerning the "Building energy simulation" and "Building energy consumption and demand" have not been yet implemented in the SCPS Ontology.

As an example, Fig. 4 shows an human-friendly representation of the semantic definition of the of "Earthquake Damaged Buildings Counter" UrbanDataset, that has been included in the SCP Ontology, and Fig. 5 provides a fragment of a JSON implementation example regarding data aggregated at city level. Note that the Region which data is refer to is expressed as code ("RegionCode" property). This code belongs to the NUTS classification (Nomenclature of territorial units for statistics) that has been adopted by the SCPS Ontology for identifying European regions.

4.3   The Three Management Scales of the Built Environment

As aforementioned, the new UrbanDatasets designed for monitoring of natural threats have been added to the SCPS UrbanDataset library. Since the "Smart City Platform Specification for Interoperability Layer" is conceived to support the development of platforms capable of collecting data from applications operating in the different contexts of the Smart city, the SCPS Ontology structures the library according to categories and subcategories suitable for representing the types of smart city applications and does not provide clear reference to the built environment scales, although the category "Built environment" is present. Nevertheless, a more comprehensive match between the two perspectives can be made, as shown in Table 2 (in the "Built environment scale" column, the "X" symbol means that UrbanDatasets are not yet available in the related subcategory; the "New UrbanDataset" column shows the UrbanDatasets relating only to the monitoring of natural threats).

UrbanDataset Identification	
Scope	Provides data on the number of buildings damaged in the specified geographic area due to a seismic event. The level of damage is indicated according to the European Macroseismic Scale 1998 (EMS-98)
Category / Subcategory	PublicSafetyPolicyEmergencyResponse / NaturalHazard
Identifier	EarthquakeDamagedBuildingsCounter-2.0
Name	Earthquake Damaged Buildings Counter
URI	https://smartcityplatform.enea.it/specification/semantic/2.0/ontology/scps-ontology-2.0.owl#EarthquakeDamagedBuildingsCounter

UrbanDataset Properties *properties marked with an asterisk require to indicate, at instance level, the adopted calculation method (e.g. "average", "total", "instantaneous",...)*					
Name	**Description**	**Mandatory**	**Format/Code list**	**Unit of Measure**	
ModerateDamageBuildingCount	Number of buildings that suffered D2 damage level ('moderate' according with EMS-98)	yes	integer	Not applicable	
NegligibleDamageBuildingCount	Number of buildings that suffered D1 damage level ('negligible' according with EMS-98)	yes	integer	Not applicable	
SubstantialDamageBuildingCount	Number of buildings that suffered D3 damage level ('substantial to heavy' according with EMS-98)	yes	integer	Not applicable	
TotalDestructionBuildingCount	Number of buildings that suffered D5 damage level ('total destruction' according with EMS-98)	yes	integer	Not applicable	
VeryHeavyDamageBuildingCount	Number of buildings that suffered D4 damage level ('very heavy damage' according with EMS-98)	yes	integer	Not applicable	
coordinates	Geographical reference of the damaged area	yes	Aggregated property	Not applicable	
subProperty: *format*	Wgs84 format in which the coordinates are expressed (optional attribute)	no	string FormatCode.gc	Not applicable	
subProperty: *height*	Altitude (optional property)	no	double	Not applicable	
subProperty: *latitude*	Latitude	yes	double	Not applicable	
subProperty: *longitude*	Longitude	yes	double	Not applicable	
timestamp	The date and time in wich the damages were detected	yes	dateTime	Not applicable	
CountryCode	A code identifying the country	no	string CountryCode.gc	Not applicable	
EventID	An unique identifier for the event	no	string	Not applicable	
ProvinceName	Province name	no	string	Not applicable	
RegionCode	A code identifying a region	no	string RegionCode.gc	Not applicable	
SchemeID	Identifies an encoding scheme	no	string	Not applicable	
SimulatedFlag	Indicates if the reported event is real (false) or simulated (true)	no	boolean	Not applicable	
TownName	Extended town name (e.g. Roma, Anguillara Sabazia, ecc.)	no	string	Not applicable	
ZIPCode	Zip Code	no	string	Not applicable	
ZeroDamageBuildingCount	Number of buildings that did not suffer damages	no	integer	Not applicable	

Fig. 4. Semantic definition of the "Earthquake damaged Buildings Counter" Urban-Dataset

```
"UrbanDataset": {
  "specification": {
    "version": "2.0",
    "id": {
      "value": "EarthquakeDamagedBuildingsCounter-2.0",
      "schemeID": "SCPS"
    },
    "name": "Earthquake Damaged Buildings Counter",
    "uri": "https://smartcityplatform.enea.it/specification/semantic/2.0/ontology/scps-
ontology-2.0.owl#EarthquakeDamagedBuildingsCounter",
    .......
  "values": {
    "line": [
      {
        "id": 1,
        "timestamp": "2024-04-24T09:30:00",
        "coordinates": {
          "format": "WGS84-DD",
          "latitude": 43.13,
          "longitude": 13.06},
        "property": [
          {
            "name": "EventID",
            "val": "SIM-001"},
          {
            "name": "SchemeID",
            "val": "MSE"},
          {
            "name": "ZeroDamageBuildingCount",
            "val": "1200"},
          {
            "name": "NegligibleDamageBuildingCount",
            "val": "60"}.
          {
            "name": "ModerateDamageBuildingCount",
            "val": "15"},
          {
            "name": "SubstantialDamageBuildingCount",
            "val": "5"},
          {
            "name": "VeryHeavyDamageBuildingCount",
            "val": "3"},
          {
            "name": "TotalDestructionBuildingCount",
            "val": "2"},
          {
            "name": "TownName",
            "val": "Camerino"},
          {
            "name": "ProvinceName",
            "val": "Macerata"},
          {
            "name": "RegionCode",
            "val": "ITI3"},
          {
            "name": "SimulatedFlag",
            "val": "true"}
        ]},
```

Fig. 5. Sample fragment of the "Earthquake damaged Buildings Counter" Urban-Dataset

Table 2. Match between SCPS Ontology's categories and subcategories and built environment scales

Categories	Sub-categories	Built environment scale	New UrbanDatasets
Built environment	Smart Home	Building	Microclimate Monitoring
	Smart Building	Building	
	Land use and management	Urban area/Territory	Urban Surface Prediction Conditions
Water and wastewater	Water collection and management	Urban area/Territory	
	Water distribution	X	
	Water consumption	X	
	Wastewater management	X	
Waste	Citizens engagement	X	
	Collection and segregation	X	
	Waste disposal	X	
Energy	Energy supply	Building/Urban area	
	Energy transmission and distribution	Building/Urban area	
	Energy demand	Building/Urban area	
Transportation	Travel demand/consumption	X	
	Traffic management	Urban area	
	Surveillance	Urban area	
Education	Learning outcomes	X	
	Learning and teaching	X	
	Service management	X	
Health	Health care systems	Building	
	Health care delivery	X	Health Monitoring
	Communication	X	
Socio-economic development	E-Governance	Urban area	
	Social Innovation and Inclusion	Urban area	
	Economy and Business	X	
Public safety, policy and Emergency Response	City surveillance and crime prevention	X	
	Communication	Urban area/Territory	
	Natural Hazard	Building/Urban area/Territory	Earthquake events, Impact Risk Indicators, Earthquake Damage Building Counter, Hydrological extremes time series

5   Conclusions and Next Steps

In this paper, with the goal of monitoring natural threats at different geographic scales, we presented a preliminary reference model, defined through public specifications for the interoperability, preparing a demonstration that use a smart city platform, based on the above-mentioned specification. The specification for the interoperability is named "Smart City Platform Specification (SCPS) for Interoperability Layer" and the platform SCPS-based is named "Smart City Platform"

(SCP). This work is the result of a process aimed to extend and customize the SCPS starting from a reference scenario depicted in the context of the MULTI-CLIMACT project and then demonstrate the interoperability with the reference model through the SCP platform. Currently, the design of the reference model has been almost finalized and the following outcomes are available: the semantic and syntax definition of the interoperability format (SCPS UrbanDataset) to exchange data for the most part of the data flows (Abstract Data Models) identified in the reference scenario, and the UrbanDataset speficifications for the missing ones will be available in the next future. The design process has demonstrated the scalability of the SCPS, adopted as reference architecture, and its applicability to the three geographic scales. The next steps involve validating the reference model and demonstrating its replicability by implementing it in a different geographic context. Validation will be conducted by demonstrating the interoperability among the MULTICLIMACT digital solutions, as previously explained, using the Italian demo site in the MULTICLIMACT project, specifically the Municipality of Camerino, as a testing ground. This site will feature an SCP instance (named SCP-Multiclimact) that will enable interoperable communication among the solutions.

Acknowledgments. The authors wish to acknowledge the Italian Ministry of Environment who founded the Project 1.7 "Technologies for the efficient penetration of the electric vector in the final uses" within the "Electrical System Research" Programme Agreements 22–24 (PTR 22–24) and the European Union who founded the MULTI-CLIMACT project (Grant Agreement No. 101123538). In particular, the first project has supported the development of the "Smart City Platform Specification (SCPS) for Interoperability Layer" and its reference implementation ("Smart City Platform" SCP); the MULTICLIMACT project has supported both the customization of the existing SCPS and the deployment of a customized SCP instance for monitoring natural threats.

References

1. Avanzi, D.D.S., Foggiatto, A., dos Santos, V., Deschamps, F., de Freitas Rocha Loures, E.: A framework for interoperability assessment in crisis management. J. Ind. Inf. Integr. **5**, 26–38 (2017). https://doi.org/10.1016/j.jii.2017.02.004, https://www.sciencedirect.com/science/article/pii/S2452414X16300929

2. Bania, A., Iatrellis, O., Samaras, N.: Information communication technologies (ICTS) and disaster risk management (DRM): systematic literature review. In: Nathanail, E.G., Gavanas, N., Adamos, G. (eds.) Smart Energy for Smart Transport, pp. 1779–1794. Springer (2023). https://doi.org/10.1007/978-3-031-23721-8_137

3. Bhatt, V., Brutti, A., Burns, M., Frascella, A.: An approach to provide shared architectural principles for interoperable smart cities. In: Gervasi, O., et al. (eds.) Computational Science and Its Applications - ICCSA 2017, pp. 415–426. Springer, Cham (2017)

4. Brutti, A., et al.: Smart city platform specification: a modular approach to achieve interoperability in smart cities. In: The Internet of Things for Smart Urban Ecosystems. Springer (2018). https://api.semanticscholar.org/CorpusID:140339889

5. Casado, R., Rubiera, E., Sacristan, M., Schütte, F., Peters, R.: Data interoperability software solution for emergency reaction in the Europe union. Natural Hazards and Earth System Sciences **15**(7), 1563–1576 (2015). https://doi.org/10.5194/nhess-15-1563-2015, https://nhess.copernicus.org/articles/15/1563/2015/

6. ENEA: smart city platform project website. https://smartcityplatform.enea.it/

7. Frascella, A., et al.: A minimum set of common principles for enabling smart city interoperability. TECHNE - J. Technol. Archit. Environ. **1**, 56–61 (2018). https://doi.org/10.13128/Techne-22739, https://oaj.fupress.net/index.php/techne/article/view/5084

8. Giovinazzi, S., et al.: Embedding resilience to climate change and natural hazards in smart services, pp. 408–420. Springer (2024). https://doi.org/10.1007/978-3-031-54118-6_37

9. Migliorini, M., et al.: Data interoperability for disaster risk reduction in Europe. Disast. Preven. Manage. October 2019. https://doi.org/10.1108/DPM-09-2019-0291

10. NIST: Nist framework and roadmap for smart grid interoperability standards, release 1.0 (2010)

11. UN-HABITAT: resilience and risk reduction, https://unhabi-tat.org/topic/resilience-and-risk-reduction

12. UNECE: people-smart sustainable cities, united nations publication issued by the united nations economic commission for Europe

13. UNHABITAT: Smart sustainable cities and smart digital solutions for urban resilience in the Arab region lessons from the pandemic, economic and social commission for western Asia

14. Villani, M.L., Giovinazzi, S., Costanzo, A.: Co-creating gis-based dashboards to democratize knowledge on urban resilience strategies: experience with camerino municipality. ISPRS Int. J. Geo-Inf. **12**(2) (2023). https://doi.org/10.3390/ijgi12020065, https://www.mdpi.com/2220-9964/12/2/65

15. WG, C.P.: Framework for cyber-physical systems, release 1.0, nist. espresso, 2016. smart city strategic growth map (2016). https://blogs.rhrk.uni-kl.de/espresso/wp-content/uploads/sites/26/2016/12/Espresso-brochure-full.pdf

Uncertain Analytic Hierarchy Process for Risk Assessment in Cyber-Physical Systems

Martina Nobili[1], Simone Guarino[1]($\boxtimes$) (iD), Luca Faramondi[1], Gabriele Oliva[1], Ernesto Del Prete[2], and Roberto Setola[1]

[1] Department of Engineering, Università Campus Bio-Medico di Roma, via Álvaro del Portillo 21, 00128 Rome, Italy
{m.nobili,s.guarino,g.oliva,r.setola}@unicampus.it,
l.faramondi@unicampus.it
[2] Department of Technological Innovations and Safety of Plants, Products and Anthropic Settlements, INAIL, Rome, Italy
e.delprete@inail.it

Abstract. This paper introduces an innovative holistic risk assessment framework that integrates Bayesian Networks (BN) with Multi-Criteria Decision Making (MCDM) to calculate and consolidate heterogeneous risk values into a single, comprehensive risk metric. Specifically, the framework employs an array of risk-specific BNs to derive a set of heterogeneous risk metrics, which are then integrated using the Uncertain Incomplete Analytic Hierarchy Process (UIAHP) technique. This approach involves soliciting pairwise comparisons of risks from a panel of experts, whose assessments are used to compute weights associated with each risk metric; further to that, the methodology incorporates information related to the degree of certainty in the experts' evaluations to enhance the robustness of the derived weights.

The effectiveness of the proposed risk assessment methodology is demonstrated through a real hardware-in-the-loop case study conducted in a laboratory environment, which simulates a scaled-down critical infrastructure for water distribution.

Keywords: Cyber-Physical Systems · Risk Assessment · Bayesian Networks · Incomplete Analytic Hierarchy Process · Experts' Uncertainty

1 Introduction

In recent years, cyber-attacks on Industrial Control Systems (ICS) have surged significantly due to the widespread adoption of open industrial protocols, enabling remote control and monitoring of industrial facilities via the Internet [12]. Such attacks pose severe threats to the physical processes under control, often causing substantial deviations from normal operations, as exemplified by the Stuxnet and BlackEnergy3 incidents, which disrupted the Iranian

This work was supported by the Italian National Project INAIL BRIC 2023 ID 44 "Industrial Cyber Shield (ICS)" under CUP C83C22001460001.

nuclear facilities and the Ukrainian power grid in 2010 and 2016, respectively [5,9]. Given the complex and potentially devastating impacts of cyber-attacks on ICSs, it is crucial to accurately assess and quantify the risks associated with these threats. However, presenting security operators with a diverse set of risk values can be overwhelming, especially when multiple attacks are detected simultaneously. Therefore, there is a pressing need to derive a comprehensive risk value that integrates individual risks, providing a clearer understanding of the overall threat to the system.

To address this need, this paper introduces a holistic risk assessment approach that integrates multiple Bayesian Networks (BN) with Multi-Criteria Decision Making (MCDM) and accounts for the uncertainty associated with the judgments of human decision-makers. Specifically, we calculate a set of heterogeneous risk values linked to detected cyber-attacks using multiple BNs, which offer a probabilistic depiction of how these attacks might propagate throughout the ICS infrastructure. These heterogeneous risks are then aggregated using a weighted sum.

In order to compute the weights in this paper we resort to the help of human decision makers. In particular, decision-makers are asked to provide an estimate of the relative impact of pairs of risks (e.g., "Risk X is twice as much impactful than risk Y"). Moreover, the decision-makers are asked to specify a degree of certainty in the provided relative information. Based on such judgments, we resort to an extension of the Incomplete Analytic Hierarchy Process (IAHP) technique [3,13], namely, *Uncertain IAHP* (UIAHP), where information on the degree of certainty is used to pose more emphasis on information associated to large certainty values. Notice that this methodology can also be adopted when objective information is available for the degree of certainty to be associated with a pairwise comparison provided by a specific expert. For instance, years of experience or specific knowledge of some of the items being compared can be the basis for associating a degree of certainty with a comparison.

The proposed risk assessment method is validated through a real hardware-in-the-loop case study in a laboratory setting, specifically the Water Distribution Testbed (WDT) for cyber-physical security testing, which simulates a scaled-down water distribution critical infrastructure [4]. We evaluate the technique against four types of cyber-attacks: Man-In-The-Middle (MITM), scanning, Denial-of-Service (DoS), and Remote Code Execution (RCE) attacks, targeting the four Programmable Logic Controllers (PLC) that manage the WDT cyber-physical process.

Notice that, while the combination of BNs and AHP has primarily been used for evaluating risks from natural disasters [8,11] and workplace accidents [10,15], cyber-attack risk assessments typically rely solely on BNs [2,14,16]. It is worth mentioning [17], which employs a single BN for system modeling and uses AHP, although not for ranking heterogeneous risks but for prioritizing ICS nodes vulnerable to attacks.

The paper is organized as follows. Section 2 outlines the preliminaries on Graph Theory, BNs, and the Incomplete Analytic Hierarchy Process. Section 3 introduces the UIHAP extension. Section 4 presents the proposed risk assessment technique. Section 5 describes the case-study setup and evaluation, and Sect. 6 concludes the paper.

2 Preliminaries

2.1 Elements of Graph Theory

Consider a *graph* $\mathcal{G} = \{\mathcal{V}, \mathcal{E}\}$ with r nodes $V = \{v_1, \ldots, v_r\}$ and e edges $(v_i, v_j) \in \mathcal{E}$, where (v_i, v_j) denotes an edge from node v_i to node v_j. A *multigraph* allows multiple edges between the same pair of nodes. A (multi)graph is termed *undirected* if $(v_i, v_j) \in \mathcal{E}$ implies $(v_j, v_i) \in \mathcal{E}$, otherwise it is *directed*. A directed graph is *acyclic* if no path exists that starts and ends at the same node. A (multi)graph is *connected* if there is a path between any pair of nodes v_i and v_j in $\mathcal{G}$. The neighborhood $\mathcal{N}_i$ of a node v_i in an undirected graph $\mathcal{G}$ is the set of nodes v_j connected to v_i by an edge $\{v_i, v_j\}$ in $\mathcal{E}$. The *Laplacian matrix* of an undirected graph $\mathcal{G}$ with r nodes is an $r \times r$ matrix $L(\mathcal{G})$ defined as $L_{ij}(\mathcal{G}) = -1$ if $(v_i, v_j) \in \mathcal{E}$, $L_{ij}(\mathcal{G}) = |\mathcal{N}_i|$ if $i = j$, and $L_{ij}(\mathcal{G}) = 0$ otherwise.

2.2 Bayesian Networks

Bayesian Networks are probabilistic graphical models represented as a directed acyclic graph $\mathcal{G} = \{\mathcal{V}, \mathcal{E}\}$, where each node $v_i \in \mathcal{V}$ corresponds to a random variable X_i, and each arc $(v_i, v_j) \in \mathcal{E}$ indicates a causal relationship between nodes [7]. These causal relationships are captured through Conditional Probability Tables (CPT). Each node v_i has an associated CPT that defines the conditional probability of each possible value of X_i given the values of its parent nodes. When new evidence is introduced, the BN updates the probabilities of all other nodes via the CPTs. The joint distribution $P(X_1, \ldots, X_n)$ for a BN is given by:

$$P(X_1, \ldots, X_n) = \prod_{i=1}^{n} P(X_i | pa(X_i)), \tag{1}$$

where n is the total number of nodes, X_i is the random variable of node v_i, $pa(X_i)$ represents the set of parent nodes for v_i, and $P(X_i | pa(X_i))$ is the conditional probability distribution for v_i.

2.3 Incomplete Analytic Hierarchy Process

In this subsection, we review the Logarithmic Least Square (LLS) method for solving the Analytic Hierarchy Process problem with multiple decision-makers when the information available is incomplete [3,13]. We consider g decision-makers, each providing an $r \times r$ potentially perturbed sparse ratio matrix $\mathcal{A}^{(u)}$, which corresponds to a possibly disconnected graph $\mathcal{G}^{(u)} = \{\mathcal{V}, \mathcal{E}^{(u)}\}$. Denote by

$$\hat{\mathcal{G}} = \left\{ \mathcal{V}, \bigcup_{u=1}^{g} \mathcal{E}^{(u)} \right\}$$

the graph representing the collective information from all decision-makers (i.e., a graph comprising the union of all edges from each decision-maker, with repeated edges allowed). The optimization problem to solve is:

$$\boldsymbol{x}^* = \arg\min_{\boldsymbol{x} \in \mathbb{R}^r_+} \frac{1}{2} \sum_{u=1}^{g} \sum_{i=1}^{r} \sum_{j \in \mathcal{N}_i^{(u)}} \left(ln\left(\mathcal{A}_{ij}^{(u)}\right) - ln\left(\frac{x_j}{x_i}\right) \right)^2. \tag{2}$$

where u iterates over all experts, i iterates over all alternatives, and for a given expert u and alternative i, j iterates over the neighborhood $\mathcal{N}_i^{(u)}$ of node i according to the graph $\mathcal{G}^{(u)}$, i.e., the alternatives for which a pairwise comparison with the i-th one is provided by the u-th expert. To simplify solving the above problem, we substitute $y_i = ln(x_i)$ and solve the equivalent problem:

$$\boldsymbol{x}^* = \exp\left(\arg\min_{\boldsymbol{y} \in \mathbb{R}^r} \frac{1}{2} \sum_{u=1}^{g} \sum_{i=1}^{r} \sum_{j \in \mathcal{N}_i^{(u)}} \left(ln\left(\mathcal{A}_{ij}^{(u)}\right) - y_i + y_j \right)^2 \right), \tag{3}$$

where $\exp(\boldsymbol{y})$ is the component-wise exponential. After substitution, the problem becomes an unconstrained convex minimization problem, ensuring that a global optimal solution $\boldsymbol{y}^*$ is found where the gradient of the objective function, evaluated at $\boldsymbol{y}^*$, is zero. Specifically, a global optimal solution satisfies:

$$\sum_{u=1}^{g} L^{(u)} \boldsymbol{y}^* = \sum_{u=1}^{g} P^{(u)} \mathbf{1}_n, \tag{4}$$

where $L^{(u)}$ is the Laplacian matrix associated with $\mathcal{G}^{(u)}$ and $P^{(u)}$ is an $r \times r$ matrix containing the logarithms of the nonzero entries of $\mathcal{A}_{ij}^{(u)}$, with $P_{ij}^{(u)} = 0$ when $\mathcal{A}_{ij}^{(u)} = 0$. Furthermore, $\exp(\boldsymbol{y}^*)$ is unique up to a scaling factor if and only if $\widehat{\mathcal{G}}$ is connected. More precisely, since the problem is an unconstrained convex minimization problem, evaluating the derivative of Eq. (3) at zero reveals that the optimal solution $\boldsymbol{y}^*$ satisfies Eq. (4).

3   Uncertain Incomplete Analytic Hierarchy Process

In this section, we extend the IAHP technique in order to take into account the uncertainty associated to the pairwise comparisons provided by the decision-makers. In the remainder of this paper, we refer to this extension as the *Uncertain IAHP* (UIAHP).

Let us consider a scenario where the u-th expert, besides providing their estimate $\mathcal{A}_{ij}^{(u)}$ for the pairwise comparison between the i-th and j-th alternative, complements their judgment with an estimate $\mathcal{B}_{ij}^{(u)} \in [0, 1]$ of their degree of certainty on the provided answer.

Based on such additional information, we modify the IAHP problem in order to give more relevance to the pairwise comparisons $\mathcal{A}_{ij}^{(u)}$ associated with the largest certainty values. In other words, we aim to solve the following weighted IAHP problem

$$x^* = \exp\left(\arg\min_{y \in \mathbb{R}^r} \frac{1}{2} \sum_{u=1}^{g} \sum_{i=1}^{r} \sum_{j \in \mathcal{N}_i^{(u)}} \mathcal{B}_{ij}^{(u)} \left(\ln\left(\mathcal{A}_{ij}^{(u)}\right) - y_i + y_j\right)^2\right). \tag{5}$$

In order to provide a closed-form solution for the above optimization problem, let us define $\mathcal{L}^{(u)}$ as a weighted Laplacian Matrix for the u-th decision-maker. Specifically, the matrix is weighted with the certainty values $\mathcal{B}_{ij}^{(u)}$, so that

$$\mathcal{L}_{ij}^{(u)} = \begin{cases} -\mathcal{B}_{ij}^{(u)}, & \text{if } (v_i, v_j) \in \mathcal{E}^{(u)}, \\ \sum_{j \in \mathcal{N}_i^{(u)}} \mathcal{B}_{ij}^{(u)}, & \text{if } i = j, \\ 0 & \text{otherwise.} \end{cases}$$

Moreover, let us define the matrix $\mathcal{P}^{(u)}$ as the matrix with entries

$$\mathcal{P}_{ij}^{(u)} = \begin{cases} \mathcal{B}_{ij}^{(u)} \ln\left(\mathcal{A}_{ij}^{(u)}\right), & \text{if } (v_i, v_j) \in \mathcal{E}^{(u)} \text{ and } \mathcal{A}_{ij}^{(u)} \neq 0, \\ 0 & \text{otherwise.} \end{cases}$$

Based on the aforementioned matrices, let us now characterize the optimal solution to the UIAHP problem.

Proposition 1. *A vector* $\exp(y^*)$ *is a global optimal solution to the UIAHP problem if and only if* $y^* \in \mathbb{R}^r$ *satisfies*

$$\sum_{u=1}^{g} \mathcal{L}^{(u)} y^* = \sum_{u=1}^{g} \mathcal{P}^{(u)} \mathbf{1}_n. \tag{6}$$

Proof. In order to prove the statement, we observe that being the UIAHP problem convex and unconstrained, y^* is a global optimal solution if and only if it satisfies

$$\frac{\partial f(y)}{\partial y_i}\bigg|_{y=y^*} = 0, \quad \forall i,$$

where

$$f(y) = \frac{1}{2} \sum_{u=1}^{r} \sum_{i=1}^{g} \sum_{j \in \mathcal{N}_i^{(u)}} \mathcal{B}_{ij}^{(u)} \left(\ln\left(\mathcal{A}_{ij}^{(u)}\right) - y_i + y_j\right)^2$$

is the objective function. By some algebra, this condition is equivalent to Eq. (6). This completes our proof. □

4   The Risk Assessment Technique

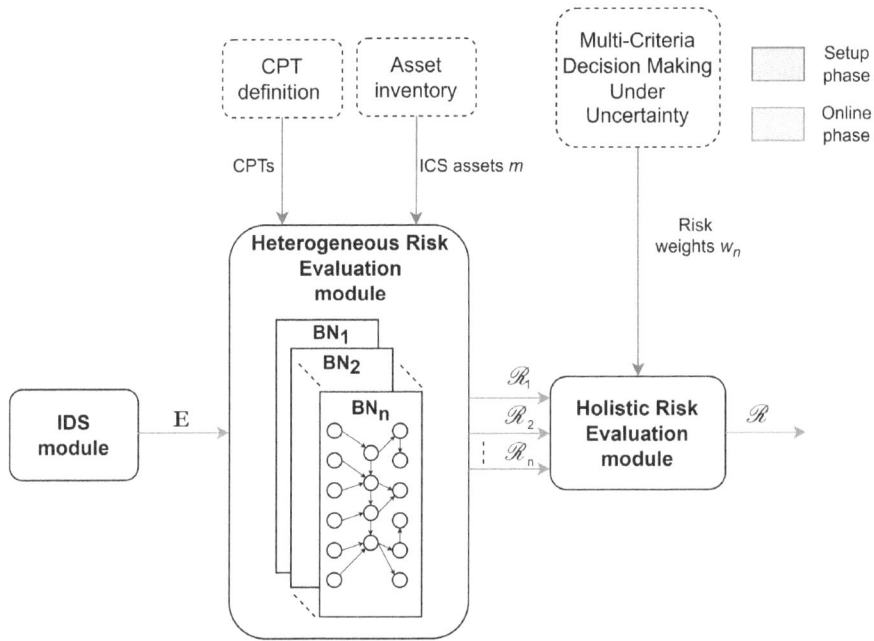

Fig. 1. The risk assessment approach for ICSs.

The proposed risk assessment technique, depicted in Fig. 1, encompasses two distinct phases: the *online phase* and the *setup phase*. The online phase is responsible for delivering a real-time holistic risk value $\mathcal{R}$ based on detected cyberattacks. It comprises three main modules: the *Intrusion Detection System (IDS) module*, which identifies cyber-attacks; the *Heterogeneous Risk Evaluation module*, which assesses the risk values associated with each detected cyber-attack using a set of BNs; and the *Holistic Risk Evaluation module*, which calculates the holistic risk by weighting the heterogeneous risk values. In contrast, the setup phase involves initializing the parameters for both the heterogeneous and holistic risk evaluation modules. This phase includes three primary activities: the *Conditional Probability Table (CPT) definition*, which establishes the CPT for each BN node; the *Asset Inventory*, which details the number and cost indices of ICS cyber and physical assets; and the *Multi-Criteria Decision Making Under Uncertainty*, which derives the cyber-attack risk weights from expert evaluations using the UIAHP methodology.

4.1   IDS Module

This module is tasked with the real-time detection of cyber-attacks on ICS cyber assets. It can implement any type of detection model to address both known attacks, through signature-based IDS, and unknown attacks, through anomaly-based IDS. By continuously monitoring network traffic among cyber assets, it generates a set of cyber events $\mathbb{E}$.

Let n denote the number of distinct classes of cyber-attacks the IDS can detect, and m_c represent the collection of cyber assets where these attacks can be identified. A cyber event $E_j^i \in \mathbb{E}$, associated with a cyber-attack class $n_i \in n$ on a cyber asset $m_c^j \in m_c$, is defined as follows:

$$E_j^i = \begin{cases} 1, & \text{if } n_i \text{ is detected on cyber asset } m_c^j \\ 0, & \text{if } n_i \text{ is not detected on cyber asset } m_c^j \end{cases} \tag{7}$$

Thus, a cyber event is triggered by the IDS when $E_j^i = 1$.

In summary, with n representing the total classes of cyber-attacks that can be detected, m_c indicating the total number of cyber assets, and $t \in [1, T]$ an online-phase time step, where T is the time horizon, the maximum number of events that may be triggered at t is $m_c \times n$, as each cyber-attack class may be detected on each ICS cyber asset.

4.2   Heterogeneous Risk Evaluation Module

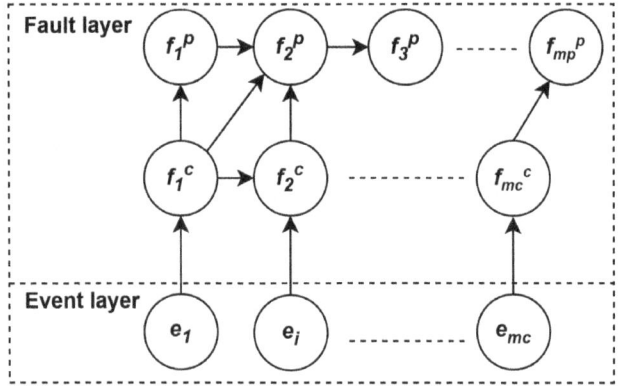

Fig. 2. BN basic topology for Event layer and Fault layer.

This module evaluates the risk value associated with each class of cyber-attack detected on the ICS cyber assets. It consists of a set of n BNs, each of which assesses the probability that a detected cyber-attack class may compromise the ICS cyber and physical assets, thereby indicating the overall risk to the entire cyber-physical system's integrity. The number of BNs corresponds to the number of detectable cyber-attack classes from the IDS module, with each BN representing the spread of a specific cyber-attack class $n_i \in n$ over the ICS assets. A small number of nodes per BN results in low-dimensional state spaces, ensuring low computational load and, consequently, low inference time.

As illustrated in Fig. 1, the heterogeneous risk evaluation module requires two inputs from the setup phase: (1) the number and cost indices associated with the ICS cyber and physical assets ($m = m_c + m_p$), and (2) the CPTs for each node within the BNs. The first input is obtained from the asset inventory, which lists all the cyber and physical items within the ICS. Each asset is associated with a specific cost index c_j, representing its criticality level: the higher the asset's weight, the more critical and important it is for the entire ICS infrastructure. The second input is crucial for evaluating the joint conditional probabilities for each BN node. Specifically, the CPTs quantify the probability that a specific cyber-attack class may propagate through the ICS infrastructure.

Figure 2 shows the basic topology for each BN, consisting of two main layers: the Event layer and the Fault layer. The Event layer includes m_c nodes that model the occurrence of events E_j^i related to the cyber-attack class n_i impacting the m_c cyber assets. Conversely, the Fault layer comprises $m = m_c + m_p$ nodes, representing the probability that the ICS cyber and physical assets are compromised, given the occurrence of cyber events detected on the cyber assets. Specifically, Fault-layer cyber nodes have one parent node from the Event layer; this relationship, encoded within the related CPT, represents the conditional probability that the occurrence of an event will cause a fault on the associated ICS cyber asset. Additionally, parent nodes can arise from the same Fault layer, modeling possible cascading failures that the disruption of one ICS asset may induce in others. This aspect is particularly relevant for the physical nodes within the Fault layer, which model the likelihood that a physical asset will be impaired as a result of failures in other assets during a cyber-attack.

Overall, each BN_i evaluates the risk value associated with each detected cyber-attack class n_i by assessing the conditional probability that cyber and physical assets will be compromised given the set $\mathbb{E}^\dagger \subseteq \mathbb{E}$ of events $E_j^i = 1$ triggered by cyber-attack class n_i and detected over $m_c^\dagger \leq m_c$ cyber assets, and the set $\mathbb{E}^\psi \subseteq \mathbb{E}, \mathbb{E}^\psi \cap \mathbb{E}^\dagger = \varnothing, \mathbb{E}^\psi \cup \mathbb{E}^\dagger = \mathbb{E}$ of null events $E_j^i = 0$ over the remaining $1 - m_c^\dagger$ cyber assets. The risk value $\mathcal{R}_i$ is calculated as follows:

$$\mathcal{R}_i = \sum_{j=1}^{m^c} c_j \, P(F_j^c = T | \mathbb{E}^\dagger, \mathbb{E}^\psi) + \sum_{j=1}^{m^p} c_j \, P(F_j^p = T | \mathbb{E}^\dagger, \mathbb{E}^\psi),$$

where m_c is the number of cyber Fault-layer nodes, m_p is the number of physical Fault-layer nodes, $m_c^\dagger$ is the number of cyber assets where cyber-attacks are detected, and c_j is the cost index associated with the j-th ICS asset. Thus, the risk value $\mathcal{R}_i$ is computed by assessing the probability that the ICS cyber and physical assets are compromised ($P(F_j^p = T | \mathbb{E}^\dagger, \mathbb{E}^\psi)$, $P(F_j^c = T | \mathbb{E}^\dagger, \mathbb{E}^\psi)$) given the set of events $E_j^i = 1$ triggered over the $m_c^\dagger$ cyber assets and the set of null events $E_j^i = 0$ over the remaining $1 - m_c^\dagger$ cyber assets.

4.3   Holistic Risk Evaluation Module

This module is designed to integrate the various risks $\mathcal{R}_1, \ldots, \mathcal{R}_n$ into a comprehensive risk measure. Specifically, during the setup phase, pairwise comparisons are obtained from g experts and decision-makers within the sector. In this phase, decision-makers are asked to evaluate the significance of different risk typologies to the cyber-physical process of an ICS. The responses collected are encoded into matrices $\mathcal{A}^{(1)}, \ldots, \mathcal{A}^{(\ell)}$. Moreover, for each pairwise comparison, the experts provide their assessment $B_{ij}^{(u)}$ of their own degree of certainty in the provided answer. These data are then aggregated via the UIAHP methodology, discussed in Proposition 1. As a result of the UIAHP methodology, we compute a weight vector $\boldsymbol{x}^* \in \mathbb{R}^n$. Since the solution $\boldsymbol{x}^*$ is defined up to a scaling factor, the weights are normalized as follows:

$$\bar{x}_i^* = \frac{x_i^*}{\sum_{h=1}^n x_h^*}.$$

Using these normalized weights, we define the *Holistic Risk* $\mathcal{R}$ as the weighted sum of the individual risks $\mathcal{R}_i$, employing the weights $\bar{x}_i^*$, which is expressed as:

$$\mathcal{R} = \sum_{i=1}^n \bar{x}_i^* \mathcal{R}_i. \tag{8}$$

5   Case Study

This section presents an evaluation of our proposed risk assessment technique applied to the Water Distribution Testbed (WDT).

5.1   Experimental Setup

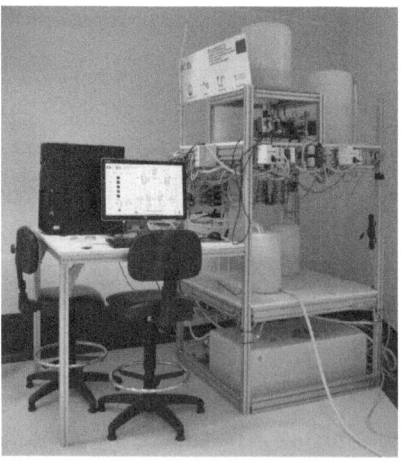

Fig. 3. The Water Distribution Testbed for cyber-physical security testing.

The Water Distribution Testbed [4] is a scaled-down version of a real ICS that facilitates cyber-physical security testing. The testbed consists of both physical and simulated components. The physical partition (depicted in Fig. 3) includes 5 tanks $(T_1^r, \ldots, T_5^r)$, 20 solenoid valves $(V_1^r, \ldots, V_{20}^r)$, 4 pumps $(P_1^r, \ldots, P_4^r)$, and 5 pressure sensors $(S_1^r, \ldots, S_5^r)$ located under each tank, all managed by a real PLC (PLC_1^r). The simulated partition comprises 3 tanks $(T_6^s, \ldots, T_8^s)$, 2 pumps (P_5^s, P_6^s), 4 flow sensors $(F_1^s, \ldots, F_4^s)$, 2 solenoid valves (V_{21}^s, V_{22}^s), and 3 pressure sensors $(S_6^s, \ldots, S_8^s)$ for each tank, with water flow controlled by three virtual PLCs $(PLC_2^s, PLC_3^s, PLC_4^s)$.

The physical process can be divided into four main subsystems, each controlled by a specific PLC. The water flow starts from the reservoir, passes to tank T_1^r, then to tanks T_5^r and T_4^r in the first subsystem. Subsequently, water from T_5^r flows to tank T_6^s in the second subsystem, then to tank T_7^s in the third subsystem, and finally to tank T_8^s in the fourth subsystem.

Table 1. CPT for Fault-layer node $F_{T_8}^p$.

$F_{T_7}^p$	0	0	1	1
$F_{PLC_4}^c$	0	1	0	1
$F_{T_8}^p = 0$	1	0.25	0.2	0.1
$F_{T_8}^p = 1$	0	0.75	0.8	0.9

Based on the WDT architecture, we derived the structure of the BNs within the Heterogeneous Risk Evaluation module. As shown in Fig. 4, the Event layer for each BN consists of $m_c = 4$ nodes corresponding to the four WDT PLCs, while the Fault layer comprises $m = m_c + m_p = 10$ nodes related to the physical and cyber assets involved in the WDT process ($m_p = 6$ tanks and $m_p = 4$ PLCs). The CPTs for Fault-layer nodes can be derived either through empirical analysis of past data or by consulting security experts with knowledge of specific ICS environments. Table 1 displays the CPT for node $F_{T_8}^p$ in the BN associated with a MITM attack; in this study, CPTs are empirically evaluated.

Tables 2 and 3 show the cost indices associated with the WDT assets. These weights quantify the criticality of each asset for the cyber-physical process. Since

Table 2. Cost indices associated with WDT physical assets.

Asset	Cost index c_j
T_1^r	0.90
T_4^r	0.70
T_5^r	0.85
T_6^s	0.70
T_7^s	0.60
T_8^s	0.50

Table 3. Cost indices associated with WDT cyber assets.

Asset	Cost index c_j
PLC_1^r	0.80
PLC_2^s	0.60
PLC_3^s	0.40
PLC_4^s	0.20

the water flow initiates from the first subsystem, the weight value is higher for assets in the initial subsystems and lower for those in the later subsystems.

The total number of BNs is set to $n = 4$, assuming the IDS module can detect four different cyber-attack classes on the WDT PLCs: MITM, DoS, RCE, and scanning attacks.

To determine the weights $\bar{x}_i^*$ for the four heterogeneous risk values associated with the four attack classes, ten decision-makers (including stakeholders, academics, and cybersecurity managers) provided pairwise comparisons of the alternatives, along with their degree of certainty in the provided answers. In particular, the experts chose the degree of certainty $B_{ij}^{(u)}$ in the scale $\{1/10, \ldots, 9/10, 1\}$. The resulting weights, obtained via the procedure outlined in Proposition 1, are reported in Table 4. Specifically, the table reports both the impacts assessed without accounting for the uncertainty and the ones obtained by taking them into account. Interestingly, in both cases, the experts' judgments indicated a higher importance for MITM attack risk value, followed by the DoS attack. The weights for scanning and RCE attack risk values were considerably lower. This situation is more evident when neglecting the experts' uncertainty, while it becomes less prominent when the uncertainty values are used for the computation of the ranking.

Notably, these results are robust and demonstrate a high degree of agreement among the decision-makers: even when any one of the ten matrices $\mathcal{A}^{(u)}$ encoding preferences was excluded, the ordinal ranking of the weights (both considering and not considering uncertainty) remained unchanged.

Table 4. Weights associated with different risk typologies, based on expert elicitation. In particular, the second column reports the weights without taking into account the experts' uncertainty (i.e., assuming all terms $B_{ij}^{(u)} = 1$), while the third column reports the weights obtained by considering the experts' uncertainty.

Attack Class Risk	Weight $\bar{x}_i^*$ (No Uncertainty)	Weight $\bar{x}_i^*$ (With Uncertainty)
MITM	0.4504	0.3950
DoS	0.2791	0.3187
Scanning	0.1274	0.1324
RCE	0.1432	0.1539

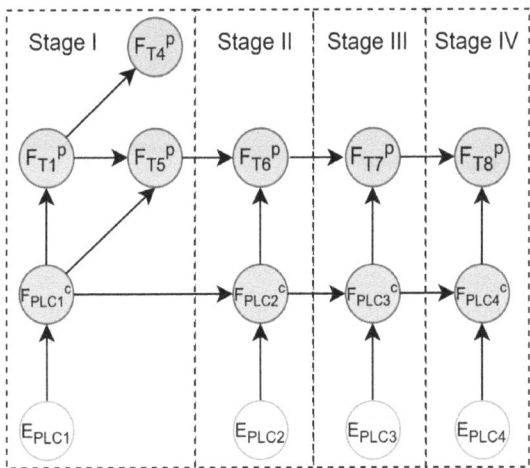

Fig. 4. Structure of Bayesian Network BN_i applied to the WDT case study. Yellow nodes represent Event-layer nodes, and red nodes represent Fault-layer nodes. (Color figure online)

5.2 Evaluation Setup

To validate the effectiveness of our proposed risk assessment technique, we conducted an experiment involving a 50-second attack scenario. Figure 5 illustrates the events detected by the IDS module for each cyber asset in the WDT. In this scenario, an attacker infiltrates the ICS network and begins scanning for PLCs. Upon locating the control devices, the attacker launches two MITM attacks on PLC_1^r and PLC_4^s, one DoS attack on PLC_1^r, and two Remote Code Execution attacks on PLC_2^s and PLC_3^s. Although the events detected for each attack were determined through experimental simulations in this study, they can also be derived using supervised or unsupervised machine learning and deep learning

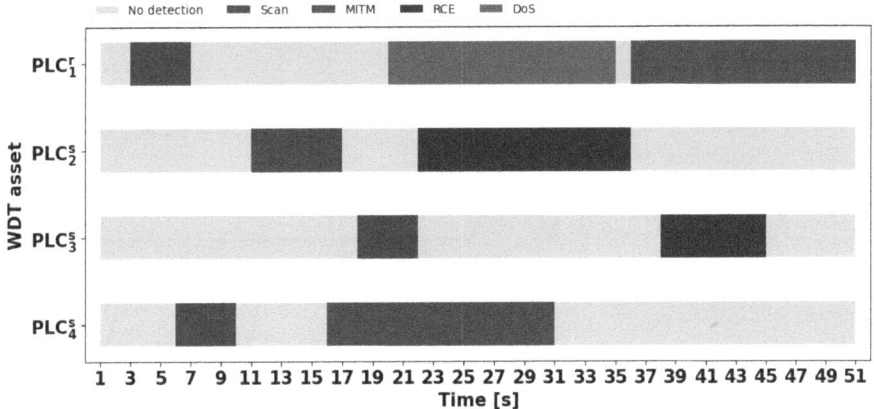

Fig. 5. Cyber-attacks detected by the IDS module for each WDT cyber asset.

algorithms, as described in [5,6]. The BNs were implemented in Python using the `pgmpy` library [1] and executed on a Windows machine with the following specifications: Intel $^{\textregistered}$ Core(TM) i9-9900K CPU @ 3.60 GHz and 64 GB of RAM.

5.3   Case-Study Evaluation

Figure 6 presents the holistic risk value, with ($\mathcal{R}^{\delta}$) and without ($\mathcal{R}$) considering experts' uncertainty, along with the heterogeneous risk values ($\mathcal{R}_{MITM}$, $\mathcal{R}_{DoS}$, $\mathcal{R}_{scan}$, $\mathcal{R}_{RCE}$) over time.

For the heterogeneous risks, it is evident that each one contributes differently to the holistic risk index, with variations directly linked to the attack class detected by the IDS module. In more detail, MITM and DoS attacks are associated with the highest risk values, surpassing four, while RCE and scanning attacks result in risk values that remain below three and two, respectively. Furthermore, the risk values vary depending on the specific PLC targeted by the attacker; attacks on more critical cyber assets yield higher risk values than those targeting less critical PLCs. For instance, the MITM attacks detected on PLC_1^r and PLC_4^s result in different risk values due to the higher cost index of PLC_1^r ($c_{PLC_1^r} = 0.80$) compared to PLC_4^s ($c_{PLC_4^s} = 0.20$), making the MITM attack on PLC_1^r more severe.

We now detail the relationship between the heterogeneous risk values and the holistic one, with ($\mathcal{R}^{\delta}$) and without ($\mathcal{R}$) considering experts' uncertainty.

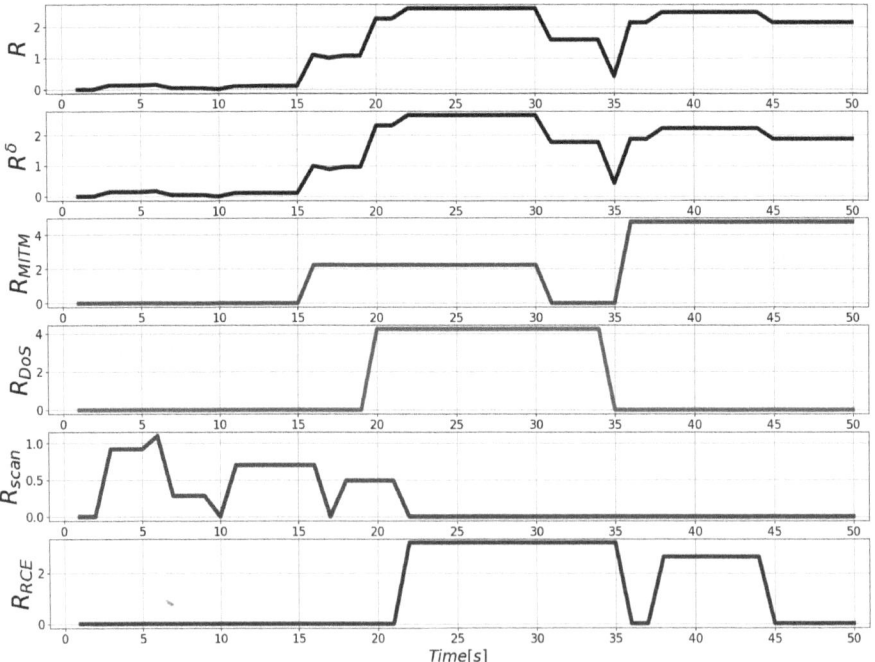

Fig. 6. The holistic and heterogeneous risk values evaluated over time, with (R^{δ}) and without (R) considering experts' uncertainty.

Examining $\mathcal{R}$, we observe that, as expected from Table 4, the most significant contributions to the holistic risk come from $\mathcal{R}_{MITM}$ and $\mathcal{R}_{DoS}$, with weights of 0.4504 and 0.2791, respectively. In contrast, $\mathcal{R}_{scan}$ and $\mathcal{R}_{RCE}$ have smaller impacts on the holistic risk, with weights of 0.1274 and 0.1432, respectively. For instance, during the time intervals $3 \leq t \leq 9$ and $11 \leq t \leq 15$, when only scanning attacks are detected, R experiences minor changes, reaching slightly above 0. On the other hand, $\mathcal{R}_{MITM}$ and $\mathcal{R}_{DoS}$ significantly influence the holistic risk, particularly when these attacks are detected on critical cyber assets. Notably, the holistic risk peaks at $t = 20$ when the DoS attack is detected on PLC_1^r, reaching approximately 2.26. The maximum value ($\mathcal{R} = 2.6$) occurs between $22 \leq t \leq 30$, coinciding with MITM, DoS, and RCE attacks detected on PLC_4^s, PLC_1^r, and PLC_2^s, respectively.

Remarkably, the holistic risk considering experts' opinions $\mathcal{R}^\delta$ shows the same shape of $\mathcal{R}$, sharing the same time intervals when the maximum and minimum values are attained. The main differences are related to the absolute values reached by $\mathcal{R}^\delta$ in specific time intervals. For instance, in $38 \leq t \leq 44$, $\mathcal{R}^\delta$ reaches the value of 2.22, slightly lower than 2.47 experienced by $\mathcal{R}$. This is due to the experts' uncertainty information which resulted in a significant reduction of the weight associated with the MITM attack ($0.3950 < 0.4504$) while slightly increasing that related to the RCE attack ($0.1539 > 0.1432$). Conversely, in time interval $31 \leq t \leq 34$, the $\mathcal{R}^\delta$ value is larger than $\mathcal{R}$ ($\mathcal{R}^\delta = 1.77$, $\mathcal{R} = 1.59$), since both the detected DoS and RCE attacks are associated to higher weight values: $0.3187 > 0.2791$ for the DoS attack and $0.1539 > 0.1432$ for the RCE attack.

6   Conclusions and Future Work

In this paper, we propose a novel risk assessment technique for ICSs that integrates multiple BNs with the IAHP methodology. In particular, we extend IAHP to UIAHP in order to account for the experts' degree of certainty in their provided answers. This technique consists of three main modules: the Intrusion Detection System module, which detects cyber-attacks in real-time; the Heterogeneous Risk Evaluation module, which computes a set of risk values for the detected cyber-attacks using multiple BNs; and the Holistic Risk Evaluation module, which synthesizes these heterogeneous risks into a single, comprehensive risk metric. The weights for this holistic metric are derived from expert evaluations using the UIAHP approach, taking into account the uncertainty in their assessments. The effectiveness of our methodology has been validated through a hardware-in-the-loop case study in a laboratory setting, specifically using the WDT testbed. This controlled environment allowed us to evaluate our risk assessment approach against four different classes of cyber-attacks targeting the four Programmable Logic Controllers that manage the WDT's cyber-physical processes: Man-In-The-Middle, scanning, Denial of Service, and Remote Code Execution. Our findings suggest that the proposed risk assessment technique can be effectively employed by off-the-shelf Intrusion Prevention Systems and Intrusion Response Systems to better understand the actual risk associated with detected attacks. This enhanced understanding can facilitate more informed decision-making regarding the selection of the most appropriate prevention or recovery actions.

Future research will focus on enhancing the proposed risk assessment technique to address zero-day cyber-attacks by introducing ad hoc Bayesian Networks tailored to unknown anomalies detected in the ICS network traffic. Additionally, we will integrate detection uncertainty from the IDS module into the risk assessment process to address potential false positive and false negative events.

References

1. Ankan, A., Panda, A.: pgmpy: probabilistic graphical models using python. In: Proceedings of the 14th Python in Science Conference (SCIPY 2015), Citeseer (2015)
2. Barua, S., Gao, X., Pasman, H., Mannan, M.S.: Bayesian network based dynamic operational risk assessment. J. Loss Prev. Process Ind. **41**, 399–410 (2016)
3. Bozóki, S., Tsyganok, V.: The (logarithmic) least squares optimality of the arithmetic (geometric) mean of weight vectors calculated from all spanning trees for incomplete additive (multiplicative) pairwise comparison matrices. Int. J. Gen Syst **48**(4), 362–381 (2019)
4. Faramondi, L., Flammini, F., Guarino, S., Setola, R.: A hardware-in-the-loop water distribution testbed dataset for cyber-physical security testing. IEEE Access **9**, 122385–122396 (2021). https://doi.org/10.1109/ACCESS.2021.3109465
5. Faramondi, L., Flammini, F., Guarino, S., Setola, R.: Evaluating machine learning approaches for cyber and physical anomalies in scada systems. In: 2023 IEEE International Conference on Cyber Security and Resilience (CSR), pp. 412–417 (2023). https://doi.org/10.1109/CSR57506.2023.10224915
6. Faramondi, L., Flammini, F., Guarino, S., Setola, R.: A hybrid behavior-and bayesian network-based framework for cyber-physical anomaly detection. Comput. Electr. Eng. **112**, 108988 (2023)
7. Guarino, S., Vitale, F., Flammini, F., Faramondi, L., Mazzocca, N., Setola, R.: A two-level fusion framework for cyber-physical anomaly detection. IEEE Trans. Ind. Cyber-Phys. Syst. **2**, 1–13 (2024). https://doi.org/10.1109/TICPS.2023.3336608
8. Joo, H., Choi, C., Kim, J., Kim, D., Kim, S., Kim, H.S.: A bayesian network-based integrated for flood risk assessment (infra). Sustainability **11**(13) (2019). https://doi.org/10.3390/su11133733, https://www.mdpi.com/2071-1050/11/13/3733
9. Lehto, M.: Cyber-attacks against critical infrastructure. In: Cyber Security: Critical Infrastructure Protection, pp. 3–42. Springer (2022)
10. Li, M., Wang, H., Wang, D., Shao, Z., He, S.: Risk assessment of gas explosion in coal mines based on fuzzy ahp and bayesian network. Process Saf. Environ. Prot. **135**, 207–218 (2020)
11. Li, M., Hong, M., Zhang, R.: Improved bayesian network-based risk model and its application in disaster risk assessment. Int. J. Disaster Risk Sci. **9**, 237–248 (2018)
12. Munirathinam, S.: Industry 4.0: industrial internet of things (iiot). In: Advances in Computers, vol. 117, pp. 129–164. Elsevier (2020)
13. Oliva, G., Scala, A., Setola, R., Dell'Olmo, P.: Opinion-based optimal group formation. Omega **89**, 164–176 (2019)

14. Peng, Y., Huang, K., Tu, W., Zhou, C.: A model-data integrated cyber security risk assessment method for industrial control systems. In: 2018 IEEE 7th Data Driven Control and Learning Systems Conference (DDCLS), pp. 344–349 (2018). https://doi.org/10.1109/DDCLS.2018.8516022
15. Xiao, L., Tang, L.C.M., Wen, Y.: An innovative construction site safety assessment solution based on the integration of bayesian network and analytic hierarchy process. Buildings **13**(12) (2023). https://doi.org/10.3390/buildings13122918, https://www.mdpi.com/2075-5309/13/12/2918
16. Zhang, Q., Zhou, C., Tian, Y.C., Xiong, N., Qin, Y., Hu, B.: A fuzzy probability bayesian network approach for dynamic cybersecurity risk assessment in industrial control systems. IEEE Trans. Industr. Inf. **14**(6), 2497–2506 (2018). https://doi.org/10.1109/TII.2017.2768998
17. Zhou, B., Sun, B., Zang, T., Cai, Y., Wu, J., Luo, H.: Security risk assessment approach for distribution network cyber physical systems considering cyber attack vulnerabilities. Entropy **25**(1) (2023). https://doi.org/10.3390/e25010047, https://www.mdpi.com/1099-4300/25/1/47

Author Index

The manufacturer's authorised representative in the EU is Springer
Nature Customer Service Centre GmbH, Europaplatz 3, 69115 Heidelberg,
Germany. If you have any concerns regarding our products, please
contact ProductSafety@springernature.com

Printed and bound by CPI Group (UK) Ltd, Croydon, CR0 4YY
29/04/2026
02099544-0013